The Many Faces of Corruption

The Many Faces of Corruption

Tracking Vulnerabilities at the Sector Level

EDITED BY
J. Edgardo Campos
Sanjay Pradhan

THE WORLD BANK
Washington, D.C.

1818 H Street NW
Washington DC 20433
Telephone: 202-473-1000
Internet: www.worldbank.org
E-mail: feedback@worldbank.org

2 3 4 5 10 09 08 07

This volume is a product of the staff of the International Bank for Reconstruction and Development / The World Bank. The findings, interpretations, and conclusions expressed in this volume do not necessarily reflect the views of the Executive Directors of The World Bank or the governments they represent.

The World Bank does not guarantee the accuracy of the data included in this work. The boundaries, colors, denominations, and other information shown on any map in this work do not imply any judgement on the part of The World Bank concerning the legal status of any territory or the endorsement or acceptance of such boundaries.

ISBN-10: 0-8213-6725-0
ISBN-13: 978-0-8213-6725-4
eISBN-10: 0-8213-6726-9
eISBN-13: 978-0-8213-6726-1
DOI: 10.1596/978-0-8213-6725-4

Library of Congress Cataloging-in-Publication Data

The many faces of corruption : tracking vulnerabilities at the sector level / edited by J. Edgardo Campos, Sanjay Pradhan.

p. cm.

Includes bibliographical references and index.

ISBN-13: 978-0-8213-6725-4

ISBN-10: 0-8213-6725-0

ISBN-10: 0-8213-6726-9 (electronic)

1. Corruption. 2. Economic development—Moral and ethical aspects. 3. Developing countries—Economic policy—Moral and ethical aspects. I. Campos, J. Edgardo. II. Pradhan, Sanjay.

HD75.M265 2007

364.1′323—dc22

2006034749

Cover design: Patricia Hord Graphik Design.

Dollar figures are current U.S. dollars unless otherwise specified.

Contents

Figures

Tables

Foreword

This project comes to fruition at an important time for the World Bank as it scales up its efforts to help countries improve governance and combat corruption. With a heightened focus on mainstreaming governance and anticorruption into its core operations, the Bank expects to engage more extensively in reforms at the sector level. This innovative volume combines analytic rigor and practical operational insights in an important and useful way. It is a "must read" for all development practitioners.

Empirical research on governance and anticorruption has made major strides in the past 10 years, providing increasing empirical evidence that corruption discourages private investment, retards growth, and inhibits poverty reduction efforts. Today, policy makers can use diagnostic instruments to make judgments about priorities for reforms across corruption-prone areas and broadly assess the potential impact over time of reform measures. But the challenge of drilling down to the operational level remains. What and where are the risk points in a given sector? When are they most likely to occur? Which ones, if addressed, might have the greatest impact on a sector's performance? For policy makers, data and information on these queries are what is missing to formulate specific, operationally tractable reforms.

This volume is the product of a successful collaborative effort among many units of the World Bank and reflects the depth of expertise and knowledge that the Bank can harness to contribute to a better understanding of complex phenomena. It includes 12 chapters plus an overview and a conclusion. The first of its three parts is on sectors. It includes seven chapters on health, education, forestry, roads, electricity, oil and gas, and water and sanitation. The second part is on public financial management, which cuts across all sectors and is critical to the operations of any sector. It includes four chapters on budget formulation and execution, procurement, tax administration, and customs administration. The third part of the book is on anti-money-laundering.

The book offers a heuristic framework for analysis to guide the integration of anticorruption measures into program development and project design. It explores prototype road maps of corruption vulnerabilities and corresponding "early warning" signals, looking at corruption from the perspective of a project manager and highlighting corruption risks that might arise at various points in the program or project cycle.

At the sector level, the road map takes on the character of a value chain. A sector produces certain outputs through a sequence of well-defined activities. In the energy sector, for example, the delivery of electricity moves from generation to transmission to wholesale distribution and finally to retail distribution. Corruption can occur anywhere along this chain. In generation, it can emerge in the contracting of power purchase agreements with private providers. In transmission, it can occur through the monopoly power of the state-owned transmission plant or in the capture of the regulatory process. In distribution, it can occur through outright theft. Given the multiple vulnerabilities along the chain, countries will likely differ in terms of the nature of corruption in the delivery of electricity. Hence anticorruption strategies will have to be tailored to fit country contexts.

This value chain approach is promising in terms of identifying specific areas where reforms may have the greatest impact on preventing and reducing corruption. Where along the chain is the weakest link? What measures can be implemented to strengthen this link? What indicators can be used to monitor and assess progress? These are critical questions that policy makers often confront in designing anticorruption strategies. Each chapter in this volume begins to address these issues and suggests possible directions for future study.

Sector performance depends crucially on a number of functions. Perhaps the most critical of these is the management of public finances. For this reason, the volume explores vulnerabilities on both the expenditure and revenue sides of public finance. Because of the complexities involved, budget management is often plagued with inefficiencies and haunted by many opportunities for corruption. In key sectors, the serious problems often start here, with diversion of budgetary allocations toward activities that have greater potential for kickbacks, bribery, fraud, or theft. But revenue management can also be—and often is—problematic. Many country-focused corruption surveys, such as the World Bank's investment climate surveys, identify tax administration and customs administration agencies as among the most corrupt. Weak tax collection has serious implications for sector performance and corruption. When revenue agencies fail to meet their collections targets, budgets have to be cut mid-year. This typically leads to a shortage of funds needed to pay contractors for projects that have been started, which in turn results in queuing, which both theory and experience suggest gives rise to corruption.

In the context of public financial management, the road map takes the form of a process flow, a heuristic device that helps guide the reader through the flow of money or goods. In procurement, for instance, the process begins with project selection and ends with contract award, with multiple steps in between. In customs, importation starts with the declaration of goods; then moves on to the assessment of origin, value, and classification of goods; to the physical inspection, examination, and release of cargo; and in most cases, to the conduct of postaudit clearances. In both cases, there is a standard step-by-step process, and each step can create opportunities for corruption. The design of anticorruption strategies must therefore consider where risks are highest along the flow and how they might be minimized.

Where there is big money, there must be channels for it to move through. The proceeds of grand corruption, where single transactions involve millions of dollars, must be laundered to be of use. The last chapter in this volume explores the murky world of money laundering and the immense challenges authorities in both the developing and developed worlds face in combating it. It is an appropriate way to end, for grand corruption cannot be addressed effectively unless laundering channels are shut down.

This volume could not have been completed without the cooperation and assistance of numerous individuals throughout the World Bank. Each chapter was coauthored by staff from the relevant sector, with support from their networks or departments, including Infrastructure, Environmentally and Socially Sustainable Development, Human Development, Agriculture and Rural Development, Finance, External Relations, Operations Policy and Country Services, the World Bank Institute, and Poverty Reduction and Economic Management. The volume is a testimony to the ability of the Bank to draw on its deep repository of global experiences and to assemble a team of experts to work collaboratively across its organizational divide.

This effort represents an initial foray into the deeper crevices of corruption. More work will be required to develop better informed, targeted reform measures at the operational level. The Poverty Reduction and Economic Management Network is delighted to have participated in and coordinated the initial leg of this long and challenging journey. I commend both the team and the initiators of this project.

Danny Leipziger
Vice President
Poverty Reduction and Economic Management Network
The World Bank

Preface

Governance and anticorruption are now high priorities in the development agenda. Empirical research over the past decade has shown convincingly that poor governance, typically manifested by different forms of corruption, is a major deterrent to investment and economic growth and has had a disproportionate impact on the poor. In-depth case studies have given form and life to these quantitative findings and have brought home the reality that corruption is indeed harmful to the individual, family, community, and society as a whole. Globally, public awareness of the detrimental impact and severity of the problem has increased markedly, as the media, policy institutes, and nongovernmental organizations worldwide have raised concerns to unprecedented levels.

Despite mounting evidence and increased awareness, governments and the development community more broadly are still struggling to find ways to more effectively translate this understanding into concrete actions and improved outcomes. Much is still unknown and subject to debate. After a decade of experience, we know that tackling corruption is politically complex but that progress can be made when appropriate reforms can be sustained. Reforms at the sector level present an important opportunity in this regard. At the sector level, users of public services meet service providers; this nexus potentially creates potent and persistent pressures for reform. The challenge for reformers is to capture this energy and usefully direct it to address the underlying drivers of corruption in the public and private sectors, domestically and globally.

The Many Faces of Corruption offers an operationally useful framework to help reformers analyze corruption and target reforms at the sector level. Through exploratory applications to several sectors, it shows that combating corruption is fundamentally about improving governance, that operationally useful indicators can be used to track corruption and monitor progress, that the private sector (particularly multinational corporations) and developed-country governments must share equal responsibility with developing-country governments in curbing corruption, and that corruption can be broken down into component parts for which tractable remedial measures can be formulated.

A central theme in this volume is the fundamental role of transparency in the fight against corruption. The aid community has only recently begun aggressively supporting reforms that enhance transparency. *The Many Faces of Corruption* will encourage donors to scale up their assistance and spur policy makers to explore innovative ways to increase transparency in both the public and private sectors. In adopting a value chain approach to sector analysis, this volume opens up many possibilities for enhancing transparency, from international agreements to policy formulation, budget allocations, regulation, procurement, and project implementation.

The Many Faces of Corruption represents only one small step in the long road toward better governance worldwide. The challenge for us today is to continue developing better ways of tackling corruption, building on the growing understanding of the problem and on lessons of experience with reform. With its focus on sectors, this volume charts a potentially promising path for both researchers and practitioners toward meeting this important challenge.

Randi Ryterman
Sector Manager
Public Sector Governance
Poverty Reduction and Economic Management Network
The World Bank

Contributors

J. Edgardo Campos is Governance Adviser for Bangladesh at the World Bank. Before this appointment, he was Lead Public Sector Specialist and Coordinator of the Bank's Governance and Anticorruption Thematic Group. Mr. Campos rejoined the Bank in 2002 after a four-year leave of absence. While on leave, he worked at the Asian Development Bank as a senior economist, providing advice and guidance on governance-related activities and programs. He also spent two years as Senior Strategy Adviser for public sector reforms at the Department of Budget and Management, Government of the Philippines. Before going on leave, Mr. Campos was with the World Bank Institute and the Policy Research Department of the Bank, where he worked on political economy, institutional reform, and governance issues. Before joining the Bank, he was an Assistant Professor of Public Policy and Management at the Wharton School of the University of Pennsylvania. He has coauthored three books and numerous papers on issues pertaining to political economy, governance, and corruption. In 1997, the Governance Committee of the International Political Science Association awarded him and his coauthor the Charles Levine Prize for the best book on comparative politics. He received his M.S. in agricultural and applied economics at the University of Minnesota and his Ph.D. in the social sciences at the California Institute of Technology.

Sanjay Pradhan is Director of the Public Sector Governance Group at the World Bank. He is responsible for leading the Bank's work on improving public sector governance and combating corruption in all member countries. Mr. Pradhan served as the World Bank's Sector Manager, Public Sector and Poverty Reduction, for the South Asia Region. Before that, he was responsible for managing the Bank's unit supporting governance and public sector reform in 26 countries across Central and Eastern Europe and the former Soviet Union. Mr. Pradhan was a principal author of the *World Development Report 1997: The State in a Changing World.* He has authored numerous publications, including articles, books, and policy papers. He received his

B.A. (magna cum laude, Phi Beta Kappa) and Ph.D. in business economics from Harvard University, where he was the recipient of the Prize Fellowship.

Vinay Bhargava is the Director of Operations and International Affairs in the External Affairs Department at the World Bank. His areas of expertise are anticorruption, global issues management, and international development and multilateral institutions. He has more than 25 years' experience designing and implementing development projects and programs in South and East Asia, Western Africa, Eastern Europe, and the Middle East. He received a Ph.D. in agricultural economics from the University of Illinois.

Pinki Chaudhuri is a Senior Infrastructure Specialist consultant with operational experience in the municipal finance, water, and transport sectors at the World Bank. She has worked on institutional and regulatory aspects of infrastructure projects, including several large public-private partnership projects. Ms. Chaudhuri contributed to the World Bank Institute's capacity development knowledge work, including the flagship study, *Capacity Development in Africa* (2005). She has also led economic, sector, and analytical work on infrastructure regulation. Before working for the Bank, she worked as a corporate attorney at Baker and McKenzie. She holds an LL.M. in international finance and a Ph.D. in utility regulation from George Washington University.

Jillian Clare Cohen is an assistant professor at the Leslie Dan Faculty of Pharmacy at the University of Toronto. She is an advisory board member of the Centre for International Health and director of the Comparative Program on Health and Society at the University of Toronto. Her research and teaching focus on drug access issues for the poor, the comparative politics of international pharmaceutical policy, and ethics and corruption in pharmaceutical systems. Before joining the University of Toronto, Ms. Cohen worked on pharmaceutical policy for the United Nations Children's Fund, the World Bank, and the World Health Organization. She has also been a consultant for a myriad of governments, international organizations, and aid agencies on topics such as pharmaceuticals, regulation, corruption, and drug access. She is the author of numerous academic and journal articles on pharmaceutical policy and is a coeditor of *The Power of Pills: Social, Ethical and Legal Issues in Drug Development, Marketing and Pricing Policies* (Pluto Press). She received her B.A. and M.A. in political science from McGill University and her Ph.D. in politics from New York University.

Piers Cross is Principal Regional Team Leader of the World Bank's Water and Sanitation Program in Africa. He has more than 25 years' experience in water and sanitation development. During his 16 years with the Bank, he has served in Africa, South Asia, and as Manager of the Water and Sanitation Program in Washington. In his current position in Nairobi, he supervises a large team of water and sanitation personnel, based in 14 African countries, that assists governments in developing sustained access to water and sanitation services by the poor. An anthropologist by training, he is the author and instigator of many publications on water and sanitation service provision, including an investigation into corruption in South Asia water agencies in 2002. He has also worked on tackling corruption and improving financial efficiency in Africa. He recently helped found the Water Integrity Network (WIN). In recognition of his work, the Water Academy made him a life member in 2003. He holds an M.Sc. in social anthropology from the University of the Witwatersrand (South Africa) and has worked for several years with the London School of Hygiene and Tropical Medicine.

Maria Dakolias is Lead Counsel in the World Bank's Legal Vice Presidency. She has worked on rule of law and good governance for 14 years, managing complex projects, advising on substantive issues, and developing policy for the Bank. She managed and developed the Legal Vice Presidency's rule of law program and built its core team. While working for the British government, she led an independent evaluation of the successes and challenges associated with rule of law and good governance reforms since 1997. Ms. Dakolias has published widely on rule of law and corruption issues. Currently, she is advancing the measurement of impacts of law and justice work and the economic and social benefits that such work brings to countries. She holds a B.A. in philosophy from Haverford College, a J.D. from George Mason University School of Law, and an LL.M from the University of Amsterdam. She was a Fellow on Justice at Harvard's Kennedy School of Government and completed the joint Harvard/Stanford Executive M.B.A. Program.

Richard Damania is a Senior Economist in the Environment and Social Unit in the South Asia Region. He has published more than 50 peer-reviewed articles spanning development economics, environmental economics, institutional economics, and macroeconometrics. His publications cross disciplinary boundaries, with papers in prestigious scientific journals, such as *Science* and the *Proceedings of the Royal Society*. Before joining the Bank, Mr. Damania was a Reader at the University of Adelaide. While working in Australia, he advised numerous international organizations, including the Organisation for Economic Co-operation and Development (OECD), the Food and Agriculture Organization, and United Nations Educational, Scientific, and Cultural Organization, as well as Australian government agencies, including the Treasury and the Departments of Justice, Industry, Environment, Fisheries, and Natural Resources. He holds a Ph.D. from the University of Glasgow.

William Dorotinsky is the Lead Public Expenditure Specialist at the World Bank and the chair of the Bank's Public Finance Thematic Group. Before joining the Bank, he spent 12 years in the U.S. Office of Management and Budget (OMB), addressing general budget management, health care reform and financing issues, and financial and performance management reforms, including implementation of the Government Performance and Results Act. While at OMB, Mr. Dorotinsky was seconded to the District of Columbia during its fiscal crisis, serving as the Deputy Chief Financial Officer. He also spent several years with the U.S. Treasury Office of Technical Assistance as a Public Finance Adviser to the governments of Argentina, Croatia, and

Hungary. He received his B.A. in economics and political science and Master of Public Policy in international trade from the University of Michigan.

Michael Engelschalk headed the World Bank's Tax Policy and Tax Administration Thematic Group from 1999 to 2004. He participated in the preparation and supervision of a large number of World Bank technical assistance operations in the areas of tax and customs reform. Currently on leave from the Bank, he advises the German government on public sector reform programs for transition economies. Before joining the Bank, he was in charge of the cooperation program with nonmember countries in the OECD Centre for Tax Policy and Administration. He organized and participated in training and technical assistance programs to build tax policy and administration capacity in developing countries and transition economies. Mr. Engelschalk began his career as an assistant professor of public and international tax law. He has published extensively on international taxation, fiscal federalism, and tax administration reform. He earned his Ph.D. degree in international tax law from the University of Munich.

Enrique Fanta Ivanovic is a consultant in the Poverty Reduction and Economic Management Department for Latin America at the World Bank. He has done operational work on institution building, tax administration, and public expenditure management in many Latin American countries and advisory work for the Europe and Central Asia Region. He headed Chilean Customs and was Auditing Director of the Internal Revenue Service. He has a degree in industrial civil engineering from the University of Chile.

Carlos Ferreira has provided consulting services on the strategic development of revenue administration since retiring from the World Bank in December 2005. While at the Bank, he coordinated the design and implementation of institutional development projects to reform and modernize the public collection of revenue, primarily under tax, customs, and social security administrations for the Europe and Central Asia Region. He joined the World Bank in 1979, after extensive experience in the public and private sectors in Brazil. Mr. Ferreira holds a bachelor's degree in electronic engineering from the Catholic University of Rio de Janeiro and graduate degrees in computer science and computer engineering from Stanford University. He also holds a graduate degree in management sciences from the Stanford Graduate School of Business, where he was a Sloan Fellow.

Theodore S. Greenberg is a Senior Financial Sector Specialist in the Financial Market Integrity Unit of the World Bank, where he helps design and implement the Bank's global technical assistance and assessment program to combat money laundering and terrorist financing. Mr. Greenberg joined the World Bank in 2003 as Senior Counsel in the Legal Vice Presidency, where he handled anti-money-laundering and terrorist-financing issues. He represents the Bank at the Eurasian Group on Combating Money Laundering and Financing of Terrorism and previously represented the Bank at the international-standards-setting Financial Action Task Force (FATF) and at the Eastern and Southern Africa Anti-Money Laundering Group. Before joining the Bank, he spent 29 years at the U.S. Department of Justice, where he served as Chief of the Money Laundering Section, Acting and Deputy Chief of the Fraud Section, Special Attorney in the Organized Crime Section, Assistant U.S. Attorney, Deputy Chief of the Fraud and Corruption Unit, and Senior Litigation Counsel.

Mohinder Gulati is a Lead Energy Specialist in the Energy and Mining Sector Unit in the East Asia and Pacific Region at the World Bank. He has managed a variety of energy projects at the Bank, promoting sector reforms and restructuring, privatization, regional electricity markets, energy efficiency, financial intermediaries, improvement in sector governance and utility management, and financing of large energy projects. Before joining the Bank, Mr. Gulati worked in the Indian financial sector, in infrastructure financing, investment banking, microfinance, and human resource management. He holds master's degrees in business management, personnel management and industrial relations, and physics from Delhi University.

Loraine Hawkins is the Human Development Coordinator for the World Bank in the Philippines. Before assuming this position, she was Lead Health Specialist in the East Asia and Pacific Human Development Sector Unit of the World Bank and spent six years with the Bank in Eastern Europe and Central Asia. Her work outside the Bank has included secondments to the U.K. Department of Health and the U.K. Treasury to work on financing reform and management of health and social services expenditure. Ms. Hawkins also spent 12 years in the New Zealand civil service, as an economist in the Treasury, as manager of a Health and Disability Services Reform Taskforce, and as manager of the Strategic Policy Directorate in the Ministry of Health. Outside of the public sector, she has worked as a strategic planner for a large service provider for people with learning disabilities. She is a graduate in economics and public policy from the Woodrow Wilson School of Public and International Affairs, Princeton University, and from Otago University (New Zealand).

Ruth Kagia is the Education Sector Director at the World Bank. She previously worked in operations in the Africa and East Asia Regions of the Bank. Before joining the Bank, she spent almost 20 years in the public sector, working on education policy, research, and management in Africa. Ms. Kagia has a long-standing interest in the role of education in socioeconomic transformation and has undertaken a longitudinal study that tracks students from home to school and into the workplace. She is a graduate of Harvard University.

Nalin Kishor is the Coordinator for the World Bank's Forest Law Enforcement and Governance Program in the Sustainable Development Vice Presidency. His research interests focus on the economics of forestry and natural resources, as well as trade, growth and income distribution, incentive compatible systems, and institutional reforms. He is a coauthor of a book on sustainable development, *The Quality of Growth*, published by Oxford University Press in 2001. He holds a Ph.D. in economics from the University of Maryland–College Park, with a specialization in natural resources and environmental economics.

Tuan Minh Le is Senior Public Finance Economist and Coordinator of Tax Policy and Administration at the World Bank. Before joining the Bank, he was with the Public Finance Group at the Harvard Institute for International Development, Harvard University, where he worked on tax policy design, tax administration reforms, revenue forecasting, and appraisal of development expenditures in Asia, Eastern Europe and Central Asia, Africa, and the Middle East. He has lectured for the Tax Analysis and Revenue Forecasting Program and the Program on Investment Appraisal and Management at Harvard University. He was Assistant Professor of Economics at Suffolk University in 2001–02. He holds a Ph.D. in public policy from the Kennedy School of Government, Harvard University.

Michael Levi is Professor of Criminology at Cardiff University and an expert on white-collar and organized crime, corruption, and money laundering. He has served as a member of the Cabinet Office Steering Group on proceeds of crime, as a scientific expert on Organized Crime to the Council of Europe, and as a parliamentary specialist adviser to a review of policing and antisocial behavior in Wales. He recently conducted metareviews of economic crime in Europe for the Council of Europe and of the nature, extent, and cost of fraud in the U.K. Home Office and the Association of Chief Police Officers. He has also examined fraud sentencing for the U.K. Government Fraud Review. He holds B.A. and M.A. degrees from Oxford University, a Dip. Crim. from Cambridge University, and a Ph.D. from Southampton Universities.

Alberto Leyton is a Senior Public Sector Specialist in the Poverty Reduction and Economic Management Department for Latin America at the World Bank. In this capacity, he has led tax administration, financial management, anticorruption, and institutional reform projects in numerous countries in Latin America. Before joining the Bank, Mr. Leyton held management positions at the Ministry of the Presidency and Ministry of Finance of Boliva, leading a comprehensive public sector modernization program that included in-depth reform of the revenue administration service. He holds degrees in sociology, statistics, and mathematics from the Universidad Mayor de San Andres, Bolivia.

Stephen MacSearraigh is a Director of Mina Corp, a private trade and finance company that pursues early-stage investment opportunities in postcrisis markets with offices in London, Kabul, Moscow, Khartoum, Rumbek, Bishkek, and Geneva. Mr. MacSearraigh has more than 15 years' experience in oil market intelligence and the geopolitics of oil. He was a Managing Director for Content and Partnerships of OILspace (London), Director of Research of Energy Intelligence Group (Washington), and Editor for Energy Compass (London). He attended the School of Communication Arts in London (U.K.) from 1987–88 and holds a B.S. in microbiology and biochemistry from the University of Cape Town, South Africa.

William Mayville provides consulting services in the areas of human capital development, strategic planning, and change management for revenue administrations. He has worked for the World Bank as a short- and long-term consultant since 1984.

Since 1990, he has worked on tax and customs reforms in Central and South America, Europe and Central Asia, the Middle East, and South Asia. Before joining the Bank, Mr. Mayville worked for management consulting firms and in higher education, as Research Associate, Adjunct Professor, and Administrator. He holds an M.A. in English literature from the American University and a Ph.D. in higher education administration and sociology from George Washington University.

Charles McPherson has recently joined the International Monetary Fund's Fiscal Affairs Department. His contribution to this book was made while he was Senior Adviser on Oil and Gas at the World Bank. His work at the Bank focused on petroleum sector reform and sector lending activities in Angola, Argentina, Nigeria, the Russian Federation, and elsewhere. Before joining the Bank, Mr. McPherson spent 15 years at two international oil companies, holding a variety of senior positions in international negotiations and government agreements. He received his B.A. in economics and political science from McGill University, M.Sc. in international economics from the London School of Economics and Political Science, and Ph.D. in economics from the University of Chicago.

Shaun Moss is the Regional Procurement Manager for the East Asia and Pacific Region of the World Bank and a procurement specialist with more than 20 years' experience in both the public and private sectors. He spent six years working in the Europe and Central Asia Region, where he led the Bank's work on public procurement reform in several countries, including the Russian Federation and Turkey. Before joining the Bank in 1999, Mr. Moss was a director of a leading U.K. consulting firm specializing in procurement. He holds a bachelor's degree in modern languages from Reading University, a postgraduate diploma in management from Kingston University, and a master's degree in marketing management from the University of Westminster.

Monique F. Mrazek is a Health Economist in the Latin America and the Caribbean Region of the World Bank. Since joining the Bank Group in 2003, she has worked in the Europe and Central Asia Region and at the International Finance Corporation. Ms. Mrazek has been involved in both public and private sector lending, as well as advisory work in the health care and pharmaceutical sectors. Before joining the Bank Group, she worked for the World Health Organization/European Observatory on Health Care Systems and the London School of Economics and Political Science. Ms. Mrazek has authored a number of peer-reviewed articles and book chapters on pharmaceutical policy. She is the coeditor of *Regulating Pharmaceuticals in Europe: Striving for Efficiency, Equity and Quality*, published by the Open University Press in 2004. She holds an M.Sc. in health economics from the University of York and a Ph.D. from the London School of Economics and Political Science.

Gregory P. Noone is a member of the Public International Law and Policy Group (PILPG), a nonprofit organization that provides free legal assistance to developing states and substate entities involved in conflicts. He also teaches international law and politics at West Virginia University and is an Adjunct Professor of Law at Roger Williams University School of Law and Case Western Reserve University School of Law. He has trained members of the Iraqi National Congress, the postgenocide government in Rwanda, the post-Taliban government in Afghanistan, civil society members in Sudan, and senior members of the Russian government. Mr. Noone appears regularly as a commentator on international and national television and radio. He received a B.A. in political science from Villanova University, an M.A. in international affairs from the Catholic University of America, and a J.D. from Suffolk University Law School.

William D. O. Paterson is Lead Infrastructure Specialist in the Transport Sector of the World Bank's East Asia and Pacific Region. He has extensive operational experience, primarily in the road sector but also in other transport subsectors and the water sector. Mr. Paterson has managed and led project operations, sector dialogue, disaster risk management, and analytical work in infrastructure in all Bank regions. In recent years, he has focused on the institutional aspects of infrastructure service delivery, including capacity development, governance, and business process modernization of public sector entities. He holds a Ph.D. in highway engineering from University of Canterbury (New Zealand).

Harry Anthony Patrinos is Lead Education Economist and the Economics of Education Cluster Leader at the World Bank. He has managed education lending operations and analytical work programs in Argentina, Colombia, and Mexico, as well as a regional research project on the socioeconomic status of Latin America's indigenous peoples, *Indigenous Peoples, Poverty and Human Development in Latin America* (Palgrave Macmillan 2006). He has published more than 40 journal articles and is one of the main authors of *Lifelong Learning in the Global Knowledge Economy* (World Bank 2003). Mr. Patrinos coauthored *Policy Analysis of Child Labor: A Comparative Study* (St. Martin's Press 1999), *Decentralization of Education: Demand-Side Financing* (World Bank 1997), and *Indigenous People and Poverty in Latin America: An Empirical Analysis* (World Bank/Ashgate 1994). He received a Ph.D. in economic development from the Institute of Development Studies, University of Sussex.

Janelle Plummer is a governance consultant working with the World Bank with operational experience in the water sector in Asia and Africa. An Associate Professional Officer with the U.K. Department for International Development (DFID) and later a Senior Specialist with the Water and Sanitation Program, her work has focused primarily on local governance, poverty reduction, and basic service delivery. She is author of numerous policy and capacity-building publications focused on development-oriented interactions among local government, the private sector, and civil society, and has authored papers on demand-side accountability, making anticorruption strategies pro-poor, and establishing anticorruption approaches in post-tsunami reconstruction. She is a founding member of the Water Integrity Network. Janelle holds undergraduate degrees from the University of New South Wales and a postgraduate degree majoring in law and development from the School of Oriental and African Studies (SOAS) at the University of London.

Shilpa Pradhan is a consultant with the World Bank Group specializing in public financial management and governance. Her operational and analytical work experience at the Bank includes contributions to public finance and public administration reforms in East Asia, South Asia, and Africa. Before joining the Bank, Ms. Pradhan was an Associate Director at the U.S. Chamber of Commerce, managing a bilateral U.S.-Singapore business development program. She also spent several years as a consultant in the private sector, working primarily in the technology and financial sectors in India, Australia, and the United States. She holds an M.B.A. from the Queensland University of Technology and an M.A. in social sciences from the University of Chicago.

M. Y. Rao has served as a member of the Indian Administrative Service, at various times as Director of Industries, Chairman of the Paradeep Port Trust, Vice Chancellor of Berhampur University, Chairman of the Orissa State Electricity Board, and Chairman and Managing Director of the Grid Corporation of Orissa Ltd. (Gridco). He has extensive experience in the electrical power sector. Since 1997, he has been a nonexecutive director of Gridco and the Orissa Power Transmission Corporation and an adviser to PricewaterhouseCoopers. He has also represented Gridco on the boards of the privatized distribution companies. In addition to his close and continued involvement in electricity reforms in Orissa, he has advised governments, electricity regulatory commissions, and utilities in Andhra Pradesh, Rajasthan, Karnataka, Assam, and Uttar Pradesh on reform matters. He was also a member of a World Bank mission that advised the government of Bangladesh on power reforms. He has a Master's degree from Kerala University.

Francesca Recanatini is Senior Economist with the Global Program Team at the World Bank Institute, where she coordinates the Governance and Anti-Corruption Diagnostic Capacity-Building Initiative in Latin America and Africa. She also serves as a technical advisor in selected governance and public sector operational projects and learning activities for policy makers and practitioners. Ms. Recanatini joined the World Bank in 1998, working in the Research Department and the Eastern Europe and Central Asia Region before joining the World Bank Institute. Before joining the Bank, she worked at the Center of Institutional Reforms and the Informal Sector, where she worked on economic restructuring and legal reforms in Central Asia. She received her Ph.D. in economics from the University of Maryland–College Park.

Glenn T. Ware is Chief Investigative Counselor with the World Bank's Department of Institutional Integrity, where he supervises fraud and corruption investigations. Before joining the Bank, he served as Managing Director of Diligence, a global risk management and consulting firm. Mr. Ware has published many scholarly articles on anticorruption and global governance. He holds a law degree from Harvard Law School.

Juan Carlos Zuleta provides consulting services on institutional development of strategic public agencies. He coordinated the design and implementation of a comprehensive organizational restructuring of the National Tax Service, customs, and the national road service in Bolivia. Before joining the Institutional Reform Project, Mr. Zuleta worked as Public Sector Management Specialist at the office of the World Bank in La Paz. A former Fulbright scholar, he holds an M.S. in agricultural and applied economics from the University of Minnesota and is pursuing a Ph.D. in economics from the New School for Social Research.

Acknowledgments

This volume could not have been written without the tireless efforts and generous support of numerous individuals. We were blessed with a highly motivated, hardworking band of coauthors who willingly took on the task of blazing a new trail through relatively uncharted territory. To Vinay Bhargava, Pinki Chaudhuri, Jillian Clare Cohen, Piers Cross, Maria Dakolias, Richard Damania, William Dorotinsky, Michael Engelschalk, Enrique Fanta Ivanovic, Carlos Ferreira, Theodore S. Greenberg, Mohinder Gulati, Loraine Hawkins, Ruth Kagia, Nalin Kishor, Tuan Minh Le, Michael Levi, Alberto Leyton, Stephen MacSearraigh, William Mayville, Charles McPherson, Shaun Moss, Monique F. Mrazek, Gregory P. Noone, Willam D. O. Paterson, Harry Anthony Patrinos, Janelle Plummer, Shilpa Pradhan, M. Y. Rao, Francesca Recanatini, Glenn T. Ware, and Juan Carlos Zuleta, it has been a great pleasure to have worked with you through all the many reviews, frustrations, joys, and long days and weekends spent in bringing this manuscript to print.

Many colleagues in the World Bank and the international development community gave precious time and effort to provide advice and guidance on various drafts. Much is owed to Randi Ryterman for her consistent encouragement and unequivocal support for this whole enterprise, to Erika Jorgensen for vetting various versions of many of the chapter drafts and her invaluable assistance on the seminar series, and to Juanita Olaya and Vito Tanzi for taking time off their schedules to participate in the roundtable discussions. Special thanks go to Charles Adwan, Anders Agerskov, James Anderson, Mario Arduz, Clive Armstrong, Felipe Barrera, Robert Beschel, Benjamin Billa, Parminder Brar, Allison Brigati, Camille Bryan, Steve Burgess, Patricio Castro, Nazmul Chaudhury, John Davidson, Luc de Wulf, Phyllis Dininio, Poul Engberg-Pedersen, Laura Esmail, Samina Esseje, Antonio Estache, Tazeen Fasih, Armin Fidler, Gita Gopal, Veronica Grigera, Jonathan Halpern, April Harding, John Howell, Imogene Jensen, Marc Juhel, Kapil Kapoor, Charles Kenny, Elizabeth M. King, Sahr Kpundeh, Sarwar Lateef, Heather Marie Layton, Knut Leipold, Katerina Leris, Maureen Lewis, William B. Magrath, Samuel Munzele

Maimbo, Saida Mamedova, Muthukumara Mani, Gerard McLinden, William McCartnen, Latifah Osman Merican, Rick Messick, Juan Manuel Moreno, Ronald Myers, Vicente Paqueo, Michael Pe, Robert Prouty, Juliet Pumpuni, Cesar Queiroz, G. P. Rao, Binyam Reja, Mike Richards, Halsey Rogers, Jamil Saghir, Harvey Salgo, Derek Schaffner, Julian Schweitzer, Richard Scobey, Andreas Seiter, Richard Stern, Helen Sutch, Bernard Tenenbaum, Seth Terkper, William Tupman, Joel Turkewitz, Wilhelm Van Egen, Rob Varley, Jonathan Walters, Donald Wong, and to numerous network colleagues from Infrastructure, Environmentally and Socially Sustainable Development, Human Development, Agriculture and Rural Development, Financial Sector, Procurement and Financial Management, and Poverty Reduction and Economic Management for their valuable comments and inputs that undoubtedly shaped the final contours of this volume.

In most endeavors of this kind, there are always unsung heroes. This manuscript stands on the shoulders of Maks Kobonbaev, who took time off from his doctoral dissertation to serve as the "master sergeant" for this enterprise, and a strong supporting cast consisting of Nisha Narayanan, Colum Garrity, Rebecca Hife, and Max Jira Ponglumjeak, without whom many things would have fallen through the cracks. Special thanks go to Stephen McGroarty, Dana Vorisek, and Martha Gottron for making the process of editing and publishing this manuscript enjoyable and exciting.

We are especially grateful to Transparency International–Berlin, in particular, Huguette Labelle, David Nussbaum, Juanita Olaya, Angela Keller-Herzog, and Katie Taft, for their support in the preparation, launch, and dissemination of this volume.

Finally, we would like to extend our deep appreciation to the Dutch Government through the Bank-Netherlands Partnership Program (BNPP) for providing the financial support for this project, to our colleagues Kai Kaiser and Doris Voorbraak for their patience and efforts in managing the governance component of the BNPP, and, most especially, to our network head, Danny Leipziger, and our constant collaborator, Dani Kaufmann, for their continued support for our work on governance and, most especially, for the publication of this volume.

To everyone, muchos gracias, merci beaucoup, dank u zeer, grazie molto, vielen dank, большое спасибо, thank you very much.

J. Edgardo Campos
Sanjay Pradhan

Abbreviations

ADB	Asian Development Bank
AIDS	acquired immune deficiency syndrome
AML	anti-money laundering
AML/CFT	anti-money laundering/combating the financing of terrorism
Cal-ISO	The California Independent System Operator
CalPX	California Power Exchange
CCSS	Caja Costarricense de Seguro Social (Costa Rica)
CEFIR	Centre for Economic and Financial Research
COC	chain of custody
CPI	Corruption Perception Index (Transparency International)
CSO	civil society organization
CVA	corruption vulnerability assessment
DFID	U.K. Department for International Development
DENR	Department of Environment and Natural Resources (the Philippines)
EDL	essential drug list
EITI	Extractive Industries Transparency Initiative
EMEA	European Medicines Evaluation Agency
EMIS	Education Management Information System
EPC	electronic product code
EU	European Union
FAO	Food and Agriculture Organization
FATF	Financial Action Task Force
FCMR	Forest Crime Monitoring and Reporting Unit (Cambodia)
FDA	U.S. Food and Drug Administration
FIU	financial intelligence unit
FLEG	Forest Law Enforcement and Governance
FLEGT	Forest Law Enforcement, Governance and Trade Action Plan
GDP	gross domestic product

GMP	good manufacturing practice
HIPCs	heavily indebted poor countries
HIV	human immunodeficiency virus
ICT	information and communications technologies
IFMIS	integrated financial management information system
IFPMA	International Federation of Pharmaceutical Manufacturers
IMF	International Monetary Fund
IOC	international oil company
IPP	independent power producer
IRP	Institutional Reform Project (Bolivia)
KDP	Kecamatan Development Program (Indonesia)
KPCS	Kimberley Process Certification Scheme
MDGs	Millennium Development Goals
MFPC	Multisectoral Forest Protection Committees (the Philippines)
MIS	management information system
MOU	memorandum of understanding
NAFDAC	National Agency for Food and Drug Administration and Control (Nigeria)
NCCTs	non-cooperative countries and territories
NGO	nongovernmental organization
NIP	National Integrity Plan (Bolivia)
NNPC	Nigerian National Petroleum Corporation
NOC	national oil company
NSWG	National Stakeholders Working Group
NTS	National Tax Service (Bolivia)
NWSC	Nairobi Water and Sewerage Company
OECD	Organisation for Economic Co-operation and Development
OPEC	Organization of the Petroleum Exporting Countries
PAC	parliamentary (or public) accounts committee
PBS	Palli Bidyut Samitis (independent electricity users' associations; Bangladesh)
PEFA	public expenditure and financial accountability
PEP	politically exposed persons
PFM	public financial management
PMO/PIU	project management office/project implementation unit
PPA	power purchase agreement
PSI	Pharmaceutical Security Institute
PWI	Procurement Watch Inc.
REB	Rural Electricity Board (Bangladesh)
RFID	radio frequency identification
SAFCO	Financial Management and Control Law (Bolivia)
SAI	supreme audit institution
SARA	semiautonomous revenue agencies
SEB	state electricity board
SFBC	Swiss Federal Banking Commission

SGS	Société Générale de Surveillance
SNPC	Société Nationale des Pétroles du Congo (Republic of Congo)
STS	sworn tax statement
T&D	transmission and distribution
TI	Transparency International
UN	United Nations
UNCAC	United Nations Convention against Corruption
UNDP	United Nations Development Programme
USAID	U.S. Agency for International Development
VAT	value added tax
WCO	World Customs Organization
WHO	World Health Organization
WSS	water supply and sanitation

Introduction
Tackling a Social Pandemic

J. EDGARDO CAMPOS AND VINAY BHARGAVA

"Corruption has a long history, but research and analysis about its causes and effects has erupted over recent years. This overview headlines the key lessons that emerge from the current state of research. It describes the landscape which that research has mapped, and illustrates how the detailed topography and diagnostics, both current and potential, gives us a basis for anticipating that the fight against corruption can be more effective in the future."

David Nussbaum,
Chief Executive, Transparency International

Electricity has finally come to Sanjiv's town, a small municipality 100 miles from the nation's capital. Today he awaits the arrival of a meter man who has finally agreed to install a connection from the main distribution line to his small but respectable house on the outskirts of town. Sanjiv has saved for almost a year to obtain this service, which will cost him one month's salary. Like thousands of his fellow citizens, he has had to pay "speed money" to get connected. Otherwise, he would have to wait another 10 years.

Not far from Sanjiv's town, a single mother, Jasinta, with four children proudly walks up to the school where her eldest daughter is to receive promotion to third grade. As she walks into the classroom, she sees other parents paying a "pen" fee to the teacher. She is told this fee is "voluntary" but has to be paid before the report is handed over—and before her daughter can proceed to the next grade. Jasinta waits until last. She has already taken out a high-interest loan to put her daughter in school and pay for overpriced uniforms and books. She does not have another day's wages to pay an unforeseen bill on the last day of the term. Her children will not eat. She argues with the teacher eventually, trying to negotiate the "fee" down. Unsuccessful, she goes to see the principal. The principal smiles at her and encourages her to simply pay, saying that it is the teacher's prerogative to ask for some payment. With no money in her wallet, Jasinta goes back to the bus dejected, wondering whom she can borrow money from to get her daughter's report card and promotion to the next grade.

In another part of the world, Carlos is meeting with four other contractors from his province. Today they are drawing lots to see who will be the "winning bidder" for a government contract to build a 10-kilometer road. If he wins, he will have to compensate the others for their bidding fees as well as give them a small share of the proceeds. He will also have to negotiate with the district official from the ministry of works on the amount of overpricing that is feasible—enough to cover the official's share, which runs to about 15 percent of the value of the contract and typically moves up the chain of command, as well as his fellow contractors' expenses and shares. As far as he can remember, collusion has been the norm in his province.

In another country thousands of miles from Carlos's province, the husband of the president is having dinner in a private room of a five-star hotel with the local representative of a large multinational engineering firm to discuss the "entry fee" for a lucrative $300 million contract to build, operate, and eventually transfer the country's new international airport. Four other multinationals are vying for this megacontract; each must ante up just to prequalify. When decision time comes, whoever wins will sit down again with the first gentleman to negotiate the arrangements needed to make the venture financially profitable for both parties. The president is up for reelection in two years and much is needed for the campaign kitty. This contract is one of several that the administration has targeted for "fund raising."

Corruption has long plagued organized societies. From ancient China to modern-day Europe and North America, governments and societies have struggled to contain this cancer. Thousands of years of literature document the presence of corruption.

> This is the "decree" or "mandate" of heaven. If the emperor or king, having fallen into selfishness and corruption, fails to see to the welfare of the people, heaven withdraws its mandate and invests it in another. The only way to know that the mandate has passed is the overthrow of the king or emperor; if usurpation succeeds, then the mandate has passed to another, but if it fails, then the mandate still resides with the king.
>
> —*The Chou,* 1050–256 BC, China

> The King shall protect trade routes from harassment by courtiers, state officials, thieves and frontier guards . . . [and] frontier officers shall make good what is lost. . . . Just as it is impossible not to taste honey or poison that one may find at the tip of one's tongue, so it is impossible for one dealing with government funds not to taste, at least a little bit, of the King's wealth.
>
> —*The Arthashastra,* Kautilya, chief minister to the king in India, circa 300 BC–AD 150

> In a state where corruption abounds, laws must be very numerous.
>
> —Publius Cornelius Tacitus, Roman historian, circa AD 56–177

> Corruption is worse than prostitution. The latter might endanger the morals of an individual, the former invariably endangers the morals of the entire country.
>
> —Karl Kraus, Austrian satirist, 1874–1936

Today corruption arguably has become the most challenging obstacle to economic development. The 1990s witnessed its emergence as a major development issue whose impact on investment, growth, and poverty reduction could no longer be ignored or rationalized. The quantum explosion of quantitative methods and research made it possible to address the problem more frontally. Indeed, much of the effort put into public sector reforms during the past 15 years has been aimed in part at reducing corruption.

BACKGROUND AND RATIONALE FOR THIS BOOK

Scholarly research into the causes and consequences of (public sector) corruption goes back several decades.[1] Scott's (1972) seminal treatise on political corruption, for instance, dealt with the various faces of corruption as it is known today: bureaucratic corruption, nepotism and patronage, and state capture.[2] Bureaucratic or administrative corruption refers to the "intentional imposition of distortions in the prescribed implementation of existing laws, rules, and regulations to provide advantages to individuals in and/or outside government through illicit, nontransparent means" (World Bank 2000, p. xvii). Bribes to tax collectors to "reduce" one's tax liabilities are a classic example.

Patronage and its close cousin nepotism refer to favoritism shown to narrowly targeted interests by those in power in return for political support. The granting of personal favors, awarding "sole-source" contracts, or making (unmerited) appointments to public office are examples.

State capture refers to the "actions of individuals, groups, or firms both in the public and private sectors to influence the formation of laws, regulations, decrees, and other government policies to their own advantage" (World Bank 2000, p. xv). The granting of a monopoly franchise to the highest bidder and the consequent protection of the beneficiary firm from competition is a typical example of this more subtle, and possibly most venal, form of corruption.

The earlier scholarly work on corruption, while extensive and illuminating, was weak on measurement and quantification.[3] The early 1990s witnessed the emergence of cross-country, perception-based assessments of country governance and corruption driven primarily by the interest of multinational firms in expanding or investing in emerging markets.[4] The Transparency International Corruption Perception Index, the best known and most referenced corruption index to date, began its annual surveys in 1995.

By the late 1990s, the World Bank Institute had developed a more comprehensive data set covering broader governance concerns. This data set covers six dimensions of governance—control of corruption, rule of law, government effectiveness, regulatory quality, voice and accountability, and political stability and the absence of violence—that provide a better picture of the overall state of governance in a country. They are derived from "several hundred individual variables measuring perceptions of governance, drawn from 37 separate data sources constructed by 31 different organizations" (Kaufmann, Kraay, and Mastruzzi 2005, p. 1).[5]

With the aid of these data sets, researchers have achieved major strides in quantifying the macro impact of corruption. Macro-level econometric-based studies have been able to establish a strong causal link between corruption and, more broadly, poor governance on the one hand and weak private investment and growth on the other (Mauro 1995; Knack and Keefer 1995; Wei 2000; World Bank 1997; Kaufmann, Kraay, and Zoido-Lobaton 1999; Rodrik and Subramanian 2003).[6] As Mauro

(1995, p. 695) estimates, "a one standard deviation increase (improvement) in the corruption index is associated with an increase in the investment rate by 2.9 percent of GDP."

More recent empirical studies have also shown that corruption distorts the allocation of resources by diverting budgetary funds toward activities where bribes and illegal commissions can be more easily made—from recurrent expenditures to capital investments, for example (Tanzi and Davoodi 2002; Mauro 1998). In many cases, the diversions impose the greatest burden on the poor (Gupta, Davoodi, and Alonso-Terme 2002; Gyimah-Brempong 2002).

These econometric findings have both heightened the awareness of policy makers, donors, the business community, and the general public of the undesirable consequences of corruption and highlighted the urgency of addressing its root causes. They have also provided the much needed impetus for policy makers to take the problem much more seriously.

The challenge today, however, lies in developing operationally effective measures for dealing with this disease. Quantitative research has not been able to provide sufficient guidance, because of the "bluntness" of perception-based indicators. As Johnston (2001, p. 163) aptly summarizes:

> Perhaps the most serious drawback of the CPI [Corruption Perception Index] and similar indices is what might be called the "single-number problem." It is a precision issue, but one with validity and reliability implications as well. Actual corruption varies in many ways: there are many forms and contrasts within most societies. No single national score can accurately reflect contrasts in the types of corruption found in a country. [7]

The implication is thus that the different shapes and forms of corruption may require correspondingly different indicators or even sets of indicators. Such indicators will be more useful in informing the formulation of area-specific remedial measures and hence will be operationally more relevant.

The early research was reasonably strong in identifying strategies for containing the spread of and eventually reducing corruption. This research essentially pointed to four general characteristics that tend to create opportunities for and increase the possibility of corruption: monopoly power, wide discretion, the lack of transparency in decision making, and the lack of accountability for decisions. The seminal works of Rose-Ackerman (1978) and Klitgaard (1988) were perhaps the first to identify these characteristics in a systematic way and were instrumental in providing policy makers with some guidance in formulating concrete and useful strategies for combating corruption, particularly administrative corruption. They were also the first to introduce a rational choice approach for understanding the motives for corruption: if the expected benefits of a corrupt transaction exceed its expected costs, an individual has an incentive to engage in this transaction.

Wade's classic work (1985) on the market for public office was the first to outline clearly the mechanics of patronage pertaining to appointments and promotions within the bureaucracy. His analysis starkly illustrated the importance of transparency and accountability in the public sector and the ill effects of discretion and monopoly control over appointments and consequently on the incentives of bureaucrats.[8]

On state capture, the rich literature on rent seeking, starting with the seminal pieces by Kreuger (1974) and Tullock (1971) and the related work by Bhagwati (1982) on directly unproductive profit-seeking activities, highlighted the centrality of government's monopoly power and discretion over laws, regulations, and policies in engendering rent-seeking behavior among narrow interests.[9] This work was instrumental in creating the strong push in the 1980s for deregulation and privatization as a means to curtail state power (and thus capture).[10] But because of its broad focus and the absence at the time of relevant empirical data, this research failed to recognize the importance of transparency and accountability in inhibiting state capture.[11]

The early research had a deep appreciation for the importance of understanding the complexity of corruption and addressing its roots. But it lacked the empirical base upon which practical measures for combating the disease could be anchored. Which areas are most prone to corruption? Given limited resources, which problem areas should a country focus on? What are the drivers of corruption in a high-priority problem area, and which ones, if addressed, could have the largest impact? These are some of the fundamental questions on which policy makers and practitioners today seek guidance.

To be sure, empirical research has made progress in this direction. Four new methodologies—investment climate surveys, report card surveys, "triangulated" governance diagnostics, and Public Expenditure Tracking Surveys—are proving useful to policy makers.[12] An investment climate survey, an instrument recently developed by the World Bank, identifies the major bottlenecks and constraints to the development of the private sector in a particular country.[13] The results are based on actual experience of survey respondents—typically a random combination of large, medium, and small enterprises and answers to a subset of questions that focuses on the extent of corruption in specific sectors or areas. Investment climate surveys have been useful in identifying the areas or sectors in a country that are most prone to and affected by corruption, at least in the context of private sector development. They help direct policy makers to areas where corruption most affects investment decisions and business activity.

A variant of an investment climate survey is the Business Environment and Enterprise Performance Survey (BEEPS), developed jointly by the European Bank for Reconstruction and Development and the World Bank.[14] The BEEPS surveys managers and owners of more than 20,000 firms across Central and Eastern Europe, the former Soviet Union, and Turkey. It is designed to examine the quality of the business environment, as determined by a wide range of interactions between firms and the state in various areas, including problems of doing business, unofficial payments and corruption, crime, regulations and red tape, customs and taxes, labor issues, firm financing, and legal and judicial issues. Three rounds of the survey have been carried out—in 1999, 2002, and 2005—providing measurement-based evaluations of progress made by countries in combating some of the pernicious effects of corruption on business activity.[15]

A report card survey is similar to an investment climate survey, but it focuses on public services and its respondents are citizens.[16] It is typically applied at a city, provincial, or state level. Report cards aggregate ratings of different aspects of service quality by a random sample of users of public services. The survey solicits information on availability of service, usage, satisfaction, service standards, major problems with service, effectiveness of grievance redress systems, corruption encountered, and other hidden costs citizens experience because of poor service. In many developing countries, the government is a monopoly provider of services. As theory and case study research has shown, this typically gives rise to corruption. Market competition tends by its very nature to constrain corruption. The report card survey was designed to simulate competition by giving citizens the ability to "grade" public services, giving them effective voice.

Both investment climate and report card surveys derive their findings from a specific class of respondents: firms for the investment climate survey, citizens for the report card survey. Like these surveys, triangulated governance diagnostics cover intersectoral governance issues. This tool differs from the other two, however, in that it targets three sets of respondents: firms, citizens, and public officials. "To provide a consistent and objective institutional map, a governance diagnostic should target more than one type of respondent and possibly triangulate, that is, use at least three types of surveys" (Kaufmann, Recanatini, and Biletsky 2002, p. 5). The World Bank Institute has conducted several triangulated surveys in Africa and Latin America.

Drilling down to the sector level, the Public Expenditure Tracking Surveys have been perhaps the most useful diagnostic instrument developed to date for evaluating the extent of corruption. First applied and tested in the education sector in Uganda, these surveys have now been conducted in other countries in Africa and Latin America.[17] Unlike investment climate or report card surveys, which are respondent based, Public Expenditure Tracking Surveys use actual expenditure data for a specific sector to estimate the extent to which funds for service providers that are determined and allocated at the central level during budget formulation actually reach those providers during budget execution. The estimates are based on objective measurements—actual expenditure data—and provide quantitative evidence on the extent of leakage of funds as they pass from the center to the final provider. These estimates provide an upper bound on the actual level of corruption in a sector or subsector. Repeated applications of this diagnostic over time can provide quantitative evidence of the impact of remedial measures on the extent of corruption.[18]

These diagnostic instruments have undoubtedly pushed the envelope to a level where policy makers can make useful judgments about relative priorities across sectors and other corruption-prone areas and broadly assess the potential impact over time of reform measures. However, they fall short of providing a detailed road map of corruption in a specific problem area, such as the sector or subsector level: they do not identify the specific vulnerabilities in the sector, suggest when and where they might occur, or indicate which problems reforms should target to have greatest impact. This is the information that policy makers need before they can craft area-specific, operationally tractable remedial measures, which in practice are what is needed to reduce corruption.

For example, to effectively address corruption in customs administration, it is necessary to understand the detailed steps an importer must go through to bring goods into the country—the "process flow" of imported goods. This process may vary with the type of commodity imported. It is one thing to conduct surveys of firms and ask them how much they have to pay in bribes to get their goods through customs, how long it takes them to complete the importation process, and so forth. It is much more challenging to inquire how bribery might be reduced and importation sped up. Doing so requires a road map of the process flow, from which indicators can be developed to warn of the relative risks of corruption at different points in the process.

OBJECTIVE OF THE VOLUME

Public opinion research shows that corruption is among the top concerns of people and leaders around the world, and it is now part of all national and international development dialogues (Tanzi 1998; Pew Research Center 2002; World Bank 2003; Transparency International 2005). Empirical research has raised public awareness worldwide of the detrimental impact of corruption on socioeconomic development. The challenge today is to develop operationally effective responses to this disease.

This volume hopes to contribute to this effort by providing prototype road maps for tracking and addressing corruption vulnerabilities in several key sectors and in core areas of public financial management. It draws part of its inspiration from the recent work of Spector (2005), which takes a sectoral cut at analyzing problems of corruption, identifies key vulnerabilities in each sector, and recommends corresponding strategies to address these vulnerabilities.[19] It takes this work forward by anchoring the analysis in an operationally useful framework that policy makers and other practitioners can adapt to different country contexts and that lends itself more naturally to measurement, monitoring, and evaluation.[20]

This volume does not pretend to provide definitive road maps or indicator sets. Rather, it humbly attempts to open the door to a promising area of inquiry that can potentially link operational concerns with theoretical and empirical work on corruption, and, in the process, motivate scholars and practitioners alike to develop more refined and informative maps and indicators.

As the reader will note, the chapters in this volume vary in the depth with which they are able to specify a road map and identify early warning indicators, partly because some areas (such as public procurement) lend themselves more easily to this approach and partly because some areas (such as the health sector and pharmaceutical industry) have had a head start. Regardless of their depth, all of the volume's chapters reflect the fact that this line of inquiry is still very much in its infancy but nevertheless holds the promise of providing the much needed link between theory, empirical evidence, and practice.

Tracking Vulnerabilities

The volume takes the perspective of a project manager who must build practical anticorruption measures into the design of a program.[21] To do so, he or she needs a good understanding of the corruption risks that might arise at various points in the program cycle—a detailed road map from beginning to end, showing indicators along the way that warn of possible problems. Two examples illuminate this perspective:

public procurement, a core public sector function highly susceptible to corruption; and the delivery of essential drugs in the health sector.

Procurement can be characterized as a process flow, starting with procurement planning and proceeding in sequence to product design, advertising and invitation to bid, bid document preparation, prequalification, bid evaluation (broken down into technical and financial evaluation), postqualification, and contract award.[22] Similarly, the delivery of essential drugs goes through a value chain beginning with the manufacturing of the drugs and proceeding through several key decision points: drug registration, drug selection, procurement, distribution, and dispensation or prescription. Each link in the chain or process flow is potentially vulnerable to corruption of some form or another. For example, in procurement, prequalification requirements can be rigged to favor a small number of potential bidders. In the distribution of drugs, cheap, substandard alternatives could be substituted for procured good-quality drugs, with the good-quality drugs withdrawn from government warehouses and sold by unscrupulous government officials in private markets for a profit. In building anticorruption measures into a program, a project manager would be greatly aided by a road map—either a process flow or a value chain—with useful warning signals along the way.

A road-map approach offers several advantages. First, it orients policy makers toward results that a sector or a core process is supposed to achieve. For example, the delivery of essential drugs to the poor, including those in remote rural areas, is a key deliverable of the health sector. The value chain discussed in chapter 1 forces the policy maker to think in terms of this output: what links in the chain impede the delivery of essential drugs? In budgeting, a clear, detailed process flow from preformulation to formulation to execution encourages reform-minded officials to focus on the effectiveness of the system in delivering funds to their intended uses.

Second, a road map provides a more structured and detailed picture of a problem area and the potential points of vulnerabilities specific to that area. It can shed light on the nature of corruption and how one type of corruption might be linked to another that occurs earlier or later in the chain. In the transport-roads sector, for example, the capture of resource allocations by vested interests (typically influential politicians) during budget formulation can underpin bid rigging during the procurement stage (when the budget is executed), which in turn can trigger "change orders" during contract implementation.

Third, the approach helps point to key vulnerabilities and thus to remedial measures that could have the greatest impact on combating corruption in a problem area. In the forestry sector, for instance, suprahigh rents (and large-scale corruption) are reaped during the stage when illegal lumber is "transformed" into legal products, such as furniture. Any serious attempt to address corruption in the sector would have to focus on this link in the chain.

Finally, in the context of program implementation, a road map offers a convenient vehicle for developing measurable indicators, or warning signals, for tracking the incidence of corruption throughout the program cycle, thus enabling program authorities to take early action anywhere along the cycle where the indicators suggest corruption may have occurred. In procurement, for example, the systematic dropping out of bidders from the initial expression of intent through the financial evaluation of bids can signal some form of collusion among participating firms. This may, of course, be just a natural process, but, like the flashing lights on a car's dashboard, it signals that something may be wrong and should be looked at as soon as possible.

Defining Corruption

Corruption, as the term is used in this volume, refers to the use of public office for private gain. It can take on a multitude of faces; its scale can be grand or petty. To make the analysis tractable, this volume classifies corruption into three broad types: state capture, patronage and nepotism, and administrative corruption, as defined earlier.[23] A road map offers a parsimonious organizing framework for identifying and tracking vulnerabilities corresponding to this typology.

State capture is often equated with grand corruption or political corruption. While these forms of corruption overlap significantly, they are not equivalent. Patronage is politically motivated, and administrative corruption can involve huge sums ("commissions" from huge, rigged procurement contracts, for example). For purposes of this volume, grand corruption refers to corruption that involves extraordinarily large side payments; political corruption refers to favors exchanged for support, financial or otherwise, to buttress or sustain the political power of individuals or groups (such as illegal campaign contributions).

Depending on the context, some chapters refer to variants of the three types of corruption. For example, "legal corruption," which tends to feature prominently in oil and gas, forestry, tax and customs administration, and roads, is a subtype of state capture, as it involves the manipulation of formal legal processes to produce laws (and thus legally sanctioned rules) that benefit private interests at huge expense to the general public. Kleptocracy and cronyism are other such variants. In these cases, political leaders use the organs of the state to enrich themselves and friends through "legal" and illegal means.

THE STRUCTURE OF THE VOLUME

This volume is divided into three parts. Part I focuses on specific sectors, with each chapter adopting a value chain perspective. Chapter 1 presents a road map of the delivery of drugs in the health sector and a relatively well-developed indicator system for assessing the vulnerabilities at key decision points along the map. Chapter 2 looks at teacher absenteeism. Chapter 3 is on forestry. In the area of agriculture and rural development, corruption in the forestry sector has arguably the most devastating and long-lasting impact on the environment and, by virtue of its links to organized crime, to society. Chapters 4 through 7 examine road maps, corresponding corruption risks, and possible indicators in four infrastructure subsectors—roads, electricity, oil and gas, and water and sanitation—that capture the range and wide variety of features and problems in this sector.

Part II deals with public financial management, a core public sector function that in most countries is especially vulnerable to corruption. Chapter 8 explores the range of possibilities for corruption throughout the public financial management cycle. Chapter 9 focuses on public procurement, a particularly problematic aspect of public financial management that affects all sectors. Chapters 10 and 11 deal with the revenue management side of public finance: taxation, and customs administration. In a majority of countries, government raises revenue by taxing income, assets, goods, and services; in most countries, corruption typically plagues tax collection and encourages tax evasion. Each of these chapters is anchored in a process flow framework, from which corruption vulnerabilities are identified, measurable indicators generated, and remedial measures derived.

Part III explores a rapidly growing problem in the financial sector—money laundering, the spout through which much of grand corruption passes. The beneficiaries of corrupt money typically want to enjoy their ill-gotten wealth. Small amounts can be spent without attracting much attention, but large expenditures and bank deposits tend to raise suspicions. Large sums of money thus tend to be exported to other countries, where they can be more easily disguised and "legalized." Chapter 12 attempts to demystify the phenomenon of money laundering and explores possible measures to address it.

All of the substantive chapters offer recommendations that may reduce, if not minimize, corruption in their respective areas. The rest of this introduction culls some implications that emerge from these chapters.

EMERGING IMPLICATIONS FOR REFORMS

The road-map approach tilts analysis toward area-specific problems and solutions and away from big picture discussions of corruption. In trying to operationalize the general principles of reform—increase transparency, improve accountability, reduce discretion, dilute monopoly power—it is necessary to get a solid practical grip on combating corruption and its varied manifestations. Administrative corruption, patronage, and state capture can take on different forms and shapes depending on context. The road map offers one such operational handhold.

Despite the narrower focus of this approach, it nonetheless offers broad implications for policy and strategy in the fight against corruption. This section attempts to cull these implications from the richly textured analyses and discussions in each of the chapters in this volume and, in the process, to illustrate the usefulness of this approach in aligning micro-level interventions with the broader aspects of reform.

One Size Does Not Fit All

The road map brings to life the well-known adage in the field of governance that "one size does not fit all." By virtue of their differences in economic structure, sectors naturally embody different road maps and thus reflect different corruption risk profiles. A sector essentially delivers a number of outputs (services). The nature of an output effectively defines an underlying value chain. The value chain for the delivery of essential drugs in the health sector differs significantly from the value chain for providing water to consumers in rural areas, and both differ from the value chain in forest products. Consequently, the vulnerabilities to corruption embodied in each of these road maps are quite different.

A road map lays out a sequential chain of activities that characterizes a problem area. While the chain itself is more or less the same across countries, the relative risks and magnitudes of corruption along each link in the chain are likely to differ from country to country. The best example in this volume comes from the electricity sector, which is broadly characterized by a three-link chain: generation, transmission, and distribution. In most countries, it is presumed that the major problems of corruption arise in power generation or transmission, primarily through the award of multimillion-dollar contracts for the purchase or construction of plants and equipment. Chapter 4 presents a case in which the greater problem resides in distribution. In South Asia petty corruption at the retail end of the chain turns out not to be so petty. The estimated losses through leakage from this link swamp by several orders of magnitude estimates of the inefficiency and corruption at the generation and transmission links. Tackling corruption in South Asia may therefore have a greater impact if it focuses on the distribution end.

The discussion in chapter 1 of the delivery of essential drugs in the health sector also suggests that countries have different pressure points. Analysis of the health-pharmaceutical value chain in Croatia indicates that drug selection is more vulnerable to corruption than is procurement; in Macedonia and Montenegro the reverse is true. The same holds for public financial management. As chapter 8 illustrates, poor management controls and oversight appear to be the weakest link in Bangladesh, while in the Kyrgyz Republic the weak link is the lack of internal control.

One way to think about the variation in profiles is in the context of the links along the value chain for a sector. For concreteness, consider that there are three links, that is, three sequential phases or stages. In some countries, the serious problems may lie in links one and three, in others in link three, and so forth. Altogether there are seven possible configurations of corruption-prone areas.[24]

The implication is that reform strategies will necessarily differ depending on the relative weights of the decision points along links of the chain. By virtue of the fact that such weights are likely to differ across sectors and countries, a road map helps align strategy with the country and sectoral context. Improving transparency in public procurement or tax administration or the delivery of essential drugs will mean different things in different countries—and may thus require different strategies.

Combating Corruption Is Fundamentally about Addressing Poor Governance Rather than about Catching Crooks

Although much of the concern voiced by international financial institutions, donor organizations, policy makers, and citizens has focused on the evils of corruption and its debilitating impact on growth and poverty reduction, the strategies to combat it essentially boil down to improving governance systems. Chapter 5, on the transport-roads sector, illustrates this point clearly, where the focus of much of the effort to curb corruption has been at the project level: procurement procedures are rationalized, disbursement processes are tightened, audits are conducted more promptly and regularly. But problems at the project level are very much driven by deficiencies and weaknesses in governance at the agency, sector, and country levels.

Strengthening Electoral Institutions Is Critically Important to Sectoral Reforms

At the country level, poor electoral laws (or weak enforcement of good laws) can make elections very expensive, inducing politicians to look for lucrative sources of campaign finance. That has implications at the sector level. In particular, policies and regulations on and annual budgetary allocations for roads are often distorted to meet this need. Even earmarked road funds, which are designed to insulate the funding of road maintenance and rehabilitation from political influence, are raided for this purpose. At the agency level, personnel appointments to the ministry of works can also be affected and influenced by this problem. In the absence of a merit-based recruitment and promotion system, unqualified personnel can find their way into the ministry through political connections. Such personnel often become the "shepherds" of their political patrons within the ministry and make it possible for bid-rigging and other corruption schemes to take place. Roads projects are thus subjected to immense pressure even before they reach the project design stage. In short, weak electoral institutions may encourage state capture, which typically occurs at the sector level, and this in turn may foster corruption at the agency and project level. Any sustained effort to reduce corruption significantly will thus require undertaking reforms of governance at all levels—project, agency, sector, and country.

The Long-Term Sustainability of Sector Reforms Depends on Improving the Legal and Judicial System

Promoting judicial and legal reform has been a priority for many donors, for good reason. In the absence of good laws and a well-functioning judicial and prosecutorial system, the rule of law remains weak, retarding investment and socioeconomic development, as empirical research has shown. The chapters in this volume strengthen that argument and heighten the urgency for legal and judicial reform. Curbing corruption in sectors depends on discouraging individuals from engaging in illegal activities. Whether it is construction firms colluding on road contracts, public officials pilfering health supplies, tax collectors harassing taxpayers, politicians protecting illegal loggers, or banks overlooking suspicious transactions, individuals will continue to engage in corruption as long as the probability of prosecution and conviction is low.

As the case studies suggest, administrative and process reforms can certainly make a dent in corruption. But such efforts will ultimately have to be complemented by improvements in law enforcement. A poorly functioning legal and judicial system creates opportunities for challenging and reversing administrative and process reforms. Establishing a semiautonomous revenue agency may improve taxpayer service and tax collection, for instance, but an inefficient, if not corrupt, court system can chip away at these gains: if convictions on and penalties for tax evasion remain low, taxpayers will be induced to revert to their old ways. That will ultimately affect the credibility of the new agency and open doors to undesirable interventions (from corruptible politicians) that undermine the reforms.

Reducing Opportunities for Corruption in Sectors Requires Substantial Reforms in Public Management

For several years a multidonor consortium (coordinated by the World Bank) has been developing a set of indicators—the Public Expenditure and Financial Accountability indicators—to help countries identify weaknesses in their budget systems and track the progress of reforms introduced to address those weaknesses. The focus of these indicators has been primarily on tracking improvements in the efficiency and effectiveness of a country's budget system, from formulation to execution. Chapter 8 shows how these indicators can be used to reflect the potential risks of corruption corresponding to specific weaknesses in governance, such as inadequate management controls and lack of external oversight. The indicators focus on shedding light on problems of governance and only indirectly on the risks of corruption. The chapter's recommendations include increasing the transparency of budgets, aligning development plans with budgets, introducing accounting and internal controls, conducting internal auditing and reporting, and providing external oversight. Reducing the risk of corruption in budgeting is thus primarily about improving governance. The implication is that the effort to "clean up" the budget system will take many years, if not decades, to complete, as it involves many governance reforms, each of which is a challenge to implement.

In tax administration, successful efforts to curb corruption have been designed not as anticorruption reforms but as governance reforms aimed primarily at increasing tax collections. Chapter 10 analyzes the efforts of the government of Bolivia to establish a semiautonomous revenue agency with the single-minded objective of increasing revenue collections. The creation of this new agency, the National Tax Service, was an outcome of the government's Institutional Reform Project, which was launched to improve the efficiency and effectiveness of the public sector in general. The National Tax Service was designed to give tax authorities the ability to hire and fire staff based on performance, offer attractive pay, introduce new business processes based on information and communication technology, and in general create a new organizational culture.

With the establishment of the new agency, tax collections increased, and as a byproduct, corruption also seems to have been curbed. The question the chapter raises, however, is whether this performance can be sustained over the longer term, given the shifting political winds in Bolivia. The experience with semiautonomous revenue agencies in other countries has been very mixed. In Peru and South Africa, indicators show a permanent upward shift in performance relative to the prereform period. But in other countries, such as Tanzania, Uganda, and República Bolivariana de Venezuela, performance has receded over time (DFID 2005). Ultimately, larger governance concerns are likely to impinge on the ability of a semiautonomous revenue agency to sustain improved levels of performance.

Broader governance concerns are also critical to addressing the problem of teacher absenteeism. Chapter 2 discusses the influence of policy and regulatory capture, procurement, personnel management, and weak monitoring systems on the behavior of school teachers, in particular on absentee rates. Policies that create or foster expenditure imbalances to the disadvantage of poorer and more remote regions (typically driven by political concerns), poorly constructed schoolhouses, the lack of textbooks, delays in salary payments, and the lack of formal supervision all affect absenteeism. Moonlighting, absence without cause, or absence to meet other extraneous demands (such as requests of local politicians) are all forms of bureaucratic corruption. But they are driven predominantly by upstream governance factors.

Corruption in "High-Rent" Sectors May Have Huge Negative Spillover Effects on Overall Governance

In sectors where rents are unusually high, corruption can lead to a gradual weakening of institutions originally designed to regulate these sectors—and in the extreme to the collapse of the governance system. A well-functioning regulatory institution limits corruption by standing in the way of potentially big money. Those who stand to gain from illicit arrangements therefore have strong incentives to weaken, if not decapitate, the institution. The forestry and the oil and gas sectors fall in this category, for in each, rents are extraordinarily high and the natural resource is geographically concentrated, making illegal extraction easy. Chapter 3 examines cases where forest regulatory agencies may have started out with reasonable capacity but over time were starved of resources and had their authority circumscribed, ultimately leading to the exodus of good staff and the deterioration of the agencies concerned, while illegal logging continued unabated. Given the rents involved, this corrosion could very well spill over into other related regulatory entities, such as those dealing with land titling and administration.

In oil-rich countries, as chapter 6 suggests, the resource curse creates immense spillover effects on governance that extend far beyond the sector. It encourages political elites and senior officials to dampen, if not eliminate, regulations that might constrain their ability to engage in corrupt arrangements. The amounts of money involved in oil transactions are so huge that commissions, legal or illegal, of $1 billion are insignificant in the grand scheme of things, indirectly making obfuscation of the money track easier. The absolute amounts are so large that there is enough money to corrupt practically all institutions in the country, including not just the regulatory agencies overlooking the sector but the bulwarks of rule of law—the police, the judiciary, and the military. This is manifested in several oil-producing countries, where the political situation has deteriorated into civil unrest, the governance system has more or less collapsed, and activities revolve around violence and the competition among factions for control of the oil. The implication of these findings is that in resource-rich countries it is essential to address the governance problems in the resource-abundant sectors.

To Be Effective, Governance Reforms Have to Be Incentive Compatible

Economists have long argued that successful implementation of any scheme requires that the preferences of all those involved be appropriately aligned with achieving the objectives or goals of the scheme. Many solutions to the classic problem of principal agency have been based on this notion of incentive compatibility. Incentive mechanisms that are compatible with the preferences of both the principal and the agent are designed to encourage agents to do what principals expect of them.[25] Several chapters in this volume identify phenomena—leadership, windows of opportunity, and the alignment of laws and policies with capacity—that in essence suggest the importance of incentive compatibility to reforms in governance.

Leadership

Many case studies on successful or failed governance reforms cite leadership of the reform effort as a critical factor. Strong and highly motivated leadership was essential to the success of the institutional reform of Bolivia's National Tax Service, the reform of the state power company in Andrah Pradesh (India), and the public expenditure tracking survey–based reforms in the education sector in Uganda. This leadership came from the head of the agency in the case of the National Tax Service, the chief minister in the case of Andrah Pradesh, and senior officials in the Ministry of Finance in the case of Uganda. All three cases illustrate the importance of leaders having strong motivations to push reforms and the political savvy to structure and sequence reform components in ways that align the incentives of various stakeholders with successful implementation. If these leaders were lukewarm toward or opposed to the reforms, the reforms would have stalled or not been launched at all, no matter how well-conceived they may have been. By necessity, leadership must want the reforms—the reforms must be compatible with their preferences.

Windows of Opportunity

Another phenomenon that often comes up in analyses of governance reforms is the so-called window of opportunity. Difficult reforms are often launched during times of crisis, as in the case of the reengineering of the public sector and the National Tax Service in Bolivia, the customs reform in the Russian Federation, and the power utility in Andrah Pradesh. A crisis is said to offer a window of opportunity that could close quickly and so must be exploited. In essence, this window reflects a realignment of incentives of different stakeholders that work in favor of envisioned reforms. It alters the balance between (individual) costs and benefits, making it possible for reformers to introduce institutional change that earlier would not have been feasible. In short, it reshapes individual incentives to make them more compatible with the reforms.

A major implication of this phenomenon is that reforms may need to be more pragmatic. So-called "first-best" reforms may be grossly misaligned with the incentives of stakeholders and therefore destined to fail. Second-, third-, even fourth-best solutions may yield better outcomes. In some cases, doing nothing may be the best option.

Capacity Matters

Perhaps one of the least appreciated constraints to the sustainability of governance reforms is the problem of capacity. Capacity refers to the capability (in terms of human and financial resources) to deliver on an envisioned task, at the agency or governmentwide level. Historical experience with governance reforms is replete with stories of best practice from the developed world being parachuted into a poor developing country and failing miserably. Chapter 3, on forestry, and chapter 12, on money laundering, both clearly illustrate this problem. Good laws on forest management and anti-money-laundering have been legislated in a growing number of developing countries but without much consideration of these countries' enforcement capacity. Courts and the police are poorly resourced, very few legal and enforcement professionals are well trained, and management systems are weak and inefficient. Faced with these handicaps, judges, prosecutors, police, and investigators can do only so much. When faced with laws that require enforcement far exceeding their capacity, their incentives are to ignore them, delay implementation, or worse, exploit the enforcement gap. In short, their incentives are not compatible with the enforcement requirements of the law.

This phenomenon is quite widespread. In many countries, complicated tax codes have been introduced in the belief that they promote fairness and cover all known loopholes. In most of these countries, however, the capacity to implement the code is inadequate (see World Bank 1991; Tanzi 2001). The country would have been better off adopting a much simpler code that, despite its deficiencies, would have been easier and thus more feasible to implement. The push toward uniform tariffs in the 1980s was in part a recognition of this misalignment.

Accounting Is Not Accountability: Supply-Side Interventions May Be More Effective When Matched with Demand-Side Mechanisms

Improving accounting and budgeting systems and processes has been a primary focus of the fight against corruption. Indeed, the fight starts with documenting, monitoring, and reporting on the flow of public money. Most donors and governments have dedicated considerable support and effort to improving the relevant systems. But while this improvement is important, performing each of these tasks effectively and efficiently requires that government, in particular the executive branch, be held accountable for the outputs and outcomes that these tasks are supposed to help deliver.[26]

In procurement and budgeting, focal areas of many supply-side reforms, the role of external stakeholders in monitoring budgetary processes and their resulting outcomes has gained increasing importance. Chapter 8 highlights the participation (and utility) of nongovernmental organizations in the full budget cycle, from formulation to execution, both at the local government level and the national level. Chapter 9 summarizes key mechanisms that have been used effectively in external monitoring of public procurement. From the adoption of integrity pacts in large-scale government contracting to the use of external observers in bids and awards committees to the dissemination of reader-friendly procurement regulations, governments have begun to engage civil society groups constructively in improving the conduct of public procurement.

At the sector level, there appears to be increasing recognition of the usefulness of engaging civil society groups in monitoring the delivery of sectoral outputs. Chapter 2 suggests a two-pronged strategy of establishing an education information management system (a supply-side intervention) and engaging parents at the community level in school management (a demand-side mechanism) as a means of reducing teacher absenteeism. Chapter 5 presents the idea of using external actors with complementary skills and experience to help contain unwarranted and undesirable political interventions that tend to occur throughout the value chain in the roads sector. Both chapter 7, on the delivery of water, and chapter 4, on the provision of electricity, recommend the use of participatory mechanisms at the local level to help curb corruption. In water, the Kecamatan Development Program in Indonesia illustrates the potential effectiveness of community monitoring combined with a complaints redressal system.[27] In electricity, the use of regular citizen fora with government to discuss policy issues and decisions in Bangalore, India, has proven effective in fostering agency-level reforms and reducing the opportunities for corruption.

In recent years, practitioners and policy makers have come to appreciate the importance of freedom of information, with an increasing number of developing countries passing relevant legislation.[28] The availability of information is indeed necessary to improve transparency in the public sector. But, as several chapters point out, this is not enough. For strengthening accountability, the information must itself be comprehensible to key stakeholders and the general public. This suggests a role for specialized nongovernmental organizations to fill in the information gap, one that is likely to become increasingly important over time.

Corollary: A Transparent and Monitorable Results Framework Provides a Foundation for Increased Accountability

Because it produces information on projected inputs, outputs, and outcomes, a strong results-based framework at the sector and project levels can sharply reduce the likelihood that monies will be diverted toward corrupt or fraudulent purposes. Such a framework typically presents disaggregated baseline and projected information down to the lowest possible unit level, so that grassroots monitoring can be done through demand-side mechanisms, such as those discussed above. Several chapters allude to the utility of producing key information that could be used to generate public demand for better services. In the electricity sector, for example, information on technical and nontechnical losses during the distribution and billing phases can help mobilize public and leadership support for reforms. Information on how much of a budget dollar actually reaches ultimate beneficiaries can generate a powerful reform momentum in the social sectors. A results-based framework typically incorporates this type of information and as such can be the foundation for strengthening accountability in the public sector.

A road map is a useful platform upon which to develop a results-based framework. It lays out the various phases of a project or program and presents early warning indicators that can often serve as intermediate outputs or outcomes. These include, for example, the actual budget for essential drugs that reach local districts, the time it takes to complete a competitive bidding process, the actual length of roads built versus the projected length, the actual value of exported lumber versus the value of reported timber cut for export, and the value of value added tax refunds for reexports versus the value of exports.

International Cooperation, Particularly Involving Multinational Corporations and Developed-Country Governments, May Be Necessary to Combat Corruption in Sectors Where Scarcity Rents Are Inordinately High and Supply and Demand Are Split Clearly along North-South Lines

Prompted by concerns that bribery involves both corruptors and corruptees, Transparency International launched its Bribe Payers Index in 1999. In so doing, it recognized the significant role that multinational firms from developed countries have played in propagating corruption, typically of grand scale, in developing countries. Chapter 3 illustrates this phenomenon very crisply. Because the worldwide demand for forest products exceeds the supply of trees, rents in the sector are very high. As economic theory would suggest, this situation creates a gold mine for corruption. Most of the demand for forest products emanates from developed countries, while much of the supply, particularly of scarce woods such as teak, comes from developing countries. As value chain analysis shows, the life of an illegally cut log goes through several distinct but interlinked stages from tree to finished product. At some point, the log is magically transformed from illegal to legal status. That stage is characterized by a market exchange between a foreign buyer and a local broker.[29] The incentive for the buyer to pay bribes in order to obtain the illegal lumber is very strong. In Indonesia, for instance, a log that is sold initially to a local broker for $2.20 per cubic meter eventually is transformed into final products sold in the United States for $1,000 per cubic meter. In that so-called "magical" middle stage, a foreign broker typically purchases the "illegal" raw lumber at $160 per cubic meter from an Indonesian broker and then resells it legally to a foreign wood processor for $710 per cubic meter. With this kind of rent, any attempt to curb corruption in the sector will need to involve both developed- and developing-country governments. The Forest Legal Enforcement Governance initiative is an attempt to achieve the necessary collaboration.[30]

Among all the sectors covered in this volume, it is perhaps in the oil and gas sector that the need for international cooperation is most glaring. As chapter 6 argues, geopolitical concerns of developed-country governments combined with unbridled profit maximization of private firms in the developed world have fostered a global arrangement that encourages and nurtures state capture and grand corruption of incomparable scale. Oil transactions globally can run upward of several trillion dollars a year, with the scarcity rent premium about four to five times the actual cost of production. The bulk of the demand comes from the developed world, with the United States alone accounting for one-quarter of that demand.

The bulk of supply comes from developing countries: 60 percent of all oil and gas reserves are in the Middle East, Nigeria, and the República Bolivariana de Venezuela. The extraordinarily high abnormal profits that can be earned in the sector make it a natural magnet for corruption. These profits encourage huge private firms in the developed world to influence the policies of their governments on oil-related transactions; they push developed-country governments to offer protection and security to oil-producing countries in exchange for access rights to oil to fuel their energy-hungry economies; they attract big-time brokers to act as mediators between these large multinationals and developing-country governments and officials; they invite developing-country officials, especially senior leaders, to "auction" access rights to their country's oil reserves to the highest bidder; and they induce international banks to turn a blind eye to corrupt transactions. In this environment, corruption cannot be curtailed without the cooperation of numerous parties in both the developed and developing countries and the establishment of an international architecture for regulating the global market for oil and gas.

In the health sector, scarcity rents stem largely from the high inelasticity of demand for essential drugs in developing countries and the small number of legitimate multinational pharmaceutical companies. This mismatch of supply and demand creates lucrative opportunities for corruption. The value chain analysis in chapter 1 suggests that bribery and fraud by drug companies can occur from drug registration to drug selection to procurement to distribution and to prescription—the chain is quite porous to corruption. At the registration and selection stage, major drug manufacturers have incentives to bribe public officials in developing-country governments. For this reason, Merck, one of the largest multinational pharmaceutical firms, has partnered with Transparency International to encourage other multinational pharmaceutical companies to jointly refrain from bribing developing-country governments. At the procurement and distribution stage, a more serious phenomenon is emerging: the production of counterfeit or substandard drugs for sale in developing countries. Because of the asymmetry of information between users and producers, it is relatively easy for producers to sell substandard or counterfeit drugs. This has encouraged the establishment of fly-by-night drug companies (both local and international) whose sole purpose is to exploit this market failure.[31] Government regulation is thus critically important. For this reason, as economic theory would suggest, it also becomes a lever for corrupt exchanges.

Any solution to this problem will require some form of international collaboration. This has been clearly recognized by the International Federation of Pharmaceutical Manufacturers, which has established a monitoring and research program to counteract the sale of counterfeit and substandard drugs, and the World Health Organization, which has recently launched an aggressive anticorruption program, in part as a step toward developing international collaborative agreements to combat fraud in drug provision in developing countries.

As chapter 9 shows, government procurement is highly susceptible to corruption. The situation is exacerbated in large-scale procurements in developing countries, typically in infrastructure, for which only established international firms qualify to bid. Given the size of such projects, the temptation for client government officials to rig the contract in return for substantial side payments is enormous. The manipulation can take place anywhere along the procurement chain, from project design to contract implementation. In the design stage, for example, the contract requirements can be structured to favor the technology of a specific firm. In the implementation stage, the contract can be "renegotiated due to unforeseen circumstances." The temptation of the few large firms to collude and share the resulting rent can likewise be irresistible.

In these instances, containing corruption can be very difficult unless all parties can credibly agree to refrain from engaging in illicit behavior. It is for this reason that

Transparency International developed the integrity pact as a credible commitment device. The organization defines an integrity pact as "a tool aimed at preventing corruption in public contracting. It consists of a process that includes an agreement between a government or a government department (at the federal, national or local level) and all bidders for a public contract. It contains rights and obligations to the effect that neither side will pay, offer, demand or accept bribes; collude with competitors to obtain the contract; or engage in such abuses while carrying out the contract. The pact also introduces a monitoring system that provides for independent oversight and accountability" (http://www.transparency.org/global_priorities/). Integrity pacts have been adopted successfully in large-scale government contracts in several Latin American countries, including Argentina, Colombia, Ecuador, and Mexico.

The proceeds from petty corruption can be laundered locally without attracting much attention. But the large sums of money involved in corruption in high-rent sectors typically need to be moved out of the country: a kickback of several million dollars is not easy to hide domestically. The money is thus likely to be laundered overseas. As chapter 12 argues, money laundering often depends on the financial systems and business practices of other countries. It is a sophisticated international mechanism designed to obfuscate and thus encourage grand corruption. The implication is that grand corruption cannot be effectively contained, let alone prevented, without the cooperation of various parties internationally on curbing money laundering.

ENDNOTES

1. For an extensive survey on research on corruption, see World Bank (2006) and Amundsen and Fjelstad (2000).
2. For a compilation of the earlier academic literature on political corruption, see Heidenheimer, Johnston, and Levine (1989).
3. Considerable theoretical and case study research on corruption has been done since the 1970s. Much of the work on rent seeking, for instance, though dealing squarely with state capture, essentially tackled conceptual issues. It was not until the mid-1990s that large cross-country econometric research began to emerge, mainly as a result of the emerging availability of usable data.
4. The International Country Risk Guide (ICRG), whose data have been used extensively in quantitative research, began its surveys in 1980. The Business Environmental Risk Intelligence (BERI) began to provide governance-related, survey-based indexes in the early 1980s. The Economist Intelligence Unit began providing related data around this time as well. For more recent additional sources, see Political Risk Consulting (http://www.asiarisk.com) and the World Economic Forum (http://www.weforum.com).
5. Through aggregation of the numerous individual variables, the six indicators tend to have significantly smaller margins of error than any individual measure.
6. A number of comparative country studies have also been conducted on combating corruption. While not statistically based, they nonetheless provide empirical analyses of reforms and strategies. See, for instance, Bhargava and Bolongaita (2004) and Quah (2003).
7. For a similar argument, see Woodruff (forthcoming).
8. For closely related articles, see Anderson, Reid, and Ryterman (2003) and Evans and Rauch (1999).
9. For an extensive discussion of rent seeking, its causes, and consequences, see Rowley, Tollison, and Tullock (1988).

10. See Hoffman (2002) for a discussion of corruption in the process of privatization in the former Soviet Union.
11. The concern with the lack of transparency and accountability arose from practitioners and academics interested in developing practical measures to reduce corruption. Theoretically, however, these concepts can be tied to basic problems of information asymmetry and imperfect information. Economists have been working on many variants and manifestations of these problems for more than two decades. But surprisingly few have taken the sophisticated analytical tools developed for such problems and applied them to problems in governance and in particular corruption (but see Tirole 1992). One exception is in the area of public procurement, where economists trained in the new industrial organization and specializing in auction theory have analyzed the inefficiencies and waste (and thus corruption) that plague government procurement from the lens of information asymmetry (bidders know more about the true cost and quality of their bids than do government procuring agents) or imperfect information (the necessity of having to write incomplete contracts when a complex product or service is being procured). See in particular Lafont and Tirole (1993) Porter and Zona (1993), Bushnell and Oren (1994), Crocker and Reynolds (1993), Bajari and Tadelis (2001), and Bajari, Houghton, and Tadelis (2006). See also Hyytinen, Lundberg, and Toivanen (2006) for an interesting empirical piece that links procurement, asymmetric information, and political structures.
12. These can be viewed as second-generation indicators, as defined by Johnston (2001)—measures that are correlated with corruption and can be quantified more objectively. The investment climate survey and the report card survey are experiential surveys—of firms or citizens having experienced corruption firsthand, for example—and thus provide richer information than perception-based surveys; the Public Expenditure Tracking Survey is based on expenditure data.
13. See the Survey Methodology section of the "Doing Business" Web site for a description of an investment climate survey and surveys (and their results) that have been completed to date: http://www.doingbusiness.org/
14. For more information, see http://www.worldbank.org/eca/econ.
15. This approach was introduced and developed in the mid-1990s by the Public Affairs Centre (PAC) in Bangalore, India, as an instrument to stimulate interagency competition among municipal public service agencies and improve performance (Paul 1995). The results of the latest survey, which are summarized in Anderson and Gray (2006), indicate that progress has been made in several areas, with corruption in general declining in a significant number of countries in the region.
16. Report card surveys have been carried out in other Indian cities, including Delhi, Kolkata, and Mumbai, as well as in 11 cities in the metropolitan Manila area. Three surveys have been conducted in Bangalore, the first in 1995, which established benchmarks; a second in 1999; and a third in 2002. The results show significant improvements over time in the quality of services, including a reduction in the incidence of bribery (see World Bank 2005 for a summary).
17. For the application of this instrument in Uganda, see Reinnika and Svensson (2004).
18. In Uganda, for instance, the first Public Expenditure Tracking Surveys, conducted in 1996, revealed that only 22 percent of non-wage-related funds allocated for primary schools in local districts actually reached the schools. The Public Expenditure Tracking Survey conducted in 2001 showed that leakage had dropped to less than 20 percent, suggesting that the remedial measures introduced in the interim had had a real and significant impact (Reinnika and Svensson 2006).
19. This report was prepared with the support of the United States Agency for International Development.

20. In the volume by Spector (2005), the chapter on the health sector comes closest to the approach proposed here.
21. Alternatively, this could be the perspective of public officials interested in or tasked with introducing anticorruption reforms in a specific context.
22. In some contexts, this might also include contract implementation, as in the case of variation orders.
23. Sometimes administrative corruption is referred to as bureaucratic corruption.
24. The total number of possible configurations (in this example, three) are $\sum_{k=1}^{3}(n-k)!k!$, where n = total number of links in the chain, k is the number of links in a specific configuration plagued by corruption, and $n! = n * (n-1) * (n-2) * \ldots * 2 * 1$.
25. In many instances, the preferences of an agent differ from those of the principal. If the principal can watch the agent 100 percent of the time, this does not pose a problem, because the agent will do the principal's bidding. However, it is costly to monitor every action of the agent, and failure to do so creates possibilities for the agent to act in ways that are counter to the desires of the principal when the principal "is not looking." To address this problem, the principal needs to design an efficient, low-cost monitoring system that keeps the agent in line—that is, an incentive-compatible mechanism.
26. The authors are grateful to Junaid Ahmed, who made this important point at a training event on governance and anticorruption sponsored by the Asia Learning Department of the World Bank, June 26–27, 2006.
27. The Kecamatan Development Program is a community-driven development (CDD) project—villagers get to choose their preferred interventions—that is predominantly focused on rural roads and water.
28. On asset and income disclosure of public officials, see, for instance, the Assets Disclosure by Public Officials section of the World Bank's Law and Justice Web site: http://siteresources.worldbank.org/INTLAWJUSTINST/Resources/IncomeAssetDisclosureinWBClientsasofJune62006.pdf.
29. Auty (2006) notes that the deterioration of institutions among resource-rich countries is more severe where rents are generated from "point-source" resources (capital-intensive and concentrated ownership) than from "diffuse-source" resources (such as land under peasant farms). Resources that require immediate processing (sugarcane, forestry, fisheries) share some point-source features. The rents from point-source resources are not widely shared throughout the population, and their presence often leads to institutional erosion.
30. The potential for using international arrangements to curb corruption is reflected in the experience of transition economies seeking admission to the European Union. The World Bank Institute Governance Indicators (2006) show that overall governance has improved in transition economies that have committed to joining the European Union (and thus have to meet the various governance-related standards set by it).
31. This is not to say that more established firms do not engage in such fraudulent activities. Some have been known to dump drugs rejected by health authorities in their home countries in the developing world.

REFERENCES

Amundsen, Inge, and Odd-Helge Fjeldstad. 2000. "Corruption: A Selected and Annotated Bibliography." Chr. Michelsen Institute, Bergen, Norway. http://www.eldis.org/static/DOC7818.htm.

Anderson, James H., and Cheryl Gray. 2006. *Anticorruption in Transition 3: Who Is Succeeding and Why?* Washington, DC: World Bank.

Anderson, James, Gary Reid, and Randi Ryterman. 2003. *Understanding Public Sector Performance in Transition Countries: An Empirical Contribution*. Washington, DC: World Bank.

Auty, R. M., ed. 2006. *Resource Abundance and Economic Development*. Oxford: Oxford University Press.

Bajari, Patrick, and Steve Tadelis. 2001. "Incentives vs. Transactions Costs: A Theory of Procurement Contracts." *Rand Journal of Economics* 32 (3): 287–307.

Bajari, Patrick, Stephanie Houghton, and Steve Tadelis. 2006. "Bidding for Incomplete Contracts: An Empirical Analysis." NBER Working Paper 12051, National Bureau of Economic Research, Cambridge, MA.

Bhagwati, Jagdish. 1982. "Directly Unproductive Profit-Seeking (DUP) Activities." *Journal of Political Economy* 90 (5): 988–1002.

Bhargava, Vinay, and Emil Bolongaita. 2004. *Challenging Corruption in Asia: Case Studies and a Framework for Action*. Washington, DC: World Bank.

Bushnell, James, and Shmuel Oren. 1994. "Bidder Cost Revelation in Electric Power Auctions." *Journal of Regulatory Economics* 6 (1): 5–26.

Campos, J. E., Donald Lien, and Sanjay Pradhan. 1999. "The Impact of Corruption on Investment: Predictability Matters." *World Development* 27 (6): 1059–67.

Crocker, Keith, and Kenneth Reynolds. 1993. "The Efficiency of Incomplete Contracts: An Empirical Analysis of Air Force Engine Procurement." *RAND Journal of Economics* 24 (1): 126–46.

DFID (Department for International Development, United Kingdom). 2005. "Revenue Authorities and Taxation in Sub-Saharan Africa: A Concise Review of Recent Literature for the Investment, Competition and Enabling Environment Team." London.

Evans, Peter, and Jim Rausch. 1999. "Bureaucracy and Growth: A Cross-National Analysis of the Effects of 'Weberian' State Structures on Economic Growth." *American Sociological Review* 64 (55): 748–65.

Gupta, Sanjiv, Hamid Davoodi, and Rosa Alonso-Terme. 2002. "Does Corruption Affect Income Inequality and Poverty?" In *Governance, Corruption, and Economic Performance*, ed. G. Abed and S. Gupta, pp. 458–86. Washington, DC: International Monetary Fund.

Gyimah-Brempong, Kwabena. 2002. "Corruption, Economic Growth, and Income Inequality in Africa." *Economics of Governance* 3 (3): 183–209.

Heidenheimer, Arnold, Michael Johnston, and Victor Levine. 1989. *Political Corruption: A Handbook*. New Brunswick, NJ: Transaction Publishers.

Hoffman, David. 2002. *The Oligarchs: Wealth and Power in the New Russia*. New York: Perseus Book Group.

Hyytinen, Ari, Sofia Lundberg, and Otto Toivanen. 2006. "Favoritism in Public Procurement: Evidence from Sweden." Research Institute of the Finnish Economy and Umea University, Stockholm.

Johnston, Michael. 2001. "Measuring Corruption: Numbers versus Knowledge versus Understanding." In *The Political Economy of Corruption*, ed. Arvind Jain, pp. 157–79. New York: Routledge Press.

Kaufmann, Daniel, Aart Kraay, and Massimo Mastruzzi. 2003. "Rethinking Governance: Empirical Lessons Challenge Orthodoxy." World Bank Institute, Washington, DC. http://www.worldbank.org/wbi/governance/pdf/rethink_gov_stanford.pdf.

———. 2005. *Governance Matters IV: Governance Indicators for 1996–2004*. Washington, DC: World Bank Institute. http://www.worldbank.org/wbi/governance/pubs/govmatters4.html.

Kaufmann, Daniel, Aart Kraay, and Pablo Zoido-Lobaton. 1999. "Governance Matters." Policy Research Working Paper 2196, World Bank, Washington, DC.

Kaufmann, Daniel, Francesca Recanatini, and Sergiy Biletsky. 2002. "Assessing Governance: Diagnostic Tools and Applied Methods for Capacity Building and Action Learning." World Bank Institute Discussion Draft, Washington, DC.

Klitgaard, Robert. 1988. *Controlling Corruption*. Berkeley, CA: University of California Press.

Knack, Stephen, and Philip Keefer. 1995. "Institutions and Economic Performance: Cross-Country Tests Using Alternative Institutional Measures." *Economics and Politics* 7 (3): 207–27.

Kreuger, Anne. 1974. "The Political Economy of the Rent-Seeking Society." *American Economic Review* 64 (June): 291–303.

Lafont, Jean-Jacques, and Jean Tirole. 1993. *A Theory of Incentives in Procurement and Regulation*, Cambridge, MA: MIT Press.

Mauro, Paolo. 1995. "Corruption and Growth." *Quarterly Journal of Economics* 110 (August): 681–712.

———. 1998. "Corruption and the Composition of Public Expenditures." *Journal of Public Economics* 69 (August): 263–79.

Paul, Samuel. 1995. "Strengthening Public Accountability: New Approaches and Mechanisms." Public Affairs Centre, Bangalore.

Pew Research Center. 2002. *What the World Thinks in 2002*. Washington, DC. http://www.pewglobal.org.

Porter, Robert, and Douglas Zona. 1993. "Detection of Bid Rigging in Procurement Auctions." *Journal of Political Economy* 101 (3): 518–38.

Quah, Jon. 2003. *Curbing Corruption in Asia: A Comparative Study of Six Countries*. Singapore: Eastern Universities Press.

Reinikka, R., and J. Svensson. 2004. "Power of Information: Evidence from a Newspaper Campaign to Reduce Capture." Policy Research Working Paper 3239, World Bank, Development Research Group, Washington, DC.

———. 2006. "Using Micro-Surveys to Measure and Explain Corruption." *World Development* 34 (2): 359–70.

Rodrik, Dani, and Arvind Subramanian. 2003. "The Primacy of Institutions." *Finance and Development* 40 (2): 31–34.

Rose-Ackerman, Susan. 1978. *Corruption: A Study in Political Economy*. New York: Academic Press.

———. 1999. *Corruption in Government: Causes, Consequences, and Reform*. Cambridge: Cambridge University Press.

Rowley, Charles K., Robert D. Tollison, and Gordon Tullock, eds. 1988. *The Political Economy of Rent-Seeking*. Boston: Kluwer Academic Publishers.

Scott, James. 1972. *Comparative Political Corruption*. Englewood Cliffs, NJ: Prentice-Hall.

Spector, Bertram, ed. 2005. *Fighting Corruption in Developing Countries: Strategies and Analysis*. Bloomfield, CT: Kumarian Press.

Tanzi, Vito. 1998. "Corruption around the World: Causes, Consequences, Scope, and Cures." *IMF Staff Papers* 45 (4), International Monetary Fund, Washington, DC.

———. 2001. "Pitfalls on the Road to Fiscal Decentralization." Working Paper 19, Economic Reform Project, Global Policy Program, Carnegie Endowment for International Peace, Washington, DC.

Tanzi, Vito, and Hamid Davoodi. 2002. "Corruption, Public Investment, and Growth." In *Governance, Corruption, and Economic Performance*, ed. G. Abed and S. Gupta, 280–99. Washington, DC: International Monetary Fund.

Tirole, Jean. 1992. "Persistence of Corruption." Working Paper 152, Institute for Policy Reform, Washington DC.

Transparency International. *Corruption Perception Index* (CPI). http://www.transparency.org/policy_research/surveys_indices/cpi .

———. 2005. *The Global Corruption Barometer 2005.* Berlin: Transparency International.

Tullock, Gordon. 1971. *The Logic of the Law.* New York: Basic Books.

Wade, Robert. 1985. "The Market for Public Office: Why the Indian State Is Not Better at Development." *World Development* 13 (April): 467–97.

Wei, Shang-Jin. 2000. "How Taxing Is Corruption on International Investors?" *Review of Economics and Statistics* 82 (1): 1–11.

Woodruff, Christopher. Forthcoming. "Measuring Institutions." In *The Handbook of Corruption*, ed. Susan Rose-Ackerman. Cheltenham, UK, and Northampton, MA: Edward Elgar Publishers.

World Bank. 1991. *Lessons of Tax Reform.* Washington, DC: World Bank.

———. 1997. *World Development Report: The State in a Changing World.* Washington, DC: World Bank.

———. 2000. *Anticorruption in Transition: A Contribution to the Policy Debate.* Washington, DC: World Bank.

———. 2003. *The Global Poll: Multinational Survey of Opinion Leaders 2002.* Washington, DC: Princeton Survey Research Associates for the World Bank.

———. 2005. *Economic Growth in the 1990s: Learning from a Decade of Reform.* Washington, DC: World Bank.

———. 2006. *Literature Survey on Corruption 2000–2005.* PREM Public Sector Governance. http://www1.worldbank.org/publicsector/anticorrupt/ACLitSurvey.pdf.

World Bank Institute. 2006. *Worldwide Governance Research Indicators Dataset.* http://www.worldbank.org/wbi/governance/govdata/.

PART 

Combating Corruption

Sectoral Explorations

1

Corruption and Pharmaceuticals

Strengthening Good Governance to Improve Access

JILLIAN CLARE COHEN, MONIQUE F. MRAZEK,
AND LORAINE HAWKINS

"Drug counterfeiting is one of the greatest atrocities of our time. It is a form of terrorism against public health as well as an act of economic sabotage. Worse, it is mass murder. Drug counterfeiting violates the right to life of innocent victims. And even though it is a global problem, it affects developing countries more seriously as the poor bear the brunt of this injustice. Corruption fuels the fake drug trade. And it is a most lethal form that plagues the health sector because it affects life directly."

Professor Dora Akunyili, Director General, National Agency for Food and Drug Administration and Control, Nigeria

According to the World Health Organization (WHO 2004a), "essential medicines save lives and improve health when they are available, affordable, of assured quality and properly used." Despite the critical importance of pharmaceuticals to health systems, poor drug access continues to be one of the main global health problems. Approximately 2 billion people, or one-third of the world's population, lack regular access to medicines (WHO 2004b). People in developing countries make up about 80 percent of the global population but represent only about 20 percent of the global pharmaceutical market by value, although this number may be somewhat higher by volume (Médicins Sans Frontières 2001). Inadequate access to essential drugs is a concern not only in the developing world. In the United States, for example, many senior citizens and uninsured people are unable to afford the drugs they need (Henry and Lexchin 2002). WHO estimates that about 10 million lives could be saved every year simply by improving access to existing essential medicines (and vaccines).

Inequalities in access to pharmaceuticals are caused by many variables, including poverty, high drug prices, and poor health infrastructure. One important variable is corruption, an issue that has been little addressed until recently by policy makers. The consequences of corruption within the pharmaceutical system are unfortunately fairly easy to identify. If quality control regulations are not sufficient or are not implemented or enforced, health and economic consequences result. At an extreme, unsafe counterfeit drugs can lead to severe health consequences, including death.

Capture of the pharmaceutical regulatory system can result in public spending on medicines that is not necessarily rational—in terms of criteria of appropriateness, safety, effectiveness and economy (Parish 1973)—and does not necessarily reflect the health priorities of a country.

Even when seemingly strong institutional checks and balances are in place, such as in the United States, fraudulent activity can still occur. Since 1986, judgments and settlements for fraud under the U.S. False Claims Act have totaled $12 billion, with most of these being against well-known drug makers. One of the largest of such settlements was against drug maker Serono, which agreed in October 2005 to pay $704 million to settle a fraud case involving its product Serostim (a human growth hormone product); the charges against Serono involved kickbacks to doctors and pharmacies, illegal off-label marketing, and sale of diagnostics for the drug that were not approved by the U.S. Food and Drug Administration (FDA).[1]

The presence of corruption in any one of the critical decision points in the pharmaceutical system from manufacture to retail sales can limit the population's access to quality medicines, thereby reducing the health gains associated with the proper use of pharmaceuticals. While corruption in the pharmaceutical system can affect a country's entire population, it is typically the poor that are most susceptible to its detrimental effects. Where the public health care system affords coverage of pharmaceuticals, it is the poor who are obviously more dependent on the system than the rich and who suffer the consequences of its mismanagement more acutely. It is estimated that in low- and middle-income countries, more than 70 percent of all pharmaceutical purchases are paid for out of pocket and that these purchases represent the largest share of household health care expenditure (WHO 1998, 2004c). Governments in these countries still have a responsibility to ensure that even the poorest can obtain quality essential drugs. Broadly speaking, good governance is a sine qua non for ensuring access of the population to essential medicines.

Governments have a responsibility to create sound institutional structures, processes, and policies and to reinforce outcomes that promote public welfare. As part of this effort, anticorruption measures, if implemented successfully, have the potential to improve access to medicines, save public money, and improve the credibility of governments and other organizations like the World Bank that are involved in drug delivery programs. Government commitment to mitigating corruption in the sector is therefore vital. Governments have two core responsibilities in the pharmaceutical system. First, they are responsible for regulating the manufacture, distribution, sale, and use of pharmaceutical products, which includes regulating all actors involved in the pharmaceutical sector. Second, where governments provide drug coverage, public purchasers are responsible for the selection, purchase, and logistical management of drugs for use through the public health care system. Both roles are of equal importance to ensure good governance in the pharmaceutical system and to ensure access to rational drugs for the population.

Given the global nature of the pharmaceutical sector, tackling corruption in it needs to go beyond any single government. Collective action is needed to address the issue of counterfeit medicines. The Declaration of Rome, adopted in February 2006, is a recent public expression of the deep concern about counterfeit medicines by the international community and the international pharmaceutical industry. The

BOX 1.1 Global Action Tackling Corruption in Pharmaceutical Systems

The World Bank has been involved in lending to strengthen pharmaceutical systems (including infrastructure, purchase of drugs, equipment, technical assistance, training, and policy advice) since the early 1980s. Because of client demand, pharmaceuticals are a growing share of the Bank's lending portfolio. Between 1999 and 2002, the total value of World Bank procurement of pharmaceuticals and medical products was $401 million, with the vast majority of these contracts (363 of 380) undertaken by the Health, Nutrition, and Population sector (Rodríguez-Monguió and Rovira 2005). This sector of the Bank has written guidance on drug procurement (World Bank 2000) and anticipates taking further action to improve governance and stem corruption.

The World Health Organization (WHO) has long been concerned about counterfeit drugs and has led the effort in developing countries to combat such medicines and promote ethical practices in pharmaceutical marketing and retailing. It has published numerous documents on combating corruption and ensuring the integrity of the drug supply; these documents are available on its Web site (http://www.who.int). WHO is also undertaking research to better understand corruption issues and is developing tools to assess vulnerability to corruption (WHO 2005b).

The European Union (EU) created a European Healthcare Fraud and Corruption Network (EHFCN) in 2004 to help member countries with enforcement activities in all areas of the health care and pharmaceutical systems (see http://www.ehfcn.org).

The International Federation of Pharmaceutical Manufacturers (IFPMA), the association of the research-based pharmaceutical industry, through its affiliate the Pharmaceutical Security Institute (PSI), monitors the sale of counterfeit and substandard drugs, including incident reporting, analytical assessments, and dissemination of reports on counterfeiting activities (see http://www.psi-inc.org).

declaration includes the statement that "counterfeiting medicines, including the entire range of activities from manufacturing to providing them to patients, is a vile and serious criminal offence that puts human lives at risk and undermines the credibility of health systems." Increasingly, international institutions are taking action to tackle corruption, including that affecting the pharmaceutical system (box 1.1).

The objective of this chapter is to explain why and where corruption is possible in the pharmaceutical sector, provide examples of how corruption occurs, highlight diagnostic tools for detecting it, and offer recommendations designed to minimize its occurrence.

WHY IS THE PHARMACEUTICAL SYSTEM VULNERABLE TO CORRUPTION?

The pharmaceutical system is susceptible to fraud and corruption for a variety of reasons. First, the sale of pharmaceutical products is lucrative, the more so because the final customers (patients and their families) are more vulnerable to opportunism than they are in many other product markets, mainly because of asymmetric information. Pharmaceutical suppliers (drug manufacturers, importers, wholesalers, prescribers, and pharmacists) are profit maximizers and will choose to behave in ways that maximize their interests. There is nothing wrong with profit maximization so long as behavior does not go beyond legal norms and, in the health sector, professional ethical norms. The illegal sale of counterfeit, substandard, unregistered, and stolen drugs is particularly attractive where the opportunity for arbitrage exists. In 2002, for example, preferentially priced HIV drugs produced by GlaxoSmithKline that were destined for poor patients in Africa were intercepted and illegally resold in Europe at a substantial markup by a Dutch wholesaler.

In the transition economies of Eastern Europe, to give one regional example, the rapid deregulation and privatization of the pharmaceutical sector, combined with an often unstable economic and political environment, not only created opportunities to engage in corruption but also became a survival strategy for many when salaries of government and health sector workers declined sharply in real terms in the early transition years. In Albania, corrupt actions included private financial interests determining the drugs to be procured for the public health system, bidders giving kickbacks or bribes to gain access to confidential information, and use of direct procurement instead of competitive bidding without sound justification (Vian 2003). In recent years, Albania has made significant strides in eliminating corruption from public procurement of hospital drugs by introducing a transparent, international tendering system that has significantly lowered the price of the average purchase contract for a given drug (World Bank 2006). However, a history of weak drug quality controls has caused consumers to equate cheap prices with bad quality, and so the low-cost generic drugs often go unused.

The pharmaceutical sector is also susceptible to fraud and corruption because it is subject to a significant degree of government regulation. If appropriate checks are not in place, individual government officials might control several core decision points in the pharmaceutical supply chain and may have discretion in making regulatory decisions. Government intervention is justified in the pharmaceutical sector given the imperfect nature of the market and the need to improve the efficiency of resource allocation. Also, regulation is rationalized on the grounds of protecting human life and public health by ensuring that only safe and efficacious medicines are made available in the market. However, the trade-off is that the incidence of corruption may be higher because the state retains a major role in the sector and its bureaucracy is pervasive (Marshall 2001). Without transparency and an accountability framework, state regulation in the pharmaceutical sector can be subject to regulatory capture, permit individual deviance from norms, and be open to corruption in general.

For example, a government may determine what drugs are included on a national essential drugs list or reimbursement list of a public health care payer. The inclusion of a drug on such a list, particularly a reimbursement list, can mean significant financial income for a drug manufacturer because it guarantees the product a relatively predictable market share. If there are no robust institutional checks and oversight mechanisms in place, government regulators may be able to make discretionary decisions about the drugs that are selected. Weak legislative frameworks result in poor outcomes, such as high prices, problems in drug quality, or availability of supply, and create opportunities for unethical and corrupt behavior.

A third reason why the pharmaceutical sector is vulnerable to fraud and corruption is because the supply chain is extremely complex, often involving up to 30 different parties before the product reaches the end user. The number of parties involved, coupled with the difficulty of distinguishing authentic pharmaceutical products from counterfeit or substandard ones, creates opportunity for the introduction of fake and low-quality drugs. In many countries with weak regulation and lax enforcement of drug distribution standards, the sale of counterfeit, unregistered, or expired drugs is very common. WHO estimates that about 25 percent of drugs consumed in poor countries are counterfeit or substandard (WHO 2005a). Controlling such practices is very difficult, particularly where counterfeiters are skillful at copying the form, color, trademarks, and packaging of legitimate products—fooling health professionals as well as patients. While patients in many markets tend to have more confidence in recognized foreign-produced drugs, the high prices of these legitimate versions drive many consumers to seek lower-cost alternatives, which in many cases are not legal, safe, or reliable. These actions have had significant social costs both in terms of access to drugs, particularly for the poor, and in terms of the quality and safety of the drug supply. Typically, it is only when there is blatant sloppiness in copying, or when serious health consequences occur, that patients and health care providers are able to identify counterfeit medicines.

FRAMEWORK FOR IDENTIFYING CORRUPTION

The pharmaceutical system is technically complex. It is made up of several core decision points, ranging from manufacture to service delivery, each of which must be recognized and understood so that corruption cannot thrive out of ignorance (Cohen, Cercone, and Macaya 2002). By understanding the multiple decision points along the pharmaceutical value chain, decision makers can determine where and how corruption can occur and implement effective anticorruption strategies to improve transparency and accountability. If best practices are known, inefficiencies and incompetence are easier to identify and address. This in turn creates a pharmaceutical sector that is less vulnerable to the risks of corruption.

Klitgaard (2000) identifies three main phases in combating corruption. The first phase involves consciousness-raising and includes educating decision makers and the public about corruption and its deleterious effects. The second phase involves adding systems analysis to consciousness-raising to determine where pharmaceutical systems are vulnerable to corruption; this chapter is proposing a framework for making such an analysis. The third phase involves determining what strategies are necessary to prevent corruption from happening in the first place.

The framework developed below is built on the rationale put forward by Klitgaard and described elsewhere in this volume: M (monopoly) + D (discretion) − A (accountability) − T (transparency) = C (corruption).[2] This corruption framework can assist decision makers in identifying circumstances that allow monopoly and discretion and situations where limited accountability and transparency could contribute to the risk of corruption. Policy makers can use the framework to diagnose potential risk points for corruption and to develop anticorruption strategies that address specific, identified risks.

While the nuts and bolts of a pharmaceutical system are similar from country to country, the vulnerable decision points may differ and may even vary within different levels within the same country. Each core decision point needs to function well so that the system as a whole offers safe, efficacious, and cost-effective medicines. If only one decision point is vulnerable to corruption, the integrity of the entire supply chain is at risk, which means that the population's access to essential medicines could be compromised. If a particular decision point is corrupted, the impact on health outcomes may also vary, depending on the institutional organization of the system and the depth of the corruption.

The following section describes these decision points, how they may be susceptible to corruption, and what prevention strategies are necessary to lessen the likelihood of corruption from occurring. The intent here is to provide early warning indicators of possible corruption. In all instances, there are clear limitations in differentiating between corruption, incompetence, and inefficiency, primarily because such distinctions are laden with complexities. What is more, incompetence and inefficiency in the management of the pharmaceutical system can foster corruption. Often, however, the same countervailing measures will reduce both corruption and incompetence or inefficiency. Nonetheless, there is a need to ascertain through case-by-case examples if a given incident is likely to involve corruption, incompetence, or inefficiency. Corruption implies the intent to do wrong, while the latter two do not necessarily entail deliberate wrong-doing.

Corruption can be minimized if institutions are transparent, public scrutiny is high, and the law and administrative processes demand accountability from public officials for their actions (Swenke 2002). The analysis undertaken here builds on Klitgaard's recommendations to disaggregate the types of corruption, determine the scope and seriousness of each type of corruption, and identify the beneficiaries and losers.

ANATOMY OF CORRUPTION: SIX CORE DECISION POINTS

Six main areas in the pharmaceutical sector are key decision points and prime targets for corruption: manufacturing, registration, selection, procurement, distribution, and drug prescribing and dispensing (table 1.1). The primary objectives here are to point out areas that allow for monopoly and discretion and to promote strategies to help solidify transparency and accountability in the system. This framework is consistent with WHO's recent work on transparency and pharmaceuticals (Baghdadi, Cohen, and Wondemagegnehu 2005).

Decision Point One: Manufacturing

Manufacturing of pharmaceutical products requires adherence to standards of good manufacturing practice (GMP) to ensure "that products are consistently produced and controlled to the quality standards appropriate to their intended use and as required by the marketing authorization" (WHO 2003). GMP is a term defined in the law of many countries and describes a set of principles and procedures of quality assurance to be followed by drug manufacturers to help ensure that the products produced meet the required quality. According to WHO, adherence to GMP helps to diminish the risks inherent in pharmaceutical production, in particular cross-contamination (including unexpected contaminants) and mix-ups caused by, for example, wrong labels being put on containers. Unless these established standards are followed throughout the manufacturing process—including handling of raw

TABLE 1.1 Key Decision Points and Related Processes in the Drug Sector that May Be Vulnerable to Corruption

Decision point	*Processes*
Manufacturing	• Adherence to GMPs[a] • Quality management • Packaging and labeling active pharmaceutical ingredients • Master, batch, and laboratory control records • Production and in-process controls • Certificates of analysis • Validation • Tracking complaints and recalls
Registration	• Full registration or abbreviated drug applications • Safety and efficacy • Labeling • Marketing • Indications • Pharmacovigilence and warnings • Batch testing • Reevaluation of older drugs
Selection	• Determine budget • Assess morbidity profile • Determine drug needs to fit morbidity profile • Cost-benefit analysis of drugs • Consistency with WHO (and other evidence-based) criteria • Pricing and reimbursement decisions
Procurement	• Determine model of supply/distribution • Reconcile needs and resources • Develop criteria for tender • Issue tender • Evaluate bids • Award supplier • Determine contract terms • Monitor order • Make payment • Quality assurance
Distribution	• Import approvals • Receive and check drugs with order • Ensure appropriate transportation and delivery to health facilities • Appropriate storage • Good distribution practices and inventory control of drugs • Demand monitoring
Prescribing and Dispensing	• Consulting with health professionals • Inpatient and outpatient care • Dispensing of pharmaceuticals • Adverse drug reaction monitoring • Patient compliance with prescription

Source: Authors.
a. Manufacturing processed section adapted from FDA (2000).

materials, storage, and packaging and labeling—there are risks to quality of drugs produced. Where such standards are not clearly defined or are weak or poorly enforced, there is a higher risk that counterfeit or substandard drugs may be in circulation.

Counterfeit or fake drugs are defined as drugs that are deliberately made to look like the original product, and they thus violate trademark or patents. Drug counterfeiting is a growing market globally. The Center for Medicine in the Public Interest forecasts that the global market for counterfeit medicines will grow more than 90 percent by 2010 to reach annual sales of $75 billion (Pitts 2005). In the United States and Europe, counterfeiting is being driven by the sale of medicines over the Internet; such sales circumvent standard controls and are insufficiently monitored (Satchwell 2004). Although often indistinguishable in appearance from the original products, fake drugs may not have the intended clinical impact, or even be unsafe, because they may contain suboptimal amounts of active pharmaceutical ingredients or none at all.

Substandard or counterfeit medicines can result in poor health outcomes and in the worst case scenario, death. One of the most tragic examples occurred in Haiti in 1995, where 89 people died when they consumed paracetamol cough syrup prepared with diethylene glycol, a toxic chemical used in antifreeze. Substandard drugs that contain less than the acceptable amount of active ingredient are of particular concern in the case of antibiotics or antimalarials, where organisms may more quickly develop resistance. One study in Southeast Asia found that 38 percent of products sold as an artesunate-based antimalarial did not contain sufficient or any active ingredient, potentially increasing resistance (Newton and others 2001). Concerns for increasing resistance to antimalarials in the Mekong region of Asia led governments there to intensify efforts to eliminate fakes and reduce the rate of resistance of the malaria parasite (box 1.2). Counterfeit and substandard drugs also damage the market for legitimately produced quality drugs by limiting their ability to compete on a level playing field.

Several steps can be taken to improve adherence to GMP requirements. First, GMP standards should be codified and appropriate consequences for nonadherence defined by law. Many countries still do not have a legal definition or legislated enforcement of GMP. Second, an international standard for GMP requirements could be adopted. Currently GMP requirements differ from country to country and among

BOX 1.2 Mekong Region Tackles Fakes to Reduce Rates of Antimalarial Resistance

In 2003, the U.S. Pharmacopeia Drug Quality and Information Program, U. S. Agency for International Development, WHO, and national and local authorities in Asia began monitoring the quality of antimalarials used in the Mekong region (Cambodia, Lao People's Democratic Republic, Thailand, Vietnam, and the Yunnan province of China) and teaching drug-testing skills to field staff. In the first year, staff tested the antimalarial quality of drugs being distributed (artesunate, quinine, chloroquine, sulfadoxine-pyramethamine) using basic tests: visual inspection, dissolution, and thin-layer chromatography. Results of testing revealed substandard or fake antimalarials in all countries; in at least two countries, 50 percent of the samples tested had no manufacturing information or expiration date. Drug regulatory authorities in all these countries have since taken steps to address these problems. In particular, communications between the regional monitoring systems and local and national drug authorities have improved, leading to swifter notification that fake drugs are circulating and faster removal of counterfeit drugs from all drug outlets.

Source: U.S. Pharmacopeial Convention Inc. (2005).

BOX 1.3 Different GMP Requirements Can Have Unintended Implications: India

In India, the current regulatory standard for manufacturing is defined in a legal document known as Schedule M. Although the introduction of Schedule M was delayed several times (from late 2002 to mid-2005), it was an important step forward for India. Nevertheless, the requirements it defines differ from the GMP standards recommended by WHO. The Indian courts have since ruled that Schedule M is the legal standard that all manufacturers presenting themselves for national procurement must follow. This ruling has created a challenge and a standoff of sorts for procurement of HIV/AIDS, malaria, and other drugs financed by international organizations and other governments for distribution in poor countries. These organizations generally demand that the WHO GMP standards must be met as a minimum requirement for the drugs procured with their financing.

Further, the fact that Schedule M is weaker than comparative GMP requirements in the United States and Europe also does not play to the favor of the growing Indian drug industry. Some of the leading Indian drug manufacturers, including some manufacturing facilities approved by the FDA, have self-imposed higher regulatory standards than are required by Schedule M. While these leading Indian manufacturers are producing international quality drugs, the fact that the Schedule M is weak and that some Indian manufacturers will continue to manufacture to these lower standards may have negative implications for the reputation of the Indian drug industry as a whole. Raising the GMP standards in India would lift the quality of the industry as a whole and be beneficial for its export markets.

enforcement agencies. Even WHO, the EU, and the FDA define GMP somewhat differently. Differences in the definition of these requirements can result in negative unintended consequences (box 1.3).

Even if a country has strong, legally defined GMP standards, adherence depends on the capacity to enforce the standards. Thus, a second step is ensuring credible enforcement. Some countries have found it effective to have both regular and random inspections not only of the manufacturing premises but also of drugs at various stages of the market process from manufacture or import to retail. Following a study in Myanmar and Vietnam, WHO concluded that inspections at various links of the pharmaceutical value chain are critical to stop the sale of counterfeit medicine (Wondemagegnehu 1995). The quality of these inspections depends on adequate financing of the regulatory agencies to ensure a sufficient number of appropriately screened, trained, and adequately paid inspectors. Inspectors should be put on a rotating schedule for the manufacturing sites to minimize the possibility that an inspector will develop too close a relationship with the manufacturer. Customs officials should also receive adequate training in identification of counterfeit products.

Even with such inspections, however, the sophistication of the counterfeiters demands more advanced means to identify and distinguish the fake or suboptimal products. Random batch testing of drugs at various stages in the market process is one method. Another is identifying legitimately registered pharmaceutical products with simple and inexpensive markers of authenticity such as bar codes or holograms. Such identifiers also can help the general public to recognize counterfeit products, as we discuss in more detail in the next section.

It is also important to engage the pharmaceutical industry in tackling fake drugs. Fourteen major research-based pharmaceutical companies have set up the PSI to deal with this problem. Through the PSI, these companies monitor the integrity of their own products in industrial countries where fake medicines are entering. In addition to tracking product flows, the members of the PSI are also engaged in educating pharmacists and other health professionals about counterfeit medicines and disseminating information on the topic more broadly to consumers. Many leading pharmaceutical manufacturers are refusing to sell their products to secondary distributors if these distributors cannot guarantee the legitimacy of all their suppliers.

The multinational pharmaceutical industry is particularly concerned about ensuring the integrity of its supply chain and mitigating reputation risks by preventing infiltration of counterfeit drugs. While bar coding and scanning have been popular methods for the past 20 years, leading drug makers are rapidly embracing more sophisticated technologies such as radio frequency identification (RFID) tags and electronic product codes (EPCs) (box 1.4). The advantage of these newer technologies over bar code systems is that the older system requires personnel to "read" the codes, while the newer systems are automated to read and store the information in ways that can easily be retrieved. In the case of RFID, this information can be easily read and retrieved from anywhere throughout a network that can extend across countries, enabling manufacturers to track and monitor their products (including storage conditions) more easily. Further, with this system a wholesaler, retailer, or even customs official, for example, could potentially read the RFID tag to check the electronic pedigree of a product and hence verify its legitimacy and integrity. However, RFID technology is relatively new, and the infrastructure to support it, particularly at the retail and regulatory level, is only at the early stages of being established. There are also privacy concerns, and the technology is not entirely foolproof (for example, a counterfeiter could conceivably replace the contents of a legitimate package bearing an RFID tag with a counterfeit or adulterated product); moreover, the technology is costly.

To further discourage counterfeiting and the production of substandard drugs, those manufacturers found to be noncompliant with standards should be named, penalized, and shamed, with their violations publicly announced. Compliant manufacturers should also be recognized and have their names posted on the drug agency Web sites, for example, to help health professionals and patients more easily recognize the manufacturers that are achieving quality.

BOX 1.4 Leading Drug Makers Embrace RFID Technology to Secure Supply

An RFID tag emits a small radio wave that can be used to identify the package that is tagged. Increasingly, leading pharmaceutical manufacturers are using RFID tags in their supply chains because they generate an electronic pedigree that allows verification of the authenticity of the product. For example, an RFID tag can be attached to a package when it leaves the drug manufacturing facility. At each subsequent point in the supply chain, the tag can be read to verify its previous location and attributes and then be updated for the next RFID reader in the network. RFID tags are machine readable and require no human intervention. These tags are also extremely difficult to counterfeit. RFID tags can also monitor other characteristics such as the temperature at which the product is being stored and can detect product diversion from the predetermined distribution path. Distributors and pharmacists that have appropriate technology can verify the integrity of the electronic pedigree, providing reassurance about the legitimacy and integrity of a given product.

Decision Point Two: Registration and Market Authorization

Drug registration and market authorization were originally introduced to protect patients from drug catastrophes like the thalidomide tragedy of the 1950s, when inadequate safety testing of the drug resulted in severe malformities in children born to women who had taken this drug during their pregnancies. The process of market authorization is generally undertaken by a national drug agency, responsible for the evaluation of a drug's safety, its efficacy against a specific disease, its possible side effects, and, in the case of a generic, its bioequivalency or bioavailability. Drug regulatory agencies are also often responsible for setting and enforcing standards relating to the manufacture, storage, and distribution of pharmaceutical products; licensing of pharmacists, pharmacies, and wholesalers; defining labeling, marketing, usage, warning, and prescription requirements; and providing postmarket surveillance and pharmacovigilence.[3] Examples of potential vulnerabilities at the registration decision point include the following: the law defining drug registration may be weak, vulnerable, or flawed; suppliers may pay government officials to register their drugs without the requisite information; government officials may deliberately delay the registration of a pharmaceutical product to favor market conditions for another supplier; or officials may deliberately slow down registration procedures to solicit payment from a supplier.

Drug registration needs to have a strong legal basis that ensures transparency as well as uniform and effective application of the defined standards. Transparency is vital to enforcing limits placed on individual discretion and minimizing risks of regulatory capture. Where the regulatory agency is dependent on the fees it receives from the drug manufacturers it is meant to regulate, independence can be difficult, and it is particularly in such circumstances that independence of the regulatory staff, separation of functions and contact with manufacturers, and transparency become even more important.

Financing an independent drug agency is a key challenge, yet one that must be met because ensuring adequate capacity is vital to the effectiveness of the drug quality control process. According to WHO, "every country regardless of its stage of development [or size], should consider investment in an independent national drug quality control laboratory," particularly given the infiltration of counterfeit drugs into local markets (WHO 1997). Yet where financial resources are limited and a full drug laboratory is not available, reliance on drugs that have gone through the WHO prequalification process can add an improved level of confidence to quality control. Another option is for poorer countries to collaborate on, say, a regional basis to finance a drug control laboratory that would serve these countries collectively. This strategy would require regional uniformity in legal requirements and might be more easily implemented in areas that collaborate in a free-trade area. The EU has adopted this approach, opting for a mutual recognition procedure, in addition to a centralized authorization procedure, so that a drug approved in one member state is granted authorization in the other member states. The EU approach has required a significant effort to harmonize legislation and procedures, but it has reduced the costs associated with drug authorization by reducing duplication both for the countries and drug companies. Some small countries have piggy-backed on the regulatory approvals of established markets by adopting an abridged application process when the same product, produced by the same manufacturer, has been authorized in established markets such as the United States, Europe, or Japan (box 1.5). Other harmonization efforts such as that of the International Conference on Harmonization or similar regional efforts are also important for standardizing approaches and improving interchange between countries to tackle counterfeiting.[4]

Various strategies can be used to lower the risk of corruption in the drug registration process. For example, to minimize the risk of individual discretion, procedures should be applied uniformly and all criteria made available to the public. The regulatory authority must operate impartially and justify its decisions clearly and openly. To facilitate this, all regulatory employees should be screened for any potential conflict of interest that could bias any decision making. Information on the drug registration process, its criteria, and results should be published regularly and disseminated in local newspapers and on the Internet. Disclosing on the Web site lists of all applications for registration and of all registered drugs (with dates) increases transparency. Overhauling the drug quality control system generally requires a multipronged approach pushed forward by strong political leadership (box 1.6).

Drug quality control requires not only a transparent drug agency but also ongoing market surveillance. To ensure the integrity of the drug supply, a market surveillance strategy should include mechanisms for monitoring the drug supply, such as random batch testing and reporting streams to ensure feedback from health professionals and users to responsible authorities when problems are identified. Additional

BOX 1.5 Approaches for Meeting Drug Registration Challenges

Many countries do not have the resources or the size to justify a full-scale drug agency such as the FDA or the European Medicines Evaluation Agency (EMEA). Instead, they have turned to alternative ways of ensuring the quality, safety, and efficacy of the drugs entering their markets, without completing all testing themselves. Common strategies include:

- *Quality.* Drugs entering the market must have documentation showing they meet standards defined in regulation, recognized pharmacopoeias, and defined guidelines.
- *Safety.* Drugs must have documentation showing they were manufactured according to regulation, scientific standards, and recognized guidelines.
- *Efficacy.* Drugs must have documentation showing that they are efficacious in treating specific conditions, according to regulation, scientific standards, and internationally recognized guidelines.
- *Essentially similar products.* Drugs must have documentation attesting to their bioavailability and therapeutic equivalency.
- *Outside documentation.* Some countries accept the documentation submitted to a recognized drug agency such as the FDA or EMEA for applicant products that have already been granted market authorization by such an agency.
- *Outsourcing:* Where documentation is not otherwise available, the country may outsource the required testing to a third-party laboratory.

These strategies save time and resources. However, having laboratory testing available, should it be required, is still necessary, particularly for otherwise undocumented products or for batch testing of marketed products. Further, ensuring that staff are independent and adequately trained to manage this process is vital.

BOX 1.6 Political Leadership and Public Engagement Essential to Tackling Counterfeit Drugs: Nigeria's Experience

Starting in the late 1980s, fake and substandard drugs began to dominate the Nigerian pharmaceutical market. Studies showed that more than 50 percent of drugs sampled in drugstores and pharmacies were not compliant with pharmacopeia standards (in one drugstore, 80 percent were not compliant). Some of these drugs had no active ingredient at all, others were mislabeled (for example, paracetamol labeled as the antimalarial drug Fansidar) or had only a small amount of active substance (50 milligrams of ampicillin instead of 250). Other samples were outdated or not registered in Nigeria at all. Unfortunately, no statistics are available on the number of people who became ill or died because of the consumption of fake drugs, although there are several anecdotal reports of fatalities. Important economic consequences also resulted from the proliferation of counterfeit dugs. Several international drug companies closed their offices in Nigeria, and Nigerian-made drugs were no longer allowed on the market in neighboring countries.

To tackle the problem of counterfeit drugs, the National Agency for Food and Drug Administration and Control (NAFDAC) introduced a multipronged strategy:

- *NAFDAC was overhauled.* Staff members were retrained and made more accountable through the use of more transparent procedures. Registration guidelines were updated and implementation capacity strengthened. The number of inspectors was increased and controls at the ports of entry were made effective, leading to many seizures of drug shipments. Illegal importers then started using airfreight, which NAFDAC countered by grounding aircraft that brought drugs into Nigeria without prior authorization. NAFDAC also ensured better control of manufacturing sites at source for GMP compliance before import certificates were issued.
- *NAFDAC engaged in a large "mopping up" exercise,* raiding local markets, manufacturers, and warehouses and seizing and burning large amounts of fake drugs. If the owner of the fake drugs could not be identified, the landlord of the premises was held accountable. Substandard manufacturing facilities and several drugstores were closed down.
- *A public campaign was started* through the media and through NAFDAC Consumer Safety Clubs at schools. The combination of publicity and pressure on the illegal trade led to a major break in 2001, when local drug sellers "outed" the largest supplier of fake drugs and helped NAFDAC to locate his warehouse, leading to the destruction of $14 million worth of fake drugs.

As a result of this campaign, NAFDAC recorded an 80 percent reduction in the incidence of fake drugs in the market in 2004. Government officials prevented 32 containers of counterfeit drugs hidden in spare car parts and imported shirts stuffed with painkillers from entering the market. Thirty convictions related to counterfeit drugs were secured, and 40 more cases were pending. The local industry experienced a turnaround with significantly growing sales and stock prices—16 new manufacturing sites have opened in the last three years. Some West African neighbors have lifted their ban on Nigerian drugs, and multinationals are coming back to Nigeria.

This campaign would not have been possible without the political leadership of the head of NAFDAC, who barely survived two assassination attempts, not to mention several death threats. Some NAFDAC officers were severely beaten and their vehicle destroyed when they confronted drug sellers, and NAFDAC buildings and labs were burned down or vandalized.

This case offers several lessons in curbing corruption in the pharmaceutical sector. Political leadership with the will and perseverance to take on corruption is absolutely necessary. It is also helpful to make an example of counterfeiters and to give small retail drug sellers incentives to act ethically. Increased inspections and credible enforcement must be among those incentives. Finally, education and training that involves the general public is critical for minimizing the incidence of corruption.

Source: Akunyili (2005).

BOX 1.7 Azerbaijan's Experience in Reducing Counterfeit Drugs

To provide patients with more certainty about the quality of the drugs they are consuming, the Central Drug Control Laboratory of Azerbaijan underwent extensive modernization and introduced several measures to tackle the problem of unregistered drugs on the market. First the lab instituted a requirement for testing each batch of drugs to be put on the market in the country. Those drugs that passed inspection were given hologram stickers, which are difficult to copy, so that doctors, pharmacists, and patients can identify them as quality controlled. The government also introduced a hotline that enables patients to call and check whether a given batch number has passed quality control. Since they were introduced in 2003, these efforts have led to a number of arrests and the seizure of unregistered drugs, and the trade in some counterfeit products has slowed.

inspection measures, including the use of field techniques (for example, the minilab used by the German Pharma Health Fund[5]) where sophisticated analysis is not available, can also be useful tools to inspectors or health professionals. Training health professionals and the public to identify counterfeit and unregistered drugs is also an important anticorruption strategy. As the experience in Azerbaijan shows, ensuring some way for consumers to identify quality-controlled drugs can go a long way toward mitigating the risks from counterfeits (box 1.7).

In Nigeria, Azerbaijan, and elsewhere, involving consumers in the identification of fake medicines has been an important part of the strategy.[6] Consumers have been informed through various media, including radio, television, print media, and the Internet, of government initiatives and ways to identify potentially counterfeit products. Consumers have been shown how to identify a product that has gone through quality control (for example, by recognizing certain demarcations on packaging) and how to identify licensed pharmacies. A critical part of these initiatives has been the development of a feedback mechanism for consumers such as a toll-free hotline number where they can ask questions or report dubious products or drug sellers. Ensuring follow-up on such tips and reporting any actions taken as a result of a consumer's involvement is important for building confidence and ensuring ongoing consumer participation.

Decision Point Three: Selection

For publicly funded drugs, the primary government task in drug selection is to ensure that the most cost-effective and appropriate drugs for a population's health needs are chosen in a fair and transparent manner through the use of impartial expert committees. WHO's essential drug list (EDL) is a helpful framework for most developing countries because it establishes priority medicines and lists the most common diseases together with effective and affordable drugs.[7] The use of EDLs has helped to increase objectivity and transparency of the selection process by listing cost-effective drugs according to their international nonproprietary (generic) names, which further stimulates generic competition (Vian 2005). However, if the selection process is not institutionally sound, even if the EDL is followed, corruption can still occur because manufacturers have a strong interest in getting their products listed.

BOX 1.8 Failure to Fully Specify Product in the Drug List Has Led to Underdosing

In the Democratic Republic of Congo, the government's failure to specify the type of quinine salt required for the treatment of malaria has led to underdosing. The country's EDL indicated the dose appropriate for using quinine hydrochloride in the treatment of malaria. But because it did not explicitly state which salt (hydrochloride or sulphate) should be used, one manufacturer began offering quinine sulfate, which must be given at a higher dosage than quinine hydrochloride to be effective. Patients who took this drug were consequently underdosed, a situation that could have potential health consequences as well as increase the threat of parasite resistance.

If institutions are weak and individuals have incentives to engage in corrupt activities, the selection process can be replete with kickbacks and payoffs so that drugs on a national drug list are not necessarily those that are appropriate and cost effective.

In some cases in the Balkans, for example, the dosage specified for a product in the essential drugs list has been set at a level that enables a favored manufacturer to secure selection, where its presentation of a given product has been different from the standard dosing offered by other manufacturers, enabling it to win the bid. In other cases, failure by the regulatory authority to carefully specify its selected products has allowed some manufacturers to behave unethically, if not illegally (box 1.8).

There are several strategies for curbing the risk of corruption in the selection process. Explicit criteria must be defined ahead of time by an expert committee and publicized so that stakeholders have clear knowledge about what criteria are being applied in the drug selection process. Members of the expert committees should be publicly identified, and their credentials and the terms of reference for membership on the committee posted publicly. Drug selection criteria should be based on international standards as set out by WHO and should include relevance to the pattern of prevalent diseases in a country; proven efficacy and safety according to sound data; evidence of performance in a variety of environments; good quality of drugs, taking into account bioavailability, stability, and a favorable cost-benefit ratio (based on assessment of total treatment cost); preference for drugs that are well known, with good pharmacokinetic properties; and public scrutiny, including regular reporting by the media of drug selection meetings. These measures would contribute to transparency and limit unethical practices.

Equally important, the deletion of a drug from the national drug formulary should be based on sound evidence that the drug is inappropriate or not cost effective for the health needs of the population. Open and formal consultations with the public should be institutionalized to ensure that all stakeholder views are taken into account in the drug selection process and in its aftermath and that no single group has undue influence.

The issues of drug pricing and rate of reimbursement by the public health system or social health insurer are closely linked to the drug selection process. Unless clear procedures are used, this area can be particularly susceptible to regulatory capture and corruption because drug pricing decisions can be subjective and vulnerable to inflation. There are a plethora of different approaches to regulating prices with varying degrees of appropriateness, fairness, and value for money. Some countries continue to negotiate drug prices directly, which clearly opens the door to much bias, regulatory capture, and potential scope for corruption.

Where generic competition is possible, and where basic conditions are met (such as a sound drug regulatory system that ensures the quality and interchangeability of drugs, and incentives for price awareness among doctors, pharmacists, and patients), then the market should be allowed to compete in price without further regulation. This is the case in successful generics markets such as the United States.

In several countries, however, the need to develop a fair pricing scheme for pharmaceutical products has led to a search for ways to set a more objective reference of fairness and appropriateness for drug prices on their own market by using the prices of drugs in other countries as a point of comparison (this practice is known as international reference pricing or cross-reference pricing). This approach has its own problems, of course, including how appropriate a selected country or its prices may be for the referent country.[8] For drugs where no competitive pricing is possible, one method that is increasingly being used is pharmacoeconomic evaluation, which gauges the cost-effectiveness of a drug relative to comparator products.[9] While one could easily engage in a full chapter on the benefits and pitfalls of the various approaches to regulating drug prices, the key here is to ensure that whatever method undertaken be as objective and transparent as possible.

As long as the methods used are uniform, publicly available, and based on objective criteria, and the process is as transparent and objective as possible, corruption can be curbed. Suggested strategies include public dissemination of written procedures for pricing; establishment of specific criteria and terms of reference for pricing committees, which should include disclosure of any potential conflict of interest; the monitoring and dissemination of prices; and creation of a formal appeals committee to hear pricing disputes. Making pricing decisions publicly available over the Internet has also helped to add transparency. Assessing the vulnerability of this process is vital to identifying a strategy to strengthen the process (box 1.9). Best practices in transparency and mitigating corruption in pharmaceutical pricing can be taken from a number of industrial countries that have learned from their own incidences of corruption to identify less vulnerable processes.

Decision Point Four: Procurement

The goal of procurement is to acquire the right quantity of quality drugs at the most cost-effective price.[10] Government functions in this decision point include inventory management, aggregate purchasing, public bidding contests, technical analysis of offers, the proper allocation of resources, payments, receipt of drugs purchased, and quality control checks. Procurement is often poorly documented and processed, which makes it an easy target for corruption. The best protection against corruption is generally international competitive procurement because it maximizes competition and minimizes opportunities for personal discretion in the selection of suppliers. Competitive procurement requires an open bidding process and clear criteria for the selection and processing of winning bids. The procurement process must include

BOX 1.9 Assessing the Vulnerability to Corruption in Pricing: The Balkans

An internal World Bank study was undertaken in selected Balkan countries (Albania, Bosnia-Herzegovina, Croatia, Macedonia, and Serbia-Montenegro) to extend and apply a corruption diagnostic focusing strictly on drug selection, procurement, and pricing. The premise for this work was anecdotal evidence suggesting that drug prices are high in many of these countries compared with neighboring countries or average international prices and that corruption may be a main reason for this problem. The working hypothesis was that a weakly developed regulatory framework in this imperfect market could create an opportunity for corruption and compromise the possibility of obtaining competitively priced drugs.[a]

With the fall of communism, the pharmaceutical sectors in all these countries went through a period of liberalization and privatization. Over the last decade, a period of reregulation has ensued as the countries have attempted to address challenges in developing a modern, safe, and affordable pharmaceutical system. But the governments lack experience in regulating in this new market context, and most professional associations and codes of ethical practice are new, absent, or weakly enforced. In addition, the legislative frameworks have tended to be weak, resulting in high prices and problems in drug quality and availability of supply and creating the opportunity for unethical and corrupt behavior. The rapid evolution of insurance funds and purchasing groups that select, price, procure, reimburse, and manage drug expenditures has added a complicating factor.

The market for pharmaceuticals in these countries is dominated by off-patent, multisourced, branded generic drugs; generic substitution is uncommon. Local or ex-Yugoslavian suppliers are dominant in many markets with favored arrangements. All countries use a form of reference pricing or tender mechanism for outpatient and hospital drugs, which should lead to competitive prices.

To assess drug selection, pricing, and procurement, a series of indicators was adapted from a World Bank study (Cohen, Cercone, and Macaya 2002) to focus on this part of the pharmaceutical chain and assess its vulnerability to corruption. The countries showed more vulnerability to corruption in pricing and procurement than in drug selection (see figure below). The least vulnerable and most transparent processes were found in Croatia, while the most vulnerable were in Macedonia. This assessment was undertaken before significant reforms were initiated in several of the countries. For example, in 2004, Macedonia introduced international tendering and a more transparent drug selection process. Montenegro also introduced reforms to increase transparency and competition in its tendering process.

Vulnerability to Corruption Indicators in Eastern Europe, 2003

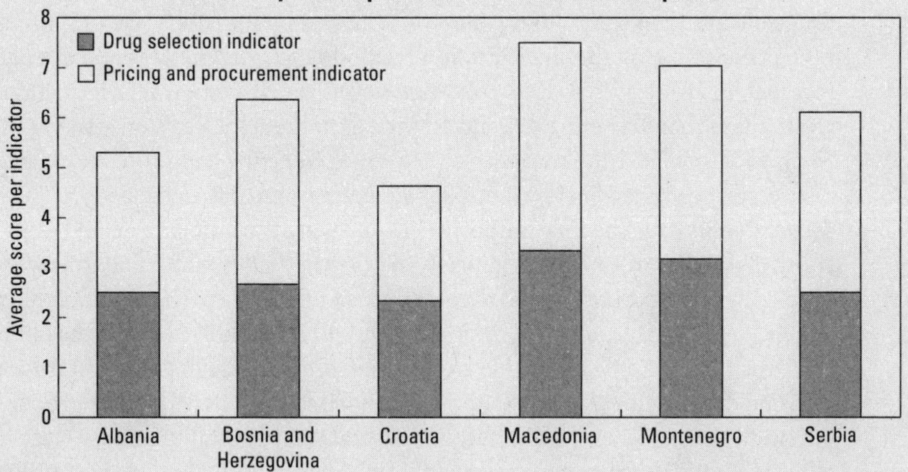

a. Imperfections in the operation of the market for pharmaceuticals generally relate to patent protection (which poses the challenge of how to balance desirable incentives for innovation with affordable access for poorer countries and patients), the process and length of regulatory approval, product differentiation and brand loyalty, as well as in information asymmetries, moral hazard, and imperfect principal-agent relationships in the demand for pharmaceuticals; demand has a four-tiered structure of the physician prescribing, the pharmacist dispensing, the patient consuming, and a third party paying.

continuous monitoring, including reviews from the inspector general's office or similar internal and external audit institutions for the public sector (USAID 1999). Reports must also be easily available for public scrutiny.

The procurement of publicly funded drug supplies is particularly susceptible to corruption because drug volumes are usually large and the value of contracts is usually high even if unit costs are low; hence contracts can be very lucrative for suppliers. Domestic or international suppliers may pay public officials bribes to gain advantage at any of several steps in the tender process. Biased procurement methods can also be employed, such as the use of direct purchase when there is no emergency to justify it. Several factors contribute to procurement corruption: The method for determining the volume of drugs needed is often subjective; there are difficulties in monitoring quality standards; coordinating procurement and product registration processes in a timely way can be challenging if the pharmaceuticals licensing agency is inefficient or corrupt; suppliers use different prices for the same pharmaceutical products and can artificially inflate prices; and specifications for drug procurement can be tailored to suit the products of one supplier. All of these factors require strong oversight mechanisms within the public procurement process. Lack of good governance in the procurement area can result in the purchase of inappropriate products and overpayment for products. To ensure institutionally strong procurement systems, some Caribbean countries have pooled their limited resources. Other countries with limited resources have contracted out some procurement functions to the private sector or to the United Nations and other development agencies with specialized drug procurement operations.

One of the core government tasks in procuring drugs is estimating the quantity needed. Preparing reliable estimates can help countries avoid having too low or excessively high inventory levels. Quantification methods are used to determine drug budgets, plan for new and expanding pharmaceutical programs, optimize drug budgets based on priority health problems and cost-effective treatments, and compare current drug consumption with public health priorities and use in other health systems.

A clear policy on the quantification methodology, preferably as part of a national, regional, or institutional drug policy, can limit the discretion that individuals and groups have to inflate estimates and provide a check on the decision-making process. As an additional institutional check, the drug therapeutic committee at the national, district, or health facility level, usually already responsible for selection of essential drugs, should have the final authority in approving the outcome of a quantification effort. This committee, however, needs to be composed of impartial experts who are selected in a transparent way and have clear terms of reference. The names of the experts and their specific roles and responsibilities should be made available to the public.

Procurement officials should concentrate on ensuring that the best price possible is paid for high-value, good-quality, priority products. A quality procurement system needs to address and monitor the actual (that is, total) purchase price of supplies, including hidden costs caused by poor product quality, poor supplier performance or short shelf-life, inventory holding cost at various levels of the supply system, and operating costs and capital requirements for the management and administration of the procurement and distribution system. Large procurement volumes generally result in better prices and contract terms for purchasers, given economies of scale. The pooling of procurement volume from many health facilities or from several states or countries, restrictions on drug selection, and the elimination of duplication within therapeutic categories can lead to higher volumes for single items and to potentially lower drug prices if the procurement process is executed sufficiently well. But such collaborative purchasing works effectively only if appropriate procedures are in place to ensure that the process is fair, that quantification is accurate, and that distribution is efficient.

Procurement procedures must be transparent, following formal written procedures throughout the process and using explicit criteria to award contracts to reduce the risk of corruption. The World Bank procurement guidelines for pharmaceuticals (World Bank 2000) provides a useful model to follow. Information on the tender process and results should be available in the public domain as a check against collusion and inflated drug prices. Brazil in recent years has posted prices paid for publicly procured pharmaceuticals on a Web site as a strategy to reduce drug prices and preclude price manipulation. Through the use of electronic bidding and information dissemination about procurement procedures and results, corruption risks there have been mitigated. These tools can be more robust when they are coupled with parallel efforts, such as ensuring that a wide range of suppliers, both local and international, is competing for each drug product that is being tendered. A large number of potential suppliers can help foster price competition and reduce the risk of collusion or price gouging on the part of the suppliers (Cohen and Carikeo Montoya 2001).

A drug procurement system should ensure that reliable suppliers of high-quality products are selected and that active quality assurance programs with both surveillance and drug testing are implemented. Pre- and postqualification procedures can help to eliminate substandard suppliers from the tendering process and thus help ensure the timely execution of tenders. Prequalification of suppliers is usually done by a broad-based procurement committee, composed of managers and technical staff, including quality assurance experts.

Establishing an initial list of prequalified suppliers for each drug product is initially a time-consuming process but saves time in the long run. The postqualification system evaluates the suppliers after bids have been received, and there may be long delays in awarding contracts while the capacity of numerous unknown suppliers is evaluated. Evaluating new suppliers may include formal registration, inspection, reference checks, test purchases, and informal local information gathering. An important component of quality assurance is "traceability," which means that suppliers must be able to trace a product to its manufacturer transparently, while the manufacturer must be able to trace the ingredients to their producers, again transparently. In any case, the selection of suppliers must be justified and backed up with appropriate evidence.

Successful procurement offices can monitor good supplier performance through a formal monitoring system that tracks lead time, compliance with contract terms, partial shipments, quality of drugs, compliance with packaging and labeling instructions, and other best practices. A good information system should also track the number and cost of tender contracts awarded and the cost of total purchases from the supplier by year and performance for each tender.

Prequalification tendering systems may keep substandard suppliers out of the tender process, but this method is not free from the risk of corruption if the suppliers included on the list are not chosen by objective and verifiable criteria. A postqualification system, conversely, may inappropriately exclude qualified bidders if a procurement agency wants to favor certain companies. In both cases, "detail" persons or company representatives may seek to influence governments to purchase drugs that may not be appropriate, either economically or therapeutically.

To mitigate corruption risks, procurement offices should strictly adhere to the announced closing date. Written records should be kept of all bids received; these records should include the date the bid was received and the name of the person who received the bid. Unopened bids should be stored in a locked, secure area until the closing date. All bids should be formally, and ideally publicly, opened on a specified date, and opened bids should be logged in a ledger and numbered for future reference. Furthermore, employees in the procurement office should assemble information for the tender board or procurement committee and make technical recommendations to them, but they should not make final contract decisions. Adjudication and awarding should be made only by the procurement committee or the tender board, with the results of adjudication, including the winning bidder and the contract price, available to all participating bidders and the public (through a posting on a Web site, for example).

The procurement office should be required to report regularly on key procurement performance indicators. Standard indicators include the planned purchase volume compared with the actual volume consumed within a specified time frame, the prices obtained compared with the average international prices, the average supplier lead time and service level, the percentage of key drugs in stock at various levels of the supply system, and a report on drug shortages. These indicators are also useful because they allow for the comparison of actual performance data with the targets over a time series. Finally, the procurement office should be audited annually by a third party that is screened for professionalism. The auditor should issue a statutory report in accordance with the legal regulations of the jurisdiction and in addition should issue a detailed letter of comment to the management of the organization and the appropriate public supervisory body. The annual audit should be available publicly through a Web site or through a government public information office.

Decision Point Five: Distribution

Whether it is done by a government agency or by a private company that has been contracted by the government, the public distribution system needs to ensure the timely and safe delivery of appropriate quantities of drugs to health facilities and pharmacies where supplies are needed. Distribution and storage costs can make up a significant amount of the retail price of a drug, especially when drugs are distributed to remote locations or where a lack of competition leads to inappropriate markups by wholesalers and retailers. Some countries have introduced codes of Good Distribution Practice that standardize requirements for distribution personnel, documentation, premises, and equipment. Poor storage conditions can lead to losses through both the diversion (corruption) and the expiration of drugs (inefficiency). A well-designed and well-managed distribution and storage system aims to maintain a constant supply of drugs, keep them in good condition throughout the distribution process, minimize drug losses due to spoilage and expiry, rationalize drug storage points, and use available transportation resources as efficiently as possible.

There are a number of models for supplying drugs. The most common in public sector supply chains is the central medical store, in which drugs are financed, procured, and distributed by the government. A second model is the autonomous or semiautonomous supply agency. This model has more flexibility than the government model, but fragmentation of purchasing volume can increase prices in comparison with a centralized purchasing system. A third model is the direct delivery system, whereby a government procurement office tenders for drugs and other supplies that are then delivered directly from the drug supplier to the health facility. This model helps reduce costs related to centralized storage and transport from the government by shifting them to private suppliers. A fourth model is the prime vendor system. In this system, a government procurement office tenders for two contracts, the first for drug sources and prices, and the second one for supplying the drugs to stores and health facilities. The party contracted for supplying drugs (prime vendor) is responsible for maintaining sufficient stocks to fill orders from regional and district stores, and health facilities. Finally, drug supplies can be purchased and distributed through a fully private supply system. There is no clear evidence to date about which model most effectively reduces the likelihood of corruption. Oversight mechanisms, clear benchmark standards, and transparent procedures are needed for each of these models.

If good practices are not in place in this decision point, direct losses can be caused by breaches in the process, including incorrect transport and storage conditions, unnecessary stocks, expired stocks, and theft of drug supplies. Opportunities for the diversion and theft of goods are present in all stages of the storage and distribution system (box 1.10). Shipments can be plundered by sea- or airport workers, or systematic crime syndicates may steal large quantities from customs warehouses, airport fields, and elsewhere. During transportation, drugs may be sold by drivers at markets along the delivery route or damaged along the way, or large quantities may be diverted to the black market. Politicians and local leaders may divert supplies to their supporters or patronage networks, and health facility staff may resell subsidized drugs or steal drugs for use in their own private practices or for their private use.

BOX 1.10 Drug Leakage and Theft in Uganda: Strategies for Prevention

Pharmaceutical distribution systems can be subject to theft, diversion, and resale of drugs. A study that focused on Uganda found that publicly funded drugs were stolen and resold on the private market, that health care workers pocketed the payments for drugs, and that service was withheld from poor people who could not afford to pay for their drugs. Altogether, the study found that 68–77 percent of revenues from formal user charges were misappropriated by workers (McPake and others 1999). Clear differentiation of the products belonging to the public procurement system through special packaging, bar coding, and holograms can help to identify public products. In some cases, standard theft prevention measures could also help reduce product loss. This includes monitoring access of personnel into and out of drug warehouses as well as sufficient information systems to monitor drug stocks.

When drugs are imported, which is common in most countries, additional steps may be involved in gaining import approvals and in testing of imported batches. These steps can be vulnerable to corruption. In Serbia-Montenegro, domestic manufacturers used legal batch-testing requirements to impose additional costs on competing imports. In one case, a noted local manufacturer was reported to have bribed both the minister and deputy minister of health in order to maintain these discriminatory provisions in a new pharmaceutical law introduced in 2003.

Strategies to reduce the risk of corruption during the distribution process include the following. Information must flow easily through every level of the distribution system to control inventory movements and deliveries. This is usually best done through the use of computerized and automated information systems, specifically those systems that use bar coding and scanners or the newer, more sophisticated systems with RFID technology and EPCs. Quality standards must be maintained in storage facilities and should include refrigeration units to guarantee the integrity of the drugs. Good security is necessary to minimize the risk of theft. The electronic monitoring of transport vehicles and careful checking of delivery orders against inventories of products delivered are some of the methods that can reduce theft. Implementing a Public Expenditure Tracking Survey is also a useful tool for assessing whether the drugs and the financing for drugs are getting to their ultimate delivery points such as the health clinics and hospitals, particularly those in rural areas. [11]

Decision Point Six: Drug Prescribing and Dispensing

Drug prescribing and dispensing involves the participation of physicians, pharmacists, nurses, and other health care providers who diagnose patients and identify what drugs a patient should consume (if any) to treat a particular disease. This is the decision point at which patients should experience the benefits of the entire system, if it is functioning well. Patients should receive the right drug at the right time at the right cost and with the appropriate information.

The main concern with drug prescribing and dispensing is that the patient may not always receive the most appropriate drug for a given condition because the prescription decision can be driven by other factors, in particular, a self-interested profit motivation. In many developing countries, it is common for a pharmacist or an unqualified drug seller to dispense drugs without a prescription. In such situations, the pharmacist takes on a critical role in drug choice and can be directly motivated to dispense the most expensive drug to earn a higher margin rather than select the most appropriate product for a patient. This inherent conflict of interest is one reason for separating the prescribing and dispensing functions. The task for a government if the prescription system is weak is to establish a regulatory environment that promotes appropriate drug choice and dispensing practices and cost-effective care.

Many advanced countries have adopted regulations to separate the prescribing role of doctors from the dispensing role of pharmacies, so that doctors do not have financial incentives to prescribe inappropriately high quantities of drugs or higher-cost drugs than are clinically necessary. Until recently, for example, the Republic of

Korea allowed doctors to prescribe and dispense medicines, which led to a high number of unnecessary prescriptions (Kwon 2006). Some countries permit exemptions for rural doctors in areas where patients may lack convenient access to a pharmacy. Evidence that prescribing practices are influenced by the profits from dispensing comes from England, where rural "dispensing doctors" have been found to be less likely than nondispensing doctors to comply with policies advocating the use of generic drugs when available (rather than using brand-name drugs) and to have a higher propensity to prescribe branded generics (Watkins and others 2003; Baines and others 1997). This may not be viewed as corruption outright, but it is certainly unethical professional behavior.

A problem area in many countries is the potential for corruption when drug companies seek to influence physicians' drug prescription practices. A 2000 study by Wazana found that physician interaction with the pharmaceutical industry was associated with increased requests for placing additional drugs in hospital formularies and for changes in prescribing practice. The influence of the industry on physician prescribing behavior is a concern globally, but it can be particularly influential in developing countries, where physicians are typically not paid well and standards of legal or professional ethical behavior are less well established or enforced. A recent WHO report on drug promotion noted that in the United States, almost $21 billion was spent on drug promotion in 2002. The same report emphasizes that the pharmaceutical industry is often the only source of drug information for health care providers in developing countries (Norris and others 2005).

Drug promotion represents a gray area in the discussion of corruption in the pharmaceutical sector. Drug promotion in itself is not a corrupt act if fair marketing practices are followed. However, the pharmaceutical industry's provision of "incentives" to physicians for prescribing particular products may border on corruption. For example, drug companies often invite physicians to "educational" seminars, which may involve travel to desirable venues and invitations for their family members (Cohen and Esmail 2005). Self-regulatory guidelines are in place to control industry marketing practices. For example, the IFPMA has had a voluntary IFPMA Code of Pharmaceutical Marketing Practices in place since 1981. Even though guidelines have been disseminated widely, their effective implementation is a major problem. Violations of basic ethical norms, even it they do not constitute a blatant breach of the law, are still a source of concern and should be a target for remedial action.

Greater effort is needed to set standards of ethical practice and legal norms for physicians and the pharmaceutical industry in drug promotion activities. The increasing body of evidence-based best practice and drug information is critical for improving rational drug prescribing, and more countries are establishing mechanisms for disseminating this information. One method for deterring unethical prescribing practice is to ensure physician compliance with clinical practice guidelines (CPGs), although this is not an easy undertaking.[12] WHO, in fact, recommends the use of evidence-based clinical treatment guidelines to develop EDLs instead of relying on experts who may be vulnerable to outside influence through bribes or kickbacks. However, even CPGs are vulnerable to corruption if the

BOX 1.11 Prescribing Guidelines and Conflicts of Interest

A survey published in *Nature* in 2005 sought to determine whether authors of the prescribing guidelines used by physicians had any conflicts of interest that might affect the content of the guideline. Guidelines may be evidence based or by consensus prepared by experts in the specific area.

Of the 90 guidelines examined in detail, no conflicts of interest were found (or acknowledged) for 31. But at least one conflict of interest was found for the remaining 59. For 45 guidelines (50 percent), at least one author had an advisory board or consultancy position with a relevant company and at least one author received research funding from a relevant company. For 39 guidelines, at least one author had a speakers' bureau position with a relevant company. And for 10 guidelines, at least one author owned stock in a relevant company.

In total, 685 authors contributed to the 90 guidelines. Of those, 445 declared they had no conflict of interest, but of the remaining 240 authors, 143 said they held an advisory board or consultancy position with a relevant company, 153 said they had received a research grant from a relevant company, 103 held a speakers' bureau position with a relevant company, and 16 owned stock in a relevant company. Clearly, some authors had more than one conflict of interest.

Source: Taylor and Giles (2005).

physicians who are defining them are influenced in their decision making by the pharmaceutical industry (box 1.11). Where more sophisticated mechanisms are possible, monitoring prescribing behavior by monitoring prescribing data can be an effective means of identifying unusual or excessive prescribing patterns and for developing strategies to improve rational prescribing.

Other methods to limit industry influence over physician prescribing patterns include placing greater emphasis on providing "detailing," or drug education, by clinical pharmacists rather than industry marketing. Physicians ideally should be educated by impartial persons through academic detailing, which can include the development of a network of prescribing advisers who visit physicians or groups of physicians to disseminate evidence-based best prescribing practice, particularly for new drugs entering the market.

Prescription fraud is a common form of medical claims fraud in public and private health insurance systems and can involve doctors, pharmacists, and patients. Prescription forms need to be treated with the same type of security features as blank checks, and systems put in place to detect, investigate, and prosecute fraud to countervail this problem. Some countries have introduced electronic systems for tracking prescriptions and dispensed drugs by patient, doctor, and pharmacist and use data analysis to identify risks of claims fraud.

Strategies to reduce corruption in this decision point could include ensuring that patients receive drugs only with the appropriate prescription. That will be challenging, however, so long as patients face a financial disincentive of having to pay for both the cost of the physician visit to receive the prescription and then the cost of the drug. Even where insurance systems are meant to cover both physician visits and drug costs, in areas where pharmacy salaries are low, additional informal payments are often charged on "free" drugs to supplement the pharmacist's income.

Pharmacies and pharmacists should be subject to appropriate licensing and inspections, and breaches should be sanctioned. Typically, these aspects of pharmacies are self-enforced through associations of pharmacists. Corruption can occur in this decision point if codes of conduct either do not exist or are ineffectively enforced. However, ensuring their enforcement is challenging, particularly for the private retail drug market in developing countries (Enemark, Alban, and Vasquez 2004).

ASSESSING CORRUPTION RISKS IN PHARMACEUTICAL SYSTEMS

This section highlights a methodology that can help policy makers create a baseline of information about each decision point in an effort to understand how susceptible each decision point is to corruption. This methodology is based on earlier work by Cohen, Cercone, and Macaya (2002) in Costa Rica and has been revised and applied in Southeast Asia and other regions by WHO.

This methodology uses questionnaires (available in Cohen, Cercone, and Macaya 2002) designed to assess the vulnerability of each decision point in the pharmaceutical system and tailored to the specific conditions of a given country. For example, is the pharmaceutical system run centrally or locally? What institutions are involved in the procurement of pharmaceuticals? What committees are responsible for the drug selection process? These questions are designed to probe decision makers about the level of transparency of each of the six decision points and solicit binary (yes or no) responses. Once all interviews are completed, indicators are rated according to the specified criteria, and an average rating is calculated for each of the questions addressing a given decision point. This average rating has a possible range from zero to one, with most cases falling somewhere in between. The sum of all the ratings of one is then divided by the number of questions in a given decision point to obtain the percent of the indicators that were rated as a one. The resulting percentage is then converted to a zero-to-ten (0.0–10.0) scale by multiplying the resulting percentage by 10. The various decision points can then be rated for the following degrees of vulnerability to corruption:

0.0–2.0	**2.1–4.0**	**4.1–6.0**	**6.1–8.0**	**8.1–10.0**
Highly vulnerable	Likely vulnerable	Moderately vulnerable	Marginally vulnerable	Minimally vulnerable

The benefit of this methodology is that it is fairly inexpensive to implement, it is straightforward, and, most important, it provides a simple rating scale that allows decision makers to determine which decision points are weaker than others. This in turn allows for more targeted interventions and can ultimately help a pharmaceutical system to function more effectively and improve drug access. The decision points that require interventions will clearly vary from country to country, which is why there is a critical need for pharmaceutical system diagnostics.

Application of the Methodology in Costa Rica

In full collaboration with government of Costa Rica, diagnostic surveys were conducted with public officials working in the Costa Rica Social Security Agency (Caja Costarricense de Seguro Social, or CCSS) and the Ministry of Health, professionals in the health system, pharmaceutical industry representatives, and customers leaving public pharmacies. The surveys were conducted by Sanigest Internacional, an international consulting company based in Costa Rica, from February to April 2002 under the World Bank's supervision. The diagnostic tools used for each group reflect recommendations by the World Bank on the formulation of tools for the diagnosis of governance. The salient features of these tools include evaluating public officials, firms, and users, complemented with hard data; specially designed and tested *closed* questions; and observation of a conceptual framework that aims to uncover the incentive structure behind governance and corruption.

The surveys included four main tools to evaluate the level of transparency and the susceptibility to corruption of each of the four principal activities involved in procuring and supplying pharmaceuticals to the general population. The surveys—evaluation interviews with public officials, industry interviews, focus groups with health care professionals, and user surveys—were conducted simultaneously. To verify answers given, the diagnostic surveys are complemented with hard data including written regulations, evidence of compliance with regulations, and documentation of transparent processes.

Overall, the Costa Rican pharmaceutical system obtained a rating of 7.7, indicating marginal vulnerability to corruption and generally good governance. The overall rating was diminished by a low rating of 5.7 in the area of procurement, indicating moderate vulnerability, and problems in the area of distribution. With minor changes in the system, Costa Rica could obtain a system that was only minimally vulnerable to corruption.

Drug Registration

The decision area corresponding to drug registration received an average indicator score of 9.4, indicating very low vulnerability to corruption. This area was well documented, and requirements for the registration of new drugs, as well as generic versions of existing drugs, are fairly well standardized. Access to information is equitable, and a formal committee makes binding decisions on new applications. This committee has a well-defined composition and clear tenure of its members; it writes reports outlining the reasons behind any decision to withhold approval of a new drug. The fee for registering a new drug is small ($500) and is therefore not a major obstacle for new companies registering drugs. Finally, regulations require that the maximum time for approving a new drug is 30 days if all documentation is in place.

Selection

Drug selection also earned a 9.4 rating, underscoring the high level of transparency that characterizes the processes and professionalism of the officials responsible for this area. This decision area was well documented, and the essential drug list appears to be updated on a regular basis. A condensed publication on official drugs in the Costa Rican health care system contains documented procedures and policies to support affirmative answers to most of the indicators; it is widely available throughout the system, being distributed free of charge to all key health officials.

A positive feature of the selection process is its consideration of cost-effectiveness in making drug selections. All drugs on the official drug list are included by their generic name, so there is no bias toward purchasing a specific brand and all suppliers are favored equally. In this regard, the official drug list follows WHO recommendations and offers no opportunity for a manufacturer to gain market share by having a specific brand listed. There are, moreover, clear criteria for the inclusion or exclusion of drugs from the list, as well as guidelines for committee membership and tenure.

Procurement

The score of 5.7 for procurement made it the segment in the value chain most vulnerable to corruption. Given the strategic and economic importance of this area—the Costa Rican government spends more than $70 million annually on purchasing drugs—problems with transparency and poor governance in this area have a significant effect on the quality of services received by CCSS users. This low ranking resulted from a combination of several factors. First, not all affirmative answers to the corresponding indicators could be validated with documents. For example, no documentation was produced to demonstrate the use of internal audits, such as prices paid and criteria used in awarding bids. Second, there was a lack of information for tracking supplier performance and product quality. Poorly performing suppliers are able to continue participating in public auctions until they are found guilty of a breach of law; such court trials typically take several years to complete. With price carrying the highest weighting in public auction decisions, a poorly performing supplier could conceivably win a public bid, despite having a poor track record. Third, no documentation was available specifying clear policies in internal procedures, membership guidelines, and tenure of key committees. In addition, purchasing decisions were based primarily on historical needs and inventory levels and did not take into account morbidity projections in a clear algorithm. This combination of structural weaknesses earned the procurement process only 12 points out of a possible 21, for a total score of 5.7 on a 10-point scale.

Complexities and inefficiencies in the procurement process may generate losses for the public health system in Costa Rica and create vulnerability to corruption. The number of personnel, offices, and committees involved in a drug purchase, together with a process that allows losers to appeal decisions and delay purchases for several weeks or months, makes the entire purchasing cycle cumbersome, error-prone, and lengthy. The cycle, from the identification of a purchasing need to the actual receipt of the drug takes 13 months on average.[13] The time-consuming nature of the procurement process means that the minimum volume of drugs purchased is equivalent to a supply of at least one year. The result is significant inventory carrying costs, generating cash flow constraints, greater problems with the control of theft, and greater possibilities of spoilage or drug expiration.

Distribution

Pharmaceutical distribution in the public health system received a score of 6.9, the second-lowest score. This area's principal weaknesses were the lack of a monitoring system to evaluate the distribution system and of an information system needed for "visibility" of inventory stock levels and movements along the distribution chain. Many storage locations also lacked security provisions, such as alarms, cameras, and constant monitoring of the entry and exit of staff or visitors into restricted areas. The most expensive pharmaceuticals and biologics did appear to have better security safeguards, but that could not be said about all drugs. In addition, the system lacked a standardized shelving system for each type of drug.

The study also included qualitative data from interviewees on their perception and experience with corruption in the system. The interviewees said there was a higher rate of corruption in the procurement and distribution segments of the value chain—confirming the survey findings on the vulnerability of those two areas to corruption. And, although the perception of drug selection was positive, the perception of drug registration was not consistent with its high rating.

Participants commented on variability in registration time, obstacles to bioequivalent products and parallel imports, and unregistered drugs on the market. The end users complained of limited inventory and unnecessary out-of-pocket payments, indicating that problems remain in the distribution and utilization of pharmaceuticals in Costa Rica. However, as a result of well-established processes and institutions and a high degree of professionalism, with a few adjustments the system could be made minimally vulnerable to corruption. As a result of these findings, policy recommendations that were categorized from high to low priority and high to low feasibility were made to the government of Costa Rica, and some changes subsequently followed.

REFORM STRATEGIES AND CONCLUSIONS

This chapter has illustrated the complexity of pharmaceutical sector, which comprises a number of critical decision points throughout the entire system from manufacturing to drug consumption. These decision points are potentially susceptible to corruption unless clear and robust countervailing measures are available. Corruption in the pharmaceutical system cannot be taken lightly—in the worst case scenario, it can lead to death. Not all corruption is equal. Discrepancies in the procurement process may not have as serious effects as breaches in the manufacturing process. For this reason, use of the pharmaceutical diagnostic tool outlined in this chapter is advantageous because it can help policy makers learn where the weaknesses lie, determine the effect of these weaknesses on health and economic outcomes, set priorities for action, and then design appropriate anticorruption strategies.

The capacity of a government to curb corruption in the pharmaceutical system also depends on other cross-cutting political economic factors that fall outside of the health sector and that are discussed in other chapters in this volume. For example, what political mandate does the government have? Is it first of all a government that will take on corruption seriously even at the risk of marginalizing some groups? Is institutional capacity in the country strong enough to underpin specific sectoral anticorruption efforts? Does the agency charged with the enforcement mandate have appropriate capacity and financial resources for undertaking this role? Corruption is a multisectoral issue and a comprehensive approach is necessary if governments are to combat it truly and forcefully. While basic elements of this framework for curbing corruption in the pharmaceutical sector should be present in all countries, some variation will be observed depending on the country's size, the resources available, the structure of the health system, and the importance of the local pharmaceutical industry to the balance of trade and employment.

The greater challenge for policy makers may be managing the global pharmaceutical industry, where raw material can be produced in one country, exported to another for manufacture into products that are then exported to still other countries. The global reach of the industry means that there is also the risk of swift export of corruption. How should the world deal with this risk? For one thing, attention needs to be paid to the larger countries, such as Brazil, China, and India, that produce pharmaceutical products and raw materials for consumption in other countries. Alliances should be formed with policy makers and manufacturers in these countries to ensure that the pharmaceutical system is robust and not easily susceptible to corruption. Major producers of products and materials are already well aware of the need to protect their reputation as suppliers of good-quality products.

Policy makers need to determine whether they will turn their first efforts on areas where anticorruption strategies can easily be implemented or instead focus on areas where an end to corruption is likely to produce the highest returns, even if these are the areas that may involve tremendous political negotiations. There is no prescriptive answer. Government preferences will vary depending on resources and commitment and can be made only after a comprehensive diagnostic of the pharmaceutical sector is undertaken. Policy makers will need to make trade-offs: should they make small gains quickly or try to implement large-scale reform with longer time horizons? Should they opt to save lives in the short term or to build service delivery institutions as a long-term solution? Ideally, there should be some combination of the two approaches. Small measures that are relatively inexpensive to undertake, such as posting pharmaceutical prices on a Web site, should be undertaken concurrently with larger measures such as investing more resources into a national drug regulatory agency; both will result in pharmaceutical systems that are more robust and less prone to corruption. To be sure, even small measures in themselves can pay off and make good governance socially "contagious."[14]

The first step toward stopping corruption in the pharmaceutical sector is to understand its structure, actors, and motivations and be able to identify the key points where corruption can occur. Only then can short-, medium- and long-term goals be mapped out clearly and appropriate strategies identified. If there is a choice, priority should be given to areas where the identified corruption is a threat to safety and health; tackling corruption that has only economic implications should not come before health concerns.

On the positive side, there is a nascent and growing body of literature and practical policy tools available that are being applied in various country contexts to diagnose or tackle pharmaceutical sector corruption. A selection of these recommended anticorruption strategies (primarily those that are highly feasible) has been described in this chapter and is summarized in table 1.2. They are not intended to represent the universe of possible anticorruption strategies but are designed to inspire thinking on the topic and to promote some concrete measures that could yield tangible results in specific areas. The common elements uniting all of these measures are transparency and accountability mechanisms. With these elements in place any movement toward corruption will be visible early on and can be stopped sooner rather than later.

TABLE 1.2 Selected Strategies to Mitigate Corruption in Pharmaceutical Systems[a]

Decision point	Selected strategies	Feasibility	Timing
Manufacturing	Ensure legal basis for GMP requirements, including appropriate and credible fines for noncompliance	High	Short term
	Improve GMP compliance by regular and random inspections	High	Short term
	Hire a sufficient number of trained and well-paid inspectors	Medium	Medium/long term
	Develop a rotating schedule for inspectors of manufacturing sites	High	Short term
	Publicly post a list of compliant manufacturers	High	Short term
	Publicly name and shame noncompliant manufacturers	High	Short term
Registration	Develop transparent, effective, and uniform laws and standards for drug registration	High	Medium term
	Ensure adequate drug quality control capacity	High	Medium/long term
	Educate public and professionals to identify unregistered drugs	Medium	Short term
	Publish drug registration information on the Internet	High	Short term
	Implement market surveillance and random batch testing	Medium	Medium term
Selection	Define and publish clear criteria for selection and pricing	High	Short term
	Make drug selection committee membership publicly available	High	Short term
	Base drug selection criteria on international standards as set out by WHO	High	Short term
	Ensure regular reporting of drug selection meetings by the media	High	Short term
	Publicly post results obtained and decisions made	Medium	Medium term
Procurement	Make procurement procedures transparent, following formal, published procedures throughout the process and using explicit criteria to award contracts	Medium	Medium term
	Justify and monitor supplier selection	High	Short term
	Adhere strictly to announced closing dates	Medium	Long term
	Keep written records of all bids received	High	Short term
	Make results of adjudication available to all participating bidders and the public	High	Short term
	Require regular reports on key procurement performance indicators	High	Short term
Distribution	Where possible, develop information systems to ensure drugs are allocated, transported, and stored appropriately	High	Medium/long term
	Establish regular communication between every level of the system to control inventory movements and deliveries	Medium	Medium/long term
	Secure storage facilities and transport appropriately	Medium	Medium/long term
	Monitor stock in distribution electronically and carefully check delivery orders against inventories of products actually delivered	Medium	Long term

TABLE 1.2 (Continued)

Decision point	*Selected strategies*	*Feasibility*	*Timing*
Pharmaceutical prescribing and dispensing	Develop and engage professional associations to improve adherence to professional codes of conduct	Medium	Long term
	Use information systems to monitor physician prescription patterns	Low	Medium term
	Impose serious penalties and name and shame for breaches of legal and ethical standards	High	Short term
	Regulate industry interaction with prescribers through explicit criteria that limit industry gifts and payments	Medium Medium	Short term Medium term
	Require physicians to post industry gifts valued at more than $25 (Vermont Model),[b] license and inspect pharmacies	Medium	Medium/long term

Source: Authors.

a. The "feasibility" and "timing" estimates in this table are for Costa Rica.

b. Under the Pharmaceutical Marketing Gift Disclosure Law 33 V.S.A 2005, the state of Vermont requires the pharmaceutical industry to report recipients of gifts over $25. Some exceptions apply.

In the final analysis, the first step in mitigating corruption in the pharmaceutical sector is intensified education. Policy makers and others need to be educated about the critical decision points in the pharmaceutical sector and the vulnerabilities that can occur within each decision point. The second step is to undertake an assessment of where corruption may be occurring. Once it is known where corruption is and how it is taking place, deterrent measures can be put in place. This assessment should include gathering baseline data (using an assessment tool as presented in this chapter) on the state of the pharmaceutical system in a given jurisdictional context. These data allow decision makers to define strategies, the third stage of this process, and set priorities for intervention. These strategies and interventions can be monitored and evaluated against baseline data to see if the appropriate change is taking place and, if it is not, to determine why and then modify the approach if necessary. These steps are crucial if access to quality and affordable medicines is to improve, particularly for the poor.

ENDNOTES

1. See a summary of the top 20 cases at the False Claims Act Legal Center, http://www.taf.org/top20.htm.
2. The original conception was $C = M + D - A$ with transparency subsumed in all three variables.
3. Pharmacovigilance, or drug monitoring, is defined by WHO (2002) as the pharmacological science relating to the detection, assessment, understanding, and prevention of adverse effects, particularly long- and short-term side effects, of medicines.
4. For information on the International Conference on Harmonization, see http://www.ich.org.
5. This is a versatile, mobile, and simple test method for identifying substandard or counterfeited pharmaceuticals that can be used by less intensively trained staff in developing countries.
6. A patient was instrumental in alerting authorities about a pharmacy in Hamilton, Ontario, Canada, that had sold counterfeit heart medication. See "Consumers Warned to Watch for Counterfeit drugs," *CBC Marketplace,* January 18, 2006, http://www.cbc.ca.

7. The WHO Model List of Essential Medicines, http://www.who.int/medicines/publications/essentialmedicines/en/.
8. For a summary of these methods and issues in the European context, see Mossialos, Mrazek, and Walley (2004, ch. 6, 14). More information about pricing best practices is discussed in Cohen (2003).
9. For an overview of the European experience with economic evaluation, see McGuire, Drummond, and Rutten (2004).
10. This section and the next section on distribution are based on Management Sciences for Health (1997).
11. The Public Expenditure Tracking Survey (PETS) is a quantitative survey of the supply side of public services, collecting information on facility characteristics, financial flows, outputs (services delivered), accountability arrangements, and the like. The surveys can serve as powerful, simple diagnostic tools for tracing the flow of resources from origin to destination and determining the location and scale of anomaly. They not only highlight the use and abuse of public money but also give insights into cost efficiency, decentralization, and accountability.
12. For a review of key issues involved in implementing guidelines and an overview of good prescribing strategies, see Chapman, Durieux, and Walley (2004).
13. According to a study by Cercone, Duran-Valverde, and Munoz-Vargas (2000), prices paid through private sector purchasing are often 10 times higher than prices paid by the CCSS through international procurement.
14. This description is taken from Gladwell (2000).

REFERENCES

Akunyili, Dora. 2005. "Counterfeit and Substandard Drugs, Nigeria's Experience: Implications, Challenges, Actions and Recommendations." Paper presented at World Bank Meeting for Key Interest Groups in Health, Washington, DC, March 11.

Baghdadi, G., J. C. Cohen, and E. Wondemagegnehu. 2005. "Measuring Transparency to Improve Good Governance in the Public Pharmaceutical Sector." Working draft for field testing and revision, Departments of Medicines Policy and Standards and Ethics, Trade, Human Rights and Health Law, WHO, Geneva (October).

Baines, D. L., P. Brigham, D. R. Phillips, K. H. Tolley, and D. K. Whynes. 1997. "GP Fundholding and Prescribing in UK General Practice: Evidence from Two Rural, English Family Health Services Authorities." *Public Health* 111 (5): 321–25.

Cercone, J., F. Duran-Valverde, and E. Munoz-Vargas. 2000. "Compromiso de gestión, rendición de cuentas y corrupción en los hospitals de la Caja Costarricense de Seguro Social." Latin America Research Network Working Paper R-418, Inter-American Development Bank, Washington, DC.

Chapman, S., P. Durieux, and T. Walley. 2004. "Good Prescribing Practice." In *Regulating Pharmaceuticals in Europe: Striving for Efficiency, Equity, and Quality*, eds. E. Mossialos, M. F. Mrazek and T. Walley. Buckingham, U.K.: Open University Press.

Cohen, Jillian Clare. 2003. "Key Pharmaceutical Policy Trends in Select Jurisdictions." Report prepared for the Drug Strategy Review, Ministry of Health and Long-Term Care, Ontario, Canada (January).

Cohen, J. C., and J. Carikeo Montoya. 2001. "Using Technology to Fight Corruption in Pharmaceutical Purchasing: Lessons Learned from the Chilean Experience." World Bank Institute, Washington, DC (February).

Cohen, J. C., J. A. Cercone, and R. Macaya. 2002. "Improving Transparency in Pharmaceutical Systems: Strengthening Critical Decision Points against Corruption." World Bank, Washington, DC (October).

Cohen, J. C., and L. Esmail. 2005. "Creating Ethical Incentives for the Pharmaceutical Industry: Reality or Fantasy?" Paper presented at a seminar on "Self-Regulation in the Pharmaceutical Industry," Basel Institute for Governance, Basel, April 21.

Enemark, U., A. Alban, and E. C. S. Vazquez. 2004. "Purchasing Pharmaceuticals." Health, Nutrition, and Population Discussion Paper, World Bank, Washington DC (September).

FDA (U.S. Food and Drug Administration). 2000. "Good Manufacturing Practice Guide for Active Pharmaceutical Ingredients" (July). http://www.fda.gov/cder/guidance/4011dft.htm (accessed August 18, 2006).

Gladwell, Malcolm. 2000. *The Tipping Point: How Little Things Can Make a Big Difference.* Boston: Little Brown & Company.

Henry, D., and J. Lexchin. 2002. "The Pharmaceutical Industry as a Medicines Provider." *Lancet* 360: 1590–95.

IFPMA (International Federation of Pharmaceutical Manufacturers). 2002. "Counterfeit Medicines: The Role of Industry and Pharmacists." http://www.ifpma.org/News (accessed March 20, 2006).

Klitgaard, R. 2000. "Subverting Corruption." *Finance and Development* 37 (June): 2–5.

Kwon, S. 2006. "Politics and Process of Health Policy Change: The Case of Pharmaceutical Reform in Korea." Seminar presentation to the Comparative Program on Health and Society, University of Toronto, April 5.

Management Sciences for Health in collaboration with the World Health Organization. 1997. *Managing Drug Supply,* 2nd ed. West Hartford, CT: Kumarian Press Inc.

Marshall, I. 2001. "A Survey of Corruption Issues in the Mining and Mineral Sector." Mining, Minerals and Sustainable Development Project, International Institute for Environment and Development, London.

McGuire, A., M. Drummond, and F. Rutten. 2004. "Reimbursement of Pharmaceuticals in the EU." In *Regulating Pharmaceuticals in Europe: Striving for Efficiency, Equity, and Quality,* eds. E. Mossialos, M. F. Mrazek and T. Walley. Buckingham, U.K.: Open University Press.

McPake, B., D. Asiimwe, F. Mwesigye, M. Ofumbi, L. Ortenblad, P. Streefland, and others. 1999. "Informal Economic Activities of Public Health Workers in Uganda: Implications for Quality and Accessibility of Care." *Social Science and Medicine* 49 (7): 849–65.

Médecins Sans Frontières. 2001. *Fatal Imbalance: The Crisis in Research and Development for Drugs for Neglected Diseases.* A Report by the MSF Access to Essential Medicines Campaign and the Drugs for Neglected Diseases Working Group, Geneva (November 30). http://www.accessmed-msf.org (accessed August 18, 2006).

Mossialos, E., M. Mrazek, and T. Walley, eds. 2004. *Regulating Pharmaceuticals in Europe: Striving for Efficiency, Equity, and Quality.* Buckingham, U.K.: Open University Press.

Newton, P., S. Proux, M. Green, F. Smithuis, J. Rozendaal, and others. 2001. "Fake Artesunate in Southeast Asia." *Lancet* 357 (9272): 1948–50.

Norris, P., A. Herxheimer, J. Lexchin, and P. Mansfield. 2005. "Drug Promotion: What We Know, What We Have Yet to Learn: Reviews of Materials in the WHO/HAI Database on Drug Promotion." WHO, Geneva.

Parish, P. 1973. "Drug Prescribing—the Concern of All." *Journal of the Royal Society of Health* 4: 213–17.

Pitts, P. 2005. "Moderator's Guide." Paper presented at the Center for Medicine in the Public Interest seminar "21st Century Health Care Terrorism: The Perils of International Drug Counterfeiting." http://politicalcap.com/Counterfeiting_Report.pdf (accessed August 21, 2006).

Rodríguez-Monguió, R., and J. Rovira. 2005. "An Analysis of Pharmaceutical Lending by the World Bank." Health and Nutrition Discussion Paper, World Bank, Washington, DC (January).

Satchwell, G. 2004. "A Sick Business: Counterfeit Medicines and Organised Crime." The Stockholm Network, Stockholm.

Swenke, S. 2002. "Cross-Sector Analysis of Corruption: Summary Report." Sectoral Perspectives on Corruption. Prepared for USAID, Democracy Conflict and Humanitarian Assistance, Washington, DC (November), http://www.usaid.gov/our_work/democracy_and_governance/publications/ac/sector/ summary.doc. [accessed 08/18/06].

Taylor, Rosie, and Jim Giles. 2005. "Cash Interests Taint Drug Advice." *Nature* 437 (October 20): 1080–81.

USAID (U.S. Agency for International Development). 1999. "A Handbook on Fighting Corruption." Center for Democracy and Governance, USAID, Washington DC (February).

U.S. Pharmacopeial Convention Inc. 2005. "Mekong Region Takes Action against Fake Antimalarials." U.S. Pharmacopeial Convention Inc., Rockville, MD.

Vian, T. 2003. "Corruption in the Health Sector in Albania." Report prepared for the USAID/Albanian Civil Society Corruption Reduction Project, Management Systems International, Boston University School of Public Health, Boston, MA, http://www.bu.edu/actforhealth [accessed 01/05/06].

———. 2005. "Health Sector" In *Fighting Corruption in Developing Countries,* ed. B. I. Spector. Bloomfield, CT: Kumarian Press.

Watkins, C., I. Harvey, P. Carthy, L. Moore, E. Robinson, and R. Brawn, R. 2003. "Attitudes and Behavior of General Practitioners and Their Prescribing Costs: A National Cross-Sectional Survey." *Quality and Safety in Health Care* 12: 29–34.

Wazana, Ashley. 2000. "Physicians and the Pharmaceutical Industry: Is a Gift Ever Just a Gift?" *Journal of the American Medical Association* 283 (January 19): 373–80.

Wondemagegnehu, E. 1995. *Counterfeit and Substandard Drugs in Myanmar and Viet Nam.* Geneva: WHO.

World Bank. 2000. "Procurement of Health Sector Goods: Technical Note." Health, Nutrition, Population, World Bank, Washington DC.

———. 2006. "Albania: Health Sector Note." Report 32612-AL, Europe and Central Asia/Health, Nutrition, Population, World Bank, Washington, DC (February).

WHO (World Health Organization). 1997. *Quality Assurance of Pharmaceuticals: A Compendium of Guidelines and Related Materials.* Geneva: WHO.

———. 1998. "WHO Public-Private Roles in the Pharmaceutical Sector. Implications for Equitable Access and Rational Drug Use." WHO/DAP.97.12, WHO, Geneva.

———. 2002. *The Importance of Pharmacovigilance: Safety Monitoring of Medicinal Products.* Geneva: WHO.

———. 2003. "Expert Committee on Specifications for Pharmaceutical Preparations," 37th report. WHO, Geneva.

———. 2004a. "Equitable Access to Essential Medicines: A Framework for Collective Action." *WHO Policy Perspectives on Medicines* 8 (March).

———. 2004b. *WHO Medicines Strategy: Countries at the Core 2004–2007.* Geneva: WHO.

———. 2004c. *The World Medicines Situation.* Geneva: WHO.

———. 2005a. "Counterfeit Medicines." http://www.who.int/mediacentre/factsheets/fs275/en/.

———. 2005b. "Measuring Transparency to Improve Good Governance in the Public Pharmaceutical Sector." Working draft for field testing and revision, WHO Departments of Medicines Policy and Standards and Ethics, Trade, Human Rights and Health Law (October), Geneva.

2

Maximizing the Performance of Education Systems

The Case of Teacher Absenteeism

HARRY ANTHONY PATRINOS AND RUTH KAGIA

"Eliminating corruption in education starts with the belief that it's not a part of our culture. Then the devolution of power to self-governed educational establishments steps in. Introducing freedom of choice and ensuring equal access follow. Last, but not least, the whole endeavor rests on strong government leadership, with vision and integrity."

Alexander Lomaia,
Minister of Education and Science, Georgia

"In spite of a lot of progress in teaching technology in recent decades, the teacher continues to be the most essential input in the learning process. When a teacher is absent, for whatever reason, cognitive acquisition suffers. The chapter documents a lot of facts on teacher absenteeism in many counties, identifies the reasons for this phenomenon, and explores solutions. It should be a required reading for country officials who, most likely, face the problem."

George Psacharopoulos, O'Leary Chair (2005–06),
College of Education, University of Illinois Urbana-Champaign

Education is essential for economic growth and social development and for reducing the intergenerational transmission of poverty. Education also interacts with other investments to raise productivity. For example, education helps make health and nutrition investments more effective. Female education yields some of the highest returns, as it is inversely related to infant and child mortality and is associated with lower fertility rates. Every additional year of schooling increases a person's productivity and increases earnings (Schultz 1997, 2002; Psacharopoulos and Patrinos 2004). Therefore, one may conclude that investments in education are a critical part of national development.

Excellent contributions were made to this chapter by Gita Gopal, Heather Marie Layton, and Veronica Grigera. Saida Mamedova provided estimates of costs. Comments from Felipe Barrera, Edgardo Campos, Nazmul Chaudhury, Tazeen Fasih, Maureen Lewis, Juan Manuel Moreno, Vicente Paqueo, and Halsey Rogers are greatly appreciated.

Despite these positive associations, the full benefits of education investments are realized only when certain conditions are in place: when there is an overall enabling macroeconomic environment (Barro 1991, 2001; Pritchett 2001); when education services reach the ultimate beneficiaries and improve learning outcomes; and when education is of good quality (Hanushek and Wößmann 2007; Hanushek and Kimko 2000).

Education investments are less effective when public spending on education is misallocated, not sufficiently focused on quality, or poorly targeted. Education effectiveness is also reduced when spending decisions are improperly guided—that is, when decisions are not based on information, tools, and mechanisms that improve outcomes. Whether through poor capacity or poor governance, misallocated spending hurts the country by not benefiting students.

Corrupt education practices around the world contribute to inefficient use of resources and ultimately prohibit the achievement of a quality education for all children. Many education stakeholders argue that the Millennium Development Goals for education (universal completion of primary school, and gender parity) may not be achieved without strengthening and building the instruments needed to control corruption in education (Transparency International 2005). Moreover, given both the increased spending on education in developing countries and the unprecedented contributions of rich countries to support education in developing countries, it is important to improve the efficiency of education systems so that taxpayers in both rich and poor countries know that their money is being well spent.

CORRUPTION AND EDUCATION

Corruption has different meanings to different people. Most broadly, it can be defined as the "misuse of office for unofficial ends" (Klitgaard 1998). Corrupt acts include but are not limited to bribery, extortion, influence peddling, nepotism, fraud, use of money to bribe government officials to take some specific action, and embezzlement. Heyneman (2004) argues that education corruption includes the abuse of authority for personal and material gain. Hallak and Poisson (2001) define corruption in education as "the systematic use of public office for private benefit whose impact is significant on access, quality or equity in education."

In a surprisingly large number of countries in all regions of the world, corruption is pervasive at all levels of education, from primary schools through tertiary institutions. It can occur at any stage and among any group of actors from policy makers at the ministerial level to providers at the school level such as teachers and contractors to beneficiaries of education such as students and parents. Corrupt practices in education can include bribes and illegal fees for admission and examination; academic fraud; withholding teacher salaries; preferential promotion and placement; charging students for "tutoring" sessions to cover the curriculum needed to pass mandatory examinations and that should have been taught in the classroom; teacher absenteeism; and illegal practices in textbook procurement, meal provision, and infrastructure contracting.

Hallak and Poisson (2001) claim that corruption seems to affect education in two key ways. The first is through the pressure corruption exerts on public resources, and as a consequence on the education budget, which represents in most countries the largest component of public spending. Corruption of this sort can cause prices to rise and the level of government output and service delivery to fall, thus reducing investment in education services. The second way is through corruption's impact on the costs of education services, their volume, and their quality; students who are educated in corrupt systems may not learn the skills needed to take advantage of available opportunities and to contribute to economic and social development. A third impact could be added to this list: corruption's impact on core values and ethics during the formative years of young people's lives. Corruption in education may undermine an entire generation's core values regarding accountability, personal responsibility, and integrity.

Corruption in education is particularly important because the sector usually accounts for a large share of public expenditures. In many countries, such as El Salvador, Guinea, Morocco, Kenya, and Yemen, one-fifth to one-third of the public budget is allocated to education (World Bank 2006b). This means that even low levels of corruption can result in the wastage or loss of significant amounts of public resources. A recent study by Transparency International (2005) documents how the leakage of resources in the education sector through corruption translates into poorly constructed classrooms, leaking roofs, dysfunctional toilets, defective furniture, and inadequate textbooks.

In his analysis of cross-country data, Mauro (1998) found that the existence of corruption causes a less than optimal composition of government expenditure. Additionally, corruption in education affects the overall access, quality, and equity of education. For example, poor families may be faced with paying illegal fees and bribes to enroll their children in free public schools. On average, the poorest 40 percent of the population in developing countries spends 10 percent of household income on costs for primary school (Oxfam 2001). Official—as well as irregular—enrollment fees and exam fees partially explain low enrollment rates (Cockroft 1998; Bentaouet Kattan and Burnett 2004).

Corruption may also reduce spending on key learning inputs. Tanzi and Davoodi (1997) found that corruption has been shown to reduce spending on textbooks. Chua (1999) found that only 16 percent of children in the Philippines received textbooks despite high public spending on them. In addition, corruption can affect the overall quality of education by reducing instructional time, in effect offering children fewer learning opportunities.

Corruption may also affect learning outcomes. Using country-level surveys, Gupta, Davoodi, and Tiongson (2000) found that countries with higher levels of corruption tend to have higher dropout rates. In fact, dropout rates in countries with low corruption and highly efficient government services are 26 percentage points lower than dropout rates in countries with high corruption and low efficiency. They found that dropout rates could be five times as high in highly corrupt countries than in countries with low levels of corruption.

A CORRUPTION FRAMEWORK FOR EDUCATION

This chapter uses a simple corruption framework for education based on Klitgaard's (1998) drivers of corruption, namely, M (monopoly) $+ D$ (discretion) $- A$ (accountability) $- T$ (transparency) $= C$ (corruption). The argument is that an organization is more likely to experience corruption when it has monopoly power over a good or service and the discretion to decide who will receive it and how much they will receive, and is not accountable for the outcome. Linked to all three drivers is the aspect of transparency. Increased transparency constrains monopoly power and the unbridled use of discretion and is essential to instilling the accountability of decision makers.

How does this framework apply to the education sector? It is relatively easy to classify most education systems as monopolies (see, for example, Friedman 1955; Becker 1964). Even in decentralized education systems, it is still the government, whether national or federal or provincial, state, or municipal, that runs education. The schools, with the exception of tertiary education systems, are essentially "branches" of the system. In most countries, public schools are a virtual monopoly despite the existence of private schools: 80 percent of schools in countries covered by the World Education Indicators were public and 89 percent of schools in the OECD (Organisation for Economic Co-operation and Development) countries were public in 2005 (UNESCO-UIS/OECD 2005). Monopoly in school systems can easily result in slow innovation, less attention to cost control, a lack of choice, and a lack of accountability. While the lack of innovation and choice may negatively affect quality, and inattention to costs may make the system much less cost-effective, it is the lack of accountability that contributes to corrupt practices.

Therefore, the impact of monopoly on corruption may not be by design, and the leaders of the education monopoly may not act in bad faith. Still the monopolistic conditions for corrupt practices exist.

Large education bureaucracies have discretion to decide who gets services. They are able to plan and allocate resources according to their own design. This can happen through the budget process, school organization, and school construction and rehabilitation, as well as through teacher appointments, promotions, assignment, and so on. In most countries, teachers are trained and licensed through a government-controlled system and are assigned by the authorities to the school in which they will teach; their employment conditions and remuneration are determined by the government. Even in decentralized systems, there is at least some government control, usually over very important matters (such as pay and overall budget control).

In some countries, large teacher unions play a role in assigning teachers and affect teacher practice in many ways (see, for example Foweraker 1993 for Mexico). Studies find that conflict between the teacher unions and the government is associated with lower academic achievement (see Murillo and others 2002 for Argentina, and Álvarez, Garcia Moreno, and Patrinos 2006 for Mexico). This could be the result of many factors, including reduced teacher attendance associated with strikes and protests initiated by teacher unions. A significant number of school days were lost to strikes in Argentina (556 days), Brazil (1,116), and Mexico (434) over the 1998–2003 period (Gentili and Suarez 2004). In Belgium, a six-month teacher strike was associated with a negative effect of 11.5 percent on the earnings of of the students affected by the strike when they entered the labor force (Belot and Webbink 2006).

Discretion on the part of teacher unions can become absolute when key processes such as budget allocation and teacher appointment, deployment, and promotion are not transparent and when systematic monitoring of such decisions is lacking.

However, monopoly power and discretion need not always lead to corruption and can be countered (balanced) in a system with high levels of accountability. That is, monopoly and discretion could exist in a system with good educational outcomes if the system were made more accountable—with sufficient checks and balances to exercising discretion, transparent decision making, access to relevant information, and effective monitoring and evaluation. Weak accountability increases the likelihood of misallocation of resources, expenditure leakages, lack of performance monitoring and evaluation, and low demand for services among the poor (World Bank 2003). Weak accountability could be manifested in poorly designed, effectively unenforceable contracts between the policy maker and the service provider—contracts that could result in an unequal power balance between the service provider (the school and its relevant authority) and the beneficiaries. Poor contracts could be exacerbated by a weak relationship between beneficiaries (students and their parents) and the policy maker (government), with the former having inadequate means to voice concerns and express preferences. The corruption vulnerabilities framework, presented in figure 2.1 as a value chain, can assist decision makers in identifying circumstances where limited accountability and transparency allow monopoly and discretion to lead to corruption.

The purpose of education can be seen as producing quality education, as well as a knowledgeable and skilled population. There is a value chain that ultimately leads to this outcome. At the higher level, national policy sets the rules and system. At the sector level, more specific strategies and goals are set, including the national budget. At the ministry level, decisions about buildings and procurement of necessary inputs are made. In most countries, decisions also are made at this level about teacher appointment, management, and promotion. At the district level—or at any other point where the education services are actually delivered, downstream on the value chain in figure 2.1—key actors, mainly teachers and directors such as headmasters and principals, make daily decisions that affect educational quality. In addition, teacher quality is an intermediate outcome of the value chain that contributes directly to final outcomes. Along all these points, from the bottom to the top, are numerous opportunities for leakages and corrupt behavior that can hamper, even block, the achievement of ultimate objectives.

A FOCUS ON TEACHERS AND ABSENTEEISM

All countries display ample scope for and some evidence of corruption in the education sector. While different forms of inefficiencies and corruption exist in education, we focus here on the most important feature of the education system: classroom teachers. That focus seems warranted since teachers are not only the gatekeepers to quality education but also account for most of the expenditures in the sector.

Teachers are the transmitters of knowledge who help ensure that children learn. They are role models to students, and in most rural communities, they are the most educated and respected personages. They are at the front line of developing pupils' understanding, attitudes, skills, learning, and core values. Teachers are, therefore, the most important element in producing quality education.

FIGURE 2.1 The Value Chain and Corruption Vulnerabilities in the Education Sector

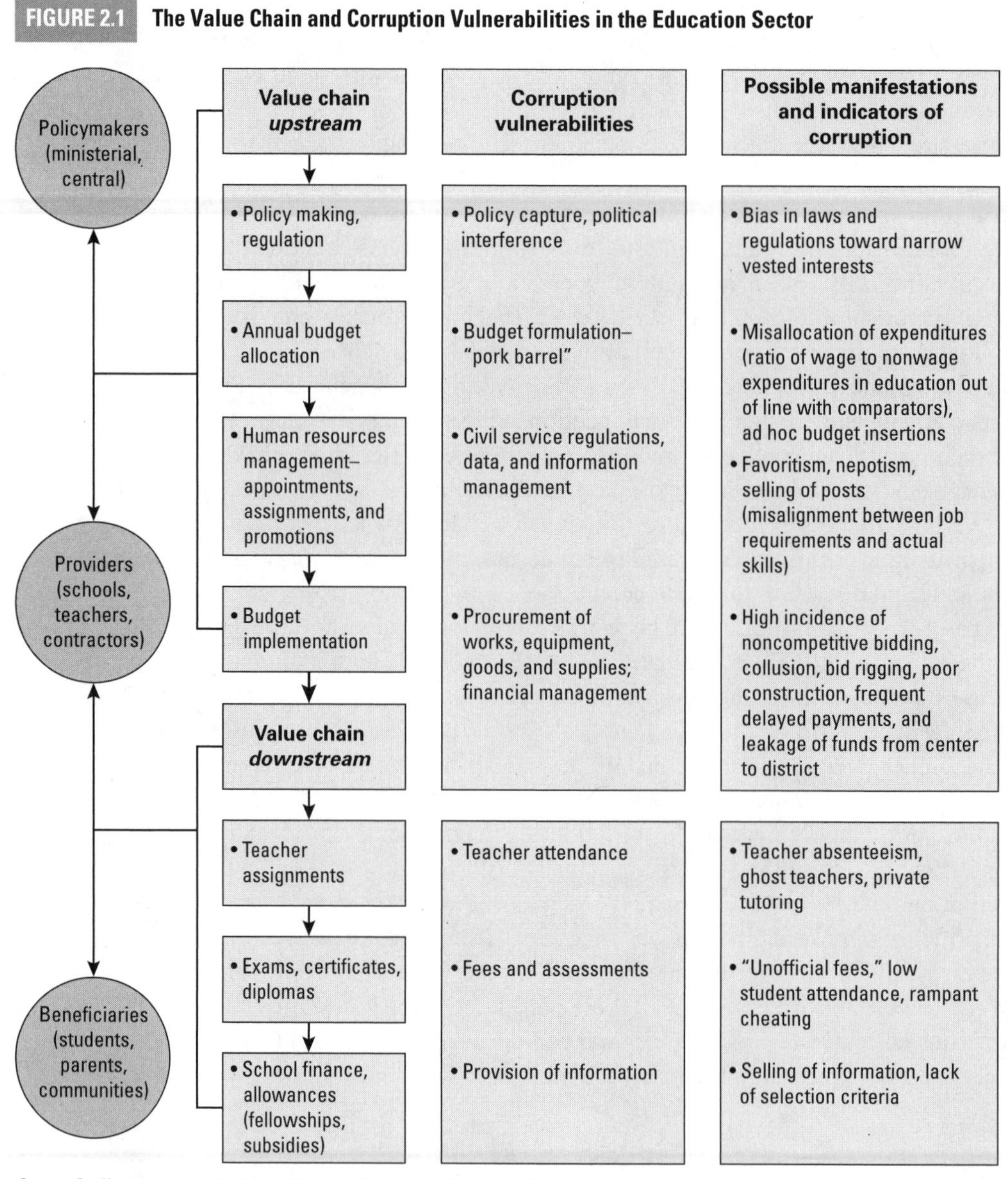

Source: Staff adaptation of Hallak and Poisson (2005) and World Bank (2003). Edgardo Campos made significant contributions to this chart.

Teacher salaries are also frequently the largest item in education budgets, often reaching more than 80 percent of the total sector budget (World Bank 2006b). One study of 55 low-income countries found that, on average, teacher salaries and benefits accounted for 74 percent of recurrent public expenditures on education, amounting on average to 4 percent of the country's GDP (gross domestic product) (Bruns, Mingat, and Rakotomalala 2003). In comparison, teacher salaries and benefits in high-income countries are generally a much lower share of total education spending. For example, mid-career salaries for primary school teachers average only 1.3 times GDP per capita in OECD countries (OECD 2005).

Several different types of teacher-related corruption practices have been systematically investigated.

- Teacher absenteeism (for example, Chaudhury and others 2006; Kremer and others 2005), which is discussed further below.
- Ghost teachers (World Bank 2004), or teachers who do not hold a teaching position but who are on the payroll and continue to receive pay, which may be cashed by other officials.
- Influence peddling and cheating, such as passing answers to students in efforts to improve results in high-stakes testing. In an influential study, Jacob and Levitt (2003) concluded that cheating occurs in 3 to 5 percent of elementary school classrooms each year in the Chicago Public Schools.
- Credential fraud (Eckstein 2003), which includes unqualified individuals obtaining academic degrees through fraudulent data, diploma mills, and other acts.
- Illegal private tutoring (Bray 2003), including cases where teachers receive illegal payments from students after hours for teaching lessons they should have been teaching during the regular school day.
- Illegal behaviors, such as child labor, abuse, and criminal offences (Human Rights Watch 2001).

Moreover, teacher wages are not typically fully responsive to local labor market conditions or to individual characteristics, so many teachers receive substantial rents in the form of wages that are higher than their outside options (Chaudhury and others 2006). Often, there are many applicants for open teaching positions, a situation that could create space for bribes and other forms of corruption in teacher recruitment and placement, especially when there is no clear and open process for recruitment.

We have chosen to focus this chapter on teacher absenteeism, one of the most serious forms of education corruption, because it appears to be pervasive, it has a lasting effect on students, and it constitutes a large burden on the education budget. The evidence we rely on comes from a few rigorous studies based on representative samples. Although we believe that the orders of magnitude these studies report are valid, it is nevertheless useful to keep in mind that the data are limited.

To give an idea of the range of the problem, a recent study by Chaudhury and others (2006) shows absenteeism rates of primary school teachers that range between 11 and 27 percent (figure 2.2). Such absenteeism rates have a tremendous impact on the education sector. In terms of direct loss of financing, it is estimated that between 10 and 24 percent of recurrent primary education expenditures are currently lost to teacher absenteeism (table 2.1). Losses from teacher absenteeism range from $16 million a year in Ecuador to $2 billion a year in India.

Teacher absenteeism causes more than economic loss. It greatly reduces the overall effectiveness of the school, diminishes pupils' achievements, damages the school's reputation, and induces pupil absenteeism (Bray 2003), while simultaneously providing negative role models for students who often see teachers as mentors.

Studies show that teacher absenteeism can influence the overall quality of education because it reduces instructional time. A study in India found that a randomized intervention that decreased the incidence of teacher absence from 36 percent to 18 percent caused test scores to increase by 0.17 standard deviations (Banerjee and

FIGURE 2.2 **Teacher Absenteeism Rates in Selected Countries**

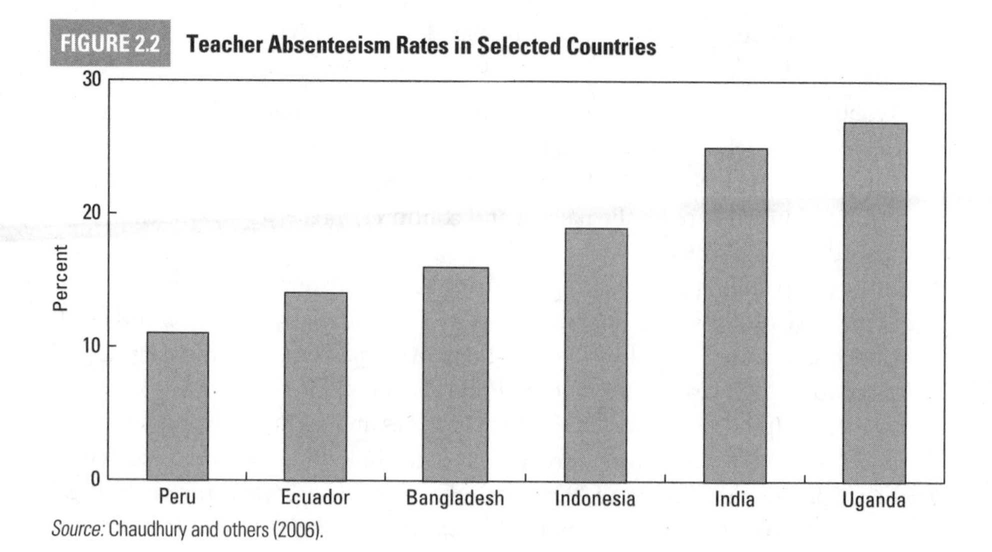

Source: Chaudhury and others (2006).

TABLE 2.1 **Estimated Direct Costs of Teacher Absenteeism, Selected Countries**

Country	*Direct cost of absenteeism as percent of public budget (current expenditure primary education)*[a]	*Direct cost of absenteeism in primary education as a percent of GDP*[b]	*GDP at market prices (current $, billions)*	*Direct cost of absenteeism in primary education (current $, millions)*[b,c]
Bangladesh	—	0.14	56.6	81
Ecuador	—	0.05	30.3	16
India	22.1	0.29	691.2	2,032
Indonesia	15.4	0.07	257.6	173
Peru	10.3	0.11	68.6	77
Uganda	23.6	0.86	6.8	59
Zambia	16.2	0.31	5.4	17

Source: Chaudhury and others (2006); Das and others (2005); UNESCO-UIS/OECD (2005); World Bank (2006b).
[a] Absenteeism rate multiplied by expenditure on teacher salaries as percent of primary current education expenditure.
[b] Absenteeism rate multiplied by public education expenditure as percent of GDP multiplied by share of public expenditure for primary education (assuming absenteeism rate is for primary level).
[c] For countries where teacher salaries are not available (Ecuador, India, Uganda), salaries for all education personnel were used; for Bangladesh, the teacher salary is an estimate from Chaudhury and others (2006) of 97 percent of recurrent education expenditures.
Note: — = not available.

Duflo 2006). An earlier study in India showed that a 10 percent increase in teacher absence is associated with a 1.8 percent lower student attendance rate as well as with a 0.02 standard deviation reduction in test scores of fourth grade students (Kremer and others 2005). Similarly, a recent study in Zambia showed that a 5 percent increase in teacher absentee rates reduces learning by 4 to 8 percent of average gains over the academic year in English and mathematics (Das and others 2005). In Bangladesh, teacher absenteeism has a significant and negative impact on primary level English language test scores (Chaudhury and others 2006). This loss of student achievement has important implications since, as mentioned earlier, education quality is the key ingredient in boosting economic growth (Hanushek and Kimko 2000).

IS TEACHER ABSENTEEISM CORRUPTION?

Not all absenteeism is necessarily a sign of corruption. Obviously, there are many valid and legitimate reasons for a teacher to be away from the classroom, such as illness, professional development, and family bereavement. But some absences are clearly illegitimate, as when teachers collect another salary by "moonlighting" when they should be in the classroom. Moreover, what might be considered official absence could be caused by inefficiencies or corruption upstream, for example, when officials use teachers for political campaigning. Reasons provided for absenteeism fall into the following key categories: official teaching and nonteaching duties, excused absence, authorized leave, sickness of self or other, unexcused absences, and tardiness (Akhmadi and Suryadarma 2004; Alcazar and others 2006; Chaudhury and others 2006; Kremer and others 2005; Rogers and others 2004) (see box 2.1).

Reported reasons for teacher absenteeism may not be fully reliable. Nonetheless, even though many teachers have a "reason" for being absent on a regular basis, it is still prima facie misuse of public resources in that services that have been paid for are not delivered. For example, a teacher who collects a government salary but does not show up to teach and instead uses the time to moonlight, thus earning more funds, is clearly abusing the system. The end result is that many students go without education. This case can be safely termed corruption.

Another example is the teacher who does not show up to work because the government has not paid his salary, and he has to travel to the payment center to collect

BOX 2.1 Reasons for Teacher Absenteeism

In South Asia, official school-related activities may include participating in immunization drives, assisting local politicians, and conducting population census work. In Bangladesh, the top reasons for absenteeism included being "away on official school-related duties" (49 percent of all absences) and "on official leave" (33 percent of absences). In India, where teacher absenteeism is 25 percent on average, only about 8–10 percent of teacher absence can be attributed to annual leave, medical leave, and other officially sanctioned reasons for absenteeism. In Indonesia, about 37 percent of absent teachers were sick or had leave permission, 19 percent reported performing official duties, 26 percent reported arriving late or leaving early, and 18 percent had unclear or unknown absences. In Ecuador, studies documented a 14 percent absenteeism rate, with 29 percent of teachers having excused and sick leave absences, 18 percent reporting being at official duties, and an astounding 53 percent of absenteeism being unexcused. In Papua New Guinea, 36 percent of teachers reported absence due to sickness, while 4 percent reported attendance in training, 11 percent reported official functions, 6 percent reported approved paid leave, 8 percent reported travel to town as a reason for absence, and 34 percent had other or unknown reasons for absenteeism.

Source: Chaudhury and others (2006); Kremer and others (2005); Akhmadi and Suryadarma (2004); Rogers and others (2004); World Bank (2004).

his paycheck. One would be wary of calling that teacher corrupt. Effectively, teachers who have to take time off to collect pay or do other official duties "misuse public office for private gain," but the misuse is caused by inefficiencies upstream. Nevertheless, the result is similar. The school lacks a teacher, the students go without learning, public funds are wasted, and learning outcomes are harmed. This sort of absence is most likely to happen in rural schools, further disadvantaging poor populations.

The situations described in these examples can occur because of a lack of enforcement, supervision, and incentives. Whatever the individual motivation, the results are the same at the school level. Therefore, using this outcome-based measure, one can consider teacher absenteeism as "corruption" regardless of the individual motivations of the teacher. The only difference is the degree of guilt or culpability (Cooter and Ulen 2000). One can think of the teachers who moonlight for personal gain at the cost of fulfilling their regular duties as being highly culpable. Further down the scale are the teachers who are absent because of illness or caring for the sick; they are "less culpable" because such absence often results from a lack of appropriate leave policy and weak central planning (combined with low salaries in some cases). Finally, there are teachers who take time off to collect their pay from the capital or are required to attend union meetings or other prescribed duties; these are perhaps the least culpable of all. In all cases, however, despite differences in intent and therefore the degree of culpability, the costs of teacher absenteeism are ultimately borne by the system and its supposed beneficiaries—the students.

INCIDENCE AND CORRELATES OF TEACHER ABSENTEEISM

Teacher absenteeism exists in all education systems. High teacher absenteeism can exist despite high salaries when teachers seem to have very low levels of motivation to do their jobs and little commitment to their profession, and when there is a lack of accountability. In addition, relatively low wages in the civil service relative to wages in the private sector can encourage corruption. When civil service pay is too low, teachers may search for additional employment as a way of supplementing their incomes, particularly when the expected cost of being caught is low (Becker 1968). This is consistent with the labor absenteeism literature (see, for example, Sapsford and Tzannatos 1993; Barmby and Treble 1991; and Allen 1981).

Several studies have attempted to determine the incidence and determinants of teacher absenteeism, but rigorous and comparable cross-country data on this subject is difficult to obtain. The evidence presented in Chaudhury and others (2006), which compares trends in teacher absenteeism in Bangladesh, Ecuador, India, Indonesia, Peru, and Uganda, offers some of the most rigorous comparable data available.

Earlier studies buttress the recent findings by Chaudhury and others (2006) regarding the prevalence of teacher absenteeism. The results of these earlier studies are not easily comparable with current findings, because different methodologies for determining teacher absenteeism were used. These studies nevertheless corroborate the fact that teacher absenteeism is (and has been) a principal drain on the education system of various countries. For example, school surveys conducted in 1995 in 14 low-income countries showed that absenteeism was especially high in Sub-Saharan Africa and South and West Asia, with teacher absentee rates ranging from 8 percent in Bangladesh to 38 percent in Tanzania (Schleicher, Siniscalco, and Postlethwaite 1995).

The findings from Chaudhury and others (2006) showing absenteeism rates for primary school teachers ranging between 11 and 27 percent might be underestimates. In countries such as Uganda, where the absenteeism rate is 27 percent, Chaudhury and others found that many teachers who were counted as present were not actually teaching. In India, 25 percent of government primary teachers were counted as absent but only about 50 percent of teachers were actually teaching. While not strictly comparable, these rates are high relative to absentee rates in the private sector of developed countries and in other industries in developing countries. For example, according to a 2000–01 Ministry of Labor Industry Survey, Indian factory workers have absence rates of about 10.5 percent, despite strict labor laws that ensure them high job security (Kremer and others 2005). Other studies also show high levels of absenteeism in Indian schools. The *Public Report on Basic Education in India* (Probe Team 1999) called attention to the disturbingly low level of teaching activity taking place in government schools. The Probe Team found that in fully one-third of schools, the head teacher was absent on the day of the survey.

Studies show that absence rates are generally higher in poorer regions (Chaudhury and others 2006). Rural teachers in India, Indonesia, and Peru have higher absenteeism rates (on average 4 percentage points higher) than their counterparts in urban areas. Teachers in smaller schools in Peru are more likely to be absent than teachers in larger schools (Alcazar and others 2006). In Papua New Guinea, the effect of a school's location on absenteeism is inconclusive, but lower teacher absence is correlated with the number of textbooks in a school (World Bank 2004). Lower teacher absenteeism is also correlated with student-teacher ratios, with teachers less likely to be absent if their classes are smaller. Different teaching methods in India do not seem to produce significantly different absenteeism rates (Kremer and others 2005). There is mixed evidence as to whether a teacher's gender is associated with higher absenteeism (Akhmadi and Suryadarma 2004; World Bank 2004; Kremer and others 2005).

The length of absence was examined in the Papua New Guinea study, where 30 percent of absent teachers reported being gone for one day while 25 percent of absent teachers reported being absent for more than seven days (World Bank 2004). This study also found that teachers began teaching well into the start of the school year: on average, they took up their posts 10 days after the official start of the school year. In extremely remote areas, teachers (not counting head teachers) began their teaching posts 27 days—almost one month—into the start of classes.

Health issues are also important determinants of absenteeism. Although illness is a valid reason for absenteeism, it is not clear why teachers would be any more absent than other workers in the country (Kremer and others 2005). HIV/AIDS has had a devastating effect on education and teacher effectiveness in Sub-Saharan Africa, although studies show that in Uganda teacher absence rates are not correlated strongly with HIV/AIDS, and in Zambia they are lower (around 17 percent) than might be expected given the country's high HIV/AIDS prevalence (Chaudhury and others 2006). Still, in 35 percent of the cases of absenteeism in Zambia, illness was reported as the reason and illness in the family and funerals accounted for an additional 27 percent (Das and others 2005).

School infrastructure appears to have a significant impact on teacher attendance in Peru and Indonesia, suggesting that poor working conditions act as disincentives for teachers. In Peru, absentee rates for teachers in schools with bathroom facilities are 21 percentage points lower than they are for teachers in schools that do not have such facilities. An increase in the availability of infrastructure is associated with a significant decrease in absences (Alcazar and others 2006). Teacher absenteeism in Indonesia was also higher in schools that did not have bathrooms and in schools that did not have enough classrooms (Akhmadi and Suryadarma 2004).

Higher-ranking officials such as headmasters are absent more often than those at the bottom of the ladder. Head teachers in Bangladesh, India, Papua New Guinea, and Peru were more likely to be absent than other teachers (Alcazar and others 2006; Chaudhury and others 2006; Kremer and others 2005; World Bank 2004). For example, head teachers are 5 to 13 percentage points more likely to be absent than regular teachers in Peru. There is some evidence from Bangladesh that official duties and administrative responsibilities may explain these higher absence rates (Chaudhury and others 2006). Head teachers may also set an example for their subordinates. In Indonesia, teacher absenteeism was likely to be higher if head teachers were absent (Akhmadi and Suryadarma 2004). In terms of corrupt behavior, it could be that these head teachers and others have the power to shield themselves from disciplinary action.

There is very little evidence that higher salaries lead to better attendance. Because reliable information on salaries is difficult to collect, age, education, and seniority are often used as proxies on the assumption that teachers who are older and more educated and who hold senior positions in schools are likely to be paid more. Better-paid teachers are absent more frequently in India and Peru (Alcazar and others 2006; Kremer and others 2005). The timing of paychecks is a factor in Papua New Guinea, where delays in salary payments are associated with greater absenteeism. Lack of teacher housing in Papua New Guinea is also correlated with higher absenteeism rates (World Bank 2004).

Contract teachers in public schools, who are not subject to civil service protection and earn a fraction of what civil service teachers earn, have the same or higher absence rates (Chaudhury and others 2006; Akhmadi and Suryadarma 2004; Alcazar and others 2006). Contract teachers may be more likely to have other jobs to supplement their teaching salaries. Or their high absenteeism could be a result of poorly designed contracts. However, private school teachers have lower absence rates than do public school teachers.

Evidence is mixed on the relationship between teachers' level of education and absenteeism (Akhmadi and Suryadarma 2004; Alcazar and others 2006; Chaudhury and others 2006; Kremer and others 2005). For example, teachers in India who hold college degrees are more likely to be absent, by 2–2.5 percentage points, than those without degrees; but the opposite relationship is found in Bangladesh. In addition, the evidence on teacher training or tenure is mixed. Again, better opportunities outside of teaching and a negligible chance of being caught for being absent—or suffering any consequence—would better explain this behavior.

Formal supervision may be one way of decreasing absenteeism. Visits from officials in the Education Ministry reduced teacher absenteeism in Bangladesh and India (Chaudhury and others 2006; Kremer and others 2005). Absence rates are 10 percent higher in secondary schools in Bangladesh that have never been visited by education officials. In India, teachers were 2 percentage points less likely to be absent if their schools had been inspected in the past three months. Moreover, teachers in districts where all schools had been inspected in the previous three months had absenteeism levels about 7 percentage points lower than those in districts where no schools had been inspected. Direct inspections in Indonesia and Papua New Guinea did not have any significant impact on teacher absenteeism, although there is anecdotal evidence from Indonesia that school inspectors are often bribed (Akhmadi and Suryadarma 2004; World Bank 2004). In Ecuador, researchers using the distance from ministry offices as a proxy estimated that absence rates for teachers at schools more than 15 miles away were 16 to 18 percentage points higher than those at schools closer to the ministry offices (Rogers and others 2004). A similar story emerges from Indonesia (Akhmadi and Suryadarma 2004).

Related to supervision is disciplinary action. In Ecuador, teachers are more likely to show up in those schools where the director imposes disciplinary action (Rogers and others 2004). That suggests that disciplinary action is needed to reinforce monitoring and supervision efforts. In fact, a lack of will or authority for undertaking disciplinary action may undermine monitoring and supervision efforts. In many places, rules for disciplinary action for repeated, unexcused absences are rarely enforced even when they exist. Teachers are almost never fired, and there are few consequences for absence. Kremer and others (2005) found that although one-fourth of India's teachers were absent at any given time, there was only one report (among a sample of 3,000 government schools) of a teacher being fired for absenteeism, and only 1 percent of head teachers reported transferring consistently absent teachers to undesirable locations. Private schools in India, whose clients may hold teachers more accountable, tend to impose more punitive action: out of 600 private schools visited, 35 reported that head teachers fired staff for repeated absenteeism. Finally, only 44 percent of head teachers in Papua New Guinea said that they play a strong role in teacher promotion, and only about 35 percent take disciplinary action (World Bank 2004).

Evidence on the impact of community and parental involvement in reducing teacher absenteeism is mixed. Predicted teacher absenteeism in Papua New Guinea fell by 50 percent when parental and community involvement was added to a model (World Bank 2004). Overall, schools in India had similar absenteeism rates whether or not they had parent-teacher associations (PTAs), although schools where PTAs had met in the past three months had lower teacher absenteeism rates (Kremer and others 2005). PTA activity was not significant in Peru, however, and parent committee activity in Ecuador was actually correlated with high levels of teacher absence, perhaps because excessive teacher absenteeism caused parents to become more involved (Alcazar and others 2006; Rogers and others 2004). An additional indicator for parental involvement in Ecuador, the share of schools in a province that had parent committees, was also insignificant. However, parental involvement in Nicaragua was thought to have reduced teacher absenteeism in community schools (Sawada 1999; see also Gertler, Patrinos, and Rubio-Codina 2006). And in Peru teachers born in the district where the school is located exhibited lower absence rates—on average, 6 percentage points lower than other teachers (Alcazar and others 2006). Community and parental involvement thus compensated to some extent for the lack of supervision and monitoring at the official level.

TABLE 2.2 Some Correlates of Teacher Absenteeism in Bangladesh, Ecuador, India, Indonesia, Papua New Guinea, Peru, and Zambia

Factor	*Indicator of level of corruption*	*Evidence (significant)*	*Potential solution*	*Proven*
Teacher education and training	High	Mixed	Link attendance to rewards Experiment with incentives and fully evaluate	Partial
Teacher tenure	High	Mixed		
Teacher ties to community	Low	Mixed	Hire local teachers whenever possible Experiment with hiring local teachers and evaluate	Promising
Teacher pay and incentives	Medium	Mixed	Publish pay rates Performance incentives	Partial Promising
Contract status	High	Negative	Contract teachers are paid at market rates when these are lower than salaries of regular teachers, making the expansion of the teaching force more financially sustainable	Promising
School infrastructure	High, medium	Mixed	Experiment with minimum standards	Partial
Remoteness	High, medium	Mixed	Experiment with transportation vouchers Experiment with incentives for working in rural areas, tied to attendance	Promising Partial
Administrative monitoring and supervision	Medium	Mixed	Formal supervision may be one way to decrease absenteeism.	Promising
Enforcement, disciplinary capacity	Medium	Positive	Disciplinary action is needed to reinforce monitoring and supervision efforts Improve the power of head teachers and school super-visors to discipline teachers that are consistently absent	Promising
Type of school (public or private)	High	Mixed	Experiment with better contracts	Promising
Community and parental involvement	High	Mixed	Experiment with school- and community-based management of schools	Promising
Lack of status for teaching	High	Little	Professionalize the teaching profession	Promising

Sources: Based primarily on Akhmadi and Suryadarma (2004); Alcazar and others (2006), Chaudhury and others (2006); Kremer and others (2005); Rogers and others (2004); World Bank (2004).

Levels of education among the beneficiary population are correlated with teacher absenteeism levels. For example, Chaudhury and others (2006) found that a 10 percentage point increase in parental literacy was correlated with a 1 percentage point decrease in the teacher absence rate. This could be the result of several factors. Greater demand for education, monitoring ability, or political influence by educated parents are likely explanations. In addition, more pleasant working conditions for teachers might be created when the children of literate parents are also better prepared for school or more motivated. There could also be selection effects, with educated parents abandoning schools with high absence rates. Finally, favorable community characteristics may contribute to both greater parental literacy and lower teacher absence.

Absenteeism results from a combination of individual and systemic issues. While some cases of absenteeism are easily categorized as individual decisions to accept pay without providing a service, in other cases systemic problems make it difficult to blame only the teacher (table 2.2). In systems that do not promote efficiency and honesty, teachers can be just as much the victims as are the students. Table 2.2 tries to categorize some of the evidence and draw tentative policy suggestions. The column on the indicator of the level of corruption presents our view on whether the reason for absenteeism is clear (or high) evidence of corruption, or less so (medium and low). The evidence column refers to whether the coefficients in the study are statistically significant and whether there is sufficient evidence from a number of countries to make a judgment. For instance, "negative" refers to cases where the factor (for example, contract status) has little impact on teacher absenteeism. Conversely, "positive" refers to factors that are likely to reduce levels of absenteeism (for example, enhanced enforcement and disciplinary capacity). Table 2.2 also has a column on whether the suggested policy response is known to work to reduce absenteeism, although we cannot say anything more at this stage than that a particular proposal may be partially proven or promising. In no case is there sufficient evidence to draw unequivocal conclusions on practices that might reduce absenteeism. The following section nevertheless draws some preliminary conclusions. It also argues that the concept of teacher absenteeism, as one form of corruption in education, needs more debate and evidence.

COMBATING TEACHER ABSENTEEISM

Combating teacher absenteeism begins with designing better systems for monitoring and reducing unexcused and invalid absences. Monopolies must be reduced or carefully regulated. Official discretion must be clarified and balanced with accountability. Transparency must be enhanced. The probability of being caught, as well as the penalties for corruption (for both givers and takers), must increase (Klitgaard 1998). Actions are needed at both the national and local levels.

Reforms at the National Level

Actions at the national level begin with political leadership and policy and civil service reforms. Improved financial management of public education spending, greater access to accurate information and awareness of the problem of absenteeism, and systematic monitoring of teacher attendance are all important ingredients of any plan to slow absenteeism. Other helpful approaches include incentives for teachers and the involvement of the private sector.

Political Leadership

The first steps in tackling teacher absenteeism are political leadership and general commitment to policy and institutional reforms to weed out corrupt practices in the use of public resources. Capable and accountable political leaders are needed to make policies, provide public services, set the rules governing markets, and oversee the use of public resources—and thus reduce poverty, promote growth, and contain corruption. Therefore, teacher absenteeism should best be addressed within the framework established for addressing overall corruption in the country. Without such an overall approach that will put all civil servants under pressure to be at their desks, it will be difficult to bring teachers back into the schools.

Policy and Civil Service Reform

The process for appointing, assigning, and promoting teachers needs to be made transparent (see Duarte 2001 on how this process is subverted in Colombia). The appointment process, for example, should encompass unambiguous selection criteria, a clear process for selection, and publication of job availability and requirements. Such a transparent process would help reduce discretion and scope for corrupt practices (Chapman 1991; Reinikka and Svensson 2006). In India and other countries where powerful teacher unions form an important voter base, policy makers should consider incentives that would reduce discretion in appointment and deployment of teachers and encourage promotions based on performance rather than on seniority and college degrees. Raising public awareness is of paramount importance in curbing abuses in appointing, assigning, and promoting teachers. Setting clear rules for teachers and responsibilities for teachers and parents are important signals that education is a national priority and that deviations are not to be tolerated. Recently, India proposed a Right to Education Bill (August 2006), which compels parents to send their children to school or face fines, such as compulsory community service. To reduce the number of teachers who perform nonacademic work, the Ministry of Human Resources Development stipulated that the only noneducational purposes teachers in state-funded schools could undertake were decennial population census; local, state, and national elections; and disaster relief duties (*Times of India 2006*). This would clearly reduce pressures for teacher absenteeism for "official duties."

The best approach for curbing teacher absenteeism would be an effective civil service reform that would enhance the accountability of all civil servants and not just that of teachers. Comprehensive reform is sometimes difficult and complex and may take time. In the interim, solutions outside of the sector can be effective. These may include better use of information throughout the system; examples are Public Expenditure Tracking Surveys (PETS)—a quantitative survey of the supply side of public services that collects information on facility characteristics, financial flows, services delivered, and accountability arrangements, designed to provide reliable administrative and financial data, to trace the flow of resources from origin to destination,

BOX 2.2 Code of Ethics for Teachers

A comparative survey undertaken by the International Institute for Educational Planning in Bangladesh, India, and Nepal argues that a teachers' code of conduct could contribute to improving outcomes and reduce absenteeism. The main elements of codes need to be:

- A clear definition of their aims
- Wide dissemination
- Establishment of both social and professional controls on their implementation
- Strict sharing of monitoring among key stakeholders
- Training of education personnel

Source: Hallak and Poisson (2005).

and to determine the location and scale of anomalies—and the posting of information on transferred resources, as is done in Kenya and Uganda, for example (see below).

Within the education sector, codes of conduct for teachers that set out clear parameters for professional behavior and performance have been found to be helpful in raising awareness of professional standards and strengthening teacher performance on the whole (box 2.2). Teachers must be seen as a crucial factor in promoting quality education. In addition to being well rewarded and well trained, the teaching profession must have dignity and recognition, as is the case in many East Asian countries.

Public Expenditure and Financial Management

Improving access to relevant and helpful information on public spending can also constrain the scope for corrupt practices, enhance transparency, and increase accountability (Bellver and Kaufmann 2005). Hallak and Poisson (2005) find that greater access to financial information is particularly helpful in situations where program administration is monopolized and where salaries of public officers are low.

In this regard, PETS can be very effective. In one study, Reinikka and Svensson (2006) documented tremendous leakage in the Ugandan education system, finding that, on average, only 13 percent of annual per student funds reached schools; local officials used the remaining 87 percent for noneducation purposes. But when information on capitation funds transferred to school districts was published in newspapers and broadcast on radio, the situation changed. Each school was also required to post a notice of all funds received on the school's bulletin board. Within three years, 90 percent of capitation funds provided by the central government were reaching the local schools (Chapman 1991; Reinikka and Svensson 2006). A PETS implemented in Kenya shows that dispersal of funds directly to schools has been efficient, with schools receiving funds allocated on time (PricewaterhouseCoopers 2005). In the past, the flow of funds to schools had been delayed or lost as the funds moved from one government office to the next. Direct dispersal has been enhanced in a large majority of the schools that have installed tracking systems that ensure transparency. These examples show that even in countries with relatively high levels of corruption, it is possible to "ring-fence" the education sector by strengthening both accountability and transparency down to the lowest delivery points. Information on resources that are supposed to reach the school, including number of teachers and information on their absences, can therefore help to reduce abuses.

Public Information Campaigns

To make any campaign to reduce teacher absenteeism more effective, awareness of the social and economic costs of absenteeism must be raised. We documented potentially very high costs from absenteeism in terms of both budget and student learning. Demand for changes, whether at the policy or institutional levels, will have to come from the population at large—from students, from parents, and even from teachers. Raising awareness is particularly important where parents and even teachers do not see teacher absenteeism as a corrupt practice or sanctionable, perhaps because it is a regular occurrence in other local service delivery institutions with which they are associated. In Uganda, a 1998 National Integrity Survey, conducted by a nongovernmental organization (Community Information, Empowerment and Transparency) in collaboration with Uganda's inspector general, found that citizens are less likely to pay "extra fees" if they have access to facts about how public service functions (CIET n.d.). Thus, while it is important to fight corruption in education, in the long term, it is equally important to use education and other programs to raise awareness of the costs of teacher absenteeism.

Systematic Monitoring

Closer oversight of local schools could help curb corrupt practices and is possible in most cases under existing regulations. Strengthening inspections, documenting the extent of ghost teachers, increasing the frequency and quality of audits, and taking corrective actions are all examples of monitoring that would help reduce teacher absence. Introducing an Education Management Information System (EMIS) program at the school level would allow collection of adequate data to better understand the problem of teacher absenteeism as well as help curb corrupt practices relating to teacher appointments and deployment (box 2.3). Not only is there is a need for learning assessments, benchmarking, and evaluations to increase school accountability (World Bank 2006a), but authorities cannot manage the education system well without proper measurement of inputs and outputs. One possible way to

BOX 2.3 Potential of an EMIS Program

The introduction of an EMIS program in The Gambia provided an objective way of tracking and ranking teachers by seniority, language abilities, subject specialization, and other factors that were supposed to be used in assigning teachers to schools. Reportedly, the availability of such information made it more difficult to deploy teachers based on personal influence or connections. A similar effort in Liberia failed after two years because head teachers refused to provide accurate data in annual school surveys.

Source: Chapman (1991).

manage accountability is to require standardized tests. Mexico, for example, expanded the use of assessments, both national and international, to hold the system accountable (World Bank 2006a).

Incentives

Incentives can help curb absenteeism, but they must be monitored to ensure that they do not become another source of corruption. For example, Kremer and Chen (2001) followed a group of preschool teachers in Kenya and found much higher absence rates during unannounced visits than were reported by headmasters, who appeared to be misreporting attendance to ensure that the teachers received salary bonuses. Chile, however, has a long history of performance-based teacher and school-based incentive programs designed to improve outcomes (Cox 2006).

Any incentives should be based on measures of performance or attendance. An external agent can be tasked with monitoring attendance and either rewarding teachers who show up regularly or penalizing teachers who are frequently absent. Technology can also be used to monitor teachers (box 2.4). Performance measures, such as test scores, have also been used, although Glewwe, Ilias, and Kremer (2003) found that this approach did nothing to improve teacher attendance.

BOX 2.4 Detecting and Reducing Absenteeism

A randomized experiment using cameras to monitor teacher attendance was implemented in a rural district in the state of Rajasthan, India, by the nongovernmental organization Seva Mandir. Because of Rajasthan's geography and the remote location of villages, monitoring schools on a regular basis is difficult. Most of these schools have only one teacher, so when the teacher is absent, children miss an entire day of school. Before the experiment began, the teacher absentee rate was 44 percent. Sixty schools were randomly selected from a group of 120 to serve as treatment schools; the other 60 served as the control group. The treatment schools were given a camera and instructions for the teachers to take a picture of himself/herself with the students at the beginning and end of each school day (cameras had a tamper-proof date and time function). Teachers received a salary of 1,000 rupees (about $22) if they were present for at least 21 days in a month and a bonus of 50 rupees (about $1) for each additional day (a day was measured as one in which the pictures were separated by five hours and a minimum number of children were present). Teachers were penalized 50 rupees for each day past the 21-day benchmark that they were absent. Depending on the teachers' attendance record, their monthly salary could range from 500 to 1,300 rupees. In the control schools, teachers received a monthly salary of 1,000 rupees and were reminded that they could be fired for poor attendance. In addition, one unannounced visit was made to each school monthly.

The absence rate fell by half in the treatment schools, much more than in control schools. Moreover, the program seemed to have an especially strong impact at the extremes of the teacher absenteeism scale: extreme absences (over 50 percent absence rate) were completely eliminated, and the number of teachers with perfect or very high attendance rose. In addition, the number of child-days per month taught increased by one-third. The experiment was also cost effective. Because of the payment structure, the average salaries in both groups were comparable, meaning that the incentives were essentially effective without an increase in net pay and the only costs incurred were the costs of the cameras and program administration. The cost of the program was $6 per child per year.

Source: Banerjee and Duflo (2006).

Bringing in the Private Sector

Absenteeism could be reduced by adopting parental choice or funding-follows-student schemes (Chaudhury and others 2006). Incentives to encourage the private sector to provide education services would break up the monopoly power of government service providers, thus limiting their ability to demand bribes. Alternative institutional forms, including hiring contract teachers, setting up community-run schools, and establishing low-cost private schools (perhaps through vouchers or scholarships) to deliver education services may reduce the incidence of absenteeism. The evidence, though, is mixed. Chaudhury and others (2006) found that contract teachers in Indonesia had higher rates of absenteeism, while Vegas and De Laat (2003) found no difference between contract and civil service teachers in Togo. Chaudhury and others (2006) also found that although alternative schools are cheaper, absenteeism is on par with government models.

Reforms at the Local Level

A national strategy for curbing corruption is a complex process that will take time to formulate and implement. Direct action to reduce corruption—even if focused only on teacher absenteeism—will be a difficult and long process. In the short term, it might make sense to focus on indirect measures at the local level that have the potential to reduce absenteeism.

Beneficiary Participation and Control Strategies

Although more evidence is needed to be certain, perhaps the most promising step would be to increase accountability and transparency at the local level, thus counterbalancing monopoly power and the unions and making official discretion more apparent. This type of reform typically relies on control strategies that are exercised by school beneficiaries, namely, students and, more important, their parents.

For beneficiary control and participation strategies to work, parents must want their children to have a high-quality education. Only when parents have a real demand for education will they have the incentive to monitor teachers and schools. To be successful, beneficiary control strategies must also give the beneficiaries the means to monitor and reward or penalize providers (as in Rajasthan and Kenya). Beneficiary control strategies include hiring and firing authority, setting salaries for providers, and simply monitoring and reporting attendance and performance. According to Banerjee and Duflo (2006), making teachers accountable to a school committee or a body of parents is the standard example of this type of reform (box 2.5).

An increasingly common approach is to involve local communities, particularly parents, in the management and monitoring of school performance (box 2.6). Typically, this involvement generates increased community "ownership" in improving education, thereby increasing accountability of school management.

Mechanisms to allow for participation of beneficiaries, especially the poor, in decision-making processes should be developed and implemented. Banerjee and Duflo (2006) note several advantages that flow from giving beneficiaries more control and decision-making power. First, this approach is cost effective. Second, beneficiaries tend to be better informed than central-level authorities, and they are

BOX 2.5 Raising Demand for Quality Services

Demand for services may be linked to teacher absenteeism in an unexpected way. In a randomized girls' scholarship intervention in Kenya (Kremer, Miguel, and Thornton 2004), both student and teacher attendance increased in treatment schools. Teacher attendance was 6.5 percentage points higher in treatment schools than in control schools and was one-third higher than it was before the program began. One possible explanation for the improved attendance is that teachers may be motivated by a class full of students. An alternative explanation may be that parents of scholarship recipients started to hold teachers more accountable than they had previously. There is indirect evidence of the second explanation in Mexico's rural school-based management program (Gertler, Patrinos, and Rubio-Codina 2006). King and Ozler (2001) found that parental involvement in schools in Nicaragua increased teacher attendance. Kremer, Miguel, and Thornton (2004) also found evidence of positive externalities associated with parental involvement: boys' attendance increased in treatment schools, as did test scores for both boys and girls.

BOX 2.6 Local Monitoring of Education Can Help Reduce Teacher Absenteeism

In some Indian villages, such as in Khetloi in Rajasthan, village leaders and parents have helped increase the quality of education by monitoring the schools. In Himachal Pradesh, too, cooperative action among parents, and between parents and teachers, has resulted in greater accountability in the system. However, in some states such as Tamil Nadu, after some misuse of power by the *panchayat* (village council) leaders, the responsibility was shifted back to the state government. In Karnataka, the state government refused to shift payment of salaries to the *panchayats,* fearing that the salaries would not reach staff. Instead the state established school improvement committees in village schools whose members consist of *panchayat* leaders and parents. Teacher's leave, for example, has to be approved by these committees. Anecdotal information suggests that teacher absenteeism has decreased.

Source: Annamalai (2001).

able to apply social pressure to providers. Finally, as long as beneficiaries have real demand for the service, they have a greater incentive to monitor and thus are more willing to punish or reward providers than are central-level or independent authorities.

Civil society organizations also can play a role in reducing corruption in education. They work at the local level, can inform the public about what is going on, and can encourage debate on corruption. They have influence over a variety of stakeholders. In addition, they can work with their clients and providers to raise awareness and ensure access to information. Such groups thus contribute more generally to greater transparency in education systems and practices (Transparency International 2005).

CONCLUSIONS

Education is a necessary condition for the achievement of the Millennium Development Goals, and thus a necessary condition for social and economic development and for personal empowerment. For education to be able to help citizens and nations reap its potential benefits, it must function in an effective manner. As this chapter shows, corruption, which hampers all development efforts, is a debilitating presence in the education sector. The focus here has been to highlight the damage from corruption in one of the most important aspects of education, teacher absenteeism. Recent, albeit limited, studies find convincing evidence that teacher absenteeism is a significant problem in many countries, wasting financial resources and shortchanging young students. Although this chapter has discussed some key determinants of teacher absenteeism and sketched out some policy options, it is quite clear that additional data from more countries are needed on issues surrounding teacher absenteeism. Effective strategies for reducing teacher absenteeism cannot be formulated until the extent of the problem is known and its determinants better understood.

Certainly, not all teacher absences are indications of corruption; but all absences have a negative impact on student learning. The costs, both monetary and educational, are just as high when absences are excusable as when they are not.

Future dialogue on issues of corruption in education is necessary. In particular, issues of teacher absenteeism require additional analyses. Priority issues include the need for more monitoring, additional research, and comparable information that can help us analyze situations of absenteeism in a number of countries. Additional experimentation and evaluation of positive approaches that show promising results is also necessary. Lessons learned from tackling the problems associated with teacher absenteeism can also be applied to other corruption issues in the education sector.

REFERENCES

Akhmadi, S. U., and D. Suryadarma. 2004. "When Teachers Are Absent: Where Do They Go and What Is the Impact on Students?" SMERU Research Institute, Jakarta.

Alcazar, L., F. H. Rogers, N. Chaudhury, J. Hammer, M. Kremer, and K. Muralidharan. 2006. "Why Are Teachers Absent? Probing Service Delivery in Peruvian Primary Schools." Development Economics Department, World Bank, Washington, DC.

Allen, S. G. 1981. "An Empirical Model of Work Attendance." *Review of Economics and Statistics* 63 (1): 77–87.

Álvarez, J., V. Garcia Moreno, and H. A. Patrinos. 2006. "Institutional Effects as Determinants of Learning Outcomes: Exploring State Variations in Mexico." Human Development Department, World Bank, Washington, DC.

Annamalai, M. 2001. "Effective Government Schools." *Journal of Literacy and Education in Developing Societies* 1 (20). http://www.servintfree.net/~aidmn-ejournal/publications/2001-11/EffectiveGovernmentSchools.html.

Barmby, T. A., and J. G. Treble. 1991. "Absenteeism in a Medium-Sized Manufacturing Plant." *Applied Economics* 23 (2): 161–66.

Banerjee, A., and E. Duflo. 2006. "Addressing Absence." *Journal of Economic Perspectives* 20 (1): 117–32.

Barro, R. J. 1991. "Economic Growth in a Cross-Section of Countries." *Quarterly Journal of Economics* (May): 407–44.

———. 2001. "Human Capital and Growth." *American Economic Review* 91 (2, *Papers and Proceedings*): 12–17.

Becker, G. S. 1964. *Human Capital.* New York: Columbia University Press.

———. 1968. "Crime and Punishment: An Economic Approach." *Journal of Political Economy* 76 (2): 169–217.

Bellver, A., and D. Kaufmann. 2005. "Transparenting Transparency: Initial Empirics and Policy Applications." World Bank Institute, Washington, DC.

Belot, M., and D. Webbink. 2006. "The Lost Generation: The Effect of Teacher Strikes on Students. Evidence from Belgium." University of Essex and CPB Netherlands Bureau for Economic Policy Analysis, The Hague, Netherlands.

Bentaouet Kattan, R., and N. Burnett. 2004. "User Fees in Primary Education." Education for All Working Paper 30108, Human Development Network, World Bank, Washington, DC.

Bray, M. 2003. *Adverse Effects of Private Supplementary Tutoring: Dimensions, Implications and Government Responses.* Paris: IIEP-UNESCO.

Bruns, B., A. Mingat, and R. Rakotomalala. 2003. *Achieving Universal Primary Education by 2015: A Chance for Every Child.* Washington, DC: World Bank.

Chapman, D. W. 1991. "The Rise and Fall of Education Management Information Systems in Liberia." *Journal of Educational Policy* 6 (2): 133–43.

Chaudhury, N., J. Hammer, M. Kremer, K. Muralidharan, and F. H. Rogers. 2006. "Missing in Action: Teacher and Health Worker Absence in Developing Countries." *Journal of Economic Perspectives* 20 (1): 91–116.

Chua, Y. T. 1999. "Robbed: An Investigation of Corruption in Philippine Education." Philippine Center for Investigative Journalism, Quezon City.

CIET (Community Information, Empowerment and Transparency). "Accountability in Health Services." http://www.ciet.org/en/documents/themes_docs/ 2006220164820. pdf.

Cockroft, L. 1998. "Corruption and Human Rights: A Crucial Link." Working Paper, Transparency International, Berlin.

Cooter, R., and T. Ulen. 2000. *Law and Economics.* Reading, MA: Addison Wesley Longman.

Cox, C. 2006. "Policy Formation and Implementation in Secondary Education Reform: The Case of Chile at the Turn of the Century." Education Working Paper Series 3, Human Development Network, World Bank, Washington, DC.

Das, J., D. Dercon, J. Habyarimana, and P. Krishnan. 2005. "Teacher Shocks and Student Learning: Evidence from Zambia." Policy Research Working Paper 3602, World Bank, Washington, DC.

Duarte, J. 2001. "Política y Educación: Tentaciones particularistas en la Educación Latinoamericana." In *Economía Política de las Reformas Educativas en América Latina,* ed. S. Martinic and M. Pardo. Santiago: CIDE-PREAL.

Eckstein, M. A. 2003. *Combating Academic Fraud: Towards a Culture of Integrity.* Paris: IIEP-UNESCO.

Foweraker, J. 1993. *Popular Mobilization in Mexico: The Teachers' Movement 1977–87.* Cambridge: Cambridge University Press.

Friedman, M. 1955. "The Role of Government in Education." In *Economics and the Public Interest,* ed. R. A. Solo. New Brunswick, NJ: Rutgers University Press.

Gentili, P., and D. Suarez. 2004. "La Conflictividad Educativa en America Latina." Foro Latinoamericano de Politcas Educativas, Chile.

Gertler, P., H. Patrinos, and M. Rubio-Codina. 2006. "Empowering Parents to Improve Education: Evidence from Rural Mexico." Policy Research Working Paper 3935, World Bank, Washington, DC.

Glewwe, P., N. Ilias, and M. Kremer. 2003. "Teacher Incentives." Department of Economics, Harvard University, Cambridge, MA.

Gupta, S., H. Davoodi, and E. Tiongson. 2000. "Corruption and the Provision of Health Care and Education Services." IMF Working Paper 00/116, International Monetary Fund, Washington, DC.

Hallak, J., and M. Poisson. 2001. "Ethics and Corruption in Education." Paris: IIEP-UNESCO.

———. 2005. "Ethics and Corruption in Education—an Overview." *Journal of Education for International Development.* http://www.usaid.gov/our_work/democracy_and_governance/publications/ac/sector/education.doc.

Hanushek, E. A., and D. D. Kimko. 2000. "Schooling, Labor-Force Quality, and the Growth of Nations." *American Economic Review* 90 (5): 1184–1208.

Hanushek, E. A., and L. Wößmann. 2007. "The Role of Education Quality for Economic Growth." World Bank Policy Research Working Paper 4122. Human Development Network, Education Unit, World Bank, Washington, DC.

Heyneman, S. 2004. "Education and Corruption." *International Journal of Educational Development* 24 (6): 637–48.

Human Rights Watch. 2001. "Scared at School: Sexual Violence against Girls in South African Schools." Human Rights Watch, New York.

Jacob, B. A., and S. D. Levitt. 2003. "Rotten Apples: An Investigation of the Prevalence and Predictors of Teacher Cheating." *Quarterly Journal of Economics* 118 (3): 843–78.

King, E. M., and B. Ozler. 2001. "What's Decentralization Got to Do with Learning? Endogenous School Quality and Student Performance in Nicaragua." Development Economics Department, World Bank, Washington, DC.

Klitgaard, R. 1998. "International Cooperation against Corruption." *Finance and Development* (March): 3–6.

Kremer, M., N. Chaudhury, F. Halsey Rogers, K. Muralidharan, and J. Hammer. 2005. "Teacher Absence in India: A Snapshot." *Journal of the European Economic Association* 3 (2–3): 658–67.

Kremer, M., and D. Chen. 2001. "An Interim Report on a Teacher Attendance Incentive Program in Kenya." Development Economics Department, Harvard University Cambridge, MA.

Kremer, M., E. Miguel, and R. Thornton. 2004. "Incentives to Learn." Development Economics Department, Harvard University, Cambridge, MA.

Mauro, P. 1998. "Corruption and the Composition of Government Expenditure." *Journal of Public Economics* 69: 263–79.

Murillo, M. V., M. Tommasi, L. Ronconi, and J. Sanguinetti. 2002. "The Economic Effects of Unions in Latin America: Teachers' Unions and Education in Argentina." Latin American Research Network Working Paper R-463. Inter-American Development Bank, Washington, DC.

OECD (Organisation for Economic Co-operation and Development). 2005. *Teachers Matter: Attracting, Developing and Retaining Effective Teachers.* Paris: OECD.

Oxfam. 2001. "Education Charges: A Tax on Human Development." Oxfam Briefing Paper 3, Oxfam, London.

Pritchett, L. 2001. "Where Has All the Education Gone?" *World Bank Economic Review* 15 (3): 367–91.

Probe Team. 1999. *Public Report on Basic Education in India.* Oxford: Oxford University Press.

Psacharopoulos, G., and H. A. Patrinos. 2004. "Returns to Investment in Education: A Further Update." *Education Economics* 12 (2): 111–34.

PricewaterhouseCoopers. 2005. "Expenditure Tracking Study: Interim Report."

Reinikka, R., and J. Svensson. 2006. "Using Micro-Surveys to Measure and Explain Corruption." *World Development* 34 (2): 359–70.

Rogers, F. H., J. R. Lopez-Calix, N. Cordoba, N. Chaudhury, J. Hammer, M. Kremer, and K. Muralidharan. 2004. "Teacher Absence and Incentives in Primary Education: Results from a National Teacher Tracking Survey in Ecuador." Development Economics Department, World Bank, Washington, DC.

Sapsford, D., and Z. Tzannatos. 1993. *The Economics of the Labour Market.* Houndmills, U.K.: Macmillan.

Sawada, Y. 1999. "Community Participation, Teacher Effort, and Educational Outcomes: The Case of El Salvador's EDUCO Program." William Davidson Institute Working Paper 307, University of Michigan, Ann Arbor, MI.

Schleicher, A., M. Siniscalco, and T. N. Postlethwaite. 1995. "The Conditions of Primary Schools: A Pilot Study in the Least Developed Countries." UNESCO and UNICEF, Paris.

Schultz, T. P. 1997. "Assessing the Productive Benefits of Nutrition and Health: An Integrated Human Capital Approach." *Journal of Econometrics* 77: 141–58.

———. 2002. "Why Governments Should Invest More to Educate Girls." *World Development* 30 (2): 207–25.

Tanzi, V., and H. Davoodi. 1997. "Corruption, Public Investment, and Growth." IMF Working Paper 97/139, International Monetary Fund, Washington, DC.

Times of India. 2006. "Send Kids to School or Else . . ." August 6.

Transparency International. 2005. "Stealing the Future: Corruption in the Classroom." Berlin.

UNESCO-UIS/OECD. 2005. *Education Trends in Perspective—Analysis of the World Education Indicators.* http://www.uis.unesco.org/TEMPLATE/pdf/wei/WEI2005.pdf.

Vegas, E., and J. De Laat. 2003. "Do Differences in Teacher Contracts Affect Student Performance? Evidence from Togo." Development Economics Department, World Bank, Washington, DC.

World Bank. 2003. *World Development Report 2004: Making Services Work for Poor People.* Washington, DC: World Bank and Oxford University Press.

———. 2004. "Papua New Guinea: Public Expenditure Service Delivery." World Bank, Washington, DC.

———. 2006a. "Mexico: Making Education More Effective by Compensating for Disadvantages, Introducing School-Based Management, and Enhancing Accountability: A Policy Note." Report 35650-MX, World Bank, Washington DC.

———. 2006b. *World Development Indicators.* Washington, DC: World Bank.

3

Crime and Justice in the Garden of Eden

Improving Governance and Reducing Corruption in the Forestry Sector

NALIN KISHOR AND RICHARD DAMANIA

"I am working to make sure we don't only protect the environment, we also improve governance."

Dr. Wangari Maathai, Nobel Laureate, 2004

The remote forests of Palindantan Harbor an exceptional array of biodiversity—rare birds, the last refuge of the country's 14 remaining tigers, and the critically endangered pygmy rhinoceros.[1] Scientists have classified the area as a global biodiversity hotspot, and in response the government has bestowed upon the forest the mantle of national park, with its own team of forest guards equipped with new vehicles and a range office. But periodically the tranquility is shattered by the sound of chainsaws. Illegal logging is big business in this area. The logs are hauled onto trucks that journey past the forest rangers' headquarters and across borders, where they are mysteriously transformed from illegal logs into legal lumber. From there the logs move into factories where they are turned into elegant pieces of furniture and sold in the retail outlets of the United States and Europe. At each stage in the journey, a lot of money passes under the table. Forest guards and local politicians in Palindantan demand their share of the plunder, the connivance of customs and transport officials is needed to export bulky illegal timber, forest bureaucrats in distant national capitals further collude in issuing fraudulent permits and certificates. And finally political lobbyists in the consumer nations play their role, vociferously resisting attempts to introduce effective log-tracking and anti-money-laundering systems. This chain of events is not uncommon throughout the global forest estate, but it is possibly most egregious in the tropical forests.

The scale and scope of corruption in the forest sector sets it apart from others. Forest-related corruption has been reported in countries as diverse as Cameroon and Canada. It can take numerous forms—petty bribery and extortion by forest officials, or payments to higher-level administrators for timber concessions, to inducements

BOX 3.1 Examples of Corruption in the Forest Sector

- Ministers, legislators, and other high officials accept bribes to shape forest laws, institutions, and procedures, and award concessions to favor the bribers.
- Officials award timber concessions to their relatives.
- Forest officers, police officers, and prosecutors take bribes to ignore violations of forest laws, including laws forbidding harvests in national parks and laws protecting endangered species.
- Forest officials extort payments from landowners for forestry services that the state ought to supply at a nominal fee.
- To avoid delays in issuance of timber transit permits, landowners bribe not only the local forester but also local tax and land officials.
- Enforcement officials stop perfectly legal log shipments on the road and threaten to charge the drivers with illegal transport unless the drivers pay a bribe.
- To win the right to cut trees on a government forest, a bidder makes cash payments to a forest officer.
- In a forest-related court case, bribes fly to the court clerks, the judges, and even opposing counsel to secure a favorable and prompt verdict.
- Officials take bribes to allow export of illegally harvested timber.
- Customs agents take bribes to allow timber to enter the country without paying duties or in violation of endangered species protections.
- A forest officer demands that his subordinates pay him kickbacks for salary increases and promotions.
- A forest officer places friends and relatives on the agency payroll, even though they are "ghosts" who do no actual work.
- Ministers use timber receipts to fund political campaigns.
- Ministers siphon money off of donor-sponsored projects for personal enrichment.

Specific examples include:

- Canada, where violations were detected in 55 percent of areas designated for protection
- Brazil, where a presidential commission concluded that fully 71 percent of the management plans in concessions did not comply with the law
- The Russian Federation, where at least 20 percent of timber logged is in violation of the law
- Papua New Guinea, where the majority of forestry operations cannot credibly be said to comply with national laws and regulations and are therefore unlawful
- Cambodia, where only 10 percent of logging in 1997 was estimated to be legal
- Cameroon, where an estimated one-third of the timber cut in 1992–93 was undeclared

Source: Rosenbaum (2005), Contreras (2002), Forest Trends (2006), and Glastra (1999).

to sanction changes in land use, and most sinister of all, to the erosion of institutions beyond the sector and across the economy (box 3.1 provides a list of corrupt practices in the forest sector).

Not surprisingly, global comparisons of governance find that the major forest producers, that is, developing economies highly dependent on forest resources, are among the most corrupt countries in the world. Figure 3.1 shows annual rates of deforestation in selected countries plotted against how the countries rate on a "control of corruption index." It is clear that economies such as Brazil, Cambodia, the Democratic Republic of Congo, Ghana, Indonesia, and others, all highly dependent on forest resources for their economic development, are also characterized by poor quality of governance. At the same time, countries experiencing either no deforestation or increases in forest cover tend to be characterized by robust governance.

FIGURE 3.1 Deforestation versus Control of Corruption

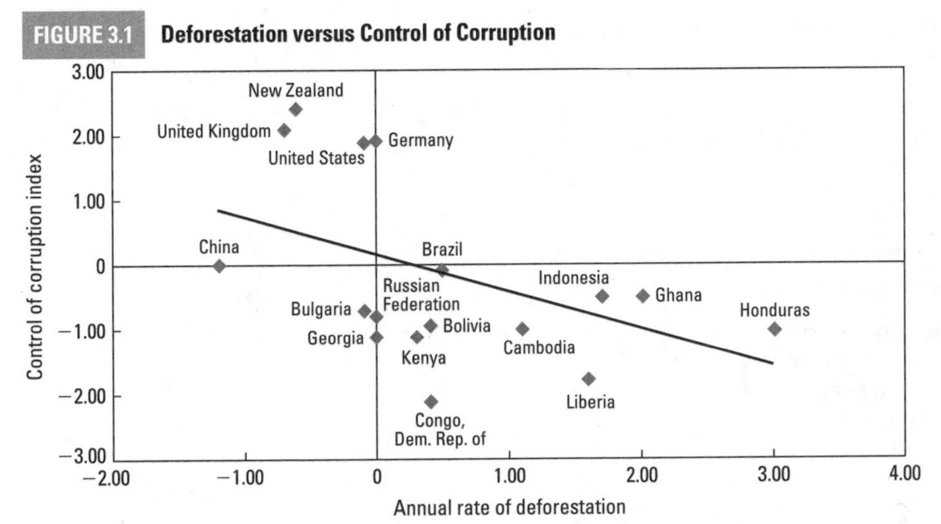

Source: Authors calculations. Corruption data from WBI (2006) and deforestation data from FAO (2006).

While causation is not formally established, the conclusion appears inescapable—corruption is likely a significant contributory factor to deforestation (and resource mismanagement) in these countries.

THE COSTS AND CONSEQUENCES OF FOREST CORRUPTION

As box 3.1 indicates, illegal acts and forest crimes of various kinds are ubiquitous; they occur in developing as well as developed nations and in all major forest types—tropical, temperate, and boreal (Callister 1999; Contreras 2002). The clandestine and varied nature of these illegal activities makes it difficult in most cases to measure the size of the problem (see annex 3A for a more detailed list of illegal acts in the context of logging). However, recent efforts have been successful in obtaining some defensible estimates. Box 3.2 is one such attempt for Indonesia, where the illegal sector (as measured by the value added) is more than seven times greater than the legal sector and accounts for 17 percent of output of the agricultural sector. At a more general level, globally an estimated $5 billion in uncollected taxes and royalties on legally sanctioned timber harvests is lost each year because of corruption (World Bank 2002). Despite the absence of accurate measures that capture all the other dimensions of corruption, it is clear that the scale and magnitude of the problem are large.[2]

In addition to direct financial losses, other negative effects emerge from illegal logging and forest corruption.

- Violation of protected areas threatens the conservation of forest resources and biodiversity.
- As many as 60 million people living in and around the forests are heavily dependent on them for their subsistence. The well-being of these vulnerable groups is at risk from illegal logging and unauthorized removals from the forest.

BOX 3.2 Earnings from Legal and Illegal Logging: A Decomposition and Analysis for Indonesia

In Indonesia, the revenues and value added associated with logging operations (legal and illegal) are staggering. The total annual turnover associated with all logging is estimated at $6.6 billion (Kishor 2004). At an estimated $1.5 billion, the legal portion of logging accounts for less than one-fourth of this total.

The estimate of the associated value added is $4.25 billion (this includes the value added to illegal log exports), which accounted for about 3 percent of Indonesia's GDP in 2000, or about 17 percent of the value added contributed by the agricultural sector.

Following are other losses associated with illegal logging in Indonesia.

- Although the government collects a large volume of taxes, significant revenues are lost because almost no taxes are collected on illegal logging.
- Informal payments and bribes in the sector are estimated to amount to more than $1 billion a year.
- Legal logging activities are not protected from bribes—more than 25 percent of the total estimated bribes originate from legally cut timber! If this corruption could be checked, estimates show that private sector return on investment (taken as the costs of extraction) would rise to about 45 percent from its current level of about 15 percent.
- Log smuggling is a highly lucrative activity, with about half of total value added in the sector being generated from the illegal export of logs.
- Small-scale illegal logging is significant, but it pales in comparison with large-scale, domestic illegal logging and illegal exports.

Source: Authors calculations; Kishor (2004). Details on calculations are available from the authors.

- Forests are a global public good and their degradation imposes global costs, such as climate change and species loss.
- Legitimate forest enterprises are subjected to unfair competition through price undercutting and are discouraged from making socially and environmentally responsible investments in the sector.
- And, as this chapter demonstrates, less visible though highly insidious costs result from the erosion of institutions, the spread of corruption across the economy (including speculative and other illegal activities), and lower economic growth.

These spillover effects of forest corruption are the most far-reaching and significant aspect of the problem. The corrosive effects of illegal logging, especially on governance, are not confined to the forest sector. Forest products are bulky, and illegal lumber could be easily intercepted by officials. So the connivance and corruption of a range of officials—customs, police, local politicians, and transport authorities—are needed for the industry to survive. Corruption in the forest sector is therefore contagious and weakens governance through other segments of the economy. The effects of corruption spread further by providing opportunities for money laundering, weakening the rule of law in forest areas, diluting the effectiveness of policies, generating trade distortions, and disrupting legitimate economic activities more generally. For Indonesia, it is estimated that as much as $5 billion is generated through illegal activities in the forest sector, all completely outside the control of fiscal authorities and free to spread corruption contagion throughout the economy (see box 3.2).

Anecdotal evidence suggests that economies of scale are probably present among illicit activities. Thus illegal logging is often accompanied by other crimes such as arms, human, and drug trafficking. Corruption contagion is probably the most significant, though least recognized, consequence of forest crime. Its impacts are transmitted through the economy, weakening governance and the rule of law, thus impeding investment in legitimate commerce and undermining faith in the legitimacy of the government apparatus.

FOREST SECTOR CHARACTERISTICS THAT ENABLE CORRUPTION

Why are forests so vulnerable to corruption and crime? To answer this question, one needs to examine some of the characteristics of forests. If forests were like farms, then producing timber would be as simple as growing wheat and the production of timber would be relegated to private enterprise. But unlike other resources, forests provide a wide range of *public* benefits (watershed protection, carbon sequestration, biodiversity protection, and ecosystem resilience) only when they are *preserved;* and they provide *private* benefits (timber rents) principally when they are *harvested.* So there is a well-recognized need for high levels of intervention to ensure optimal and sustainable levels of harvesting as well as adequate protection of the public benefits.

The state is typically responsible for a nation's forests, and it either owns or regulates the management of forests through a forest department. Globally, governments own or control an estimated three-quarters of all forest resources, and in many countries, the government is the monopolist owner of forested lands (White and Martin 2002). In addition, governments regulate private and community-owned forest lands as well as hold principal responsibility for the supervision of forest production.

Forest management agencies are entrusted with the onerous responsibility of managing the conflicting objectives of conserving global assets of value and generating resource rents. A commonly followed approach to managing the public and private benefits from forests is to demarcate the forest estate into *protection areas* (to ensure the environmental and public goods contribution of forests) and *production areas* (to create sustainable economic wealth from the resource). In a continuum approach to forest management, *mixed-use areas* are also specified. Such a demarcation by itself does not solve and may in fact exacerbate the problem of forest corruption. Government forest officers work for meager salaries, yet they are responsible for protecting a resource with a high commercial value. And since timber is scarce and the costs of harvesting are low, the rents from depleting forests remain high, and there are strong incentives to subvert regulations and pay bribes to capture a greater share of the resource.

In addition, forestry officials usually operate in remote forests, far from public scrutiny, with *broad discretionary powers.* Thus, unsupervised local forest officers may have a great deal of latitude to certify compliance with the law or collude in illegal acts. The propensity for malfeasance and the incentive to accept bribes in these circumstances is clearly high.

Rarely do governments have adequate information for proper forest management, including its monitoring.[3] Despite advances in modern remote sensing and mapping technology, the capacity of the responsible agencies, especially in tropical countries, to monitor and enforce the law over large forest areas is limited. Forest inventories are often incomplete or nonexistent (bin Buang 2001). There is seldom adequate information on existing volumes, quality of forest resources, the distribution of species, and their geographical location. Thus, the lack of information compromises transparency and provides a convenient cover for plunder and malpractice.

With limited oversight and abundant rents, opportunities for corruption abound.[4] As a result, illegal felling is widespread in almost every tropical country. Neither production areas nor protected areas are immune from corrupt practices and illegal logging.

DRIVERS OF FOREST CORRUPTION: A TYPOLOGY

The existence of high scarcity rents, coupled with wide discretionary powers and low accountability, create a climate ripe for corruption in the forest sector, as elsewhere. However, the driving forces for forest corruption are more complex and often more "institutionalized" than suggested by the Klitgaard "corruption equation." To identify the actors and kinds of corruption that plague the forest sector, this section develops a typology of corruption.

State Capture: Institutional Erosion and Rent Seizing

State capture refers to the actions of individuals or interest groups (in both the public and private sectors) to influence the formation of laws, regulations, statutes, and other government policies to their own advantage (World Bank 2000a). Institutional structures are endogenous and are shaped by the interests of those in authority. However, timber rents are also a lucrative source of revenue to those in authority. To capture a greater share of these rents, it may be necessary to undermine the institutional safeguards that impede the process. Most arguments about corruption assume that it is made possible because existing institutional structures are weak or flawed and thus enable rent seekers to strip the economy of its assets. The argument here is that even when institutions are strong, the presence of high rents unleashes powerful incentives for those in government to weaken the institutions that constrain rent capture, that is, the existence of the high rents results in institutional erosion.

Ross (2001) reports that in a variety of countries such as Indonesia, Malaysia, and the Philippines, the dismantling of legal and regulatory mechanisms that had previously served to protect forests and their inhabitants occurred during timber booms. Ross argues that in all three countries it was a resource boom that paradoxically caused a decline in the quality of the institutions. The windfalls generated by the booms encouraged greedy and unscrupulous politicians to engage in a type of rent-seeking behavior called rent seizing, which is an effort by state actors to gain the right to allocate rents. When timber prices begin to create supernormal profits (rents) for logging firms, state officials have typically responded by dismantling the legal and regulatory mechanisms that had previously served to protect the forests and its inhabitants—mechanisms that kept logging in line with sustained yield levels, guarded the traditional rights of forest dwellers (as in Indonesia and Malaysia), and insulated the forestry bureaucracy from political interference. At the moment when these institutions are most needed, they are taken apart (see box 3.3 for proposed remedies.)

BOX 3.3 Potential Solutions to End Resource Windfalls, Rent Seizing, and Institutional Erosion

Between 1950 and 1995, Indonesia, Malaysia, and the Philippines each experienced periods of booming timber exports, based on their immense resources of trees from the *Dipterocarpaceae* family. While Malaysia and the Philippines had strong forestry institutions, those in Indonesia were relatively weak. Yet, over time, and concomitant with the timber booms, the forestry institutions broke down in all three countries. The forest departments lost their political independence and the quality of the forest policies dropped sharply—the state sanctioned timber extraction at rates far in excess of annual sustainable cuts.

Ross (2001) suggests four possible approaches to mitigating the problem of rent seizing. First, reduce the incidence of windfalls by stabilizing international commodity prices. However, the experience with commodity price stabilization has not been encouraging, and the weight of the evidence suggests that creating a stabilization fund for tropical timber is not a practical matter. Second, protect the windfalls by shrouding them in secrecy. For example, the government of Cameroon placed its oil windfalls in secret offshore funds controlled by the president's office. However, this is a risky approach, open to corruption by a small group of very powerful state actors. A third, and (according to the author) more plausible, option is to keep the windfall out of the hands of the state and to distribute it as widely as possible among the stakeholders in the country. The fourth option consists of using third-party enforcement to help curtail rent seizing. When the state's normal enforcement mechanisms become endogenous to the rent-seeking process, third parties can help force the government to use its windfalls prudently. The World Bank, the International Monetary Fund, and the Asian Development Bank have all performed the role of third-party enforcer at one time or another.

Institutional erosion and state capture are ubiquitous in the forest-dependent economies. Both general and robust statistical evidence show that point resources (such as minerals and forests) are enticing targets for rent seizure, which weakens institutional structures, leading to poor governance and high levels of corruption. Additionally, governments that rely on natural resource rents tend to be less responsive as well as less accountable to their polity than those that depend upon taxation of the polity to raise resources. Weak institutions in turn lower the growth rates and impede development (Dixit 2004; Isham and others 2004; Damania, Deacon, and Bulte 2005). The hidden contagion of forest corruption is clearly a broader economic issue that deserves much greater attention from scholars and policy analysts.

Grand Corruption and Rent Seeking

While unlawful logging may account for a large proportion of deforestation, the vast majority of forests are lost to "legal" activities. Logging companies routinely pay bribes and (legal) political contributions to parties for preferential access to forest resources. This is termed grand corruption and typically involves high-level officials and substantial amounts of money changing hands (as bribes, kickbacks, speed money, and the like).[5] Bribes and contributions are also paid to sanction changes in land use, which can have a substantial impact on forests. Perhaps the most widely publicized example is the (often subsidized) expansion of cattle ranching into the deep forests of the Amazon. Local communities are seldom consulted in the process and their role is restricted to supplying cheap labor. This is unsurprising as the ability of large firms to pay bribes is considerably greater than that of small, poor, and dispersed communities.

BOX 3.4 Alchemy through International Trade: Transforming Illegal to Legal in the Forest Sector

The United States is the largest consumer and importer of wood products. In addition, rapidly expanding demand for timber and wood products from fast-growing countries, such as China and India, provides a strong impetus to import from "producer" countries and consequently creates pressures for illegal harvesting of timber. In other words, trade in timber is an important driver of illegal logging in producer countries such as Brazil, Cambodia, Cameroon, Indonesia, Myanmar, Papua New Guinea, and the Russian Federation. A report commissioned by the American Forest & Paper Association (Seneca Creek Associates 2005) estimates that as much as 17 percent of all round wood traded internationally may come from illegal sources. The trade of timber products is often routed through third countries, with important implications for the value chain. The example below illustrates the value chain of a log, given as value per cubic meter; gains are higher the closer one gets to final demand.

Logger (Tanjung Putin National Park, Indonesia):	$2.20
Broker (buying illegally in Riau province, Indonesia):	$20.00
Broker (selling in Melaka, Malaysia):	$160.00
Buyer (of ramin sawn timber in Malaysia):	$710.00
Exporter (of sawn ramin, in Singapore)	$800.00
Buyer (of molded ramin in the United States):	$1,000.00

Source: EIA and Telapak (2001).

Where is grand corruption most likely to occur? To answer this question, it is instructive to follow the life of a log through its value chain from source to destination. Box 3.4 shows the rents accruing at each stage of the process. In producer countries, there is intense lobbying and bribery all designed to gain access to scarce timber resources. And yet as the box shows, somewhat paradoxically the rents earned at this stage are relatively low. The bulk of profits seems to accrue at the final stages where the product is consumed (Malaysian broker to Malaysian buyer and the final destination—the United States in this case). Does grand corruption mysteriously vanish at the export border despite the high rents?

A distinguishing feature of the global timber trade is that crossing a border is often all that is needed to transform illegal timber into legal product. (By contrast, illegally manufactured goods, such as DVDs, textiles, and computers, retain their illicit status wherever they are sold.) A report from the Environmental Investigation Agency (EIA and Telapak 2001), an international advocacy organization committed to investigating and exposing environmental crime notes that, "A sophisticated network operates to move ramin stolen from Kalimantan and Sumatra onto the international markets, with Malaysia and Singapore effectively laundering the plundered timber." The huge rents shown in the box table are probably illustrative of corruption associated with greasing this network and obtaining fraudulent permits (for the origin of timber as well as for exports) for the illegally logged ramin. While the evidence presented here is necessarily anecdotal rather than statistical, it does indicate the corrosive impacts of forest crime across the economy.

Table 3.1 provides one reason why this anomaly of high rents persists, at least in the United States. The table compares campaign contributions made by industry public affairs committees across sectors. Taken together, the contributions of the

TABLE 3.1 **Campaign Contributions in the United States, by Sector, 2000**

Industry	*Contribution ($ millions)*	*Percent of total 2000 contributions*
Medicine and pharmaceuticals	4.32	13.5
Tobacco and cigarettes	2.46	7.7
Timber and pulp	2.27	7.0
Wines and liquor	1.46	4.5

Source: Authors' calculations, based on industry public affairs committee data made available by Kishore Gawande.

timber and timber-processing industry rank third largest in the country. Clearly, then, the timber industry remains a highly significant player in the lobbying process, and consequently its interests remain well-represented among policy makers, which may explain why implementing a system to track the legal status of logs has not been a priority for the U.S. government.

Even though the United States has few mechanisms in place to prohibit the imports of illegally logged timber, it is seeking to enter into free-trade agreements with countries which are significant sources of illegal timber either directly or as transshipment points. Clearly such free-trade agreements will further expand the scope for imports of illegal timber and timber products into the United States, unless adequate safeguards are built into the agreements (EIA and Telapak 2006).

Corruption and Illegal Commercial Logging

Illegal logging is big business, amounting to at least $10 billion a year globally, according to a World Bank estimate. It usually involves commercial operators with presumed links to organized crime. Illegal logging is simply a market response to the gap between legally sanctioned supplies and escalating demand.

The commonly proposed remedy is strengthened law enforcement. Improved law enforcement, including better detection of forest crimes and their suppression, is an important part of the solution. It has seldom worked on its own, however, because improving enforcement is difficult in systems with weak institutions, poor governance, and low oversight. More important, it neglects the fact that illegal logging thrives because the law enforcers are captured by the interests they are supposed to regulate. For example, the government in Cambodia has improved its capacity to detect forest crimes, but the judicial system is weak and prone to corruption and delays, so the potential deterrent effects of prosecution are close to nonexistent.

So, there is a need to address the fundamental causes of corruption (high rents, unsustainable demand, and weak oversight), rather than the symptoms (bribes, theft, and illegal logging). Demand for timber in a producer country (which could be from domestic or international sources) that outstrips the annual allowable (sustainable) cut creates excessive rents and therefore encourages illegal logging and corruption. Indonesia is a good illustration of this point. It is estimated that, catering to domestic and international demand, the annual domestic processing capacity in Indonesia is about 70 million cubic meters, whereas the annual allowable cut is only about 15 million cubic meters. This dramatic excess demand has sustained the pressure to supply logs from illegal cuttings and supports an entire value chain of illegal and corrupt activities.

Petty Corruption and Extortion Related to Need-Based Illegal Logging

Illegal felling is often motivated by need, taking the form of subsistence harvesting by locals who depend on forests for their livelihoods and lack feasible alternative sources of income. Thus, the heavy dependence of the rural poor on fuel wood to meet their energy demands puts forest resources under huge pressure and creates incentives for illegal extraction. Often, the rural poor may extract more than they need and sell the surplus as a means of supplementing their meager incomes. But seldom is such harvesting on a scale comparable to the illegal commercial operations.

Several reasons exacerbate illegal logging for subsistence. These include the over-harvesting and consequent degradation of traditional (legal) sources of fuel wood, reduced access to forest resources because of commercialization and development of concessions without consideration of local rights, population pressures, and inadequate investments in the development of woodlots. Forest law often does not recognize the legitimate rights of the local people to use of forests. As a result, forest rangers who are charged with upholding the law and protecting the forests need to be bribed to look the other way so that the rural poor can meet their fuel wood needs from the forests. This situation is defined as petty or need-based corruption, and anecdotal evidence supports the widespread nature of this phenomenon.

The countries of the former Soviet Union provide a good example of how rapid economic changes and institutional evolution can create a situation of illegality and opportunities for petty corruption. The fall of the communist regime led to the elimination of energy subsidies and a sudden rise in the price of alternative energy sources, which rapidly increased the demand for fuel wood. Because the legal supply was insufficient, illegal production expanded as people scrambled to meet their basic needs.

This type of corruption may be called petty, but the impacts on the poor are likely to be far from trivial. The poor are least able to afford such payments, and, from any moral or ethical standpoint, they should not have to pay for use of traditional lands. Solutions need to be based on protecting the rights of the poor, not on criminalizing them. In fact, solutions to illegal subsistence harvesting are relatively straightforward and involve providing alternative and affordable sources of fuels to meet legitimate rural household energy. A "technical fix" such as the development of community woodlots, or provision of solar cookers or more efficient wood-burning stoves, can effectively address the problem. However, the political will and social commitment need to be solidly in place for these alternatives to take hold (Blaser and others 2005).

CONTAINING THE CANCER: A SEARCH FOR ANSWERS

There is no silver bullet for the problem, which calls for a range of solutions that tackle the fundamental drivers of corruption: excess demand and scarcity rents, weak or flawed institutions, and the lack of accountability of forest officials and politicians.

TABLE 3.2 Supply Value Chain and Corruption Vulnerabilities

Stage of production	*Type of vulnerability*
Forest estate	• Policy capture for legal but unsustainable supply of timber • Bribery of politicians and forest guards for illegal supplies • Bribery of officials to evade royalties and timber taxes • Bribery in forest service for transfers to remote estates with high timber resources
Transport and export of illegal logs	• Bribery of customs and transport officials, local police • Bribery of transporters to carry illegal logs • Bribery of bureaucrats for fraudulent permits for laundering illegal logs
Milling and processing	• Bribery of police and bureaucrats when processing illegal lumber
Destination, retail outlets	• Policy capture to resist log-tracking and anti-money-laundering legislation

A common suggestion, as discussed earlier, is to reduce corruption by improving enforcement through deterrence, suppression, and monitoring. The recipe is intuitively appealing and if implemented would no doubt be highly effective.[6] But like so many other reforms, it runs into problems of incentive compatibility: it asks government leaders to introduce reforms that undermine their self-interest—it seems unlikely that the beneficiaries of corrupt timber rents would adopt policies that erode their power and incomes. The focus of policy should thus be on seeking solutions that *address the fundamental causes* of corruption, which would eliminate the incentives to resist reform.

Table 3.2 summarizes the key corruption vulnerabilities along the life of a log from the angle of resource supply. This table is helpful in thinking about measures to address the problem. The discussion that follows highlights a range of initiatives that have targeted one or another type of vulnerability (from both the demand and supply aspects) as a way of controlling corruption in the sector and attempts to assess their impacts and possibility for replication elsewhere.[7]

Demand-Side Interventions

Part of the solution to corruption may lie in reducing or eliminating scarcity rents by altering patterns of demand.[8] This proposed solution implies reducing the demand for illegal produce and requires implementing environmentally and socially responsible procurement policies in consumer countries. Because the trade of timber products is often routed through third countries, these issues must also be addressed at the international level and involve all countries in the forest products value chain in the control efforts.

Corporate codes of conduct are one promising initiative whereby corporations, either independently or as members of associations, commit themselves to follow self-defined principles of social and environmental responsibility. These pledges also often include committing to comply with the laws of countries in which they operate.

IKEA, the giant Swedish furniture maker, has developed a "staircase model approach" to promote legal and sustainable forestry among its suppliers. Requirements include the legal sourcing of wood products. IKEA, in partnership with the World Wildlife Fund, has developed a wood-tracking system to ensure that there are no leakages along the chain of custody.[9] The partnership has also established producer groups committed to extracting only legally sanctioned harvests.

Many examples of industry codes also exist. The Confederation of European Paper Industries has declared a set of principles committing its members to the purchase and use only of wood coming from legal logging (CEPI 2005). Similar declarations have been made by other associations that are prominent users of timber, such as the International Council of Forest and Paper Associations, the Interafrican Forest Industries Association, the Japanese Federation of Wood Industry Association, and the American Forest & Paper Association (FAO 2005).

Fostering responsible consumption is also of paramount importance in closing the demand-supply gap. The experience in this regard is mixed. While green consumerism has been in vogue for quite some time, it is not widespread. Nor are there significant price premiums attached to legally produced timber and timber products. At the same time, however, countries such as Denmark, Japan, and the United Kingdom have pledged that their public procurements would use only legally sourced timber. But in the absence of a significant price premium, certification is unlikely to do any more than cater to niche markets of environmentally conscious consumers. Influencing incentives in producer countries will necessitate much bolder remedies that reward sustainable harvesting and penalize unsustainable logging. That can be achieved more directly by taxing uncertified timber, at least in export markets. Such a tax would provide multiple benefits: it would reduce incentives for corruption, improve governance by reducing the corrosive effects of forest crime on institutions, promote economically prudent and sustainable use of scarce natural resources, and generate environmental benefits.

Increasing Timber Supplies

Scarcity rents can also be eliminated by augmenting the supply of timber potentially available for the market. An expert study on the global demand and supply of wood and fiber indicates that plantation forests managed exclusively for fiber and timber production on just 4 percent of the forest lands could meet 50–60 percent of the world demand in 2050.[10] Clearly, countries such as China and India, with significant amounts of degraded (and relatively worthless) land and high demand for wood and wood products, are prime candidates for investing in fast-growing industrial plantations. Trees, even fast-growing varieties, take time to grow and thus any strategy to combat corruption and illegal logging must invest in the development of plantations now. Between 1990 and 2000, plantations increased by about 5 percent and stand at almost 190 million hectares for industrial and nonindustrial uses. China accounts for 45 million hectares, and China, India, and the Russian Federation together accounted for half of the world's forest plantations in 2000 (FAO 2001).

Forest certification is one approach for controlling illegal logging and other forest crimes by increasing the supply of timber from well-managed forests. Under the

BOX 3.5 The Kimberley Process Certification Scheme for Conflict Diamonds

In May 2000, diamond-producing states met in Kimberley, South Africa, to come up with a way to stop the trade in conflict diamonds and to assure consumers that the diamonds they purchase have not contributed to violent conflict and human rights abuses in their countries of origin. The Kimberley Process Certification Scheme (KPCS) came into effect two-and-a-half years later, in November 2002. The KPCS outlines the provisions by which the trade in rough diamonds is to be regulated by countries, regional economic integration organizations, and traders in rough diamonds.

The KPCS imposes stringent requirements on all participants to guard against conflict diamonds entering the legitimate trade. Participation is voluntary, and there is no legally binding treaty or agreement to which countries are signatories. Participants are required to implement internal controls, as outlined in the KPCS document, and attach a Kimberley Process certificate to all shipments of rough diamonds. While each participant is required to implement the Kimberley Process in its respective territory, sharing information and insight is an integral part of making the certification scheme work. Annual plenary meetings are held to give participants the opportunity to converse with one another and with industry and civil society members to improve the effectiveness and integrity of the regulatory regime. Today, the KPCS is an important instrument in the global fight against trade in conflict diamonds.

Source: http://www.kimberleyprocess.com:8080/site/?name=home.

scheme, an independent organization develops standards of good forest management, and independent auditors issue certificates to forest operations that comply with those standards. This certification verifies that forests are well managed—as defined by a particular standard—and ensures that certain wood and paper products come from forests that are managed to meet a predetermined set of environmental, social, and economic standards. Currently, about 140 million hectares of forests are under various forms of certification schemes. Of this, tropical forest countries account for only about 10 million hectares, a small fraction of the total production area. There is thus an urgent need to extend the certified area, especially in tropical countries (ITTO 2002). (For a successful voluntary international certification initiative, for the case of diamonds, see box 3.5.)

Rent Capture

The persistence of supernormal rents in the sector is an important underlying cause of corruption. Widespread evasion of taxes and royalties contributes to this aspect. Often, legislatively complex rules and procedures for capturing rents make evasion easier and lead to low rent capture (World Bank 2004a). Illegal activities and bribery associated with low rent capture by the government reinforce wasteful logging and inefficient resource allocation and hinder sustainable forest management.

Development of proper forest resource accounting and forest valuation systems are necessary measures for improving rent capture and preventing windfall gains. Rent collection should be strengthened at the level of the forest concession itself, so that opportunities to misreport on timber volumes and species can be minimized. When capacity and resources are limited, it may be more advantageous for the government to implement administratively simpler approaches such as an area tax (levied as an annual charge per hectare of the concession) as distinct from a volume-based tax (which is based on the actual timber volume being harvested) (Gray 2002). While country-specific conditions will determine the final approach adopted, reforming the forest rent capture system is a critical element of any strategy to control corruption and improve the efficiency of forest resource use.

Transparency and Detection

The remoteness of forests offers rich opportunities for plunder away from public scrutiny. So transparency and information are part of the defense against corruption. Detection, monitoring, and surveillance are crucial for setting priorities and for evaluating other elements of the enforcement program. Successful detection of illegal acts depends closely on the existence of proper baseline data, including indicators that will enable a regular monitoring of the state of forests. Baseline data are needed for a detection system to operate effectively, and monitoring of such data will provide the foundations for eventual prosecution of wrongdoers (Magrath and Grandalski 2001; Melle and Beck 2001).

Cost-effective methods include the use of satellite data to monitor forest cover. Synergistic advances in technology and institutions have the potential to reduce dramatically the cost of forest monitoring and to enable civil society (for example) to use this information to more fairly balance interests in the forest (Chomitz 2006). In Brazil, the state of Mato Grosso set up a system that registers the location of large properties and uses remote sensing to track the properties' compliance with land-use regulations. In Cameroon, nongovernmental organizations are using remote sensing to correlate the construction of new logging roads with logging concessionaires' reports of timber extraction (Global Forest Watch 2005). Similar initiatives are being developed in other countries, including India, Indonesia, and Russia.

Where the existing local capacity is inadequate to provide an effective level of monitoring, it may be advantageous to hire an independent forest monitor to initiate the process. In Cambodia, Cameroon, and Ecuador, independent monitors have not only initiated critical detection efforts but also built up local capacity over time (box 3.6).

Different stakeholders can provide help in detection activities, and multistakeholder collaborative models have worked effectively in many instances (see box 3.7). The contributions of the EIA for Indonesia and, more broadly, in East Asia, and of Greenpeace in Brazil are noteworthy, as are the efforts of the World Resources Institute, which monitors forest developments in several key countries through its Global Forest Watch Initiative (EIA and Telapak 2001, Greenpeace 2001, Barreto and others 2006). The continuing contribution of these institutions will be a critical element in future efforts to control forest crimes.

Accountability

The mechanisms for establishing accountability will vary with country-specific traditions and institutions. Although vested interests will resist such reforms, experience shows that change can be initiated and promoted by external support (such as

BOX 3.6 Strengthening Detection and Suppression in Cambodia: Achievements and Pitfalls

To control rampant corruption in the forest sector, the government of Cambodia established the Forest Crime Monitoring and Reporting Unit (FCMR) in October 1999 to develop the government's capacity to detect and suppress illegal logging.

The FCMR consists of three components: an office in the Department of Forestry and Wildlife, known as the Forest Crime Monitoring Office (FCMO), to monitor crimes in production forests; an office in the Ministry of Environment, known as the Department of Inspection, to monitor forest crimes in protected areas; and an independent monitor, Global Witness, an international nongovernmental organization, to independently monitor the performance of the two new government agencies to protect them from manipulation, self-censorship, and physical risk (Magrath and Grandalski 2001).

A national tracking system was established, under which the two government offices operate parallel information tracking systems. Provincial and district offices feed information, on a monthly basis, into the monitoring units. According to the terms of the contract, Global Witness is empowered to carry out independent field inspections in concessions and review production and export records and other data. A case tracking system has been developed to serve as a database of all forest crimes. The case tracking system is also an important tool for prioritizing action, for cataloging the actions taken, and for increasing the transparency and accountability of the two government agencies. (Global Witness 2000, 2001, 2005; Sokhun and Savet 2001).

The FCMR's efforts to control illegal logging have been generally positive, resulting in the suspension of corrupt forestry officials, on-the-spot investigations of allegations of illegal logging by high-ranking officials, and destruction of illegal sawmills (UNDP/FAO 2002). But the experience has been mixed. The project has been plagued by a lack of full information sharing among the three entities; external funding has been available only in fits and starts rather than on a longer-term programmatic basis, a rather top-down approach has seen little involvement of local people, and a poorly functioning legal system has failed to move against the big offenders.

The Société Générale de Surveillance (SGS) replaced Global Witness as the independent monitor in 2003. The SGS had been contracted for a period of three years, but the contract was suspended prematurely in February 2006 because of lack of funding. The latest assessments of the SGS suggest that while the government has been doing a competent job of monitoring and detecting forest crimes, the prosecutorial system is weak and prone to excessive delays.

General lessons to be learned from this experience include the importance of defining with precision the role of the independent monitor, as well as the legal standards to be verified, and of integrating the management structure with the rest of the control system (Luttrell and Brown 2006). At the practical level, ongoing discussions between the government and Cambodia's development assistance partners will determine future steps in reestablishing a streamlined and robust system of independent monitoring of Cambodia's forests.

donor agencies) and nongovernmental organizations. Bolivia and Ecuador have introduced systems that allow for independent surveillance and monitoring by the public, thereby promoting accountability to the ultimate stakeholders. Box 3.8 illustrates these approaches.

Streamlining, Simplifying, and Reforming Forest Legislation

A number of illegalities in the forest sector stem from inadequate legislation. A commonly occurring situation is the failure to recognize in law the traditional rights of access and use (let alone ownership) of forest resources by indigenous

BOX 3.7 Involving Local Communities in Forest Protection in the Philippines

The World Bank funded the Environment Sectoral Adjustment Lending Program initiated in 1991 in the Philippines. This program supported a widespread public awareness campaign on the negative impacts to society of forest destruction and the creation of Multisectoral Forest Protection Committees (MFPCs) to reinforce detection and suppression efforts in the Philippines. These committees are considered to be one of the most important institutional legacies of the project (Acosta 1999).

The original MFPCs were organized under the initiative of the Department of Environment and Natural Resources (DENR) and were established initially in areas where illegal logging was rampant and in areas with significant wood-processing and -trading activities. The committees included representatives from the DENR, local government, military, police, church, business groups, media, and civil society organizations. The functions of these committees were to serve as a collection center for information about illegal activities by tapping into the members' formal and informal networks; regularly read and discuss reports from the DENR on its routine and special monitoring, apprehension, and prosecution of illegal logging operations and advise the DENR on ways to enhance their effectiveness; and mobilize members' networks in support of forest protection activities.

The 16 original MFPCs, organized in 1994, grew in number to more than 400 nationwide by 1999. They range from a national MFPC federation to regional, provincial, and municipal committees. The impacts have been significant—confiscation and seizure of thousands of board feet of logs worth about 350 million Philippine pesos, destruction of illegal minisawmills, closure of large illegal sawmills, the arrest and prosecution of big-time illegal loggers. Altogether, 360 cases had been filed by 1999, with 285 convictions (Embido 2001).

Several important lessons have been learned from the operation of the MFPCs. First, the committees provide an acceptable venue for people to report illegal activities in their areas, particularly when they do not trust the law enforcement officials or fear retaliation from those perpetrating the illegal acts. Second, the MFPCs have been effective in mobilizing public opinion against forest crimes and have proven to be an effective deterrent to violators, especially if the latter are prominent public figures who fear exposure. Third, the MFPCs and law enforcement agencies have collaborated effectively and often to take action against forest crimes. Finally, the MFPCs have had a "virtuous" impact in encouraging other civil service organizations not covered by the World Bank programs to form their own forest protection programs in the Philippines.

communities; as a result, the forest activities of these communities tends to get criminalized.

Rosenbaum (2004) classifies two types of failure in the legal system that lead to criminal behavior: failures of law and failures of implementation. Failures of law include clashes of norms, where "the rights to the resources as set out in law are not the same as the rights that people or communities believe that they are entitled to have"; undetectable violations, where the law is written in a way that makes it difficult to enforce; and weak penalties, resulting in insufficient punishment to deter criminal behavior.[11] Failures of implementation, in contrast, include poor dispute resolution; unfair application of the law, including bias, patronage, and corruption; failure on the part of forest agencies to follow the law; lack of capacity to administer and enforce the law; lack of coordination among government agencies; and lack of enforcement of laws outside the forest sector (such as banking or immigration laws) that have an effect on the forest sector.

Clearly, there is a need to scrutinize the legal systems in any country and to ensure that the "right" laws are in place and are enforceable (see box 3.9 on experience with legislative reforms in Bolivia).

BOX 3.8 Improving Transparency in Forest Administration in Ecuador

In 1999, after a national participatory process, Ecuador's Ministry of the Environment developed a new forest policy that recognizes the need to manage the country's forests to maximize the full range of services—harvesting of timber and nontimber products and the conservation of ecological functions (ITTO 2002).

Recognizing that transparency and accountability were essential to the success of the policy, the government issued Executive Decree 346 in April 2000, substantially revising the regulations for applying the existing Law on Forestry and Conservation of Protected Areas and Wildlife. Three new features are noteworthy. First, the new Standards for Sustainable Forest Management enable the forest authority to monitor logging activities on the basis of verifiable indicators. This has provided a sound basis for sustainable management of natural forests and prevention of illegal and destructive logging in Ecuador.

Second, the decree established the country's Outsourced Forestry Supervision System. A supervisory organization, known as the Green Surveillance (*Vigilancia Verde*) and including representatives from the armed forces, the police, and five nongovernmental organizations, is responsible for controlling the transport of round wood between the forest and marketing and processing locations via checkpoints on major transport routes. (In its first year, the Green Surveillance seized five times more illegal timber than had been seized the previous year, attesting to its effectiveness.) Another element of the Outsourced Forestry Supervision System is the Forest Steward (*Regencia Forestal*) program. Forest stewards, licensed by and working under state authorization, ensure that harvesting activities authorized by the forestry administration are fully consistent with the management plans (FAO 2005).

The third innovative change called for the Ministry of the Environment to contract out a major portion of its administrative and verification responsibilities to a supervisory entity. This entity was to be in charge of awarding forest logging licenses, granting timber transport permits, overseeing the performance of forest stewards, supervising the mobilization of forest products, and collecting stumpage fees and transferring them to the government, among other duties. The idea was to improve forest administration services and make them more transparent. Being freed of some of its traditional responsibilities, the Ministry of Forestry can then concentrate its resources in law enforcement and other strategic services.

The system became operational in 2003, when the Ecuadorian branch of the SGS was contracted to carry out the ministry's administrative services, and in only a few months, the amount of confiscated timber doubled. But the government's attempt to outsource was challenged as unconstitutional, and the challenge was upheld by Ecuador's Constitutional Tribunal. Hence the SGS's services were terminated and the administrative and supervisory activities reverted to the Ministry of the Environment. Thus, at this point, Ecuador does not have any effectively functioning verification system, and a key pillar of its forest management strategy cannot be implemented (Navarro, Del Gatto, and Schroeder 2006).

Institutional Reforms and Incentive Compatibility

Deep institutional reforms across the economy are crucial to any lasting approach to combating corruption and controlling illegal logging. These need to be incentive compatible, which implies that public officials must be adequately motivated (through a clearly defined system of rewards and sanctions) to implement tasks for which they are responsible.[12] A growing literature on the broader issue of institutional structures appropriate for growing market economies (World Bank 2002, 2004b) provides useful guidance in this context.

Focusing more narrowly on the forest sector itself, we know that forest departments (or equivalent agencies) control three-quarters of all global forest resources. Yet inadequate staffing, poor training, lack of economic incentives, and lack of equipment and other resources makes them poorly placed to manage the resource properly. With such crippling constraints, it is unlikely that forest departments would be

BOX 3.9 Legislative and Administrative Reforms in Bolivia

In Bolivia, a law approved in 1996 contained a number of innovative provisions to ensure forest law enforcement and reduce the impact of forest crime and corruption. One innovative procedure authorized the forest superintendent to grant special warrants to private citizens to inspect forest field operations (*libramiento de visita*). Now any party, public or private, can denounce an illicit act. The law has also sanctioned the legal establishment of local community associations as a way to establish a more effective system of checks and balances at the local level by integrating local populations in decision making about forest law enforcement. The associations are composed of traditional forest users, peasant communities, and indigenous populations that depend on forests within a municipality (Contreras and Vargas 2002).

The law also makes professional foresters liable for any illegal actions they take in implementing forest management plans. To eliminate one important source of corruption, the new law set flat fees for timber concessions. This procedure has the great advantage of being transparent, and not subject to the discretionary (arbitrary) interpretation that had led to so much corruption in the past.

New procedures also make it mandatory for the forest superintendent to hold public hearings to explain work carried out and provide an opportunity for the public to raise questions about performance. Any citizen can request copies of official documents. To increase transparency and reduce the scope for corruption, open auctions will govern the allocation of all new concession contracts and will also be the method for disposing of confiscated forest products and equipment. Since the Office of the Superintendent was open to political manipulation, the new legal system required that the superintendent be selected by the president of Bolivia from a list of three names submitted by the Congress. The period of the superintendent's appointment is six years, thus straddling the presidential period, which is five years. Finally, the new law gave the forestry agency financial independence by allowing it to keep 30 percent of the forest concession fees (Contreras 2002; Contreras and Vargas 2002; FAO 2005).

able to perform their service delivery functions to any reasonable standard of efficiency (PAF 2004; ECSSD/PROFOR 2005).

A recent publication on the experiences and lessons from reform of forest institutions in transition economies (ECSSD/PROFOR 2005) provides valuable (and sector-specific) lessons and approaches dealing with more competition and accountability, greater service-provider orientation, separation of technical forest management functions from law and order and crime prevention functions, promoting meritocracy, salary reforms, and sustainable financing of institutional activities, among other issues.

While these are useful suggestions, they are unlikely to resolve the fundamental problems of political will and state capture that are key to effecting durable changes in the sector. These problems require other powerful measures, including international processes such as the Forest Law Enforcement and Governance (FLEG) process, described in the next section. Nor will these sector-specific approaches fully resolve the problem of petty bribe taking by forest officials. To address this problem, the fundamental incentives for corruption must be tackled, which requires a more nuanced approach to salary reforms. Forest officials, especially the field staff, receive paltry salaries, barely enough to keep them above the poverty line.[13] So, it is no surprise that corruption and extortion abound on the forest estate. With advances in remote sensing technology, it would be quite feasible to introduce systems of pay related to performance. All that would be required is to link a performance bonus to objective evidence of forest cover and crown density. That in turn would require high-resolution, satellite-based forest cover information, which is available, relatively cheaply, in most instances. To be effective, the payment would need to be sufficiently large to dilute the gains from bribery.[14]

The Forest Law Enforcement and Governance Ministerial Processes

The Forest Law Enforcement and Governance (FLEG) process is an umbrella initiative catalyzed by the World Bank (strongly supported by development partners and key country governments). It is a powerful first step in providing a targeted framework for addressing governance failures in the forests in a collaborative process that promotes dialogue and development of action programs between consumers and producers.

On the demand side, FLEG recognizes the responsibility of "consumer nations" to place controls on the demand-side pressure and has built up on initiatives such as the adoption of G-8 Forest Action Program (with a key focus on illegal logging) and the European Union's Forest Law Enforcement, Governance and Trade Action Plan (FLEGT). Broadly speaking, these initiatives emphasize support for developing an understanding between producing and consuming countries to develop licensing schemes to ensure that only legal timber enters the markets of consumer countries (World Bank 2006b). On the supply side, the FLEG process addresses the underlying causes of corruption and illegal logging related to domestic, international, and poverty aspects.

The approach of the FLEG ministerial processes, supported by the World Bank since 2001, has been to convene a regional preparatory conference followed by a high-level ministerial conference. This approach has allowed for a joint approach by producer and consumer countries, a multistakeholder technical meeting where experiences with FLEG issues are shared, intergovernmental negotiations for the drafting of a declaration or action plan, and other stakeholder discussions and development of statements for consideration by the intergovernmental negotiators. The processes aim to create the political "space" and will at national and regional levels to address these complex and politically sensitive issues. Partnership and consensus building with major stakeholders from civil society and the private sector to design and implement concrete actions at the national and regional levels are also key features of the process (World Bank 2006b).

The FLEG process has emphasized the need for reliable information as a key for informed discussion and consensus building. At the same time, it has pointed out serious gaps in the availability of such information. Thus, collection of baseline information has been initiated within the regional FLEG processes, including through surveys of public officials and households.[15]

Broadly, all three FLEG regional ministerial processes have been successful in eliciting high-level political commitment and in creating partnerships between various donors and development agencies sharing a common concern with improving forest governance (box 3.10). They have fostered a spirit of collaboration among governments, the private sector, and stakeholders and have also promoted a sense of joint responsibility between producer and consumer countries for tackling the problem. The ministerial processes have also been successful in drawing the attention of policy makers to new and innovative tools, such as anti-money-laundering laws, to combat illegal logging and forest corruption (see chapter 12 in this volume).[16]

BOX 3.10 Experience with Regional FLEG Processes

Three regional FLEG ministerial processes have been conducted so far—in East Asia (2001), Africa (2003), and Europe and North Asia (2005). They have been cohosted by forest producer and forest consumer countries and the Bank (World Bank 2006b).

Southeast Asia. In September 2001, the East Asia Ministerial Conference took place in Bali. The conference adopted the Bali Declaration, whereby participating countries committed themselves to intensifying national efforts and strengthening bilateral, regional, and multilateral collaboration to address forest crime and violations of forest law. The Bali Declaration and the follow-up discussions it spawned have led to agreements on specific national and regional efforts needed to address forest threats. A memorandum of understanding (MOU) between Indonesia and the United Kingdom to improve FLEG and combat illegal logging and international trade in illegally logged timber, and MOUs between Indonesia and Japan, Indonesia and Malaysia, and China and Indonesia, with similar objectives, are noteworthy in this context. The U.K. initiative to modify its public procurement policies to purchase only legally sourced timber is also a significant step forward in controlling a source of demand pressure.

Africa. The Africa Forest Law Enforcement and Governance (AFLEG) Ministerial Conference took place in October 2003 in Yaoundé, Cameroon, and resulted in the AFLEG Declaration and Action Plan. In the declaration, governments pledged to mobilize financial resources for FLEG, promote cooperation between law enforcement agencies within and among countries, involve stakeholders in decision making, and explore means of demonstrating the legality and sustainability of forest products. An AFLEG Support Group of active producer, consumer, and donor governments was established in May 2004, with the purpose of maintaining momentum for action to implement the declaration, especially through national-level action plans.

Europe and North Asia. Concerned about rampant illegal logging, the Russian Federation in May 2004 announced its interest in initiating a FLEG process for Europe and Northern Asia in collaboration with regional partners. An international steering committee has been established to provide advisory inputs to the process. A FLEG preparatory conference was held in June 2005, and the ministerial conference was held in November 2005. Attendees endorsed a Ministerial Declaration and Indicative List of Actions, which differentiates between poverty-driven and commercial illegal logging and addresses each in a balanced way. The declaration emphasizes that combating illegal logging is a shared responsibility of both exporting and importing countries, that it requires high-level political commitment and collaboration across sectors, and that it should engage governments, civil society, and the private sector.

Source: World Bank 2006b.

CONCLUDING REMARKS

This chapter has established that corruption and crimes in the forest sector are extensive and their effects pernicious. According to the World Bank (2002), illegal logging in public lands alone costs $10 billion a year in lost assets and revenue more than six times the total official development assistance for the sustainable management of forests. That figure does not take into account the effects illegal logging has on institutions, poverty, the environment, or climate change. The economic, social, institutional, and environmental reasons to control forest crimes are compelling.

The chapter identifies the major motives driving illegal activities and argues that high rents in the forestry sector, which act to undermine already inadequate institutions and reduce transparency and accountability, create a fertile ground for lawlessness. To reduce forest crime, the rents from corruption must be lowered, institutions strengthened, countervailing ones built where none exist, and innovative approaches explored.

While traditional efforts to control corruption have tended to be mandatory in nature, promising voluntary control measures such as corporate codes of conduct, certification, and voluntary (trade) partnership agreements have emerged in the forestry sector. While important in themselves, voluntary initiatives are unlikely to be sufficient to address the problem. The precise combination of instruments to control corruption will depend on institutional, historical, and biological pressures in each country and on capacities. But a common theme is the need for a broad, multipronged approach that addresses the root causes of corruption—scarcity rents and weak institutions, including lack of transparency and low levels of accountability. Solutions need to focus on mechanisms that curb the demand that generates high rents, increase the supply of sustainable legal timber, improve the incentives to enforce existing laws against corruption, and build effective and robust governance institutions for addressing corruption both inside and outside of the sector. Finally, it must be acknowledged that poor governance and corruption in the forestry sector are problems of long standing that will likely take a long time to overcome. Patience and willingness to stay the course are key to making progress in this difficult and complex area.

ANNEX 3A: EXAMPLES OF ILLEGAL LOGGING AND ASSOCIATED ILLEGAL PRACTICES IN FORESTRY

Illegal logging

- Logging protected species
- Counterfeit duplication of felling licenses
- Girdling or ring-barking to kill trees so that they can be legally logged
- Contracting with local entrepreneurs to buy logs from protected areas
- Logging in protected areas
- Logging outside concession boundaries
- Logging in prohibited areas such as steep slopes, riverbanks, and water catchments
- Removing under- or oversized trees from public forests
- Extracting more timber than authorized
- Passing off logs extracted from unauthorized areas outside the concession boundaries as legally harvested
- Logging without authorization
- Obtaining logging concessions through bribes

Illegal timber transport, trade, and timber smuggling

- Transporting logs without authorization
- Transporting illegally harvested timber
- Smuggling timber
- Falsifying or reusing timber transport documents
- Exporting and importing tree species banned under international law, such as the Convention on International Trade in Endangered Species of Wild Flora and Fauna (CITES).
- Exporting and importing timber in contravention of national bans

Transfer pricing and other illegal accounting practices

- Declaring lower values and volumes exported
- Declaring higher purchase prices above the prevailing market prices for inputs such as equipment or services from related companies
- Manipulating debt cash flows to transfer money to a subsidiary or parent company, for example, by inflating debt repayment to avoid taxes on profits
- Colluding in submitting bids to obtain timber concessions cheaply
- Avoiding royalties and duties through undergrading, undervaluing, undermeasuring, and misclassifying species exported or for the local market
- Nonpayment of license fees, royalties, fines, and other government charges

Illegal forest processing

- Operating without a processing license
- Ignoring environmental, social, and labor laws and regulations
- Using illegally obtained wood

Source: Based on Callister (1999) and Contreras (2002)

ENDNOTES

1. A hypothetical, though not untypical, location.
2. Estimates for East Asia suggest that evasion of royalties and timber taxes range from a low of 50 percent in Myanmar to 100 percent in Cambodia (World Bank 2006a).
3. An assessment commissioned by the International Tropical Timber Organization (Poore 1989) indicated that the extent of tropical forests being managed under sustainable yield systems was negligible. An assessment a decade later found that while significant progress had been made, the challenges of full and coordinated implementation of management plans had still to be adequately addressed (ITTO 2000).
4. Klitgaard's (1988) suggested approach in diagnosing corruption is relevant here, namely, M (monopoly) + D (discretion) − A (accountability) − T (transparency) = C (corruption) and the underlying incentive structures are precisely those that Rose-Ackerman (1999) cites as the principal drivers of corruption.
5. It is useful to make a distinction between "state capture" and "administrative corruption": state capture focuses on *distortion* in legislation and regulation to suit private interests, while administrative corruption involves corruption in the *implementation* of laws and policies (World Bank 2000a). Grand and petty corruption belong to the latter category.
6. The *expected* loss (and therefore its deterrent effect) to a criminal depends upon: (Probability of detection) × (probability of prosecution) × (probability of being found guilty) × (level of the penalty) × (discount factor related to the duration of the process). Clearly, this chain is only as strong as its weakest link, and in practice, links are quite weak in forestry, especially because law enforcement is lax and corruption rampant (for empirical evidence from several countries see Akela and Cannon 2004; for evidence from southern Cambodia, see Claridge, Chea-leth, and Chhoan 2005).
7. It may be hypothesized that, as one follows up the value chain (from the forest to the consumer), rents grow larger and the countervailing forces to corruption weaker, thereby necessitating implementation of strong exogenous measures of the sort described here. But this requires further analysis for validation.

8. Demand-side interventions are perhaps unique to the forest sector; in other sectors, such as water, there is little scope for lowering rents by manipulating demand.
9. A "chain of custody" (COC) refers to the custodial sequence that occurs as ownership or control of the wood supply is transferred from one custodian to another along the supply chain. A COC system comprises a set of technologies, procedures, and documents that are used to provide information useful for managing the wood supply chain (Dykstra and others 2003). COC systems can be used to expose log theft and to prevent unscrupulous operators from commingling illegally harvested logs with others of legal origin. Modern techniques such as bar coding and computerization have reduced the costs of COC systems and made them less susceptible to corruption.
10. Global Vision for Forests 2050 Project, http://www.worldwildlife.org/alliance/pdfs/gar/5_Influencing_Attitudes.pdf.
11. Ecological crimes are rarely viewed as seriously as traditional criminal acts, such as murder or house break-ins. Thus, it is common for penalties for illegal forest-related acts to be small in comparison with the rewards of forest crime. Often, penalties are so light that they do not have the potential to act as a deterrent to would-be miscreants.
12. Incentive-compatible institutions are institutions capable of achieving compatibility among individual, organizational, and societal objectives. In the absence of efficient incentive-compatible institutional design, the transaction costs associated with ad hoc approaches to achieve social goals are likely to be enormous and can even cripple the achievement of key social objectives. (Ruttan 1992).
13. In Cambodia, forest guards are paid the equivalent of $23 a month. Assuming the guard has a family of three, she is significantly below the World Bank poverty line of a $1 a day and is unlikely to have any incentive to prevent crooks from stealing from the forests.
14. At the same time, one should not make light of the difficulties with the proposed approaches. Navigating through an entrenched system of patronage, nepotism, and corruption to linking results to fair pay will be tough. Any generous system of remuneration could conceivably be overturned by increased corrupt payoffs, and forest officials may not have the money to carry out inspections, even though they have the right incentives to do their job. Thus, pay reforms need to be seen within a wider set of reforms (and political will) to make them work.
15. The World Bank has developed and implemented the Governance and Anti-Corruption Diagnostic Assessment, which consists of in-depth, country-specific surveys of thousands of households, firms, and public officials on information about vulnerabilities within a country's institutions (http://www.worldbank.org/wbi/governance). This information, when complemented with forest sector diagnostics information, could be a powerful way to address the problems of corruption, weak governance, and illegal logging.
16. Anti-money-laundering and asset forfeiture laws can be powerful instruments in combating forest crimes, especially in those cases of large-scale corruption, where illegal money flows through the financial system within a country, and when it flows across national borders (World Bank 2006b).

REFERENCES

Acosta, R. T. 1999. "Forest Management and Protection: The Philippine Experience." Paper prepared for the Regional Symposium on Strengthening Cooperation for Forest Law Enforcement in Mekong Basin Countries, Phnom Penh, Cambodia, June 14–15.

Akella, Anita Sundari, and James B. Cannon. 2004. *Strengthening the Weakest Links: Strategies for Improving the Enforcement of Environmental Laws Globally*. Washington DC: Conservation International.

Barreto, Paulo, Carlos Souza Jr., Ruth Noguerón, Anthony Anderson, and Rodney Salomão (in collaboration with Janice Wiles). 2006. *Human Pressure on the Brazilian Amazon Forests.* Washington, DC: IMAZON, Global Forest Watch, and World Resources Institute.

bin Buang, Amah. 2001. "Forest Management Experiences from East Asia." Paper delivered at the Forest Law Enforcement and Governance: East Asia Ministerial Conference, Bali, Indonesia, September 11–13. http://lnweb18.worldbank.org/eap/eap.nsf/2500ec5f1a2d9bad852568a3006f557d/c19065b26241f0b247256ac30010e5ff?OpenDocument.

Blaser, Juergen, A. Contreras, T. Oksanen, E. Puustjarvi, and F. Schmithusen. 2005. "Forest Law Enforcement and Governance (FLEG) in Eastern Europe and Northern Asia (ENA)." Reference paper prepared for the St. Petersburg Ministerial Conference, November 22–25.

Callister, Debra J. 1999. "Corrupt and Illegal Activities in the Forestry Sector: Current Understandings and Implications for World Bank Forest Policy." Discussion draft (May). http://wbln0018.worldbank.org/essd/forestpol-e.nsf/HiddenDocView/ BCE9 D2A90FADBA73852568A3006493E0?OpenDocument.

Chomitz, Kenneth. 2006. *At Loggerheads? Agricultural Expansion, Poverty Reduction, and Environment in the Tropical Forests.* Washington, DC: World Bank.

Claridge, Gordon, Veasna Chea-leth, and In Van Chhoan. 2005. "The Effectiveness of Law Enforcement against Forest and Wildflife Crime: A Study of Enforcement Disincentives and Other Relevant Factors in Southwestern Cambodia." East-West Management Institute, Conservation International, and U.S. Agency for International Development, Washington DC (September).

CEPI (Confederation of European Paper Industries). 2005. *Illegal Logging: Codes of Conduct for the Paper Industry.* Brussels.

Contreras-Hermosilla, A. 2002. "Law Compliance in the Forestry Sector: An Overview." WBI Working Papers, World Bank Institute, Washington, DC, http://lnweb18.worldbank.org/eap/eap.nsf/2500ec5f1a2d9bad852568a3006f557d/c19065b26241f0b247256ac30010e5ff?OpenDocument.

Contreras-Hermosilla, A., and M. T. Vargas. 2002. "Social, Environmental and Economic Dimensions of Forest Policy Reforms in Bolivia." Forest Trends, Washington, DC. http://www.forest-trends.org/whoweare/pdf/BoliviaEnglish.pdf.

Damania, R., R. Deacon, and E. Bulte. 2005. "Resource Abundance, Poverty and Development: An Empirical Assessment." *World Development* 33: 1029–54.

Dixit, Avinash K. 2004. *Lawlessness and Economics: Alternative Modes of Governance.* Princeton, NJ: Princeton University Press.

Dykstra, Dennis P., George Kuru, Rodney Taylor, Ruth Nussbaum, William B. Magrath, and Jane Story. 2003. "Technologies for Wood Tracking: Verifying and Monitoring the Chain of Custody and Legal Compliance in the Timber Industry." Discussion paper, Environment and Social Development, East Asia and the Pacific Region, World Bank, Washington, DC.

ECSSD/PROFOR (Europe and Central Asia Socially Sustainable Development Department/Program on Forests). 2005. "Forest Institutions in Transition: Experiences and Lessons from Eastern Europe." World Bank, Washington, DC (February).

EIA (Environmental Investigation Agency) and Telapak Indonesia. 2001. "Timber Trafficking." (September). http://www.eia-international.org.

———. 2006. "America's Free Trade for Illegal Timber: How US Trade Pacts Speed the Destruction of the World's Forests." http://www.eia-international.org/files/news312-1.pdf

Embido, Oscar. 2001. "Forest Law Enforcement and Investigation Techniques in the Philippines." Paper delivered at the Forest Law Enforcement and Governance: East Asia Ministerial Conference, Bali, Indonesia, September 11–13. http://lnweb18.worldbank.org/eap/eap.nsf/2500ec5f1a2d9bad852568a3006f557d/c19065b26241f0b247256ac30010e5ff?OpenDocument.

FAO (Food and Agriculture Organization). 2001. "Global Forest Resources Assessment 2000." FAO Forestry Paper 140, FAO, Rome.

———. 2005. "Best Practices for Improving Law Compliance in the Forest Sector." FAO Forestry Paper 145, FAO and International Tropical Timber Organization, Rome.

———. 2006. "Global Forest Resources Assessment 2005." FAO Forestry Paper 147, FAO, Rome.

Forest Trends. 2006. *Logging, Legality and Livelihoods in PNG: Synthesis of Official Assessments of the Large-Scale Logging Industry,* vol. 1. Washington, DC: Forest Trends.

Glastra, R., ed. 1999. *Cut and Run: Illegal Logging and Timber Trade in the Tropics.* Ottawa: International Development Research Centre.

Global Forest Watch. 2005. *Interactive Forestry Atlas of Cameroon (Version 1.0). An Overview.* Washington, DC: Global Forest Watch, Ministry of Environment and Forestry, Cameroon, and World Resources Institute—a Global Forest Watch Report.

Global Witness. 2000. "Chainsaws Speak Louder than Words." Briefing document, Global Witness, London. http://www.globalwitness.org/campaigns/ forests/cambodia/reports.html.

———. 2001. "The Credibility Gap—and the Need to Bridge It." Briefing document, London. http://www.globalwitness.org/campaigns/forests/cambodia/reports.html.

———. 2005. *A Guide to Independent Forest Monitoring.* London: Global Witness.

Gray, John. 2002. "Forest Concession Policies and Revenue Systems: Country Experience and Policy Changes for Sustainable Tropical Forestry." Technical Paper 522, World Bank, Washington, DC.

Greenpeace. 2001. "Partners in Mahogany Crime: Amazon at the Mercy of 'Gentlemen's Agreements.'" Greenpeace International, Amsterdam (October).

Isham, Jonathan, Michael Woolcock, Gwen Busbly, and Lant Prichett. 2005. "The Varieties of Rentier Experience: How Natural Resource Endowments Affect the Political Economy of Economic Growth." UC Berkeley Discussion Paper, University of California, Berkeley.

ITTO (International Tropical Timber Organization). 2000. "Review of Progress towards Year 2000 Objective." ITTO, Yokohama, Japan.

———. 2002. "Ecuador's New Approach to Enforcing Forest Law." *Tropical Forest Update* 12 (1). http://www.itto.or.jp/newsletter.

Kishor, Nalin. 2004. "Review of Formal and Informal Costs and Revenues Related to Timber Harvesting, Transporting and Trading in Indonesia." Informal note, World Bank, Washington, DC.

Klitgaard, Robert. 1988. *Controlling Corruption.* Berkeley: University of California Press.

Luttrell, Cecilia, and David Brown. 2006. "The Experience of Independent Forest Monitoring In Cambodia." VERIFOR Country Case Study 4 (May). http://www.verifor.org.

Magrath, W., and R. Grandalski. 2001. "Forest Law Enforcement: Policies Strategies and Technologies." World Bank, Washington DC.

Melle, Ann, and DeAndra Beck. 2001. "The U.S. Forest Service Approach to Forest Law Enforcement." Presentation at the Forest Law Enforcement and Governance: East Asia Ministerial Conference, Bali, Indonesia, September 11–13. http://lnweb18.worldbank.org/eap/eap.nsf/2500ec5f1a2d9bad852568a3006f557d/c19065b26241f0b247256ac30010e5ff?OpenDocument.

Navarro, Guillermo, Filippo Del Gatto, and Martin Schroeder. 2006. "The Ecuadorian Outsourced National Forest Control System." VERIFOR Country Case Study 3 (June). http://www.verifor.org.

PAF (Public Affairs Foundation). 2004. "Benchmarking Public Services Delivery at the Forest Fringes in Jharkhand, India." Public Affairs Foundation, Bangalore (October).

Poore, Duncan. 1989. *No Timber without Trees: Sustainability in the Tropical Forest.* London: Earthscan.

Rose-Ackerman, Susan. 1999. *Corruption in Government: Causes, Consequences, and Reform.* Cambridge, UK: Cambridge University Press.

Rosenbaum, Kenneth L. 2004. "Illegal Actions and the Forest Sector: A Legal Perspective." In *Illegal Logging in the Tropics: Strategies for Cutting Crime,* ed. Ramsay Ravenel, Ilmi Granoff, and Carrie Magee. New York: Haworth Press Inc.

———. 2005. "Tools for Civil Society Action to Reduce Forest Corruption: Drawing Lessons from Transparency International." World Bank, Washington, DC.

Ross, Michael L. 2001. *Timber Booms and Institutional Breakdown in Southeast Asia.* Cambridge, UK: Cambridge University Press.

Ruttan, Vernon. 1992. "Issues and Priorities for the Twenty-First Century." In *Sustainable Agriculture and Environment: Perspectives on Growth and Constraints,* ed. V. Ruttan, pp. 177–83. Boulder, CO: Westview Press.

Seneca Creek Associates LLC and Wood Resources International LLC. 2004. "'Illegal' Logging and Global Wood Markets: The Competitive Impacts on the U.S. Wood Products Industry." Prepared for the American Forest & Paper Association, Washington, DC.

Sokhun, Ty, and E. Savet. 2001. "Cambodia Forest and Wildlife Law Enforcement Experience in Cambodia." Presentation at the Forest Law Enforcement and Governance: East Asia Ministerial Conference, Bali, Indonesia, September 11–13. http://lnweb18.worldbank.org/eap/eap.nsf/2500ec5f1a2d9bad 852568a3006f557d/c19065b26241f0b247256ac 30010e5ff?OpenDocument.

UNDP (United Nations Development Programme)/FAO. 2002. "Forest Crime Monitoring and Reporting Project." Report of the Evaluation Mission, CMB/99/A05/6M/12. Royal Government of Cambodia, United Nations Development Programme, and Food and Agriculture Organization, Rome (December).

WBI (World Bank Institute). 2006. *Governance Matters V: Governance Indicators for 1996–2005.* http://www.worldbank.org/wbi/governance/govmatters5.

White. A., and A. Martin. 2002. "Who Owns the World's Forests?" Forest Trends and Center for International Environmental Law, Washington, DC.

World Bank. 2000a. "Anticorruption in Transition: A Contribution to the Policy Debate." World Bank, Washington, DC (September).

———. 2000b. "Reforming Public Institutions and Strengthening Governance: A World Bank Strategy." Public Sector Group, Poverty Reduction and Economic Management Network, World Bank, Washington, DC (November).

———. 2002. *World Development Report 2002: Building Institutions for Markets.* Washington, DC: World Bank.

———. 2004a. "Reforming Forest Fiscal Systems: An Overview of Country Approaches and Experiences." PROFOR, World Bank, Washington, DC (February).

———. 2004b. *World Development Report 2004: Making Services Work for the Poor.* Washington, DC: World Bank.

———. 2006a. "East Asia Region Forestry Strategy." World Bank, Washington, DC.

———. 2006b. "Strengthening Forest Law Enforcement and Governance: Addressing a Systemic Constraint to Sustainable Development." Report 36638-GLB, World Bank, Washington, DC (August).

4

Corruption in the Electricity Sector
A Pervasive Scourge

MOHINDER GULATI AND M. Y. RAO

"The infrastructure sectors are seen as being particularly vulnerable to corrupt practices given inter alia the large and lumpy expenditures involved (therefore easier to hide bribes), the reality that there are often relatively few qualified contractors (which can, in turn, lead to collusion) the presence of natural monopolies and the limits to competition (even with reform), the prevalence of 'regulatory capture,' and the numerous opportunities for discretionary decisions and 'rent taking' by public and private officials. The problem is compounded by the long tradition of corrupt practices in infrastructure in many countries and its embodiment in the political and social infrastructure. This chapter offers a promising approach to better understanding and tackling corruption in the electricity sector."

Richard Stern, Managing Director, Adalcorp

Electricity is probably the most versatile, widely used, and consumer-friendly form of energy. It can be generated from a wide variety of fuels such as coal, lignite, petrol, naphtha, fuel oil, diesel oil, vegetable oil, alcohol, natural gas, and biomass. Almost any form of energy occurring in nature can be converted into electricity: energy from wind, waves, steam, and water rising from geysers; from tides, flowing water, sunlight, and the vast energy lying locked in the heart of the atom. Its myriad applications and the simple way it can be put to use (or taken out of use) at the flick of a switch have made it a basic necessity for the economic and social life of much of the world. Life in a large part of the world would be unthinkable without electricity: pumps that operate drinking water supply lines or dispose of sewage or pump out storm water; the telecommunications network that crisscrosses the globe; the mass transport of goods and people on land, water, and across the skies; the provision of cooling in hot weather and heating in cold weather; the storing of medicines, foods, and other perishables at a given temperature; the provision of artificial light that extends the natural day, making more time available for work or leisure. The entire infrastructure of a community—its homes, offices, agriculture, industries, hospitals, banks, shopping malls, transport, communications, and recreational facilities—depends on this form of energy.

The electricity sector is made up of three technically separate activities—the generation of electricity, its transmission through high-voltage lines, and its sale to a large number of retail consumers through a distribution network. Most electricity is generated from fossil fuels, flowing water (hydroelectricity), or atomic energy, with nonconventional sources of energy like wind or solar power contributing a small but increasing share. Once generated, electricity is usually transmitted over long distances and then distributed to most consumers at low voltage, although large consumers may opt to obtain their supply at higher voltages.

In many countries, these activities are carried out by vertically integrated, state-owned monopolies. Often, governments use these utilities to pursue political, social, and economic objectives, thereby obfuscating the commercial aspects of the utilities. In the process, the management controls, the accountability of the utility managers, and the transparency of their operations are compromised. Over the years, this can lead to inefficiency, corruption, overstaffing, poor standards of supply and service, weak financial performance by the utilities, and fiscal burden. In many countries, these conditions have resulted in a climate of poor accountability and weak monitoring institutions that facilitates corruption until it becomes a fact of life pervading every stage and every level of the electricity business, from government at the apex to meter readers and linemen (responsible for operating and maintaining the low-voltage network) serving the consumer.[1] Often, the electricity utilities are very large enterprises compared with the state's economy and other commercial entities as measured by investments, revenue, number of people employed, and the size of the customer base. Hence corruption in the electricity sector in such countries, if left unchecked, could bleed the utilities, impoverish the community, and even corrode its moral fabric.

Before proceeding further, let us define "corruption" as it is used in this chapter. While the word usually has a cluster of associations including fraud, bribery, moral turpitude, misappropriation of funds, acquisition of illegal wealth, and venality, in this chapter, corruption has the somewhat narrower meaning of "the offering, giving, soliciting or acceptance of an inducement or reward that may influence the actions taken by any authority, its members or officers" (as defined in the United Kingdom's Prevention of Corrupt Practices Act of 1916). However, the sector also has its share of corporate fraud and financial malfeasance. Many reports use a broad-ranging definition of fraud that includes theft, false accounting, bribery and corruption, deception, and collusion. Although not categorized as corruption, some actors may try to take advantage of deficiencies in regulatory regime and defects in market design.

Monopoly, conflicting objectives imposed as a matter of public policy, and populist politics that present electricity supply as a public good characterize power utilities in many developing countries and provide fertile ground for inefficiency and corruption. Among other factors, the extent of corruption is correlated to the discretion held by decision makers, the absence of clear and enforceable accountability, and the lack of transparency in the decision-making process.

Recognizing that an effective international legal instrument against corruption was necessary, the UN General Assembly adopted the United Nations Convention against Corruption in October 2003. The convention emphasizes that while corruption can be prosecuted after the fact, the first and foremost step should be prevention. Suggested preventive measures include model policies such as the establishment of anticorruption agencies and enhanced transparency in the financing of election campaigns and political parties. States must endeavor to ensure that their public services, especially in critical areas like public procurement and the judiciary, are subject to safeguards that promote efficiency, transparency, and recruitment based on merit. The convention calls for active involvement of nongovernmental and community-based organizations as well as other elements of civil society in raising public awareness of corruption and what can be done about it. One of the fundamental principles agreed at the convention relates to the legal and procedural formalities to be followed for the recovery and return of corruption-funded assets to the countries that request such restitution. This is a particularly important issue for many developing countries, where high-level corruption has become a serious problem.

This chapter deals with corruption in the electricity sector. The chapter is divided into three sections: the first section discusses the pervasiveness of corruption in the electricity sector and its magnitude among utilities and countries. Corruption has affected every process and every activity of the electricity business, raising serious questions about its long-term viability. However, a few utilities that have been successful in maintaining a high level of probity even in an environment of corruption offer useful lessons in combating corruption. Two such case studies, *Palli Bidyut Samitis* of Bangladesh and the state-owned electricity utilities in Andhra Pradesh in India, are presented in annex 4A. Another success story worth mentioning is from Africa, where in 1997 the government of Gabon awarded a 20-year concession to a private entity, the Société d'Energie et d'Eau du Gabon, to operate both water and electricity services throughout the country (Tremolet 2002). The concessionaire has performed well in established service areas, often overachieving targets, but has made less progress in more isolated areas.

The second section provides a diagnosis of corruption in the electricity sector—how it occurs, how big a problem it is across the spectrum of activities in the sector and across different countries, who its beneficiaries are, and what makes corruption possible. It identifies the activities that are vulnerable to corruption and suggests which vulnerable points, if addressed, might have a relatively larger impact on curtailing corrupt activities. It shows that countries with high corruption generally have weak governance and a low human development record, pointing to a possible inverse relationship between corruption and human development.

The third section discusses strategies for combating corruption. These include strengthening accountability through access to information, codes of conduct, consumer rights statements, conflict of interest rules, and public participation; strengthening institutions such as audits and independent regulation; and stimulating employee commitment through progressive human resource policies. Constraints and obstacles blocking implementation of these strategies and an assessment of the costs involved are also covered in this section.

CORRUPTION: A PERVASIVE SCOURGE

Corruption in the electricity sector can range from petty corruption at the level of meter readers and linemen to grand larceny by the political executives who award lucrative concessions or require state-owned utilities to sign unfavorable power

BOX 4.1 Cost of Corruption: Eliminating Losses Could Also Eliminate Supply Gap

In Bangladesh, consumer payments account for only 55 percent of the power generated (Lovei and McKechnie 2000). Mismanagement and corruption in billing and collection alone is estimated to account for about half the losses of Bangladesh Power Development Board and the Dhaka Electricity Supply Authority, costing more than $100 million every year.

Orissa, an Indian state, privatized its electricity distribution in 1999, and since then there have been significant all-around improvements, including improvement in billing and collection. Even so, a review of the performance of the utilities conducted by the Orissa Electricity Regulatory Commission for the year ending March 2005 showed that the aggregate technical and commercial losses were about 46 percent (OERC 2005). The purely "technical" losses accounted for about one-third of the losses. The commission attributed the remaining losses primarily to corruption (mainly stolen electricity but also some inefficiency in metering, billing, and collection). The cost of this corruption was estimated at about $240 million.

Similar annual losses for the whole of India could be in the range of $4 billion to $5 billion.[a] This is a recurring loss and, if eliminated, would be sufficient to finance generating capacity of 4,000 to 5,000 megawatts every year. To look at it another way, elimination of this loss would release enough resources for India to meet the bulk of its commitment to provide "electricity for all by 2012."

a. Address to the nation by Indian Prime Minister Atal Bihari Vajpayee on August 15, 2002, in which he said that Rs 250 billion were lost through electricity theft.

purchase agreements (PPAs) or manipulate policies to suit favored parties. Utility managers are in the middle, getting their share from suppliers and contractors. Petty corruption, in aggregate, turns out to be anything but petty. Although reliable data are difficult to obtain, rough estimates by industry experts show that the amounts involved in so-called petty corruption are multiples of that involved in grand larceny and are large enough in their totality to bleed the utility and sometimes even the government to near-bankruptcy. Petty corruption in the electricity sector is a recurring, not just a one-time phenomenon; it erodes the work culture of the utility; and it becomes a major source of harassment of the consumers. Sometimes the direct cost of corruption in the electricity sector can be so large that its elimination can generate enough resources to eliminate substantial supply shortages (box 4.1).

Corruption cuts across countries and cultures, and petty corruption, which is arguably its most pervasive manifestation, thrives at the consumer interface. Nonpayment by consumers in connivance with the utility staff at the grass roots is the starting point for much of this petty corruption. Nonpayment slowly chokes the flow of funds to the utility, reduces its ability to expand or properly maintain the system, leads to poor and erratic power supply, and eventually results in consumer dissatisfaction. An example of this vicious circle was observed at the state-owned Baku Electricity Company in Azerbaijan, where household collection from electricity consumers in the second half of 1999 was only 12 percent of what it should have been (Lovei and McKechnie 2000). In the countries of the former Soviet Union (FSU), revenue collection by electric utilities ranges from 16 percent of what is owed in Azerbaijan to 98 percent in Bosnia and Poland (Komives and others 2005). Consumers and utility staff both benefit from their collusion in the short term, but predictably, the consumers' attitude changes to ire when the quality of supply deteriorates steeply. Noncash transactions (such as bartering), which are common in FSU countries, provide a fertile ground for corruption. Exchanging electricity (for fuel) and gas (for electricity) at inflated rates is one of the methods utility managers adopt to enrich themselves illegally. Power theft was so serious in Pakistan that in 1999 the government had to deploy the army to supervise metering and billing. What surprised the authorities was the sheer scale of the theft and the extent to which it benefited rich customers such as industries, shopping complexes, and large residential consumers.

Corruption and inefficiency in public services are linked to weak governance. The political and economic environment of a country determines, to a large extent, the quality of its public services. Governance issues such as accountability and responsiveness of the government, freedom of the press and the media, the right of the citizens to dissent and protest, the probity of institutions for maintaining law and order and for dispensing justice, the extent of delegation of effective power to local government institutions, and the level of public participation in decision making, all have a vital bearing on corruption in a country. Transparency International (TI) has conducted extensive surveys that show a strong link between weak governance, poor development, and corruption. One of these surveys (Transparency International 2002) examined seven sectors (education, health care, power, land administration, taxation, police, and judiciary) across five countries (Bangladesh, India, Nepal, Pakistan, and Sri Lanka). Education, health care, and power emerge as the three most commonly used public services across the region, and for a large percentage of the population, public institutions are the sole providers of these services. The study shows a high incidence of corruption in all these countries in the electricity sector as well as in other public services.

Another Transparency International (India Chapter) report (2005b) on corruption in India devoted one chapter to the pervasiveness of corruption in the electricity sector. Its conclusions are revealing:

- Nearly three-fifths of households in the country claimed to have interacted with their respective power utilities in the past year. Interaction was higher in urban households (70 percent) than in rural households (55 percent).
- More than one-tenth (12 percent) of all households in the country claimed to have paid bribes to obtain services in the past year.
- Nearly two-thirds (65 percent) of those who sought a service perceived that the utility was corrupt.
- Even private utilities are perceived as corrupt. Nearly three-fifths of the households served by private power utilities think their respective utilities are corrupt.
- Nearly half (49 percent) of those who interacted with the utility felt that the corruption in the utility had increased in the past year.
- More than one-fourth (27 percent) of those who had approached the utility had adopted means like paying bribes, using influence, and approaching middlemen.
- More than one-third (35 percent) of those who claimed to have paid bribes had paid money to linemen, while one-fourth (25 percent) had paid money to an agent or middleman.

Usually it is the poor who bear the brunt of corruption. In many countries, only the wealthy—a small percentage of the population—can afford access to electricity. Even when government policies may enable the poor to get electricity through the provision of capital and tariff subsidies, the benefit is generally limited to a lucky few. In such a situation, the impact of corruption is hardest on the poorer sections of society: they have low rates of access to the power grid, and power sector subsidies crowd out expenditures on other public services that primarily benefit the poor (box 4.2).

When a utility fails to bill and collect even the minimum revenue required for its operation, it can turn to a variety of means for survival such as borrowing, taking advantage of government subsidies, deferring payments, and obtaining credit from other government agencies for fuel, transportation, and other operations. But such measures merely postpone the inevitable. When all these measures are exhausted, the utility resorts to power rationing or load shedding. This may take the form of

BOX 4.2 The Poor Bear the Brunt of Corruption

Consumers bear the costs of poor-quality electricity supply resulting from wide fluctuations of voltage and power surges. In Bangladesh, where voltage in distribution networks is unstable, observers in rural areas have noticed that light bulbs last only a few days because of voltage surges. A low-income rural household might spend as much on light bulbs as on electricity. A survey funded by the World Bank (Lovei and McKechnie 2000) revealed that power outages in Bangladesh cost about $1 billion a year and reduced economic growth by about half a percentage point.

Subsidies for weaker sections of society form part of the social and political agenda of most governments. Poor consumers may receive subsidies for obtaining new power connections (capital subsidies) or for lowering the tariff (revenue subsidies) to make consumption affordable. Utilities usually administer the subsidies, but they lack the institutional mechanisms for accurately targeting the beneficiaries. As a result, the benefits largely bypass the poor and go to those who have no need for them. A World Bank study (World Bank 2001) on the supply of free power to the farmers in two states in India shows that only a small percentage of poor farmers benefited from the scheme. Supply to agriculture in these states was unmetered and provided a convenient camouflage to the utilities to hide the losses from corruption and mismanagement. A substantial part of the subsidies actually went to fund these losses.

The loss to the poor is twofold: they receive hardly any benefit from the subsidy, and the subsidy to the power sector drains away the resources of government that, had they been utilized for social welfare programs, could have qualitatively improved the lot of the poor. The case of Andhra Pradesh in India in fiscal 2002 is illustrative:

Transmission and distribution losses of the utilities	30.2 percent
Subsidy to power sector	Rs 24 billion ($525 million)
Subsidy/gross state domestic product	1.6 percent
Subsidy/government revenue	11.0 percent
Subsidy/revenue deficit	80.0 percent

Opportunity Cost of Power Subsidy

Program	*Capital cost*	*Annual operating cost*
Primary health care for rural areas in the state	Rs 12 billion	Rs 1 billion
Clean drinking water per village	Rs 10 million	Rs 0.4 million
Primary schools for all rural areas	Rs 9 billion	Rs 9 billion

TABLE 4.1 A Comparison of the Human Development Index (HDI) and the Corruption Perception Index (CPI)

Country	*HDI country rank, 2003*	*CPI country rank, 2004*
Malaysia	61	39
Sri Lanka	93	67
Iran, Islamic Rep. of	99	87
Indonesia	110	133
India	127	90
Pakistan	135	129
Nepal	136	90
Bangladesh	139	145

Source: Transparency International (2004); UNDP (2005).

rotational power cuts (which may affect all consumers in a locality at a given time) or the switching off of particular classes of loads at given times (such as domestic or agricultural pumping loads), depending on the configuration of the lines and the rules followed for effecting power cuts. Often, the utilities prefer to spare industries and other high-value customers the rigors of power cuts and instead switch off the lines supplying power to the poorer areas. Shortage of funds affects the quality as well as the coverage of the supply, and the rising costs of refurbishing the system can discourage if not deter the poor from even applying for an electricity connection. In such a context of inadequate supply and absence of alternatives, the scope for corruption among utility employees goes up. The consumers and the community are caught in a vicious circle of spiraling corruption.

There seems to be an inverse relationship between corruption and human development. Transparency International has been publishing a Corruption Perception Index (CPI) since 1995. The index measures the degree of corruption perceived by businesspeople and country analysts and ranks countries according to perceived corruption, from least corrupt to most corrupt. It is interesting to study the CPI for 2004 side by side with the UN's *Human Development Report* (UNDP 2005), which ranked 145 member countries of the United Nations on a number of indexes such as life expectancy at birth, per capita income, adult literacy, and nutrition. Countries with a high CPI ranking (that is, countries perceived to be more corrupt) are almost invariably rated low in human development, indicating a possible relationship between corruption and development. Details relating to a sample of developing countries are presented in the table 4.1.

CORRUPTION VULNERABILITIES

Even in a fairly liberalized economic environment, the government has a vital say on a whole range of issues. Often the main agencies for implementing government policy are state-owned enterprises. This arrangement blurs the distinction between policy, ownership, and operation. In the electricity sector, government policies typically cover matters such as estimation of demand and the need for adding capacity, licensing, statutory and administrative clearances, sourcing of the plant and machinery, acquisition of land, and resettlement of people affected by electricity projects. Often, these policies are made without any detailed study of the issues and with little or no consultation with the stakeholders. As a result, such policies may turn out to be unsound. This infirmity in policy making is exacerbated by the government officials who are not subjected to public scrutiny when they grant licenses or award contracts. The situation facilitates corruption. The beneficiaries are the politicians, senior bureaucrats, utility staff, and the entities, usually from the private sector, that win the license or the contract.

Government institutions and agencies such as state electricity boards or government-owned corporations invariably mirror the ethos and attitudes of the political and bureaucratic executive. In its survey of corruption in South Asia, Transparency International (2002) documented the perceived reasons for corruption in public services, including the power sector. An overwhelming majority of the respondents rated lack of accountability as the most important reason. Second in order of importance was the monopoly power enjoyed by the utility, followed by lack of transparency and the discretionary powers of the utility staff. It is significant that the low pay of staff came only fifth in order of importance. Other causes identified in the report include acceptance of corruption as a way of life, the ineffectiveness of the judiciary in punishing corruption, and inadequate training and orientation of officials. This report concludes that lack of transparency and accountability in the system is the primary cause of corruption. Corruption in public interfaces, especially in South Asian countries, has more than an element of extortion about it, with individuals hesitating even to protest against malpractices because of fear of retribution by the utility employees. The next section reviews a few key areas of vulnerability in the sector and then analyzes the underlying causes.

Key Areas of Vulnerability: Identification, Magnitude, and Beneficiaries

Levels of corruption in the electricity sector as well as its manifestations can vary greatly from country to country depending on local conditions. As a general proposition, however, a few key areas are particularly prone to corruption in many developing countries: government policies, investment and financing decisions, customer-interfacing activities, commercial operations of the utilities, procurement, and human resource management.

The following paragraphs provide more details on these areas, as well as point out the indicators of corrupt practices (red flags) that a practitioner should look for in a diagnostic analysis. However, it is important not to jump to quick conclusions. A more rigorous analysis of any specific situation is necessary before one can establish corruption as the underlying cause of the symptom, which may indicate inefficiency, inadequate skills, faulty organizational structure, inefficient business processes, poor judgment and decisions by policy makers, or expediency-driven choices in public policies rather than outright corruption. Further analysis of the decision-making process, incident analysis of a few cases, user perception surveys, and use of other diagnostic tools are always necessary before one can conclude that the indicator reflects corruption.

Government Policies

The activities usually covered by government policy on the electricity sector and the areas that are vulnerable to corruption in such a policy framework are described in table 4.2. The beneficiaries of corruption at this level are politicians, senior bureaucrats, and senior managers of the utilities. Often an informal nexus develops among the politicians, bureaucrats, utility managers, and utility staff. While benefits of corruption flow to the top, dilution of accountability flows to the lowest levels.

TABLE 4.2 Vulnerability to Corruption: Government Policies

Activity	*Areas vulnerable to corruption*	*Red flags*
Estimates of the additional capacity required to meet demand	Manipulation of the estimates[a]	No or inadequate analysis of demand No public consultation Lack of transparency in demand forecasting
Norms and procedures for licensing	Alteration of licensing criteria to favor particular interests	Ad hoc revisions or exceptions made to the criteria Nontransparent process for revising norms
Statutory and other clearances	Dilatory and repetitive procedures with no time limit for final decision	Vague procedures Authorities with overlapping jurisdictions
Sale of the energy generated	Restrictions on who may buy the energy and the price payable PPAs	Noncompetitive procurement of independent power producers (IPPs)
Acquisition of land and rehabilitation of project-affected persons	Payment of compensation to landowners Payment to and resettlement of project-affected people	High level of activity in land transactions before government notification for zoning or land acquisition A few transactions registered at inflated prices to raise the benchmark for rates of compensation Opaque procedures for payment of compensation Several partial payments
Subsidies to specified consumer groups	Administration of subsidy, including selection of beneficiaries	Unmetered supply Absence of or weak linkage with means criteria
Selection of regulators and top management of utilities	Manipulating selection criteria Corruption in appointments	Undue delay in appointments Lack of transparency in the selection process

a. When the demand is deliberately underestimated, an opportunity for future shortages is created that will justify "emergency" arrangements to purchase electricity from expensive sources; an overstated demand can justify the setting up of a favored new IPP.

TABLE 4.3 Vulnerability to Corruption: Different Stages of Project Development

Activity	Areas vulnerable to corruption	Red flags
Project formulation	Technoeconomic studies to establish feasibility and viability Surveys and site investigations Estimation of costs and implementation schedules Statutory and other clearances Land acquisition for the plant Rights-of-way for transmission lines Rehabilitation of persons affected by the project	A perfunctory study (or no study at all) Omitting surveys and site investigations or leaving them to be done later by the contractor Estimation of costs Vagueness about procedure for obtaining clearances Not allocating sufficient resources for paying compensation to project-affected persons
Project implementation	Procedure for selection of contractor Type of contract (works, labor, turnkey) and contract documents Monitoring and supervision of contractor's work Purchase and supply of plant, machinery, and materials Stage payments to contractors Completion and commissioning	Procedure not spelled out in bid documents Lack of specificity in the contracts Failure to designate supervisors with clear responsibilities Not allocating sufficient funds for payment, leading to disputes and claims of escalation of costs
Project operation	Performance of plant and machinery during initial guarantee stage Execution of operations and maintenance (in-house or outsourced) Emergency repairs Purchase and use of materials, stores, and consumables Emergency purchases Payments to contractors, suppliers, and vendors Employee-related issues, such as promotion, transfer, payment of employees' dues such as provident funds, various allowances, and reimbursement of expenses Adherence to relevant codes and licensing conditions	Failure to specify the performance parameters and methodology of verification Failure to spell out clear procedures for routine as well as emergency purchases Requiring multiple certifications (thus diluting individual responsibility) before payments can be made Absence of codified and transparent procedures Failure to specify responsibilities of individual officers to ensure compliance with license conditions

Investment Decisions

In many developing countries, utilities frequently must deal with inadequate investment planning, capital shortages, and absence of political incentive for the decision makers because of the time lag between the capital investment and the payout of benefits, which may not accrue during their tenure in office. Underinvestment provides the scope for gaming, which thrives on emergency works taken up in a hurry when a power crisis occurs. Strengthening the planning process in the utility and adhering to least-cost expansion plans can minimize the ad hoc nature and risk of corruption in investment decisions as well as bring significant economic benefits. A master plan for least-cost expansion prepared sufficiently in advance also leaves ample time to organize a competitive process for procurement.

Once a proposal for investment meets government policy requirements, the stage is set for the planning and implementation of the project. This stage covers a large number of activities—each providing its own niche for corruption. Cataloging every one of them is unnecessary, but the more important vulnerable areas common to generation, transmission, and distribution are presented under a few generic headings in table 4.3.

Bad faith should not be read into every instance of poor planning or poor implementation resulting in delays in project completion, escalation of costs, and claims from contractors. These could occur simply because trained personnel were not available to the utility or the government. Before deciding whether corruption has played any role, the circumstances of each case must be examined on their merits. Wherever corruption has featured in these activities, the beneficiaries are usually the middle- and senior-level executives of the utilities. In large projects, the main beneficiaries are often the politicians, who may share the spoils with compliant government officials or senior utility managers who are used as a conduit. Poor decisions, whether stemming from corruption, lack of technical capacity, or poor judgment, impose a heavy cost on the utilities, the government, and the consumers (box 4.3).

Customer-Interfacing Activities

Policy implementation involves politicians and executives at the top and middle levels. But it is at the consumer interface that corruption is most blatant and widespread. Utility staff members at the consumer interface are poorly paid, but they

BOX 4.3 Cost of Poor Investment Decisions and Less than Transparent Procurement

The government of Tanzania and the Tanzania Electricity Supply Company entered into contractual agreements with Messrs. Independent Power Tanzania Limited (IPTL) of Malaysia for the supply of 100 megawatts of power over a 20-year period. This transaction was believed to have been made during a power crisis and was hotly contested by some government officials and by the international donor community and other interested stakeholders on the grounds that it was the wrong technology (heavy fuel oil instead of indigenous gas), that it was not part of the least-cost generation plan, that it was not procured on a transparent and competitive basis, and that the power was not needed. The government ultimately submitted the case to arbitration. Under the final arbitral ruling, the project costs were reduced by about 18 percent, and the utility company was not to be held responsible for any claims for damages arising from the plant sitting idle for several years. Nonetheless, the cost of this project to the electricity consumer and the government has been significant, including the payment of capacity charges when energy for the grid was not required, and the high cost of generation using heavy fuel oil when much cheaper alternatives (indigenous gas) were available.

Source: Juliet Pumpuni, World Bank Institute Global Programs.

exercise large discretionary powers. They freely exercise this discretion in providing (or refusing) a connection, billing (or not billing) a consumer, revising a bill upward (or downward), or changing (or not changing) a defective meter. As providers of the services that are often subsidized, these staff members are also seen as the representatives of the government. Consumers, reluctant to look a gift horse in the mouth, lower their expectations of the utility regarding quality of service. This attitude further weakens the stigma attached to corruption. Table 4.4 shows the activities at the consumer interface that are vulnerable to corruption, the causes of this type of corruption, and its beneficiaries.

TABLE 4.4 Vulnerability to Corruption: Customer-Interfacing Activities

Activities	*Areas vulnerable to corruption*	*Red flags*
New connection, additional load	Information on procedure not clear or not available Harassment by utility staff	Undue delays in giving connections Lack of periodic data reconciliation between new connections, meter-reading book, and consumer ledger
Meter reading	Poor quality of meters Irregular meter reading	Tampered-with meters Meters not tested according to norms Wide variations in consumption by similarly placed consumers High electricity losses in some feeder lines High incidence of broken meter seals
Payment and correction of bill	Errors in bill Collusion between utility staff and consumer Billing based on factors other than actual use (such as average consumption or load factor)	High incidence of billing disputes or bill corrections Fall in collection while consumption remains the same
Repair service, fuse call	Supply interruptions caused by accidents Routine maintenance work	Poor maintenance of complaints record Undue delay in attending to complaints Frequent burning of transformers
Meter installation, replacement of defective meters	Inadequate protection devices for meters Delay in issuing and installing meters	High volume of complaints regarding quality of service High incidence of burnt meters of large consumers (who may be charged a flat rate for consumption during the period the meter is not replaced)
Disconnection	Nonpayment of bill Delay in receipt of bill Pilferage by consumer	High level of receivables Frequency and amount of default in bill payment
Reconnection	Delay even after rectification of cause of disconnection	High incidence of deviation from the normative standards of service

Commercial Operations: Theft of Electricity

Theft of electricity takes place in a variety of forms and thrives with the support of people from different walks of life: utility staff, consumers (acting individually or in powerful groups), labor union leaders, political leaders, bureaucrats, and high-level utility officials. While almost every operation in the electricity sector is vulnerable to theft, be it generation, transmission, or distribution, some of the more common varieties of theft, the mode of theft, and its beneficiaries are described in table 4.5.

Absence of accountability and internal controls is possibly the single most important factor leading to theft. Electricity is a commodity, and its sale and purchase should be regulated by the commercial procedures that govern such transactions. Basic to this proposition is that what is sold should be measured, what is measured should be billed, what is billed should be collected, and what is collected should be remitted to the treasury. State-owned power utilities that suffer from power theft are generally slack in this respect. Power from the generating plant is measured and delivered to the high-voltage transmission network at the grid

TABLE 4.5 Vulnerability to Corruption: Theft of Electricity

Activities	*Mode of theft*	*Beneficiaries of corruption*
Generation	Theft of fuel camouflaged as auxiliary consumption in thermal generation plant Unauthorized use in the homes of generation plant staff	Staff of the generation plant Labor union leaders
Transmission	Tapping of overhead transmission lines by large consumers Defective meters	Large consumers Politicians Bureaucrats Utility managers Transmission line staff
Distribution	Tapping of distribution lines	Consumers Distribution utility staff
	Unauthorized supply of energy	Consumers Utility managers Distribution utility staff
	Organized resistance to paying for electricity	Labor union leaders Politicians Groups of consumers acting in concert (farmers, industries, residential areas, and the like), Local mafia with political protection
	Nonbilling and underbilling of energy	Consumers Billing staff
	Tampering with or bypassing meters	Consumers Linemen
	Billing the consumer at a lower rate	Consumers Billing staff Utility managers

BOX 4.4 Who Wants Accountability?

One distribution utility in India took a series of steps to tighten procedures and plug the leakage of revenue. Metering was given high priority on this agenda. Utility staff enthusiastically supported the purchase of about 400,000 meters to be installed in consumer premises. The process of drawing up specifications, issue of tender notices in newspapers, choice of turnkey contractors, and visits abroad to inspect the meters before they were shipped was completed promptly. But when it came to buying about 600 meters to be installed at the feeders, troubles started. Unions of linemen and section officers saw the step as a move to victimize their members by making them specifically responsible for the energy received and sold. They argued that accountability should be ensured across the utility at all levels and not confined to a few low-level employees. It took the utility another two years and a change in the management to get all the feeders metered.

substation. This power is then stepped down at distribution substations and released into distribution feeders. It is at the distribution substations that the first major theft of power takes place. All substations are required to have meters to measure the flows of energy into the feeders, but these meters are often erratic and unreliable. Replacement of defective meters is deliberately delayed, with utility officials citing various problems such as lack of finances, need for "bulk purchase" to obtain competitive rates, and elaborate tendering procedures. There is anecdotal evidence that utility employees and their union leaders steadfastly resist efforts to put meters on feeders (box 4.4).

Measuring the energy received and sold is the starting point in curbing this sort of power theft. Not many utilities have reliable reporting and monitoring systems, however. As a result, there is usually no way of reconciling the energy received against energy billed or the amount billed against the amount paid by the consumers. The inability of many utilities to segregate current consumption and charges from the arrears adds a further layer of complication. Since collection is invariably low in poorly run utilities, the arrears climb higher every year until they are eventually written off.

Some influential consumers steal electricity by raising bogus disputes about bills and stalling payment by resorting to litigation and then taking advantage of delays in court procedures. Once the litigation has dragged on long enough to ensure that utility personnel pursuing the case are no longer there, the consumer will move to settle the dispute. Politicians and senior bureaucrats who would not like to be seen interfering in the affairs of a utility are nonetheless willing to use their good offices to settle the matter through negotiation in which the utility takes the hit in various forms: forgoing part or all of the interest on delayed payment, providing a large number of easy installments, and even writing off part of the payments owed in "one-time settlements."

A combination of employee resistance and slack management has impeded many utilities from taking advantage of innovations, technological or otherwise. Computerized billing, online monitoring of consumers (beginning with the large consumers), and provision of insulated electricity lines in areas prone to tapping of wires fall into this category. Efforts by some utilities in India to have their utility bills processed by hired computer firms provide an interesting insight into the pitfalls of poor management (box 4.5).

BOX 4.5 Outsourcing without Monitoring Is No Solution

Some utilities in India turned to computerized billing as the first step toward the introduction of a management information system (MIS). Because of internal resistance to computerization, many utilities decided to outsource this activity. The terms of engagement provided many safeguards against malpractices, but because of slack supervision, a disconnect developed between the consumer databases maintained by the utility and those used by the computer firms. The firms established a nexus with the consumers and provided them "concessions in billing" without the knowledge of the utility. When the utility tried to terminate the contract, the firms blackmailed them into giving them concessions in exchange for their database.

BOX 4.6 Community Participation and Good Governance

Sagar Island in the Sunderbans in India is supplied with electricity generated by solar panels provided by the West Bengal Renewable Energy Development Authority for the use of the community. A typical unit serves about 120 to 150 households grouped in a cluster. A local committee oversees all operations, including delivery of bills, collection from consumers, and monitoring the system. Consumers pay more than twice the amount mainlanders pay the state-owned utility for electricity. The supply is restricted to a few hours in the evening. Consumption is limited to about 7–10 kilowatt hours a month, and overdrawals are blocked by miniature circuit breakers installed in homes. Theft is almost nonexistent and defaults very few, thanks to enormous peer pressure and self-monitoring by the user-group.

An age-old tenet holds that "it is immoral to steal from your neighbor but perfectly legitimate to steal from the state." State-owned utilities are identified in the people's mind with the state, and electricity is viewed as state property. Many communities perceive the state as remote, unresponsive, and exploitative. In the public mind, stealing from such an entity is no crime, but rather is seen as one way of getting back at a powerful antagonist. This attitude is in sharp contrast to the way the people perceive irrigation water (flow irrigation). Local committees closely watch the sharing of the irrigation water, and any theft of water is perceived as theft from a neighbor, which is taboo. A similar attitude is at work in isolated communities that are served by electricity generated and sold locally (box 4.6).

People's attitude to private electric utilities reinforces these observations. Private utilities have been serving the cities of Kolkata and Mumbai, in India, for decades. Despite changes in management, their commercial procedures are much better than those in state-owned utilities. Accountability is enforced and theft is strongly discouraged. Commercial losses, including losses from theft, are about 12–15 percent, half as large as those incurred by the state-owned utilities, which typically are in the range of 30–35 percent. The public recognizes this better performance and treats the private utilities quite differently from the way they treat the state electricity boards (SEBs) that serve adjoining areas. Even the government respects the private companies' operational imperatives, and as a result, political interference in their working is minimal. In sharp contrast with SEBs, these utilities are profitable.

Procurement

The utilities regularly spend large amounts on purchasing a variety of things: equipment for capital projects, inventory for operation and maintenance, power purchases through long-term agreements as well as short-term purchases in the market, fuel for generation plants, and outsourcing of services. Competitive bidding is generally accepted as the best way of ensuring transparency. But even with competitive bidding, opportunities for corruption abound in procurement activities. They generally appear in unsolicited bids; suppliers' credits; and "emergency" procurement where there is little or no competition among suppliers, the quality is negotiable, and reputable firms may be reluctant to participate. Even where competitive bidding processes are used, broad (rather than detailed) specifications and manifestly impractical terms and conditions leave scope for posttender negotiations with bidders and consequent bribes. A combination of managerial venality and incompetence may be seen in a wide range of activities. Contracts awarded without obtaining legal possession or right-of-way over the land, without getting necessary environmental or other clearances, and without furnishing clear data giving topographical details and soil conditions open up a rich field for litigation with the contractor. Sheer incompetence may partly explain such poorly drawn contracts, but given the powerful links between the contractors and the utility managers, there is a strong possibility that these loopholes are deliberate. Eventual settlement of these disputes, irrespective of whether they are through court intervention, arbitration, or mutual discussion, invariably favors the contractor at the expense of the utility.

Despite elaborate rules and procedures in most utilities, procurement of equipments, spare parts, and consumables is vulnerable to corruption for many reasons. The technology is growing more complex, and utility managers making decisions about a tender are generally one step behind private contractors and suppliers who are able to access better technical expertise. Procurement managers may deliberately keep the technical specifications and the bidding documents ambiguous, impose unrealistic schedules on the bidding process and contract execution, and use subjective or nontransparent qualification and evaluation criteria for the bidders. During contract execution, the certification of quality, delivery, and stage payments also offer opportunities for corruption.

Contracts with IPPs as well as contracts for purchase of large equipments are very complex. Such contracts quickly become the domain of a few experts; dissemination of relevant information and its use by the public become difficult, creating opportunities for grand corruption by the decision makers. Experience in several developing countries shows that often the PPAs they sign are not in the interest of the utilities or the consumers. According to a study by the World Bank (Albouy and Bousby 1998), the IPPs often inflate supply prices for utilities. Often, the contracted generation capacity exceeds the demand, but the government is bound to buy the agreed quantity of power.[2]

Many of these contracts are arranged through a memorandum of understanding with the electricity generators rather than through a transparent and open competitive bidding process. Governments and state-owned utilities sometimes advance the most specious reasons for failing to engage in competitive bidding, holding, for example, that the procedure has no relevance where a private sector investor chooses to set up a project using its own resources; that it would be counterproductive to insist on competitive bidding when the foreign consortium involved is composed of internationally reputed companies in the field of energy, power equipment manufacture, and engineering; that competitive bids require costly and time-consuming preparatory work; and that the expert knowledge and experience required for evaluating bids as well as for identifying and allocating risks is not available. It is also true that the wide variety of fuels and the rapidly changing technologies available for electricity generation renders the decision-making process difficult for many developing countries that may not have the expertise to assess the full implications of a plant using a particular fuel or technology.

Large contracts, signed with IPPs in an environment of weak watchdog institutions, offer attractive opportunities to influential decision makers for making illegal gains. The negotiations are held in secret, and minutes are not kept at all or are very sketchy. The costs to the country and the illegal gains for those entering into the contracts are enormous. A few examples illustrate the size of the amounts involved.

A PPA was negotiated for an Enron project (Dabhol Power Company) in the state of Maharashtra, India. After the agreement drew widespread protests and litigation, it was renegotiated by the successor government, which was headed by a different political party that was highly critical of the original PPA (Energy Review Committee 2001). During litigation over the project, the High Court of the state of Maharashtra observed that the state committee involved in the renegotiation "forgot all about competitive bidding and transparency." The annual cost of this project to the state was computed at Rs 60 billion ($1.3 billion). A settlement was reached among Indian financial institutions, offshore lenders, and foreign investors, and claims of foreign investors settled. The plant was taken over by a consortium of government-owned companies, but it continues to remain idle because of the high cost of generation.

Another example comes from Indonesia, where most IPPs provided the family and friends of politicians with "loan-financed" shares in the company (Bayliss and Hall 2000) The loans were to be repaid with the dividends from the shares, but the shares were essentially gifts camouflaged to escape the anticorruption legislations.

Often, government uses a crisis situation to justify contracting for excess capacity or taking on more risk in terms of technology, fuel, financing terms, or capacity payments. The Philippines signed 42 IPP contracts between 1990 and 1994, much in excess of demand, resulting in financial burdens for the utility and the government, which had to make payments for unused capacity. The Gujarat Electricity Board in India sustained a similar financial burden when it was forced to continue making capacity payments for naphtha-fired private generators even after increasing naphtha prices rendered these plants uneconomical. These examples could reflect risky or bad decisions arising from a lack of capacity in the governments and their agencies to negotiate complex contracts. However, lack of transparency, the governments' frequent unwillingness to use competent advisers to help in negotiations, and the failure to disseminate information to the public tend to support the allegations of corruption.

In some regions, such as East Asia, where the utilities operate reasonably efficiently and theft of electricity may not be an issue, procurement of equipment and

BOX 4.7 OPCOM Power Exchange: Improving Governance of Public Utilities in Romania

The Power Exchange operated by OPCOM, the electricity market operator in Romania, provides a benchmark for the regional electricity market in Southeast Europe. In addition, it provides a tool to improve governance of public sector generators and to address "second-generation" issues in power sector reform emerging from market liberalization.

In the late 1990s, the Romanian power sector was restructured through unbundling of the vertically integrated power company RENEL into separate generation, transmission, and distribution companies. An independent power sector regulator, ANRE, was established in 1998. Distribution has been organized into eight regional companies. Transelectrica is in charge of transmission and system operations, and its fully owned subsidiary OPCOM is the electricity market operator. As of 2006, five of the eight electricity distribution companies have been privatized and the remaining three are expected to be offered for sale in 2007.

Market liberalization started in 2000 and has now reached 83 percent, with all but residential consumers now being "eligible" (having the freedom) to choose their electricity supplier. Within the liberalized market, eligible consumers and suppliers are free to enter into bilateral contracts for the supply of electricity. In July 2005, OPCOM launched a day-ahead market based on demand- and supply-side bids, followed by centralized auction of bilateral contracts in December 2005.

The government, ANRE, and the electricity companies addressed a number of major issues through the reform process. But market liberalization raised a new issue about the way public sector generators executed bilateral contracts. Prices in some of the bilateral contracts were allegedly set below true market value, and corruption was alleged in the case of bilateral contracts with some government-owned generation companies. In response, the top managers of two companies were dismissed and the government required public sector generators to use OPCOM's competitive auction for bilateral contracts. OPCOM's Power Exchange thus not only facilitates electricity trading but also provides a tool to improve governance of public sector generators.

services and contract awards could still be open to corruption. In some other regions, such as Southeast Europe, trading of power has allegedly been a source of corruption at high levels in both the utility and the political leadership (box 4.7).[3] The benefits of corruption often flow directly to the senior levels in utility management, trade unions, and government bureaucracy. Large contracts can also be a source of side payments for financing elections.

Human Resources

Even staff functions like human resource management fall prey to corruption. Interference by politicians is not limited only to appointments to the utility boards or senior management. Quite often, the politicians and senior managers of the utilities can turn routine personnel decisions such as recruitment, transfer, promotion, and disciplinary action into a fruitful source of corruption. It is quite usual for utility managers to award "lucrative" postings to compliant employees in the expectation of getting a share of their illegal earnings. Newspapers occasionally write about this "industry," which calls for no capital investment and yet accounts for regular and hefty dividends. The mere threat of a transfer from a lucrative position or a transfer order cancelled on the basis of a representation from the employee is enough to open a channel for the illegal flow of money. The price of the bribes extorted in these ways is ultimately paid by the consumer in the form of higher utility bills and poorer service.

Diagnosis: The Causes of Corruption

The preceding overview illustrates several areas within the electric utility sector that are vulnerable to corruption. Seen through the lens of outcomes or a utility's performance, it is difficult to separate the impact of inefficiency, corruption, and sometimes public policy. However, Klitgaard's (1988) formulation, M (monopoly) $+ D$ (discretion) $- A$ (accountability) $- T$ (transparency) $= C$ (corruption), presents a useful framework for diagnosis of corruption.

In most of the developing world, government is the sole provider of electricity. In an environment of low responsiveness, weak accountability, and inactive civil society, the relationship between the government and the governed is one of master and servant, where the citizen's right to a basic service is hardly ever recognized. Basic services are seen as a favor conferred by government functionaries at their will and pleasure and subject to whatever terms they choose. These services are provided either directly by the government or through quasi-governmental agencies like corporations or boards managed, by and large, by professionals with a broad charter and considerable operational freedom within a specified policy framework.

Transparency and access to information are keys to good governance. Agreements executed by governments (or government-controlled utilities) to purchase power from generators selected other than through open competitive bidding provide a fertile ground for corruption. Even tax holidays, subsidies, and other types of concessions given to IPPs as part of government's policy to encourage investment in the sector easily lend themselves to misuse and corruption unless they are administered in an open and transparent manner. The controversies and the continuing legal wrangles surrounding the Dabhol Power Company, set up by Enron in India in the mid-1990s and commissioned (phase I) in 1999, is a case in point. The California power crisis of 2000–01, which siphoned off billions of dollars of public money, provides an interesting example of how powerful corporations with political influence can manipulate markets and regulators to fleece the public. The part played by Enron and others in the California scandal may not be termed corruption, since collusion by government or government instrumentalities has not been proved. But it is a reminder that even sophisticated systems of governance and oversight are not adequate safeguards against massive frauds (annex 4B).

Weak governance and supply shortages create fertile grounds for corruption. In developing countries, the electricity supply system experienced substantial expansion in the last few decades. The system worked reasonably well in the early stages of the expansion, when the beneficiaries of the services were few and belonged to the affluent or influential classes. In the course of time and as a result of development initiatives taken by governments, electricity began to become available to the general populace. In the 1970s, for example, India launched a program to electrify hamlets and homes of the poor and other socially disadvantaged segments of the population. Policy initiatives like this called for a major, and in many cases sudden, change in the way these government agencies conducted their business, and few of them managed the transformation smoothly.

The sudden spurt in demand for electricity led to scarce supply, thus preparing the ground for large-scale corruption. Staff hired in large numbers without adequate attention to quality or training and the unplanned and rapid expansion of electricity networks led to a general weakening of the control and monitoring systems. Lack of accountability and transparency became the rule rather than the exception among utility employees who became a law unto themselves, especially in rural and remote areas.

Governments in developing countries typically spend a large part of their scarce resources on providing basic amenities like primary education, health care, drinking water, and electricity. Governments claim success in these areas on the basis of inputs (how much money has been budgeted for them and how much has been spent) and outputs (such as completion of projects, length of network, and the number of villages electrified), but almost never by outcomes (whether the money has been spent prudently and efficiently to improve the quality of life of the people). The lack of effective mechanisms for monitoring outcomes of governmental action shields corruption from public scrutiny.

COMBATING CORRUPTION

The money involved in grand larceny in the electricity sector is substantial, but what is even more damaging is the acceptance of corruption as a way of doing business. When high-profile politicians and government functionaries routinely engage in corrupt practices, the stigma begins to wear away. Gradually, what is a misdemeanor in the higher echelons becomes an entitlement to the levels below. At the grassroots level, utility employees find nothing wrong in supplementing their modest pay by what they have come to consider the perquisites of office. The day-to-day petty corruption faced by the public breeds cynicism, steadily erodes faith in the system, and eventually gnaws away the very moral foundations of the society.

If corruption is pervasive, as happens in some countries, combating corruption in the sector requires mutually reinforcing improvements in public governance. Eminently desirable though this may be, it is a long-term process requiring sustained political commitment, changes in the incentives of stakeholders, and new standards of transparency and accountability—in short, a paradigm shift in public governance and management of the sector. To make a positive impact on the fight against corruption in the short and medium term, it is more useful to focus on those vulnerable points that, if addressed, can have a relatively large effect. The starting point for combating corruption could range from introducing transparency in the procurement process, to seeking expert consultation in investment decisions and enforcing accountability of public officials and utility managers, to fighting petty corruption in order to build public support.[4]

In some countries, corruption in procurement and contracting may be a larger problem than electricity theft, in which case an anticorruption strategy should focus on transparency and competition in procurement and contracting by externalizing accountability of public officials through public participation and independent regulatory institutions. Petty corruption in the electricity sector has not received much attention from the media, civil society, organizations promoting transparency, or international financial organizations, which have tended to focus more on corruption in large contracts. Because of the sheer magnitude in terms of the money involved and the number of people affected, combating petty corruption at the consumer interface of the electricity supply utility may assume more importance in some cases.

Conditions Precedent for Launching an Anticorruption Strategy

The last few years have seen a growing demand from the public for measures to address the epidemic of corruption, a demand that has been reinforced by the requirement of the international donor community to ensure that the funds it provides are properly used. In view of the magnitude and pervasiveness of petty corruption at the consumer interface, a strategy for combating corruption in the sector should focus on improving governance in the utility. Participants in this campaign should include top government officials, who should provide demonstrable evidence of commitment, resources for implementation, and the legal and institutional framework; the utility, which can make reforms acceptable by simplifying procedures, using technology to improve performance, and adopting suitable measures to ensure employee support; the employees, who will have to relearn many practices and attitudes; civil society institutions, whose role is to engender transparency and accountability; and the consumers and the general public, who by their active participation in all aspects of governance will ensure the continued success of the reforms.

Committed Leadership at the Top

A change process requires a crisis to trigger action, a "champion" for change, and a core team backed by necessary resources to build and sustain support. When the political cost of the status quo starts rising because of disaffection among stakeholders or a burgeoning fiscal burden, political commitment for change can increase. But the initiation of change by the political executive is largely dependent on timing. Governments may be willing to start reforms in the first year or so of coming to power, so that the benefits of reform in the remaining period of their tenure will outweigh its immediate (and unpleasant) impact. Quite apart from this, the electorate expects a new government to come up with innovative policies in the initial phase of coming to power. Even relatively harsh innovations can pass muster during this period because of the people's willingness to endure some hardships in the expectation of improvements in their well-being. The lesson seems to be: governments can be persuaded to introduce reforms during the early stages of their tenure, but not later, when reforms will be too much of a political gamble.

The importance of firm and sustained commitment to the reforms by government and its political leaders cannot be overstated. A country may enact anticorruption laws or create institutions because it has been urged to do so by the donor community or international pressure, but a government that lacks commitment to cleaning up corruption can find ways to neutralize those laws and institutions that it sees as potential threats to its political control. Common neutralizing tactics include not disseminating information to the public, rendering the laws inoperative by not establishing the detailed rules and procedures, and depriving the institutions of necessary budget, funds, and staff. Sector regulators and utilities boards are sometimes packed with pliant officials who can be relied upon to anticipate what government wants and act accordingly. Or key positions in utilities and the regulatory agencies can be left vacant for long periods, inviting confusion and lack of accountability. Government policy directives can curtail the independence of regulators.

Professing commitment to anticorruption efforts is not enough, however. The government needs to "walk the talk" through sustained actions such as an effective communication campaign led by the chief executive and reinforced regularly by other members of the political establishment, thereby giving political visibility to reforms. The political leadership must also be prepared to provide an appropriate legal and regulatory framework to carry forward the reform and to appoint persons of proven integrity and ability to key positions; make adequate funds available to meet the projected costs over the entire reform period; establish regular monitoring to remove bottlenecks impeding reforms and to smooth the way forward; support the institutions, such as independent regulators, set up to further reforms; and facilitate law enforcement even when the offenders are politically influential.

Commitment of the senior utility managers to rooting out corruption is also critical for success. The quality and commitment of the managers empowered to implement strategies to combat corruption are strong indicators of political commitment. New managers may have to be brought in from outside the utility to initiate the reforms and introduce measures that encourage probity and actively discourage any infraction. Pressure from civil society and the international donor community can nudge utilities to reform. Initiatives by the utility need to be fully supported by government through a package of enabling laws, institutions, and executive actions.

Establishing Good Governance

An enabling legal and regulatory framework is a necessary but by no means sufficient condition for fostering accountability. Combating corruption calls for a range of actions that go far beyond the passing of laws or the pronouncement of policies. It requires establishment of good governance at all levels of society. Introducing good governance in electricity-related matters amounts to inculcating a new culture among the employees, the consumers, and the general public. Introduction of good governance will be resisted by all who have benefited by its absence. This includes, in varying degrees and on different issues, politicians, utility executives, utility employees, labor unions, and sections of the public. But that is only part of the problem. People in many parts of the developing world have traditionally conformed to the prevailing practices in their society governing the use of community resources such as river water or communal grazing lands. Electricity is a phenomenon of fairly recent origin to many of them, and the body of laws relating to electricity, itself an area of rapid growth and increasing complexity, has not been understood or accepted by them. Political parties often promise electricity free of charge (or at a nominal rate) and condone nonpayment. It takes time and persistent effort to reorient the attitudes and behavior of consumers, utility employees, and civil society who perceive electricity as a public good to be enjoyed free or at best by making a nominal payment.

Admittedly, creating a constituency for reform cannot be achieved overnight. Some countries may attempt to do so by using "shock therapy"—a sharp and wholesale change—while others may undertake a more gradual approach to building consensus. The choice of approach depends largely on the social and political context, the judgment of the reformers, and the commitment of the political and bureaucratic leadership.

Design and Implementation of an Anticorruption Strategy

Subject to the basic conditions described in the preceding paragraphs being satisfied, several important measures have been found to be effective in combating corruption. Because implementation of an anticorruption strategy may amount to a major cultural and attitudinal change in public governance and sector management, reformers may need to begin with a campaign to mobilize the support of the passive majority; deft political management of the process is required. Consultation, communication, and participation are critical elements of the strategy, as are perseverance, an adequately resourced plan, and timeliness—hence the need to sequence and prioritize the actions. Designing an anticorruption strategy and prioritizing and sequencing its implementation begins with a good-quality technical analysis of the problem (figure 4.1). The strategy should be informed by the judgment of opinion

FIGURE 4.1 A General Framework for the Implementation Process

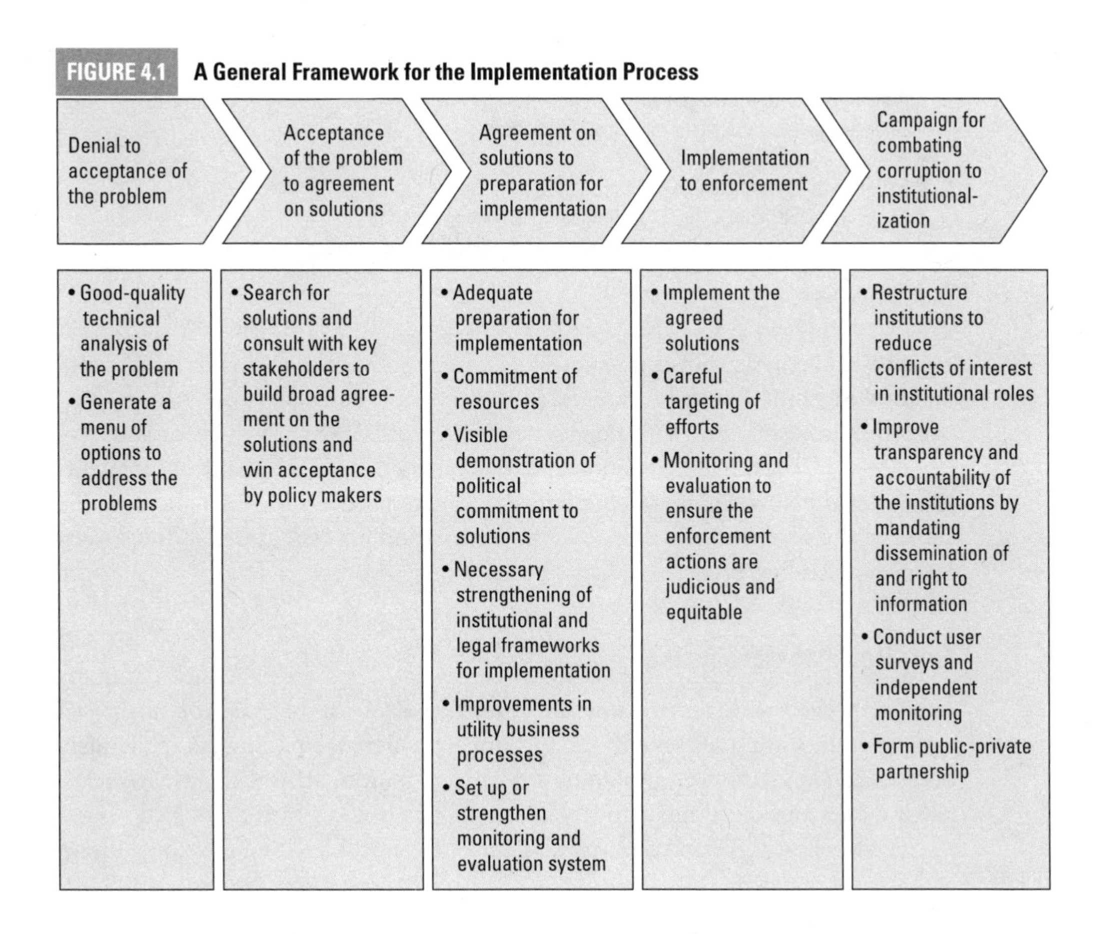

TABLE 4.6 Five Key Elements of an Anticorruption Strategy

1. **Move from denial to acceptance of the problem and build a broad agreement among policy makers and key stakeholders**
   - Undertake analytical and diagnostic work to identify the causes of the problem, its severity and effects, and the political cost of maintaining the status quo
   - Consult on the diagnosis to create an authorizing environment for implementation of the strategy
   - Disseminate diagnostic information without blaming the actors
   - Launch a communication campaign with strong and visible involvement of senior politicians
2. **Build a coalition**
   - Ensure buy-in by utility management and employees by addressing employee issues
   - Secure employee commitment to reforms
   - Improve customer service by establishing effective customer support centers
   - Reduce the political cost of reform through better-targeted, transparent, judicious, and equitable enforcement
   - Ensure that service improvements precede tariff adjustments
   - Engage in meaningful consultation with and participation of civil society
3. **Improve utility business processes**
   - Simplify and codify procedures
   - Introduce modern technology in selected areas
   - Foster efficiency and effectiveness of customer service and compliance with service standards
   - Make procurement transparent
4. **Strengthen institutional mechanisms for accountability**
   - Separate commercial from regulatory functions
   - Strengthen audit and internal integrity units
   - Prosecute offenders in courts and confiscate their illegal gains
5. **Encourage public participation**
   - Sponsor open discussions on all important matters
   - Institutionalize user surveys
   - Put in place a mechanism to redress public grievances
   - Implement an effective "right to information" program
   - Persuade client governments to adopt reforms suited to their countries

makers and analysts with deep knowledge of the political economy of the country and of the technical operations of the sector.

Any successful anticorruption strategy in the utility sector will encompass five key elements. These five elements are listed in table 4.6, and their major components are outlined below. Figure 4.2 presents a seven-step process for implementing the strategy, and annex 4A describes the implementation process, as well as the lessons learned, in Andhra Pradesh, India.

From Denial to Acceptance

Analytical work is necessary to counteract denial of the problem or misplaced assumptions about it, its severity, and its impact. Often, the problem is deliberately obfuscated to push for technical solutions (such as additional investments, new technology, and subsidized financing) that are politically convenient. It is critical that the key decision makers accept the existence of the problem and develop a broad

FIGURE 4.2 **A General Framework for Controlling Corruption in the Electricity Sector**

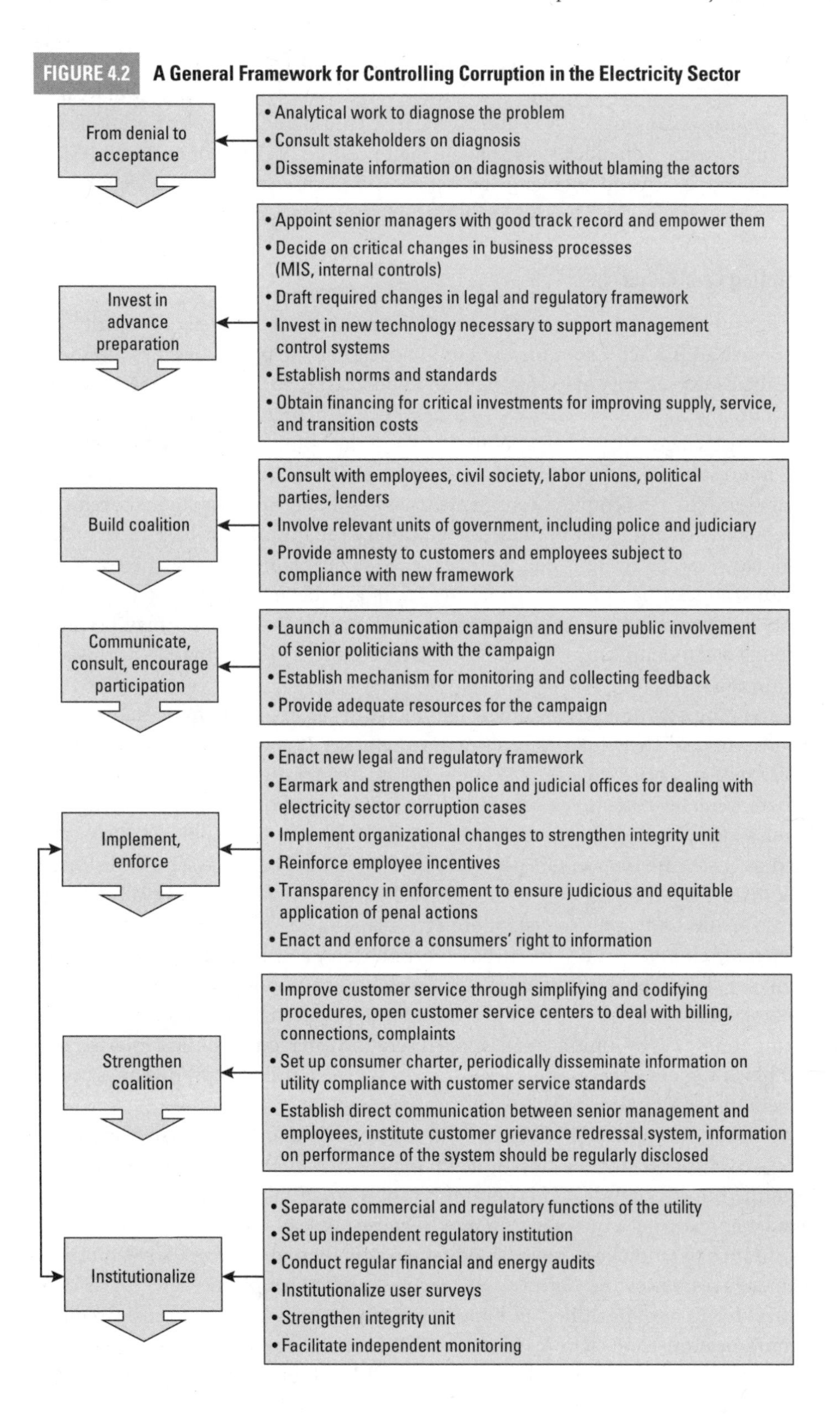

agreement on the diagnosis. Even if the existence of the corruption is common knowledge, lack of good-quality analytical work to buttress the strategy will weaken the "reform champions" when difficulties are encountered in implementation, and the "opponents" will quickly consolidate their position. It is also important to take a systemic approach and not blame the actors, who themselves may have been the victims of the system. An objective technical analysis helps depoliticize the strategy.

Building Coalitions

No reform is likely to succeed unless employee concerns about their job security and career are addressed. In countries that do not have a safety net for employees who lose their jobs, security of livelihood is all important. Reforms in many sectors have cut jobs, and if employees believe reform will cost them their jobs, they will firmly resist any change. A categorical assurance from the political executive that reforms will not result in the retrenchment of existing staff, together with provision of necessary funds to meet employee entitlements, is absolutely necessary to make reforms acceptable. An attractive package for voluntary separation can help in reducing staff. However, competent staff members need to be retained through better career options and compensation. Sometimes that can be managed by encouraging them to compete in the selection process for new managers who may be hired through a competitive process and by linking compensation to market norms and performance.

Creating a working environment conducive to career growth for employees can secure workers' continued commitment to reforms. It is wrong to assume that all utility staff are corrupt. Generally, one may find a small proportion of workers who are irredeemably corrupt, an equally small proportion who fight against corruption in the system, and a large majority who are indifferent to the problem or passively corrupt. These are the workers who have quietly acquiesced in a system of distorted incentives where corruption goes unpunished and is sometimes rewarded. An objective and participatory system of performance assessment, training programs to upgrade employee skills, merit-based promotions, and incentives linked to performance should be put in place. Penalties should be imposed for misdemeanors, especially those involving corruption and collusion. A transparent system for transferring employees by limiting managerial discretion can reduce political interference and block the emergence of a corrupt nexus between utility staff, dishonest consumers, and local politicians.

Direct communication between the top management and the staff is a very effective way of keeping the employees up to date on accurate information "straight from the horse's mouth." This communication could take the form of a regular newsletter featuring a message from the chief executive of the utility on a matter of importance to employees, queries and letters from employees together with management's responses and clarifications, requests seeking employee views on various matters relating to the utility, and updates about the progress of reforms. Credible communications and actions by management can help secure the support of a majority of the employees who may otherwise be ambivalent in the fight against corruption.

Improving Utility Business Processes

A first step in improving the business practices of utilities is to simplify the procedures. Many consumers are baffled by the prolixity and obscurity of the forms utility companies use. This puts them at the mercy of middlemen and the utility employees who may be tempted to collude with them. Lack of clarity in the procedures (for example, vagueness about what exactly the utility needs to provide a new service connection or repair a meter) often means the consumer must make repeated visits to the utility office and endure occasional harassment. Simplification of the forms and procedures would reduce these hassles, save employee time, and increase customer satisfaction.

Internal procedures should be codified and responsibilities specified. Internal operational policies, business procedures, and decision-making processes are seldom reviewed and updated and over time lose internal coherence. Further, lack of clarity opens procedures to abuse. Utilities should periodically review and update their procedures and inform the staff of the changes, giving them any additional training they might need to eliminate confusion and improve efficiency in implementation.

Utilities would benefit from the use of modern technology. A comprehensive database of consumers linked to a suitable MIS can improve efficiency and reduce fraud. Software such as the "customer analysis tool" can help track theft and nonpayment. Many utilities use remote metering, prepaid meters, spot billing, and remote control of substations. The costs involved in installing new technology are offset by improved efficiency throughout the utility. Payment of bills electronically and by check is gaining popularity among customers in developing countries. Utilities should encourage such practices, which will improve their cash flow and reduce the scope for corruption. Various technology-enabled features such as toll-free telephone numbers, Web sites, or SMS (short messaging service)-based applications can also be developed for better service delivery.

Utilities can also improve efficiency and stem corruption by outsourcing certain services. Outsourcing management functions has generally not been very successful in the sector, but many utilities have successfully used performance-based contracts to outsource services such as meter reading, bill preparation, and bill distribution. Greater flexibility in deployment, reduced costs, and greater discipline are among the features that make outsourcing attractive. Resistance by staff and unions can often undermine the effectiveness of such initiatives, but properly structured alternative delivery mechanisms can succeed, as demonstrated by franchisee operations in some rural areas in the Indian state of Orissa.[5]

Contracts, especially major contracts for purchase of equipment, fuel, or power, involve large amounts of money and are areas where corruption thrives. An effective anticorruption strategy must ensure that procurement processes are transparent. This is an area where technology can make a significant qualitative improvement.

The first priority should be the creation of a Web site where all information about the contracting principles and procedures of the utility, details of forthcoming contracts, and progress in the contracts already awarded are regularly shown and updated. Use of a Web site for such purposes has been found to be more transparent and more cost effective than other methods such as publicity through newspapers or notice boards.

The utility should have a clear set of contracting principles. Admittedly, these may vary from utility to utility and from time to time. While open competitive bidding should be the overarching criterion, some utilities, in response to state policy, may reserve contracts of certain types or magnitudes for "local" players, though all other contracts may be open to national or international competitive bidding. Multilateral aid agencies such as the World Bank favor international competitive bidding except for small contracts for which national bidding may be acceptable, but some bilateral donors may restrict the competition to the lending and receiving countries. Some utilities may empanel suppliers or vendors for specified periods for certain items of supplies or works. Some may have provision for blacklisting contractors or suppliers on the basis of poor performance. Many utilities resort to short-time tenders to meet emergency requirements. Prequalifying contractors for large or technically sophisticated works is quite common. So is the adoption of "two-part bidding" involving a technical and a financial bid. Some utilities may have a procedure for holding negotiations with the bidders under certain conditions. These are matters of policy that may vary widely across utilities and countries, but whatever they may be, they should be widely disseminated and easily accessible to anyone interested.

For each specific contract, the Web site should put out clear and unambiguous information on the prequalification criteria for taking part in that contract; the quantities, specifications, and milestones for completion of different phases of the work; any other information about the worksite such as access to the site, survey maps, soil, and topographical details; and a complete set of contract documents that will eliminate the need to visit the office of the utility. It is important that tender documents are available online and that online documents be treated the same as the documents collected manually from the utility.

Publication of all contract-related information on the Web site will provide a built-in safeguard against changing the rules of the game after the process has started. Adoption of the standards laid down by the relevant bureau of standards, third-party inspection of works and equipment before making payments, assistance from qualified consultants in the various stages of complex contracts, the provision of funds to complete the work within schedule, timely payments to contractors, and regular review of the works by senior management are a few other steps that can bring additional transparency to contract procedures.

Strengthening Institutional Mechanisms for Accountability

Several different steps can be taken to strengthen accountability.

Separation of Regulatory and Commercial Functions

To ensure fair play, the players must be separate from the umpires, but state-owned electricity utilities routinely violate this principle. Quite often, the utilities regulate the technical standards as well as competition to the utility, such as investment by consumers in self-generation. The government ministry responsible for the performance of the state-owned utility may also be responsible for regulating the sector. Separation of regulatory and commercial functions and ensuring independence and accountability of the regulatory institutions should be key elements of any anticorruption strategy.

Independent Regulatory Regime

Creation of an effective regulatory regime that is independent of the government calls for a major shift in the attitude of the governments that have always wielded a great deal of control over the entire sector either directly or through the utilities they own. The following list enumerates the important features of an independent regulatory regime.

- The regime should be established by law (not by executive decree), with the role of the regulators, the mode of their appointment, service conditions, powers, immunities, and responsibilities defined in law and implemented in a transparent manner.
- The regulatory budget should be independent, and funding should be secure.
- All regulatory procedures (on licensing, tariff setting, grievance redressal, and the like) should be well defined and widely publicized, and the scope of government intervention in regulatory processes should be clearly specified by law.
- All regulatory decisions should be thoroughly explained and made after a transparent and participative process that is open to all stakeholders. Decisions should be subject to appeal before an appellate forum.
- Decisions should be legally enforceable, and penalties should be set for noncompliance with regulatory orders.
- Information on the regulatory regime should be made available to civil society in an easy-to-understand format.
- The rights and obligations of the utility as well as those of the consumers should be clearly spelled out, given wide publicity, rigorously monitored, and firmly enforced.
- Regulatory decisions should be predictable and timely.
- Regulators should be held accountable for their actions, and mechanisms for appealing regulatory decisions should be established.

It needs to be emphasized that the creation of an independent regulatory regime by itself will not have any significant impact on corruption. Several other conditions need to be fulfilled before the regulator can be effective. For example, the government must choose the right persons as regulators, give them sufficient financial autonomy to do their work, and demonstrate a willingness to uphold regulatory decisions even when they are politically inconvenient.

Consumers' Charters

The right to information, enshrined in law and enforced through regulatory institutions, can help reduce opacity and abuse of discretionary powers by the utility. Citizens' charters, wherever they have been publicized and enforced, have helped improve governance. Such charters spell out the rights and responsibilities of consumers and confer on them the right to receive service of good quality from the utility. Such a document may specify the standards to be followed by the utility for various services, the fees chargeable, and the time frame for providing them. Regulatory bodies are usually empowered by law to penalize deviations from the specified norms. A well-informed and empowered public armed with the right to critically examine the working of a utility is a powerful safeguard against corruption.

Regular Financial Audits

Regular audits are a mandatory requirement of all utilities, whether government-owned or otherwise. Most utilities also have systems for both internal and external audit. Most poorly run utilities, however, give little importance to these audits and fail to take prompt follow-up action on the audit report. Utilities that have a corporate structure should have audit committees consisting of independent directors with the authority to investigate any activity of the utility and seek information from any employee. The audit committee should report to the board of directors, and action taken on the recommendations of the audit committee should be included in the agenda of the board meetings.

Norms and Standards

The remit of regulatory bodies should include establishing the technical standards for generation, transmission, and distribution; laying down the norms for operational efficiency of the utilities; and regularly reviewing the performance of the utilities. The commercial (efficiency) standards could specify the time taken by a utility to provide a new connection, rectify a defect, or replace a meter. The utilities may have to be allowed a transition period to reach the envisaged standards of performance. These standards, both technical and commercial, should be given due publicity to enable consumers to demand quality service from the utilities. These documents, which would provide an objective framework for assessing the performance of utilities, are an important means of establishing accountability.

Penalties for Offenders

Utility employees collude or assist in the theft of electric energy only at the behest of the consumer. The law should mandate punishment both for theft of energy and for connivance in such activities. To break free from the prevailing inertia in enforcement agencies, some governments have found it helpful to set up special police stations and fast-track courts to handle such cases. The recurring expenditure for such mechanisms is quite small and can be recovered through tariffs.[6]

Confiscation of Assets

Enacting and enforcing laws to confiscate the assets derived from corruption will send a powerful signal to would-be wrongdoers. It will also help the state recover resources that were plundered.

Regular Energy Audits

A business process that reconciles quantities of energy generated and sold with the money collected from consumers will reduce the scope for fudging and help fix responsibility on the staff at various levels. A four-step reconciliation of generation, billing, collection, and remittance to the treasury should be a standard management control system. Accurate and regular metering at the interfaces between generation and transmission and transmission and distribution and at consumers' premises is a precondition for such reconciliation. The cost of such metering (integrated with a fairly basic but effective MIS) will vary depending on many factors, but experience shows that the payback period for such investment is typically under two years. Estimation of losses by an independent auditor, contracted by the regulator and making all its reports public, can be used to set tariffs and benchmark the utility's performance, putting pressure on both the utility and the government to improve their accountability.

Institutionalize User Surveys

Public feedback obtained through surveys is a powerful tool to ensure public accountability. Results from user surveys give a very strong indication to the utility about the services rendered by them. Surveys may be conducted by the utilities themselves, consumer organizations, nongovernmental organizations, or regulatory agencies. The costs may vary depending on the sampling size, the questionnaire, and the survey method adopted (door-to-door or electronic). Utilities and regulators should institutionalize periodic user surveys.

Customer Grievance Redressal Mechanisms

All utilities should put in place effective customer grievance redressal mechanisms spelling out types of grievances, the forum competent to redress them, the time frame, and an appellate forum for deciding unresolved matters. Public confidence in the utility can be enhanced by displaying information on the complaints received, solved, and pending. With computerization, customers can track the status of their complaints and shift the onus of explaining the delays to the utility staff. It would also be useful to set up an ombudsman's office to settle complaints that cannot be resolved by the utility. Consumer courts can also be empowered to adjudicate disputes between consumers and utilities, although utility regulators may exercise jurisdiction over such forums under different legislation.

Integrity Units

An integrity unit (sometimes called an internal vigilance unit), set up by the utility, suitably staffed, and empowered to call for records or investigate utility officials, can provide an effective check to corruption. It should be headed by a senior functionary with a specified term, either from within the utility or brought in from outside. Care, however, should be taken to see that the integrity unit does not deteriorate into another source of corruption or an ineffective bureaucratic entity that stifles the managers and the employees.

Independent Monitoring

The performance of the utilities should be monitored regularly and the results given wide publicity for the benefit of the consumers and other stakeholders. The credibility of such monitoring will be enhanced if it is performed by the regulator or by a nonpartisan and expert body.

Encouraging Public Participation

Developing countries often fail to fully recognize or utilize the power of civil society to improve governance. Public participation in making and implementing decisions should be encouraged through forums like standing committees (which are required to be consulted on a wide variety of matters), ad hoc committees (which spontaneously come into being in the face of specific issues), public hearings conducted by regulatory bodies (on matters such as tariffs, licensing, investments, financing, large contracts, and performance reviews of utilities), "open houses," nongovernmental organizations, and panel discussions in the media. Use of the local language at these forums as well as in all documents meant for the information of the public (notices, performance standards, grievance redressal mechanisms, consumer rights statements) or to be used by the public (consumer bills, application forms, disconnection notices) will stimulate public participation and reduce the mischief value of middlemen.

An important benefit of public participation is that it can remove the disconnect between what the people want and what their representatives think they want. For example, given a choice between a free but erratic power supply, with burnt transformers, long power cuts, and uncertainty about the availability of water when it is needed most, and good quality power supplied at an affordable cost, most farmers prefer the latter. Giving consumers a real voice in policy making can reduce the clout of the "free power" lobbies that pretend to speak for them. Corruption is deeply rooted and pervasive, but it can be fought successfully through empowering consumers and civil society by providing them access to information and the opportunity to participate in policy formulation and decision making. Consumers and civil society organizations acting in tandem with select members of the utility staff can form a powerful and effective coalition against corruption.

Role of Donors and Multilateral Agencies

Power sector reforms in the past generally focused on matters such as industry and market structure, corporatization, and privatization. This approach overlooked the fact that many of the ills of the sector are the result of neglecting other dimensions of governance. There is now increasing realization that improvement in public and corporate governance should be an integral part (if not precede) the process of corporatization, commercialization, and privatization. With private sector interest in power utilities declining in developing countries, it is critical for the governments and the donor community to pay attention to improving governance and accountability of utilities.

Most of the steps for combating corruption outlined here can be implemented with a modest level of expenditure. However, in some cases, investments in infrastructure may be needed to improve the quality of supply and service to the consumers. Similarly, many of the institutional mechanisms (such as audits and vigilance) already exist. What is needed is a reduction in the political cost of reform through innovation and a phased approach to change; an increase in the political cost of the status quo through empowerment of consumers and civil society by increasing access to information; and financing of the transition costs so that cost recovery and efficiency improvement move in tandem.

Irrespective of the issues of ownership or corporate structure of electric utilities, the donor community has an important role to play in eliminating corruption by persuading client countries to enact laws, establish institutions, and adopt procedures that improve governance. For example, the steady and substantial support provided by the World Bank and the United Kingdom's Department for International Development to the government of Andhra Pradesh, India, and its electrical utilities played an important part in the success story there (see annex 4A). Patience, perseverance, and a sympathetic understanding of the local environment on the part of the donors can help reduce the politicization of implementing decisions. Donors should also devise strategies specific to the particular place and time, in consultation with the client government, and not rely on broad-spectrum strategies based on a model that worked in a different place and in a different socioeconomic environment.[7] In developing reform strategies, donors must also be mindful to act in ways that are consistent with the dignity of the client governments and their national pride.

Before launching a campaign for eradicating corruption it is important to analyze the interests of various stakeholders. One of the important dimensions is the time disconnect between the political costs and the benefits of such reforms—costs are incurred upfront while the benefits flow much later—for the politicians whose decision horizons are short term. In addition, the voice of beneficiaries is diffused while the vested interests act in a more concerted manner and capture the political space. Political economy issues cannot, need not, and should not be ignored.

In this chapter, we have attempted to identify the vulnerabilities and the beneficiaries of corruption and glean lessons from some successful examples of campaigns against corruption in the electricity sector. Plans need to be ready, and resources committed, for institutionalization of benefits of campaigns. We have also proposed certain methods for successfully fighting—if not eliminating—corruption. Much of what we have suggested is neither new nor particularly expensive or difficult to implement. But it is a timely reminder to all of us that instead of wringing our hands in despair, it is well within our power to fight and defeat corruption, provided we, the stakeholders, have the will to do it.

ANNEX 4A: TWO CASE STUDIES

Andhra Pradesh, India: Controlling Electricity Theft in Electricity Distribution Companies

Many developing countries confront widespread theft of electricity from government-owned power utilities (Bhatia and Gulati 2004). In India, electricity theft leads to annual losses estimated at $4.5 billion, about 1.5 percent of India's GDP. Who are the losers? Honest consumers, poor people, and those without powerful connections who bear the burden of high tariffs, system inefficiencies, and an inadequate and unreliable power supply.

What stops governments from eliminating electricity theft? Vested interests of such stakeholders as politicians, bureaucrats, labor unions, utility employees, and consumers. Because of political interference and weak accountability, state-owned utilities have little incentive to improve their performance. Privatization could be a solution, but high political risk, low cost recovery through tariffs, and large-scale theft make the power distribution business in developing countries unattractive to the private sector.

Can utilities improve efficiency even under government ownership? Yes, as shown by the example of Andhra Pradesh, where state-owned power companies reduced theft and losses.

The Context

The Andhra Pradesh State Electricity Board, a government-owned, vertically integrated power utility serving about 12 million customers, suffered large and growing financial losses in the 1990s, amounting to Rs 40 billion ($0.9 million) by 1997. The utility's operational and financial performance deteriorated, adversely affecting the power supply. Power subsidies grew to 1.6 percent of state GDP, while public spending on health and education fell from 4.7 percent of state GDP in 1987 to 3.6 percent in 1998.

In 1998, the government of Andhra Pradesh initiated a comprehensive reform in the power sector—a phased program to establish a new legal, regulatory, and institutional framework; develop a new industry and market structure; and privatize distribution. So far, Andhra Pradesh has enacted an electricity reform law; unbundled the utility into one generation, one transmission, and four distribution and supply companies; and established an independent regulatory commission responsible for licensing, setting tariffs, and promoting efficiency and competition.

The new distribution utilities inherited a weak system of energy accounting—and rampant electricity theft—that, together with revenue leaks and other factors, undermined financial performance. In fiscal 1999, only 42 percent of the electricity flowing into the distribution system was billed on the basis of metered consumption. The balance was counted as consumption by about 2 million unmetered agricultural customers or as transmission and distribution losses. The unverifiable estimates of sales and losses allowed the utilities to camouflage inefficiency and theft and thus to deflect public scrutiny of their poor performance, hide political and bureaucratic corruption, and obscure the public debate about agricultural subsidies. The theft occurred in several ways, including tapping power lines and tampering with or bypassing meters, often with the connivance of utility staff. Revenue leaks resulted from weaknesses in metering, billing, and collection; in internal control systems; and in enforcement of the disconnection policy.

The first step to reform was to move beyond denial and accept the existence of theft. An energy audit program led to more realistic estimates of transmission and distribution losses (at 38 percent in fiscal 1999, up from an earlier estimate of 18 percent) and recognition of "nontechnical losses"—a euphemism for electricity theft. Public expectations of the reform program, and regulatory reviews that increased accountability, brought the theft and losses under sharper public scrutiny. In January 2000, the government launched a major campaign to control theft.

The Plan

The plan focused on four measures: enacting a new law to address electricity theft, strengthening enforcement mechanisms, reorganizing the anticorruption function in the utilities, and reengineering business processes to improve management control and customer service.

In July 2000, the state government amended the Indian Electricity Act of 1910 to make electricity theft a cognizable offense and impose stringent penalties. A separate law, unprecedented in India, provided for mandatory imprisonment and penalties for offenders, allowed the convening of special courts and tribunals for speedy trial, and recognized collusion by utility staff as a criminal offense.

Advance preparations ensured that the government was able to set up special courts and appellate tribunals as soon as the new law came into force. The utility service areas were divided into 24 "circles" coinciding with the state's 24 administrative districts. A special court and police station were established for each circle to ensure rapid detection and prosecution of electricity theft. And the state police and anticorruption units of other government departments were directed to support utility employees in inspections to control theft.

The government also initiated institutional changes in the utilities. The anticorruption department for the transmission and distribution operations was strengthened by promoting its head from an advisory position to an executive position on the board and by modifying the organizational structure to strengthen the department's coordination with other departments. In addition, the anticorruption department's procedures were simplified and made transparent. Inspecting officers were required to provide an inspection report with an identification number to customers on the spot and carry numbered receipts so that they can accept payments of fines. Police stations will have to provide public notification of all theft cases, and a new tracking system would follow the progress from inspection to payment of fine or prosecution. More than 2,000 inspection teams were deployed throughout the state to launch the theft control drive.

To reengineer business processes, a new management control system, the "customer analysis tool," was developed. The system uses a centralized customer database to analyze metering, billing, and collection performance—allowing monitoring of actual staff performance against collection targets—and generates focused management reports useful for initiating corrective action. The substantially faster processing for analyzing data and generating reports allows quick action.

A key capability is the generation of risk profiles of customers based on their payment history, enabling utility staff to prioritize and target nonpayers. While the past practice was to inspect entire neighborhoods to detect a few thieves, the new system helps target inspections to defaulting customers and high-loss service areas. The paradigm shift from "inspect and detect" to "detect and inspect" has significantly increased the detection of irregularities. Most important, it has reduced the alienation of honest customers, who no longer have to suffer the indignity of police raids and neighborhood searches.

Consulting with Stakeholders

The government launched a communication program through media ads, posters, and videos, and a public outreach program through visits by special teams and regular public meetings with utility managers. The outreach campaign deployed about

600 teams to conduct town hall meetings in all settlements with more than 200 residents. The teams informed people about the proposed new law and the penalties for electricity theft and gave everyone the opportunity to obtain an authorized connection on the spot after paying a connection fee. They also explained the utilities' deteriorating financial situation and the effect of electricity theft on their costs and tariffs.

In addition, teams held consultations with the labor unions about the proposed legal provisions for making collusion by utility staff a criminal offense. Assurance that old cases would be excluded under the new law helped secure the unions' consent to punitive action against staff caught colluding in theft in the future. The credibility of the communications, and the government's political resolve to combat theft were tested when some politically powerful people (including a member of the legislature) were charged with electricity theft. The cases went forward, and the proof that even the most powerful were subject to the new law, and that utility officials would be protected from government and political interference, generated broad support for the program among the public as well as utility employees.

Providing Adequate Resources

Adequate funds were provided for advertising, holding public meetings, purchasing high-quality meters and remote meter reading instruments, and adopting advanced communications technology—all of which helped to sustain the momentum and credibility of the change.

More than 2 million high-quality meters for energy customers were installed in two years, compared with a past average of 600,000 a year. High-accuracy meters were installed for high-value customers, and the old meters recalibrated and installed for low-value customers. To support energy auditing, electronic meters with data-logging devices and facilities for transmitting the data through a satellite communications system were installed on all 11-kilovolt distribution feeders. While agricultural customers remain unmetered for sociopolitical reasons, meters were installed on the transformers serving mainly these customers to allow better estimation of sales to agriculture.

Setting Priorities

In the initial phase, the theft control program focused on high-value customers. Dedicated feeders were constructed to supply large industrial customers, which were also provided with high-quality, tamper-proof electronic meters. Protective boxes were installed on transformers. Meter-reading instruments were provided to inspection teams to download monthly data, allowing analysis to identify customers whose monthly consumption varied by more than 2 percent. Irregularities in metering and billing were found for about 15 percent of the 23,000 industrial connections—and 10 percent of the 36,000 commercial connections—inspected in fiscal 2001. For residential customers, inspections focused on 11-kilovolt feeders with high line losses and on 114 towns accounting for 53 percent of consumption and 60 percent of revenue.

Building a Constituency for Change

The campaign also gave high priority to connection delays and poor customer service—two major reasons for customer dissatisfaction. Utilities introduced a spot billing system to allow meter reading in the presence of customers and thus minimize billing complaints, established a special cell in each operation circle to authorize new connections and address customer complaints, and opened collection centers at convenient locations (mobile collection centers were made available in rural areas). Utilities also set up computerized customer care centers serving as one-stop windows for handling complaints, receiving payments, and following up on electricity supply problems.

Monitoring Results

The campaign was closely monitored, including at the highest level of the government. All district offices were linked to headquarters through a satellite network for quick transfer of data, and district administrators and engineers submitted daily reports on the number of connections regularized and the amount of fees collected. The information system developed to monitor the campaign was improved and integrated into the management control systems of the companies and continues to be used for monitoring.

The Results

The campaign has made a big difference in the utilities' bottom line. Monthly billing has increased substantially, and the collection rate has reached more than 98 percent. Transmission and distribution losses were reduced from around 38 percent in 1999 to 26 percent in 2003, in large part through theft control, with the utilities regularizing 2.25 million unauthorized connections. Moreover, enforcement of the new antitheft law has proved effective. Disciplinary action has been taken against 218 employees, and criminal cases were launched against 87 employees allegedly involved in stealing electricity and misappropriating funds and materials. In the first three years after the law's enactment, the authorities pursued more than 150,000 cases of electricity theft, compared with 9,200 in the previous 10 years, and arrested more than 2,000 defaulting customers.

In an environment of limited commercialization, deeply entrenched vested interests, and politicized operations and management in the power sector, Andhra Pradesh's efforts to control electricity theft are impressive. The program, now in its fourth year, has sustained the improvements. Whether the program will remain immune to political interference has yet to be seen; there is always a risk that populist electoral politics will undermine governance and accountability. But the program includes actions that, together with strong political commitment, are key to sustaining any such initiative:

- Creating a constituency for change through effective communication with key stakeholders and building confidence in the government's assurances by following up the communication with appropriate actions.
- Modifying the legal framework and enforcement mechanisms to remove legal impediments and empower enforcement authorities.
- Ensuring that punitive actions are seen as judicious and equitable, and giving those with illegal connections a chance to become lawful customers.

- Institutionalizing new business processes by adopting modern technology, improving management information systems, and introducing new management control systems.
- Changing the incentives of managers and staff by punishing collusion and poor performance.

Bangladesh: A Participatory Approach

The Bangladesh Rural Electricity Board (REB) started its operation in January 1978. The REB electrifies rural areas through *Palli Bidyut Samitis* (PBSs), which are independent users' associations. By 2002, the REB and 67 PBSs had jointly established 96,000 kilometers of distribution lines, set up 165 substations, and supplied power to an estimated 22 million rural residents. The rural electrification project was supported from the beginning by technical assistance from the National Rural Electrification Cooperative Association in the United States, along with soft loans from the U.S. Agency for International Development (Nexant 2000). The project has also received sponsorship from 15 international donors that contributed more than $1.1 billion through 2002.

Each PBS is a cooperative organization managed by its participants and beneficiaries. It has a board of directors consisting of 12 to 15 members elected by the entire membership of the PBS. Directors have a three-year term with one-third retiring every year. The president of the association is elected for a term of one year. Directors must meet stringent qualification criteria: they must be between the ages of 30 and 70, should have completed secondary school at a minimum, should not be an office bearer of any political party, should never have been convicted for any criminal offence, should be a permanent resident of the PBS area, and must have paid all electricity bills. Voting rights are confined to nondefaulting members. PBS employees are prohibited by law from unionizing. Many employees, including all meter readers, are appointed on contract. The meter readers are frequently rotated to prevent them from developing relationships with the consumers and can serve in one or more PBSs provided that the total period as meter reader does not exceed three years. Those who perform well during this period can look forward to being absorbed in other jobs like lineman, supervisor, and electrician.

The REB keeps a strict watch over all the activities of PBSs. The management process could be called "martial," and the head of the REB has generally been drawn from the Army. The REB must approve each PBS budget, and the annual Performance Target Agreement between the REB and the PBS is rigorously enforced. Boards of directors and the general manager of the PBS can be dismissed by the REB for nonperformance or gross misdemeanors. Targets are based on 20 parameters covering areas like reduction of system losses, improving on accounts receivable, and increasing the number of connections. If the targets are not met, the PBS can be penalized with salary reductions; if targets are met, bonuses are awarded to all the PBS employees.

Even though a PBS is established in a village, not all households in the village are supplied with electric power. In Bangladesh, only 15 percent of all households have power supply on average. Electrification of every household is not an objective of the REB. All new PBS service areas must satisfy revenue requirement standards. Some communities may remain unelectrified for several years until population and the associated potential for productive use of load grow to the point where they will qualify to be included in the PBS system. Customers must be prepared to spend the equivalent of $6 or $7 as an initial investment on lead-in wires and interior wiring. Only households that can afford such initial cost and a monthly electricity bill can become PBS members.

Under the PBS system, several members form a community group within a cooperative. If a member in the group taps electricity illegally, all the group members must pay for the cost. This means that an entire group is subject to a penalty if they cannot prevent stealing of electricity. This method of dealing with power theft brings to bear enormous peer pressure on potential power thieves. Any member who defaults on payment is removed from the association, and his meters are taken away. The transmission and distribution losses in PBS areas are about 10–12 percent, which is half of the loss in other areas of the country. The PBS average tariff collection is also much higher, at about 95 percent.

The REB purchases power in bulk from the Bangladesh Power Development Board at a negotiated price, which is far below the board's price to industrial consumers. The tariff for each PBS is set by the REB in an attempt to balance the perceived ability of PBS customers to pay for electric service and the need for the program to sustain itself economically. The PBS tariff is about 40–60 percent higher than normal average tariffs charged in urban areas. Even so, only about 18 out of 54 PBSs that are fully operational have achieved financial viability. The REB has its own training facilities and provides extensive training for PBS staff. The PBS also has staff training facilities as well as a special division for member education and for informing beneficiaries of the rights and obligations of cooperative members.

The success of PBSs in the rural areas prompted the Bangladeshi government to attempt bringing some of the urban areas under the PBS scheme. The REB took over six urban areas, but the success of PBSs in these areas was initially patchy. Although losses were reduced from 56 percent to 18 percent in three years in one of the areas (Narasingdi), in another area (Manikganj), resistance from consumers and staff initially stood in the way of much improvement. By 2006, however, the losses in Manikganj were brought down to 10 percent and were reduced to about 13 percent in the other five areas.

By the middle of 2006, the REB had succeeded in establishing all 70 PBSs that it had originally planned to set up in the country. The consumer strength in the rural areas has grown to about 29 million (of which over 80 percent are domestic consumers) with corresponding expansion of the delivery system. The chief executive of the REB is no longer drawn from the armed forces, but comes from the civil service. To deal with the increasing size and complexity of its operations, the REB designed a system to give greater autonomy to financially strong PBSs in the areas of budget, procurement, and recruitment of staff. In July 2006, three PBSs were given such autonomy. If the experiment succeeds, the REB's role in relation to such autonomous PBSs would be limited to monitoring their performance, leaving it free to concentrate on nurturing and strengthening the weaker PBSs.

While the average losses in the 70 PBSs were still only about 13 percent in 2006 (with a collection efficiency of 98 percent), there were indications of greater political interference in the decision-making process of the PBSs. The REB is less "martial" in its approach, but compared with other organizations in the country, it still has a better esprit de corps, which it tries to keep going in a difficult environment.

ANNEX 4B: CALIFORNIA POWER CRISIS: CORPORATE FRAUD AND REGULATORY FAILURE?

To develop a competitive electricity market, and to respond to energy problems in 1995, California initiated restructuring of its electricity industry. The aim was to convert California's investor-owned, regulated utilities into a deregulated market in which the price of electricity would be established by competition, and consumers could select their electrical power suppliers. A transition period was allowed for divestment of generation plants by the investor-owned utilities, recovery of stranded costs, and establishment of an auction market (California Power Exchange, or CalPX) in 1998 and The California Independent System Operator (Cal-ISO), which was authorized to procure "imbalance energy" to balance the grid as well as operating reserves (also called "ancillary services"). The utilities were required to buy most of their power through CalPX, at prices paid by CalPX even though retail tariffs were capped. By 2000, the market design started to unravel, and the states was hit with rolling blackouts.

Under the new structure, over 80 percent of the transactions were being made in the spot market (CalPX), and energy sellers quickly realized that the spot market could be manipulated by withholding power from the market to create scarcity and demanding high prices to meet the created scarcity. Traders engaged in anomalous bidding practices, including "hockey-stick bidding," in which an extremely high price is demanded for a small portion of the market, and "round-trip trades," in which an entity artificially creates the appearance of increased revenue and demand through continuous sales and purchases.

One of the major traders, Enron Corporation, allegedly gamed the California market with impunity, using manipulative corporate strategies with nicknames like "FatBoy," "Get Shorty," and "Death Star." Under the "Death Star" strategy, Enron allegedly sought payment for moving energy to relieve congestion without actually moving any energy or relieving any congestion. All of the demand was allegedly created artificially, giving the appearance of congestion, and then satisfied artificially, without the company providing any energy. "FatBoy" refers to a strategy through which Enron allegedly withheld previously agreed-to deliveries of power to the forward market so that it could sell the energy at a higher price on the spot market. The company would overschedule its load, supply only enough power to cover the inflated schedule, and thus leave extra supply in the market, for which Cal-ISO would pay the company spot prices. Using the "Get Shorty" strategy, traders allegedly were able to fabricate and sell operating reserves to Cal-ISO, receive payment, then cancel the schedules and cover their commitments by purchasing through a cheaper market closer to the time of delivery.[8]

On June 19, 2001, the Federal Energy Regulatory Commission (FERC) reaffirmed that the electric market structure and the rules for wholesale sales of electric energy in California were seriously flawed and imposed price caps on all spot market sales from June 20, 2001, through September 30, 2002, and took steps to prevent power generators from withholding supply. The prospective price mitigation plan applied to all sellers that voluntarily sold power into the Cal-ISO and other designated spot markets or that voluntarily used Cal-ISO's or other interstate transmission facilities subject to FERC jurisdiction. These moves brought the rolling blackouts, catastrophically high prices, and near-continuous power emergencies under control.

The California power crisis of 2000–01 is a powerful example of market manipulation and possible fraud in a highly developed economy with sophisticated sector governance. While the causes of that crisis are complex, a good part of the blame is likely to fall on prominent players in the power sector that indulged in market manipulation in violation of the relevant laws and that deliberately caused shortages so as to benefit from the sale of power at very high market prices.

ENDNOTES

1. For example, in India, the annual reports on the performance of SEBs, published by the Planning Commission, routinely showed that "transmission and distribution losses" (or T&D losses) in the SEBs were in the range of 21–25 percent. The reports make no mention of "commercial losses," which are largely the result of theft and corruption. Even the SEB audit reports prepared by the independent office of the Comptroller and Auditor General of India, while commenting on the T&D losses, seldom report commercial losses, except in footnotes.
2. The buyer is required to pay for the entire output of the plant computed at a very high plant load factor irrespective of the real need or the capacity of the transmission lines to evacuate the power. In case of a shortfall in the power drawn, the generator gets "deemed generation charges."
3. The Energy Financing Team Ltd., a United Kingdom–based electricity trading company active across the Balkans, faced allegations that it engaged in corrupt practices in power projects in Bosnia, Montenegro, and Serbia. See Leigh and Evans (2005).
4. In the 1990s, New York City successfully used an approach called "take back the streets" to fight street crime. This strategy was based on the premise that letting petty criminals get away establishes a norm of "anything goes" in the society and creates a perception that governance has broken down.
5. The distribution companies in Orissa, India, have entered into agreements with franchisees for rendering specific consumer-related services in many places within their license area. So far, these arrangements have been limited to serving rural consumers. The franchisee, usually a local person, functions as the executive officer of a local committee of electricity users. The lineman in charge of the area is also an ex officio member of the committee. The franchisee functions as the single contact point between the utility and the consumers of the village and facilitates activities such as providing new connections, repairing and replacing meters, collection of dues, and disconnecting nonpayers with the help of the village committee. Franchisee remuneration consists of a fixed component to meet minimum expenses and a variable component linked to performance. The

experience so far has been encouraging, with steep reductions in demand, reduced costs, improved billing and collection, better voltage, reduced theft, and improved customer satisfaction. But most important of all, the franchisee movement has been welcomed by the users and even by the utility employees who are suspicious of privatization.

6. In Orissa, the recurring cost of setting up 27 energy police stations and 8 special courts was an estimated Rs 80 million ($1.8 million), accounting for 0.3 percent of the utility's annual billing of Rs 22 billion ($480 million).
7. One example of a specific strategy evolved to counter a specific threat was a covenant in a World Bank loan for the Orissa Power Sector Reform Project that saved Orissa utilities from entering into agreements with IPPs under political pressure. Many IPPs sought to enter the Indian market through these agreements rather than through competitive bidding. The loan covenant essentially made that route unpalatable for the IPPs.
8. United States Court of Appeals for the Ninth Circuit, June 17, 2006 (2006 U.S. App. LEXIS 19476).

REFERENCES

Albouy, Yves, and Reda Bousby. 1998. "The Impact of IPPs in Developing Countries: Out of the Crisis and into the Future." Public Policy for the Private Sector Note 162, World Bank, Washington, DC (December).

Bayliss, Kate, and David Hall. 2000. "Independent Power Producers: A Review of the Issues." Public Services International Research Unit, University of Greenwich, United Kingdom (November).

Bhatia, Bhavna, and Mohinder Gulati. 2004. "Reforming the Power Sector." Viewpoint Note 272, Public Policy for Private Sector, World Bank, Washington, DC (September).

Energy Review Committee, chaired by Dr. Madhave Godbole. 2001. "Report of the Energy Review Committee, Government of Maharashtra, India" Mumbai (April).

Gulati, Mohinder, Bhavna Bhatia, and Joseph D. Wright. 2003. "Developing a Diagnostic Toolkit for Institutional and Governance Review of the Power Sector." World Bank, Washington, DC (October).

Klitgaard, Robert. 1988. *Controlling Corruption*. Berkeley, CA: University of California Press.

Komives, Kristin, Vivien Foster, Jonathan Halpern, and Quentin Wodon with support from Roohi Abdullah. 2005. "Water, Electricity and the Poor: Who Benefits from Utility Subsidies?" Energy and Water Department, World Bank, Washington, DC.

Leigh, David and Rob Evans. "Fraud Office Looks into British Energy Firm's Role in Balkans," *The Guardian*, February 15, 2005. http://www.guardian.co.uk/uk_news/story/0,,1414765,00.html.

Lovei, Laszlo, and Alastair McKechnie. 2000. "The Costs of Corruption for the Poor, Energy Sector." Viewpoint Note 207, Public Policy for Private Sector, World Bank, Washington, DC (April).

Nexant. 2000. "Rural Energy Services, Best Practices." Paper prepared for the U.S. Agency for International Development and SARI Energy, San Francisco, CA (May).

OERC (Orissa Electricity Regulatory Commission). 2005. "Review of the Utilities for the Year 2004–2005." Bhubaneshwar, Orissa, India.

Tremolet, Sophie. 2002. "Can Private Multi-Utilities Help Expand Service to Rural Areas?" Viewpoint Note 248, Public Policy for the Private Sector, World Bank, Washington, DC (June).

Transparency International. 2002. "Corruption in South Asia." Transparency International, Berlin.

Transparency International and ORG-MARG Research Private Ltd. 2002. *Corruption in India: An Empirical Study.* New Delhi.

Transparency International, India Chapter. 2005a. *Corruption in Electricity.* New Delhi.

———. 2005b. *India Corruption Study, 2005.* New Delhi.

———. 2005c. *State Report, Kerala.* New Delhi.

UNDP (United Nations Development Programme). 2005. *Human Development Report 2005.* Geneva: United Nations.

World Bank. 2001. "India. Power Supply to Agriculture." Energy Sector Unit, South Asia Regional Office, World Bank, Washington, DC (June).

5

Making Inroads on Corruption in the Transport Sector through Control and Prevention

WILLIAM D. O. PATERSON AND PINKI CHAUDHURI

"Roads connect food, goods, markets, people, families, communities, and lives. They connect politicians, civil servants, the police and the military, the judiciary, and governments. But roads can lead from heaven to hell, as the ugly heads of greed and envy often seize the material opportunities for graft and corruption in the development, maintenance, and operations of roads."

Manolito Madrasto, Former Secretary General,
International Federation of Asian and Western Pacific
Contractors' Associations (IFAWPCA)

The financial rationale for combating corruption in transport infrastructure is very strong. Budgets are large, often making up 10–20 percent of a country's national budget. The road subsector alone may constitute the majority of a developing country's annual infrastructure budget. Additionally, the large numbers of tangible goods and services in the transport sector—such as permits and contracts with multiple points of entry at central and local levels—lend themselves to corruption. The prevalence and style of corruption varies considerably between countries and agencies. Leakage from corruption may be as low as 5 percent but can often amount to 20 percent of transaction costs in corrupt countries or even more in some instances. Similar levels of wastage are possible through inefficiency and ineffective resource use, so collectively strengthening governance and capacity in the transport sector could potentially save 10–40 percent of sector expenditures.

Beyond the direct costs of resource leakage, corruption frequently diverts funds to projects with lower economic rates of return. Corrupted construction is often substandard, reducing project sustainability and increasing the need for maintenance and rehabilitation. Transport infrastructure is fixed and subject to considerable local influence on land use and social and economic development, so not only are the opportunities for extracting rent potentially high but the impacts are also significant and long term. These economic losses may be as large or larger than the direct financial costs of corruption. Furthermore, significant institutional costs are often associated with corruption. Corruption is rarely, if ever, limited to one sector, and the effects of corrupt practices in the transport sector are likely to spill over to other sectors and the broader economy. Thus, there is a broad rationale for combating corruption to ensure institutional integrity and sustainability within and across sectors.

Despite the considerable financial, economic, and institutional costs of corruption, within government departments the capacity for due diligence in combating corruption is often low. In the engineering profession, which constitutes a major part of transport infrastructure spending, rigorous systems of checks and balances exist regarding the roles of owner, supervisor, and supplier; contract provisions; regimes for testing and certifying quality; measuring and payment for quantities; and obligations and sanctions. Many of these systems have legal status, but where they are weakly applied or individuals conspire, corruption may emerge. Even within international financial institutions and donor agencies, institutional integrity and anticorruption practice areas remain nascent. At the same time, the transport sector has substantial potential for stemming corrupt practices where they may exist.

This chapter explains the risks and forms of corruption throughout the value chain of public expenditures for transport infrastructure and services, offers tools for identifying fraud and corruption as well as remedies, and develops strategic management mechanisms to combat corruption in the transport sector. The focus of this chapter is thus geared to strengthening integrity in the transport sector and, toward that goal, to helping establish operational practices for institutional strengthening and anticorruption work in the sector. The first section reviews the political and transactional anatomy of corruption by mapping key risk areas in the transport sector that are vulnerable to corruption at the national, sector, and project levels. The second section analyzes remedial options in a twin-pronged strategy—first with a focus on short-term controls, investigation, fraud detection, sanctions, and their enforcement in the transport sector; and second, through a longer-term preventive approach that aims to build internal controls and capacity in ways appropriate to local conditions and the prevailing modes of corruption.

WHAT CORRUPTION LOOKS LIKE IN THE TRANSPORT SECTOR

The working definition of corruption adopted by the World Bank Group is "the abuse of public funds and/or office for private or political gain." Corrupt practices in the transport sector thrive in an environment of weak institutions, but not all such instances result in corrupt activity. For instance, during budget preparation, agencies may inflate their needs, distort priorities, or identify and cost programs and projects inaccurately—all of which lead to inefficiency but not necessarily to corrupt practices (for a discussion on the legal status of a variety of seemingly suspicious acts, see Søreide 2005). Thus, it is important to distinguish between corruption—intent and action to abuse public office for private gain—and a range of institutional weaknesses that result in waste and inefficiency (that may also provide opportunities if not incentives for rent-seeking behavior and policy bias). This chapter maintains this distinction throughout as the connection is very tight between poor governance, process weaknesses and abuses, state capture, and project-specific administrative corruption. In tackling corruption, this distinction becomes important, because the response may differ somewhat depending on whether the source of the problem is incompetence or corruption. Enforcement-oriented remedies can only tackle downstream effects, and thus a broader sector integrity approach is needed for long-term and upstream impact on both corruption and incompetence.

Typology of Governance Failure and Corruption in the Transport Sector

The governance-corruption spectrum in the road sector illustrates the close nexus between state capture at the national and sectoral levels, a range of governance failures at the agency and department levels, and administrative corruption at the project level. Governance failure is the broadest level of analysis and action, covering all corrupt activities as well as noncorrupt but inefficient processes and systems. State capture involves the manipulation of rules, laws, policies, and public entities other than for their intended purposes for private or political gain. A subset of corruption, state capture is often associated with grand corruption because it involves the wholesale distortion or exploitation of public entities, elections, or broad government functions such as national budgetary processes. Administrative corruption involves the abuse of public office or funds for private gain through the manipulation of specific transactions. This kind of behavior, which involves bribes, kickbacks, and the like, is what has traditionally been considered to be corrupt behavior.

Broadly speaking, in the transport sector, governance failures at the country and sector levels relate to arbitrariness in decision making, to discretion in the spending of public funds, and in some cases, to poorly defined original mandates. At the agency level, the governance failures in the road sector tend to stem from the absence of appropriate business processes and mechanisms that can increase efficiency and reduce discretion. These mechanisms include information technologies as well as automated planning and financial tools and applications that replace individual discretion with objective and automated criteria for decision making, thereby making it much harder for unintended or corrupt purposes to prevail, and if attempted, making corrupt acts much easier to detect. Figure 5.1 depicts the levels of governance failures and corrupt activity and some of the typical indicators of both.

A bare-bones typology of corruption in the transport sector would thus comprise:

- State capture often involving grand corruption at the country and sector levels, a high level of political discretion over transport expenditures, poorly defined entities and structures, and subversion of public entities and resources other than for their intended purposes. Grand corruption also includes capture of the legislative process of transport policy making through aggressive lobbying processes that can often involve various forms of corruption, including illicit quid pro quo favors, kickbacks, and outright bribery.
- Administrative corruption refers to capture of the government's supply and demand chain for goods and services that are intended for public/taxpayer benefit but are diverted by government officials. In transport, this includes pilferage of materials and equipment; manipulation of contracts for works, goods, or services; or award of concessions for private sector operation of rail, port, air, or road facilities and services.

Corruption in the transport sector involves a variety of strategic behaviors from improper influence in budgeting and the choice of projects at the level of state

FIGURE 5.1 State Capture versus Administrative Corruption in the Road Sector

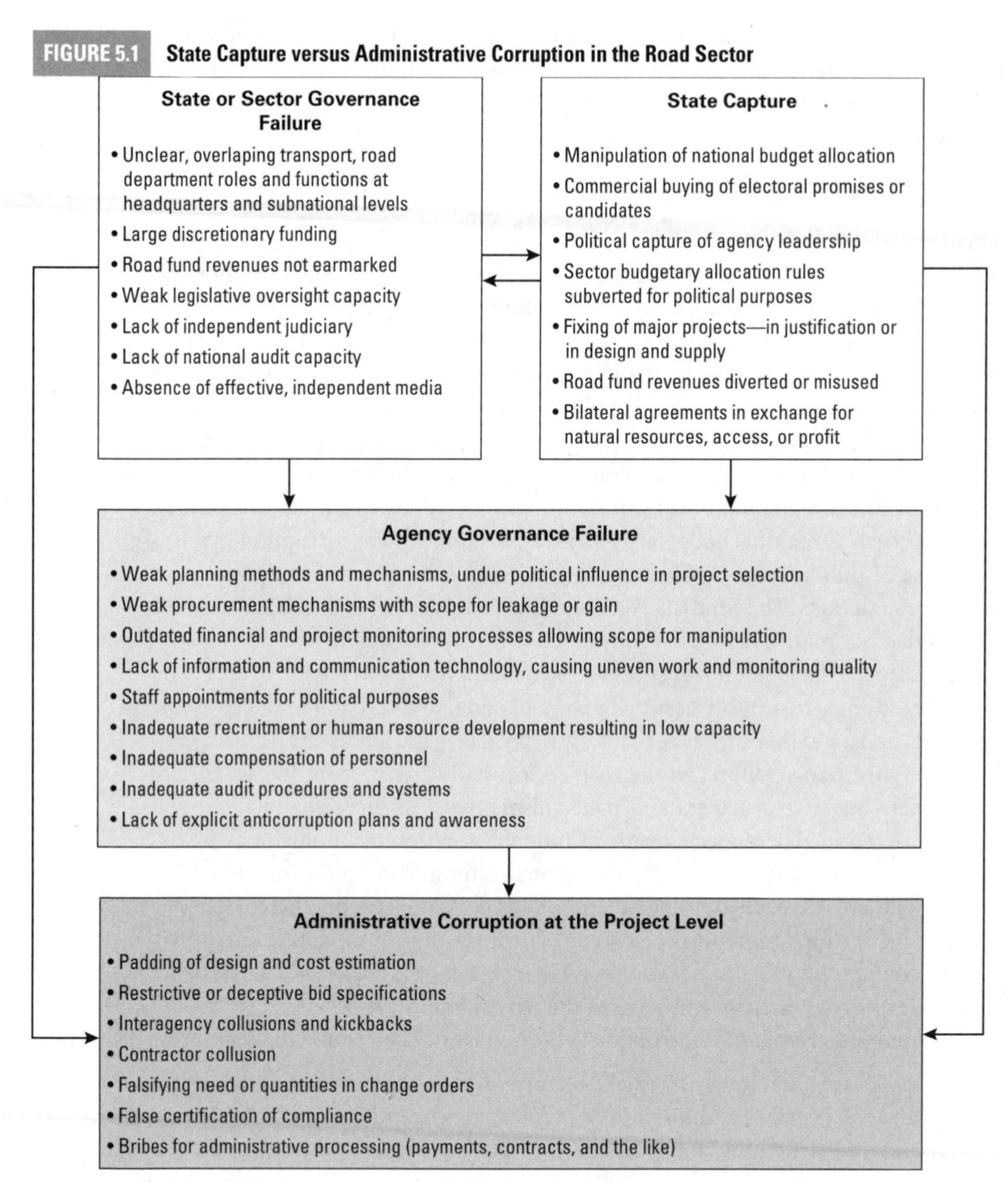

Source: Authors.

capture to a range of activities to extract rent, or "something of value," in return for a public good such as a carriage permit, a construction contract, or a concession or lease (table 5.1 lists such activities, along with operational definitions). Public officials at all levels may be involved, from ministers to clerks. Administrative corruption almost always involves an explicit transaction, whereas the transaction in state capture may be indirect, as for example, in cases where ministers choose policies that will benefit firms in which they have an interest. Even in the case of administrative corruption, the kickback may be remote from the administrative decision—a beneficiary firm might pay for the education or other benefits for a member of the

TABLE 5.1 Types of Corrupt Activity Prevalent in the Transport Sector

Corrupt activity	*Definitions and examples*
Bribe	Payment to a government official for any type of favor. Bribes are paid by firms to be "short listed" or prequalified, to win contracts, to approve contract amendments and extensions, to influence auditors, to induce site inspectors to compromise their judgment regarding quality and completion of civil works, and to avoid cancellation of contracts for poor performance. Bribes are typically paid on a one-off basis for a specific task or favor performed. They are often a percentage of the contract or benefit desired. The amount of the bribe is often negotiated, sometimes causing significant delays in contract awards, project implementation, or the payment of invoices.
Kickbacks	Payment made by a successful bidder to a third party as a result of an arrangement made prior to bidding. This is typically regarded as a share of proceeds from a bid that has been padded sufficiently to cover the payoffs and kickbacks to the parties involved. Kickbacks are usually arranged as a percentage of the bid amount and increase in size with the status of the party concerned.
Collusion	Agreements among bidders to manipulate the bidding process or its results in a manner that is mutually satisfactory. Public officials may orchestrate or be involved in the collusion in return for a bribe. Collusion often involves bid rigging (see below).
Bid rigging	Actions that influence a bid price in a noncompetitive way to achieve a prearranged objective. All forms of bid rigging include some type of information or procedural asymmetry to tip the scale in favor of a contractor or consortium. Two common forms are manipulation of bid specifications and sole-source contracts, both of which unfairly exclude competition. In bid rigging involving collusion, parts of a bid may be deliberately raised in order to create a losing bid. The "winning" bid may be set above the known cost estimate ("highball") in order to finance kickbacks after award. In noncollusive bid rigging, contractors may submit a "lowball" bid, where the price is set low to win the contract, only to be increased after the contract award through change orders or addenda, often with the help of officials.
Fraud	Illicit documentary practices to subvert qualification requirements, such as commercial registration or financial capacity, or to cover up poor performance and corrupt practices, such as billing for works never performed, failing to meet contract specifications for road construction, and inflated billing for goods and services, among other actions. Fraud by project officials includes diverting project assets such as computers or vehicles, documenting "ghost employees," and setting up front companies (to create the illusion of competition or conceal the identity of the principal owners or beneficiaries for taxation avoidance, usually working in concert with selected complicit firms).

official's family, for example. Most bribe givers are contractors, private firms, or a consortium of firms. These activities, in most if not all types of legal jurisdictions, are actionable offenses and are punishable under the law. Importantly, even though the corrupt acts can be broken down into actionable offences, the larger evidentiary chain may reveal complex connections with state capture. Other than pilferage, corruption in modal transport sectors is as likely to conjoin administrative and state capture—including policy capture at the legislative levels—as it is to be unraveled by a discrete "smoking gun" or proverbial "hand in the cookie jar." In terms of solutions, this signals a need for an integrated approach to control, through internal control systems, detection techniques, and external monitoring.

Corruption in Transport at the Sector Level

At the sector level, corruption typically occurs in the context of the capture of the policy-making process. Private interests, often through politicians, exert influence on the direction and content of policies to favor their own activities or investments. This then affects sectoral planning and the annual allocation of budgetary resources.

State Capture

In transport, state capture tends to occur in two forms. The first form involves the allocation of high-level responsibilities, appointments, and mandates pertaining to the planning and funding of transport infrastructure. Political or vested interests may determine the allocation of resources to transport and other major investments with little regard to objective planning criteria, forecast of needs, or expected rates of return. New investments may be favored over maintenance because they offer more and larger opportunities to cream off or divert funds. The extent to which these top-level decisions are the mandate of a few appointed or elected officials without adequate interaction with a rigorous planning process, impact analysis, or consultation can provide an opportunity for influencing the disposition of a substantial amount of public resources and the potential for incurring substantial damage or social costs. Collusive alliances rely on higher-level cover, and appointments may foster an oligarchic or corporate influence over the planning and funding processes. The rules relating to major private sector investment in transport may allow indirect involvement of public officials through participating companies, or oversight arrangements may have loopholes that give officials opportunities for private gain. Revenues collected through a state-owned port operator or toll road company or through other means may be directed to political party funding.

The second form of state capture involves bilateral concessions, wherein the government may grant substantial benefits—through preferential access to scarce natural resources or another concession—in return for investment in a major transport asset, such as construction of a port, airport, or highway, or for supply of particular commodities such as rail cars or aircraft. These schemes take numerous forms. The construction of a border road may be offered in return for access to logging of hardwood forests. Undue influence may be exerted on the shaping of national policy on the privatization of rail, ports, or airports, such as the packaging of rail networks and services; or of port and airport facilities and services, which would confer a special benefit to the concessionaire. A related form of state capture at the legislative level involves the power of industry lobby groups—such as the automobile and road construction industries—that attempt to bias legislation in their favor, such as in emissions control, fuel economy, and safety regulations.

Discretionary Influence in Resource Allocation

The allocation of national resources to and within the transport sector typically involves a combination of fiscal criteria, economic planning and development criteria, and political discretion. For transport systems, established methods for planning, evaluating, and prioritizing capital investments integrate socioeconomic, spatial, and environmental considerations at a network level. These methods are complex, and their results can also be manipulated, misrepresented, or ignored in order to elevate the priority of a project.

In some governments, elected representatives are allowed line-item or allocation privileges that are entirely discretionary, with little legislative or technical scrutiny. Line-item budgets, sometimes referred to as "pork barrel," may indicate that an objective planning process is being bypassed.[1] Such discretionary power may be used to seek direct gain through kickbacks to allies or indirect gain through increased business and rising land prices in the representative's constituency.

Recurrent expenditures include operations and maintenance, where total spending may be small but is widely dispersed. These funds are handled by local jurisdictions and may be given lower levels of scrutiny. Allocations may be directed to support political influence, including withholding funds from disfavored areas. This overriding of technical and objective criteria in program allocation effectively undermines the government's ability to be a prudent asset manager.

Where objective criteria have been established for budget allocation or prioritization (based, for example, on an inventory of assets), the corruption risk may extend to manipulation of the information on which decisions are based. An example would be the overreporting of road and bridge inventory, where funding allocations are based on length of road and bridges, or overreporting of staff by including temporary staff in the count. Another example would involve reclassification of local roads to national road status in order to qualify for national funds and thus a larger budget allocation than would otherwise be warranted on functional grounds. Such a change of road status would also result in eligibility for greater maintenance funds, which may receive lower scrutiny or be jurisdictionally targeted.

Role of Institutional Structures and Policies

The nature of sector institutions can significantly change the nature of corruption. Traditionally, the transport sector has been vertically integrated. Transport infrastructure is typically delivered through a public works department, and transport services are regulated, and in some cases provided, through a transport department. The probity of such a model depends considerably on internal controls and the integrity of individual officials.[2] In corrupt environments, the nature of the work, weak controls, and weak accounting mean that a public works director or engineer could easily direct the use of heavy equipment and staff to tasks of little public priority or even private gain. The purchase and maintenance of equipment also provide ample opportunities for private use and pilfering. In transport operations and services, the power afforded to officials for granting permits or licenses could also permit external influence.

Since the mid-1980s, sector reforms have focused on the separation of operations from policy-making and regulatory functions with the aim of greater efficiency in service delivery and often lower cost of service. Major gains were achieved through separating service provision from infrastructure management, especially in air- and seaports. It is expected that such deconcentration of power allows for greater impartiality and transparency and, depending on the legislative and contractual mandates of the parties involved, likely provides stronger incentives and controls for accountability. The resulting structure is considered less vulnerable to state capture than a vertically and functionally integrated public sector agency. Commercialization of service delivery in the sector, by separating management and operations and by procuring works and services under contract and through competitive processes, was advanced mainly to achieve efficiency gains in quality and cost. Where effective competition and oversight exist, this approach has improved the accounting of works and services—both technical and financial—as well as the quality and cost. Corruption remains a risk, however, because it has shifted to transaction management—the procurement process, quality control, and financial control—exploiting weaknesses in each process. These weaknesses are often exacerbated at subnational levels where the capacity of local government units may be thin, staff are close to local vested interests, influence engenders alliances, and scrutiny may be light.

The mixed performance of these unbundled structures in recent time offers important lessons. For the unbundling of the functions to perform effectively, there needs to be both adequate capacity in each of the new sector entities and effective market forces. Where the transport sector is small, professional capacity is weak, or corruption spans public and private sectors, such unbundling is likely instead to increase the opportunities for corruption and governance failure and is especially vulnerable to influence over staff appointments or high-level alliances among officials. For example, under early road fund models, corrupt officials were sometimes able to capture road boards, which were given additional autonomy over substantial funds that were often treated as "off-budget" because of their dedicated revenue stream from road users. Under "second generation" road funds, the oversight has been made stronger and more transparent by involving road users and diversifying the composition of the board; however, where appointments are subject to high-level political authorization, the process can still be compromised through a directed appointment of corrupt "players" and relaxation of controls. Similarly, corruption has flourished in semiautonomous port authorities and services where the appointments have been political or controls have been weak. Thus, sector restructuring will reduce corruption only to the extent that critical assumptions and caveats on the governance environment and institutional capacity are realized.

Corruption at the Agency Level

Poor governance at the sector level often results in problems at the agency level that lead to corruption. Business processes and control systems may be inadequate and inefficient because leadership at higher levels is less concerned about sectoral outcomes and more with generating private returns: the impetus for agency officials to establish or improve effective procedures and more efficient systems is weak. A common corollary is a perversion of personnel management in which recruitment, transfers, assignments, and promotions are based less on merit and more on favors and connections. The resulting environment thus leads to ample opportunities for administrative corruption to emerge and thrive.

Weak Business Processes and Controls

Corrupt practices at an agency level generally thrive with two facilitating factors—weak internal controls and processes, and an alliance or network of cooperating agents. Accounting methods and financial management processes are critical to the tracking of funds and transactions. When these are in paper form, the difficulty of verifying authenticity, tracking individual transactions, and retrieving or auditing transactions in a corrupt environment rises steeply, and corrupt agents have developed many fraudulent schemes, ranging from petty cash theft through substantial internal transfers or manipulation of book entries. Standard internal controls and audits can be subverted by falsified documents or co-opted staff at critical but not necessarily visible or senior positions. Fund transfers between offices may be destined for a local office where scrutiny and document control are more lax than at headquarters, or they may be billed to bulk or general tasks that are plausible but typically not measured, such as routine repairs, landslide removal, safety repairs, and earthworks. Emergency maintenance is typical of a category that few would dispute but is rarely subject to explicit measurement and control. In return for fraudulent documentation, payments may be made to local officials or agents, or claims for expenses may be misrepresented. Revenue collection is a notorious point of leakage, especially in remote locations or in enforcement situations, such as traffic or vehicle infringements, toll or tariff collection, and registration or testing.

Other perversions of agency processes may involve the use of agency or public assets, usually with the connivance of and protection by officials in key positions. The use of heavy equipment for private or nonpublic purposes is a common feature of some public works agencies—sometimes to further arguably good social or community interests. Some equipment scams involve renting out equipment in return for receipts that are not documented, the billing of multiple repairs to a single vehicle, the retention of scrapped vehicles on the inventory to which are charged various maintenance and overhaul costs, and similar schemes that provide cover for stealing funds. Theft of materials from warehouses and quarries, where bulk materials are rarely inventoried, or of spare parts is another example. Critical to these schemes is a cadre or small network of agents who manage the scheme, usually with an identifiable leader. Often, however, the appearances of normal operation are such that nonparticipants in the scheme may be set up or targeted for blame in the event of an investigation, especially if senior officials are involved.

Personnel Appointments

Staff appointments and promotions may be used as rewards or incentives for cooperation with corrupt practices. Sometimes staff positions may be sought not for the pay or prestige they bestow but for the rent-seeking opportunities they offer. In the case of technical management positions, entry rules such as technical qualifications may be relaxed or waived in order to place a favored ally; such hirings also compromise the quality of professional decisions in that jurisdiction. These employees or "agents" are co-opted or placed in critical nodal points within the bureaucracy to facilitate corrupt transactions. They may be embedded in the procurement or disbursement chain with relevant authorization, or they may be the collection agents for bribes and kickbacks. A recent study on corrupt practices reveals that the entry fee paid to obtain a "lucrative" position, such as in transport, can be very high and may be financed by an informal network of creditors—family, neighbors, community—at high rates of interest, thereby generating a significant bloc of stakeholders who are directly or indirectly invested in and rely on corrupt practices (CESIFO 2004).

Lack of Oversight, Monitoring, or Independence

In corrupt environments, even the institutional watchdogs, such as the national auditor or a departmental inspector, may be compromised and provide clearances in return for a share in kickbacks. In cases where annual audits reveal substantial amounts of undocumented transactions, the typical explanation is loss or lack of documentation, which is a governance failure, whereas some cases are as likely to be signs of corruption but with no evidential material to detail the transactions or identify the parties involved. Weak investigative and judicial capacity—or quiescent or complicit agency management—means that few of these cases are likely to be solved and prosecuted. In certain situations, even external groups that have been brought into the process to enhance transparency because of their supposed independence, such as nongovernmental organizations or other civil society representatives, have been compromised. Where the incentives are sufficient—whether in terms of payments, or through the cultural pressures of respect for authority or of harmony and cooperation, or from fear of reprisals—there are examples of the so-called independent monitor being co-opted with payments or acquiescing without objection. Improved transparency is important in securing the trust of users as well as in adding another oversight mechanism. At a minimum, the subversion of outside monitors adds to the cost of the corrupt transaction.

Mechanics of Transport Corruption at the Project and Transaction Level

Corruption at the sector and agency levels invariably "cascades down" to the project level, beginning with the processes for preparing the project, to the bidding and implementation phases, and to the payment process.

Preparation of Projects

While most corrupt activities at a transaction level are found during the bidding phase of procurement, several forms of corruption can be inserted during the preparation phases of study, design, and prebid documentation. In the feasibility study or design stages of a project, consultants may overdesign a facility if their fee is based on a percentage of project cost. Or they may bias a decision for a project option that could involve higher income for them from design and supervision services downstream. They may also be influenced at this stage by political or vested interests who may benefit financially from a specific option. Adverse impacts on environmental and social safeguards such as land acquisition or terrain stability may be deliberately understated, or traffic demand and similar benefits overstated, to influence the feasibility or cost estimates of the project. Provisions for minimizing conflict of interest are common in consulting assignments, but these controls do not necessarily eliminate design bias.

When controls are imposed to ensure that bids conform closely to the agency cost estimate, the designs or cost estimates may be manipulated through the quantities or unit costs used in preparing the design in conjunction with various bidding games. Agency officials may inflate the project cost estimate with the knowledge that the output can be provided at a lower cost so that the margin is available for distribution as kickbacks. Overestimation can occur when the decision maker is certain of the contract award—guaranteeing the awardee a comfortable margin, part of which is shared with the decision maker. Alternatively, the project cost can be underestimated to facilitate the authorization of a project, only to be inflated later through variations or cost overruns.

The specification of goods, equipment, or materials to be procured may incorporate critical features that favor a particular product or supplier, including the use of trade names. Especially in regard to equipment or materials, corrupt officials may collude with contractors to specify design or material requirements that give a certain contractor advantage (through proprietary rights, for example, or through location or access rights), often in return for kickbacks. Information asymmetry is also deliberately created to conceal corruption. Favored contractors may be tipped off regarding incomplete or inaccurate information deliberately inserted into the specifications, thereby enabling the firm to disregard a particularly onerous condition in its bid and thereby submitting a winning low bid. Tip-offs may also permit the submission of an alternative high bid with options that may be used during evaluation to override the specifications and give the award to a higher bidder.

Bidding Phase

Several opportunities for corrupt actions occur during the bidding phase. One of the most pernicious involves bid rigging and access. Informal conditions can be imposed on firms for participation in bidding for a project, either by officials of the contracting employer or by external individuals such as a local politician, official, or influential party. These conditions can include a requirement to pay a certain portion of the contract value in return for being allowed to sign the contract or gain access to the site and to continue operations unimpeded. The margins to cover these kickbacks are generated in two ways. If the specifications and cost estimate are accurate, kickbacks can be generated downstream by firms bidding substantially above the cost estimate, by generating large variation or change orders and cost overruns during implementation, or by compromising the quality of construction in ways that are not apparent. If awards are forced to be close to the cost estimate, kickbacks can be generated upstream by agency officials through manipulation of the design and cost estimates. Frequently these margins are well established and known among the industry and may be distributed according to an established hierarchy of shares to nominated officials and agency directors; these payments are often regarded as supplemental income where the remuneration of government officials is particularly low. In most cases, these amounts may be up to 10 percent of the contract price, but in some countries and where political influences are strong, they can be as high as 30 percent of the contract price. Kickback schemes can exist without overt signs of collusion and, especially if the margins are relatively small, on the order of 10 percent or less, they may not be apparent in an examination of bid prices.

Another form of corruption in this phase is collusion (box 5.1). It is common practice in the construction sector in some countries for contractors to share work among firms by taking turns as the "favored" contractor. Under this arrangement, everyone "wins" over the long haul. Collusive practices involve the outright rigging

BOX 5.1 Case Study Examples of the Mechanics of Collusion in Road Civil Works

The examples of corruption summarized here are generalized from actual instances of corrupt transactions in road construction projects involving World Bank and other multilateral donor funds that have been uncovered, some of which are currently under investigation.

Construction cartels involve agreements between competitors that make procurement less competitive, whether through tenders or quotations. They may include any or all the following, which are not mutually exclusive: collusive tendering, market sharing, and price fixing. In one instance, a highly organized and institutionalized cartel set the contract price with the agency for projects with international financing. The cartel controlled all aspects of the bidding process so that the procurement controls appeared to be ineffective. For many years the cartel operated with impunity, with high-level political influence ensuring the "anointed" contractor would be successful. The losing bidders complied with the collusive practice so that they could obtain government agency contracts in the future. Politicians, losing bidders (contractors), and government officials were party to the scheme and received kickbacks. These illicit payments were referred to as shares, and the collusive scheme was known as the SOP—standard operating procedure. The person who arranged the cartel activity or collusive scheme was known as the fixer or coordinator, and the cartel was so institutionalized that it was an open secret among contractors, government officials, politicians, and the construction industry generally.

Typically such collusive practices operate under "silent guidelines." The winner is supposed to set aside 3 percent of the contract to be shared by the other prequalified and losing bidders. The "matchmaker" asks contractors if they are interested in a particular project. At a follow-up meeting, the anointed winner, who always has local political support in exchange for corrupt payments, arranges the price markup and negotiates the payments for the politicians (two-thirds of their share on winning the contract and one-third on implementation). Contractors add 20–28 percent to the estimate depending on the circumstances of each project. The losing bidders receive the price they are to bid one day before the bid deadline. The arrangers check the losing prices right before they are submitted to make sure they are correct and conform as pre-arranged. "Divers" (contractors who deliberately reduce their price to win a contract) can avoid the pre-arranged bidding but will be punished by not winning government work in the future. If a particular contractor "dives," the system is so controlled that project officials can counter the lower bid, for example, by extending the bid date, should they desire to do so. If a diver does win the bid, the company will either make no money and will have trouble with politicians or will have to make some compromise agreement with the politicians.

"Shares" refers to the percentage of the contract paid corruptly. In one case, these shares were distributed as follows: One share each went to the bid committee members, the bid committee chairman, the legal advisers, the local nongovernmental organization or media (to look the other way), the coordinator or mediator, and the winning bidder; four to five shares went to the project management unit; and three to five shares went to the losing bidders. In another example, 6 percent of the contract price was paid to the executive office and representatives, 5 percent to national politicians, 1 percent to agency personnel, 1 percent to the agency project director, and 3 percent to local government officials, including the mayor. Inspectors were paid relatively small amounts. Some of the kickback funds came from a 15 percent mobilization payment to contractors at the outset of the contract because the kickbacks have to be paid up front.

of bid prices; "losing" contractors do not submit bids even if expressions of interest are extended, submit intentionally high bids, or withdraw their bids before the final stage of the bidding process when the lowest evaluated bidder is determined. The designated "winning" contractor structures his bid to accommodate the payments he will need to make after he is awarded the contract. Besides collusion among contractors, corruption in the procurement process can also take place through the inconsistent application of prequalification or eligibility screening. Contractor collusion can also involve a large number of firms either structured as a consortium or as subcontractors. "Cascade subcontracting," as it is called, may occur at any stage of construction (such as groundwork or materials transport) and can radically transform the initial financial estimate.

Corrupt agents may also circumvent regulations involving contract packaging and bid invitations. Splitting large construction contracts into smaller contracts with weaker or streamlined regulation may offer more opportunity to influence the award, even for one firm or patron. It also allows the same firm to do the work and submit bills under phony company names. In other instances, corrupt agents may restrict publicity by publishing a bid announcement in a journal with limited circulation under false claims of urgency. A restricted call for tenders such as limited international or national bidding, while justified under certain circumstances, may be used to eliminate rivals (Bueb and Ehlermann-Cache 2005).

At bid openings without adequate oversight, a false price may be read out or a discount not read out, which could prevail over the accurate prices during bid evaluation (see, for instance, box 9.2 in chapter nine). During bid evaluation, a large arithmetic correction may be contrived to favor a desired firm or to penalize a disfavored firm. After the winning bidder has been selected, the bid price or conditions may be changed when either a corrupt agent or official or the firm may impose new conditions before starting the job. Even without corrupt intentions, the official or the firm could agree to the coerced modification of the bid price in order to start the work. These ex post change orders are justified by the corrupt officials on a variety of grounds, mostly based on alleged change in prices, inflation, unavailability of certain materials or equipment, and the need to substitute more expensive alternatives, among others. In consultant technical evaluations, which carry the most weight in a quality- and cost-based selection system, selections can be manipulated to favor a particular firm, often through a knowledgeable or informed person on the evaluation panel.

Implementation Phase

Once project construction begins, another mode for generating additional kickbacks is through a proliferation of change orders, variation orders, or amendments, which may collectively increase a contract price by 10–50 percent above the original contract price and extend the delivery period. Variations are essential changes that are agreed between the implementing parties—supervisor, contractor, client—but may be used to conceal substantial excess quantities or unnecessary services that would be billed but not delivered. This approach may be used to enrich a different set of people from those involved in the original award, especially if the project staff, management, or local officials have changed in the interim.

Supervisors are another point of vulnerability. Certification by quality assurance inspectors, either during implementation or once a work is completed, may be used to extract rent from the contractor. On one hand, materials or quality that does not comply with the specifications may be permitted with the complicity of officials, who provide such latitude for a price. Field or laboratory test results may be made to reflect compliance with specifications even when they failed or the tests were not actually conducted. Testing staff are frequently very junior and often may be housed and fed by the contractor they are monitoring, so it can be difficult for them to act independently or to reject work. On the other hand, corrupt officials may fabricate deficiencies in materials or construction to exert pressure on the contractor for a bribe. In developing countries, lax supervision may frequently result from weak skills or experience. However, where corruption is rife in an agency, even an independent quality assurance team can be susceptible to bribe or capture in such instances.

Payment to Firms

Bribes may be sought for processing claims for payment after certification of quantities and quality of works, goods, or services in compliance with stipulated standards. This is often evident from long payment delays, which may be caused by negotiations for a bribe or a particular result. The multiple layers of approval required may provide more opportunity to extract rents to expedite processing than do short, focused approvals. Some payment delays, however, simply reflect long approval paths and slow manual procedures or inefficiency—all governance failures but not intentionally corrupt.[3]

A PROPOSED REMEDIAL FRAMEWORK

As the pressure to develop strong anticorruption interventions has intensified, a variety of approaches has emerged in the transport sector. These usually have focused on transactions and fiduciary processes at the level of a development project and have been enforced through a project-specific legal agreement. While these approaches are a necessary short-term step for development aid partners, the ultimate goal must be to increase the resilience of the sector to corruption and to reduce the incidence of corrupt activity in the sector as a whole at the country level. With this long-term goal in mind, this section outlines a twin-pronged strategy of prevention and control to be applied at each of the core levels of the sector—sector institution, organization, and transaction.

The goal of the preventive paradigm is one of good governance that has the direct and indirect effect of preventing opportunities for corruption to thrive. The objective is to prevent, monitor, and deter corruption as well as to educate all stakeholders on its costs and on approaches to prevention. In a prevention framework, the interventions are ex ante, using strategies, policies, and tools that seek to prevent, preempt, and deter corrupt acts based on the mapping of risks and vulnerabilities in sector entities and transactions. However, just as good medical practice must combine preventive health care with aggressive treatment of existing virulent disease, combating corruption will need to stem the current flow of corrupt activity while improving overall sector governance. Thus the goal of the control paradigm is to rigorously confront, prosecute, and punish corrupt acts. Ex post interventions use strategies, policies, and tools that help confront corrupt acts that are suspected—either while in progress or once they have been alleged, investigated, or proven. Table 5.2 summarizes the core remedial framework that is proposed, and specific options and activities within each strategic category are discussed below.

TABLE 5.2 Remedial Framework and Menu of Response Options

Levels of governance and incidence of corruption	*Goal: Improve governance to prevent and reduce corruption* *Objectives: Prevent, monitor, educate, deter* *Outputs: Ex ante interventions*	*Goal: Rigorously confront and punish corrupt acts* *Objectives: Control, law enforcement* *Outputs: Ex post interventions*
State capture at the sector level	Undertake dialogue and remedies at the CAS (country assistance strategy) level Reduce discretionary spending of revenues Adopt improved, objective, and transparent national budgetary allocation rules Reduce areas of discretion with good rule making Earmark revenues for special purpose entities Increase appropriate civil society interventions at sector entities Adopt appropriate legal reforms Restructure sector to allow for incentive-based reforms; reward reform-oriented staff and entities, activities Improve public access to information Increase judicial independence, reform, and accountability Mount educational campaigns on anticorruption	Take strong, coordinated donor action, sanctions in event of country- or sector-level scandal Bring donor pressure to investigate appropriately Engage in damage control, restore perception of integrity, send strong message of due process Publicize trials, enforce court orders
Agency process and capacity failure	Modernize business planning and fiduciary tools Improve human resource development and management Reform procurement system, including improved automated processes Upgrade information technology Train employees, raise awareness, change management Plan and implement institutional anticorruption Set up complaints hotline at agency Monitor performance Establish integrity indicators, collect baseline data, monitor	Investigate staff and firms aggressively Prosecute all parties involved Establish or review institutional anticorruption plan, make changes based on recent events Review agency processes based on integrity indicators
Transactional integrity compromises	Install effective internal fiduciary, audit controls Implement project management and supervision controls Set up project audits by ombudsman or auditor general Establish project monitoring in-house and by a third party Solicit civil society oversight Forge integrity pacts with private firms Train staff in basic investigative requirements	Train staff to detect suspicious activity Coordinate project teams and investigative teams Conduct rigorous investigations to collect evidence Follow up with due process and trials Apply criminal and professional sanctions (such as debarment of firms) aggressively

Controls and Enforcement-Based Integrity Restoration Options

Project and management staff in government agencies and among bilateral and multilateral donors cannot be expected to undertake some of the detailed investigations that are required for strong control, nor do they have the technical and legal expertise to conduct such forensic tasks. This discussion is intended to give guidance on indicators of suspicion, fraud, and abuse of public funds in the transport sector, so that staff can be proactive in detection and know when to call the authorities or ask for investigative assistance and how to establish monitoring processes so that actionable evidence is not lost. Some legal distinctions are important. As noted in the earlier discussion on state capture, not all governance failures are crimes—government officials can engage in many acts that are inept or inefficient and cause enormous losses without intending to defraud, extort, or commit a crime. In detection and investigation, the issue of actionable evidence, that is, evidence that establishes intent to commit a crime, becomes critical to the forensic process.

Detection: Recognizing Red Flags

Increased controls and investigation work by donor agencies and some governments have begun to narrow the wingspan around corrupt agents and the scope of their transactions. Operational teams can learn from the collective experience of investigative efforts undertaken so far that reveals patterns of events and behavior in the procurement process. For bribes and kickbacks, teams should be alert to the existence of local "agents" that provide generic, ill-defined services. Often such agents have boilerplate contracts with no clear definition of services to be delivered, and the agent's compensation is calculated as a percentage of the contract rather than on a time or services basis. Unexplained delays, bidding irregularities in favor of a small group of contractors, or unjustified sole-source awards are also common signs that bribes and kickbacks are being offered and extracted.

Some obvious indicators of bid rigging include selection of unqualified contractors, unreasonable prequalification requirements, unreasonably short times to submit bids, selection of other than the lowest qualified bidder, multiple contract awards just under the bidding threshold, and selection of the low bidder followed by a change order increasing the price or scope of the project. Questionable disqualification of the winning bidder and extension of an expired contract rather than a rebidding process should also alert project teams that some impropriety may be occurring. Contractor collusion can often produce indicators such as persistently high bid prices, relatively few bidders, and the same bidders, with losing bidders becoming subcontractors. Bid cartels may be operating if bid prices drop when new bidders enter, or when there are apparent connections between bidders' affiliated companies, such as the same fax numbers on two bidders' bidding documents. Indicators of fraud in project implementation include poor quality of works, frequent repairs, bogus inspections, and complaints from users, as well as inadequate supervision and inspections.

Investigation: Gathering Actionable Evidence

As noted above, red flags may be the tip of the iceberg and are useful to alert project staff; however, they do not constitute actionable evidence. The process of gathering proof to indict and prosecute perpetrators of fraud and corrupt transactions requires labor-intensive forensic work. This is typically undertaken by law enforcement authorities or by institutional integrity teams that are trained and qualified to uncover corrupt payments and receipts. Typically, such an investigation entails working from either the point of payment or the point of receipt to prove that an illegal payment occurred. Both involve financial investigations of givers and receivers. To prove fraud, investigators often test prices of inputs for reasonableness and compare the actual quantity and quality of goods received with those claimed in official invoices. Proof of receipt of a bribe often involves "lifestyle checks" of suspected officials to demonstrate that they are living beyond their legitimate means or have unexplained financial resources.

In recent years, donors' internal investigative units have detected some fraud and corruption by maintaining databases containing series of bid-related information and searching the database for indications of corrupt transactions. For instance, internal database queries to detect bribes and kickbacks may analyze high prices, high-volume purchases, or unusual approval patterns. One detection method involves searching on the basis of improper or excessive change orders. The typical anticorruption or fraud investigation begins with a tip, report, or discovery of a red flag and is then followed by a detailed investigation of the transaction. With the new genre of financial investigative software, investigators can test the allegations of tipsters by querying the database, interviewing officials, interviewing contractors such as losing bidders, tracing illicit funds, and other financial forensic techniques.

For donor project or program staff, the issues are likely twofold. First, staff will need to address the burden of an additional layer of due diligence in an environment of scarce time and resources. Second, staff will need to assess risk and make judgments when considering the gravity or veracity of a suspected red flag. Some may have a tendency to refer cases to the organization's investigative arm—if there is one—at the first sign of a red flag, which would overload investigative units and create backlogs. The challenge for them is to begin monitoring a range of red flags, assess which ones are actionable and which may be indicative of more general weakness in capacity, and pursue those that are likely to yield the highest payoff—in this case, prevent the larger diversion of funds. This approach will include increased communication between project and investigative units in the government and in donor agencies and training of operational teams to learn basic evidentiary rules and investigative techniques. In addition, forensic tools such as detection software will need to be increasingly incorporated into the procurement process in-house, to reduce dependence on the investigative arm of the organization. These new forensic tools will involve resources, training, and a learning curve in the immediate term.

Enforcement of Sanctions: Legal Regime and Political Will

Aggressive enforcement of sanctions against corrupt officials and contractors, such as debarment and blacklisting, is important and has been undertaken by a growing number of transport agencies and donors. Ample evidence shows that major sectorwide changes are usually implemented only after a "big fish"—either a senior government official or a major firm—has been caught and prosecuted. Thus, the effectiveness of a preventive strategy may depend on first achieving successful enforcement and sanctions in a major case. In the ultimate analysis, the effectiveness of sanctions will depend on the broader legal and judicial framework of the country and the type of legal, judicial, and procurement reforms the government is willing to undertake. This is a generic issue affecting all sectors and not unique to transport. What may be useful is for the transport sector to proactively engage in the reform process within the country to identify specific sector-related amendments and adjustments in laws, regulations, and procedures that seek to plug evidentiary loopholes in the country's enforcement structure that is peculiar to transport contracts.

Preventive Strategy for Enhancing Institutional Integrity

A preventive strategy for combating corruption focuses on strengthening the governance environment at each of the levels of the sector and the value chain in ways that specifically target and limit the various forms of corrupt behavior. The structure of a particular strategy will need to be adapted to address the prevalent risks evident in a specific situation. Thus, it may begin with the more easily achievable aims (the low-hanging fruit) and progressively focus on the more important issues and finally on the longer-term issues. Ultimately, however, the strategy must be complete, as the forms of corrupt behavior will adapt over time, like a virus, to bypass the remedial measures until the costs of corruption once again outweigh the incentives.

The key factors that engender good governance are transparency, accountability, and efficiency. To sharpen the focus on corruption, several key elements of a preventive anticorruption strategy are outlined in table 5.3. Transparency is enhanced through the power of information and communications technology, mechanisms for sharing and revealing information, and incentive structures. Accountability is enhanced through formal institutions such as the legal and judicial environment, external forces such as the effective voice of citizens and users outside the public sector, and internal drivers such as incentives. Sector efficiency is enhanced when firms compete openly and the preference or power of the elite is harnessed, institutional operations have been reformed, and external markets provide a higher incentive than local rewards. The following discussion provides examples of actions that can be developed under each of these nine elements, together with typical tools that can be used in the transport sector and applied at each institutional level.

Information Power

Information on assets, costs, and performance provides crucial evidence that enables and facilitates accountability and transparency. The power of data for demonstrating what was intended and what was actually delivered, whether costs are reasonable or high, whether qualifications are fraudulent or not, lies at the heart of reducing the space for discretion, subjectivity, and ambiguity in the decisions on which corruption thrives. Traditional decision making relies strongly on status, experience, or skill with significant use of subjective criteria and discretion. While that works well in the

TABLE 5.3 Elements of a Remedial Anticorruption Strategy

Strategic element	*Focus*	*Explanation*
Data power	Metrics	Information on assets, costs, and performance provides crucial evidence that enables and facilitates accountability, transparency, and incentives.
External accountability mechanism	Effective voice	To be effective, external mechanisms (such as civil society) need to be coherent and have adequate power and integrity.
Transparency mechanism	Reduced discretion, improved confidence and integrity	Use of information and communication technology, computerization, e-procurement, e-governance, and access to asset inventory and management data can all improve transparency.
Incentives	Drivers of good behavior, prevention	Rewards and recognition can be offered to compensate for loss of revenue.
Roles of the firm and the elite	Reducing the incidence of capture	Disempowering agents of the elite provides a more level playing field and enhances competition.
Judiciary and legal environment	Consistent enforcement, protection of integrity	A well-functioning judicial system strengthens prosecution and discourages corrupt behavior.
Political reform	Improving the enabling environment for a sector	Political reforms provide leadership and example as well as foundation blocks, such as procurement legislation, streamlined institutional structure, and efficient business processes.
Capital market development	Requires governance discipline	The protocols and standards of international business impose governance discipline and efficiency.
International donors and financing agencies	Incentives for international acceptance	Harmonization of donor approaches improves transparency, accountability, and efficiency, making it easier for donors and third parties to enforce discipline within the donor community and in donor projects

Source: Adapted from material by Daniel Kaufmann, World Bank Institute, 2004.

hands of honest and informed agents, it provides open space for the corrupt to manipulate results to their own advantage. In this information age, the power of data and information needs to be appreciated as a critical tool for making decisions more objective and thus consistent and transparent. These information tools are available for and useful at each step in the process cycle.

- *Inputs.* Reliable data on the inventory of existing assets or stock, and their current condition, use, and costs, are critical as a baseline for decisions on where and how further investments should be made and on evaluating actual delivery. Reliable data on finances, qualifications, and past performance are critical in evaluating the capacity of firms for delivering services under a competitive process. Examples abound where data on existing conditions have been distorted to justify needs or a procurement award or to cover up the undersupply of new goods.

- *Options.* Knowledge of alternatives and comparison of options are crucial to good decision making and cost saving. An insistence on defining options and obtaining market information on alternative products or treatments, and making this information available, can reduce the influence that a corrupt vendor or buyer may have on restricting the market to a predetermined choice.
- *Evaluation and selection.* The use of systematic methods and objective information is critical to transparency and needs to span several dimensions, such as technical, economic, financial, social, environmental, and value. System-based tools for asset management and budget programming provide a quantitative and objective frame of reference against which political or corruptly motivated alternatives can be evaluated.
- *Outputs.* The accurate measurement of the products or services delivered—in quantity, quality, location, and compliance with specifications—and of the payments for them is one of the most important tools for eliminating wastage, underdelivery, or diversion. Pay items that are notoriously difficult to measure, such as freight damage, earthworks in emergency road works, and routine or general maintenance of vehicle or assets, are favorite targets of the corrupt, and measurement is generally more accurate when it is based on performance or results.
- *Results.* Where payment is based on outputs, the benchmarking of output costs on the basis of average unit costs—with a defined unit of output—can be used to compare across jurisdictions or over time (this may be a key indicator when prices are being rigged and funds diverted). Where the measurement of outputs may be corrupted, it can be useful to shift the control to a measure of outcome or result. Examples are performance-specified contracts and longer-term contracts where the contractor or supplier is responsible for ensuring quality and where payment is based on actual results rather than outputs per se. In this case, the measurement of performance criteria and results themselves becomes highly critical because it is directly linked to payment for the services provided.
- *Monitoring and evaluation.* The amounts of information involved in this entire process cycle are often large, complex, and technical; possibly widely dispersed; and either change over time or involve multiple transactions. The format and design of reports need to be very practical and targeted on critical measures for monitoring to be effective, either by internal or external parties. Moreover, managing the data to keep them current and reliable is critical to the success of an information-based approach.

The tools for implementing these objectives need to be designed to fit individual cases, but the following examples indicate the range of tools that have been found to be effective in the transport sector.

- A computer and communications network supporting the agency is crucial for managing and exchanging information, for comparing and analyzing data, and for generating reports. While paper-based tools have an important place in some situations and in some subnational governments or small agencies, the reality is that digital media and technology have rapidly become a given in management of the sector. Careful and appropriate design of the computer systems must take into account the operating budget, the technical capacity of staff, system performance, stability, and security. Systems do not need to be large or complex to be effective, but they do need to be stable and secure.

- An asset inventory eliminates gaps, duplication, and ambiguity. The inventory should begin with an explicit definition of assets, the quality of the data must be ensured and the asset data regularly updated. Video images in the database allow a virtual review and verification of road, port, or airport assets.
- Accounting and financial management reports should cover cost centers to reconcile transactions and inputs against project outputs, include account balances to control exceptions and diversion, and provide a means for verifying the use of budget transfers.
- Annual or regular reports should be prepared in readable format with explicit data on various performance measures—physical assets or stock (vehicles, roads, bridges, port facilities), outputs, costs of delivery (including average output cost), safety, staffing—compared with benchmarks and trends.
- Specific reports aiding interpretation of inventory or transactions help nonprofessionals monitor or review performance and manage results. For example, a straight-line diagram of a road that indicates current and previous inputs by location allows unambiguous interpretation of outputs.

Transparency Mechanism

Enhancing transparency involves reducing the areas of discretion and ambiguity by the consistent use of objective criteria and processes, keeping sensitive information secure, and making access to general information available to stakeholders in an appropriate way. These actions improve the integrity of the processes and the confidence of participants in the results. The power of information and communications technology for managing and processing large amounts of data and providing access to information is huge and plays a large role in making transport operations transparent. The basic elements include guidelines, Internet-based tools, computerized applications for procurement, procurement monitors, and independent procurement agents.

Clear, agreed, and announced guidelines on the processes to be followed in public procurement and project management are the basic tool of transparency. The guidelines set the rules of the game, the eligibility to participate, and the way it will be administered. Many of the improvements in the fight against corruption have come through upgrading and harmonizing the guidelines that government and various financing agencies apply to procurement. The most successful guidelines incorporate best practice and set standards that are applied during the selection, evaluation, and award of contracts. This area is the first and primary element for an agency to review, examining it against the evidence of prevalent corrupt practices and strengthening the weak links. However, compliance with the guidelines rests on the integrity of those administering it, and infiltration or co-opting of staff can occur. Also some types of corruption, such as bribes and collusion, occur behind the official process, and special techniques are required for detection.

The use of Internet- or Web-based communication technology, such as e-procurement, to address the transparency issues is powerful and developing quickly as the computerization of agencies and the transport sector evolve. A major advantage is that the same information is available to all participants. Usually this step is introduced progressively as the information technology capacity of the agency and the industry evolves. It is important that the coverage, reliability, and security of the systems are adequate and that the literacy of the industry is sufficient for the information to enhance and not limit competition. Typical Internet-based communications include advertisement of bid opportunities and information, announcement of contract awards and prices, announcement of bid prices and evaluation results, availability of bid documents on line for downloading, and direct submission of expressions of interest, eligibility, or bid documents.

In addition to improving the efficiency of the procurement process, computer applications can also enhance transparency in the evaluation process. One example involves the production of notices and bid documents. Computerization of these documents can improve their quality by ensuring integrity of mandatory text and selected optional text, consistency of data, compliance with guidelines on specific requirements, and completeness. Similarly, computerization can help process evaluation results and generate evaluation reports. A computerized registry of civil works contractors has proved successful in improving the integrity of prequalification processes: the legal, commercial, and financial data of firms in the database are compared with the qualifications profile of a project, and a list of eligible firms is generated together with a list of those firms not qualifying and the reasons for disqualification. Various provisions for due diligence are applied to the data entry process and to a right of review for disqualified firms.

A common approach to enhancing transparency has been the use of a nonagency person as a monitor in key stages of the procurement process in order to introduce an element of independent review of compliance of processes with the guidelines. This is typically applied to public stages such as bid opening, and it guards against some missteps. However, these monitors typically need to have their participation costs covered and may also be prone to capture by corrupt agents (see box 5.1). Attention must be paid to their selection, funding, and training; to inserting them into evaluation parts of the process; and to using techniques of rotation and undercover review to preserve their integrity in the process.

In extreme cases where capacity is weak or corruption is extensive, enhancing transparency may require instituting a parallel process for conducting procurement through an independent procurement agent appointed outside the implementing agency. Results would be provided to the agency responsible for making and implementing the decisions. While this approach is similar to the use of procurement agents in the past, it represents a significant departure from the development aid principles of internal capacity and ownership.

External Accountability Mechanism

The structure and design of accountability mechanisms is one of the primary and most important controls and preventive tools in combating corruption. Accountability mechanisms involve parties external to those involved in the transactions and ostensibly independent of them. Their purpose is to ensure the integrity of the process and to see that the rules are followed, with an absence of corruption. A widening array of tools is being employed as the limitations of traditional mechanisms are discovered. These tools fall into four categories—financial audit, technical audit, fiduciary review, and third-party monitoring—and a comprehensive accountability framework would include all four.

A financial audit is a periodic inspection of accounts to determine whether all funds and assets have been used for their legitimate and intended purpose and are fully accounted for. The integrity and extent of the financial audit, which is a mandatory requirement of public agencies and financing agencies, is critical to its effectiveness as an anticorruption tool. Steps to ensure the independence and impartiality of the auditor are critical, whether the auditor is public or private, and thus the selection process needs careful attention. The substance of an audit is in the management report, where specific accounting issues and anomalies are identified and explained, and project teams should use this report to require correction of specific weaknesses in accounting and internal controls. Often, the audit does not extend down to subnational offices, except on a sample basis or if a comprehensive computer-based financial management system is in place. Targeted audits should be conducted where corrupt activity is suspected. The quality of documentation identifying the purpose of the transaction and the person responsible for it may become key evidence in a forensic investigation of the paper trail. The scope should include an audit of the asset register to determine the location, disposition, and deployment of assets owned and procured by the agency. This is particularly important in relation to items such as vehicles and computers that are particularly liable to theft, numerous, and periodically written off and are thus notoriously difficult to monitor at an agency level.

A technical audit is a periodic inspection to determine that the assets and services provided with the funds were appropriate to their intended purpose and were delivered in the quantity, quality, and location or disposition specified. A relatively new but powerful tool, technical audits inspect the implementation of projects; they are essentially auditing the quality of operation, supervision, and project management by a transport agency. A technical audit's primary purpose is to verify that the goods or assets purchased under an expenditure program were delivered as specified to the place and persons legitimately intended. It can also extend to evaluating the appropriateness of the specifications and standards applied in the projects or transactions. To be credible, the audit must be conducted by a technical professional qualified and experienced in the subject and independent of the implementing agency. Because this audit strikes at the core business role of an agency and requires extensive cooperation and access to data, the auditor can be placed under considerable pressure to understate or overlook certain aspects or even be misled through nondisclosure. Thus, the selection and administration of the technical auditor sometimes can present difficulties, especially if the corrupt network extends to the leadership of the agency. In some cases, it may be necessary to employ the auditor or administer the audit through a separate public agency, such as an ombudsman, inspectorate, or other impartial oversight body. A particular version of this audit, originating from nontechnical sectors but of potential application to the transport sector, is a Public Expenditure Tracking Survey (PETS). This survey combines financial and technical aspects by tracking the expenditure of funds on a specified program through every step of the process from national authorization down to delivery and use at the local and individual level.

A fiduciary review is a comprehensive review of an implementing agency's procurement, financial management, and project management processes, including their internal controls and oversight. The review is conducted by an independent group periodically or as warranted. In implementing environments where the risks of corruption are high and extensive, a comprehensive fiduciary review provides an intensive inspection and evaluation of all the financial, procurement, and implementation processes of an implementing agency. Its outputs assess the level of corruption risk in each process, identify the points of weakness and required remedial actions, and adjust the review and authorization thresholds. Because of the degree of access to information required, such reviews are typically undertaken by a multidisciplinary team of specialists with extensive participation by government officials.

Third-party monitoring is a continuous mechanism for monitoring the execution of sector expenditures, including the procurement and implementation of projects. The third party is either a public agency external to the implementing agency, a civil society group, or a private agent employed by the government in an independent role. In transport agencies, the integrity of fiduciary processes has generally been secured by requiring parallel independent evaluation by a panel of individuals from different sections of the agency. These individuals are accountable to each other, and the panel itself is accountable to agency management. When the evaluation panel or the agency management becomes corrupted, these provisions are not enough, and third-party monitoring by a person or group independent of the agency is introduced. Public sector models for third-party monitoring include an inspectorate within the sector ministry but independent of the subsector being monitored, a national auditor, or a national agency with the role of monitoring for corruption. When these, too, are corrupted, the involvement of civil society and the private sector—independent of the government—may be needed to provide the process with a measure of independence and accountability. Some of the effective models for third-party monitoring and their related issues include the following.

A common option is the appointment of an independent observer, typically from a nongovernmental organization or other representative citizens' group, to attend bid openings, observe bid evaluation, or participate in technical audit inspections. This may be a mandated requirement for the agency, or it may result from an external demand from a watchdog organization. For this model to be effective, observers need to be actively engaged, from the unsealing of the bid box to actual sighting and posting of the bid amounts, and be trained and competent in all aspects of the bid process or the construction-delivery process. Issues experienced with the observer model include the logistics and costs of attending the process and pressures of co-option and collusion by threat or a share in kickbacks. In addition, the signs of collusion may not be apparent without specialized tools, and the observer may not wield enough authority to influence acceptance of the result.

Outsourced monitoring is a second option. Auditors or monitors trained in fraud detection and financial forensics may be employed in-house or hired from the private sector. Where internal auditors may be susceptible to corruption, the hiring of a monitoring or forensic accounting service from private sector firms with an arm's length relationship to the agency and the appropriate incentives may yield higher payoffs in terms of investigation, detection, actionable evidence, and results. Stronger audit clauses can be inserted in contracts that provide for review of a contractor's financial records. Administrative rules can also require annual financial disclosures by project and government officials, as well as require contractors and subcontractors to disclose all fees and commissions. Compliance with the rules would be ensured through rigorous audits.

A variant of the independent observer model is the appointment of an independent evaluator—an individual or firm with the requisite professional skills to conduct an independent evaluation of the bids or proposals in parallel with the official committee. In this model, one set of bids would be set aside and sealed at bid opening for later review against evaluated documents. The evaluator would be present in the bid evaluation meetings to receive all information but would conduct an independent evaluation and submit it as a separate report to an independent official, either above the evaluation committee or in a monitoring agency. A final recommendation must include a reconciliation or explanation of differences between the official and independent findings. Issues with this model include the authorizations needed to give the evaluator access to confidential information, the difficulties in defining and managing the reporting and conclusion of recommendations, the sensitivity of an agency to exposing dissent, and the cost and financing of the service.

The most stringent of the third-party monitoring options is to hire an independent private sector agency to undertake all aspects of procurement on behalf of the agency. In this model, the independent agent would manage the process from start to finish. He would conduct parts of the process in public, as in the public model, involve agency officials in the evaluation process and public meetings, and make recommendations to the agency for official authorization. Normally with this model, the implementing agency financially responsible for the output signs the contract for the works or services. Issues with the independent agent model include hiring, financing, and monitoring the independent agency and the acceptance by government of the need for such a high level of control and independence. In other respects, the model is similar to the hiring of engineering or other transport services.

For sector-level issues, such as accountability for the allocation and expenditure of funds, the external accountability mechanism operates in parallel with the formal government budget process. In this instance, the public agency and a cohort of groups representing civil society and stakeholders agree on a social compact covering a range of expenditure programs, agency performance standards, and obligations to the community. In the case of the road sector, the concept views all interventions—whether they involve asset preservation or network expansion—as part of a larger dynamic process involving diverse stakeholders. The thrust of a "road social contract" is one of public accountability and transparency: the road agency holds itself accountable to road users for efficient expenditure management and road service conditions through a published annual compact with a representative civil society group to achieve a stipulated level of performance that is derived from and monitored through a participatory process. Operationally, the road social contract can take the form of a memorandum of understanding (MOU) between the agency and civic organizations representing the general public. The process could also be applied to a semiautonomous sector, fund such as a road fund, through the annual report and an MOU between the fund's oversight board and a representative civil society group.

At an organizational level, an agency can be held accountable for a range of performance measures through a tool such as an agency report card, in which citizens or transport users are able to articulate their assessment of agency performance and value for money in a range of measures. This assessment is then publicized and formally addressed by the agency. This tool has been used in a growing number of applications for infrastructure and municipal services, and while it focuses more generally on organizational capacity and efficiency issues, it can have an impact on certain forms of corruption, such as those associated with redirection or subversion of funds, underdelivery or overpricing, and various transparency measures. This tool could be particularly useful in monitoring a road social contract.

Incentives

The choices made by any person at any point in the value chain are driven very much by individual incentives and how these might be influenced by external or institutional factors. This is an intersection between formal rules, informal rules of the game, and values. To break a cycle or pattern of corrupt behavior, the incentives for good behavior must outweigh the rewards for engaging in or acquiescing to corrupt behavior. Likewise, the risks and cost of corrupt behavior must outweigh its rewards. While incentives are a generic and not very sector-specific issue, some examples as they apply in the transport sector include the following.

At the state level, any personal gain a politician may receive by arguing for an inappropriate allocation or budget line item can be counterbalanced by calling attention to the politician's position in a way that might cost him votes or loss of reputation among his constituency. For example, a strong civil society or media voice could make information available on the socioeconomic benefits of alternative transport allocations or projects or reveal "white elephant" projects sponsored by the politician.

At the transport agency level, incentives are driven by the perception of the effectiveness of internal controls, protection afforded by senior management or elite patrons, threats to job security, protection of whistleblowers, and the risks of exposure. Changing these incentives to reduce corruption requires the strengthening of internal controls, enforcing penalties for violation of controls, appointing staff of integrity to critical positions, rotating staff to avoid formation of collusive alliances, affording agency protection against external influences, and providing whistleblower protections, especially to lower-ranked personnel who are usually the most vulnerable in the process.

At a transaction and individual level, incentives can be improved by emphasizing transparency, employing systems that limit the areas of discretion, speeding up the processing time to limit the risks of deal negotiation, and preventing or discouraging any interaction of staff with interested stakeholders (such as bidders, local authorities, or politicians). Here, too, leadership by example is important. Leaders who display integrity and act ethically can provide powerful incentives. For individuals, the opportunity to report malpractice to a hotline or ombudsman in confidence or anonymously is essential to counter the likelihood of threats and reprisals. The adequacy of remuneration is an important factor in some situations. Where salaries are very low, individuals are vulnerable to bribes and gifts in kind, such as vehicles or mobile phones, often given in exchange for silence and complicity. At this level, a restructuring of salaries can assist in reducing the vulnerability. However, at the manager level where the deals are organized, the sums changing hands may be substantial—a 1 percent share of a $20 million contract, for example, may represent 10–30 years of salary. At this level, only severe sanctions, such as loss of employment, pension, and forfeiture of assets, may be sufficient to shift the incentives from bad to good. For a firm bidding for a contract, the price to be paid for patronage and the right to operate within a given constituency may become too high if the sanctions imposed for collusion, such as prolonged blacklisting, preclude it from a substantial portion of its regular income.

Roles of the Firm and the Elite

When an oligarchy or elite faction dominates a corrupt culture, all players, whether government or private sector, may be beholden to the power of the elite for survival, patronage, or compliance with the one establishing the informal rules of the game. One or a few powerful and possibly corrupt firms may likewise exert a dominant control of the market. Curbing such power can be very difficult, and a combination of powerful tools is typically required. First, benchmarking of prices or independent verification of agency estimates is important to reveal and publicize the markup or margin that is likely to typify the take from a bid. Second, strict adherence to a range of transparency provisions to allow open, level competition and to protect contesting firms is crucial. Third, the process must be supported by a monitoring power approaching or exceeding that of the elite; this may be achieved by mobilizing civil society into a coherent strong voice (in ways noted earlier), by applying international norms (such as ISO—International Standards for Organizations—and accounting standards) or by the intervention of an international organization (such as international financing institution) that imposes both rules and oversight. Fourth, the process needs a credible and strong investigative and deliberative body, such as a credible anticorruption commission where cases can be brought against the elite or powerful firms. Finally, there are tools for making major or international firms more accountable to an industry or international monitor than to local elites in ways that could affect the worldwide or national business of the firms unless they refrain from participating in local corruption. An example in the transport sector is the integrity pact (box 5.2).

Industry associations in several industries are proposing and adopting sector agreements, such as the Business Principles for Countering Bribery in the Engineering and Construction Industry. The core principles for these sector agreements are often developed in partnership with Transparency International or under the auspices of the World Development Forum in Davos, Switzerland. Under this approach, signatory companies commit themselves to certain rules of market behavior, including a zero tolerance policy on bribery. At this time, such sector agreements among private sector providers do not contain mutual monitoring and sanctioning provisions; peer pressure is expected to promote compliance.

BOX 5.2 Private Sector Integrity Pacts

The integrity pact instrument developed by Transparency International is relevant to the transport sector. Under an integrity pact, a principal and all the bidders in an investment project mutually commit to refrain from and prevent all corrupt acts and submit to effective sanctions in the event of noncompliance. The Korean Public Procurement Service has implemented an integrity pact for all contracts since March 1, 2001. The pact is meant to remind the private sector that business values originate from business ethics and to exhort businesses to join the campaign against corruption. The Korean Integrity Pact is unique in that it requires contractors to submit an "integrity pledge" within 10 days of award of the contract, or forfeit the contract award. Contractors must also agree to strict penalties for violation of the integrity pact, including debarment. Contracting officials are also required to submit an integrity pledge to their respective procurement heads agreeing to strict sanctions in the event of violations.

National and Cross-Sectoral Factors

Anticorruption efforts in the transport sector also are dependent on simultaneous efforts in its external operating environment. A strong legal and judicial environment is essential for legal controls and remedies to be effective; contract provisions need to be upheld and fraud and other infractions prosecuted if any of the sectoral legal framework is to be effective. The availability of commercial information on registered businesses, including financial information on tax returns, through freedom of information legislation can greatly assist in the detection of fraud. Procurement legislation that promotes competition, accountability, and transparency and that strengthens the provisions for monitoring and remedial action is also essential. Finally, a climate of political and commercial reform is invaluable in encouraging the transport sector to be restructured, to separate and commercialize functions, to reduce or refocus regulation, to shorten and clarify the lines of accountability, and to enhance transparency and focus on performance. Usually, the progress of reform in the transport sector must align with public sector reform initiatives at the national level, but the commercial implications in the sector also make it a good one for piloting and driving reforms.

International Drivers

In countries where corruption is prevalent in the public sector and much of society, it is evident that international factors can be strong incentives for controlling corruption. In addition to the influence that international agencies can place on a national government, international drivers such as international financing and trade agencies can also exert significant influence on the integrity and efficiency of the transport sector. Regulatory reform in transport logistics ahead of accession to the World Trade Organization can reduce corruption losses due to pilferage, bribes, and fraud. The procurement and project management guidelines imposed by multilateral development banks can raise competitiveness and transparency in the sector and, if the guidelines are applied consistently, can help overcome national cartels. For maximum impact, bilateral agencies could also adopt open processes. The current move for harmonization of procurement and project management procedures in the sector under international development aid effectiveness initiatives is important for reducing the opportunities for corruption involving international firms and internationally financed goods and services.

Measuring Progress: Relevant Indicators and Baseline Data

As the strategy for governance reform and anticorruption plans in the transport sector is implemented, appropriate indicators to measure the results need to be defined. Emphasis to date has been placed on the formulation of tools, approaches, and investigative techniques. Going forward, more attention will need to be paid to relevant indicators of institutional integrity that can be incorporated into projects and CASs. The initial emphasis may be on implementation and compliance with anticorruption plans, where monitoring teams can review and refine the indicators through projects.

Examples include comparing variances of bid award prices with agency cost estimates across the agency or by division; looking at the average or unit prices of standardized items of works or goods, such as the price for handling containers or the cost of asphalt overlay per square meter; and comparing indicators by administrative or political district to reveal possible individual variances or biases. Other examples include looking at the duration of preparation, bidding, and implementation phases of procurement relative to norms, as well as the duration of contract processing stages, such as signing or clearances, relative to norms. Other measures include the percentage of all contracts awarded following modernized procurement tools and processes (or the percentage of agency expenditures implemented by contract); progress in the implementation of an e-procurement action plan; and measures of results of internal investigations, such as the number to cases sent to an ombudsman or investigative body.

More analytical work is needed in formulating indicators of institutional integrity, and in this area donors and development partners will need to harmonize their approaches from the outset to be able to measure and take stock of the incremental progress collectively.

CONCLUSION

As traced throughout this chapter, the transport sector is prone to corruption in many developing countries. The political value, the high value of some contracts, numerous small contracts and projects distributed locally, and weak or obsolete business processes are all points of vulnerability in the sector. A distinction is made, which can often be blurred in reality, between the results of weak sector governance (inefficient business processes and ineffective policies) and corruption (deliberate acts for illegal private gain or influence), but it is clear that corruption can thrive where governance is weak. However, the sector has well-established tools and processes for planning, designing, procuring, implementing, and monitoring programs and expenditures in the sector, so there are fertile opportunities for increasing the level of detection and control of corruption.

An understanding of the prevalent modes of operation of corruption in each subsector in a particular country is a necessary precursor to strengthening control and reducing the incidence of corruption. To that end, the chapter has identified common forms of fraud, corruption, and collusion that can be found in transport infrastructure projects and in transport agencies. Finally, guidance is provided on a twin-track strategy for curbing corruption: strengthened enforcement and a preventive strategy. The preventive strategy identifies several key elements to guide the design of an approach appropriate to local circumstances, including using the power of information; providing external accountability, transparency, and incentives; controlling the role of the elite and firms; and taking advantage of national and cross-sectoral factors (legal and judicial environment, political and commercial reform) and international drivers (the roles of international markets, agencies and related standards and protocols).

The complexity and, in some places, the deep roots of corruption in the sector mean that reducing corruption may take time as anticorruption plans are developed, implemented, and strengthened and as anticorruption efforts in all levels of government across sectors are mainstreamed. In all cases, attention to preventive measures and capacity-building efforts will be part of a long-term strategy. In those situations where corruption is endemic, a menu of stronger preventive measures will be needed in both the short and medium terms, together with active prosecution of substantial cases. The potential dividends from success in the transport sector are incentive enough for all development partners to actively pursue anticorruption efforts in transport.

ENDNOTES

1. Pork-barrel funding per se is not indicative of corruption, either in transport or in any other sector, as it is part of a broader democratic culture in which elected representatives are expected to provide aggressively for their constituents, and it can even allow for healthy performance-based competition in the electoral process. However, in many countries, the share of the national budget for transport can be disproportionately high in terms of such discretionary funding compared with transport funding that is subject to legislative scrutiny.
2. Modal operations, especially air, rail, and sea, are usually managed under separate entities in most countries, and the issues differ somewhat in each case.
3. This may also result from poor budget planning where revenue forecasts prove too optimistic and agency budgets have to be cut as a result of midyear shortfalls. However, because they create queuing among contractors for payment, these incidents do create opportunities for bribery.

REFERENCES

Bueb, Jean Pierre, and Nicola Ehlermann-Cache. 2005. "Inventory of Mechanisms to Disguise Corruption in the Bidding Process and Some Tools for Prevention and Detection." In *Fighting Corruption and Promoting Integrity in Public Procurement*, 161–75. Paris: Organisation for Economic Co-operation and Development.

Center for Economic Studies [CES], Ifo Institute for Economic Research, and CESifo GmbH [Munich Society for the Promotion of Economic Research] (CESIFO). 2004. "The Political Economy of Corruption and the Role of Financial Institution." CESIFO Working Paper Series 1293:1–32.

Søreide, Tina. 2005. "Grey Zones and Corruption in Public Procurement: Issues for Consideration." In *Fighting Corruption and Promoting Integrity in Public Procurement,* 51–58. Paris: Organisation for Economic Co-operation and Development.

6

Corruption in the Petroleum Sector

CHARLES McPHERSON AND STEPHEN MacSEARRAIGH

"We know what corruption has cost us—it has denied us the value of our resources, both human and natural. It breeds injustice. It causes killings. It causes the diseases that ravage us almost everywhere."

Nuhu Ribadu, Head of Economics and Financial Crimes Commission, Nigeria (Address to World Bank and International Monetary Fund Annual Meetings, Singapore, September 2006)

"The so-called resource curse and specific petroleum industry dynamics make the oil and gas sector particularly prone to corruption, from the first speculation about potential oil in the ground through all stages ending in the spending (or misspending) of oil revenues. A recent oil corruption scandal in the Middle East involving a European oil giant reminds us that no country is immune to the malign dynamics of corruption and that it takes at least two to tango: the foreign investor and the host government, the state oil company, and/or local business. Overall, Norway has limited oil-related corruption, largely thanks to decades of investment in transparency, a bureaucracy with high integrity, and a political culture that frowns on corruption. Through the Oil for Development program, Norway continues to share its experience in this field—its successes as well as its shortcomings—with developing countries eager to take the corruption curse out of the oil and gas sector."

Poul Engberg-Pedersen, Director-General, Norwegian Agency for Development Cooperation (NORAD)

Resource wealth is widely distributed among developing countries and economies in transition. While the potential of such wealth to contribute to poverty reduction and growth is clearly significant, the offsetting temptation for corruption and abuse appears to be similarly great, perhaps never so great as when the wealth in question derives from petroleum.

This chapter opens with a brief description of the often observed inverse relationship between oil and gas wealth and a country's economic, social, and political performance. It then discusses industry-specific features that contribute to this underperformance by encouraging corruption, introduces a typology of sector corruption, and identifies major actors and their roles. The several stages of the oil value chain and their respective vulnerabilities to corruption are described along with examples. Finally, the chapter suggests, with appropriate caveats, possible remedies and responses to sector corruption. Special attention is paid to the Extractive Industries Transparency Initiative (EITI), a promising approach to corruption issues strongly supported by the World Bank Group. The chapter closes with a summary table, or policy maker's road map, plotting stages of the sector value chain against susceptibilities to corruption, corruption warning signals, and recommended responses.

THE "PARADOX OF PLENTY"

Some 32 developing countries and transition economies are considered petroleum rich, measured in terms of the importance of petroleum revenues and exports to overall fiscal revenues, GDP, and total export earnings. These countries are listed in table 6.1.

Petroleum wealth on the scale experienced in these countries might reasonably be expected to deliver sizable developmental benefits. Yet, more often than not, the same countries experience low growth relative to their nonoil peers, poor performance against human development indicators, and more than their fair share of social and political unrest and even violent conflict. This counterintuitive result is referred to as the "resource curse" or "paradox of plenty."[1]

Nigeria provides just one example of the paradox of plenty. Assessed against desirable developmental outcomes, the performance of this oil-rich country has been significantly below its potential and even below that of many of its non-oil Sub-Saharan African neighbors. GDP per capita is $400 per year, 60 percent of the population lives on less than $2 per day, 78 out of every 1,000 infants dies at birth, 35 percent of the population under five years of age is malnourished, barely 50 percent of the adult female population is literate, and so on. The oil-related civil war in Biafra, Nigeria's well-documented suppression (until recently) of democratic institutions, escalating violence in the Niger Delta, and the environmental degradation that has characterized oil operations in the delta complete the picture painted by the summary statistics on development. The record is dismal, yet over the past 35 years, oil rents accruing to Nigeria have amounted to an estimated $300 billion. Nigeria, however, is not unique. Its experience is replicated throughout African oil-producing countries and in other regions of the world where there is similar dependence on oil and gas.[2]

OMINOUS CORRELATIONS

A large body of literature and analysis is devoted to the paradox of plenty.[3] While the explanatory factors put forward are numerous, they appear to fall neatly under technical and political headings. The most important technical factors are revenue volatility and the phenomenon known as the Dutch disease. Revenue volatility derives primarily from the notorious swings in oil prices on international markets.[4] Difficult to cope with under any circumstances, swings in oil prices are especially challenging when unpredictable. The Dutch disease occurs when inflows of oil revenues overheat the domestic economy, causing an appreciation of the real exchange rate, which results in a loss of competitiveness of traditional nonoil exports and erosion of diversification of the domestic economy. When pronounced, these outcomes can put serious strains on a country's economic and social fabric. These technical factors are better understood, and macroeconomic policies to deal with

TABLE 6.1 Petroleum-Rich Developing Countries

	Average annual hydrocarbon revenues, 2000–03		*Average annual hydrocarbon exports, 2000–03*
Country	*As percent of total fiscal revenues*	*As percent of GDP*	*As percent of total exports*
Algeria	69.9	25.8	97.1
Angola	80.9	33.9	90.3
Azerbaijan	47.0	11.9	88.3
Bahrain	71.2	23.5	72.1
Brunei Darussalam	85.8	52.7	88.2
Cameroon	26.6	5.3	44.9
Colombia	9.0	2.7	27.8
Congo, Rep. of	70.6	20.2	89.5
Ecuador	26.4	6.9	43.5
Equatorial Guinea	84.0	21.6	93.4
Gabon	60.5	19.6	79.9
Indonesia	31.3	6.1	22.6
Iran, Islamic Rep. of	59.3	16.8	82.0
Iraq	58.4	93.1	—
Kazakhstan	21.0	5.1	49.7
Kuwait	68.4	47.6	91.9
Libya	72.5	36.1	97.0
Mexico	32.2	7.0	14.9
Nigeria	77.2	32.6	95.8
Oman	78.3	32.4	80.1
Qatar	71.3	25.3	83.0
Russian Federation	39.7	6.8	52.8
Saudi Arabia	81.6	27.4	89.2
Sudan	43.0	4.6	73.3
Syrian Arab Rep.	45.7	13.4	69.5
Trinidad and Tobago	27.4	6.6	60.6
Turkmenistan	42.8	8.7	83.6
United Arab Emirates	76.1	32.4	49.1
Venezuela, R. B. de	52.7	14.3	79.9
Vietnam	31.8	7.1	21.4
Yemen, Rep. of	68.6	25.0	91.5
Average	**52.7**	**20.8**	**67.2**

Source: IMF (2005, annex 1).
Note: — = not available. Table includes all countries that are considered rich in hydrocarbons and/or mineral resources on the basis of the following criteria: an average share of hydrocarbon fiscal revenues in total fiscal revenue of at least 25 percent during the period 2000–03 or an average share of hydrocarbon export proceeds in total export proceeds of at least 25 percent during the same period. Countries with potential large medium- and long-term hydrocarbon revenue: Bolivia, Chad, Mauritania; São Tomé and Príncipe; Timor-Leste.

them are better appreciated than they once were. Corrective policies include exchange rate management; expenditure smoothing, possibly through the use of special petroleum revenue funds; and enhanced fiscal discipline.[5]

Much more daunting and, as many students of the phenomenon would now argue, with greater explanatory power, are the nontechnical, political drivers behind the paradox of plenty. Within the political sphere, good governance has been identified as essential to success in combating the resource curse. Unfortunately, oil-rich developing countries do not score well under this heading. In World Bank surveys of a wide range of governance indicators among countries, oil-rich developing countries and transition economies typically find themselves in the bottom one-third of the governance rankings.[6]

Certainly weak governance existed before oil development in many countries, and it is arguable that causality runs from weak capacity to mismanagement of oil. That said, there is growing evidence in support of the argument that causality runs primarily in the other direction, that is, that oil itself erodes governance.

Good governance has several dimensions, including clear and stable laws; the rule of law; high levels of capacity in government; fiscal, monetary, and budgetary discipline; and open dialogue between government and society. The absence of corruption, however, is one of good governance's cornerstones. Unfortunately, oil is widely recognized as a lightning rod for corruption, and, not surprisingly, data on corruption corroborate the broader findings on governance. Oil wealth and dependence on oil revenues are closely linked with perceptions of corruption.

Table 6.2 is extracted from Transparency International's most recent survey of perceptions of corruption. Perceptions of corruption are closely correlated with resource wealth. Once again, major petroleum producers in developing countries and transition economies are clustered in the bottom one-third of the country rankings.[7]

TABLE 6.2 Oil and Perceptions of Corruption, 2006

Countries ranked from 1–50

Rank	*Country*	*2006 CPI*	*Rank*	*Country*	*2006 CPI*
1	Finland	9.6	24	Barbados	6.7
1	Iceland	9.6	24	Estonia	6.7
4	Denmark	9.5	26	Portugal	6.6
5	Singapore	9.4	28	Slovenia	6.4
6	Sweden	9.2	28	Uruguay	6.4
7	Switzerland	9.1	31	United Arab Emirates	6.2
8	Norway	8.8	32	Bhutan	6
9	Australia	8.7	32	Qatar	6
9	Netherlands	8.7	34	Israel	5.9
11	Austria	8.6	36	Bahrain	5.7
11	Luxembourg	8.6	37	Botswana	5.6
11	United Kingdom	8.6	39	Oman	5.4
14	Canada	8.5	40	Jordan	5.3
15	Hong Kong	8.3	41	Hungary	5.2
16	Germany	8	42	Mauritius	5.1
17	Japan	7.6	42	South Korea	5.1
18	France	7.4	44	Malaysia	5
18	Ireland	7.4	45	Italy	4.9
20	Belgium	7.3	46	Czech Republic	4.8
20	Chile	7.3	46	Kuwait	4.8
20	United States	7.3	49	Latvia	4.7
23	Spain	6.8	49	Slovakia	4.7

TABLE 6.2 ***(Continued)***

Countries ranked from 50–100

Rank	*Country*	*2006 CPI*	*Rank*	*Country*	*2006 CPI*
51	South Africa	4.6	79	Burkina Faso	3.2
51	Tunisia	4.6	79	Lesotho	3.2
54	Greece	4.4	79	Moldova	3.2
55	Costa Rica	4.1	79	Morocco	3.2
55	Namibia	4.1	79	Trinidad and Tobago	3.2
57	Bulgaria	4	84	Algeria	3.1
57	El Salvador	4	84	Madagascar	3.1
59	Colombia	3.9	84	Mauritania	3.1
60	Turkey	3.8	84	Panama	3.1
61	Jamaica	3.7	84	Romania	3.1
61	Poland	3.7	84	Sri Lanka	3.1
63	Lebanon	3.6	90	Gabon	3
63	Thailand	3.6	90	Serbia	3
66	Belize	3.5	90	Suriname	3
66	Cuba	3.5	93	Argentina	2.9
69	Croatia	3.4	93	Armenia	2.9
70	Brazil	3.3	93	Eritrea	2.9
70	China	3.3	93	Syrian Arab Rep.	2.9
70	Egypt	3.3	93	Tanzania	2.9
70	Ghana	3.3	99	Dominican Republic	2.8
70	India	3.3	99	Georgia	2.8
70	Mexico	3.3	99	Mali	2.8
70	Peru	3.3	99	Mongolia	2.8
70	Saudi Arabia	3.3	99	Mozambique	2.8
70	Senegal	3.3	99	Ukraine	2.8

Countries ranked from 100–160

Rank	*Country*	*2006 CPI*	*Rank*	*Country*	*2006 CPI*
105	Bolivia	2.7	138	Cameroon	2.3
105	Iran, Islamic Rep. of	2.7	138	Ecuador	2.3
105	Libya	2.7	138	Niger	2.3
105	Malawi	2.7	138	Venezuela, R. B. de	2.3
105	Uganda	2.7	142	Angola	2.2
111	Guatemala	2.6	142	Congo, Rep. of	2.2
111	Kazakhstan	2.6	142	Kenya	2.2
111	Lao PDR	2.6	142	Kyrgyzstan	2.2
111	Paraguay	2.6	142	Nigeria	2.2
111	Timor-Leste	2.6	142	Pakistan	2.2
111	Vietnam	2.6	142	Sierra Leone	2.2
111	Yemen, Rep. of	2.6	142	Tajikistan	2.2
111	Zambia	2.6	142	Turkmenistan	2.2
121	Benin	2.5	151	Belarus	2.1
121	Gambia	2.5	151	Cambodia	2.1
121	Honduras	2.5	151	Côte d'Ivoire	2.1
121	Philippines	2.5	151	Equatorial Guinea	2.1
121	Russian Federation	2.5	151	Uzbekistan	2.1
121	Rwanda	2.5	156	Bangladesh	2
130	Azerbaijan	2.4	156	Chad	2
130	Burundi	2.4	156	Congo, Dem. Rep. of	2
130	Ethiopia	2.4	156	Sudan	2
130	Indonesia	2.4	160	Guinea	1.9
130	Togo	2.4	160	Iraq	1.9
130	Zimbabwe	2.4	163	Haiti	1.8

Source: Transparency International (2007). Available at http://www.transparency.org/policy_research/surveys_indices/cpi/2006.
Note: Rank means global country rank (inverse to CPI score). CPI means Corruption Perception Index, ranging from a score of 10 (lowest perceived corruption) to 1 (highest perceived corruption). Petroleum-rich developing countries (see Table 6.1) are shaded.

SPECIAL FEATURES OF THE PETROLEUM INDUSTRY

Against this background, we now turn to a description of the characteristic features of the petroleum industry that help explain what makes it so susceptible to corruption.

Volume of Transactions

Oil is often referred to as "the biggest business." Dollar volumes in the industry are huge. The International Energy Agency has estimated that $3 trillion will be invested in the oil and gas sectors globally over the next 25 years. While large, these investments will amount to less than 6 percent of projected revenues over the period. Annual gross revenues on crude oil sales are currently running at an estimated $1.5 trillion per year. Assuming conservatively that along the value chain, each barrel is sold three times, the actual volume of global oil market transactions will be many times larger (International Energy Agency 2005).

Estimates for Angola illustrate the scale of investments and revenues involved for just one emerging oil producer. The investments required in Angola's petroleum sector over the next 5 to 10 years are on the order of $8 billion to $10 billion annually. Gross revenues generated by these investments are estimated in the range of $70 billion to $80 billion annually at current prices during peak producing years 2010–15. Corresponding annual government receipts would range between $50 billion and $55 billion.[8]

What these global and country-specific numbers reveal is that very small fractions of transaction values in the petroleum sector can equate to very large sums of money, representing a very serious temptation to corruption. What is more, because they are such small fractions, they are very difficult to detect should they go missing, thus adding to temptation.

Rents

There is scarcely an industry that can touch oil for the magnitude of the rents it generates. Largely because of the oligopolistic character of the industry, prices are typically vastly in excess of cost.[9] The average price of a barrel of crude oil on international markets during 2006 has been in the range of $65–$75, while costs per barrel range from $3–$5 in the Middle East, through $12 in the Gulf of Mexico, to $15 in the North Sea (International Energy Agency 2005, p. 11). These numbers result in margins of $50 to more than $70 a barrel—an obvious corruption risk.

Concentration of Revenue Flows

Certainly at the production level, petroleum revenue flows to the government tend to be concentrated, coming from relatively few taxpayers, mostly foreign rather than domestic. In this sort of environment, the accountability to the populace of government agencies in receipt of the revenue flows is limited. Concerns of the general public, in particular challenges to account for the use of the revenues, can be ignored with impunity. Furthermore, given the likely scale of revenues, it is not difficult for government authorities to either buy off or intimidate those who would challenge their behavior.[10]

Complexity

The oil industry is technically and structurally complex, and the legal, commercial, and fiscal arrangements governing revenue flows are typically even more complex. This makes it relatively easy for those who manipulate revenue flows for political or personal gain to conceal their activities.

Natural Monopolies

The sheer scale of the oil and gas industry and its supporting infrastructure often result in natural monopolies in areas such as pipeline transport, terminaling, and port facilities. Monopoly control creates opportunities for corrupt abuse through discretionary control of access and through the setting of fees or tariffs for use.

Strategic Significance

Oil is almost universally regarded as being of strategic significance.[11] From the standpoint of producing-country governments, oil is one of the "commanding heights" of the economy, an argument that is used in support of wide-ranging government involvement in the sector. Government intervention ranges from ownership of the resource through policy formulation and legislation, control of access to infrastructure, and regulation of operations to the establishment of national oil companies. Each of these areas of government involvement may spawn innumerable opportunities for corruption.[12]

From a consuming-country government's standpoint, the perceived strategic importance of oil heightens concerns over security of supply. These concerns often lead to engagement with producing-country governments with the intent of ensuring supply security. The terms of engagement may or may not involve varying degrees of corruption. Powerful new developing-country consumers have made no secret of their pursuit of oil supply security through typically opaque arrangements with developing-country producers.[13] Major developed-country consumers have similarly allowed supply security concerns to, if not involve them in directly corrupt activity, at least use their considerable economic, political, or military leverage to influence the behavior of developing-country producers in their favor. At the same time, they may adopt an attitude of tolerance in the face of corrupt behavior on the part of the producing-country government to avoid prejudicing supply security. The apparently ambivalent attitude of developed country governments toward alleged corruption and human rights abuse in key oil-producing states has been referenced in the press as an example of such behavior.[14] The supply security interests of the two consuming-country groups—developing and developed countries—are increasingly coming into competitive conflict.[15]

Spillover Effects

Corruption in a sector as rich and as powerful as petroleum can be expected to have major negative spillover effects on the governance not only of other sectors but also of the economy as a whole. Hence the sector vulnerabilities listed above have an importance for policy makers that goes far beyond oil. Before turning to specific corrupt practices in the petroleum sector, the next two sections of this chapter provide a stage-setting review of the categories of corruption encountered and of the cast of actors involved.

CORRUPTION TYPOLOGY

Oil sector corruption can be characterized in a variety of ways, descriptive of the channels through which it is achieved. Four useful distinctions are listed below.

Policy Corruption

Policy corruption involves corrupt influence on the design of sector policies, as well as the enactment of sector laws and taxes in a manner intended to provide political or personal gains at the public expense. Foreign policies, tax breaks, price controls, awards of exclusive rights, special accounting procedures, and the myriad of special industry or regional incentives characteristic of the petroleum industry might all fall under the policy corruption heading. Blatantly illegal corruption such as bribe paying may or may not play a role. So-called legal corruption is often more important in this area.[16] Legal corruption of policy decisions may result from carefully cultivated close relationships between policy makers or legislators and special interest groups. The "revolving door" is just one aspect of legal corruption; in exchange for policy or related favors, for example, policy makers may expect or find a "home" with key interest groups, such as a seat on the board or a corporate executive position, when they leave politics. Oil company boards commonly include high-ranking former politicians with continuing access to senior policy makers. Clearly a spectrum of activity may be involved, from legitimate lobbying to something next door to criminal corruption.[17]

Administrative Corruption

One step down from policy corruption, this type of corruption refers to the abuse of administrative office to extract illegal benefits in exchange for approvals covering a wide range of commercial and operational activities, for "looking the other way" in the face of corrupt behavior, or for a favorable interpretation of fiscal regulations. As with policy corruption, the concept of legal corruption may apply. A recent U.S. dispute is illustrative. Four lawsuits have been brought against the U.S. Department of Interior, charging that it blocked auditors from pursuing more than $30 million in underpayment of oil royalties in the Gulf of Mexico. The inspector general for the Interior Department told a U.S. congressional subcommittee that "short of crime, anything goes" (Andrews 2006). Administrative corruption may also involve direct action by administrative agencies in their own interest, when, for example, such agencies become involved in trading government oil or in regulating access to infrastructure.

The more heavily regulated the system, the higher the degree of government control, and the greater the scope for administrative corruption.

Commercial Corruption

The broad area of procurement abuse, including tender rigging, kickbacks, and cost inflation, would come under this heading. Given the scale of industry transactions, the scope for corruption in this area is stunning. The widely reported cost-inflation scandals associated with the rebuilding of Iraq's petroleum sector by primarily U.S. contractors provides a recent example of procurement abuse on a major scale (Walker 2004).

Grand Corruption

Direct theft of massive amounts of money through diversion of production, products, or revenues would qualify as grand corruption. Investigators say General Sani Abacha, president of Nigeria in 1993–98, diverted to offshore bank accounts or companies controlled by his family tens of millions of U.S. dollars in oil revenues on a monthly basis from the government accounts for which they were otherwise destined.[18]

RELEVANT ACTORS

A wide range of institutions and individuals may be involved in oil sector corruption. The main relevant actors and their respective roles are listed below.

Government

Producing-country governments—broadly defined to include all branches of government, executive, legislative, and judiciary—have all at one time or another been implicated in sector corruption, under the full range of corruption channels listed in the preceding section.

Consuming-country governments are rarely blameless either. As suggested earlier, driven by supply security concerns, or simply out of an interest in promoting the commercial success of their companies abroad, they may use simple bribes or their leverage—economic, political, or military—in the form of either carrots or sticks to influence outcomes in producing countries in their favor. Transparency International's Bribe Payers Index, the flip side to its Corruption Perception Index, puts China and Korea, both oil-hungry consuming countries active in oil sectors outside their own territories, near the bottom of the country rankings in terms of desirable performance. When bribes are more broadly interpreted to include not just money but promises of economic assistance and political or military support, countries such as France, Japan, the United States, and the United Kingdom, again all countries with serious oil supply security concerns, move into the culpable zone. Box 6.1 provides a graphic illustration of the corrupt and quasi-corrupt relationships that can develop among powerful consuming-country governments, oil-producing-country governments, and the oil industry itself.

BOX 6.1 ***L'Affaire Elf***

In 2003, the so-called *L'Affaire Elf* broke in France, exposing a tangled web of political ambitions, influence peddling, oil, and corruption. Court proceedings refer to Elf, the former French oil giant, as having been created in 1965 to secure French oil independence, primarily by maintaining French influence in oil-producing countries. From the outset, Elf was very close to the French presidency, which appointed several of its key political executives. The company became equally close to political leaders in its "client" states. Bribery at Elf ultimately extended to nearly all countries in which it operated. In 2003, 37 defendants, including the company's former chief executive and former general affairs director, were convicted of channeling €305 million from Elf to secure business contracts in Africa, South America, Russia, Spain, and Germany between 1989 and 1993.

West Africa was a particular focus of Elf's efforts. The company's former long-time Africa administrator told the court that annual transfers of about $20 million were made to the president of Gabon, while other huge sums were paid to leaders in Angola, Cameroon, and the Republic of Congo. The multimillion-dollar payments were partly aimed at guaranteeing Elf's (France's) preferential access to oil in these states, but they were also designed to ensure the African leaders' alignment with France. Elf's corruption apparently was not confined to its foreign operations. The company was a major domestic French political force, contributing money to Gaullist parties. According to testimony from Elf's former chief executive, the company paid "at the very least" €5 million a year to all of the main French political parties to buy their support. Elf, in other words, was not only a French asset not only in the global competition for access to oil, but also in the domestic competition for political power. It developed into a cancer at the heart of France and spread to every country in which Elf operated. "The whole oil system operates in an opaque way," Elf's former chief executive told the court. While *L'Affaire Elf* is perhaps an extreme example, similar operations can probably be found in other countries of the developed world.

Sources: Robert-Diard (2003a, 2003b); Fitchett and Ignatius (2002); Henley (2003).

Oil Companies

There are several categories of oil companies. Private sector oil companies fall into two categories, the international oil companies (IOCs) and the typically much smaller local firms. There is no shortage of examples of corruption on the part of IOCs, such as buying privileged access to resources, legislation, and favorable regulatory or tax treatment. Although they are still not above pressing host and home governments for favorable treatment, IOCs today have strong incentives to stay away from direct corruption. These incentives take the form of severe home-country laws, such as the U.S. Foreign Corrupt Practices Act; international codes, such as the Organisation for Economic Co-operation and Development (OECD) Convention against Bribery and the United Nations Convention against Corruption; civil society or shareholder oversight, and reputational risks. Allegations or instances of direct corruption by IOCs can still be found, but these appear to be fewer than in the past.[19]

Local private companies appear to be less constrained. Many indigenous start-up companies may be serious in their stated intent to become genuine oil and gas companies. Too often, however, local companies are shell companies owned by influential local investors with no interest in building real oil companies but a strong interest in skimming profits. Nigeria has in the past been notorious for this kind of behavior. Indigenous companies with little or no relevant experience or capacity regularly obtained valuable exploration rights on a favored, nontransparent basis, only to turn around and "farm out" these rights to qualified international operators for very significant sums.[20]

Most oil-producing developing countries have their own national oil companies (NOCs). Although reform seems to be under way in a number of countries, the NOCs have enjoyed a notorious reputation for corruption and waste. Past audits have estimated that waste and corruption caused annual losses from these two sources of $1 billion at the Nigerian National Petroleum Corporation (NNPC) and of $2 billion at Indonesia's Pertamina (World Bank 200b; PwC 1998). Losses on this scale have a macroeconomic impact and are not to be ignored. The corruption involved is often commercial, through influence on procurement, sometimes under the guise of promoting local content, but in actuality promoting the interests of the NOC or its affiliates. NOCs may also play an important role in administrative corruption, where, as a result of failure or weak capacity in the nominal regulatory agency, they have captured regulatory authority. Finally, in countries where they handle large revenue flows on behalf of government, NOCs may be involved in grand corruption. Box 6.2 profiles the corruption that for years pervaded Pertamina, culminating in its radical restructuring and reform. The NNPC has also undergone major reform and restructuring in response to the same pressures.

A subcategory of NOCs deserves special attention, namely, the NOCs of oil-importing countries. These NOCs are often the, or one of the, instruments used to implement these countries' supply security strategies (Andrews-Speed and Ma 2005). As might be expected, the NOCs of China, India, and Korea come up regularly in this context. Concern has been expressed that their typically opaque agreements with oil-producing countries may act in some cases as a cover for corrupt practices.[21]

Oil service companies are another critical category of companies. A very high percentage of oil industry work is performed not by the oil companies themselves or by government but by their contractors. These are legion in number and cover all stages of the industry value chain, from seismic and drilling contractors and geological and geophysical consultants in the exploration phase; to drilling services, material suppliers, and engineering and fabrication contractors in the development and production phase; to pipeline and refinery engineering and construction firms further along the chain. Service companies are very frequently caught up in the tangle of corrupt petroleum sector practices, especially as they relate to procurement.

Big Men

Powerful individual influence peddlers or "arrangers," referred to in Africa as "big men," are common to all regions of the world and to most economic sectors. They have become permanent features of the petroleum sector, particularly but by no means exclusively in developing countries and transition economies. Big men often operate through local and international networks involving players from both consuming and producing countries. Where bribes are used, corruption is clear. However, the activities of big men may take place along a continuum that ranges from acceptable lobbying to criminal dealings and from policy corruption through to grand corruption. The operations of a classic international oil industry big man are described in box 6.3. The box also illustrates the dilemma a major oil-importing

BOX 6.2 Corruption in Pertamina

In the late 1960s and early 1970s, Indonesia's NOC, Pertamina, was the epitome of national pride among Indonesians and a role model for NOCs in many other developing countries. With capital from American banks, expertise from independent oil companies, and all-embracing government support, Pertamina grew rapidly. Adding to its significant oil production and revenues, the company became a gigantic conglomerate with, among other things, its own drilling equipment, tanker fleet, gasoline outlets, petrochemical complex, tourism complex, stadium, and steel mill.

Pertamina's overextension led to a financial crisis not only for the company but for the country as a whole. In response to public criticism, a high-level review committee (the Commission of Four) was appointed in January 1970 by President Suharto to investigate corruption in Indonesia in general and Pertamina in particular. The investigation revealed serious and deep-rooted problems of mismanagement, corruption, and capture of the petroleum industry by powerful vested interests. Pertamina was found to be in violation of Indonesian legislation in multiple areas. The company's defense was that many of the laws were not pertinent because of Pertamina's strategic importance and special place in Indonesia.

According to the commission report, revenue management was not transparent; balance sheets were never published, and profits were never revealed. An audit by the U.S. accounting firm Arthur Young found that the company was operating six uncoordinated accounting systems—a breeding ground for corruption. Only a fraction of payments by foreign exploration and production contractors to Pertamina were reaching the government. Tax evasion was standard. The costs of Pertamina's projects were often inflated several times, enriching people close to the company. Corruption on such a scale was only possible with the complicity of top political circles. By some accounts, President Suharto's rise to power was attributable to financing from Pertamina. Suharto's family and friends became involved in every stage of the oil industry, and Pertamina supported the military in all aspects. Pertamina was also asked to provide subsidized fuel to the public and to buy off political opponents.

The Commission of Four report provoked a wave of anticorruption measures, but unfortunately Pertamina's appeal as a cash machine proved irresistible and continued unabated. Only after President Suharto's resignation in 1998 did it become possible to trace the full extent of corruption in the company. A parliamentary investigation in 2003 revealed that Suharto and his closest allies, including Pertamina's top executives and a range of ministers, gained some $1.7 billion from Pertamina.

The upshot of all these findings was a new law, enacted in 2001, that radically restructured Pertamina, stripping it of its special privileges and monopoly powers, and introduced measures to make the company more competitive and transparent, thus setting the stage for a turning point on corruption.

Sources: Kobonbaev (2006). See also Glassburner (1976), Mackie (1970), "Indonesia: Perils of Pertamina" (2003), Oxford Analytica (2000), Muljadi (2002), and Hari (2004).

developed country can face in balancing the priority it assigns to energy security with a professed interest in the promotion of good governance.

Banks

When large amounts of money from corrupt sector activities need to be hidden away or transferred, banks enter onto the stage. Their role is examined elsewhere in this book in chapter 12. A highly publicized example of alleged participation in questionable transfers of oil revenues involved the Riggs Bank of Washington, DC. A 2004 U.S. Senate investigation found that in the case of Equatorial Guinea, Riggs "turned a blind eye," perhaps because of the importance of its client, "to evidence suggesting the bank was handling the proceeds of foreign corruption." Another bank, BNP Paribas, a major

BOX 6.3 The Giffen Case

"In February 2007, the U.S. Attorney General's Office in Manhattan is scheduled to go to trial in the largest foreign bribery case brought against an American citizen. The case involves a labyrinthine trail of international financial transfers, suspected money laundering and a dizzying array of domestic and international shell corporations. The criminal case names President Nazarbayev of Kazakhstan as an un-indicted co-conspirator. The defendant, James Giffen, a wealthy American merchant banker and consultant to the Kazakh Government, is accused of channeling more than $78 million in bribes to Mr. Nazarbayev and the head of the country's oil ministry. The money, doled out by American companies seeking access to Kazakhstan's vast oil reserves went towards the Kazakh leadership's personal use.

The case against Mr. Giffen has opened a window onto high stakes, transcontinental maneuvering that occurs when Big Oil and political access overlap—a juncture marked by intense and expensive lobbying, overseas deal-making and the intersection of money, business and politics. It is a shadow world that people like Mr. Giffen establish and define.

Prosecutors accused Mr. Giffen of overseeing a tangled web of bribery networks in the 1990's designed to buy access and influence in Kazakhstan for oil giants like ExxonMobil, BPAmoco (now BP) and Phillips (now ConocoPhillips). The payment, prosecutors said, violated the Foreign Corrupt Practices Act which forbids American citizens or corporations from paying bribes to foreign officials to obtain business. None of the oil companies have been accused of wrongdoing.

The case also illustrates the U.S. Government's struggle to reconcile its short term energy interests with its long term political goal of encouraging democracy in countries the international community has deemed corrupt. Mr. Giffen's lawyers have maintained that he did not act alone. 'Mr. Giffen was working with the knowledge of our Government,' Mr. Giffen's lawyer said. Mr. Giffen's lawyers say he cannot be found guilty because 'his actions were part of his official duties as an adviser to the Kazakh Government and received the blessing of senior American officials.' That contention has prompted a blizzard of motions, memorandums and filings between the federal government and Mr. Giffen's lawyers. Federal prosecutors have sought to block Mr. Giffen's access to documents on the grounds that discussing them could breach national security interests."

Source: Stodghill (2006). © 2006 by The New York Times Co. Reprinted with Permission.

French banking firm, has been named in oil-related money transfer scandals in the Republic of Congo and Iraq. Ideally, anti-money-laundering responsibilities of the banking sector should be extended to avoid any other actions that facilitate corruption.

THE OIL VALUE CHAIN: VULNERABILITIES TO CORRUPTION

This section examines the vulnerability to corruption of each segment of the oil sector value chain from the award of exploration rights through to the sale of gasoline at the retail pump. This section also indicates the red flags, or warning signals, that suggest the presence of corruption.

Exploration

The exploration phase comprises the award and negotiation of exploration and production rights, approvals and the permitting of exploration operations, and oversight of any relinquishment or extension of exploration rights. Enormous amounts of money may be at stake, given that a successful exploration could lead to production worth hundreds of millions or even billions of dollars.[22] With sums like this, it is no surprise that the exploration stage of the value chain has been vulnerable to corruption. Corruption has been especially associated with the awards process itself and the subsequent negotiation of contract terms, the most important of which relate to the work to be performed, the recovery of costs, sharing of profits, and the rate and extent of obligatory relinquishments to the state. Past practice, still widespread, awarded exploration acreage on the basis of a direct negotiation, with or without competition. Oil companies and governments often argued that these negotiations should be confidential to protect commercially sensitive information and to allow terms to be tailored to individual country and company requirements. Unfortunately, the opacity of these negotiations also left the door wide open to corruption.

Warning signals include absence of competition, awards to companies without demonstrated ability to perform, waivers of bid bond requirements, seriously unbalanced contract terms, and unexplained contract extensions. Growing concerns over corruption at the exploration phase have led several new oil-producing countries to opt for full transparency of awards. One or two established oil-producing countries with negative track records are now trying to follow suit.

Timor-Leste, the world's newest country and a new petroleum producer with major liquid and natural gas reserves opted from the outset for full transparency of the awards process. The government published drafts of applicable legislation and model contracts for comment, public hearings were held, and the licensing rounds and their terms were publicly advertised. A prequalification process screened potential bidders for technical and financial capacity. Contracts were awarded on an international competitive bid basis with one-bid variable (the offered work program), sharply narrowing opportunities for discretionary behavior. Final awards were publicly announced and explained. More recently, past "bad boys" Angola and Nigeria have adopted similarly transparent awards procedures. Although not without flaws, the new procedures represent a vast improvement on past practice, winning widespread if cautious international commendation.[23]

Elsewhere, unfortunately, nontransparent award procedures are still common. One startling, relatively recent case of corruption at the exploration-production awards phase involved Statoil, Norway's national oil company, and Iran. In June 2004, Statoil was fined the equivalent of $2.9 million after paying substantial consultancy fees, aimed at securing oil and gas contracts in Iran, to a politically well-connected investment firm. Similar recent episodes have occurred in other countries. Prosecutors in the Giffen case profiled in box 6.3 asserted that senior Kazakhstan government officials received $78 million in illegal payments in connection with six separate oil transactions, mostly related to the acquisition of exploration and production rights.[24]

Certain practices in the award of petroleum exploration licenses in Equatorial Guinea, while allegedly legal in that country, represent a conflict of interest at best and a probable opportunity for corruption. Licenses are awarded by direct negotiation in Equatorial Guinea, and according to a senior government official, companies owned by government ministers often bid for licenses in consortia with foreign groups. If successful, they receive "a percentage of the total contract the company gets. This means that a cabinet minister ends up with a sizeable part of the contract price in his bank account."[25]

Development

Once a commercial discovery is declared, the development phase kicks in. While administrative corruption almost certainly exists in relation to approvals of development plans, well locations, environmental permits, and the like, perhaps the greatest vulnerability to corruption at this stage lies in the procurement process. Capital and operating costs, along with the potential for abuse of the procurement process, begin to skyrocket. The full range of industry actors and procurement tricks comes into play.

Kickbacks to officials—a form of success fee dependent on contract award—appear to be the most common form of corrupt payment in procurement. Payments can be made equally to government or private contractors—the same principles apply. In 2000, Nigeria Liquefied Natural Gas Limited selected a consortium of four major engineering service companies known as TKSJ, including Technip of France, Snamprogetti of Italy, JGC of Japan, and led by Kellogg, Brown & Root, a subsidiary of the U.S. firm Halliburton, to build a $2 billion production facility at Bonny Island in the Niger Delta. A current French investigation alleges that, in connection with the award, a TKSJ subsidiary paid $171.5 million to TriStar, a company registered in Gibraltar and headed by a London lawyer who had long worked for Halliburton and had close ties with officials in the Nigerian government (Isikoff 2004). The TKSJ charges are simply illustrative; other examples abound.

While most examples of procurement abuse fall under the heading of commercial corruption, policy and administrative corruption can play a role as well. Government agencies, NOCs among them, are often able to use their influence to direct procurement toward government-favored or government-affiliated suppliers. Companies may be "advised" that awards to certain local firms, connected with senior officials, could have a favorable impact on their business. Open exercise of this influence is less common now than it once was, but it is still found, often under the guise of the promotion of domestic or local content, supported by contractual provisions or laws that leave latitude for abuse. Taking advantage of local content requirements, local or indigenous firms may present themselves to international suppliers as essential partners, regardless of whether they possess the skills or capacity required to do anything more than lend their names and share in any profits. This comment is not meant to belittle the importance of achieving progress on local content, but simply to underscore the need for caution or oversight in the implementation of local content policies.

Host countries and their NOCs are not the only parties accused of engaging in these practices. IOCs are frequently charged by host governments and at times by their own partners with favoring affiliated service companies or companies from their home countries in procurement.

Procurement abuse raises costs, but relative to the scale of industry expenditures, especially in the development phase, these cost increases may be overlooked or attract less attention than they deserve. Taxes provide a second important explanation for this less than merited attention. Oil companies, while normally resistant to procurement-related cost inflation, may not lose significantly in the end, since inflated costs are all recoverable against taxes, often with an "uplift." (An uplift is a form of investment incentive, common in the petroleum industry, that allows recovery of more than 100 percent of costs for tax purposes.) The losers are finance ministries, whose coffers are lower as a result of lower tax revenues, and ultimately the public as a consequence of reduced budgetary allocations to health, education, transport, and other essential services.

Red flags during the development phase might include unreasonable permitting and approval delays, nontransparent or opaque procurement, limited or no use of international competitive bidding for major contracts, awards to firms with limited demonstrated capacity, aggressive "national interest" local procurement rhetoric, unusual repeat awards, and persistent rumors of abuse.

Production

On completion of development, production begins. This phase is particularly vulnerable to grand corruption—theft on a major scale, involving serious criminal elements. This may occur through underreporting and diversion of production volumes or through more direct means, such as tapping into producing wells or pipelines and carrying off the oil.

Hossein Shahrastani, Iraq's Minister of Oil, counts production theft as one of the most important current problems facing his country. Theft is achieved by the underreporting of production volumes and the diversion of oil by local mafias for clandestine sale. Recognizing the problem, Iraqi authorities sought to put in place production metering devices, but their installation was long stalled, almost certainly by those who stand to gain by their absence (Reuters 2006). In one case documented by the UN investigation of mismanagement and corruption in Iraq's Oil-for-Food Program, theft of Iraqi oil was made possible after the independent quantity-control expert appointed specifically to prevent such thefts was bribed. In its final report issued in October 2005, the investigating committee alleged that significant volumes of stolen oil were illegally added to cargoes approved for export under the Oil-for-Food Program. According to the committee, Iraqi officials bribed the quantity-control expert, who worked for Saybolt, the Dutch inspection firm, to disregard the unauthorized oil loadings in exchange for 2 percent of the proceeds of the operation.

In the Niger Delta, thieves have made little effort to hide their activities, tapping into production flow lines, removing production to barges standing by, and delivering the stolen oil to tankers waiting in the Gulf of Guinea. The volumes lost range between 30,000 and 40,000 barrels a day. At $65 to $75 a barrel, these losses equate to considerable fortunes. As in Iraq, part of the problem is lack of adequate metering, and one of the priority recommendations of a physical audit of oil industry operations recently commissioned by the Nigerian government is a substantial upgrading of metering capacity. The problem almost certainly goes deeper, however. It seems inconceivable that theft on this scale could happen without the complicity of big men, senior politicians, and enforcement agencies.[26]

As the examples suggest, volume discrepancies, between producing field and export measurement points, for example, would provide a clear indication of production theft. Any breakdown in metering or apparent weakness in the volume inspection process should also raise suspicions.

Trading

Trading involves the sale and purchase of oil production. Theft under this heading often involves the underinvoicing of the value of the oil sold, allowing its purchaser to resell the oil at an inflated margin. The parties involved in corrupt transactions of this type are typically a government agency or NOC as the first seller and an oil trader as the first purchaser and onward seller. World Bank audits of crude oil sales by the NNPC during the Abacha years revealed consistent underpricing relative to market values, thus creating significant margins for those middlemen, frequently well-placed big men, with contracts to sell on the crude (World Bank 2000a). The practice has since been corrected, and prices for Nigerian oil sold by the NNPC on behalf of the government now closely track international market values.

More recently, financial audits of Société Nationale des Pétroles du Congo (SNPC), the Republic of Congo's NOC, uncovered a similar phenomenon. SNPC was selling the state's share of crude oil production at prices that were 5 to 6 percent below market. Sales were made to an unknown oil trading firm called Sphynx, which turned out to be owned by the president of SNPC. This has led to allegations of corruption, although the government has denied such charges.[27]

One of the more notorious examples of oil trading corruption was unearthed by the Volcker Committee in its investigation of the United Nations' Oil-for-Food Program in Iraq. Under the program, the United Nations allocated certain volumes of crude oil for sale on international markets. The proceeds were earmarked to purchase food and other necessities for Iraqis, who were suffering under the worldwide embargo placed on Iraqi oil in the 1990s in the wake of Iraq's thwarted invasion of Kuwait. The United Nations determined a "fair market price" at which the Iraqi crude oil could be sold. As it happened, this was below international market prices, creating an immediate premium for access to Iraqi crude. Because Iraq, not the United Nations, chose its buyers, Iraq had considerable political and economic leverage, which it exercised first by selling oil to recipients capable of influencing foreign policy and international public opinion in its favor, and later by demanding that illicit "surcharges" be paid into Iraqi-controlled banks in Jordan and Lebanon and to selected Iraqi embassies. Companies named in the Volcker Committee report (2005) include Glencore, an oil trading firm based in Switzerland, which was identified as being a leading provider of kickbacks to Saddam Hussein's regime under the oil-for-food program, and the French bank BNP Paribas, the leading financier of Oil-for-Food deals, which the Volcker Committee accused of turning a blind eye to the use of front companies to hide the real identity of Iraq's partners.[28] Very recently, Total, the French oil and gas group, has been named in connection with the Oil-for-Food trading scandals. A Paris judge has charged the incoming chief of Total with payment of kickbacks to the Iraqi regime from 1996 to 2002 to gain better access to Iraqi crude during the UN embargo. Total has denied the charges (Arnold 2006).

Oil trading, whether in crude oil or petroleum products, thrives on cheating, and the list of corrupt practices is long. In addition to the examples given here, the list includes inappropriate pricing benchmarks in contracts, a common practice that can increase trading margins and that is difficult to detect. Above all, traders benefit from administrative restrictions, whether sanctions or price controls, because the profits that derive from breaching the barriers created by those restrictions can be enormous.

Warning signals for corruption in oil trading include lack of transparency in sales of government oil, official sales at prices below readily determined international benchmarks, and unusual reliance on middlemen.

Transport

Transport—the delivery of oil to market by pipeline or tanker—presents additional opportunities for illegal gain. Transport infrastructure, including pipelines, storage or transfer terminals, and port jetties, are often correctly characterized as natural monopolies. Owners of infrastructure, which may be the state itself, are in a position to extract monopoly rents and commonly do so. Corruption enters when rents are extracted not as official, published tariffs payable to the state but as clandestine payments to officials in control of access. Access to Russian export pipeline capacity was greatly coveted in the 1990s, when Russian crude oil prices were substantially below those in neighboring European markets. Terms of access to pipeline capacity were far from transparent at the time, and it was widely suspected that gaining access involved not open payments to state agencies but rather significant secret sharing of the domestic-international price disparity between producers eager for access and those officials in administrative control of it.

Tip-offs of possible corruption at this stage of the value chain are nontransparent rules of access to infrastructure, nontransparent administration of access, long queues, and favored customers.

Refining and Marketing

Refining and marketing, the downstream segment of the oil industry, may not enjoy the same lucrative margins as the upstream exploration and production business, but the volume of transactions is large, and, as suggested earlier, any illegal activity that takes even a fraction of a percent may be very tempting.

Refining is the industrial process that converts crude oil into usable petroleum products—gasoline, kerosene, diesel, jet fuel, and fuel oil. Distribution or marketing involves moving the petroleum products from refineries to the final consumer. Opportunities for illegal profits are often created by official policies. Price controls on refined petroleum products represent perhaps the most important, common, and invidious driver of corruption in this segment of the oil value chain. Policies that control domestic petroleum product prices below market levels may well be responsive to populist pressure, particularly in countries that produce and export oil, but they may also reflect the influence of those who stand to gain from the space for illegal activity that the price controls create. Imposition of petroleum product price controls and the resulting product shortages are almost invariably followed by a rapid expansion in black market activity and smuggling. Populist pressure and corruption at the policy level create the opportunity, while corruption at the administrative level allows it to thrive.

An example occurs in Iran, where gasoline sells at a controlled price of $0.40 a gallon. To meet resulting demand, which far outstrips its domestic refining capacity, Iran buys foreign gasoline for more than $2 a gallon, one of the highest gasoline subsidies in the region. However, a very high percentage of gasoline imports purchased domestically at the control price go right back out of the country. According to a parliamentary report, the cheap gasoline is smuggled out to other countries at a rate of 2 million gallons a day (Fathi 2006). The story is much the same in Iraq, where smugglers are suspected of hampering rehabilitation of Iraq's refineries in order to maintain their lucrative trade.[29] Similarly, in Nigeria, those profiting from price controls through black market activity and from the smuggling and kickbacks associated with large product import contracts are suspected of being behind the lack of any progress in the rehabilitation of domestic refining capacity, which would put more product on the market at official, controlled price levels. Continued vandalization, widely believed to be aided by the collaboration of refinery officials, has kept Nigerian refinery output low. Theft for delivery to the black market of whatever product is available at the refineries has also been a problem under price controls (Economist Intelligence Unit 2004).

In addition to these difficulties, differential price controls among petroleum products can create opportunities for illegal activities and will be encouraged by those who stand to profit. For example, the control price for kerosene is typically low, ostensibly to meet the needs of the poor. Often, however, the low control price results in the withdrawal of kerosene from the market and its subsequent use to criminally adulterate higher-priced gasoline. These operations are typically controlled by organized crime syndicates, and collusion of administrative or enforcement agencies is common (Kojima and Bacon 2001).

The chairman of the Indian Oil Corporation recently testified to a parliamentary committee that his inspectors were "helpless in checking the diversion of kerosene for adulteration in diesel." The reason given was that it was very "dangerous," referring to the murder of one of his officers.[30] He might well have added that poor pay of inspectors makes it very easy for illegal elements to persuade those inspectors to look the other way.

For many developing countries, taxes on petroleum products constitute a major share of government revenues (Bacon 2001). Tax evasion is common, often achieved by undermeasuring volume. Effective metering is an issue downstream, as much or more as it is upstream. The Tanzanian government recently vowed to curb massive tax evasion on oil product imports caused by tampering with flow meters at the Dar es Salaam port. Collusion between the country's importers and meter operators is thought to be behind the frequent breakdown of meters (Xinhua News Agency 2005).

Clues to possible corruption at the downstream end of the business should be evident from the foregoing: product price controls, product shortages and queues, stories about the black market and smuggling, volume discrepancies, absence of transparent competitive tendering for import contracts, and metering "difficulties."

Corporate Accounting, Taxes, and Finance

Corrupt activities under this heading apply to all stages of the petroleum value chain and are by no means unique to oil. Discussion of the topic in any detail is beyond the scope of this chapter. Suffice it to say once again that the petroleum sector is a favored target because the money it generates offers huge returns to accounting fraud, tax evasion, and illegal financial manipulation and because the complexity of the sector reduces the risk of detection. The widely publicized case of the American energy trader Enron is a prime example of the scale of fraud that can occur, but there is no shortage of other examples. Accounting practices of most NOCs should be a cause for concern. Often, the books are unavailable or, if available, they are nontransparent and confusing. In general, lack of transparency, weak or nonexistent audits, and unnecessarily convoluted accounting, tax, or financial structures should be taken as signals of possible problems.

REMEDIES AND RESPONSES

The foregoing sections suggest why corruption is so endemic in the petroleum sector, identify the channels through which it operates and the principal players involved, and provide an abbreviated and selective catalogue of the corrupt practices found in each segment of the oil value chain. In this final section, we consider possible remedies and appropriate responses to corruption in the sector. Before turning to specific recommendations, however, several caveats are in order.

First, it should be apparent that the attraction of the sector to corruption is extraordinarily strong. Vested interests opposed to reform will be very powerful and well financed. Every investigation cited here implicates networks of corruption, not just individuals, and these networks are likely to be transnational. Networks spawn networks, spreading much like an infectious disease. Hence rooting corruption out of the oil sector will be exceptionally difficult, even dangerous, and can be expected to take a long time. Sustained, high-level, high-profile commitment will be essential to success.

Second, anticorruption campaigns in the oil sector stand a much better chance of succeeding if they are part of a wider country program promoting good governance and attacking corruption across the board. The good news is that both the international community and local communities, through the Internet and other means of communication, are very aware of the damaging influence of corruption, and there is now broad-based pressure for reform.

Third, as in other sectors, success in tackling corruption in the petroleum sector will depend on the concerted effort of all stakeholders—government, industry, civil society, the financial community, and development agencies such as the World Bank and the IMF.[31] Because they are often overlooked in this context, special mention must be paid to the roles and responsibilities of the developed countries. There is a tendency, particularly in the context of development, to view corruption in the oil sector principally as a problem in the developing world. However, this ignores several realities. As the examples quoted in this chapter show, the companies and institutions of the developed world, and the governments that host them, are frequently complicit, passively and actively, in developing-world corruption cases. While multiple objectives, diplomatic or otherwise, may make it difficult, governments of developed countries should make a special effort to avoid sending mixed signals to countries struggling with petroleum sector corruption.

The strategic nature of oil seems to have a deranging effect on the moral compasses of the world's most powerful developed nations. Too often, the effectiveness of campaigns to roll back sector corruption, which may well be endorsed or supported by developed countries through bilateral or multilateral channels, is undermined in part by simultaneous praise for the governments in whose countries the corruption occurs—praise motivated by developed-country self-interest in security of oil supplies or the protection of commercial interests. And when it comes to more active roles, the behavior of too many players in developed countries shows that corruption is not simply an exotic disease to which Westerners are exposed when they go abroad. On the contrary, corruption has deep roots in the developed world, and whenever sophisticated greed from the West ties up with the immature polities of the developing world, the result is toxic. Any putative remedies to petroleum sector corruption that focus their attention solely, or even primarily, on the developing world are destined to fail.

Fourth, fighting corruption in any sector, but certainly in the petroleum sector, requires resources—the right skills and adequate funding. The resources needed range from moderate for informational campaigns, through serious for technical assistance to and capacity building in government agencies and civil society, to significant, where complicated investigations and surveillance are called for. Rhetoric without these resources will not go far.

Last, circumstances make a difference, and a crisis may be the most favorable environment in which to launch an anticorruption campaign. The case of Nigeria is illustrative. President Olusegun Obasanjo's second administration put the fight against corruption at the top of its "to do" list because corruption had become so pervasive that it stood in the way of all other progress. The oil sector received priority attention as a result of domestic and international public perception that it was the most corrupt sector of all, and that petroleum sector corruption was infecting not only other sectors of the economy but also society as a whole.

With these caveats or challenges in mind, desirable features in any anticorruption effort would include credible leadership or sponsorship, a reform context broader than just the petroleum sector, stakeholder coalitions, adequate resources and funding, favorable circumstances and a willingness to "seize the day." These dimensions of an anticorruption program are well illustrated by the global Extractive Industries Transparency Initiative and by its specific and promising application to the petroleum sector in Nigeria.

Launched in 2003 by U.K. Prime Minister Tony Blair, the initiative has gained considerable traction internationally among all stakeholders. It is designed to address the paradox of plenty in resource-rich countries by requiring transparency of payments made by companies and of revenues received by governments, thereby limiting opportunities for corruption and promoting accountability. Technical assistance in support of implementation is provided by an EITI Multi-Donor Trust Fund managed by the World Bank through bilateral aid programs, and, in some cases, by implementing countries themselves. Box 6.4 describes the initiative, its principles and objectives, and the criteria applied to assess performance.[32]

BOX 6.4 Extractive Industries Transparency Initiative

Principles and Objectives

- Ensure that all resource revenues are properly accounted for and contribute to sustainable development and poverty reduction
- Provide guidelines to stakeholders on auditing, reporting, and disseminating information on resource payments and revenues
- Facilitate technical assistance in support of EITI implementation

Implementation Criteria

- Credible, independent audits of payments made (by companies) and revenues received (by governments) and reconciliation thereof
- Publication and widespread dissemination of audit results in an easily accessible format
- Comprehensive coverage of all companies, including NOCs
- Engagement of civil society in the process
- Public, financially sustainable, time-bound plan of implementation.

Source: http://www.eitransparency.org.

Some 20-plus countries are now implementing the EITI program; another 5 to 10 countries are in the early stages of engagement. More than half of the oil-rich developing countries listed in table 6.1 have endorsed or are actively pursuing EITI compliance criteria. Industry is well represented in the initiative by the major international oil, gas, and mining corporations, as is civil society not only at the international level but, most important, at the local level. Donor countries, the financial community, and the international development institutions are also active backers.

The modalities adopted for implementation of the initiative are instructive guides to combating corruption in the petroleum sector and are well illustrated by Nigeria's particular version, known as NEITI. Nigeria, as noted earlier, was ready for EITI and was quick to adapt it to its own particular circumstances. NEITI contains all of the recommended features of an anticorruption campaign. In fact, it goes well beyond the minimum requirements of the global EITI. The following elements deserve specific mention:

- Prominent involvement in and endorsement of NEITI by the country's president, as well as by program "champions" at the ministerial level.
- Engagement of all key stakeholders—government, industry, and civil society—acting both independently and as a coalition. A 16-member National Stakeholders Working Group (NSWG), established by presidential decree, meets monthly. Subcommittees have been created to address specific topics, such as training, legislation, and outreach.
- Promotion of a sustained commitment through establishment of a permanent, professionally staffed NSWG secretariat and submission to the National Assembly of a draft NEITI bill to anchor the initiative and its funding in legislation. While legislation is pending, the secretariat and related NSWG activities listed

here are supported by donors on a bilateral basis (especially the United Kingdom) and by the World Bank administered EITI Multi-Donor Trust Fund.

- Dialogue with major developed-country consuming states on corruption issues, exemplified by the anticorruption pact that was agreed at the 2004 G-8 summit at Sea Island, Georgia, in the United States and that addresses a wide range of governance issues, Nigeria's commitment to EITI among them.
- Focus on transparency regarding not only revenues but also a wide range of additional policy and operational areas, including the adequacy of fiscal and cost audits; volume audits; the monitoring, reconciliation, and reporting on the flow of funds in the sector; and licensing procedures.[33]
- Broad dissemination of information related to the sector in an easily accessible format. Outreach activities include a Web site and regular Internet reports, detailed monthly newspaper reports on revenues, simple brochures, regional and local workshops, and petroleum information centers.
- Significant emphasis on governance-related capacity building in key government and sector agencies and in civil society. Topics addressed include petroleum industry basics, petroleum economics, accounting and taxation, fiscal administration, and budget analysis.

Nigeria still has a long way to go to rein in corruption and correct past abuses in its petroleum sector, but the steps it has so determinedly taken show promise and offer a model to other countries dependent on petroleum revenue. While not as far along as Nigeria, several other countries are well on their way toward establishing credible revenue transparency programs.

Focused as it is on one item—revenue transparency—EITI represents only a first step toward successfully addressing petroleum sector corruption. That said, as the example of Nigeria suggests, the initiative, once under way, can be easily extended into other relevant dimensions of good governance. For example, revenue transparency can be expected to encourage demands for policy and administrative transparency, transparency in licensing and procurement, and transparency in sector operations. And the availability of credible revenue numbers will surely increase the demand for transparency on expenditures. All of this will raise the bar on accountability and reduce the scope for corruption, not only at the sector level, but also at the economy-wide level. Transparency may be only a first step, but it is a very powerful one.

This closing emphasis on EITI and transparency should in no way detract from the importance of other measures or recommendations designed to tackle corruption. For example, while not specific to the petroleum sector, the international anticorruption conventions adopted over the past few years are impressive in their scope. Rigorous action to ensure their effective application should be encouraged and supported. Governments can also do more to target observed persistent corruption by certain companies and individuals, by "naming and shaming" or by taking more active steps to disqualify such companies and individuals from bidding on public contracts or holding public office. Finally, the increased awareness of corruption issues that can be expected to result from all these initiatives should be enlisted to help in addressing more elusive shades of corruption such as legal corruption, the revolving door, and the use of diplomatic nonmonetary pressures and inducements.

TABLE 6.3 Petroleum Sector Corruption: Summary Table

Petroleum value chain	*Corruption vulnerability*	*Warning signs*	*Recommended response*
Exploration	• Policy formulation • Laws, contracts, fiscal terms • Licensing, contract awards • Permits, approvals	• Lack of policy clarity • Opaque, incomplete legal, fiscal framework • Direct, nontransparent negotiation of licenses • "Unbalanced," "odd" awards • Delays on permits, approvals	• Clear, publicly announced policies • Best practice legal, fiscal framework • Transparent, simplified bids for license awards, published results • Transparent public reports on permitting approvals
Development and production	• Permits, approvals • Procurement • Theft of production or revenues	• Permitting delays • Limited international competitive bidding, nontransparent bids • "Odd" or repeat procurement awards • Rumors of abuse • Aggressive local content rhetoric • Volume discrepancies • Absence of metering	• Transparent public reports on permitting • Transparent, competitive procurement • Publication of results • Credible channels for complaint or challenges • Regular volume audits and reconciliations
Trading and transport	• Underreporting of value or volume • Illegal rent extraction for infrastructure access	• Prices below reference benchmarks • Volume discrepancies • Opaque or lack of reporting on sales • Unusual reliance on middleman • Rumors of abuse • Queues for access to infrastructure	• Full transparent reporting of trades, sales • Transparent bidding for selection of middleman • Regular audit of sales • Volume audits, reconciliations • Transparent public rules and tariffs for infrastructure access • Appeal, complaint procedures
Refining and marketing	• Downstream policy formulation, such as price controls • Black marketers, smuggling • Product adulteration • Product procurement	• Price controls • Nontransparent product procurement • Queues for products, product shortages • Volume discrepancies	• Policy clarity • Price liberalization (transparent allocation of proceeds) • Competitive transparent tendering
Corporate accounting and finance	• Inaccurate reporting • Tax evasion • Diversion of funds • Money laundering	• Limited transparency, secrecy • Tax immunity or unusually low tax burdens • Inadequate audit	• Full, transparent, publicized audits • Qualified, independent tax and cost audits

Source: Authors.

SUMMARY AND CONCLUSIONS

Table 6.3 provides in summary form the policy makers' road map promised at the beginning of this chapter. The table breaks down the petroleum sector value chain into its several parts, identifies their vulnerability to corruption, suggests warning signals, and recommends responses. The challenge of petroleum sector corruption is immense, but the payoff to success ought to be equally impressive and is surely worth the effort. Better understanding of the phenomenon, new initiatives, and a changing context less tolerant of corruption are all encouraging signs that the effort is well under way.

ENDNOTES

1. See Gelb and Associates (1988). This influential book is the starting point for much of the literature on petroleum governance and revenue management issues. The phrase "paradox of plenty" was coined by Terry Lynn Karl (1997) in her ground breaking book of the same name, which examined the economic and social troubles experienced in major petroleum-rich developing countries. A third standard reference is Sachs and Warner (2001). Dissenting views to the inevitability of the paradox can be found in Lederman and Maloney (2006). Through a series of case studies, the authors in that volume argue that resource wealth, if coupled with appropriate institutional and policy choices, can be a significant advantage in achieving long-term economic growth.
2. A good discussion of oil's negative influence on democracy can be found in Ross (1999). Links among oil, violent conflict, and civil war are examined in Bannon and Collier (2003). A broader assessment of oil's impact on Africa is contained in Catholic Relief Services (2003). It should be noted that the Obasanjo regime in Nigeria has put in place a wide range of initiatives to combat corruption and address other aspects of the paradox of plenty. See Sacker (2006).
3. See endnotes 1 and 2.
4. New discoveries and changes in reserve or production estimates may also produce sharp revisions to revenue projections. Angola, Equatorial Guinea, Mauritania, and Timor-Leste have all experienced dramatic windfalls as a result of new discoveries. Cambodia is the latest country facing a bonanza from a major new find. See "An Oil Find to Enrich or Corrupt Cambodia," *International Herald Tribune,* November 4–5, 2006.
5. For an excellent treatment of the technical issues contributing to the paradox of plenty and of corrective policy options, see Katz and others (2004) and Davis, Ossowski, and Fedelino (2003).
6. The World Bank Institute surveys cover six broad dimensions of good governance and represent a statistical compilation of responses by all significant stakeholders. Over 150 countries are covered. See http://www.worldbank.org/wbi/governance.
7. For the basis of Transparency International's rankings, see http://www.transparency.org/policy_research/surveys_indices/cpi/2005. The perceptions may occur with a lag relative to actual performance. For example, several of the countries listed have recently launched anticorruption campaigns, in some cases complementary to commitments to the Extractive Industries Transparency Initiative, described later in this chapter.
8. See Wood Mackenzie presentation to government of Angola, World Bank workshop, Luanda, May 2006. The reference price assumed is $75 a barrel for Brent North Sea crude oil, based on September 2006 market prices. Angolan prices are adjusted for transport and

quality differentials. Production estimates are based strictly on discoveries already under development or committed to development, that is, no estimates of possible future discoveries are included. The price of $75 a barrel is likely to prove a relative high. More conservative price estimates still generate large numbers, however. At $45 a barrel, peak gross revenues would come in at $45 billion a year, with corresponding government revenues of $30 billion annually. In addition to illustrating scale, this example provides a dramatic illustration of the vulnerability of revenues to oil price movements, one of the technical challenges of oil wealth and dependency.

9. The Organization of Petroleum Exporting Countries (OPEC) has for years successfully limited the flow of oil to world markets, thus maintaining high margins or rents.
10. A succinct presentation of the risks of resource wealth to accountability and the development of modern political institutions can be found in Zakaria (2004, pp. 73–76). See also Moore (2004) and Karl (1997). Buying off the opposition may equate to direct transfers or, less directly, to funding of the ruling party's electoral campaign.
11. This perception persists even though oil is now a widely traded commodity on international markets. The "commanding heights" reference in the next sentence comes from Lenin and is the title of a book on the history of international oil; see Yergin and Stanislaw (1998).
12. The often tangled and nontransparent relationships between government and NOCs can provide particularly fertile ground for corruption. See box 6.2 and McPherson (2003).
13. See, for example, Carola Hoyas, "China and India Fill Void Left by Rights Campaigners," *Financial Times,* March 1, 2006; David White, "The China Factor," *Financial Times,* November 21, 2006; and Rowan Callick, "China Promises Bonanza for Africa," *The Australian,* November 6, 2006.
14. These themes are taken up in "Oil Clouds West's Dealings with Africa Strongmen," Reuters, July 20, 2006. An instructive analysis of the nexus of U.S. politics, commercial interests, and corruption in Kazakhstan can be found in Ron Stodghill, "Oil, Cash and Corruption," *New York Times,* November 5, 2006. The U.S. government's mixed signals on Equatorial Guinea are highlighted in "With Friends Like These . . .," *Washington Post,* April 18, 2006; and Chris McGreal and Dan Galister, "The Tiny African State, the President's Son, and the $35 Million Malibu Mansion," *The Guardian,* November 6, 2006.
15. See Pascal Fletcher, "China Muscles in to Africa Oil Scramble", *Reuters,* December 15, 2005, and Steven Mufson, "As China, U.S. Vie for More Oil, Diplomatic Friction May Follow," *Washington Post,* April 15, 2006.
16. The concept of legal corruption was developed by Daniel Kaufmann and Pedro Vincente at the World Bank. See Kaufmann and Vincente (2005).
17. Oil and gas companies in the United States spend an enormous amount on exercising their constitutional right to get a hearing before their elected representatives. According to the Center for Public Integrity, which collects data on corporate spending on lobbying based on public records, oil and gas companies paid out more than $480 million in 1998–2004 in government lobbying and campaign contributions. Ten companies spend more than $1 million annually. It is unimaginable that they should do so without a reasonable expectation that the investment will produce a return in terms of the crafting of legislation. Data from http://www.opensecrets.org. Edmund Andrews, "Vague Law and Hard Lobbying Add Up to Billions for Big Oil," *New York Times,* March 27, 2006, provides a detailed account of successful legislative lobbying by the oil industry to win major royalty incentives resulting in a significant industry windfall.
18. Nigerian investigators estimate that Abacha embezzled some $2.2 billion during his time in office. 1A.215/2004/col, Arret du 7 fevrier 2005, Ire Cour de droit public, http://www.polyreg.ch/bgeunpubliziert/Jahr_2004/Entscheide_1A_2004/1A.215_2004.html.

See also "Swiss Freeze a Dictator's Giant Cache," *International Herald Tribune,* January 26, 2000.

19. The track record indicates a very high morbidity for corporations tainted by corruption allegations. Elf, Mobil, Triton, Yukos, Enron, Arthur Andersen, and Saybolt—all implicated in high-profile petroleum industry corruption cases—either no longer exist, are severely reduced in size, or have been taken over by competitors.
20. The most recent example involves the sale in June 2006 of a 45 percent interest in a highly prospective oil license by South Atlantic Petroleum to the Chinese NOC, CNOOC, for a colossal $2.3 billion. South Atlantic, an obscure Nigerian firm, was awarded the block by the late General Abacha's military regime.
21. The same concerns have been voiced in the past with respect to the IOCs whose homes are the developed countries of the West. As noted earlier, however, these concerns have been increasingly allayed by legislative and civil society oversight of IOC performance and by the IOCs' own internal policies.
22. Signature bonuses, that is, bonuses paid simply on award of an exploration concession without any guarantee of exploration success, reached record levels in the most recent Angolan offshore licensing round, with the three top blocks attracting payments of $910 million, $1.2 billion, and $1.2 billion. Clearly, bidders expected the risk-weighted value of exploration success to be well in excess of these already staggering sums.
23. All three countries mentioned in this paragraph put up Web sites covering the exploration awards process. See http://www.transparency.gov.tl, http://www.thecwcgroup.com/UserFiles%5CCon_File%5CNigeria%20Licensing%20Round.pdf#search=%22nigeria%20petroleum%20licensing%20round%22, and http://www.sonangol.co.ao/sonangolEP/concessions_en.shtml
24. See box 6.3 and http://www.usdoj.gov/criminal/fraud/giffenpr.pdf.
25. See "African Minister Took Cut of Oil Contracts," *Financial Times,* October 25, 2006. The admission of this practice is contained in a sworn affidavit to Capetown High Court by Teodorin Nguema Obiang, the son of the president of Equatorial Guinea. Nongovernment groups have long contended that officials in other oil-rich West African states have made substantial sums from foreign business contracts, often in contravention of local laws, but statements to that effect by African officials are rare. Mr. Obiang contends that the practice is legal in his country.
26. Beyond the oil that is stolen, production of another 450,000–470,000 barrels per day has been "shut in," or deferred, as a result of violent conflicts in the delta, which stem mainly from ethnic tension and local resentment of oil company operations but are attributable in good part to deliberate chaos introduced as a cover for oil theft.
27. The government contends that its peculiar crude oil trading arrangements were a necessary protection against creditors who had bought up Republic of Congo debt at a discount and were preparing to seize Congolese oil as payment. Global Witness, an investigative nongovernmental organization, is skeptical. See Global Witness, "The Riddle of the Sphinx: Where Has Congo's Oil Money Gone?" December 13, 2005, http://www.globalwitness.org. The SNPC's trading practices are detailed in two U.K. court judgments. See, for example, *Kensington International* v. *Republic of Congo, Walker Holdings Ltd.,* Queen's Bench Division (Commercial Court), 26 November 2005 *[2005] EWHC 2684 (comm.) 2005 A11 ER (D) 370 (Nov) (Approved judgment).* See also Sebastian Mallaby, "A Corrupt French Connection," *Washington Post,* March 13, 2006. Mallaby reports that one of the creditors, Kensington International, has also brought a case in New York, alleging that BNP Paribas colluded with officials in the Republic of Congo to hide revenues. "Whatever the French bank's role," writes Mallaby, "Congo's corruption does not appear to offend the French

Government which has led the charge to grant Congo debt relief." Mallaby notes that this has happened notwithstanding an article in the French press detailing missing millions in oil sector revenue flows. The French paper *La Tribune* remarked that "President Jacques Chirac and Congolese ruling strongmen are old friends."

28. In addition to the Volcker Committee report itself, Meyer and Califano (2006) provide a good discussion of oil operations under the Oil-for-Food Program. See especially chapter 4, "Saddam's Slush Fund; Oil Allocations and Surcharges."
29. Jonathan Finer and Nelson Hernandez, "Iraqi Bust Nets Ring Smuggling Oil to Syria," *Washington Post,* April 15, 2006. The Iraqi government spends nearly $500 million a month to import refined fuels, which it sells at heavily subsidized prices. It estimates that as much as 30 percent of the imported fuels, purchased at the subsidized price, are then illegally spirited out of the country and resold.
30. Combating corruption has become a major focus of attention at the World Bank, as this book suggests. Particular attention has been paid to the petroleum and mining sectors through internal programs and support to external programs such as the Extractive Industries Transparency Initiative.
31. "My Poor Sales Officers Are Helpless..." 2005. *Indian Express/Financial Times,* November 26.
32. Major donor support to the fund is provided by the governments of France, Germany, the Netherlands, Norway, and the United Kingdom, and has been promised by Australia. The World Bank also provides implementation support directly through country programs and through its Development Grant Facility.
33. The results of a major three-part study on these topics, commissioned by the NSWG, can be found at http://www.neiti.org.

REFERENCES

Andrews, Edmund. 2006. "Suit Says U.S. Impeded Audits." *New York Times,* September 21.

Andrews-Speed, Philip, and Xin Ma. 2005. "The Overseas Operations of China's National Oil Companies." *Oil, Gas and Energy Law* 3 (December).

Arnold, Martin. 2006. "Total Chief Charged in UN-Iraq Oil Graft Case." *Financial Times,* October 21–22.

Bacon, Robert. 2001. "Petroleum Taxes: Trends in Fuel Taxes and Subsidies." World Bank Viewpoint Note 237, World Bank, Washington, DC (September).

Bannon, Ian, and Paul Collier, eds. 2003. *Natural Resources and Violent Conflict,* Washington, DC: World Bank.

Catholic Relief Services. 2003. *The Bottom of the Barrel.* New York: Catholic Relief Services.

Davis, J. M., Rolando Ossowski, and Fedelino Annalisa, eds. 2003. *Fiscal Policy Formulation and Implementation in Oil Producing Countries.* Washington, DC: International Monetary Fund.

Economist Intelligence Unit. 2004. "Nigerian Economy: Fuel Price Rises Reversed," Economist Intelligence Unit, August 31.

Fathi Nazila. 2006. "Iran, an Oil Giant, in a Gasoline Squeeze." *New York Times,* July 16.

Fitchett, Joseph, and David Ignatius. 2002. "Lengthy Elf Inquiry Nears Explosive Finish." *International Herald Tribune,* February 1.

Gelb, Alan, and Associates. 1988. *Oil Windfalls: Blessing or Curse?* New York: Oxford University Press for the World Bank.

Glassburner, Bruce. 1976. "In the Wake of General Ibnu: Crisis in the Indonesian Oil Industry." *Asian Survey* 16 (12): 1099–112.

Hari, Vandan. 2004. "Pertamina under Scrutiny form the Corruption Panel." *Platts Oilgram News,* June 23.

Henley, Jon. 2003. "Gigantic Sleaze Scandal Winds Up as Former Elf Oil Chiefs Are Jailed." *Guardian,* November 13.

IMF (International Monetary Fund). 2005. *Guidelines for Resource Revenue Transparency.* Washington DC: International Monetary Fund.

"Indonesia: Perils of Pertamina." 2003. *Energy Compass,* June 26.

International Energy Agency. 2005. *World Energy Outlook.* Paris: Inernational Energy Agency.

Isikoff Michael and Mark Hosenball. 2004. "Another Halliburton Probe." *Newsweek,* February 4.

Karl, Terry Lynn. 1997. *The Paradox of Plenty: Oil Booms and Petro-States.* Berkeley: University of California Press.

Katz, Menachem, Ulrich Bartsch, Harinder Malothra, and Milan Cuc. 2004. *Lifting the Oil Curse.* Washington, DC: International Monetary Fund.

Kaufmann, Daniel, and Pedro Vincente. 2005. "Legal Corruption." Working paper, World Bank, Washington, DC (October). http://siteresources.worldbank.org/INTWBIGOVANTCOR/Resources/Legal_corruption.pdf.

Kobonbaev, Maks. 2006. "The Case of Corruption in Pertamina." Internal note, World Bank, Washington, DC (July).

Kojima, Masami, and Robert Bacon. 2001. "Abuses in Fuel Markets." World Bank Viewpoint Note 220, World Bank, Washington, DC (September).

Lederman, Daniel, and William Maloney, eds. 2006. *Natural Resources: Neither Curse nor Destiny.* Stanford, CA: Stanford University Press.

Mackie, J. A. C. 1970. "The Commission of Four Report on Corruption." *Bulletin of Indonesian Economic Studies* 6 (3): 87–101.

McPherson, Charles. 2003. "National Oil Companies: Evolution, Issues, Outlook." In *Fiscal Policy Formulation and Implementation in Oil Producing Countries,* ed. J. M. Davis, R. Ossowski, J. Daniel, and S. Barnett. Washington, DC: International Monetary Fund.

———. 2004. "Petroleum Revenue Management in Developing Countries." *Oil and Gas Energy Law* 2 (April).

Meyer, Jeffrey A., and Mark Califano, with an introduction by Paul A. Volcker. 2006. *Good Intentions Corrupted; The Oil-for-Food Scandal and the Threat to the UN.* New York: Public Affairs.

Moore, Mick. 2004. "Revenues, State Formation, and the Quality of Governance in Developing Countries." *International Political Science Review* 25 (3): 297–319.

Muljadi, Kartini. 2002. "The Indonesian Oil and Gas Sector: Light at the End of the Tunnel." *International Financial Law Review* October (Energy and Power 2002 Supplement).

"My poor sales officers are helpless....". 2005. *Indian Express/Financial Times,* November 26.

Oxford Analytica. 2000. "Indonesia: Jakarta Drafts Energy Deregulation Bill" *Oxford Analytica* (June 21).

PwC (Price water house Coopers). 1998. "Pertasmina's Restructuring Blueprint: The Roadmap Towards a World-Class Oil and Gas Company." PwC.

Reuters. "Work. Set On Long-Delayed Iraq Oil Metering System." Reuters News, March 24.

Robert-Diard, Pascale. 2003a. "Elf, une histoire francais." *Le Monde,* November 18.

———. 2003b. "Procès Elf: trois hommes un systeme et des moeurs politiques." *Le Monde,* June 1.

Ross, Michael. 1999. "The Political Economy of the Resource Curse." *World Politics* 51 (2): 297–322.

Sachs, Jeffrey, and A. M. Warner. 2001. "Natural Resources and Economic Development: The Curse of Natural Resources." *European Economic Review* 45 (4–6): 827–38.

Sacker, Stephen. 2006. "Nigeria: Curing Corruption," BBC interview with Ngozi Ikonjo-Iweala, former finance minister of Nigeria, October 27.

Schloss, Miguel. 1993. "Does Petroleum Procurement Matter?" *Finance and Development* 30.

Transparency International. 2006. "Corruption Perception Index." http://www.transparency.org/policy_research/surveys_indices/cpi/2005.

U.S. Senate, Permanent Subcommittee on Investigations. 2004. *Money Laundering and Foreign Corruption: Enforcement and Effectiveness of the Patriot Act, Case Study Involving Riggs Bank*, Report of the Minority Staff, July 15.

Volcker Committee (Independent Inquiry Committee into the United Nations Oil-For-Food Programme, chaired by Paul A. Volcker). 2005. *Report on the Manipulation of the Oil-For-Food Programme.* October 27. http://www.iic-offp.org/documents/IIC%20Final%20Report%2027Oct2005.pdf.

Walker, David. 2004. "Contracting for Iraq Reconstruction and Global Logistics Support." Statement of the Comptroller General of the United States before the Committee on Government Reform, House of Representatives, GAO-04-869T, Government Accountancy Office, Washington, DC.

World Bank. 2000a. "Analysis of the Flow of Funds in Nigeria's Petroleum Sector." Oil and Gas Policy Unit, World Bank, Washington, DC.

———. 2000b. "Nigerian National Oil Company Management Audit." Oil and Gas Policy Unit, World Bank, Washington, DC.

World Bank Institute. 2006. *A Decade of Measuring the Qualty of Governance: Governance Matters 2006.* Washington, DC: World Bank Institute.

Xinhua News Agency. 2005. "Tanzania Probes Tax Evasion on Oil Imports." Xinhua News Agency, April 25.

Yergin, Daniel, and Joseph Stanislaw. 1998. *The Commanding Heights.* New York: Simon and Schuster.

Zakaria, Fareed. 2004. *The Future of Freedom.* New York: W. W. Norton & Co.

7

Tackling Corruption in the Water and Sanitation Sector in Africa

Starting the Dialogue

JANELLE PLUMMER AND PIERS CROSS

"Kenya was the first country to sign the UN Convention Against Corruption: we have made an international commitment to tackle this scourge. Corruption leaks valuable finance that could be used elsewhere; it undermines our institutions and puts a burden on the poor. The Government of Kenya has committed itself to reforming the water sector through introducing new water laws and restructuring the governance of its water institutions. Increasing transparency and accountability and fighting corruption are integral to these reforms. Now the reforms are in place, national anti-corruption efforts must be stepped up, fast. Corruption has no place in the water sector and we need to scrutinize all transactions, large and small, in cities, towns and rural areas."

Hon. Mutua Katuku, Minister for Water and Irrigation, Kenya (Water Week, Stockholm, Sweden, August 2006)

For the past three decades, a substantial number of governments, donors, and nongovernmental organizations (NGOs) have focused efforts on a range of institutional, financial, technical, and social interventions aimed at bringing about much-needed improvements in the delivery of water and sanitation services in rural and urban areas in developing countries. Recognizing the adverse impacts of low levels of access for the poor, approaches have become increasingly targeted and service-oriented: responding to demand from users, identifying entry points with clients, reacting to signals in a developing water and sanitation market, and of course steering this course with the ebb and flow of donor funding. In more recent years, governments have embarked upon a process of establishing road maps that plot the long paths of sector reform and service improvement needed to meet the Millennium

This chapter is a revision of an earlier paper also titled *Tackling Corruption in the Water and Sanitation Sector in Africa*. We are particularly grateful to Ed Campos for his ongoing support; to the Roundtable reviewers of this version, Randi Ryterman, Francesca Recanatini, and Vinay Bhargava; to Scott Guggenheim and Steve Burgess for so many more insights than could be referenced; and to Charles Kenny, Jean Doyen, Fook Chuen Eng, Alain Locussol, Antonio Estache, Clarissa Brocklehurst, Patrik Stalgren, Donal O'Leary, Chris Heymans, Juliet Pumpuni, Vivek Srivastava, and Jonathon Halpern for helpful comments on earlier drafts.

Development Goals (MDGs). In a number of well-performing states, it looks like steady progress is being made.

Yet the attainment of the water and sanitation MDGs is unlikely in the majority of African countries, where the stability, investment, and capacity needed to meet significant and growing demand is inadequate (JMP 2002). Even if additional finance were to become available, an unacceptable level of leakage of existing resources in some settings brings into question current processes, and perhaps the wisdom, of increasing resource flows to the sector in those settings. Much of the funding available in ministries, local governments, utilities, and village administrations is being used by public officials for private gain. Whether in decision making on the allocation of water resources, or bribery and fraud in procurement or construction, corrupt practices are endemic to many water supply and sanitation (WSS) institutions and transactions in Africa. This corruption varies substantially in size and incidence, but it is clear that significant WSS sector finances are being lost to those charged with making decisions about, and delivering, water and sanitation services.[1] If the estimated $6.7 billion needed annually to attain the water and sanitation MDGs in Sub-Saharan Africa were actually mobilized, a 30 percent leakage would represent a loss of more than $20 billion from the sector over the next decade.[2]

The struggle with corruption in the water sector is of course fundamentally part of a broader governance problem and is characterized by the dynamics of reform processes at both the sector and national levels. Policy reform promoting decentralization and private sector participation, as well as new funding paradigms such as sectorwide approaches (SWAps) and direct budget support (DBS), may have provided a more fertile environment for new (sometimes higher) levels of corruption involving national or donor funds. Simultaneously, however, WSS sector reform in many African countries has removed conflicts of interest in sector management, improved transparency and accountability, and created the potential for models and the promise of change. Placing sector-specific anticorruption initiatives in the broader context of governance and anticorruption reform is therefore key to understanding the opportunities and limitations of sector anticorruption reform.

Notwithstanding the importance of the governance framework, the sector also needs to focus on diagnostics and solutions specific to WSS service delivery if it is going to improve progress toward the MDGs. The dysfunctionality and failure of the water and sanitation sector in Africa is distinctive. The sector is characterized by widespread financial disorder, few service providers are accountable to their customers, and resources are frequently not separately ring-fenced to create transparent financial management. Sector providers are also characterized by diversity: formal and informal, large and small, delivering different types of services in small and large towns and villages. In addition, the sector shares high-risk vulnerabilities to corruption with a number of other sectors. Because the sector provides a basic service, is predominantly public, and frequently requires expenditure on capital-intensive infrastructure, corruption in WSS is multifaceted. Evidence suggests that the WSS sector is vulnerable to massive distortion in resource allocation and significant procurement-related corruption (as a construction sector), to the daily opportunities for petty corruption (as a service delivery sector), and to the opaque budgeting and financial management practices of weak institutions, typical of the civil service.

Despite this complexity, leakage, and the potential impacts on the poor—and despite significant reform efforts by a range of supporting agencies—the current understanding of the extent and nature of corruption in the water and sanitation sector in Africa is limited, as is knowledge of the policies and mechanisms that are required to tackle it. There are virtually no data, and the data that do exist are piecemeal, often produced for other purposes. The need to launch the dialogue and begin the required diagnostics and reforms is urgent.

This chapter synthesizes the known dimensions of sector corruption and anticorruption activity. It first gives an overview of the water sector in Africa, looking specifically at access to water supply, perceptions of corruption in the sector, and reforms. It then describes the plural nature of corruption in the sector, setting out in a structured framework the network of corrupt practices prevalent in the sector. This framework categorizes the many types of WSS corruption into a typology of *public-to-public, public-to-private,* and *public-to-consumer* interactions and considers these interactions at each stage of the WSS value chain. The chapter then describes the range of anticorruption policies and mechanisms that have emerged over recent years, maps these over the corrupt interactions, and thus links the framework of corrupt practices to a menu of existing solutions. The chapter concludes with a discussion of key concerns the WSS sector will need to address as it moves forward with the anticorruption agenda.

Notwithstanding this effort to promote a comprehensive understanding of corruption in the sector in Africa, the chapter emphasizes the need for sound diagnostics to identify areas of concentrated corruption, as well as a focus on understanding appropriate and viable anticorruption strategies for the sector. It suggests that more targeted efforts should be made to improve mechanisms for instilling greater transparency and accountability in the sector, and it argues for more data and learning, for context specificity, and for efforts to develop appropriate methodologies and models for interventions tailored to the different economic, governance, and sector contexts of the African region.

ACCESS, CORRUPTION, AND REFORM IN THE WSS SECTOR

More than 42 percent of all Africans—some 300 million people—lack access to an improved water supply, and 64 percent, or 477 million Africans, lack access to adequate sanitation (JMP 2002). Averages for the continent hide a wealth of problems and gaps. In Ethiopia, for example, only 22 percent of the population has access to improved drinking water and 6 percent to adequate sanitation. Many of the poorest African states recovering from natural disasters and humanitarian crises are still politically and economically unstable and have few functioning assets, little capacity, and high levels of corruption; in these countries, access to WSS services is propped up by relief measures that are highly susceptible to leakage, or service delivery is nonexistent. Yet the story of corruption, reform, and limited access in the WSS sector in Africa is not restricted to these postcrisis countries. At any one time, 30 to 50 percent

FIGURE 7.1 Corruption, Water Reform, Gross National Income per Capita, and Access to Water

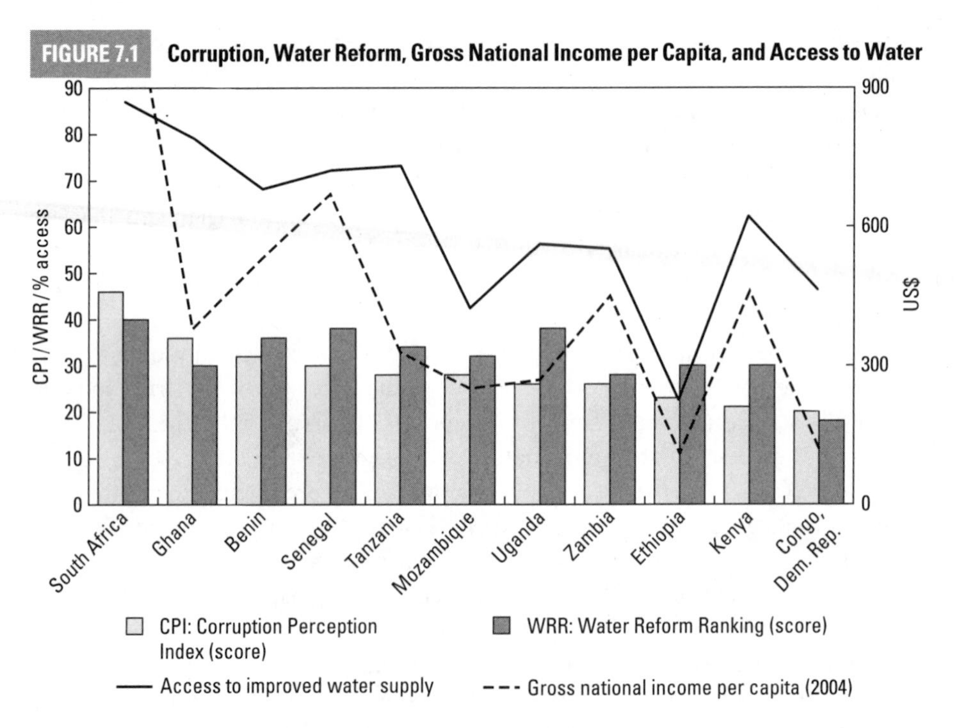

Source: Transparency International (2005); WSP-Africa (2006); JMP (2004); World Development Indicators database (2004).

of rural water supplies are out of order, and 80 percent of urban water utilities in Africa are considered financially unviable.[3]

Corruption in Africa is significant, unabated, and country specific, driven by conditions ripe for unaccountable and less than transparent behavior. Of the 34 African countries ranked in the Corruption Perception Index (CPI) published by Transparency International in 2005, only six were ranked in the least corrupt half of the 146-country index, 15 countries were ranked in the next 25 percent, and 13 countries, many of them postconflict states, were ranked among the most corrupt in the bottom 25 percent.[4] In Africa, the correlation between corruption (as measured by the CPI) and growth (as measured by gross national income per capita) is variable.[5] While South Africa and Ethiopia show correlations at either end of the scale, in an (unrepresentative) basket of countries, the country-by-country correlation between corruption and growth is less steady, perhaps supporting the thesis that a range of country-specific factors determines the growth-corruption relationship.

In this set of African countries, a general correlation is also found between perceived corruption levels and water reform. Notwithstanding the range of other influencing factors, countries with less corruption seem to have made better progress in WSS sector reform.[6] Figure 7.1 shows the CPI together with a water reform ranking for 11 African countries (WSP-Africa forthcoming).[7] While South Africa leads the region in water sector reform, Benin, Senegal, and Uganda also show significant progress, whereas the Democratic Republic of Congo has only recently initiated the reform process and struggles with postconflict levels of corruption.

Stronger water reforms and lower corruption correlate with higher levels of access to water supply. The limitations of the indexes or the existence of a range of factors influencing access notwithstanding, the available information shows an expected correlation between higher levels of access to water supply and countries that have made progress in WSS sector reform. Analysis also reveals that it takes time for reforms to be translated into better outcomes. Uganda stands out as an example of a country where water reforms have not yet been reflected in increased levels of access.

The correlation among sector reform, lower corruption, and higher rates of access is supported by utility-specific studies and cross-cutting global studies. Evidence provided in investment climate surveys that measure the perception of petty corruption in WSS delivery (Kenny 2006) supports the finding that corruption seems to be strongly correlated with lower levels of WSS coverage.[8] In their assessment of the efficiency of African utilities, Estache and Kouassi (2002) found that corruption is significant. Controlling for other variables, they estimated that if water utilities were operating in corruption-free environments, efficiency would be 64 percent higher (or costs would be reduced by 64 percent).[9]

The vast differences in the African continent suggest the need for country specificity and better understanding of regional patterns and trends. Regional typological differences are apparent in terms of economies (be they coastal, landlocked, or resource-rich), governance (be they fragile, emerging, or capable) and political systems (authoritarian, established democracies, and emerging democracies). This variation creates a multitude of contexts and suggests a mixed basket of solutions. The variation is also evident at the WSS sector level. Institutional capacity and frameworks vary (national and decentralized, regulatory and provider agencies with and without autonomy), as do service delivery models (public or privately managed utilities, municipal and district water departments, large and small towns, small local providers, and community management). Understanding what can be done in the best and worst economic or governance cases, and how these differences affect potential action at the sector level, will be useful lessons for the region.

DIAGNOSING CORRUPTION IN THE WSS SECTOR IN AFRICA

The corruption that occurs in the WSS sector can generally be understood in terms of bureaucratic, or *petty,* corruption, in which a vast number of officials abusing public office extract small bribes and favors; *grand* corruption, involving the misuse of vast amounts of public sector funds by a relatively small number of officials; and *state* capture, seen in the collusion between public and private actors for private benefit (Shah and Schacter 2004). In the WSS sector, these corrupt practices, big and small, take the form of abuse of resources—theft and embezzlement from budgets and revenues, corruption in procurement, administrative corruption in payment systems, and corruption at the point of service delivery.

Corruption in the WSS sector varies by country (and regions within a country), by governance, by WSS systems, and by a multitude of other local conditions. In urban areas, the type, size, and incidence of corruption in service delivery may be a function of the path of legislative reform or of the leadership that the sector has seen. Or it might be an outcome of decentralization and the role of social structures and civil society, or the nature of the water market in difficult locations. In rural and periurban areas, similar factors, plus the structural shift toward community-driven development approaches, the highly opaque construction and management processes, the isolated nature of remote areas, and the nature of traditional social structures potentially contribute to local-level corruption, capture, and collusion.

Who Is Involved?

Corruption in the water and sanitation sector involves a vast range of stakeholders. The list includes international actors (donor representatives, private companies, and multinationals), national and local construction companies, consultancy firms and suppliers, large and small operators, a range of middlemen, consumers, and civil society organizations, national and subnational politicians, and all grades of civil servants and utility staff. Corrupt activities between these stakeholders occur at a range of institutional levels, with different stakeholders often involved in one or more types of corruption.

What Are the Causes?

Like all corruption in developing and transitional economies, corruption in WSS in Africa is founded in historical, political, and social realities—the causes of corruption are not sectoral. Corrupt practices take hold and are manifest in different contexts in very different ways, and legal frameworks, institutional structures, and bureaucratic systems strongly influence how elected, managerial, and technical officials behave. Klitgaard's (1988) definition of the factors that cause corruption: M (monopoly) $+$ D (discretion) $-$ A (accountability) $-$ T (transparency) $=$ C (corruption)—is very relevant to an understanding of the WSS sector in Africa in that it highlights the aggregate effect of monopoly and discretionary power.[10] The WSS sector has long grappled with its monopolistic past and the traits (such as high capital costs and economies of scale) that tend to keep it that way. A strong characteristic of agencies and officials involved in the sector is their enormous discretion in the planning, design, contracting, implementation, and monitoring of water and sanitation service delivery (compounded by a lack of clarity of rules and regulations). To this it must be added that demand for accountability for services, although improving in many contexts, is typically a missing element in service provider (Gray and Kaufmann 1998) and water user relationships in Africa.

Is the Water Sector Prone to Corruption?

It is difficult not to follow the lead of other sectors and emphasize the enormity of the problem of corruption in the WSS sector.[11] While corruption in water and sanitation is known to be significant, it is not clear whether the sector is currently more or less prone to corruption than other sectors, or whether such a generalization should even be made when country contexts, institutions, and policies vary so greatly.[12] Nevertheless, it is possible to posit a number of characteristics that make WSS services susceptible to corruption and a cause for grave concern for all stakeholders.[13] Many of the fundamental characteristics, such as low institutional capacity, low wages, dysfunctional institutions, and large-scale procurement, are common to delivery of all sorts of public services, but the WSS sector is also part of the construction sector, globally thought to be the most corrupt of all sectors (Transparency International 2005), and it encompasses several other dimensions that suggest high potential for corruption. These include, among other things, a large flow of public money, often including uncoordinated donor, national, and local funds; the opacity of, political interference in, and discretion for investment decisions; the monopolistic nature of service delivery, coupled with the failure of sector financing and cost recovery, problematic tariffs and subsidies, and the increasing role of the informal market; the cost of sector assets;[14] the asymmetry of information between user and provider; and the complexity of sector stakeholders, systems, levels of service, and institutional roles and functions.

How Much Is Corruption Costing the WSS Sector?

Hypotheses on the cost of corruption in the WSS sector in Africa are largely untested. Leakage can be roughly estimated through comparative and limited sector studies, but to date it has not been measured in the WSS sector in Africa in any systematic way.[15] As a proportion of sector expenditure, the high levels of petty corruption, in the aggregate, constitute a substantial figure across the continent, but there are no regional or country estimates based on empirical studies. The figure of 20–35 percent provided by Davis (2003) for service delivery in South Asia provides a sectoral, not a regional, indication, and it should be noted that this estimate is limited to petty corruption and does not account for high-level abuse or diversion of resources. Measuring corruption is an urgent area of future work.

Promoting a Comprehensive View of Sector Corruption

A comprehensive approach to sector diagnosis and action first requires recognition that water service delivery is heterogeneous at the sector, city or district, and household levels, and it involves a number of formal and informal stakeholders from the public and private sectors and civil society. Figure 7.2 provides a simplified picture of the water marketplace. While a utility may be producing half of the water consumed, only a proportion of the population is connected formally from source to consumption (illustrated by the top arrow to point A), which might represent the means by which a majority of nonpoor are served in urban areas. In practice, however, water produced by a utility might be distributed either by the utility or bought or stolen during the secondary or tertiary distribution (illustrated by the diversion to point B).

Alternatively, water might be diverted immediately after production, being bought or stolen by other providers willing to distribute it from the point or near the point of production and following a series of lines along a route of nonutility distribution to point C. Under the fourth alternative, shown by the arrow at the bottom of the diagram reaching point D, the water source and production are from individual or private producers, typical of wells and rural boreholes that might have no

FIGURE 7.2 The Spectrum of Utility and Nonutility Water Providers

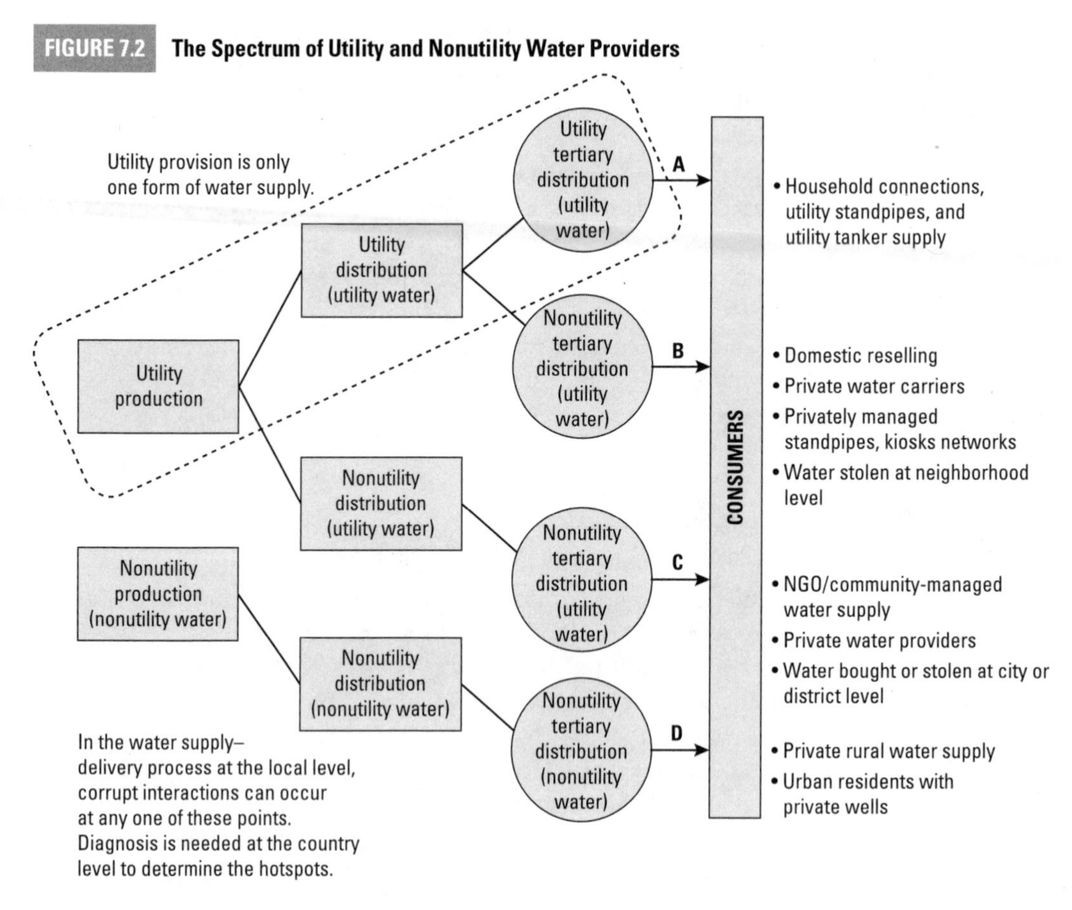

Source: Adapted from Plummer (2003).

direct public role after construction. The typical forms of delivery for each of these supply chains are shown at the right-hand side of the diagram. They include the utility, community-managed provision, formal intermediate providers, informal providers, and household self-supply. Corruption can occur at any interaction on these supply lines.

One of the problems this chapter addresses, and the key issue motivating its structure and content, is that perceptions of corruption among WSS stakeholders tend to be very narrow. Individual stakeholders seem to hold subjective views on what corruption is, often focusing more on one type of corruption than another; the formal corruption debate has mostly focused on procurement and the operational inefficiencies of utilities, leaving aside a range of other forms of corruption and failing to address the linkages between them.[16] This narrow understanding limits the development of effective reform. To move forward with a pro-poor strategy for anticorruption action in WSS in Africa, it is necessary to consider the whole network of corrupt practices. Notwithstanding the need for project-level intervention, the need for *sector-level* analysis and action is key to a coordinated and meaningful sector response.[17]

DEVELOPING A CORRUPTION INTERACTION FRAMEWORK

To help meet this objective, the following comprehensive framework is set out to unbundle and differentiate types of sector corruption. This framework can be used to identify the corrupt practices that exist in different settings, who is involved, and at what stage of WSS service delivery they occur. The framework can also be used in each country context to locate concentrations of corruption, to identify unknowns, to plot shifts in corruption activity, and to identify links within the corruption matrix. Ultimately, the goal of this sort of information-organizing exercise is to provide a robust framework that is relevant and applicable to the sector, integrates project-level and cross-cutting governance diagnostics, and is usable as a tool for understanding and promoting change.[18]

The corruption framework, illustrated in table 7.1, is structured around *interactions* and a *value chain.* This interactions approach is driven by a need to build broad stakeholder commitment and a coalition for change and by a strong belief that the corruption problem in the WSS sector should be articulated in terms of the actions of all public, private, and civil society actors and institutions. It is also pursued knowing that policy actions are more likely to influence the public sector than other actors and that more policy options are available to this end.[19] Beginning with the definition of corruption as *the use of public office for private gain,* the approach places the public or entrusted office at the core of the interaction framework and notes that the public officer or agency interacts with three types of actors: other public actors and agencies; private actors and companies; and consumers, civil society, and its representative organizations.[20] The framework highlights these interactions as they relate to functions to be performed in water and sanitation services—a cycle of policy making and regulation, budgeting and planning, financing, program design and management, tendering and procurement, construction, operation and maintenance, and monitoring functions.

Public-to-Public Interactions

The public actor in WSS includes actors from international, national, and subnational governmental departments and agencies in both water and nonwater functions. Corrupt practices within government typically involve interactions between public actors, although in rare cases, an individual may act alone. These interactions can be described as vertical, when they occur within the hierarchy of water institutions, and as horizontal, when they involve various line departments and agencies at a similar level of government (table 7.2). At the higher levels of government, corruption is opaque and complex, but distortions in the allocation of resources can be achieved only by collaboration within water departments and between line departments such as finance, planning, and water affairs or public works. Officials are expected to "play the game," and their status and power base are dependent on their willingness to work within the established system.

Public-to-public corrupt practices are often concentrated in *policy-making* functions. Politicians and officials responsible for water sector policies seek to set up future opportunities for rent seeking by influencing the focus of policy and

TABLE 7.1 Value Chain Framework: Corrupt Interactions in the Water Sector

	Public-to-public	*Public-to-private*	*Public-to-consumers*
Policy making and regulation	• Policy capture (competition and monopolies)	• Policy capture • Regulatory capture (waivers to regulations and licensing) • Extortion over licensing	
Planning and budgeting	• Distortions in decision making by politicians (affecting location and type of project investments) • Corruption in national and sector planning and budget management (misuse of funds, interministerial bribery for fund allocation, collusion or bribery in selection and project approval) • Corruption in local budget management (fraud, falsification of accounts or documents, village-level collusion)	• Bribery to influence allocation of resources • Bribery in sector budgeting management (influencing, distortions in funding allocation) at national and local level	
Donor financing	• Donor-government collusion in negotiations to meet spending/funding targets • Donor-government collusion/fraud with respect to progress and quality.	• Donor and national private operator collusion (outside legal trade agreements)	
Fiscal transfers	• Bribery, rent seeking, and kickbacks to ensure fund transfers between finance ministry and WSS sector ministries, or subnational levels		
Management and program design	• Corruption in personnel management, such as payments for preferred candidates (e.g., utility directorships); payments for promotions, transfers, and salary perks • Distortionary decision making (collusion with leaders in selection and approval of plans) • Corruption in local government in program design		• Influence project decision making • Bribery for preferential treatment, elite capture • Distortionary decision making (project-level site selection, equipment, construction)

TABLE 7.1 (Continued)

	Public-to-public	*Public-to-private*	*Public-to-consumers*
Tendering and procurement	• Administrative corruption (fraud, falsification of documents, silence payments) • Interdepartment or agency collusion over procurement	• Bribery to influence contract/bid organization • Corruption in delegating management: fraud involving over/underestimating assets; selection, type, award of concessions; decisions over duration, exclusivity, tariffs, subsidies • Corruption in procurement: inflated estimates for capital works, supply of chemicals, vehicles, equipment • Falsification of documentation	
Construction	• Administrative corruption (fraud, falsification of documents, silence payments)	• Corruption in construction: bribery and fraud involving failure to build to specification; concealing substandard work materials; failure to complete works; underpayment of workers — Fraudulent invoicing, including marked-up pricing, overbilling by suppliers	• Corruption in community-based construction (with similar types of practices as for public-private interactions)
Operation and maintenance		• Overbilling by suppliers, theft/diversion of inputs (chemicals) • Avoiding compliance with regulations, specifications, health and safety rules • Extortion to gain permits and licensing (speed money) • Falsification of accounts	• Administrative corruption to obtain access to water, such as installing or concealing illegal connections, avoiding disconnection, illicit supply using utility vehicles • Administrative corruption for speed (or preferential treatment) in obtaining repairs or new connections
Payment (for services)			• Administrative corruption regarding payment and billing: fraudulent meter reading, avoidance or partial payment, overcharging

Source: Authors.

investment priorities. In those countries where a regulatory function has been defined, politicians and other stakeholders may pay regulators to formulate biased or favorable standards and regulations (a practice known as regulatory capture) or to allow projects to bypass established standards or procedures.

TABLE 7.2 Key Public Actors Involved in the WSS Sector

	General public actors	Public actors within water sector
National political actors	Government leadership Policy makers Judiciary	
National agencies	Enforcement agencies Anticorruption forums	Regulators
National line departments management	Directors in finance, planning, health, interior/home departments	Directors in public works, water ministries
National planning and implementing staff	Deputy directors (finance, planning)	Deputy directors (finance, operations, customer support) Departmental heads at national or provincial levels (planning and budgeting) Procurement staff
Provincial/local *Political actors* *Management*	District/ local-level leaders Mayors/town clerks	Public works officials Municipal engineers
Utility staff *Midlevel local implementing staff*	Municipal procurement staff Engineering staff	Utility directors Utility procurement and project management staff Senior operations staff Technical managers Engineers, technicians, supervisors, facilitators
Community leaders and quasi-government officials	Village leaders Lower-level public officials	Management user committees Lower-level public officials

Source: Authors.

Grand corruption occurs among politicians and senior officials in the selection of WSS projects: during *planning and budgeting* processes, capital investment projects may be favored over more effective and lower investment alternatives; sector investments that guarantee higher levels of personal return are favored over those that do not. In other words, public resources may be being diverted to WSS projects with greater potential for kickbacks at the lowest possible risk. Experience suggests that, more often than not, these projects are regressive in their impact—benefiting the rich more than the poor. Sourcing water from surface rather than groundwater alternatives where they are available is a typical illustration of decision making that, while legal, creates opportunities for both grand and petty corruption. Surface water projects that require the construction of costly water treatment plants and ongoing procurement of chemicals (as seen in Kinshasa, for instance) can provide opportunity for bribery, extortion, and fraud and are characteristic of the types of decisions made within the water sector that have long-term effects on corruption. The use and abuse of resources found in the manipulation of budgets and in dubious decision making in planning processes is exacerbated by a disconnect between policy objectives, planning, and implementation. In delivery agencies (or communities), this type of corruption might involve the diversion of the inputs themselves (such as the chemicals for water treatment) for resale or other use. All these practices result in lower quality or quantity of water supply.

In some countries, *fiscal transfer* systems present a series of opportunities for fraud and extraction of funds from the system, as well as extortion by public departments and units that have funding approval authority for WSS spending. In some cases, approval must pass through several units in a number of ministries, such as planning, finance, public works, and water departments, before passing through a similar series of subnational agencies and their own subdepartments.

Corruption between the tiers of government, irrespective of the sector, frequently concerns *personnel management:* bribes paid for promotions, appointments, transfers, and a multitude of perks. Buying senior appointments is thought to be common throughout the region, and the prices paid for utility directorships or municipal engineers are often common knowledge and calculable, based on sector norms.[21] Corrupt politicians and managers might also appoint willing personnel to lucrative positions on the condition that they pass back a portion of the illegal income the office earns. Many argue that these types of practices, common throughout the civil service, lie at the core of the incentive and patronage system and propagate other forms of corruption.

Public-to-public interactions might also include collusion between government officials and international donor representatives in the targeting of *donor financing.*[22] International donors are under pressure to disperse loans or grants and to maintain relationships with government partners. In the water sector, this pressure can lead to an emphasis on quantity over quality and speed over specification. Furthermore, donor representatives, like all employees, have incentives to deliver and to be seen to be managing successful projects delivered on time and on budget. On the government side, donors channel large levels of funding through inadequate financial management systems, often dwarfing annual budgets and the capacity of recipient departments, utilities, or district offices. Funding for capacity building can also have a multitude of perverse personnel management effects, giving senior public officials discretion to top up staff salaries with donor-funded allowances, often by an order of magnitude, and developing unhealthy incentive structures and relationships within recipient agencies and departments.

Public-to-Private Interactions

Procurement requires interaction between the public and private sectors and is the most publicized face of corruption. Every level of government and every type of government agency has to purchase goods and services, normally from the private sector. In WSS, a number of public actors may be involved, depending on the size and type of project: national and local government politicians and managers, municipal engineers, operations staff, project managers, and procurement officers. The set of private actors might include suppliers, contractors, utility operators, and local and national consultants. In the case of large loans or grants, procurement corruption might also involve the collusion of donors seeking preferable terms for donor-country firms or operators.[23]

It is a norm of economic life for private actors to seek to reduce competition, and private stakeholders do so in the WSS sector at all levels. It is also clear that the supply chain creates a number of concentrated opportunities for private and public actors to gain from public-to-private transactions.[24] (The Lesotho Highlands project provides useful insights into procurement-related corruption in the water sector, see Darroch 2004; Earle and Turton 2005.) Corruption in public procurement seeks to influence the selection of contracts for WSS services and supplies, payment schedules, profit margins, and the outcomes of the regulatory process. In urban water supply, much of the attention given to public-private interactions has focused on transactions for operating water and sanitation services. The practice of creating public-private partnerships behind closed doors has created unworkable agreements in Africa and elsewhere, has muddied incentive structures, and has undermined the possible benefits of reform attained through private sector efficiency and effectiveness.

The *design, tendering, and negotiation* phases in the procurement of WSS infrastructure and facilities offer substantial opportunities for corrupt action.[25] High-level officials can influence the way a contract is let, determining the nature of the project and then the type of contract. Purchasing officials for a utility, municipality, or district office can tailor specifications to suit favorite suppliers. During tendering, corrupt practices can either restrict or influence the flow of information to favored and unfavored competitors, create excuses for sole sourcing or uncompetitive selection, breach confidentiality or disqualify suppliers, and accept or solicit bribes to influence tender lists or selection procedures. Contractors and operators may falsify records and documentation to ensure that bids look competitive, and officials may either encourage them to do so or turn a blind eye. It is also common for private contractors, consultants, and suppliers of pipes, chemicals, and other inputs to collude in taking turns in bid winning or to mark up pricing. Collusion and the falsification of records are often known to the public procurement official who receives a kickback for silence.

Corruption in *construction* can also be concentrated at several points. Those responsible for licenses and permits can demand bribes or slow down licensing procedures affecting the performance of contractors. Oversight officials are bribed or extort payments to provide fraudulent documentation when specifications (such as the depth of pipe work) are not met, when works are not completed, or when lower-quality materials are used. Typically, these practices help contractors minimize costs and result in substandard works, affecting sustainability and quality of WSS service delivery. Supervising officials may also be bribed or extort payments to agree to falsified claims or accounts and to facilitate the speedy approval of payments. Regulators may be bribed or extort payments to keep silent or permit waivers of works not completed to standard.

Corruption in *operations and maintenance* can occur in all service arrangements; the practices vary according to the actors involved. Be it in large or small towns, the public sector is responsible for operating and maintaining most if not all of the water treatment and distribution systems and the sewerage or sanitation services.[26] Public utilities, municipalities, district governments, and lines departments interact with the private sector through the supply of goods (chemicals, pipes, meters, and other hardware) or in the delegation of services that can be unbundled from the main water supply function. These include earthworks, billing and collection, security, cleaning,

BOX 7.1 Utility Officials Extort Bribes from Small Water Providers in Nairobi

The sprawling squatter settlement of Kibera lies in an area of Nairobi not served by the city water utility. Instead, small private providers buy water from the utility and sell it from water kiosks. These tanks with taps provide a neighborhood source of water for Kibera's half-million residents. Householders queue for water during the times it is available. The price is fixed and competitive within the squatter settlement, although at 3–20 shillings a vessel, it is many times the price of utility water, and it varies according to the season and availability of water.

Water bills for the private providers are erratic and hugely inconsistent, and the irregular delivery of the bulk water supply gives utility officials leverage over the providers, who have little choice but to "tip" the officials in order to receive their water or to get their bills revised to something approximating the true charges. The losers are the poor who pay a higher price for their water each time this "surcharge" is levied.

The small-scale private providers are becoming increasingly organized and have now formed an association and developed a code of ethics to ensure that they all follow a set of agreed rules; the association also gives them a platform with the capacity and leverage to interact effectively with the utility. The private providers see their association as a critical vehicle to counter the regular petty corruption engaged in by Nairobi Water Utility officials.

Source: WSP-Africa (2005); author interviews with Kibera providers (May 2005).

and the like. The interactions between the contractors and suppliers providing these goods and services can fall prey to the same types of corrupt practices seen in procurement and construction.

In large cities where the water supply function itself has been delegated to private operators, opportunities for bribery and fraud are created by the way the deal is structured at the outset and played out throughout the duration of the contract. Experience suggests that public-private negotiations can influence the types of contract (design-build-lease contracts, concessions, leases, management contracts), the concession area and bundle of services, and their duration and conditions (such as exclusivity), all areas in which the potential for corruption is high. The capacity needed can be over- or underestimated, assets over- or undervalued, the level and process of tariff setting manipulated, and the targets and subsidies for serving the poor determined through public-private deals that benefit the deal makers.

In large and small towns and periurban areas, an alternative set of corrupt interactions may occur in the water market involving local government and utility officials and small private providers of water. Investigations into the actions of small private water providers in squatter settlements reveal that their ability to function is often dependent on the deals they make with local officials. For example, as box 7.1 reports, legal water kiosk operators in squatter settlements in Nairobi say they must bribe utility officials to keep billing inconsistencies at tolerable levels (Plummer, Collignon, and Mehrotra 2005). Legal operators bribe officials to obtain more reliable and longer daily bulk supply, while those functioning illegally pay officials to connect into the network or deliver bulk water that they then distribute in a competitive market. In the sanitation sector, small-scale private operators pay local government officials to allow them to dump waste on inappropriate sites irrespective of health and environmental consequences.

Public-to-Consumer/Civil Society Interactions

Corrupt interactions between consumers and public officials, mostly in the form of bribery, are typically petty, frequent, and systemic. For the consumer who pays the bribe, water is the desired outcome, and the incentive is to obtain a much-needed basic service. The public official may extort the payment from consumers, or the consumer may voluntarily pay the bribe to gain access to the service.[27] Common corrupt practices at the point of service delivery in the operations and maintenance of water services include providing illegal connections, reselling utility water and utilizing utility vehicles, and giving preferential treatment for repairs or new services in exchange for so-called "speed money."

In rural areas, corruption affects the delivery of community-based and NGO-supported water supply and sanitation projects in their design, implementation, and ongoing maintenance.[28] Although systematic assessment in Africa is lacking, collusion between village leaders and government overseers is frequently visible and adversely affects the poor. Pumps or tanks may be located where they benefit the elite, or efforts by community leaders to increase profit may reflect typical public-private fraud such as theft of materials and failure to build to specification. Project management may involve fraudulent documentation or accounting and reporting by the same people charged with managing finances. The cost of rural boreholes in Africa—at up to four times the cost in some parts of Asia—is considered by sector professionals to be a prime hotspot for further investigation (WSP-Africa 2005).

In urban areas, community-based WSS projects suffer from similar patterns of behavior. Where the poor are served by utilities, they frequently pay bribes to officials to obtain access to services, household connections, sewage disposal services, and repairs off the utility books. In squatter areas, the bribe may be pitched at a level the poor can afford—it may be similar to the cost of obtaining other informal forms of water supply. In other situations, where the poor live in mixed-income settlements and the water market is differentiated, higher-income households are prepared to pay more, and the bribe price can be higher, marginalizing the poor and placing them at the end of the queue.

Other common public-consumer interactions concern administrative corruption in *payment systems,* irregular billing, falsification of meter readings, and overcharging are typical utility practices that can be avoided or mitigated by the payment of bribes (Davis 2003). Typically, where poor consumers are involved, the bribe is demanded rather than offered. Most of these practices result in commercial leakage, adding to the inefficiencies of dysfunctional agencies. In surveys conducted in Mozambique, 12 percent of households reported that they always had to bribe officials for services, more than 20 percent of user-enterprises reported that they paid bribes in more than 25 percent of transactions, and almost half reported that it made no difference which official was involved, suggesting an institutional norm (Austral Consultoria 2004). Moreover, these figures appear to be low. In a Transparency International survey conducted in Nairobi, more than 60 percent of households and institutional customers reported they had dealt with corrupt utility officials (Transparency International Kenya 2006).

Public-to-consumer corruption is a part of a series of failures. Weak policies and institutions lead to a lack of services and inevitably create a market for corruption at the point of service delivery. It is vital that this corruption be viewed as a part of this broader, failed system because the problem is far more complex than a simple picture of officials forcing consumers to pay bribes to obtain a service they are entitled to obtain free of charge. Where there is no alternative water supply (and especially where no informal supply market has developed), it is common for poor and non-poor households to create a demand for "corrupt water." They need the water and are not so concerned with the terms that unofficial providers set. Similar to costly "informal" water (water provided by informal suppliers), corrupt water fills a gap created by ineffective agencies: corrupt officials, acting as informal providers, provide the poor with services they may not have otherwise obtained (Plummer and Cross 2005).[29] This presents the sector with a dilemma, at least in the short term, that needs to be carefully managed to ensure that poor households continue to have access to water even as sector corruption is reduced.

Identifying Concentrated Areas of Corruption

In practice, each water and sanitation context will experience different areas of concentration or vulnerability to corruption in policy making, planning and budgeting, fiscal transfers, procurement, personnel management, construction, and service delivery, all of which respond to the factors determining the local and sector corruption scene. Rather than advocate for a total system of reform, this section promotes the need for comprehensive diagnosis, to provide a picture of the range of corrupt practices in WSS, on which vulnerable spots can be located, and to stress the importance of links and connections.

In practice, too, corruption varies significantly between countries, within countries, between agencies and institutions, and within sectors.[30] Understanding the weighting (intensity and incidence) of corruption at any one point in this matrix in the sector, as well as the institutional context, is vital to ensure that anticorruption efforts concentrate on major points of leakage. Good policy and effective mitigation efforts can therefore come only from good diagnosis. Country-level diagnosis specifically in the WSS sector is vital.

TACKLING CORRUPTION IN THE WSS SECTOR IN AFRICA

Over the last decade, a number of theories and mechanisms have been developed and tested to tackle corruption in its various forms. Policy changes that support anticorruption activity generally range from removing trade barriers, to more targeted actions streamlining or eliminating unnecessary regulation and licensing, and strengthening accounting and auditing standards. Institutional reform strategies have included the strengthening of judicial and legal systems; improving budgeting procedures and financial management; mainstreaming civil service reform; and focusing on incentives, competition, and internal checks. More specific anticorruption strategies have dealt with enforcement, watchdogs and ombudsmen, awareness campaigns, and anticorruption commissions. Despite this menu of options and the increasing resources from development agencies devoted to the fight against corruption, many commentators highlight the lack of rigor and specificity in the development of anticorruption programs (Shah and Schacter 2004).

This section briefly considers the array of instruments for tackling corruption and positions them in relation to the WSS corruption interaction framework. To focus the discussion, it concentrates on the most prevalent area of corruption for each of the public-to-public, public-to-private, and public-to-consumer/civil society interactions. This is done with some caution, knowing that generic lessons are continually emerging, that sector lessons are few and far between, and that any anticorruption strategy would inevitably need to be developed at the country level to respond to the country-specific nature and causes of corruption.

Understanding and Addressing Incentives: A Key Starting Action

Irrespective of the actors involved, corruption flourishes when the incentives exist for it to do so. Corruption is driven by need, greed, or opportunity for money or power (Klitgaard, Maclean-Abaroa, and Parris 2000); for poor consumers, it may be driven by the simple need for water (Plummer and Cross 2005). Public incentives might suggest that lower-level, poorly paid officials have a need to supplement their income; midlevel managers have ample opportunity; and politicians, senior managers, and directors are driven by greed. Yet public officials at all levels shoulder a range of responsibilities and must meet the obligations that come with their position. Individual and organizational incentives are complex, closely aligned with sociopolitical and institutional structures, and often driven by factors outside the sector.

An understanding of incentive structures developed in governance and civil service reform initiatives (Huther and Shah 2000) can be applied to water sector institutions and relationships. The key concern for any corrupt official is that the potential gains from the corrupt actions outweigh the potential losses. To change behavior of officials, the expected gains must be lowered and the expected penalties increased. Expected gains can be lowered by reducing both the incidence of corrupt transactions and the gain from each single transaction. The incidence of corrupt transactions can be lowered through policies and organizational reforms that reduce discretion, monopolies, and bureaucratic procedures and that clarify functional responsibilities for regulation, policy making, and delivery. Increasing service standards and decentralizing government services can also help lower the incidence of corruption. The gain to be had from a transaction can be lowered by scaling down large projects or improving the contract management of those projects (through transparent decision-making processes, for example), by demonopolizing public services, and by promoting competition in the sector.

The probability of detection or penalty can be enhanced by clarifying procedures and streamlining operational roles, increasing accountability and transparency through citizen or consumer participation and monitoring of WSS services, establishing citizen charters, specifying standards, ensuring media independence, promoting transparency in interactions between public and private sectors, and providing support for whistleblowers. The magnitude of the penalties for corrupt actions should also be increased. The key to enforcement is meaningful penalties, but these are currently rare at the sector level in developing countries.

Key Dimensions of Good Governance in WSS Sector Anticorruption Activity

Experience with anticorruption activity has provided a set of mechanisms fundamental to good governance and applicable to anticorruption reform in the water sector. Best practice suggests that demand-side efforts are needed to support the technical approaches to improved sector performance carried out in many countries over the last decade (UN-Habitat and Transparency International 2004). Careful consideration must be given, however, to the applicability and impact of these various approaches within any given context in the water sector, as well as to their blending and sequencing. Key areas of action include the following.

Diagnosis and Measurement

Effective anticorruption policy depends on sound diagnosis and understanding of the sector context, as outlined earlier. In addition, measurement systems that enable sector benchmarking and that monitor relative progress can be used to raise awareness and focus efforts. There is much debate over the appropriateness and accuracy of corruption indexes. Possible approaches for sector consideration include the Global Corruption Perception Index (Transparency International 2006), the corruption measurement approach (Olkren 2005), and the measurement of anticorruption instruments and policies such as the Global Integrity Index, which is similar in objective to the water reform ranking system developed by WSP-Africa (2006).[31]

Transparency and Access to Information

On the demand side, promoting greater transparency around the actions of politicians and water sector officials creates disincentives for their engagement in corrupt transactions. Transparency can be developed in various forms at the project, community, and sector levels—publicizing utility accounts, budgets, contracting arrangements, and annual reports, and holding public hearings by regulators are all tangible mechanisms for improving transparency. Access to information is essential to improve demand for accountability. Typically, consumers have no knowledge of recurrent and capital costs, making it possible for public officials to deliberately misallocate resources or tap into limited budgets without detection. Consumers also should be able to access information about complaints mechanisms and their rights as consumers and citizens. A significant contribution to political accountability and a transparent operating environment can also be made by increasing the role of the media (Stapenhurst 2000) and by utilizing e-government for transparent record management.

Accountability

The development of accountability, be it through transparency, professionalism, honesty, or competence, is central to tackling corruption in WSS and applies to all parts of the service delivery framework.[32] Efforts focused at improving accountability occur on both supply and demand sides. On the demand side are the institutionalization of surveys, mechanisms to strengthen civil society's role in monitoring (such as the Bangalore citizen report card), and consumer associations (Thampi 2005). These efforts must be supported by building the capacity of the government officials involved and by educating consumers about the role they can play in thwarting corruption. This is particularly important in Africa, where civil society tends to be relatively immature, struggles to be heard, and is low in capacity.

Education and Advocacy

Lack of awareness is currently a key factor preventing action in Africa. Politicians, high-level officials, the media, and the general public all need to be more aware of the causes and consequences of corruption. But a truly effective means for generating that awareness in countries with weak governance has yet to be found—most advocacy campaigns have failed.[33] Evidence from rural India also suggests that higher levels of education and literacy correlate with lower corruption, more accountability, better targeting, and less political capture.[34]

Institutional and Policy Reform

Anticorruption efforts need to look beyond the demand side, however. Reforms addressing the complexities and ambiguities of country policy, regulatory, and institutional frameworks and decentralization are vital and must be underpinned by civil service reform, particularly in the areas of organizational and financial management. Efforts to create an environment of accountable service provision are central to these reforms, all of which will create the structural change needed in WSS service delivery systems and reduce opportunity for corruption. These technical approaches include better sector planning and policy making; aligning the functions of different tiers and departments; separating provider, regulatory, and financing responsibilities; improving corporate governance within water utilities; improving internal procedures, such as contract management; addressing monopolistic and uncompetitive systems; establishing partnerships with private operators to improve efficiency; and adopting results-based performance approaches. Among these steps, efforts to strengthen the accountability between WSS service providers and policy makers, better allocation of functions, and adoption of results-oriented approaches (such as output-based aid mechanisms) are gaining momentum in Africa (Halpern and Mumssen 2006; Trémolet and Halpern 2006).

Leadership

The need to embed the anticorruption struggle in broader reform, strong leadership, and good management is critical.[35] Central to the anticorruption institutional reform agenda is leadership: the struggle will be carried by leaders who cast the drive against corruption as a part of their effort to expand and improve services. One outstanding example is the successful attack against corruption led by the mayor of La Paz from 1985 to the late 1990s as part of municipal reforms (Maclean-Abaroa 2006).

Integrity

Efforts to promote integrity and ethical behavior among government officials, utility managers, and others working in the water sector have been developed and tested with some success in developed countries and are gaining momentum in developing countries. The integrity pact promoted by Transparency International pledges contractors, suppliers, and government agencies to refrain from offering or accepting bribes in connection with public contracts. Government and professional associations have developed codes of conduct or ethics and training on ethics issues with the aim of binding members to corruption-free behavior. Other mechanisms include establishment of business principles, laws and rules governing conflicts of interest, and protection for whistleblowers. Most of these approaches are potentially useful for cleaning up the multinational private sector that operates in developing-country water sectors, but they may have limited applicability in developing countries until transparency and accountability frameworks are established.

Enforcement and Regulation

A large number of countries have introduced anticorruption legislation, regulations, rules, and procedures aimed at controlling corruption. In most developing countries, however, these sanctions-based approaches are rarely accompanied by effective enforcement, and many have proven ineffective, in part because the police and judiciary are themselves riddled with corruption. Ombudsman and complaints offices, oversight committees, watchdog agencies, independent auditing introduced to formalize processes and enforce punishment, and special anticorruption and fraud agencies have all been tested but have had little success in the context of weak governance (Shah and Schacter 2004). At the international level, the UN Convention against Corruption offers a common framework for countries to tackle corruption and provides for cross-border cooperation. International finance institutions have also established rules and sanctions, but to date a lack of harmonization between financiers and donors has made efforts less than effective.[36]

Aligning Potential Anticorruption Mechanisms to Corruption in the WSS Sector

Anticorruption instruments work at and across general, sector-specific, and project levels. They often improve governance generally and may be effective in creating an enabling environment that discourages corruption in all sectors. To provide an overview of the tools available and their relevance, the following discussion describes the types of mechanisms that might be applicable to each of the corrupt interactions mapped in the WSS sector (see table 7.1) at each of the relevant points in the value chain.

Tackling Corruption within Government (Public-to-Public Interactions)

To date, there has been little *direct* effort to tackle corruption involving water sector officials. In the past, corrupt interactions internal to the public sector—within or between government tiers, departments, WSS agencies, and individuals—have generally been addressed through *indirect* initiatives aimed at civil service reform and improved accountability through decentralization and other political reform processes.[37] While the extent to which these efforts have been successful in

TABLE 7.3 Tackling Hotspots in Public-to-Public Corruption

	Public-to-public interactions	*Early warning indicators*	*Potential responses*
Policy making	• Bribery of decision makers to influence policy priorities	• Low tariff structures Monopolies and a resistance to competition	• Policy and tariff reform
Regulating	• Influencing regulations and licenses • Bribery to bypass constraining regulations • Influencing appointment of regulator	• No division of regulator and provider roles • Renegotiation of contracts (frequency and timing)	• Separation of regulator and provider roles, including private sector participation. • Development and publication of minimum standards. • Public oversight of negotiations with operators
Planning and budgeting	• Distortions in decision making by politicians (affecting location and types of project investments) • Corruption in national and sector planning and budget management (interministerial bribery for fund allocation, collusion/bribery in selection, and project approval) • Corruption in local budget management (fraud, falsification of accounts, village-level collusion)	• Lack of coordination between ministries of planning and finance (number of inconsistencies) • Speed and complexity of budget allocation (number of approved plans and budgets, time taken) • Overlapping roles and responsibilities in delivery stage • High share of spending on capital-intensive and large projects • Use of inappropriate discretion by finance and planning officers	• Independent auditing of decisions made • Organizational and procedural change in budgeting and finance functions • Decentralization of functions • Review options for alternative delivery systems (such as, PSP community) • Citizen involvement and demand for accountability in planning and budgeting • Media involvement
Donor financing	• Donor-government collusion in negotiations to meet funding targets • Donor-government collusion/fraud in progress and quality	• Unexpected change in donor support/choice	• Transparency in negotiations, budgets, and proposed plans
Fiscal transfers	• Bribery and kickbacks to ensure fund transfers	• Long process time for fund transfers • Unexpected release of funds	• Performance standards • Auditing
Management and program design	• Corruption in personnel management • Appointments and transfers, salary perks • Distortions in decision making (at and between central, local, and village levels	• High number of unqualified senior staff • Poorly paid staff with significant extras, living beyond means • High number of unplanned transfers • Lack of local government and utility management autonomy • Conflict of interest on management board • Increase in price of informal water	• Staffing reforms promote competition, performance/merit-based career structures. • Disclosure of assets • Transparent appointment of qualified administrative leaders (and election of political leaders) • Ring-fencing finances of utilities, separation of roles between local government and utilities

Source: Authors.

combating corruption in the water and sanitation services is unclear, action has been focused in four areas (table 7.3).

- *WSS sector restructuring, policy reform, and organizational change.* Specific actions include openness to leveraging private sector and other local stakeholder involvement; increased competition; reduced civil service size; stronger leadership; better sector coordination; separation of policy, regulation, and implementation; and more clarity in the allocation of functions.
- *Decentralization reform and improving accountability.* Reforms have aimed at improving political accountability and the adoption of mechanisms to emphasize the need for accountability for basic services among service providers and local government. Specific efforts include citizen report cards, service surveys, and increased public awareness, as well as improved accountability among tiers of government.
- *WSS planning and financial management.* Specific actions include more rational financial policies; ring-fencing; increased transparency; and cost recovery and improvements in metering, billing, and collection as well as stepped-up oversight, reporting, and auditing processes.
- *Personnel management reforms.* Staffing reforms include pay structures; processes to regularize promotions, appointments, recruitment, and transfers; adoption of performance-based management approaches, standardized terms and conditions of employment, and enforcement and sanctions for noncompliance.

These instruments may have mixed impact in reforming sector agencies, especially where authority is limited. In practice, the hierarchies of officials from a ladder of agencies within and outside water agencies (illustrated in table 7.2) interact with each other at various points in the value chain. In many countries, trying to build capacity and accountability in service delivery agencies such as utilities, district administrations, and village water committees will be futile without also tackling reforms at higher levels of government or among influential local government leaders. Similarly, it may be unproductive to work on developing accountability in a ministry of water without the implicit agreement or participation of political leaders and the ministry of finance.

Tackling Corruption between the Government and the Private Sector

In its tendering, supply, construction, and operating roles, the private sector is a key actor with the potential for involvement in corruption in the WSS sector. Cleaning up the interface between the public and private sectors is paramount in corruption reform. Corrupt interactions between government and private sector companies have been addressed implicitly in the sector through reform efforts that strengthen the policy and enabling environment and through specific contracting and procedural mechanisms within the construction sector in public procurement, construction, and operations (table 7.4).

To date general efforts to curb corruption in *procurement* have focused on prescriptive improvements to procurement environments: introducing anticorruption

TABLE 7.4 Tackling Hotspots in Public-to-Private Corruption

	Public-to-private interactions	*Early warning indicators*	*Potential responses*
Tendering and procurement	• Bribery to influence contract/bid organization. • Corruption in delegating management: fraud to over/underestimate assets; selection and type, award of concessions; decisions over duration, exclusivity, tariffs, subsidies • Corruption in procurement for: — capital works — supply of chemicals, vehicles, equipment — marked-up pricing • Falsification of documentation	• Same tenderers short-listed, selected (possible cartels) • Dropping out of bidders • Share of sole-source suppliers • Share of standard design unchanged • Share of higher unit costs • Lowest tender repeatedly not selected • Share of immediate renegotiation of contracts	• Transparency in public-private interactions • Independent tender evaluation • Integrity pacts and sanctions • Simplification of tender documentation • Review of role of middlemen and local consultancy commissions • Audits and reporting • Reduced size of contracts • Citizen oversight • Support for improving integrity of business (professional associations, codes of conduct)
Construction	• Not building to specification, concealing substandard work, materials Failure to complete works • Underpayment of workers • Fraud and bribery in invoicing: marked-up pricing — Overbilling by suppliers	• Resistance to meeting standard specifications • Number of changes in specification • Number of variation orders in site works	• Citizen role in oversight • Technical auditing • Citizen auditing, public hearings • Performance-based management contracts
Operations and maintenance	• Corruption in operations • Corruption in supply chain (e.g., fraud and bribery in the supply of chemicals, vehicles, and other inputs) • Avoiding compliance with regulations, specifications, health and safety rules • Falsification of accounts, evidence Small, informal providers • Inconsistent, irregular billing to small-scale providers • Extortion to enable businesses to continue	• Share of sole-source supply • Share of change in quality or coverage • Increase in informal price of water	• Integrity pacts (in countries with capacity for sanction) • Demonopolizing operations and maintenance • Financial and technical audits and reporting • Performance-based contracts with defined minimum standards • Transparency in operations and management • Citizen role in oversight • Benchmarking utility performance Small/informal providers • Improve interface between formal and informal • Legitimization • Formal bulk supply, pricing, competitive tenders for franchises

Source: Authors.

laws, charters, and performance standards, and establishing rules, principles, and practices dictating procurement procedures and auditing (see chapter 9; Transparency International-Pakistan 2003). Ideally, these efforts would mean that public and private project and procurement staff are working at a new level of professionalism, with less discretion, in a commercial environment where actions are overseen and sanctions enforced if necessary. In practice, however, reform of the procurement environment is difficult and takes a great deal of time to become effective (box 7.2).

BOX 7.2 Institutional Reforms Improve Utility Performance in Nairobi

For decades, the Nairobi City Council Water and Sewerage Services Department was responsible for delivering water and sanitation services to the city's residents. In 2002, after corruption in the department caused widespread public outrage, the water service functions and assets were turned over to a newly founded private company, the Nairobi Water and Sewerage Company (NWSC). The NWSC is run by a board of 12 directors drawn from private sector organizations and professional bodies and a number of officials from the former city water department.

Supportive national legislation (the Water Act of 2002 as well as the provisions of the Local Government Act) provided for the reform of the institutional framework and enabled the establishment of an independent entity for water supply in the city. The essential institutional reforms separated policy, service provision, and accountability, creating seven autonomous water boards who appoint water service providers. The new private company in Nairobi inherited 2,200 staff and the operational structures from the old water department, but creation of the new company brought new leadership, clearer accountabilities, introduction of a commercial culture with improved service conditions, greater transparency of operations, and better communication policies.

Despite these improvements, the new company's management still saw corruption as a major obstacle to efficiency and profitability and wanted more information about the scale and incidence of corruption. Although the sample was small, an assessment conducted by Transparency International exposed a number of potential corruption hot spots:

Corrupt practices involving consumers. The assessment revealed that consumers were still being solicited for, and paying bribes, at two points. The first was at the point of service delivery, where bribes were sought and paid to avoid being disconnected or to get reconnected, or to establish illegal connections. The second was in relation to billing and collection, where bribes were solicited and paid to adjust inflated bills or resolve billing disputes. About 65 percent of those domestic and institutional customers surveyed said they experienced corrupt practices with the NWSC, mostly with low-level employees. Inflated billing was also found to be a major reason why domestic consumers sought illegal connections. Survey respondents routinely charged that the NWSC, like the city water department before it, took advantage of its monopoly status and insisted on payment of inflated bills without record or justification. The assessment pointed toward the need for immediate improvement in record keeping and in accuracy and frequency of water meter reading and practical steps toward better dispute resolution over inflated bills. To this end Transparency International recommended the design and implementation of a consumer liaison process and strategy.

Corrupt practices involving private suppliers. Transparency International also surveyed NWSC suppliers to see how they were faring under the new company in comparison with the old water department. Overall, suppliers indicated that the incidence of corrupt practices has decreased since the NWSC took over operations, but that there were still a lack of transparency and possibly corruption in the way tenders were awarded. Some of the suppliers admitted to having inside information. As a result of the assessment, the NWSC was urged to reform its procurement procedures, to ensure that all staff comply with the company's code of ethics and conduct and to take upfront action concerning conflicts of interest.

Source: Transparency International-Kenya (2006).

A second set of efforts focusing on either the project or departmental level aim to improve the localized procurement "space." These include the introduction of integrity pacts dissuading contractors and officials from offering and accepting bribes, together with sanctions for noncompliance. Transparency in public-private interactions, such as the publication of tender documentation and tenders received, independent evaluation of tenders, auditing, monitoring of unit rates, and public participation in negotiations, creates a different environment from the opacity that characterized private sector participation in the 1990s. In Pakistan, a clean and open bidding process promoted by the Karachi Water and Sewerage Board and monitored by Transparency International showed how the application of a no-bribes integrity pact could be applied to contracts for consultancy services and all physical works and supplies. It resulted in an estimated net saving of about 75 percent of the cost of the contract (Transparency International-Pakistan 2003).

A third set of efforts, initiatives with multinational companies and national companies operating in developing countries, have focused mainly on achieving a greater level of integrity and professionalism among members through professional associations, codes of conduct, monitoring and benchmarking, and integrity pacts. (In Latin America, the integrity pact has been used successfully in the water sector in Argentina and Colombia and is being adopted by other countries in the region.) Transparency International has spearheaded efforts to establish minimum standards for public contracting. The World Economic Forum's Partnering against Corruption Initiative (PACI), the Extractive Industries Transparency Initiative (EITI), and construction industry initiatives in the United Kingdom and Europe seek to improve integrity in private companies, national governments, and construction companies, respectively.[38]

Anticorruption measures to clean up the corrupt practices associated with *construction* in the water and sanitation sector have been limited in developing countries, where "looking the other way" is still common practice. Contractors are mostly, although not all, domestic (large or small) and working within sector norms. There is little possibility that either corrupt contractors or public officials would be brought to justice, and those exposing fraud or bribery often find themselves in a worse position by doing so. Some efforts to measure and control corruption in construction provide lessons for African village water supply. Evidence from Indonesia suggests that technical audits such as spot checks on pipe work, community oversight and monitoring, and even the simple announcement or threat of an audit (when combined with community participation) seem to reduce corruption in rural development projects (Olkren 2005). In both small and large projects, urban and rural, the introduction of performance-based projects that define minimum standards and requirements and reimburse only after the water is flowing show promise in improving accountability and outcomes (Halpern and Mumssen 2006).

In *operations*, little explicit focus has been given to reducing corruption but significant effort has been made to improve efficiency. Reforms at the sector and utility levels have focused on improving leadership and management, financial management, and ring-fencing; clearly defining and delegating roles for operations and maintenance; and increasing citizen participation in planning, budgeting, and monitoring to improve accountability. Separation of providers from policy makers and regulators has been pursued in conjunction with decentralization to some degree, although roles are still cloudy at the local level, where local government and utility boundaries are less than defined. Monitoring and measurement has improved, and benchmarking approaches that compare utility performance (as seen in Uganda) aim to promote efficiency through competition. All such mechanisms aim at establishing an environment less susceptible to corruption.

Although it forms a relatively small segment of the WSS sector in Africa, privately operated utilities provide some lessons for consideration. In Côte d'Ivoire, for example, the delegation of operations to a privately operated utility in the late 1980s led to a shift in investment from capital-intensive production units to the rapid extension of distribution networks; what had once been 100 percent debt financing became 100 percent cost recovery; and public-private deal making was replaced by commercial procedures (WUP 2003).

Efforts at the interface between local private providers and those operators authorized to provide service delivery have begun to emerge in different forms in many cities in Africa and are central to developing more effective and efficient links between public and local private water sector actors. Efforts to form associations of suppliers, develop constitutions and mechanisms for dialogue, install formal bulk supply and other technological solutions that result in better access for the providers (and revenue for the utility), and implement competitive tender processes for area franchises formalize the interface between utilities and municipal water departments and create more predictable environments for honest water businesses to flourish (WSP-Africa 2005; Plummer, Collignon, and Mehrotra 2005). The local private sector is also the home of the middlemen who facilitate bribes between large national and multinational companies and governments. Much greater focus is needed on understanding and developing the integrity of the local private sector.

Tackling Corrupt Interactions between Public Officials and Consumers

To date, anticorruption mechanisms tackling corrupt interactions at the point of service delivery have largely focused on improving the efficiency of the utility or delivery agency. The sector has long been aware of the various types of corruption that occur "at the tap." The problem of illegal connections has been addressed through efficiency drives or, in more innovative situations, legitimization programs, while a focus on improved meter reading, billing, and collection has implicitly addressed some of the leakage that occurs through payment systems.

Interactions between public officials and consumers over operation and maintenance of the water system can be tempered by citizen oversight and monitoring as a part of water governance efforts aimed at stimulating accountability of service providers. On the consumer side, the important work on report cards developed by the Public Affairs Centre in Bangalore (Thampi 2005) has been applied specifically to the WSS sector in Nairobi, Mombassa, and Kisumu in Kenya (WSP-Africa forthcoming). Still in the development stage, this consumer report card initiative, sponsored by Water and Sanitation Program–Africa (WSP-Africa), encourages households, both poor and nonpoor, to provide public feedback on the quality of water supply, sanitation and solid waste services, and, with the results in hand, then underpins a national campaign to publicize and advocate for change. A critical aspect of the report card approach is the existence or development of an effective complaints redressal system. At a broader level, corruption surveys such as those conducted by the World Bank Institute, have provided some insights into community perceptions of bribery between officials and consumers in the water services sector (Austral Consultoria 2004; Center for Democracy and Development 2000). These are invaluable inputs for policy makers.

Despite efforts by utilities, only an estimated 23 percent of the African population is served by utilities, and few of these are poor (WSP-Africa 2006). Community-based delivery systems, the preferred donor approach to water and sanitation service provision, has escaped the attention of sector efficiency drives and has been bypassed in the debate over sector corruption. This model of WSS service delivery has suffered from a somewhat naive assumption that community involvement will, by definition, produce accountable and efficient outcomes. Investigations into community-managed rural development programs with sizable WSS components have found, however, that community management often results in high levels of corruption. Poorly paid, quasi-public officials frequently act in a nontransparent and unaccountable manner; collude with the project overseers, contractors, and suppliers; and engage in a range of practices and decisions regarding procurement, construction, and payment that distort project benefits (Woodhouse 2002).[39] Surveys, report cards, and other forms of citizen monitoring can also be applied to community-managed water supply.

The innovative introduction of corruption mapping, community monitoring, and complaints redressal in the Kecamatan Development Program (KDP) in Indonesia provides a model for strengthening citizen voice, improving accountability, and reducing corruption (box 7.3). This initiative raises important issues for WSS public-consumer interactions and community-based service delivery in all continents. Assessments have shown that corruption varies depending on whether the goods and services bring public (common) or private benefit. For private goods (such as rural water supply) with mainly individual benefits, information and participation have proven successful in reducing corruption. For public goods (such as sanitation and roads), the use of audits, sanctions, and enforcement has proven more effective. The KDP has also raised the understanding of "corruption horizons" in community-managed development programs: as corruption is tackled in observable spheres, it moves elsewhere. In the case of the KDP, corruption shifted to less detectable but perhaps also less profitable forms of nepotism (Olkren 2004).

The development of more effective payment systems in WSS delivery has been an integral part of utility efficiency improvements. These include meter replacement programs and professionalization of billing and collection systems. Designed to reduce fraud and bribery, these programs change the nature of the customer interface. In some utilities, efforts have been made to ensure that these systems are appropriate to poor households (battery meters, collective billing, localized payment offices). Taking the corruption out of payment systems requires better-informed consumers, however. More effort is needed to provide households and communities with the information and capacity they need to know if billing is correct, and the systems for appealing if it is not.[40] Some innovative approaches in

BOX 7.3 Intensive Efforts to Curb Corruption in Village Infrastructure Development: Lessons from Indonesia

The Kecamatan Development Program (KDP) is a $1.2 billion World Bank-financed and community-driven development project in Indonesia, begun in 1998 during the East Asia financial crisis. It now funds significant infrastructure development and provides small loans to villages. The program has been rapidly scaled up and now serves more than 20,000 villages nationwide.

The two-pronged approach to combating corruption in the KDP is based on an analysis of the political economy of corruption in Indonesian villages. First, it aims to change the conditions that breed corruption in villages by breaking existing monopolies over information, resources, and access to justice. Second, it aims to prevent corruption in the project itself by skewing the incentives of the project structure against corrupt behavior. The KDP experience is useful for understanding what works to limit corruption in a large, rural development project in a country with endemic corruption, a weak legal system, and a history of top-down political control by a powerful state bureaucracy.

At the heart of the KDP's anticorruption approach is the principle that villagers themselves should have decision-making power over planning, procurement, and management of funds. Some of the concrete measures of its approach include:

- simplifying financial formats so that they can be understood easily by villagers
- transferring funds directly into collective village bank accounts
- insisting that all financial transactions have at least three signatures and that at least three quotations are found for the procurement of goods, to be shared publicly at village meetings
- insisting that details of all financial transactions are posted on village notice boards
- requiring that project funds be accounted for at regular village meetings, at which villagers have the right to suspend further disbursements of funds if irregularities are found
- providing village-level sources of information and channels for complaints independent of local government
- providing intensive field-level supervision by elected village facilitators and subdistrict project facilitators
- providing independent monitoring of the project by NGOs and local journalists.

Although these measures have had some success, corruption in KDP projects persists. Assessments (including in-depth ethnographic interviews, field experience reviews, and analysis of the incentive structures throughout the project cycle) determined actors' interests, motivations, and constraints. The study found that corruption is primarily a problem of incentives and can be fought effectively only by changing the costs and benefits attached to corrupt behavior; local context and social norms are key to understanding how these incentives can be changed.

Corruption in KDP projects takes several forms, including budget markups, collusion, bribes, and kickbacks to local officials. The elements found to be most effective in limiting corruption are transparency, community participation, and the provision of independent channels for resolving complaints. Information and local control are key elements in both preventing and fighting corruption: the most successful strategies for fighting corruption in the KDP have hinged on publicizing anticorruption activities, garnering wide local support, and using sanctions credibly. Project facilitators are also key to fighting corruption: they provide a channel of information to villagers that is independent of local government and, because facilitators are backed by the central KDP structure, they have more protection from threats and intimidation than ordinary villagers. There is also evidence that villagers have used their experience with KDP projects to protest against corruption in other projects.

The incentives analysis of the project cycle identified three stages of the project cycle most vulnerable to corruption. These were proposal preparation (formation of false borrower groups for small loans), release of funds (collusion among bank account signatories to embezzle funds), and implementation (collusion and corruption in procurement). The analysis highlights several ways in which corruption could be better prevented, including improving information dissemination; working with social sanctions to make the incentive structure less conducive to corruption; increasing incentives for KDP staff to fight corruption; instituting measures at specific stages of the project cycle intended to limit monopoly, clarify discretion, and improve accountability; and supporting the capacity of project facilitators to come up with flexible local solutions to their problems.

Source: Woodhouse (2002).

TABLE 7.5 Tackling Hotspots in Public-to-Consumer/Civil Society Corruption

	Public-to-consumer interactions	*Early warning indicators*	*Potential responses*
Construction	• Community-based construction and management: — Fraud and bribery — Theft of materials by village leaders — Fraudulent documentation, accounting, and reporting	• High loss of materials • Resistance to meeting standard specifications	• Citizen role in oversight and monitoring • Technical auditing, spot checks of infrastructure constructed • Performance-based contracts
Operations and maintenance	• Bribes for access to water: installing or concealing illegal connections, avoiding disconnection, non-network (tankers) illicit supply using public assets • Bribes for speed or preferential treatment for repairs, new connections	• Changes in unaccounted-for water • Unofficial usage of tankers • Lack of interest in connection campaigns • Low reporting of faults • Number of faults reported • Number of connections versus increase in water consumed • Unexplained zonal variations	• Legitimization of illegal connections • Legitimization of public officials extending services • Review of connection costs • Performance contracts for speed of repairs • Citizen participation in monitoring and oversight • Transparency and reporting of performance requirements • Report cards and other survey and feedback mechanisms • Complaints redressal
Payment systems	• Billing corruption: fraudulent meter reading, avoidance or partial payment, overcharging	• Unexplained variations in payment • Complaints from consumers • Complaints from small-scale providers	• Information and awareness campaigns • Citizen participation in monitoring and oversight • Participatory corruption assessments, corruption mapping • Commercialization • Reform to customer interface: metering billing, collection • Performance contracts • Complaint redressal • Women cashiers

Source: Authors.

Benin and Côte d'Ivoire have delegated billing and collection to private firms that work on a performance contract (although their use of entrusted office is equally susceptible to corruption); these systems also have introduced women cashiers, who have shown they are less inclined than men to accept bribes or defraud the utility (WUP 2003).

A Cautionary Tale for the Water Sector

Despite the variety of anticorruption instruments relevant to the sector, there is still much debate over what works and what does not in developing countries. Cross-cutting activity over the last decade has provided lessons, but a much greater understanding of how it will all work at the sector level is still needed.[41] Models and pilot programs are needed in the WSS sector to test approaches that promise change in the context of weak African institutions and civil society.

Meanwhile, a number of anticorruption mechanisms have failed or backfired in developing countries. The World Bank Institute and others have analyzed the performance of specific anticorruption instruments. Overall, this work has found that the proliferation of anticorruption commissions, corruption watchdog agencies, and ethics agencies across Africa and the drafting of new anticorruption laws, decrees, and codes of conduct have had little impact, being more appropriate in countries where public accountability and transparency have already been established (Kaufmann 2005). A second key lesson is that a focus on the public sector alone is not enough; the private sector must be included in any anticorruption effort. The problem with "getting it wrong" is that anticorruption activity, if wrongly focused, can result in significant "fallback" in the reformed institutions because corruption adapts, reestablishes elsewhere, and even grows more robust when old opportunities are closed down (Shah and Schacter 2004).[42] For instance, stepped-up enforcement might lead to less incidence of bribery, but the bribes might be larger. Or firms adhering to integrity mandates might be marginalized within the market, providing strong disincentive for others to follow suit.

More constructively, experience has illustrated that the level of governance is key to making decisions about what anticorruption activities to undertake (Kaufmann 2005; Shah and Thompson 2004); different anticorruption mechanisms are applicable in different governance contexts (Shah and Schacter 2004). Prescriptive anticorruption efforts need to be treated with caution in countries where the rule of law is weak, the state has little legitimacy, institutions responsible for service delivery are not accountable, and the commitment of national leaders is questionable.

What is the message for future anticorruption activity in the water sector in Africa? The cautionary tale is to look before you leap (Shah and Schacter 2004). Little direct anticorruption reform has been undertaken in the sector, and while it is possible to learn lessons from other sectors, those lessons will need to be tailored to the specific circumstances of country, sector, and even local contexts. The African WSS sector needs to approach the anticorruption agenda cautiously, draw on lessons from the broader governance agenda, continue to expand knowledge about WSS sector institutions, and focus on the means to demand reform.

The sector needs to learn how to identify and prioritize interventions. Before undertaking reforms at the country level, it is important to first understand capacity and governance, as well as incentives and the impact of corruption. Only then can one determine the effectiveness of differing processes (shock or gradual change) and choose the appropriate anticorruption mechanisms (prescriptive, preventive), the combinations of anticorruption mechanisms needed (such as matching transparency reforms with increased citizen roles), and the sequencing of interventions that will work best.

The sector needs to test, build, and disseminate experience: Working within this broader sphere of governance, accountability and transparency efforts to get sector governance right will be critical in any context. Strategy development should look at the best way to prioritize demand activities such as improving voice and participation, transparency and access to knowledge and information, and institutional reform. Understanding how these areas of activity can be more effectively focused on anticorruption ends seems a critical step for the sector.

MOVING FORWARD

Several issues should be kept in mind as the water and sanitation sector embarks on anticorruption reform.

First, there is a notable lack of information on the scope, nature, impact, and costs of corruption in the WSS sector. For decades, donors and other supporting agencies have carried on regardless of endemic corruption that has distorted decision making and leaked sector investment. As a result of this tolerance, few attempts have been made to define, unpack, or delve into the key dimensions of sector corruption. While there are islands of information, most stakeholders acknowledge that this lack of comprehensive information on the scope and nature of corruption hinders future action. Furthermore, little is known about the impacts and costs of WSS sector corruption. Understanding of the degree of corruption in water supply and sanitation, when compared with other water subsectors such as irrigation, is limited, and no accurate measure has been made of the relative levels of WSS sector corruption between countries in the region. Data are urgently needed to support proposed actions.[43]

Second, corruption in the water sector is linked with overall and sector governance: few would argue that the main challenges for improving water sector governance and tackling sector corruption do not lie in the water sector at all (Estache and Kouassi 2002) or that corruption is embedded in the problems of a dysfunctional sector. Yet while many dimensions of governance, such as the rule of law and political stability, lie outside the remit of any single sector, many solutions, such as strong leadership and the emergence of social groups demanding change, are common to all. A key to effective sector anticorruption activity thus lies in an understanding of the primary "interaction space" in which corruption takes place—in particular, how far corrupt water interactions extend beyond water institutions and stakeholders.[44] Developing a better understanding of the scope and content of viable sector action, in particular, what is possible with ring-fenced service providers, will be important to sustainable interventions.

Third, decentralization has created a new set of risks and opportunities, and more effort is needed to develop accountability at the outset. Decentralization provides a window of opportunity for the development of transparency and accountability in subregional governments. To date, the effects of decentralization on water service delivery and on corruption levels in the water sector have been mixed and unpredictable.[45] This can be attributed at least in part to the heterogeneity of the reforms in the region. Decentralization in Africa is a mix of political, fiscal, and administrative delegation carried out through very different processes (big bang, gradual, top-down, bottom-up, in different time frames) (Shah and Thompson 2004). In practice, too, local, often poorly skilled, sector officials, previously without access to decision making or budgets, have seized the opportunity for rent seeking created by the delegation of finance and function, and the lack of clarity around functional allocations and relationships and the lack of transparency have created failures in accountability. Better understanding of the links between corruption and decentralization processes is urgently needed at the sector level. In particular, how has decentralization affected sector corruption, which areas are most prone to corruption, and how can the momentum presented by decentralization be harnessed to prevent corruption from reemerging?

Fourth, it takes two or more to bribe: anticorruption efforts need to include the briber(s) involved in WSS transactions. Because of the potential for significant profits, many private WSS sector stakeholders (be they international, national, or local companies or individuals) have strong incentives to ensure that their companies are included in tenders, win contracts, avoid unnecessary delays in construction, and find ways to cut corners to create higher profit margins. But this is not always the case—not all companies and not all individuals join in. Understanding incorruptible behavior might provide pointers for actions to reduce private sector bribing.[46] More detailed knowledge is also needed about the role of the middlemen who facilitate payments. Anticorruption efforts have generally focused on cleaning up offending governments, but efforts to promote accountability in government are undermined if pressures on staff come from outside government. It is vital to develop anticorruption mechanisms that tackle the actions of bribers soliciting and paying bribes in water sector transactions.

Fifth, the political realities of fighting corruption in the water sector are sobering: many constraints and opposing stakeholders block the way forward. Despite increasing political rhetoric and high-profile commissions and investigations, there is still a reticence in many countries to discuss corruption and anticorruption activity at the sector level in Africa.[47] Only a few stakeholders are interested in analyzing corruption, sharing their knowledge, or proposing anticorruption tools and techniques, and advocacy is hindered by the absence of a strong civil society in Africa.[48] Outside government, a strong set of incentives and disincentives affects stakeholders' willingness to engage in anticorruption activity: large construction and engineering companies are concerned with shareholder profit, consultants with their client base; individuals fear reprisals for not going along. Bilateral and multilateral agencies need to meet spending and lending targets and maintain the status quo, but they also fear anticorruption activity will sour their relationships with government partners. At the sector level, in WSS organizations, the advocacy base is also narrow—not everyone in the sector is persuaded that corruption is something that should be confronted. Acknowledging that corruption is a problem, developing a broader platform of advocates, building awareness, and creating a safe space for dialogue will all be critical to effective sector action.

Sixth, the net effects of corruption and anticorruption activity in WSS for the poor are not really known. The structural impacts of corruption on the poor

TABLE 7.6 Next Steps

Actions at the country and regional levels

1. Diagnose the sources, extent, and impacts of corruption, especially as it affects the poor. Develop an understanding of the sector context for corruption and its causes and incentive structures that can be used to forge effective anticorruption measures.
2. Establish robust tools and indicators at the sector and subsector levels for measuring and monitoring corruption and setting baselines against which to measure the effectiveness of specific anticorruption strategies.
3. Build a platform of informed anticorruption advocates among public, private, and civil society stakeholders, including working groups at the country and regional levels to promote an anticorruption agenda.
4. Develop country-level anticorruption strategies that are coordinated with MDG road maps and sector reforms.
5. Launch advocacy, awareness-building, and capacity-building drives at all levels to develop committed leaders in the fight against corruption and informed communities. Identify and build capacity of appropriate civil service organizations.
6. Create channels for disseminating anticorruption tools, methodologies, best practices, and lessons learned.

Thematic areas of investigation

1. *Understanding decentralization and corruption in the water service and sanitation sector.* How has decentralization affected the regulatory environment? How can decentralization frameworks mainstream anticorruption objectives?
2. *Unbundling and diagnosing corruption in WSS delivery systems.* What are the areas of concentration and modalities of corruption in public utility supply systems, private concessions, large- and small-town systems, donor-led or community-based projects?
3. *Understanding the impacts of corruption in WSS on the poor.* What types of corruption have the most negative impact on the poor? How much do they pay? What are the net effects on the poor? Are there any benefits in unofficial rather than official supply? How can the detrimental impacts on the poor of both corruption and anticorruption actions be mitigated?
4. *Enhancing transparency in the water sector.* How can current reform approaches be strengthened with a significant focus on transparency? What are the dynamics and constraints of increasing sector transparency in differing contexts? In what situations would transparency in the sector harden corruption?

summarized by Kaufmann and others,[49] are now well disseminated—lower investment and economic growth, less pro-poor growth, less progress in service delivery and the development of human assets. To this can be added the many noneconomic consequences of corruption—weakening of new and emerging democracies, social injustices, environmental degradation, heightening of insecurity, and undermining trust in public institutions. But at the sector level, more detailed analysis is needed on the short-, medium-, and long-term impacts on the poor. Medium- to long-term impacts on the poor result from distortions and delays created by corrupt officials steering water sector investment away from the poor toward opportunities that are likely to bring them the most personal gain. Typically, this means inappropriate investment in large, capital-intensive infrastructure projects such as water treatment plants, bulk supply, or networks. In the short term, however, corrupt activities by low-level officials who sell or provide illicit utility water might fill gaps in the services available to the poor households, providing them with a service they could not otherwise obtain. In some cases, providing private service with public assets may not necessarily be inefficient when considered at the sector level and in the short term.[50]

Finally, developing pro-poor anticorruption activity within the water sector should be informed by more widespread and detailed demand-side assessment.

Much of the anticorruption activity launched to date has proceeded on the assumption that any anticorruption intervention will automatically improve efficiency and effectiveness and thus create benefits for the poor. But this is not always the case, and while corrupt water is clearly not optimal in the long run, focusing reform on the misuse of assets by low-level officials may have immediate negative effects on those who need water services most. Complementary demand-side assessments and actions are vital to reveal and mitigate against any likely negative impacts of anticorruption mechanisms at the local level. To ensure that reforms are pro-poor, anticorruption advocates need to understand the interactions between long-term structural changes and short-term contingent ones and plan for both positive and negative impacts on water supply to the poor. With this recognition, legitimization rather than eradication or supplementary instruments that provide the poor with water in the short term might, for instance, become an important pro-poor aspect of tackling corruption at the point of service delivery.

Table 7.6 provides a set of country, regional, and thematic actions for anticorruption stakeholders able and willing to take the agenda forward. Donor engagement is essential for funding, harmonization, and creating a stronger motive for reform.

CONCLUDING REMARKS

Although the challenges in tackling corruption in the WSS sector in Africa are significant, a number of opportunities have emerged in recent years that have heightened the issue of corruption on the WSS agenda. First, a growing number of governments are indicating their willingness to discuss corruption openly and engage in discussion of anticorruption programs. Second, the World Bank, the African Development Bank, sector donors, and other sector agencies have strengthened their commitment to addressing corruption in donor-funded initiatives and in their own systems. Third, there is growing commitment to government and donor harmonization on the anticorruption agenda.[51]

Most of what is being done now in the water governance agenda—introducing policy, institutional, and financial management reforms; reducing inefficiencies; improving leadership; and building demand-side capacity—is central to anticorruption activity, but so far these activities have had little effect on corrupt practices in the sector. It is vital that the sector come to understand what adjustment is needed to recharge these efforts and focus them more effectively on tackling corruption.

This chapter has aimed to start the dialogue over corruption in WSS in Africa. It has described, through a framework of corrupt interactions among public, private, and consumer/civil society actors, the types of corruption that occur in the various stages of sector policy making, planning and budgeting, financing, delivery, and implementation. It has argued that corruption is neither singular nor homogenous in any one setting, and that understanding the network of corrupt activity and identifying the areas of concentration of corruption within this larger framework are critical to effective policy making and strategy development. Over this framework of corrupt interactions, this chapter has laid out the many and varied anticorruption mechanisms, including those that are generic and create an environment that deters or mitigates against the risk of corruption and those that target specific types of anticorruption activity. This menu of actions should be considered with caution, because it is not yet known conclusively what works in which situations, what combinations of interventions are needed, and what sequencing of reforms will optimize anticorruption efforts. This is the task that lies ahead. Most of all, the water and sanitation sector in Africa urgently needs to undertake the diagnosis and testing that can provide the empirical basis for action.

ENDNOTES

1. A key task in the next stage of work is to ascertain a clearer estimate for different WSS contexts and countries of Africa.
2. This figure is based on an estimate of $6.7 billion for annual expenditure requirements to meet the MDGs in Sub-Saharan Africa. Of this, $2.6 billion is intended for capital investments (Mehta, Fugelsnes, and Virjee 2005). Of course, not all these leaked funds would necessarily make their way into sector investment, and there is no way to measure how much would.
3. Depending on the country and regions within each country, hand pump failure rates can be anywhere from 15–50 percent, averaging around 30 percent continent-wide (Sutton 2004).
4. The Transparency International Corruption Perception Index (CPI) ranks countries by the degree to which corruption is perceived to exist among public officials and politicians. It is a composite index, drawing on corruption-related data in expert surveys carried out by a variety of reputable institutions. It reflects the views of businesspeople and analysts from around the world, including experts who are locals in the countries evaluated. The CPI provides a snapshot, with less capacity to offer year-to-year trends. See, for example, Transparency International (2005, 2006). The limitations of these indexes are recognized in the broadbrush overview provided here, and efforts are needed to develop more robust sector indicators. For limitations on the CPI, see http://www.transparency.org.
5. There are many exceptions to the general trend that growth is stronger in less corrupt countries. Indonesia's economic miracle occurred in the context of historically unprecedented corruption and an authoritarian state (Timmer 2006). Kaufmann and Kraay (2003) examine the links between growth and governance and find a strong causal effect of better governance on higher per capita income, confirming the importance of good governance and economic development. But they found no virtuous circle whereby higher incomes result in better governance.
6. These findings are not statistically significant; such analysis has not been systematically carried out in the sector, but should be undertaken.
7. The water reform ranking has been drawn from data obtained from 16 Country Status Overviews in Africa conducted by WSP-Africa to ascertain sector progress toward meeting the MDGs. The criteria for this ranking include sector restructuring to create transparency and to separate policy, regulation, and implementation; financial policies and ring-fencing for viability; openness to leveraging private sector and other local stakeholder involvement; policy toward servicing the poor; and sector coordination and sector financing instruments (WSP-Africa 2006).
8. In 16 recent country-level Investment Climate Surveys carried out by the World Bank, companies were asked if they made informal payments to get a water connection. Although statistically insignificant, results in all 16 countries (controlling for GDP per capita) suggest a strong correlation between corruption and low levels of WSS coverage. Interestingly, however the microlevel survey (with firms, not households) did not confirm that *sector*

corruption (as measured by bribe payments for a water connection) is correlated with *general* measures of country corruption, but the fragility of the results further highlights the recommendation for improved measurement at the sector and subsector level.

9. This exceeds the total gain achieved from privatization; see Estache and Kouassi (2002), quoted in Collier and Hoeffler (2005).
10. A number of anticorruption advocates, including Klitgaard and Rose-Ackerman, have identified the key factors that engender opportunities for corruption. These include monopoly power, wide discretion, weak accountability, and lack of transparency.
11. On health, see Transparency International (2006); on power, see World Bank (2006); on forestry, see the Forestry Integrity Network initiative at http://www.transparency.org/fin, and on the construction industry, see Transparency International (2005).
12. There are some comparative findings in the World Bank Institute country governance and corruption surveys. In Mozambique, for instance, water is perceived to be the most corrupt basic service (above health and education, significantly higher than sanitation); see Austral Consultoria (2004).
13. The need to disaggregate water and sanitation is well recognized. Some contend that sanitation in rural projects is subject to less corruption than water because sanitation is a public good (author discussion with Scott Guggenheim, Addis Ababa, January 2006). The Mozambique survey indicates that the public perceives water services as being significantly more corrupt than sewerage (Austral Consultoria 2004). More research is needed before any conclusions can be drawn. Future analysis should disaggregate not only water and sanitation but the type of service delivery system (community-based, utility, or household).
14. The very specific nature of equipment and infrastructure of assets in the water industry makes the cost three to four times than that of the telecommunications and power, and a higher cost when compared with electricity (Kirkpatrick, Parker, and Zhang 2004).
15. The limitation of the figures commonly quoted in the sector is a key concern addressed in this chapter. These figures are often derived only from leakages in utilities, but they are similar to the levels of corruption quoted generally and in similar programs (such as rural development programs, roads projects) elsewhere.
16. This observation comes from discussions with a wide range of stakeholders and sector professionals, who say that few in the sector have acknowledged the many and varied types of corruption that exist. Perceptions of corruption are not homogenous, but they are narrow, limiting the development of effective reform.
17. Governance, sector, and project levels of anticorruption mechanisms were used to describe post-tsunami reconstruction efforts in the WSS sector in Aceh in Plummer (2005).
18. In the absence of meaningful sector data, the purpose of this framework is to open up understanding and areas of investigation. Many corruption documents focus on one form of corruption or another without the data to justify that focus. A broad matrix is needed that can be used in specific settings to identify local areas of concentration. Other diagnostic work has informed the approach. Focusing on areas of activity, the first version of this chapter provided a framework of these interactions structured by the levels of the delivery agency. One very useful initiative developed for the World Bank–funded KDP in Indonesia (which supports village-level, community-based infrastructure) is the "corruption map." This mapping tool walks through the project cycle, considering the design, implementation, and monitoring stages, and setting out the incentives of actors, the forms of corrupt behavior, and the risks associated with each potential leakage. The project uses this map to develop specific responses to each medium- to high-level risk. Facilitators use

it to structure their oversight of the various processes. The mapping process has been critical in establishing transparency and empowering communities to monitor implementation (and ongoing operation and maintenance) at the project level. Several roads projects have taken a similar approach, using the project cycle as the foundation for assessing potential areas of corruption. The approach is similar to that originally presented by Klitgaard in the participatory diagnosis approach he developed for the municipality in La Paz, Bolivia, that focused on corrupt systems and aimed to identify the size, winners, losers, causes, and cures of the different types of corruption identified through the participatory process (Klitgaard 1998). These maps are not carried out at the sector level, however. Another useful conceptual approach is the adaptation of the accountability framework presented in the *World Development Report 2004* (World Bank 2004), which examines the relationships between key stakeholders in the service delivery process, highlighting the importance of the "voice"-accountability relationship between citizens and politicians, the "compact" relationship between politicians or managers and service delivery agents, and the "service/client power" relationship between the service provider and the citizen/consumer. Each side of this triangular framework explores a set of complex interactions enabling corruption and the key mechanism for improving accountability.

19. This issue is taken up in the evaluation method used in Huther and Shah (2000).
20. While it is possible that private-to-private interactions, such as bribery or fraud between contractors and subcontractors, as described in Rocío Balcázar (2006), are also prevalent in the sector, it is also the case that one private party is entrusted with office and that this type of practice is embodied in public-to-private interactions. For instance, in those situations where the private sector has been granted concessions, they have "entrusted office." In other cases, the practice may be fraudulent and may be illegal and harmful, but care should be taken before describing it as corruption.
21. Informal feedback in more than one African country suggests that this could be as much as a few years' salary for large utilities—the larger the utility, the larger the bribe. Bribes for appointments are thought to be made to both politicians and to management staff, although it is not known in what proportion. Davis (2003) found that in South Asia, most bribery of politicians and local leaders was intended to exert influence on decision makers.
22. For a decade or more, governance has led the agenda of bilateral and multilateral development agencies, and support for anticorruption has been recognized as a key concern in meeting both development and risk management objectives. At the same time, few would argue that development assistance, by its nature, does not exacerbate inherent corruption by injecting cash into weak institutional systems.
23. This practice was perhaps more associated with the letting of concessions to international firms during the 1990s, but it still applies to large construction contracts.
24. The lack of detailed knowledge of public-private interactions in the water sector is exacerbated because diagnosis has not always included the right actors—those paying the bribes. There has been inadequate critical analysis of how mechanisms work on the ground and why it is likely they will continue to do so (author conversation with M. Sohail Khan, Water Integrity Network Preparatory Meeting, Delft, The Netherlands, November 2005.). The sector is acutely aware that addressing the bribing and solicitation process that some private firms engage in is as important as addressing government actors, but more diagnosis of public-to-private interactions is needed.
25. Bribery in procurement and construction is described in detail in Transparency International (2005). Much of this information is pertinent to the water sector.
26. Only 5 percent of water delivered in Africa is delivered by the private sector, predominantly in West Africa in concession-type arrangements (WUP 2001).

27. *Extortive* behavior reflects an imbalance of power and typically can mean officials are exploiting the poor. For the poor, the outcome may be access to water service, but the transaction price is high. This widespread behavior often occurs in a monopolistic situation where consumers are dependent on decision-making officials. *Collaborative* transactions between the poor and public service delivery officials are voluntary transactions that often provide the poor with a service they would not have otherwise, and often at a price that is competitive with local alternatives. In squatter settlements, for instance, officials provide illegal connections or tanker water at a price and arrangement the consumer is willing to pay. See Kaufmann, Montoriol-Garriga, and Recanatini (2005).
28. Although NGOs are more limited in Africa than elsewhere, NGO service delivery is one way to mobilize services to the poor. But one should not assume that all government-NGO transactions are free of corruption; the assumption that NGOs are corruption-free and accountable is naive. Government-to-NGO corruption is emerging as a key area of investigation, as it occurs concurrently with government-to-private corruption in many areas.
29. It is recognized that this practice may in some, but not all, cases also contribute to the inefficiencies of the utilities. To some extent, the problem is caused outside the water sector. Typically, tenants and illegal squatters have fewer WSS options and are more likely to tap into the service a corrupt official (or a landlord) might offer. The illegality of their dwelling makes this group vulnerable and susceptible to extortion and high-priced water. Other households with changing needs and capacities are also susceptible as they may wish to opt in or out of a higher level of service, creating the opportunity for extortive or collaborative bribery.
30. Author communication with Scott Guggenheim, Addis Ababa, January 2006. See also Recanatini, Prati, and Tabellini (2005).
31. The Global Integrity Index provides a quantitative scorecard of governance practices in each country, assessing the institutions and practices that citizens can use to hold their governments accountable to the public interest. It is currently developed in fewer than 30 countries worldwide. See http://www.globalintegrity.org.
32. The *World Development Report 2004* (World Bank 2004) provides a triangular framework of accountability relationships among policy makers and politicians, service providers, and citizens. It highlights the need to shorten and strengthen accountability relationships of voice, compact, and client power.
33. Shah and Schacter (2004) argue, for example, that corruption awareness campaigns have universally failed in developing countries and that advocacy is useful only in countries where governance is strong.
34. The social accountability movement in India has provided a range of lessons on the constraints and opportunities for strengthening the demand side that are all relevant to anticorruption.
35. Corruption is closely linked to legal but misguided policies such as low tariffs for water sources, and many basic remedies for corruption are synonymous with efforts effective utilities are making to improve performance.
36. For example, not all bilateral and multilateral donors blacklisted the companies found guilty in the Lesotho Highlands corruption case (Earle and Turton 2005).
37. Work by Recanatini, Prati, and Tabellini (2005) highlights a number of features as being characteristic of less corrupt institutions and agencies, including regular audits by external or internal auditors of decision making, open and transparent procedures, and personnel decisions based on merit and professional competence. These features all strongly reinforce reform efforts in the water and sanitation sector.

38. More information on PACI can be found at http://www.weforum.org/. More information on EITI may be found at http://www.eitransparency.org.
39. The line between civil society representatives or leaders and village public officials is typically unclear, with individuals frequently playing both roles.
40. The supporting role of consumer associations has been explored in East Africa. A first set of lessons on capacity building of consumer bodies to engage in WSS sector reform has been developed by the WSP-Africa in collaboration with Consumers International (WSP-Africa 2004a).
41. Over the last five years, focus has shifted from supply- to demand-side efforts.
42. See Shah and Schacter (2004), in which they warn against ad hocism in anticorruption work and suggest that the lack of progress in eradicating corruption could be due to misguided strategies.
43. The need for a stronger analytical basis than for anticorruption basis has long been recognized (Kaufmann 1998).
44. There are very mixed views on the level to which anticorruption activity can be ring-fenced within the WSS sector, and models and strategies urgently need to be tested. Some argue that efforts can proceed at the local (delivery agency) level, while others argue that anticorruption efforts are likely to be futile, counterproductive, or at the margins, if sector efforts are not coordinated with the broader governance agenda. The Kenyan experience too is sobering, where reforming one branch of government and not another created serious problems, deepening levels of corruption; see Nussbaum (2006).
45. Fisman and Gatti (2002), for instance, argue that no country has ever solved its corruption problems through decentralization.
46. Author communication with M. Sohail Khan.
47. In other countries (such as Indonesia), the situation is more nuanced; there may be dialogue about corrupt practices, a group of anticorruption champions, and public willingness to speak openly about corruption, but there also might be reticence to speak about installing anticorruption mechanisms that may affect friends, colleagues, or family income.
48. Best practice in anticorruption activity underscores the importance of civil society organizations (CSOs) taking a lead role in demanding change. This is more difficult in the African region, where the CSO movement is weak, especially in the government-dominated water sector. Even where the state cannot deliver, there is the public perception that WSS provision is a state responsibility with no role for civil society. CSO support in the Africa water sector generally consists of scattered, specific projects. These may develop momentum in stimulating public demonstration, as in Ghana, where a CSO led a movement against water privatization, but African CSOs do not play a central role in large-scale service provision as they do, for example, in Bangladesh, and social accountability is only emerging. Efforts will be needed to work with and develop the capacity of nonwater CSOs such as the country chapters of Transparency International.
49. See the Synthesis Matrix on Poverty and Governance in Kaufmann (2000).
50. See the overview of the types of water available to the poor, including corrupt water, in Plummer and Cross (2005).
51. As embodied in the Paris Declaration on Aid Effectiveness, signed in Paris in March 2005. The Paris Declaration is an international agreement under which more than 100 ministers, heads of agencies, and other senior officials committed their countries and organizations to continue to increase efforts in harmonization, alignment, and managing aid for results with a set of monitorable actions and indicators.

REFERENCES

Austral Consultoria a Projectos. 2004. "Governance and Anticorruption Diagnostic Survey: Mozambique." Paper prepared for World Bank Institute, Washington, DC.

Center for Democracy and Development. 2000. "The Ghana Governance and Corruption Survey: Evidence from Households, Enterprises and Public Officials." Report commissioned by the World Bank, Washington, DC (August).

Collier, P., and A. Hoeffler. 2005. "The Economic Costs of Corruption in Infrastructure." In *Global Corruption Report* 2005. London: Transparency International and Pluto Press.

Darroch, F. 2004. "Lesotho Highlands Water Project: Corruption and Debarment." Prepared for the Information Research Institute, London.

Davis, J. 2003. "Corruption in Public Service Delivery: Experience from South Asia's Water and Sanitation Sector." Massachusetts Institute of Technology, Department of Urban Studies and Regional Planning, Cambridge, MA.

Earle, A., and A. Turton. 2005. "No Duck, No Dinner: How Sole Sourcing Triggered Lesotho's Struggle against Corruption." Paper presented at the World Water Week seminar, "Corruption in the Water Sector: How to Fight It?" Stockholm, August 23.

Estache, A, and E. Kouassi. 2002. "Sector Organization, Governance, and the Inefficiency of African Water Utilities." Policy Research Working Paper 2890, World Bank, Washington, DC.

Fisman, R., and R. Gatti. 2002. "Decentralization and Corruption: Evidence across Countries." *Journal of Public Economics* 83 (3): 325–45.

Gray, C., and D. Kaufmann. 1998. "Corruption and Development." *Finance and Development* 35 (1): 7–10.

Halpern, J., and Y. Mumssen. 2006. "Lessons Learned in Infrastructure Services Provision: Reaching the Poor." Working Paper 6, Global Partnership for Output-Based Aid, Washington, DC. http://www.gpoba.org.

Huther, J., and A. Shah. 2000. "Anticorruption Policies and Programs: A Framework for Evaluation." Operations Evaluation Department, World Bank, Washington, DC (December).

JMP (Joint Monitoring Project). 2002. *Meeting the MDG Drinking Water and Sanitation Targets: A Mid Term Assessment of Progress*. Geneva: WHO/UNICEF.

Kaufmann, D. 1998. "Challenges in the Next Stage of Anti-corruption." In *New Perspectives on Combating Corruption*, ed. D. Kaufmann. Washington, DC: Economic Development Institute.

Kaufmann, D. 2000. "Governance and Poverty: A Brief Note on the Power of Empirics, Quality of Growth, Governance, and Corruption." Unpublished paper, World Bank, Washington, DC.

———. 2005. "Back to Basics: 10 Myths about Governance and Corruption." *Finance and Development* 42 (3).

———. 2006. "Debunking Myths about Governance and Corruption Lessons from Evidence and Initial Applications to Water Sector." Presentation for the Workshop on Anticorruption Practices in the Water Sector in Africa, World Bank, May 15, Kampala, Uganda.

Kaufmann, D., and A. Kraay. 2002. "Growth without Governance." *Economia* 3 (1).

Kaufmann, D., and A. Kraay. 2003. "Governance and Growth, Causality Which Way? Evidence for the World Bank in Brief." World Bank Institute, Washington, DC.

Kaufmann, D., J. Montoriol-Garriga, and F. Recanatini. 2005. "How Does Bribery Affect Public Service Delivery? Micro-Evidence from Service Users and Public Officials in Peru." Working Paper, World Bank Institute, Washington, DC.

Kaufmann, D., and P. C. Vicente. 2005. "Legal Corruption." World Bank Institute, Washington, DC.

Kenny, C. 2006. "Corruption in Infrastructure." Unpublished paper Energy and Water Department, World Bank, Washington, DC.

Kirkpatrick, C., D. Parker, and Y. F Zhang. 2004. "State versus Private Sector Provision of Water Services in Africa: A Statistical, DEA, and Stochastic Cost Frontier Analysis." Paper 70, University of Manchester, United Kingdom.

Klitgaard, R. 1988. *Controlling Corruption.* Berkeley, CA: University of California Press.

———. 1998. "International Cooperation against Corruption." *Finance and Development* (March): 3–6.

Klitgaard, R., R. Maclean-Abaroa, and H. Lindsey Parris. 2000. *Corrupt Cities: A Practical Guide to Cure and Prevention.* Washington, DC: World Bank and Institute for Contemporary Studies.

Maclean-Abaroa, R. 2006. "Workshop on Anticorruption Practices in the Water Sector in La Paz, Bolivia." May 15, Kampala, Uganda.

Mehta, M., T. Fugelsnes, and K. Virjee. 2005. "Financing the Millennium Development Goals for Water and Sanitation: What Will It Take?" *International Journal of Water Resources Development* 21 (2): 239–52.

Nussbaum, D. 2006. "Building Accountability for Shared Growth." Presentation at PREM Week, World Bank, Washington, DC, (April).

Olkren, B. 2004. "Monitoring Corruption in CDD: Main Findings and Implications." KDP Note, Kecamatan Development Project, World Bank, Jakarta, Indonesia.

———. 2005. "Corruption Perception versus Corruption Reality." Harvard and NBER, for the DFID–World Bank Strategic Poverty Partnership Trust Fund, Jakarta, Indonesia.

Plummer, J. 2003. "Small-Scale Providers in Water and Sanitation." Background paper for *World Development Report 2004,* World Bank, Washington DC.

———. 2005 "Anti-corruption Efforts in the Post-tsunami Reconstruction of Water and Sanitation Infrastructure and Services in Aceh, Indonesia." Water and Sanitation Program, East Asia and the Pacific (WSP-EAP), Jakarta, Indonesia.

Plummer, J., B. Collignon, and S. Mehrotra. 2005. "Supporting the Market that Serves the Urban Poor: Emerging Responses to Enhance the Role of Local Private Sector Providers." Background paper for the WSP-Africa Domestic Private Sector Participation Initiative Workshop, Nairobi, June 20–21.

Plummer, J., and P. Cross. 2005. "Combating Corruption: Developing an Anti-corruption Strategy for the Water and Sanitation Sector in Africa." Paper sponsored by WSP-Africa and presented at the preparatory meeting of the Water Integrity Network (WIN), Delft, November 18.

Recanatini, F., A. Prati, and G. Tabellini. 2005. "Why Are Some Public Agencies Less Corrupt than Others? Lessons for Institutional Reform from Survey Data." Paper prepared for the Sixth IMF Jacques Polak Annual Research Conference on Reforms, International Monetary Fund, Washington, DC, November 3–4.

Rocío Balcázar, Alma. 2006. "Development of an Anti-corruption Agreement with the Water Pipe Manufacturing Companies in Colombia." Presentation at the International Anti-corruption Conference, sponsored by Transparencia por Colombia, Guatemala City, November 16.

Rose-Ackerman, S. 1999. *Corruption and Government: Causes, Consequences, and Reform.* New York: Cambridge University Press.

Shah, A., and M. Schacter. 2004. "Combating Corruption: Look Before You Leap." *Finance and Development* 41 (4): 40–43.

Shah, A., and T. Thompson. 2004. "Implementing Decentralized Local Governance." Policy Research Working Paper 3353, World Bank, Washington, DC.

Stapenhurst, R. 2000. "The Media's Role in Curbing Corruption." World Bank Institute, Washington DC.

Sutton, S. 2004. "Preliminary Desk Study of Potential for Self Supply in Sub-Saharan Africa." WaterAid and the Rural Water Supply Network, London (October).

Thampi, G. K. 2005. *Community Voice as an Aid to Accountability: Experiences with Citizen Report Cards in Bangalore.* Bangalore: Public Affairs Foundation.

Timmer, P. 2006. "Paying Suharto as if He Were an American CEO." Center for Global Development, Washington DC.

Transparency International. 2005. *Global Corruption Report.* London: Pluto Press.

———. 2006. *Global Corruption Report.* London: Pluto Press.

Transparency International-Kenya. 2006. "Nairobi Water and Sewerage Company Ltd. A Survey." Nairobi, Kenya.

Transparency International-Pakistan. 2003. "Integrity Pact: A Pakistan Success Story. Greater Karachi Water Supply Scheme Phase V, Stage II. 2nd 100MGD, K-III Project." Karachi (November).

Trémolet, S., and J. Halpern. 2006. "Regulation of Water and Sanitation Services: Getting Better Service to Poor People." Output-Based Aid Working Paper 8, Washington, DC.

UN-Habitat and Transparency International. 2004. "Tools to Support Transparency in Local Governance." Urban Governance Toolkit Series, United Nations, Nairobi.

Woodhouse, A. 2002. "Village Corruption in Indonesia: Fighting Corruption in the World Bank's Kecamatan Development Program." World Bank, Jakarta, Indonesia.

World Bank. 2004. *World Development Report 2004: Making Services Work for the Poor.* Washington, DC: World Bank.

———. 2006. "An Anticorruption Agenda for the Power Sector: A Suggested Bank Approach Discussion Draft." Energy and Water Department, World Bank, Washington DC.

WSP-Africa (Water and Sanitation Program–Africa). 2004a. "Moving from Protest to Proposal: Building the Capacity of Consumer Organizations to Engage in Urban Water Supply and Sanitation Sector Reform in Africa." WSP-Africa, Nairobi.

———. 2004b. "Solutions for Reducing Borehole Costs in Rural Africa." Field note, WSP-Africa, Nairobi.

———. 2005. "Rogues No More? Water Kiosk Operators Achieve Credibility in Kibera." Field note, WSP-Africa, Nairobi.

———. 2006. "Getting Africa on Track to Meet the MDGs on Water and Sanitation: A Status Review of Sixteen African Countries." Final Report, WSP-Africa, Nairobi.

———. Forthcoming. "A Citizen's Report Card Initiative for the Water Sector in Kenya." Final Report, WSP-Africa, Nairobi.

WUP (Water Utilities Partnership). 2001. "Status of Reforms in the Water and Sanitation Sector in Africa." Abidjan, Côte d'Ivoire.

———. 2003. "Better Water and Sanitation for the Urban Poor in Africa." European Union and WSP-Africa, Nairobi.

PART 

Corruption and the Public Financial Management System

8

Exploring Corruption in Public Financial Management

WILLIAM DOROTINSKY AND SHILPA PRADHAN

"Corruption has its own motivations, and one has to thoroughly study that phenomenon and eliminate the foundations that allow corruption to exist."

Eduard Shevardnadze, Former President of Georgia

"Public financial management has become very complex in modern economies, because of the wide scope of governmental action. Complexity has created various nontransparent areas and niches that facilitate the development of principal-agent problems. These problems often lead to corruption. For this reason, effective controls and oversight of public financial management systems are essential. This chapter identifies some of the areas at risk and some of the problems and suggests ways to deal with them. It should be required reading for policy makers and managers who want to improve these systems and for experts who want to understand the phenomenon of corruption."

Vito Tanzi, Former Director, Fiscal Affairs Department, International Monetary Fund, and Former Deputy Minister of Finance, Government of Italy

Corruption in public financial management (PFM) is a problem faced by countries throughout history and across the globe. Coincident with government responsibility for managing public funds are the risks that resources may be diverted for private use, that governments will not receive the resources owed them, that collected resources are lost before proper use, or that once approved for use, the funds are not used as intended. Corruption in PFM diverts scarce resources away from public purposes, jeopardizes the ability of governments to achieve their agenda, directly affects spending on priority sectors such as education and health, and can have a particularly damaging impact on growth.

In many developing countries, the conditions of public service and institutions of PFM often create an environment that enables corruption to flourish. The nature and quality of a country's PFM system to a large extent determine the ease with which public corruption can occur. Weak regulatory and control environments offer the best opportunities for corruption in public spending. The challenge is creating a robust public finance system that maximizes detection and remediation of corruption, thereby minimizing opportunities for corruption.

Corruption in the public sector is defined as "the misuse of public office for private gain."[1] Its manifestations and legal or operational definitions vary from country to country. Corruption is often broadly characterized as grand or political corruption and administrative corruption. Political corruption typically includes influence peddling on resource allocations and projects that benefit the decision maker, friends, and acquaintances; campaign-financing abuses; vote rigging and directing resources to special projects; and abuse of privileged information. Grand corruption is the large-scale transfer of public resources for private interests. Administrative corruption includes (a) petty corruption such as bribery, direct theft of cash, goods, equipment, and services; (b) direct abuse of office, including misappropriation and misuse of public funds or assets, illegal fines, duties, taxes or charges, misprocurement or contract steering; manipulation of regulations and licensing; cronyism and nepotism; and (c) indirect abuse of office where regulatory authority is used to extract rents from civil society, such as taking bribes for favorable treatment or rulings. Administrative corruption is also often referred to as "fraud, waste, and abuse" of public resources.

Successful strategies to mitigate the risk of corruption should seek to strengthen institutions that govern PFM as well as systems of checks and balances designed to manage conflicts of interest. Bulwarks against corruption lie as much with the actual management of public resources as with the institutions of accountability within and outside the government. This chapter provides a broad framework for understanding corruption in relation to PFM, for assessing vulnerabilities to corruption, and for designing reform strategies to reduce the risk of corruption in public spending. It examines corruption in all stages of PFM, including budget preparation, budget execution, accounting and reporting, internal control, and external audit and oversight. (Corruption in public procurement and revenue administration are introduced in this chapter and are discussed in detail in chapters 9 and 10, respectively.) The chapter then applies the proposed framework to address potential risks of corruption in public spending in Ghana. Throughout the chapter, lessons learned are highlighted in italics.

ASSESSING VULNERABILITIES FOR CORRUPTION IN PFM SYSTEMS

Countries with better-performing PFM systems have lower corruption perception indexes. Strong PFM counters corruption by increasing the likelihood of detection and corrective action. Examples include performance-oriented budget formulation, which provides a benchmark for assessing results;[2] predictable budget execution, which minimizes irregular procedures used to justify discretionary decisions; good record keeping, which furnishes an audit trail; and accurate reporting, which enables management to oversee spending, detect anomalies, and take corrective measures. Sound internal auditing ensures the integrity of control processes and assures management that its policies are being followed. A sound PFM system assists in the detection and prevention of corruption by minimizing the opportunities for fraud, highlighting potential causes of anomalies (such as poor training or weak capacity), establishing rules, and implementing appropriate disciplinary action against violations.[3] A strong PFM system increases both the risk of detection and the cost of misbehavior.

FIGURE 8.1 Perception of Corruption and Quality of PFM

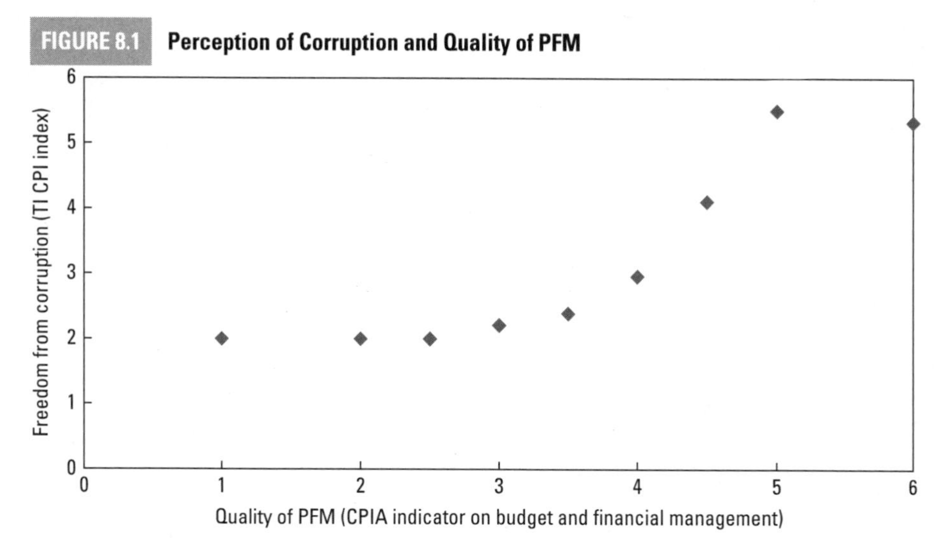

Source: Transparency International and World Bank Country Policy and Institutional Assessment.

For public finance practitioners, the correlation between sound PFM systems and lower risk of corruption is self-evident and proven by experience. However, since corruption cannot be directly measured, a robust statistical correlation between PFM system quality and corruption cannot be established. Using perception of corruption as a proxy measure, figure 8.1 maps freedom from corruption (using average scores from Transparency International's Corruption Perception Index [CPI]) against the quality of the PFM system (using the World Bank's Country Policy and Institutional Assessment, or CPIA, ratings). The figure suggests that higher-quality PFM systems correlate with reduced perceptions of corruption, at least for PFM systems above the median quality. Experience reinforces that lack of adequate spending controls, lack of checks and balances for public resources, limited transparency of fiscal information, and low probability of being detected and penalized create an enabling environment for corruption (World Bank 1998). Strong, transparent PFM systems with well-defined and uniformly applied controls, oversight, and accountability can reduce the risk of corruption.

Systemic factors that increase the risk of corruption in PFM are weak capacity, inadequate internal controls, limited transparency, weak management and supervision, and weak external accountability in public spending. Institutional weaknesses can be analyzed within the four generic stages of the budget cycle, namely, budget formulation, budget execution, accounting and reporting, and external audit and oversight. The prevailing balance of interests, incentives, and institutional norms affects all stages of the budget process. Figure 8.2 illustrates the basic budget cycle and key functions of the four stages.

Budget Formulation

Budget formulation takes place in a broad political context and is influenced by the country's policy, regulatory, and institutional context.[4] The budget process is inherently a political process. The executive has a dominant role in drafting the budget and

FIGURE 8.2 **The Budget Cycle**

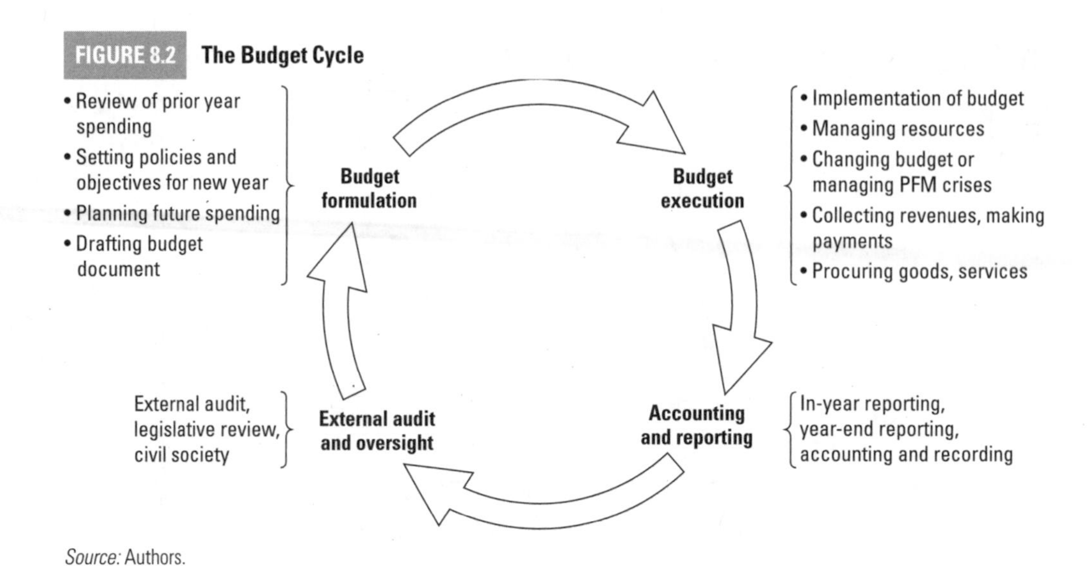

Source: Authors.

presenting the budget proposal to the legislature. The central budget offices of the finance ministries are responsible for coordinating the budget-drafting process within the executive and overseeing its execution by spending ministries. Once agreed within the executive, the budget proposal generally must be approved by the legislature.

Without adequate legislative oversight, discretionary power granted to the executive could be misused, paving the way for significant corruption. Legislative activism during budget formulation has ebbed and flowed over time and is on the rise (Schick 2002). The extent of legislative involvement depends on the constitutional nature of the state itself. The constitutional form of government defines the legislative power to amend the budget, the veto power of the president, and the power of the legislature to amend or override the budget. The legislative process and structure, time allocated for legislative review, and the quality of legislative engagement vary across countries (Dorotinsky and Barraclough forthcoming; Santiso 2005; Stapenhurst 2004). Legislatures in presidential systems are in theory designed to play a more significant role in budget formulation than those in parliamentary systems, where the executive by definition commands the majority in the parliament. Legislative influence over the budget is significantly influenced by factors including the electoral system (such as proportional representation, "first past the post," direct election, or party lists) and the number and nature of political parties (strong parties, coalition governments).

Corruption during budget formulation is primarily grand or political corruption and is influenced by the distribution of budgetary powers between the executive and the legislature. Unchecked and excessive executive discretion in the budget process tends to create opportunities for political corruption, as can unchecked legislative involvement. Politicians or senior-level bureaucrats are able to provide subsidies or favorable tax treatments to favored citizens or groups or allocate budget resources to projects or areas based on political affiliations (Martinez-Vazquez, Arze, and Boex 2004).

Political corruption during budget formulation influences resource allocations for public investments, including their choice, location, and design. Tanzi and

Davoodi (1997) show that corruption is associated with higher levels of public investment, reduced investment quality, lower government revenues, lower expenditures on operations and maintenance, and lower quality of public infrastructure.

Nontransparent systems of decision making, lack of comprehensiveness of resources included in the budget, and lack of transparency of budgetary information reduce opportunities for accountability and enable corruption to flourish. For example, discretionary off-budget accounts enable government officials to divert resources and circumvent budget disciplinary controls and sectoral lobbying over those resources. Similarly, unilateral, unlimited executive decisions to approve spending through in-year adjustments without reporting create environments for corruption. At the same time, unrestrained parliamentary involvement could also create opportunities for politicians to leverage their positions to support special interest or elite lobbying, giving rise to the "tragedy of the commons." Each member of parliament could demand a largest possible claim on the common resource pool, despite preferences of the government to maintain aggregate fiscal discipline and long-term sustainability.

The budget formulation stage is also an opportunity for the government to plan the scope and structure of public revenues. Poor planning for revenues, systemic overestimation of revenues, lack of transparency in revenue estimation and collection (by source and type), and weak accountability give rise to significant opportunities for corruption. Systemic overestimation is often as much a result of weak technical capacity as of internal institutional incentives that drive the planning process (World Bank 1997). Overly optimistic planning during formulation results in cutbacks in allocation of funds to agencies and encourages reallocation of resources to the highest bidder during budget implementation.

PFM system weaknesses during budget formulation can increase the risk of administrative corruption during budget execution. Key weaknesses that increase vulnerabilities include weak budget estimates or underspecified plans for using the funds; lack of comprehensiveness of budget information, including both revenues and expenditures; and lack of transparency in budget documents. Unreported government operations, incomplete fiscal information, and poor budget classification reduce comprehensiveness of the budget, affecting the ability of the government to report on, monitor, and audit public spending. A robust budget classification enables more transparent information on government activities for reporting, control, audit, and ex post accountability for revenue collection and public spending. The ability of key stakeholders to hold the government to account requires that budget documents and in-year and year-end fiscal reports are transparent, comprehensive, and easy to understand.

Budget Execution

The central budget offices and treasuries of the finance ministries are responsible for overseeing budget implementation by the spending ministries during the fiscal year. Although the budget execution process varies substantially from country to country, broadly speaking it covers cash management, procurement (contracting), and revenue management. Cash management includes the commitment stage, when purchase orders are placed or contracts are signed; the verification stage, when the spending agencies confirm the delivery of the goods and check the bill; payment authorization, in which a public accountant authorizes the payment; and the payment stage, when the bill is paid by cash, check, or electronic transfers.

The budget execution stage, where resources actually flow and assets change hands, is the most fertile ground for corrupt activities. Lack of comprehensiveness and transparency of budgetary information, weak controls on revenue and expenditure management, and lack of penalties for deviations from planned revenue and expenditure targets provide incentives and opportunities for corruption during implementation of the budget. Poor cash planning and predictability of funds often create opportunities for manipulation of rules for personal gain or the benefit of close associates. Public procurement is a common area of fraud and corruption, typically involving large amounts of public funds, that affects the efficiency of public spending and donors' resources and ultimately the quality of public service delivery. Revenue administration also provides significant opportunities for corruption, either in direct skimming of receipts, collusive administrative reductions in tax liability, selective enforcement of tax obligations or unjustified writing off of tax arrears. Aside from the direct losses from corruption in revenue administration, there are secondary effects as revenue shortfalls create opportunities for corruption in spending through in-year discretionary adjustments to spending or favoritism in invoice payments.

Extractive industries, such as oil, where the sector is publicly owned or there are large concession payments to government, provide significant opportunities for loss of public revenues to private hands (receipts never reach the treasury, for example, or payments are made directly from the treasury but outside the accounting system). State-owned enterprises, frequently unregulated and nontransparent, also provide opportunities for profit transfer to private interests through weak procurement, transfer pricing, or misallocation of profits.

Sound cash management ensures that the government has liquidity to meet payment obligations at as low a cost as possible and that financial assets obtain the highest return. A consolidated treasury fund (sometimes mislabeled a single account) is good practice,[5] and in some countries, the cash management function is outsourced to the central bank. Electronic payments made through the banking system reduce the opportunities for corruption by establishing records and an audit trail. In countries where the banking system is not well developed, payments are often made through the cashier's office. A cash-based system increases the risk for corruption, as cash can be directly skimmed and frequently leaves no audit trail. Regardless of whether a cash-based or electronic payment system is used, sound record keeping of all transactions is essential for management control and oversight. Fraudulent schemes may include pocketing payment of fines, customs duties, or fees; payment of salaries to ghost workers; extraction of bribes for salary or benefit payments; and manipulation of cash allocations to favor specific line ministries and agencies (commonly the chief executive's office, defense, and internal security) from which kickbacks may be arranged (Isaksen 2005). Box 8.1 provides examples of corruption and fraud during budget execution.

Weaknesses in cash and expenditure management processes and controls manifest throughout the stages of commitment, verification, payment approval, and payment processing. The commitment control stage ensures that resources are

BOX 8.1 Corruption Patterns

The Pakistan National Accountability Bureau annual report for 2003 noted misuse of authority as the most common allegation for decided cases, but did not define this in the report. Of the 382 cases decided between 1999 and 2003, 144 involved misuse of authority; 102, corruption and corrupt practices; 88, assets beyond known sources of income; 22, willful bank defaults; and 4, living beyond means.

A 2002 Public Sector Fraud Survey by the South African Institute of Government Auditors found that bribes and inventory theft were the most common types of employee fraud, and "time fraud" (people not contributing a full day's work) was a major fraud category for employees and management.

The United Kingdom's Treasury fraud report for 2005 found that fraud related to personnel management, theft of assets and information, and procurement fraud were the most common types of fraud, in that order of magnitude (see figure below). By monetary value, the top three in order of magnitude were theft of assets and information, procurement, and travel and allowances fraud.

Types of Public Sector Corruption, United Kingdom 2005 (Percentage of total reported cases)

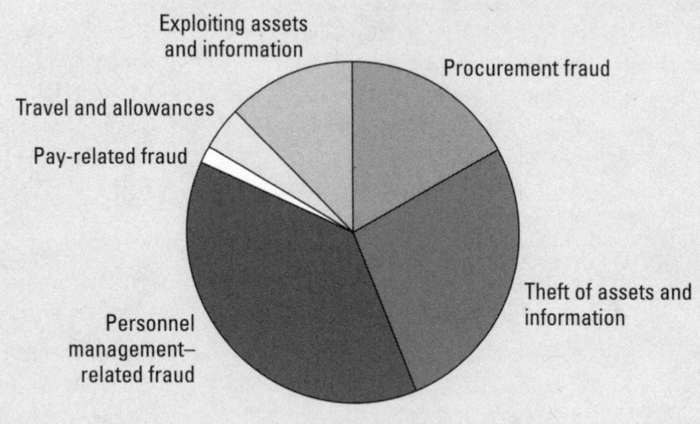

Source: Her Majesty's Treasury (2005, pp. 7–8).

committed to an approved purpose and do not exceed the approved budgeted amount. Corruption during the commitment stage may take the form of ordering goods and services not authorized in the budget. Collusion between officers in charge of commitment, verification, and payment authorization can lead to corrupt activities being overlooked because of a breakdown in internal controls and lack of separation of duties among officers in charge. Without adequate controls and management oversight, payment officers can use their discretionary powers to extract bribes from suppliers. Uncertainties in revenue collections and inflation-related cost escalation increase the unpredictability of resources during budget execution and increase opportunities for fraudulent activities in public procurement. Payment for goods and services, payments of consultant fees, and other accumulated payment arrears are then processed based on kickbacks received by the payment officers.

In many developing countries, complex tax and trade regimes—including multiple discretionary exemptions, confusing and nontransparent procedures for tax compliance, and excessive discretionary power of tax inspectors—increase opportunities for corruption in revenue collection during budget execution. Poor wages, lack of professionalism, inadequate reward and penalty structures, and weak internal and external controls and accountability mechanisms are persistent systemic weaknesses that foster corruption.

Weak management supervision, weak transparency and accountability, limited capacity to detect and monitor corruption, and limited enforcement capabilities also give rise to significant opportunities for corruption in public procurement. Examples include contract steering, kickbacks, or bribes to government officials, bid rigging to manipulate contract recipients, use of fictitious companies, and misuse of public assets. Other opportunities for corruption during budget execution include abuse of travel expenses and abuse of portable assets such as vehicles and computers. Table 8.1 provides a more extensive, though not exhaustive, list of administrative

TABLE 8.1 PFM System Weaknesses and Patterns of Administrative Corruption

Economic class	*Systemic contributing factors*	*Examples of corruption*
Employee compensation	• Absence of clear rules on hiring • Absence of management controls, internal controls • Absence or weakness in internal audit, external audit • Absence of treasury payroll matching • Absence of records, weak record keeping • Absence of management mandates for and review of regular financial reports	• Ghost employees • Nepotism • Absenteeism • Queue jumping in payments and consultants fee
Goods and services	• Absence of nonpayroll expenditure controls • Absence of inventory control, asset registry • Weak procurement system • Absence of management oversight and review of payment and procurement practices	• Contract steering • Collusion • Fraudulent invoices • Payment for goods and services not received • Theft of government supplies
Capital expenditures	• Absence of nonpayroll expenditure controls • Absence of inventory control, asset registry • Weak procurement system • Absence of management oversight and review of payment and procurement practices	• Favoritism in payments or contract awards • Use of substandard material or practices in construction • Collusive pricing • Underpricing bids and using change orders to raise cost • Theft of stocks
Transfers	• Cash or in-kind transfers • Weak or no record keeping • Absence of clear procedures for processing applicants • Failure to follow procedures • Absence of clear laws, regulations, rules for eligibility, criteria	• Transfers to unauthorized, fictitious, or deceased individuals • Transferring less than approved levels and pocketing difference • Kickbacks • Favoritism in approving eligibility

Source: Authors.

corruption by economic classification as well as some factors that contribute to corruption.

Major vulnerabilities that increase the risk of corruption during budget execution are weak internal controls and weak management control and oversight of public spending. Internal controls include payroll controls, nonpayroll expenditures controls, and internal audits that increase the possibility of detection and reduce incentives for engaging in fraudulent activities (assuming there are real costs after detection).

Management control and oversight of system performance and fiscal information to hold others to account provides a strong deterrence to fraudulent behavior. Management includes the chief executive (president or prime minister, cabinet), ministers, permanent secretaries, and senior ministry management. Management control and oversight place senior and mid-level ministry managers and elected officials at the front line during budget formulation, execution, and oversight. Their role in analyzing data, examining trends, raising issues, holding staff to account for performance, following up on errors, and ensuring disciplinary action is often neither understood nor exercised.

Budget Accounting and Reporting

Accurate, timely, and transparent record keeping, accounting, and reporting of revenue and expenditure information is essential for enforcing accountability in the budget process. Modern integrated accounting systems facilitate tracking of revenue and expenditures and the matching of information from alternative sources. Accounting officers in spending ministries, the treasury, and the accountant general play a key role in preparing financial statements on a regular basis.

Budget accounting and reporting generally do not offer direct opportunities for corruption; however, corruption during the budget execution stage is often detectable through strong accounting and reporting systems, especially if computerized with integrated financial management information systems (IFMIS) or a management information system (MIS).[6] Inaccurate and incomplete recording of transactions because of technical weaknesses or intentional disregard for accuracy and comprehensiveness can obscure fraudulent activity, impede auditing, and restrict management control and oversight. Every transaction should be recorded, including loans, disbursements, commitments, and payments. The accounting system is at the heart of the IFMIS. Weaknesses in accounting practices and in reconciliation of bank accounts introduce vulnerabilities into the budget process by decreasing the comprehensiveness of fiscal reports and data essential for audits and management control. Similarly, fiscal reporting that is not timely, regular, accurate, and comprehensive increases the risk of corruption during other stages of budget execution. Strong accounting and reporting systems are powerful deterrents to fraud and corruption.

Weaknesses in this stage typically include lack of transparency, accuracy, and comprehensiveness in in-year and year-end fiscal reports, weak capacity of accounting systems and record-keeping processes, and irregularities in reconciliation processes between public bank account data held by commercial and central banks and accounting records. Weak accounting and record keeping, disregard for accounting procedures, weak capacity of staff, and excess fragmentation of procedures for accounting and reporting make information consolidation and management control difficult.

Internal transparency of fiscal information to ensure that information is timely, understandable, and available to all executive decision makers is essential for internal accountability and oversight. Information asymmetries can cut many ways, but absence of reasonable information in a timely fashion prevents management from being in control and blocks active monitoring of or fighting fraud and corruption.

External Audit and Oversight

Strengthening transparency and accountability to key external stakeholders in the management of public finances is an important dimension of promoting fiscal responsibility in developing countries. Legislatures, legislative committees such as parliamentary (or public) accounts committees (PACs), legislative audit agencies such as supreme audit institutions (SAIs), the judiciary, civil society, and the media are key players in enhancing transparency and accountability in the management of public finance. Legislatures may hold the executive accountable by reviewing the annual budget, conducting oversight hearings on government revenue administration and spending (annual accounts), reviewing financial and performance audits, and incorporating results into legislation or requests for executive action.

Following the implementation of the budget, government accounts and financial statements are audited by SAIs. The quality of audits, legal mandates on the scope of audits, and follow-up on audit recommendations, including detail investigation and penalties for identified fraudulent behavior, are essential elements of effective oversight. The interaction between an SAI and the legislature depends on the model of SAI used and its reporting structure. In most commonwealth systems, the SAI reports to the PAC, which reviews the findings and reports to the parliament. SAIs in Napoleonic systems have both judicial and administrative authority and are independent of the legislature and executive (Stapenhurst and Titsworth 2001). As agencies responsible for auditing government income and expenditures, SAIs can be the linchpin of the country's public integrity system.

External audit and oversight may themselves be a source of corruption where vulnerabilities may arise if excessive political influence over external accountability institutions results in underreporting of fraudulent behavior and inadequate investigation into allegations of corruption. The ability of SAIs, PACs, and legislatures to hold the government to account depends on several factors, including the constitutional form of the government; its independence from political pressures, in particular from the executive; clear mandates; a supportive institutional environment; adequate financial resources; and qualified staff.

Civil society and the media can play a significant role in increasing accountability in every stage of the budget process. Active civil society participation provides an effective mechanism for monitoring decisions of elected parliamentary officials, influencing budget decisions (an example is participatory budgeting in Porto Alegre, Brazil),

TABLE 8.2 PFM Roles and Anticorruption

Institution	*Internal to executive branch*	*External to executive, but in government*	*Civil society (external to government)*
Political stakeholders	President, prime minister, cabinet, minister of finance	Legislature	Media, citizens
Management	Permanent secretary, senior and mid-level management in line ministries	Anticorruption commissions, ombudsman, vigilance committees, legislative committees	
Accountability institutions	Ministry of finance and economy, internal audit, treasury	SAI, criminal courts	Nongovernmental organizations, business or trade associations

Source: Authors.

and increasing transparency in budget implementation (monitoring of public school expenditures in Uganda, for example). Although recognition of civil society involvement in developing-country budget processes is fairly recent, there is some evidence that civil society organizations can have a positive impact on budget decision making and implementation. Table 8.2 summarizes the roles of key stakeholders in the budget process.

Administrative corruption in PFM manifests primarily during the implementation of the budget. However, vulnerabilities across all the stages of the PFM cycle contribute to the risk of fraud and abuse of public funds. The absence of rules and regulations for payroll and nonpayroll expenditures, general disregard for existing rules, high levels of unreported government expenditures, incomplete fiscal accounting and reporting, weak capacity of staff in key public finance offices (including line ministry budget, accounting, and audit offices), inadequate management oversight over public spending, weak institutions of accountability, and inadequate oversight of public resources are common weaknesses of PFM systems in developing countries.

All of the PFM system vulnerabilities noted can be summarized into five system dimensions:

- weak capacity of staff and systems to capture all government activities
- limited internal transparency of fiscal information
- limited internal transparency of fiscal information
- poor management control and oversight
- weak external audit and oversight.

This framework has been used to design reforms to reduce corruption and strengthen PFM.

STRENGTHENING MANAGEMENT OF PUBLIC RESOURCES

Mitigating the risk of corruption in PFM requires creating robust public finance systems that are open to internal and external scrutiny that minimize opportunities for corruption and maximize detection and remediation. This section addresses entry points for strengthening internal PFM systems and processes. External accountability and oversight mechanisms are discussed in the following section.

Identifying the potential weaknesses in PFM systems is the critical first step in mitigating the risk of corruption. This chapter uses the Public Expenditure and Financial Accountability (PEFA) assessment tool to identify the weak links in management control and oversight, capacity, internal transparency, and internal control.[7] While the PEFA indicators do not directly measure corruption in PFM, they do measure PFM system performance and hence identify weaknesses in the management of public resources. Figure 8.3 analyzes the strengths and weaknesses for five developing countries along the four internal dimensions using recent PEFA assessment and suggests potential entry points to strengthen PFM. The figure compares the quality of the capacity, internal controls, internal transparency, and management control and oversight within countries and identifies the weakest link among the four dimensions within the country.

The figure suggests significant variations in PFM system performance along the four dimensions. For example, in Mozambique and Zambia, internal control and management control and oversight are the weakest links, lagging behind capacity of PFM systems and internal transparency. The figure also suggests a number of operationally relevant entry points for reform activities along the four dimensions. For example, in Bangladesh, reform should focus on strengthening management control and oversight, which is the weakest among the four dimensions.

While mitigating the risk of corruption in developing countries requires substantial reform in all four areas, immediate efforts to reduce the risk of corruption should focus on the weakest link. A system of interdependent parts is only as strong as its weakest link. PFM systems will provide better results if all dimensions of the system operate

FIGURE 8.3 Analyzing PFM along the Four Dimensions, Selected Countries

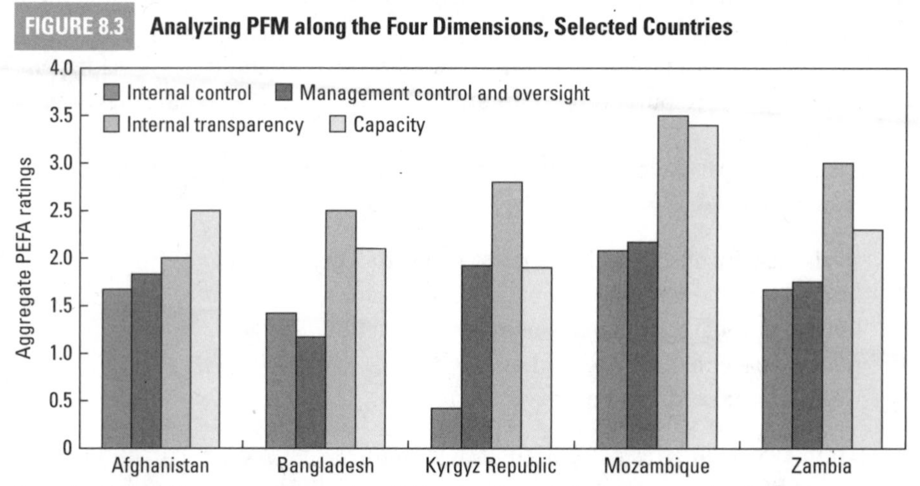

Source: Performance Measurement Framework, available at http://www.pefa.org/about_test.htm#Application.

together at any given level. Mitigating the risk of corruption requires that management control and oversight, internal controls, capacity, and transparency complement one another to identify questionable transactions and deter fraudulent behavior. Reforms that strengthen PFM systems and processes should be incrementally implemented according to country circumstances. A useful guide to sequencing PFM reforms in low-capacity settings is the "platform approach" to reform, sponsored by the PEFA program (Brooke 2003). Each platform focuses on an improved outcome to which individual reform activities should contribute. For instance, in developing countries with overall weaknesses in PFM, the platform approach recommends strengthening capacity and internal controls before increasing transparency and accountability. The entry point should focus on the weakest link in the four dimensions and build on the improved outcome to strengthen other dimensions in PFM. For example, in Papua New Guinea, the PEFA assessment indicates that reform activities should focus first on strengthening internal control and then build on improved internal control to improve internal transparency, capacity, and finally management control and oversight in PFM.

Capacity

Capacity of PFM systems and processes includes systems for comprehensive and accurate record keeping, reporting, and accounting as well as the capacity of budget staff. In many developing countries, budget laws, rules, and regulations that govern public spending are often in place but not commonly known by staff or followed in practice. Basic accounting systems that help track and report fiscal transactions are usually not developed or integrated. Automation of financial information systems is often overly complex and does not provide quality reports. Capacity constraints in many developing countries are often compounded by the scarcity of qualified domestic staff in key positions in the government. For example, in Afghanistan and Timor-Leste, day-to-day budget activities are carried out by international consultants.

Activities that strengthen the capacity of PFM systems include hiring qualified staff; implementing competitive wage levels;[8] training existing and new staff on budget issues and ethical conduct; implementing a robust classification system that allows tracking of expenditures along administrative, economic, functional, and programmatic dimensions; improving budget and process comprehensiveness; and progressively implementing a more purpose- or objective-oriented budget. Eventually, a multiyear perspective in budgeting can be introduced.

Internal Transparency

Internal transparency of fiscal information ensures that information is recorded and reported accurately and in a timely manner and that it is available to executives and decision makers. Transparency of budget documents and the availability of budget information in a clear and understandable format are essential elements for reducing corruption in PFM. The absence of reasonable and timely information prevents management monitoring and oversight of activities and detection of fraudulent and corrupt activities. Lack of transparency of fiscal information reduces the risk of detection and remedial action.

Improving internal transparency of fiscal information should aim to increase frequency of in-year fiscal reports, accuracy of fiscal reports, timeliness and accuracy of year-end fiscal reports, comprehensiveness of accounting and reporting, and the distribution of reports to make them available to all stakeholders (internal to government). It should also ensure that the report format is easily understandable by all users and improve timeliness and accuracy in accounting and record keeping of all fiscal transactions.

Internal Control

Internal control is commonly understood as the procedures within government to streamline processes and prevent or detect improper use of funds. Modern internal control is understood more as a process designed to provide reasonable assurance regarding achievement of organizational objectives in effectiveness and efficiency of operations, reliability of financial reporting, and compliance with statutes and policies. Internal control processes involve the control environment, assessment of risks from various operations or expenditures, control activities (what most view as internal control), information and communication, and monitoring. Typical internal control activities include formally recorded transaction approvals, authorizations, verifications, reconciliations, reviews of performance, security of assets, segregation of duties, and information system controls.

Key issues that affect internal control are weak control activities on payroll and nonpayroll expenditures, poor adherence to the control regime, limited or weak capacity of internal audit functions, and overwhelming audit mandates. Weaknesses in the capacity of internal audit departments and limited or no follow-up of audit recommendations by management are major reasons often cited for ineffectiveness of internal audit. For example, the Local Fund Audit unit of the state of Punjab has 562 employees and is responsible for auditing 17,382 organizations (World Bank 2005). The unit's annual report for 2000–01 states that more than 103,000 of its audit objections had been ignored and that almost half of them were more than 10 years old. In such cases, institutionalizing departmental response to internal audit findings would be a high-priority reform activity.

Internal control and formal quality assurance mechanisms over spending, revenues, recording, reporting, and payroll can prevent fraud and corruption. Activities to strengthen internal control mechanisms should include effective measures for taxpayer registration and tax assessment, effective payroll controls, internal controls for nonsalary expenditure, procedures for timely and regular accounts reconciliation, clearly defined and simple audit standards, training to improve capacity of audit staff, increased authority for internal audit bodies, strengthened payroll audits, a strengthened treasury system (or the creation of one if it does not exist), and automated payment systems (if a cash-based system is still in use).

Management Control and Oversight

Management control and oversight of public expenditures is often weak because of the limited understanding and capacity of management to analyze spending. Analyzing and reviewing details of spending is frequently undertaken in a perfunctory manner.[9] The role of senior management in formalizing and institutionalizing the response to fraud and other corrupt practices is essential to mitigate the risk of fraudulent behavior. Management responsibility for overseeing system performance, using information, holding others to account, or accepting responsibility for failure of the system to operate properly provides strong incentives for deterrence of fraudulent behavior. Traditional bureaucratic practices and lack of incentives to take the initiative in responding to and following up on internal audit findings significantly impede the fight against corruption. A note (World Bank 2005) on the workings of the public financial management system in Punjab, India, identified lack of accountability (and a weak internal control environment) as key challenges that need to be addressed. Recent Ghanaian and U.K. SAI reports also site weak management control and oversight as a key recommendation to reduce fraud and corruption in public spending.

Management oversight of budgeted expenditure, deviations from the approved budget for expenditures and revenues, expenditure payment arrears, or aggregate fiscal risk from other public sector entities can be the first step in flagging potential occurrences of fraud and corruption. Improving management oversight in reforming countries includes training senior managers on their role in fiscal oversight, the detection of fraudulent behavior, and responding to fraud; instituting procedures to follow up on audit findings and recommendations; strengthening the planning and monitoring of tax, expenditure, and payroll audit and fraud investigation programs; and implementing procedures to identify and hold fraudulent behavior to account.

STRENGTHENING EXTERNAL CHECKS AND BALANCES

Countries with stronger participation of external stakeholders in the public spending have lower corruption perception indexes. Figure 8.4 maps Kaufmann-Kraay voice and accountability scores against Transparency International's Corruption Perception Index. The Kaufmann-Kraay voice and accountability indicator developed by the World Bank measures various aspects of the political process, civil liberties, and political rights, including the extent to which citizens of a country are able to participate in

FIGURE 8.4 External Stakeholder Participation and Perception of Corruption

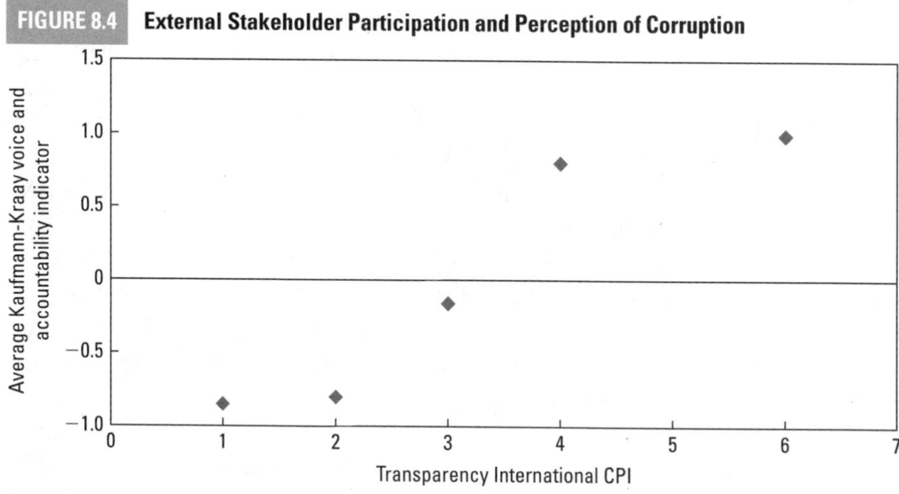

Source: Authors.

the selection of governments. It also measures the independence of the media, which serves an important role in monitoring those in authority and holding them accountable for their actions. The results suggest perception of lower corruption in countries where external stakeholders are actively engaged in the public sector processes.

In identifying entry points for participation of external stakeholders in the budget process, it is essential to balance external demand-side pressures for increased accountability with supply-side measures to improve PFM. Anticorruption reforms are inherently political. The politically acceptable pace of reform requires careful balancing of demand-side pressures for increased transparency and accountability with supply-side measures to strengthen PFM performance. Increasing the demand for accountability from governments with limited capacity could result in a politically unstable environment. Basic technical capabilities need to be in place before demands for improved accountability can be met. In politically sensitive environments, technical reforms, regardless of whether they are called anticorruption reforms, will help combat corruption in PFM. Reforms that increase external demand-side pressures in PFM should be incrementally implemented according to country circumstances. The platform approach to reform (Brooke 2003) can prove helpful here. Each platform focuses on an improved outcome to which individual reform activities should contribute. The platform approach suggests that to be successful, reform strategies should sequence technical budget reforms to achieve basic budget functionality as well as reforms increasing external transparency of fiscal information and strengthening capacity of key external stakeholders to engage in the budget process and reforms increasing external accountability in PFM. Entry points for technical budget reforms to fight corruption were discussed earlier. This section looks at external transparency and accountability mechanisms and their role in mitigating the risk of corruption.

Increasing External Transparency and Capacity of External Stakeholders

Effective involvement of institutions of accountability requires greater transparency of fiscal information. Tanzi (1998) suggests a strong correlation between lack of transparency and corruption. Transparency of budgetary information includes access to budgetary documents, in-year financial reports, and year-end fiscal reports. Public access to regular, accurate, and timely fiscal information in easily understandable formats is an essential requirement for effective legislative as well as for civil society engagement.

Depending on the constitutional form of the government, the legislature is often viewed as the primary institution through which governments are held to account. Effective participation of legislatures and legislative committees is often constrained by limited understanding of the budget process, unclear understanding of their role in the budget process, undefined legal mandates, and weak technical capacity and political incentives to exercise their budgetary responsibility effectively (Alesina and Perotti 1994, 1996). Strengthening legislative committees, legislative audit, and research organizations and establishing a well-structured budget that allows sufficient time for legislative engagement during policy-level decision making are possible reforms for improving legislative capacity for participation in the budget process.

Civil society participation in the budget process in developing countries is limited by weak capacity, unfamiliarity with the budget process, unclear understanding of the ability of external organizations to influence the budget process, and excessively complex budget documents. Key reform strategies should include increasing the awareness, understanding, and capacity of civil society and media to participate in the budget process and improving the presentation of budget information into an easily understandable format. For example, the Public Service Accountability Monitor (PSAM) in South Africa, established in 1999 to track actions taken by the government in response to reported corruption cases, has became an active source of information for citizens. Over time, PSAM shifted its focus on the structural context of weak financial management that was responsible for the mismanagement of funds and corruption and began to monitor the compliance of spending agencies with public finance regulations and administrative directives.

Strengthening External Accountability Mechanisms

Legislatures posses a wide range of responsibilities and budgetary powers that affect fiscal outcomes. By increasing scrutiny of the budget, legislative oversight can redress informational asymmetries between the government and society and open the debate on the underlying policy choices and budgetary allocations, reinforce public scrutiny, and create conditions for improved government accountability (Santiso 2005). Institutional arrangements underlying the budget process have a significant impact on budgetary restraint and fiscal discipline (Baldez and Carey 1999). Stein. Talvi, and Grisanti (1998) and Alesina and others (1999) have shown that budgetary institutions contribute to variances in budgetary outcomes in Latin America.[10]

Legislative committees, such as PACs, are arguably the most effective mechanism to support ex post scrutiny of audit findings and improve legislative oversight of budget implementation. Strengthening external audits and improving links with legislative committees such as PACs can enhance external accountability. Factors that enable PACs to successfully oversee public expenditures and hold the government accountable include a broad mandate to cover all past, current, and committed expenditures; freedom to identify expenditures for scrutiny without government interference; capacity for detailed analysis and reporting; and authority to make recommendations and publish conclusions (Stapenhurst and others 2005). In parliamentary systems, PACs frequently have limited credibility as an agent of accountability where the majority (government) party chairs the PAC. In Westminster parliamentary systems, tradition gives the PAC chair to an opposition party member, increasing the potential for accountability as the opposition has more natural incentive to hold the government to account than a member of the governing party. Box 8.2 illustrates the importance of key features of the PAC in Canada.

Independent external audit institutions, such as SAIs, are widely viewed as the watchdogs of the public interest. The role of SAIs includes ensuring that the executive complies with the budget as approved by the legislature and promoting sound financial controls to reduce the opportunity for corruption and foster efficiency in public spending (Dye and Stapenhurst 1998). The performance of SAIs in

BOX 8.2 An Effective PAC: The Canadian Example

The federal PAC in Canada has nine government and eight opposition members and is chaired by an opposition member. About 25 years ago, the PAC engaged in an independent investigation beginning with a short reference in the auditor general's report to unsubstantiated payments made by Atomic Energy of Canada Limited (AECL), a state-owned enterprise. The AECL had paid more than C$20 million to agents abroad in the hopes of selling its nuclear reactors. The PAC conducted its own investigation beyond the audit report and concluded that the corporation followed unacceptable business practices and suspected some payments were used for corrupt practices. PAC recommended major changes in the accountability structures for state-owned enterprises that were subsequently implemented. The media reported the proceedings as front page news and were able to uncover additional evidence that the committee could not have obtained by itself.

Source: Stapenhurst and others (2005).

BOX 8.3 Key Factors for SAIs and Examples

Experience in developed countries suggests that developing the capacity of an SAI to control for corruption requires that SAIs be given clear mandates free from government interference; clear auditing mandates; recruitment of high-caliber auditors; competitive compensation for auditors to attract qualified staff; adequate training for audit staff; transparent and easily available audit reports to all stakeholders, including the media; high-quality audit control; and quality assurance mechanisms for auditing.

In 1996, the comptroller general's office in Puerto Rico recovered $28 million in unlawfully disbursed funds by aggressively modernizing the office. In 1987, most workers had typewriters and maintained manual ledgers. A decade later, the office had become the best-equipped and most updated of all government departments in Puerto Rico.

Before 1938, the general accounting office in República Bolivariana de Venezuela was weak and powerless and located in the executive branch. With assistance from the United States, the office of the comptroller general, which was only loosely affiliated to the congress, was established. As in Puerto Rico, this office is undergoing extensive modernization and is moving toward a system of comprehensive ex post financial and performance audits.

Source: Dye and Stapenhurst (1998).

developing countries is often affected by inadequate independence to select issues for investigation; inadequate funding sources and legal mandates; inadequate capacity to undertake financial, compliance, and performance audits; and limited transparency and impact of the audit findings (because of limited willingness of the executive to follow up on the findings and limited coordination between the SAI and the parliamentary oversight agencies) (World Bank 2004). Box 8.3 discusses the factors for developing and improving external audit capacity and improving ex post detection of corruption and examples.

Clear laws and independent, competent judiciaries are also important deterrents to corruption in public spending (Lambsdorff 1999). Specific laws that prevent unauthorized spending or spending over the appropriated limit and that clearly define corrupt practices are important elements of effective anticorruption efforts. For example, the U.S. Anti-deficiency Act prevents authorization of expenditures over the approved limit or processing payments before an appropriation is made. The penalty for violating this act is a fine and imprisonment.[11] The penalties have never been applied. The requirement that any violation must be reported to the president and Congress provides a strong deterrent. The U.S. state of Virginia is even clearer; there, overspending or unauthorized spending is not the responsibility of the state to pay but the personal responsibility of the officers approving such spending. Factors that assist in creating capable and predictable judiciaries include independence from political influence, meritocratic recruitment and promotion of judges, adequate compensation, efficient court administrative systems and record keeping, and accountability for performance.

Successful anticorruption initiatives can also benefit from a politically independent anticorruption commission with clear legal mandates. In practice, however, national anticorruption agencies are difficult to set up and often fail to achieve their goals once they have been established. A primary challenge is mobilizing the political will to establish an effective, politically independent anticorruption agency. Governments that have established successful independent anticorruption agencies have done so in response to significant pressures from a majority of the domestic stakeholders (Heilbrunn 2004). Such agencies must be subject to review by a free press and by civil society. Successful anticorruption agencies are reported in Australia, Botswana, Hong Kong (China), Malawi, and Singapore (Heilbrunn 2004).

Although recognition of civil society involvement in the budget process is fairly recent, there is some evidence that it has a positive impact on increasing accountability in public spending. Examples include the Mazdoor Kisan Shakti Sangathan (MKSS) in Rajasthan, India. The MKSS uses innovative forums called public hearings or social audits to facilitate structured discussion among residents on government expenditures of public funds in their communities. The Institute for Democracy in South Africa, a civil society organization, helped to strengthen a new financial management act by insisting on the inclusion of stronger *virement* rules and on a provision requiring direct departmental responsibility for overspending (Ramkumar and Krafchik 2005).

The news media—television, radio, newspapers, and the Internet—all increase demand-side pressures on the government to hold to account those involved in corrupt practices. By exposing fraudulent behavior or publishing corrupt activities identified by SAIs, the media can increase public awareness of leakages in public expenditure, identify weaknesses in the system, identify corrupt officials, and publish follow-up actions taken regarding those officials. Public awareness and demand for effective follow-up measures can provide an effective deterrent and prevent others from acting corruptly for fear of similar public exposure, humiliation, and embarrassment (Islam 2002). For example, the role of the Philippine Center for Investigative Journalism in 2000 in exposing corruption and wrongdoing by Joseph Estrada, then the president of the Philippines, played a key role in forcing him out of office in 2001. The center did very thorough research, obtained evidence, and produced several reports to show that Estrada had far more wealth in money and property than he had declared in a sworn written document.

THE CORRUPTION CONUNDRUM IN GHANA: ASSESSING VULNERABILITIES IN PFM

The Ghanaian government is committed to reforming its PFM systems and processes; however, corruption continues to be an issue. The Ghanaian government has been the driver of change in building capacity and has implemented reforms ranging from macroeconomic and structural reforms to changes in PFM systems. However, the African Peer Review Mechanism (2005) cites high levels of corruption in Ghana's public sphere at both the national and regional levels. Transparency International rates Ghana as a 3.5 (on a scale of 0 to 10, where 0 is the highest level of perceived corruption and 10 is the lowest) in its 2005 Corruption Perception Index.[12] Cases of administrative corruption in Ghana include the presence of ghost workers, misappropriations in the privatization processes, bribery, procurement fraud, and general leakages in public spending that result from corruption (Transparency International 2003; U4–Anticorruption Resource Center 2002).[13] The Transparency International *Global Corruption Report* for 2003 found that underdeveloped expenditure controls, accounting procedures, and reporting were insufficient to curtail misuse of public resources or to stop leakages of transfers to local government units.

In his report on the public accounts of Ghana for 2004, the country's auditor general highlighted several recurrent and serious irregularities in "tax administration, unsatisfactory cash management, and inadequate procurement and inventory control procedures." The financial impact of these irregularities for the year ending December 31, 2004, was estimated at $1.6 million, or 1.23 percent of the total expenditures for 2004. Tax irregularities included nonpayment of national development levies, nonpayment of rent tax, and undercollection of duties. Cash irregularities increased by 99.4 percent from 2003. More than three-fifths (61.5 percent) of disbursements were made without receipts and other requisite documentation to authenticate the transaction; other cash irregularities included failure to submit payment vouchers, misappropriation of revenues and other receipts, misapplication of funds, bank balances not promptly transferred into the consolidated fund, and payment vouchers not returned to the treasury. Procurement violations included inappropriate purchase of items and inaccurate vehicle logs. Other fraudulent transactions included payroll overpayment; outstanding loans, debts, and fees (representing uncollected fees, staff advances, and outstanding utility bills); and contract irregularities (including unexecuted contracts and payment of advances without signed contract documents).

The auditor general's report also noted limitations in the transparency of fiscal information and in participation of external stakeholders in the accountability of fiscal information. The auditor general reported that a total of ₵ (cedis) 1,453 billion in project grants (82 percent of total grants) received from donors in fiscal 2004 was not disclosed in the financial statements for the year ending December 31, 2004. The report also stated that the Ministry of Finance did not seek parliamentary approval before issuing ₵27,339 billion (and redeeming ₵24,032 billion) of securities during the fiscal year.

FIGURE 8.5 Assessing PFM Performance in Ghana

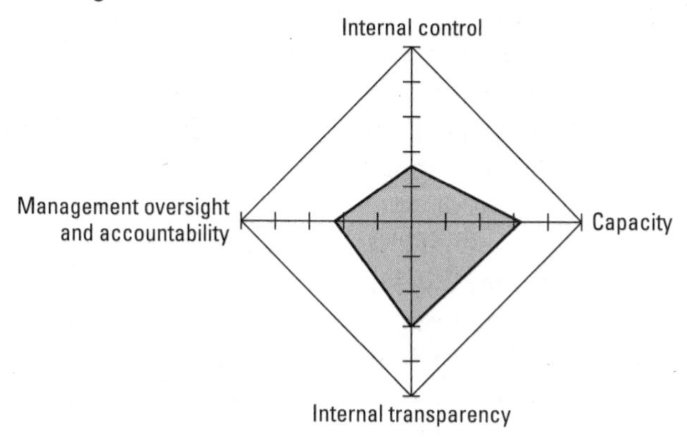

Source: Authors.

Strengthening PFM in Ghana

Strengthening internal controls and management oversight and accountability are key priorities for mitigating the risk of corruption in public spending in Ghana. The June 2006 PEFA assessment of the PFM system in Ghana indicates that despite improvements, substantial upgrading is still required in the areas of internal control and management control and oversight.[14] Figure 8.5 compares the performance of internal control, capacity, internal transparency, and management control and oversight in Ghana. When compared with the scores for its internal control and management oversight and accountability, Ghana scores relatively well on capacity and internal transparency. Both areas have significantly improved since 2002 under government leadership, but further improvements are possible. However, mitigating the risk of corruption and fraud in Ghana requires a focus on strengthening internal controls and management oversight and accountability mechanisms in the short term to levels compatible with the stronger dimensions.

Formal internal control institutions are the weakest link in PFM in Ghana. While the government has introduced internal controls, the implementation of rules and regulations that govern the PFM process can be substantially strengthened. Timeliness and comprehensiveness of internal audit and management follow-up of audit findings require substantial improvements. The last payroll audit was conducted in 2003, and while reasonable controls underpin the payroll process, the auditor general has documented a few cases of personal emoluments funds being used for other purposes, and the effectiveness of payroll controls has been hampered by weaknesses in security controls.

Activities to strengthen internal control should focus on implementing the recently enacted updates to the PFM regulatory framework, which include procurement, financial administration, and internal audit agencies acts; training to improve capacity of audit staff; increased authority for internal audit bodies; follow-up procedures for audit recommendations; strengthened planning and monitoring of tax audit and fraud investigation programs; strengthened payroll audits; and improved timeliness and regularity of accounts reconciliation.

The auditor general's report specifies that the violations and the general disregard for financial regulations primarily result from underlying weaknesses in management oversight and accountability. The ability of senior management to identify and respond to fraud is limited. Although management has responded to some audit findings, formal procedures to follow up on audit actions are currently in the process of being established. Activities to improve management oversight and control over public spending should include training for senior and mid-level management in all ministries to detect fraudulent behavior, establishment and implementation of formal mechanisms to report and investigate fraudulent behavior (and disseminate those procedures) and to implement disciplinary actions where warranted, and implementation of formal mechanisms to respond to audit findings.

Maintaining a balance in the development of PFM capacity, management control, transparency, and accountability is essential for an effective PFM system and the long-term sustainability of reforms. While efforts to strengthen internal controls and management oversight and accountability are under way, improvements to capacity and internal transparency of fiscal information can be planned. Improvements to the system capacity can focus on timely approval of the budget. The 2006 budget was the first since Ghana achieved independence in 1957 to be approved in the parliament before the beginning of the fiscal year. While some reports such as the budget are made public in the *Ghana Gazette*, the format of the budget information is difficult to understand, and general access to the gazette is limited. Improvements to the format, simplicity, timeliness, and accuracy of all fiscal information will assist key stakeholders to engage in the budget process effectively. Similarly, reports and assessments of fiscal impact of aggregate expenditure outcomes, composition of expenditure outturns, aggregate revenues outturn, payment arrears, and aggregate fiscal risks for other public sector entities should be made available to the parliament.

In sum, strengthening PFM in Ghana could include activities that help strengthen internal controls and management oversight and accountability, including capacity building (in particular, improving the budget classification system, increasing the effectiveness of tax collection, and improving the recording and management of cash balances), staff training, refining record keeping and reporting, improving budget information, and improving the quality and timeliness of in-year and year-end reports. Complex reforms such as a multiyear perspective in budget formulation and execution should be considered in the medium term.

Strengthening External Participation in the Budget Process

While strengthening internal control and management oversight are the first order of business in Ghana, parallel efforts to increase transparency and the ability of external stakeholders to understand fiscal issues and engage constructively in the future might be useful. The ability of key stakeholders to engage effectively in the budget process is constrained by the limited external transparency of budget documents and fiscal reports and weak understanding of the budget process. The International Budget

Project rated Ghana above the cross-country average in availability of budget documents to the executive, but Ghana's scores for the other two categories of "monitoring and evaluating reports" and "encouraging public and legislative involvement" were below the cross-country averages, indicating weaker practices in these areas.[15] Actual spending reports are not always submitted to parliament as required, and when produced, their accuracy cannot be guaranteed. Budget priorities, macrofiscal policy, and constraints are not well documented and generally not detailed enough to allow meaningful engagement of the parliament (The International Budget Project 2002).

Similarly, civil society has limited understanding of the budget process and is not well organized to effectively participate in the budget process. Existing civil society organizations in Ghana, such as the Center for Budget Advocacy in Integrated Social Development Centre, are participating in the budget process, but lack of resources and poor understanding of the budget process impedes effective monitoring of the public spending.[16] Limited access to fiscal information in a format that is easy to understand also inhibits their participation.

Activities to increase participation of external stakeholders in public spending can focus on increasing transparency of fiscal information in an easily understandable format and on improving parliamentary and civil society understanding of the budget process.

CONCLUSION

Corruption in PFM is not new, nor are the efforts to curb it. Various procedures and institutions have been developed over time as essential elements for combating corruption. This chapter has provided an overview of types of corruption that occur in PFM systems, introduced an indicator-based tool for assessing PFM system vulnerabilities, and provided a framework for developing a PFM anticorruption reform strategy.

Going forward, the challenge will be implementing PFM reforms. The budget process and anticorruption reforms are inherently political. In environments where anticorruption reforms are politically sensitive, technical reforms that strengthen PFM systems and processes can have a significant and long-lasting impact on reducing fraudulent behavior and corrupt activities. For instance, a better treasury system would help combat corruption, whether it is labeled as a technical reform or an anticorruption reform.

Recent work by the World Bank and the International Monetary Fund (IMF) using an abbreviated indicator set in 24 heavily indebted poor countries (HIPCs) for 2001–04 clearly illustrates the remaining weaknesses in many country PFM systems.[17] Subsequent work by the World Bank in conjunction with PEFA partners has yielded a new program designed to assess progress in PFM system performance over time.[18] That program entails three pillars: a country-led PFM reform strategy, donor coordination at the country level in support of that strategy, and a common framework for assessing PFM system performance (the PEFA PFM performance indicators). This approach holds promise for better monitoring and oversight of PFM improvements on the ground, which should also assist in improvements in the quality of PFM systems.

Keeping expectations realistic is key. Building effective, individual institutions takes time, and building systems of institutions that function together takes more time. Drawing from the World Bank–IMF HIPCs assessments, countries in the sample improved their PFM system performance by an average of 3 percent a year in the two years from 2002 to 2004. Development of PFM systems is dependent on existing system capacity and the environment in which these systems operate. While the rate of reform varies, consistent improvement in the quality of PFM systems over time will reduce corruption in public financial management.

ENDNOTES

1. Klitgaard, Maclean-Abaroa, and Parris (2000, p. 2). It is important to distinguish between political corruption and political leveraging or bargaining. Political bargaining is at the heart of all political and economic exchanges in contemporary society and is the very essence of politics itself; it should not be interpreted as corruption. An example of political leveraging occurred in Peru under the first Fujimori administration, when service delivery resources were shifted from Lima and urban areas toward rural areas to create a base of support for the administration and rectify historical inequities in resource distribution.
2. Accountability is enhanced where ex ante objectives of spending are specified, against which results can be measured. There are many ways of accomplishing this. Common approaches include program budgeting, performance budgeting, results-oriented budgeting, and policy-based budgeting.
3. Penalties may be administrative (dismissal, fine, repayment) or criminal (prosecution in court of law, with fines or incarceration). For criminal sanctions to be effective, elements of the judicial system—from public prosecutors to courts and prisons—need to function well. But effective deterrents also include administrative dimensions, and frequently loss of employment and income is the single greatest cost.
4. Institutions are the formal and informal rules that shape the behavior of organizations and individuals in a society (North 1990, p. 3). Formal rules include the constitution, laws and regulations, contracts, and internal procedures; informal rules are the values and norms that drive bureaucratic behavior.
5. Generally, a greater number of accounts makes it harder to monitor all spending, complicates consolidated financial reporting and auditing, and, from a purely cash management perspective, prevents pooling of cash balances to meet payment obligations—debt may be issued to meet a payment while idle cash remains in some accounts.
6. For example, assuming that invoices are recorded correctly and in a timely fashion, the IFMIS should record the date due as well as when paid for all invoices. A data query comparing length of time between receipt and payment, by type of payment, can detect anomalies that should be further investigated. In addition, where a commitment must be registered before a payment can be made, the IFMIS should record cases where the commitment and payment order were registered the same day, flagging transactions for audit. In both examples, information technology enables targeting of audits to higher-risk transactions, improving the marginal return to limited audit resources.
7. The PEFA performance framework for assessing and monitoring country PFM systems was formally issued in June 2005 by the PEFA Secretariat. Indicators are mapped to the five dimensions of internal control, management control and oversight, internal transparency, and capacity, based on a review of the description of the indicator. In many

cases, each indicator measures a combination of management control, capacity, internal transparency, and internal and external accountability. Each indicator is mapped to the dimension that has the largest focus in the description. Indicators are mapped to the four internal dimensions of this section as follows: Capacity includes classification of the budget (PI-5); predictability in the availability of funds for commitment of expenditures (PI-16); extent of unreported government operations (PI-7); multiyear perspective in fiscal planning, expenditure policy, and budgeting (PI-12); effectiveness in collection of tax payments (PI-15); and recording and management of cash balances, debt, and guarantees (PI-17). Internal control includes effectiveness of measures for taxpayer registration and tax assessment (PI-14), effectiveness of payroll controls (PI-18), effectiveness of internal controls for nonsalary expenditure (PI-20), effectiveness of internal audit (PI-21), and timeliness and regularity of accounts reconciliation (PI-22). Internal transparency includes transparency of intergovernmental fiscal relations (PI-8); comprehensiveness of information included in budget documentation (PI-6); orderliness and participation in the annual budget process (PI-11); competition, value for money, and controls in procurement (PI-19); availability of information on resources received by service delivery units (PI-23); quality and timeliness of in-year budget reports (PI-24); and quality and timeliness of annual financial statements (PI-25). Management control and oversight include aggregate expenditure outturn compared to original approved budget (PI-1), composition of expenditure outturn compared with original approved budget (PI-2), aggregate revenue outturn compared with original approved budget (PI-3), stock and monitoring of expenditure payment arrears (PI-4), and oversight of aggregate fiscal risk from other public sector entities (PI-9). PEFA ratings have been converted to numerical values where D is 1, D+ is 1.5, and A is 4. Ratings have been normalized and aggregated for each dimension.

8. Among public finance practitioners, it is a common rule of thumb that those handling public funds should be well paid, if not paid slightly more than the average civil servant, to reduce the incentive for corruption. From an enforcement view, loss of a good salary is a significant opportunity cost for most people, particularly in developing countries, and the risk of losing such a position permanently for a momentary gain through fraud provides a strong counter to corrupt behavior in environments where detection and accountability mechanisms work.
9. In some Central and Eastern European systems, the minister of finance personally signs each and every adjustment to the budget during execution, regardless of amount. While appearing to be a strong system of accountability at the highest levels, this practice does not ensure adequate review of transaction.
10. Budgetary institutions are defined as all rules and regulations according to which budgets are drafted, approved, and implemented (Alesina and Perotti, 1996).
11. United State Code, Title 31.
12. Ghana is ranked 65th among the 159 countries voluntarily included in the 2005 rankings. The recent *Global Monitoring Report* (World Bank 2006b) rates Ghana as a country with better corruption control, compared with other International Development Association countries, but one that still requires significant improvements to policies and institutions.
13. In Ghana, the deputy auditor general disclosed in March 2002 that more than $20 million had been paid to about 2,000 ghost names in the previous two years. In response, the finance minister ordered a head count of civil servants; however, Ghana's government faced growing criticism of its failure to address corruption within the civil service. In his inaugural address in 2002, President John Kufuor promised to establish an office of

accountability under the direct supervision of the presidency that would oversee a code of conduct for public servants. Neither the office nor the code of conduct has yet been established. In 2002, a former national insurance commissioner, Samuel Appiah-Ampofo, was found guilty of accepting a $96,500 bribe from a broker working for a subsidiary of Aon, the U.S.-based insurance company. See Transparency International (2003).

14. In 2002 and 2004, HIPC assessments of the PFM systems were conducted. These assessments identified significant improvements in the PFM systems since 2002. Government-led reforms after the 2002 assessment, which rated Ghana to be the weakest among 23 HIPCs measured, resulted in a substantial increase in the performance of the PFM systems, measured as the number of benchmarks met in 2004. The PEFA indicators build on the HIPC indicator set to provide a more comprehensive and detailed assessment of PFM systems. See World Bank, IMF, and the government of Ghana (2004).
15. The International Budget Project was formed in 1997 within the Center on Budget and Policy Priorities (a U.S. nongovernmental organization) to nurture the growth of civil society capacity to analyze and influence government budget processes, institutions, and outcomes globally.
16. For more information, see http://www.isodec.org.gh/budget-advocacy/index.html.
17. See World Bank–IMF Board HIPC Assessment Board Papers 2001, 2002, 2003, and 2005. http://web.worldbank.org/WBSITE/EXTERNAL/TOPICS/EXTPUBLICSECTORAND-GOVERNANCE.
18. See http://www.pefa.org for more information.

REFERENCES

African Peer Review Mechanism. 2005. "Country Review Report of the Republic of Ghana." New Partnership for Africa's Development (NEPAD). Midrand, South Africa.

Alesina, Alberto, Ricardo Hausmann, Rudolf Hommes, and Ernesto Stein. 1999. "Budget Institutions and Fiscal Performance in Latin America." Inter-American Development Bank Working Paper Series 394. Washington, DC (September).

Alesina, Alberto, and Roberto Perotti. 1994. "The Political Economy of Budget Deficits." NBER Working Paper 4637, National Bureau of Economic Research, Cambridge, MA.

———. 1996. "Budget Institutions and Budget Deficits." NBER Working Paper 5556. National Bureau of Economic Research, Cambridge, MA.

Allen R., and D. Tommasi. 2001. *Managing Public Expenditure: A Reference Book for Transitions Countries.* Paris: Organisation for Economic Co-operation and Development.

Baldez, Lisa, and John Carey. 1999. "Presidential Agenda Control and Spending Policy: Lessons from General Pinochet's Constitution." *American Journal of Political Science.* 43 (1): 29–55.

Brooke, Peter. 2003. "Study of Measures Used to Address Weaknesses in Public Financial Management Systems in the Context of Policy-based Support." PEFA Secretariat, Washington, DC (April). http://www.pefa.org.

Dorotinsky, William, and Katherine Barraclough. Forthcoming. "The Role of the Legislature in the Budget Drafting Process: A Comparative Review."

Dye, M. Kenneth, and Rick Stapenhurst. 1998. "Pillars of Integrity: The Importance of Supreme Audit Institutions in Curbing Corruption." Economic Development Institute, World Bank, Washington, DC.

Heilbrunn, John R. 2004. "Anticorruption Commissions: Panacea or Real Medicine to Fight Corruption?" World Bank Institute, Washington, DC.

Her Majesty's Treasury (United Kingdom). 2005. "2004–2005 Fraud Report: An Analysis of Reported Fraud in Government Departments." Her Majesty's Treasury, Norwich, United Kingdom.

The International Budget Project. 2002. "Africa Fiscal Transparency: Ghana." http://www.internationalbudget.org/resources/GHANA.pdf.

Isaken, Jan. 2005. "The Budget Process and Corruption." Utstein Anti-Corruption Resource Center at the Chr. Michelsen Institute, Bergen, Norway.

Islam, Roumeen. 2002. *The Right to Tell: The Role of Mass Media in Economic Development.* Washington, DC: World Bank Institute.

Klitgaard, R., R. Maclean-Abaroa, and H. L. Parris. 2000. *Corrupt Cities: A Practical Guide to Cure and Prevention.* Oakland, CA: Institute for Contemporary Studies Press.

Lambsdorff, J. G. 1999. "Corruption in Empirical Research: A Review." Also published as a Transparency International Working Paper.

Martinez-Vazquez, Jorge, F. Javier Arze, and Jameson Boex. 2004. "Corruption, Fiscal Policy, and Fiscal Management." Working Paper fr1003, United States Agency for International Development, Washington, DC.

North, Douglass C. 1990. *Institutions, Institutional Change, and Economic Performance.* Cambridge: Cambridge University Press.

PEFA Secretariat. 2005. "Public Financial Management: Performance Measurement Framework." World Bank, Washington, DC.

Ramkumar, Vivek, and Warren Krafchik. 2005. "The Role of Civil Society Organizations in Auditing and Public Finance Management." The International Budget Project, Center for Budget and Policy Priorities, Washington, DC.

Republic of Ghana. 2005. "Report of the Auditor-General on the Public Accounts of Ghana for the Year Ended 31 December 2004." Accra.

Santiso, Carlos. 2005. "Budget Institutions and Fiscal Responsibility: Parliaments and the Political Economy of the Budget Process in Latin America." World Bank Institute, Washington, DC.

Schick, Allen. 2002. "Can National Legislatures Gain Effective Voice in Budget Policy?" *OECD Journal on Budgeting* 1 (3): 15–42.

Stapenhurst, Rick. 2004. "The Legislature and the Budget." World Bank Institute, Washington, DC.

Stapenhurst, Rick, V. Sahgal, W. Woodley, and Riccardo Pelizzo. 2005. "Scrutinizing Public Expenditures: Assessing the Performance of Public Accounts Committees." Policy Research Working Paper 3613. World Bank, Washington, DC.

Stapenhurst, Rick, and Jack Titsworth. 2001. "Features and Functions of Supreme Audit Institutions." PREM Note 59, Poverty Reduction and Economic Management Network, World Bank, Washington, DC.

Stein, Ernesto, E. Talvi, and A. Grisanti. 1998. "Institutional Arrangements and Fiscal Performance: The Latin American Experience." NBER Working Paper 6358. National Bureau of Economic Research, Cambridge, MA.

Transparency International. Various years. *Global Corruption Report.* London: Pluto Press.

U4 (Utstein Anti-corruption Resource Center). 2002. "Ghana Internal Audit Report."

Tanzi, Vito. 1998. "Corruption around the World: Causes, Consequences, Scope, and Cures." *IMF Staff Papers* 45 (4): 559–94.

Tanzi, Vito, and Hamid Davoodi. 1997. "Corruption, Public Investment, and Growth." IMF Working Paper 97/139, International Monetary Fund, Washington, DC.

World Bank. 1997. *World Development Report 1997: The State in a Changing World.* Washington, DC: Oxford University Press and World Bank.

———. 1998. *Public Expenditure Management Handbook.* Washington, DC: World Bank.

———. 2004. "Supporting and Strengthening Supreme Audit Institutions: A World Bank Strategy." Financial Management Network, Operational Policy and Country Services, World Bank, Washington, DC.

———. 2005. "Punjab State: Note on the Workings of the Public Financial Management System." Poverty Reduction and Economic Management Unit and South Asia Region, World Bank, Washington, DC.

———. n.d. "Responses to Corruption: The Role of the Media." Youth for Good Governance Distance Learning Program Module, Washington, DC.

———. 2006b. *Global Monitoring Report 2006: Strengthening Mutual Accountability.* Washington, DC.

World Bank, International Monetary Fund, and the government of Ghana. 2004. "Ghana: Public Expenditure Management Country Assessment and Action Plan." World Bank, Washington, DC.

9

Corruption in Public Procurement
A Perennial Challenge

GLENN T. WARE, SHAUN MOSS, J. EDGARDO CAMPOS, AND GREGORY P. NOONE

"Because of the stakes involved and despite an increased effort invested in procurement reform, procurement continues to be an area of heightened corruption risk across the globe. This calls for a continued approach to curb corruption that is wise in understanding the nuances that the characteristics of each sector brings about. This chapter is an important contribution in this direction."

Juanita Olaya, Programme Manager for Revenue, Transparency International

Corruption is a worldwide scourge that afflicts both developed and developing countries alike and that requires constant attention by many sectors of society if it is to be kept in check. It has its most damaging impact, however, on those weakened systems that have the least capability to prevent, detect, and stop its debilitating effects (Transparency International 2006). The African Union estimates that approximately one-quarter (or $148 billion) of Africa's GDP is "lost to corruption each year" (Thachuk 2005, p. 149). In Kenya alone, international donors estimate that since 2002, nearly $1 billion has been stolen as a result of corruption (Wax 2005). The Asian Development Bank (ADB 1998) reports that in the Philippines, approximately $48 billion may have been lost to corruption over a 20-year period. And in Latin America, the Inter-American Development Bank estimates that on average about 10 percent of GDP is lost to corruption annually (Mora 2004).

This social pandemic has been pervasive in public procurement. It distorts public finance, impairing the delivery of public services, such as the building of schools and the provision and quality of medical care; ultimately, it retards efforts to reduce poverty. Globally, Transparency International estimates that at least $400 billion a year is lost to bribery and corruption in public procurement, increasing government

This chapter could not have been completed without the efforts of Nisha Narayanan, who provided invaluable, just-in-time research assistance, and Dr. Diana Noone, who provided advice and inputs on legal and investigative aspects.

costs by about 20–25 percent (Transparency International 2006a). In Asia, the ADB (1998) has noted that corrupt public procurement has led several countries to pay 20–100 percent more for goods and services than they would have had to otherwise. And, in Uganda, it is estimated that approximately $107 million is lost annually to corruption, mostly through public procurement (Mugazi 2005).

Public procurement is particularly susceptible to corruption because of the high level of funds involved and because of the expenditure profile of public procurement programs.[1] In contrast to the other major components of a country's public expenditure, public procurement usually involves a relatively low volume of high-value transactions (typically a few hundred procurement transactions conducted annually by each public institution, the most valuable of which may involve millions or even billions of dollars). By contrast, expenditures on public sector salaries, for example, invariably involve a much higher volume of low-value transactions, each of which is less attractive to potentially corrupt public officials.

The susceptibility of public procurement to corruption is further exacerbated by the relatively high degree of discretion that public officials, politicians, and parliamentarians typically have over public procurement programs in comparison with other areas of public expenditure. For example, in a typical annual public investment planning cycle, parliamentarians, through their influence over and voting on public expenditure bills, usually get to decide which roads are funded from the public purse and in which locations. Invariably parliamentarians have strong incentives to promote "pork-barrel" projects in their own constituencies to stimulate economic activity and thus bolster their chances of reelection. Likewise, it is typically a senior civil servant who gets to decide, often under pressure from those same parliamentarians, which contractor wins the contract to build the publicly funded road, even under circumstances where a competitive tender is conducted. In either case, it is the existence of individual discretion that exponentially raises the risks of corruption. By contrast, other large chunks of public expenditures such as salaries and public debt are paid directly to recipients based on set rules and involve very little discretion. The corruption risks inherent in discretion tend to be elevated in developing countries, where the legislative, regulatory, and institutional frameworks put in place to curtail the discretionary aspects of public procurement tend to be weaker than those in developed countries.

Given the amounts of money at stake, public procurement is often typified by cut-throat competition between bidding companies that rely heavily on public contracts for their survival. The dependency of many private sector companies on public sector business is often disproportionately greater in developing countries, where public procurement may amount to more than 20 percent of GDP, where the state is the largest economic actor, and where the private sector may be relatively underdeveloped. The juxtaposition of high volumes of expenditure, excessive and unbridled discretion afforded to public officials, and the presence of dependent private sector contractors often creates a ready market for corruption in public procurement.

The causes and impact of corruption vary from country to country. Generally, the less capacity a country has to prevent, detect, and punish corruption—through checks and balances, controls, and monitoring, and enforcement of laws and regulations more broadly—the greater the likelihood of corruption. Most experts agree that the monopoly of power, wide discretion, weak accountability, and little or no transparency magnify opportunities for corruption (Klitgaard 1988; Rose-Ackerman 1978, 1999; Ware and Noone 2003). These opportunities are rooted in a distorted incentive system that entices individuals, often including very capable ones, and institutions, both public and private, to engage in corrupt activities.

Just like a computer hacker who can intrude into a computer system at many points in the network, so too can corrupt actors intrude into a procurement procedure at many points along the procurement chain. The U.S. government has developed one of the most sophisticated procurement systems in the world. Guided by many laws and regulations, as well as monitored by administrative and legislative bodies, this system manages the massive U.S. defense and executive agency budgets.[2] Nevertheless, numerous incidents of corruption still occur annually. One of the most recent cases involved a senior Department of Defense acquisition official, who pleaded guilty to criminal conspiracy for secretly arranging a job with Boeing, a major defense contractor, at the same time she was negotiating with Boeing in her official capacity to make a $23 billion acquisition for the U.S. Air Force (Merle and Markon 2004; Merle 2004). The sheer magnitude of the funds at stake and the relative ease with which the criminal conduct occurred indicates that even the most advanced procurement systems are prone to control breakdown, particularly when the controls rely on human judgments. For its part, Boeing accepted responsibility for the misdeed, agreed to pay more than $600 million in fines, and fired its chief financial officer, who had agreed to the deal with the Defense Department official.[3]

To control corruption in public procurement, it is imperative first to understand how public procurement procedures operate and which methods may be effective in reducing corruption risks. This chapter explores how corruption attacks public procurement, identifies red flags that might indicate the operation of corruption schemes, and examines potential vulnerabilities that exist along the procurement chain. The chapter also discusses various instruments that can be helpful in preventing corruption in public procurement. It concludes with a discussion of comprehensive vulnerability assessments as a new, potentially promising instrument to reduce the risk of corruption in public procurement.

THE AIM OF PUBLIC PROCUREMENT

To be effective, public procurement must be responsive to the demands of its stakeholders, namely, the public, the government, and the private sector. A country's public procurement system must provide the required inputs to the delivery of public services—typically, goods, civil works, and services—at low cost and with appropriate levels of quality. To achieve this objective, most public procurement systems attempt to emulate the operation of the market, primarily by requiring competitive tendering procedures for major acquisitions (competitive bidding is not always required; see, for instance, the case of emergency procurement in annex 9A). A truly competitive process enables the country to effectively use public funds—whether they be domestic revenues, foreign aid, or loans—for developing infrastructure, promoting human capital, reducing poverty, and enhancing economic growth. A sound public procurement system is governed by several key principles.[4]

- *It must be based on rules.* Countries should have a clear and adequate legal and regulatory framework in place to guide public procurement. The laws, regulations, policies, and implementing rules must promote fairness (and be seen as fair by all potential bidders) and thus discourage discrimination (primarily between national and international companies) and favoritism. Equal treatment of bidders in the public procurement process promotes greater certainty and predictability in the awarding of contracts, which are essential to fostering healthy competition.
- *It should encourage competition in bidding for government contracts.* In most cases, competition results in better quality and lower cost, both of which are desired outcomes of a well-functioning system. Under some special circumstances, alternative modes for letting contracts may yield better results. The rules and regulations should be clear on the circumstances that justify the use of such alternatives and should limit discretion in deciding when to use them.
- *It should promote transparency.* The public procurement process should imbue the public with confidence that the government is providing legitimate services for citizens rather than increasing private wealth of government officials and narrow private interests. The easiest way to accomplish this objective is to ensure transparency in decision making throughout the entire procurement process, that is, to show that the government is spending taxpayer monies responsibly. Transparency "refers to the ability of all interested participants to know and understand the actual means and processes by which contracts are awarded and managed. This requires the release, at a minimum, of information sufficient to allow the average participant to know how the system is intended to work, as well as how it is actually functioning" (Wittig 2005, p. 111).
- *The system should strengthen accountability.* Public officials should be held responsible for the proper implementation of rules and regulations governing public procurement and thus for the procurement decisions they make. Accountability requires the existence of a credible sanctioning system for violations of the rules, consistent with due process. Such a system entails the adoption of adequate internal controls and audit procedures, a complaints system for bidders to challenge decisions, as well as appropriate administrative and judicial review bodies that have the authority to impose corrective measures and remedies.
- *The system must be economic.* A key element of the implicit social contract between the government and the citizenry is that the government will spend taxes prudently and effectively. For public procurement, this means the government should procure goods, works, and services at a reasonable cost and with reasonably good quality, that is, it should obtain good value for money spent.
- *The system should be efficient.* Time is money, and time wasted is money lost. Rules and procedures should thus encourage the completion of the procurement process within a reasonable length of time as well as the timely delivery of the goods, services, and works procured.

CORRUPTING PUBLIC PROCUREMENT

In public procurement, corruption schemes are often similar in form, shape, nature, and anatomical structure worldwide (Ware and Noone 2005). This section examines some of the most common corruption schemes, with a particular emphasis on procurement in the development context, and identifies corresponding red flags that indicate the possible operation of a particular scheme.[5]

Bribes, or kickbacks, are one of the most common features of corruption schemes in public procurement (Ware and Noone 2005). A kickback typically occurs when a company that wins a public contract "kicks back" a bribe to the government official(s) who influenced the awarding of the contract (either voluntarily or under duress) to that company. Generally, the kickback is a percentage of the value of the contract and, in highly corrupt environments, it becomes an added cost that all bidders must take into consideration when bidding on public contracts, which makes it all the more insidious. The authors, for example, have uncovered elaborate "commission-sharing agreements" between multinational companies engaged in joint ventures, allocating kickback amounts among the partners based on the percentage of interest in the company. Bidders pay kickbacks both to buy influence over the procurement decision-making process and to solicit direct and immediate rewards (Volcker Committee 2005b). For example, an urban transport project in Africa, costing more than $100 million, was cancelled after investigators working for an international financial institution discovered systemic corruption. The officials involved in the scheme used their control over the procurement process to extract bribes from contractors who were willing to participate in both the project and the corruption scheme.

Scheme 1: Kickback Brokers

Kickbacks in large public procurement projects are typically brokered by someone with good connections to the parties involved. These so-called kickback brokers are often the local agent, representative, or joint venture partner of a foreign company seeking a procurement contract. Local representatives, or "business development agents," as they are often called, are a common feature of international trade and are used by many large companies who want to do business in a country where they do not have a local office. Typically, a business retains the services of an agent to market, distribute, or resell its goods, products, and services. Because of their expertise, local knowledge, and connections, these agents have proven invaluable to companies seeking to enter new markets.

Foreign companies have also turned to local agents for assistance in helping them bid on public procurement contracts. The agent typically represents the foreign company locally, obtains the bidding documents, submits the required financial and technical bid, and attends all meetings relating to the procurement, including prebid meetings and public bid-opening meetings. By using a local agent, the foreign company obviates the need to maintain a permanent presence in the purchaser's country.

But local agents can also play the role of kickback broker.[6] In corrupt transactions, the local agent is compensated for "capturing" the contract for the foreign bidder by exerting influence on the local public officials, including by arranging and paying kickbacks to them. Success fees may be built into the agency agreement between the multinational company and the local agent, which has the effect of providing the agent with a powerful incentive to be as aggressive as possible in helping to win the contract for the foreign bidder.

This incentive structure is a fertile breeding ground for corruption. It has become all too common for local agents to share a portion of their success fee with the officials who are awarding the contract. These fees can range from a few percentage points to a significant percentage of the contract value. The ability of the purchasing government to detect these illicit transactions is often constrained by the fact that the agency agreement between the foreign company and the agent appears legitimate and customary.[7] In fact, the agent may be nothing more than a legalized conduit for money to flow between a foreign bidder and those in government responsible for awarding the contract.[8] In other cases, a multinational company may not specifically authorize the local agent to pay bribes but is nonetheless prepared to turn a blind eye to the business methods, including bribe paying, which the local agent has to employ to win the contract. In such cases, the multinational company may use the local agent to keep itself at arm's length from corrupt practices; this is a particular consideration for multinational firms registered in countries with legislation that prohibits and penalizes bribing foreign officials. In still other circumstances, a multinational company may hire a local agent for legitimate marketing purposes and be unaware that the local agent is engaging in corrupt practices to help it win a given contract.

In a recent case reported by Transparency International (2006b), a U.S. manufacturing company retained as a local agent a company owned by the son of a prominent government official to assist it in winning state-funded contracts in the local agent's country. The relationship of the local agent to government officials was not known to the U.S. company at the time it hired the local agent, nor was the U.S. company aware that its local agent was sharing its fee with government officials responsible for awarding the contract. The U.S. company's robust internal compliance program, however, spotted a red flag regarding the agent's relationship with government officials, which led to a forensic examination and the dismissal of the local agent.[9]

In the procurement process, project overseers should be aware of typical red flags that may signal kickback-related problems:

- Bidder selection is improper; for example, repeated contracts are awarded to the same supplier without competition, often at higher-than-market prices.
- An unnecessary middleman or local agent is involved in a public contract, where the local agent adds no obvious value to the performance of the contract.
- Procurement officials accept inappropriate gratuities, such as expensive meals or gifts, from bidders or their local agents.
- Government officials who are responsible for overseeing or implementing public procurement, particularly in countries where public sector salaries are low, display unexplained or conspicuous wealth.
- Government officials are known in the local community for demanding or accepting bribes.

- Underdelivery or poor performance of a public contract by a favored contractor is followed by recurrent contract awards to the same contractor.
- Former government officials act as suppliers to a public sector institution on projects for which they were previously responsible or as local agents of a foreign company bidding on contracts awarded by that institution or project.
- Close personal relationships, including family ties, exist between suppliers or local agents and government officials with authority over public procurement.

Scheme 2: Bid Rigging

Bid rigging occurs when a competitive public tender, which has as its purpose open and fair competition between all interested bidders, is manipulated in such a way that a preselected bidder wins the tender.[10] In some cases, this manipulation takes place among some or all of the bidders participating in the tender without the knowledge of the public officials responsible for conducting the tender. In other cases, public officials actively participate in the manipulation, sometimes with the willing collaboration of some or all of the bidders or, at other times, by coercing some or all of the bidders to participate in the bid-rigging scheme.[11]

Bid rigging can take subtle forms.[12] For example, specific requirements can be written into certain sections of the bidding documents, such as the technical specifications or the qualification requirements, so that only a particular product will meet the specification and competitors offering other products will be rejected. Or the contract may be drawn up so that only one particular bidder will qualify and all others will be rejected as being unqualified. For example, Transparency International (2006b) reported that the bidding document for a contract for printing an educational book stipulated the use of a specialized paper; an investigation found that specialized paper was not needed and that only one bidder—the favored bidder—had access to that paper.

Alternatively, a favored bidder may be given inside information, not made available to all other bidders, which enables the favored bidder to enter the lowest-priced bid. In another variation, the public officials responsible for conducting the public tender may give the favored bidder access to the bidding documents before they are formally disseminated, so that the favored bidder has more time than other bidders to prepare his bid. Following are brief descriptions of five common bid-rigging schemes identified by enforcement officials engaged in investigating fraud and corruption in public procurement.

Bid Suppression

One or more competitors agrees not to bid or is coerced by another bidder or, in some cases, by a public official into not bidding or withdrawing a previously submitted bid, so that a designated bidder will win. In return, the nonbidder may receive a subcontract to the winning bidder or a payoff for not bidding.

Complementary Bidding

Coconspirators submit token bids that are intentionally high or that deliberately fail to meet all of the requirements of the tender in order to allow a favored bidder to win.

Typically, these "losing bidders" are compensated by the winning bidder; they may, for example, be given a small share of the "premium" on the contract, which is made possible by the collusion. Complementary bids are designed to give the appearance of real competition in a public tender.

Bid Rotation

Coconspirators submit bids, but by agreement they take turns being the low bidder on a series of related contracts. In a recent series of tenders for civil works to rehabilitate rural roads in four remote provinces of a small Asian country, it was found that a group of four local contractors had prearranged to rotate the contract awards among them. Given the rural location of the work, the four companies were well known to each other, and because of the remote location and the small value of the contracts, contractors from other provinces were not interested in competing for the contracts. These circumstances facilitated the rotation of the bids among the conspirator firms.

Customer or Market Allocation

Coconspirators agree to divide up customers or geographical areas. The result is that the coconspirators do not bid against each other or submit only complementary bids when a solicitation for bids is made by a customer or in an area not assigned to them. This scheme is most commonly found in the service sector and may involve quoted prices for services as opposed to bids (USDOJ n.d.).

Lowballing

In this case, the designated company submits the lowest bid with the understanding of the public official responsible for awarding the contract that, once awarded, the contract will subsequently be amended and the contract price increased to enable the winning bidder to complete the work and to inflate his profit margin, part of which may be shared with the public official. A corollary but related feature is the abuse of the "change orders" process. In such instances, the favored bidder "lowballs" his bid with the understanding or expectation that he can eventually make up for the low bid by submitting change orders to the contract that are then approved by the involved public official. The change orders materially change the contract price. In a recent construction project, a contractor was able to increase the price of its contract by submitting change orders alleging that a site inspection conducted after the contractor started work revealed unexpected conditions not foreseen in the specification contained in the bidding documents. The acquisition officials approved the change order in exchange for a facilitation payment.

Red Flags in Bid Rigging

Following are some common indicators of bid rigging identified by leading enforcement officials:

- Identical bids are submitted by different bidders either for individual line items in the bids or for the total bid.
- All bids submitted are substantially higher than the procuring entity's cost estimate of the contract or than comparable bids submitted by the same bidders for similar work or in other areas.

- A winning bidder subcontracts performance of part of the contracted works to one or more losing bidders with or without the client's knowledge.
- There is indication of a physical alteration of one or more bids, particularly at the last minute or after submission.
- The prices quoted by some bidders for particular line items are substantially higher than the prices quoted by other bidders for the same items and bear no relation to cost. (This is a common technique for hiding excessive profits within a winning bid, which is subsequently used to pay bribes to the awarding public official.)
- The range of bid prices shows a wide gap between the winner and all other bidders, which may indicate that all but the winning bidder were instructed to price their bids above a certain predetermined price.
- The bid prices of all bidders vary from one another by the same increment, such as the winning bid price plus 1 percent or the winning price plus 2 percent.
- A bidder submits different bid prices for the same line item on different contracts that are tendered close together in time.
- There is physical evidence of collusion in the bids submitted, such as different bidders submitting bids with the same handwriting or in the same type of envelope, or containing the same mathematical or spelling errors, or with the same contact information, such as telephone or fax numbers.
- Qualified bidders do not bid, especially if they initially took steps to bid, such as applying to prequalify (this may be a sign that they have been coerced by the procuring entity or another bidder not to bid).
- When a contract is rebid—for example, because all the bids submitted in the original tender were unacceptable—the new bids result in the same ranking order of the bidders or some bidders fail to submit new bids.
- In rebids, most bidders make significant increases in the prices of certain items over their initial bids even though there has been no commensurate increase in the cost of those items.
- Prices mysteriously drop when a new bidder begins participating in public tenders; this may indicate that bidders were colluding among themselves to keep prices artificially high in the absence of competition from a bidder who had not been part of the collusion scheme (USDOJ n.d.).[13]

It should be noted that bid rigging is not unique to developing economies but a vulnerability of all procurement systems. For example, in a case in New York, 11 public school officials were arrested for receiving kickbacks and arranging bid rigging on maintenance contracts for public schools. The officials would fake competition by requiring the selected bidder to provide phony bids from other potential bidders in order to meet bidding rules requiring the submission of at least three competitive bids for the tender to be considered valid. The kickbacks received by the public officials amounted to 10 percent of the contract price (New York State, Office of Attorney General Eliot Spitzer 2001).

Scheme 3: Use of Front or Shell Companies

Corrupt public officials commonly use front or shell companies, generally in conjunction with other schemes, such as kickbacks, to disguise their illegal influence over contract awards for which they are formally responsible (see figure 9.1). Using

FIGURE 9.1 Common Kickback Scheme

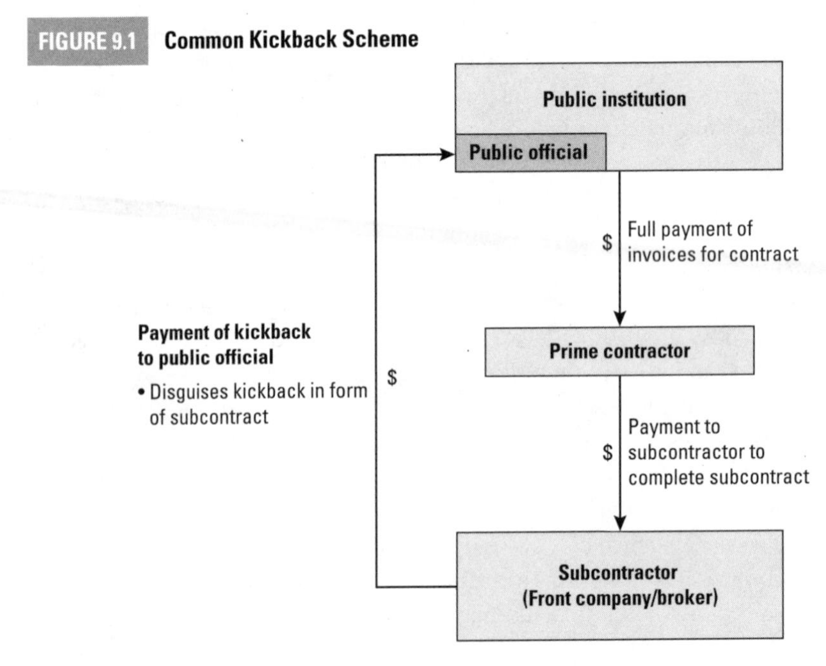

Source: Authors.

a front company enables a corrupt public official to rig the tender and, commonly, to exert coercive influence over other, genuine bidders, to ensure that his front company wins the contract and he enjoys the resulting illegal gain. Frequently, the official has no intention of having the front company actually implement the contract. A typical trick is to supply old, used, or refurbished equipment to the public procuring entity under the contract, and in some cases, the goods or services may not be delivered at all.

Alternatively, a front company may appear as a subcontractor to a prime contractor and actually function as a broker or intermediary between the prime contractor and the corrupt public official. In this way, the subcontract disguises the kickback paid by the prime contractor to the public official, while no real performance is rendered under the subcontract. While the prime contractor may be coerced into agreeing to participate in such a scheme, it is often the case that the corrupt public official who demands the bribe may also have control over the payment of the prime contractor's invoices; the public official provides a benefit to the prime contractor by ensuring that its invoices are paid promptly and in full, without dispute, thus enabling the prime contractor to funnel the bribe through the subcontract back to the public official.

Money can be easily disguised in subcontractor shell company arrangements that provide a mechanism for laundering money or moving it offshore. In a case investigated by one of the authors, a West African company was acting as an intermediary for a West African public official. To disguise and launder the kickback, the intermediary acted as a subcontractor to the bribe-paying prime contractor, a prominent European company. The subcontractor invoiced the prime contractor for "technical data" amounting to 30 percent of the contract value. The subcontractor was later discovered to be passing money to public procurement officials. The prime contractor paid the invoice but did not receive any "technical data" in return for the payment. When questioned why they paid, executives of the European company replied that "this is the way business is done here" and shrugged off further questions by investigators.

Front companies can be stacked up in layers, making detection of the ultimate beneficiary extremely difficult. Detection is even more difficult when the front company or companies are created in so-called "secrecy jurisdictions" that may cloak company ownership with privacy rules.[14] A recent report by the U.S. Government Accountability Office (GAO 2006, pp. 30–31) noted the significance of shell companies in facilitating criminal activity: "Law enforcement officials and other reports indicate that shell companies have become popular tools for facilitating criminal activity, particularly money laundering."

Perhaps the starkest example of the pervasive use of front companies is the well-publicized UN "oil for food" investigation conducted by the Volcker Committee (2005a). High-ranking Iraqi officials under Saddam Hussein created scores of front companies to steal funds for the regime's own use instead of spending the funds on much-needed humanitarian services, as intended. The front companies were using the funds to procure weapons, fund the Intelligence Service, and otherwise support the regime of Saddam Hussein (U.S. Department of the Treasury 2004).

In many developing countries, legitimate companies owned by prominent families, some of whose members may include government officials, are awarded contracts to provide legitimate services to the government. Often, the ownership of these companies is general public knowledge and the award of contracts is not necessarily done in secret.[15] But because of their high-level connections, these enterprises have the power to divert public resources to projects that may not actually be in the public interest.[16] In a case investigated by one of the authors, the director of an urban transport project had awarded several contracts to a consulting company of which he was the listed principal owner. Even more startling, no attempt had been made to hide the ownership of the consulting company and no government overseers of the project had ever checked to ensure that contracts were not let in this fashion (Transparency International 2006b).

Following are some of the red flags that indicate the existence of shell or front companies:

- Previously unknown companies, with no track record of implementing government contracts, serve as subcontractors to foreign or local prime contractors on a project.
- A subcontractor company is registered in a secrecy jurisdiction.
- Payments are made against invoices to accounts held by companies registered in a secrecy jurisdiction.
- The subcontractor company has an opaque ownership structure.
- The owners of the subcontractor company are listed as law firms or as incorporation agents, rather than as named individuals; this form of listing may be used to hide the identity of the individuals who benefit financially from the company's business operations.

- The subcontractor company lacks visible corporate facilities, such as a headquarters building.
- The phone number provided by the subcontractor company is a personal residence or an answering service.
- Companies winning sizable or recurrent government contracts have opaque ownership structures.
- Family members of senior government officials hold ownership or management roles in companies that win government contracts.
- Recurrent appearances of government officials at company headquarters.

Other Schemes

Although kickback schemes are the primary vehicles through which corruption is perpetrated in public procurement, there are other schemes that do not involve kickbacks but nevertheless result in the manipulation of public procurement for private gain. (Still other corruption schemes only indirectly linked to procurement involve fraudulent use of public funds; see annex 9B.)

Misrepresentation of Facts

Public officials may subvert public procurement procedures and steal money from the government simply by misrepresenting facts. Public officials may collude with a favored bidder to enable that bidder to win a contract resulting from a public tender that it would not have won had the rules of the tender been correctly applied.

In a recent public tender in an Asian country, the chairman of a bid evaluation committee in a government ministry colluded with a corrupt bidder to steal $56,000 in public funds in the award of a public contract for the supply of equipment in two lots, by allowing the bidder to withdraw the bid that it had originally submitted by the bid submission deadline and to replace it with a high-priced bid, to which the contract was then awarded.

Table 9.1 shows how the scheme worked. Bidder A is corrupt. The price of the original bid that bidder A submitted by the bid submission deadline for lot 2 was $91,168. The bid evaluation committee found that the bid submitted by bidder B for that lot was technically nonresponsive, because the equipment offered by bidder B failed to meet the technical specifications in the bidding documents. As a result, B's bid for lot 2 was correctly rejected. This created a price difference of $57,372 between bidder A's bid price for lot 2 and the price of the next-ranked bid, submitted by bidder C ($148,540 less $91,168). The chairman of the bid evaluation committee spotted the opportunity presented by this situation, approached bidder A, and arranged to allow A to withdraw his original bid and submit a new, fraudulent bid, priced at $147,168, a few days after the bid submission deadline. The report on the bid evaluation process, which was submitted to the government for its approval, made no mention of bidder A's first bid but recorded only his second, higher bid. The corrupt public official attempted to conceal his fraud by failing to keep written records of the bid-opening meeting, at which the bidders' prices were read out, including bidder A's initial bid.

TABLE 9.1 Discretion and Corruption in Bid Rigging

Prices of bids as originally submitted

	Bid price				
Bidder	*Lot 1*	*Lot 2*	*Total*	*Bid security amount*	*% of bid price secured*
Bidder A	$81,176	$91,168	$172,344	$3,446.88	2.00
Bidder B	$100,105	$112,056	$212,161	$4,300.00	2.03
Bidder C	—	$148,540	$148,540	$3,000.00	2.02
Bidder D	$58,120	$163,907	$ 222,027	$4,441.00	2.00

Bid evaluation report as submitted for government approval

	Bid price				
Bidder	*Lot 1*	*Lot 2*	*Total*	*Bid security amount*	*% of bid price secured*
Bidder B	$100,105	$112,056	$212,161	$4,300.00	2.03
Bidder A	$81,176	$147,168	$228,344	$3,446.88	1.51
Bidder C	—	$148,540	$148,540	$3,000.00	2.02
Bidder D	$58,120	$163,907	$222,027	$4,441.00	2.00

Amount of public funds stolen: $56,000.

Source: Authors' construction based on classified information and documents.

In this case, there was a telling red flag, which the government failed to spot. The bidding documents required each bid to be accompanied by a bid security equal to 2 percent of the total bid price for the two lots. The total price of A's original bids was $172,344, and the bid correctly contained a bid security in the amount of $3,446.88. The amount of the bid security was correctly recorded in the bid evaluation report, which was prepared by the bid evaluation committee and reviewed and cleared by the government. However, bidder A's second bid price for lot 2 made his total bid price $228,344, which would have required a bid security of $4,566.88 (2 percent of $228,344). Unfortunately, the government's reviewing authority failed to spot this discrepancy in the bid evaluation report and approved the award of contract, thereby allowing the corrupt public official and bidder A to complete their fraud. It was only later, when one of the other bidders complained, that the government authorities detected the fraud.

Following are some red flags that may indicate deliberate misrepresentation of facts:

- The procuring entity fails to keep written minutes of the public bid-opening meeting.
- The minutes of the public bid-opening meeting are not signed in their original form by all the members of the bid-opening committee or by the representatives of the bidders who attended the bid opening.
- There is a time delay between the public bid opening and the dissemination of the minutes of the bid opening to all the bidders.

- The procuring entity fails to keep adequate written records of the procurement process, such as a written report on the bid evaluation process, minutes of the bid-opening meeting, copies of the bids submitted, or copies of correspondence with the bidders.
- The bids submitted contain written corrections, deletions, or interlineations that alter key information contained in the bid, such as prices or the bid validity period (it may be impossible to tell whether such revisions to a bid were made before or after the bid was submitted).

CORRUPTION VULNERABILITIES IN THE PROCUREMENT SYSTEM

Procurement-related corruption is perpetrated in a variety of ways, as the previous section showed, and very often corruption schemes are interrelated and used in a complementary manner that reinforces the effectiveness of each scheme and makes them more difficult to combat. A well-designed and well-regulated system can reduce the risk of corruption, but no public procurement system is totally corruption-proof. Like a computer software program, the system may contain structural holes, gaps, or weaknesses that allow corruption to seep into the procurement process.[17] A procurement system has numerous portals or entry points, each having a "responsive control adjustment" that seeks to secure it from attack, much like a patch on a software program that ostensibly closes a particular entry point to a hacker.[18] The loopholes may be unintentional or, in their worst form, deliberately designed by corrupt officials to create vulnerabilities for later exploitation.

To minimize the risk of corruption, government officials should examine their procurement system for potential vulnerabilities. To this end, an overview of the system is instructive. This section presents the four phases of the procurement process and identifies the possible vulnerabilities associated with each phase. Identifying these vulnerabilities permits the formulation of remedial measures and control mechanisms that strengthen the procurement system and reduce the risk of corruption.[19] Indicators of corruption risks, corresponding to the vulnerabilities, are also presented. These indicators have been drawn from the World Bank's extensive experience in preventing, detecting, combating, and investigating corruption in its projects. The Bank has conducted numerous such investigations and from this experience has identified "yellow flags," or early warning signals, to watch for throughout a project's cycle.[20] Many of these flags have appeared in several investigations regardless of country or sector.

The four phases of procurement are typically project identification and design; advertising, prequalification, bid document preparation, and submission of bids; bid evaluation, postqualification, and award of contract; and contract performance, administration, and supervision.

Project Identification and Design

This phase includes the selection of projects as well as the identification of funding sources for the project. The preliminary phase is critical in setting the tone for the subsequent phases. In several countries, projects face the challenge of political influence. For example, the selection of roads projects is often heavily influenced by politicians, who use their approval authority over the annual agency budgets to pressure the procuring entity—typically the ministry of public works or ministry of transport—to insert their favored projects into the ministry budget proposal. Road projects are thus identified and selected less on the basis of the public's transportation needs and more on the basis of political expediency: the projects serve as a source of campaign financing. This distortion at the outset of a project may set up a dynamic that leads to bid rigging or collusion in later phases (see chapter 5 in this volume). Budgetary insertions guarantee that there will be funding for the project; bid rigging or collusion guarantees that the expected diversion of funds to political and other unintended uses is realized.

The following indicators are yellow flags that merit further investigation before proceeding to the next phase:

- The project approval process lacks clear, objective criteria for selecting projects.
- In the case of physical works, selected locations are not based on a demonstrated public need, or the component parts of the project are too numerous and small to take advantage of potential economies of scale.
- The government does not have sufficient capacity to monitor decentralized units responsible for conducting the procurement.
- The procurement plan relies too heavily on local competitive bidding, so contracts are not tendered internationally.
- No affirmative anticorruption control plan is built into the project design.
- Cost estimates are inconsistent with market rates.
- Least-cost solutions have not been considered.

Advertising, Prequalification, Bidding Document Preparation, and Submission of Bids

This second procurement phase begins once a project has been identified and the responsible public institution decides that a public procurement contract is necessary to achieve the desired outcome. Multiple yellow flags exist at this phase.

Advertising

The widespread public advertisement of an invitation to bid for public contracts is an essential element of transparency. Not only should the invitation be widely publicized, it should be disseminated sufficiently ahead of the bid submission deadline to give potential bidders adequate time to obtain the bidding documents and prepare and submit their bids. Widespread public advertising is essential to maximize competition and therefore to undermine would-be cartels or other bid-rigging schemes, as the colluding bidders have no way of telling which other bidders intend to bid. The participation of bidders from outside the collusive scheme is key to disrupting the scheme's operation, which is why colluding bidders often try to limit the public advertisement of invitations to bid or to ensure that tenders are not advertised at all.

Here are some of the more common yellow flags regarding advertising of bids:

- An invitation to bid on a public contract awarded by competitive tendering is not advertised.
- An invitation to bid is advertised but only on a restricted basis; for example, a provincial government tender is advertised only within that province and not throughout the country.
- An invitation to bid on a high-value contract, which is likely to be of interest to foreign bidders, is advertised only in the procuring country's local or national press, not internationally.
- An invitation to bid is advertised in only one newspaper and, even then, in only one edition, the number of copies of which is limited and sell out rapidly.
- The advertisement does not include all the information that a potential bidder needs in order to decide whether to bid; it may not give the name and address of the official or organization from which the bidding documents may be obtained or state the deadline for bid submission.
- The advertisement contains all the required information, but the tender is conducted in a manner that is inconsistent with the published information; for example, the location of the office where bids are required to be submitted is changed at the last minute and not all bidders are notified of the change.
- An invitation to bid is published only three or four days before bids must be submitted or other qualifying steps taken.
- An invitation to bid is advertised on the procuring entity's Web site, but access to the site is controlled by a password requirement or is otherwise restricted.

Prequalification

For high-value or technically complex public contracts, it is common for the procuring entity to prequalify bidders to ensure that only those that have the necessary experience, capability, and resources to perform the contract successfully are allowed to bid. Bidders must meet certain contract-specific qualification requirements to be prequalified. This stage is designed to screen out frivolous, unreliable, or unqualified firms. However, it may also be used as a device to favor a small subset of bidders or to screen out other qualified bidders. Following are yellow flags applicable to this stage:

- The invitation to prequalify is insufficiently advertised (see advertising yellow flags, above).
- Inadequate time is given for preparing and submitting prequalification applications.
- Prequalification requirements are stated in vague terms or are unrelated to the contract to be awarded. For example, for a construction contract estimated to cost $10 million, to be constructed over a period of two years, applicants are required to have access to $15 million in cash, whereas a much lower level of cash flow would be adequate to perform the contract satisfactorily.
- Prequalification documents require applicants to submit voluminous administrative documentation in multiple copies, and the absence of a single document results in the rejection of a firm's application.

- Applicants are required to be preregistered, on a government-approved register, before being allowed to apply to prequalify.
- The prequalification requirements are deliberately exclusive. The prequalification documents for the construction of a dam in an Asian country, for example, required applicants to have built two dams of similar size in the past five years, but no dam had been built in the country in more than a decade.
- The method for evaluating applicants' qualifications is not stated in the prequalification documents, or it is subjective, such as being based on an arbitrary merit points system.
- Bidders are prequalified for certain contracts but subsequently fail to bid for all contracts for which they have been prequalified (box 9.1).

Preparation of Bidding Documents

The bidding documents for a particular contract perform several essential functions, including defining the rules bidders should follow when preparing and submitting their bids; defining the technical requirements of the procurement, including the technical specifications of the goods to be procured; and defining the criteria that will be used to evaluate the bids and select the winning bidder. Bidding documents are usually composed of standard sections, such as instructions to bidders and general conditions of contract, and contract-specific sections, which vary according to the contract being tendered. In the absence of appropriate checks and balances, bidding documents may be manipulated to favor a few bidders or a single bidder or manufacturer. The following are yellow flags in bidding documents:

- Contracts for similar or related goods or works are not packaged together into a single bidding document but are split into several separate tenders. Splitting contracts may indicate a desire to discourage foreign bidders or large companies, thus allowing small, often local, companies to minimize competition or to rig the tenders among themselves.
- The fee charged to potential bidders to obtain the bidding documents is excessive in comparison with the value of the goods to be procured, for example, a fee of $5,000 for a bidding document to procure goods estimated to cost $200,000. Excessive bidding document fees may be intended to deter certain bidders, particularly small companies, from purchasing the bidding documents.
- The procuring entity issues bidding documents in a form other than the standard bidding documents approved for official use; this may enable the procuring entity to use arbitrary evaluation criteria or to avoid imposing standard contract conditions on favored bidders, thereby harming the public interest.
- Technical specifications in bidding documents contain brand names or are based on a single manufacturer's products, thus limiting competition to that manufacturer or its authorized distributors and discriminating against other manufacturers' products.
- Bidding documents do not provide clear instructions on how bidders should prepare their bids or structure their bid prices.
- Bidding documents fail to disclose the criteria that will be used to evaluate bids and how those criteria will be applied to identify the winning bid.

BOX 9.1 Prequalification: What Could Go Wrong?

A provincial government in an Asian country carried out prequalification of bidders for two contracts for the construction of urban roads. Contract 1 had an official cost estimate of $11,621,500, while contract 2 was estimated to cost $12,000,000. During prequalification, eight bidders applied to prequalify, and six of them, bidders A through F, were prequalified to bid for both contracts. When bids were submitted, it turned out that three of the prequalified bidders bid only on the first contract and the other three bid only on the second contract. The bid evaluation report indicated the following submitted bids and bid prices:

Contract 1

Bidder	Read-out price	Read-out discount	Final read-out price
Bidder A	$12,549,756	$0	$12,549,756
Bidder B	$12,401,759	$0	$12,401,759
Bidder C	$15,190,019	$3,568,528	$11,621,499

Contract 2

Bidder	Read-out price	Read-out discount	Final read-out price
Bidder D	$13,933,488	$0	$13,933,488
Bidder E	$13,795,146	$0	$13,795,146
Bidder F	$12,008,765	$0	$12,008,765

The procuring entity recommended that the first contract be awarded to the lowest evaluated bidder, bidder C, at a contract price of $11,621,499, which was $1 lower than the official cost estimate for the contract, and that the second contract be awarded to bidder F at a contract price of $12,008,765.

Yellow flags in this prequalification:

- While six firms were successfully prequalified to bid for both contracts, each applicant purchased the bidding documents for and bid for only one of the two contracts. This is a clear indicator that either the prequalified firms colluded to reduce competition for each contract or perhaps even to rig the tender and determine the winning bidder in advance, or that the procuring entity coerced each of the six prequalified firms into bidding for only one contract.
- The price discount offered by bidder C for contract 1 results in that bidder's bid moving from the highest-priced bid to the lowest-priced bid, which was just $1 lower than the official cost estimate. This is an indicator that the procuring entity had informed bidder C of the official cost estimate before it submitted its bid. It may also indicate that the three bidders for contract 1 colluded to arrange the award of contract to bidder C or that either the procuring entity or bidder C, or perhaps both of them, had coerced bidders A and B into allowing bidder C to win contract 1.
- The discount offered by bidder C for contract 1 is dubious and may be fraudulent. It is also possible that, if bidders A and B were not involved in collusion, this discount may not have been included in bidder C's bid when it was originally submitted nor read out at the public bid opening, but that the procuring entity allowed bidder C to introduce the discount after the submission and opening of bids, thereby changing the ranking of the bids, once the prices of the bids submitted by bidder A and bidder B were known.

Source: Authors' construction based on classified World Bank documents.

Submission of Bids

As discussed earlier, the bidding process itself may involve collusion among bidders with or without the participation of government officials; inside information may be sold so that a few select companies are able to cheat the process. Bidders in collusion may also agree among themselves that certain bids will be won by a designated company and that contracts are shared among members of the cartel (box 9.2). The following yellow flags may indicate this kind of collusion:

- One or more favored bidders are informed of the procuring entity's cost estimate for the contract, while other bidders are not.

BOX 9.2 Dirty Tricks at Public Bid Openings

The public opening of the bids submitted in response to a public tender, at which representatives of all bidders are entitled to attend to witness their bids being opened and the prices publicly read out, is an indispensable element of transparency in public procurement. Nevertheless, it is one of the phases of the procurement process that is most frequently targeted by corrupt public officials and bidders to try to undermine the integrity of the procurement process.

The example below involves a public opening of bids for the supply of computer equipment to a government department of a Central Asian country. the chairman of the bid opening committee had entered into a corrupt relationship with one of the bidders, bidder D.

Bidder	Bid prices as read out	Bid prices as written in bids
Bidder A	$2,450,650	$2,450,650
Bidder B	$2,226,730	$2,226,730
Bidder C	$2,725,000	$2,725,000
Bidder D	$2,190,525	$2,583,760

In the conduct of a public opening, bids are required to be opened in random order, and to facilitate this, bidders are required to submit their bids in unmarked envelopes, so that nobody attending the meeting can tell what envelope contains which bidder's bid. However, the chairman of the bid opening committee had prearranged for bidder D to submit his bid in an unmarked envelope as required, but to cut off a small section of the corner of the envelope so that his envelope could be identified before the envelopes were opened.

While conducting the public opening of the bids, the chairman made sure that he first read out the prices of bidders A, B, and C and left bidder D's bid until last, by which time the other three bidders' prices were known to him and to everyone else attending the meeting; they also had been written on a board on prominent display in the meeting room. When he opened bidder D's bid, he immediately saw that that it was priced higher than those of bidders A and B and that it would, therefore, be unlikely to win the contract award. So, instead of reading out bidder D's price as written in the bid ($2,583,760), the chairman read out a fictitious price of $2,190,525, which was lower than the prices of the other three bidders. The representatives of bidders A, B, and C did not notice anything wrong with the process, as neither they nor anyone else attending the meeting could see that the chairman had not read out the price of bidder D's bid as it was written in the bid. Bidder D's representative at the public bid opening, who was complicit in the fraud, noted down the new, fictitious price of his bid and, a few hours after the conclusion of the bid opening proceedings, was allowed by the chairman to alter his bid form to indicate the read-out price of $2,190,525 and to substitute his bid security with one that matched the lower bid price.

Source: Authors' construction based on classified World Bank documents.

- The procuring entity fails to provide clarification of the bidding documents, as sought by bidders, or circulates the clarification only to one or more favored bidders.
- There is an unusual time delay between the deadline for submission of bids and the public bid opening.
- The location for submission of bids or bid opening, or both, is switched at the last minute and not all bidders are informed of the switch.
- Certain bidders or groups of bidders are prevented from submitting their bids. For example, in a tender for a high-value provincial construction contract in a small country in southeastern Europe, a cartel of bidders from the province where the works were to be constructed placed armed gunmen outside the provincial government office where the bids were to be submitted to forcibly prevent bidders from outside the province from submitting their bids.
- Bids are submitted and accepted after the bid submission deadline.
- Bids are not opened in public.
- The procuring entity fails to keep accurate minutes of prebid meetings, including questions and answers, and to distribute them promptly to all bidders.
- Price discounts in one or more bids are not read out at the public bid opening, but are subsequently evaluated, altering the ranking of the bids.
- The procuring entity fails to provide secure storage of bids submitted before the deadline, leaving such bids at risk of being prematurely opened and information about their prices being shared with competitor bidders.

Bid Evaluation, Postqualification, and Award of Contract

The evaluation of bids is the most important phase of a public procurement procedure, as it is at this juncture that the procuring entity decides which bidder will be awarded the contract. The reliability, integrity, and transparency of this key step in the process depends mainly on how clearly the bid evaluation criteria were originally expressed in the bidding documents and whether those criteria are faithfully applied in the selection process.

Not all evaluation systems are created equal. Some types of evaluation systems give public officials excessive discretion in decision making and thus are particularly prone to exploitation by corrupt public officials and the bidders who influence them. Although price is the most widely used evaluation criterion in public procurement, other, nonprice criteria are also commonly applied. These may include the delivery time, payment schedule, costs of operating the equipment, efficiency, the compatibility of the equipment offered with equipment already owned and operated by the procuring entity, the availability of after-sales service and spare parts, training, safety, and environmental impact.

The extent to which these nonprice evaluation criteria are quantified and expressed in monetary terms in bid evaluation—as they must be, for instance, under the World Bank's Procurement Guidelines—often largely dictates the extent to which the evaluation process is prone to undue or corrupt influence. The most vulnerable evaluation systems are those that convert evaluation criteria, and sometimes, inexplicably, even price itself, into notional points, which are then awarded to each bid by one or more evaluators based on his or her own subjective assessment of the worth of the bid against each criterion. Under such evaluation systems, there is often no right or wrong answer in the decision-making process, as the winning bid is simply the one that receives the most points; in such a situation, the decision is wide open to corrupt influence, and it becomes all but impossible to hold the evaluators accountable for the correctness of their decision.

Another stage vulnerable to corruption in this phase of the procurement process is postqualification. In some countries, the prequalification process has been streamlined to foster greater competition. With an e-procurement system, this takes the form of an electronic supplier registry where firms interested in bidding on government contracts must electronically submit documents that are typically required during prequalification and that attest to their qualifications. The information is then stored in the registry and retrieved when a firm has bid on a contract. Once the winning bidder has been selected, its qualifications to perform the contract, including in particular those submitted to the supplier registry, are subjected to evaluation, that is, postqualification. If the bidder does not pass this postqualification, it is declared "disqualified," and the firm with the next best bid is selected for postqualification.

Depending on the postqualification criteria and decision-making arrangements, the most qualified and cost-effective bidder may be prevented from receiving the award. When the best bidder fails to win the award, price of delivery increases, quality decreases, and the destructive consequences of corruption take shape. Yellow flags in this phase are numerous; they are presented in box 9.3.

Contract Performance, Administration, and Supervision

This phase begins immediately after the contract is awarded, when the contractor or vendor is then "on the clock" and expected to make progress in fulfilling the terms and conditions of the contract. It includes the management of the contract by the procuring entity, in particular the monitoring of proper implementation. The monitoring procedures must be established in advance and should include complete documentation and accurate records to ensure that the money is being used as specified in the contract; default procedures should also be spelled out. Numerous vulnerabilities exist during the performance of the contract itself as well as in the oversight during the performance.

Weak accounting systems are a common problem in many developing countries, permitting financial irregularities to go undetected as well as illicit conduct to occur (such as "ghost names" of fictitious personnel listed on the payroll) (Werlin 2005, p. 521).

Monitoring the contract and work completed is important for controlling corruption. A contract that is not properly and frequently monitored leaves opportunity for individuals to siphon money without completing the necessary work or providing the quality of work expected. It is essential to conduct forensic spot checks to ensure the work is being completed in accordance with the contract. The spot checks should be conducted at random; if they are done in a predictable and routine manner, opportunity still exists for the contractor to disguise illegal activity. Yellow flags for this phase are presented in box 9.4.

BOX 9.3 Monitoring Bid Evaluation: Early Warning Indicators

- Unreasonable delays occur in evaluating the bids and selecting the winner.
- The evaluators use evaluation criteria other than those specified in the bidding documents.
- The evaluators use the same criteria as specified in the bidding documents but apply them in a manner other than stipulated in the bidding documents.
- Bid evaluation committee members do not have the technical expertise necessary to evaluate bids correctly.
- The bidding process is controlled by a small number of persons in the procuring entity.
- A high-level public official or politician, senior to the members of the evaluation committee, intervenes in the process and the ranking of bids changes as a result.
- Two or more versions of the bid evaluation report are circulating within the bid evaluation committee, each recommending award of contract to a different bidder, and factors within the evaluation committee are lobbying for their version to prevail.
- Qualified bidders drop out voluntarily as the bidding process progresses so that only one firm is left at the postqualification stage.
- High numbers of complaints about bid process and evaluation are received from losing bidders, especially when lower-priced bids are declared nonresponsive.
- Complaints received from bidders during evaluation include a high degree of specificity about the evaluation process, including details of other bidders' bids, indicating that members of the evaluation committee are feeding confidential information to their preferred bidder.
- The same bidder repeatedly wins similar types of contracts.
- The prices of all but one of the bids submitted are close to each other and significantly above the purchaser's cost estimate, while the remaining bid is significantly lower in price than all the others and close to the cost estimate.
- Similarities occur between competing bids (such as format of bid; type face; identical unit prices; identical spelling, grammatical, and arithmetic errors; photocopied documents).
- Bid securities are acquired by competing bidders from the same financial institution.
- Bid securities submitted by several bidders bear the same date of issue or sequential serial numbers or both.
- A bidder lists multiple addresses.
- Unit prices in competing bids vary inconsistently by amounts greater than 100 percent.
- Unit prices in competing bids are identical.
- Bidders propose identical items, such as the same make and model (may indicate the specification was based on a single product).
- Competing bidders have common ownership.
- The bid evaluation report is revised or reissued.
- An arithmetic check of the bid(s) is not performed or results in a bidder being favored inappropriately.
- An evaluated bidder should have been disqualified based on the information submitted in its bid.
- The lowest bidder is disqualified, and the explanation provided, if any, is weak.
- Clarification of the bid is used to disguise financial negotiations with the winning bidder.
- Vested interests are identified among members of bid evaluation committee.
- Curricula vitae in consultant services proposals are falsified.
- Delays in negotiating and executing the contract are unreasonably long.
- Contract is not in conformity with specifications in bid documents.
- Contractor's name differs between contract and bid evaluation report.
- Contract amount is different than amount in bid evaluation report.
- Contract includes allowances for variations that are not part of the bidding documents.
- Subcontracting requirements are imposed.
- There is a rigorous system for handling contract variations, and evaluating claims are not defined in the contract.
- Staff involved in contract award decisions become involved in contract supervision (award and supervision are with the same procuring entity).

Source: Authors' construction based on classified World Bank documents

BOX 9.4 Tracking Contract Administration: Yellow Flags

- Contract specifications or scope of work are altered after contract is awarded.
- Site inspection indicates that work performed was not in accordance with the technical specifications (below-specification civil works, goods, and services are accepted).
- Site inspection indicates that project completion is less than that certified or that a completed project is not operational.
- Goods or services are not being used, or are being used for purposes inconsistent with intended purposes.
- Wrong quantities of goods and materials are delivered.
- Delays in the delivery of goods or services occur in any part of the contract implementation process.
- Substitution of nominated consultant staff with less qualified and inexperienced personnel.
- Key staff of project management office/project implementation unit (PMO/PIU) frequently changes.
- PMO/PIU responsible for postprocurement verifications changes.
- Oversight of the physical works is low or nonexistent.
- Verification of scope of work and physical inspections is absent or insufficient.
- Site diaries and meeting minutes are not maintained.
- Written instructions are not given to contractors; instructions given to contractors, particularly to alter the contract, are given orally and not recorded in writing.
- Incomplete records in PMO/PIU; the number of missing documents is significant.
- Change orders are made to the contract with high frequency.
- "As-built" drawings are photocopies of technical specifications in the bidding documents.
- The detailed drawings, "as-built" drawings, and backup data sheets contain errors or repetitive entries.
- Progress payments and invoices are not paid on a timely basis.
- Excessive numbers of signatures are required to approve progress payments.
- Evaluations of contractors' performance are not recorded.
- Cost overruns are inadequately explained or justified.
- Customer or client is dissatisfied with completed facilities.

Source: Authors' construction based on classified World Bank documents.

Broader Governance Concerns

Three critical, overarching factors that underpin the procurement system may engender or heighten possible risks of corruption throughout the procurement chain: budget management, personnel management, and staff capacity. Chapter 8 deals with budget management. The second and third factors are discussed in several of the sector chapters but are worth highlighting in the context of procurement.

In many developing countries, civil service reform has proved to be a major challenge, and the results of donor assistance for such efforts have not been very encouraging (Nunberg 1997; Manning and Parison 2004). Recruitment, promotion, and assignments are typically not well defined, and even if there are clear rules guiding personnel matters, they tend to be overridden by political concerns. Promotions are rarely based on performance. Such conditions provide fertile ground for patronage and nepotism to emerge. Over time, an informal market for civil service jobs can be created where the "price" of a position is derived from the potential corruption returns that it can generate for the person holding the position. In the area of procurement, this could imply the "purchase" of positions for district engineers, internal auditors, external auditors, and others that would allow them to participate in corrupt deals (Trepte 2005).

To target corruption specifically within the procurement system, introducing reform for the entire civil service may be the necessary starting point. A well-functioning procurement system, with lower incentives for corruption, is typically achieved through methods that foster accountability, establish true market conditions within the civil service system that allow governments to develop competitive and skilled employers, and inculcate a code of ethics that promotes the value of public goods more than private interests (Odhiambo and Kamau 2003). Such a system also pays appropriate compensation to maintain capacity (OECD 2005, p. 12) and establishes public independence for public procurement officials to alleviate pressure from high-ranking political officials so they can make balanced decisions based on merit and the proper application of procurement regulations.

Staff capacity is another issue that requires attention but often is ignored in the context of anticorruption. Where staff lack training and experience in procurement, auditing, accounting, and reporting, the procurement process will be inefficient and possibly confusing (and thus opaque). This too creates pressure for corruption; one example is contractors who pay bribes to get the agency to release payments. Increasing both initial and on-the-job training on procurement rules and mechanisms for both public personnel and the private sector engaged in procurement is extremely important to sustaining a well-functioning procurement system. Policy officials should be required to review programs continually and undergo and provide training when the need arises (Burton 2005, p. 28). Training should include techniques for identifying suspicious patterns of corrupt procurement practices (Sacerdoti 2005). With adequate training and well-defined objectives, both efficiency and accountability are enhanced.

TOOLS AND REMEDIES

Tackling corruption in procurement requires a multifaceted approach that extends beyond controls and attacks the problem from many different angles. This section explores several promising measures that can help reduce corruption in public procurement. These measures can be classified broadly into two categories, supply-side interventions and demand-side mechanisms; each typically addresses problems of monitoring, reporting, and enforcement. Supply-side interventions are measures that governments can adopt to improve internal processes; demand-side mechanisms are designed to complement and strengthen these interventions.

Supply-Side Interventions

Four interventions that have shown substantial potential for reducing corruption are e-procurement, forensic audits, selective sanctioning, and voluntary disclosure programs.

E-Procurement

Perhaps one of the most promising recent innovations in the area of public procurement is the use of information and communication technologies (ICTs). Given an appropriate and supportive legal and regulatory framework, adequate training of staff, and sufficient support from the political leadership, ICT solutions in the procurement field, so called e-procurement, can increase competition, enhance transparency, reduce administrative costs, improve government efficiency, and in the process help control corruption in public procurement.[21] For instance, the introduction of an electronic public tender board where all invitations to bid have to be posted greatly reduces the incidence of collusion. Field investigations of the World Bank into corruption in its projects suggest that, in some countries, firms have developed a round-robin system in which each takes turns as the "winning bidder." But for collusion to work, the number of firms with express intent to bid on a contract needs to be restricted. The larger the number of firms, the smaller the side payments that the "winning bidder" can offer, and thus the less the incentive for the other potential bidders to buy in.

In one case that the authors were made aware of, firms and public works officials in a particular municipality connived with the regional newspaper to produce two editions of its daily for a period of two weeks, an early edition and the regular edition. The advertisement for municipal contracts was placed in the early edition, and the firms purchased all of these copies. Publication of the early edition met the legal requirement that an invitation to bid be placed in a newspaper with at least regional circulation for a period of two weeks, but no one other than the colluding firms was made aware of the contract. An electronic public tender board counteracts schemes of this sort and expands the potential number of bidders for any given contract, thus reducing the risk of corruption through collusion.

Several countries have adopted e-procurement systems primarily to cut down on costs and generate savings for the government. Their experience suggests that e-procurement can indeed lead to substantial savings and, by implication, reduce corruption. Box 9.5 summarizes the e-procurement experiences in Chile, Mexico, and the Republic of Korea.

Note, however, that ICT can improve performance and reduce corruption only if systemic weaknesses or problems are addressed adequately. First, laws and regulations governing procurement have to be simplified. Two of ICT's potential benefits are increased transparency and improved efficiency. If the laws and regulations are complex, these benefits may not be realized. Second, management systems have to be streamlined in ways that enhance transparency, accountability, and efficiency, and procurement staff need to have adequate training in operating them. Third, implementation rules and practices for procurement have to be standardized, that is, there must be standard bid documents, uniform rules for advertising, and so on. Fourth, procurement officials have to adopt more businesslike attitudes in managing the procurement process, such as efficiency in inventory management, fairness in contract management, and ethical practices. And fifth, adequate oversight mechanisms have to be put in place (World Bank forthcoming). E-procurement can be an effective tool for reducing corruption, but it must be complemented by these institutional reforms.

Forensic Audits

An appropriately structured e-procurement system can improve the monitoring and reporting capabilities of government and thus oversight of the procurement process.

BOX 9.5 Three Examples of the Potential Benefits of a Well-Functioning E-Procurement System

The Republic of Korea introduced e-procurement in the late 1990s primarily to enhance transparency and reduce human contact between government officials and private firms bidding on government contracts. Procurement regulations were streamlined, and a new information technology system was introduced as the anchor for these new regulations. Before this reform, both government and suppliers were engaged in time-consuming and convoluted processes. There was no consistency in supplier information across agencies, and many suppliers were involved in prearranged bidding practices. The new system has served as a focal point for more than 30 procurement-related external agencies to obtain information and gain access to over 420,000 standardized products, documents, and expedited payments. Online access has allowed suppliers to prequalify, in addition to being able to retrieve all the relevant information on the bidding process, including comparative assessments across agencies. The wide availability of relevant information and the increased number of participating bidders has most likely mitigated the risks of collusion and bid rigging. Specifically, e-procurement has led to a decrease in procurement staff and speedier conduct of disbursements/payments. In 2002,the system counted over 25,000 public agencies and 87,000 companies involved in conducting close to $20 billion worth of transactions. And the government has saved more $2.5 billion by using the more efficient system.

With an estimated 25 percent of the public budget directed toward procurement expenditures in the 1990s, the Mexican government felt compelled to address inefficiency and corruption in public procurement: high surcharges were incorporated by bidders to compensate for these costs. CompraNet, the Mexican e-procurement system, was born out of this recognition. Over 250 federal agencies and municipalities have conducted $25 billion worth of transactions through CompraNet. Administrative costs have decreased by 20 percent as a result of the reduction in both paperwork and previously required face-to-face interaction. And, because the invitations to bid, awards, and payments are published online, interested firms and the general public, particularly concerned civil society groups, can now easily view procurement records "on demand." This feature has increased transparency, competition, and accountability. For example, the so-called "Towelgate" scandal was discovered in online information on CompraNet's transactions that revealed large discrepancies in the value of towels purchased for the presidential palace.

Through the Public Procurement System Strategic Plan, the government of Chile streamlined its regulations on public procurement, establishing standard rules and an online national information system. Chile's Public Purchasing Law required that all public procurement services be conducted through this system. ChileCompra established an electronic, interactive marketplace for suppliers and buyers to initiate and complete their transactions in one central location, accessible to several government institutions. This led to the standardization of all documents relevant to public procurement process, which were made available on line, and to the creation of a registry for all participating bidding companies. In 2001, the public procurement market in Chile was valued at close to $7 billion a year, with 10 percent of the gross national product allocated to public procurement expenditures. The introduction of ChileCompra has allowed more users to participate in the public procurement process (thereby increasing competition), reduced the transaction time of a bid cycle, and led to a more cost-effective way of doing business for the government. The efficiency gains, coupled with the decrease in the cost of procurement advertisements, have contributed to savings of over $70 million annually for the government.

Sources: For information on Korea's e-procurement system, see http://siteresources.worldbank.org/INTPEAM/Resources/premnote90.pdf. Information on Mexico's system can be found at http://www.undp.org/surf-panama/egov/docs/programme_activities/bpractices/e-procurement_in_mexico-compranet.pdf. Information on Chile's system is available at http://www.chilecompra.cl.

Oversight also can be strengthened through the conduct of random forensic audits. Audits are a routine control in the public procurement process. However, most audits focus on process controls and do not sufficiently drill down to determine whether the funds are being used appropriately. Accordingly, routine audits should have forensic features built into their terms of reference. These forensic features drive auditors to "look behind the paper" and verify, for example, that invoices submitted by contractors are authentic, or that material noted on the invoices has been delivered or installed. Such verification might include site visits to determine if contractors actually exist or are shell enterprises. Random selection puts potential fraudsters on guard and reduces their expected gain (and thus their incentives to perpetrate corruption).

Selective Sanctioning: Leveraging Investigative and Enforcement Capacity

Reporting and auditing are critical to identifying corrupt transactions and to increasing the risk of detection. In turn, effective enforcement increases the risk of punishment.[22] Effective enforcement begins with independent investigators who have authority to look into present and future contracts. There must be a system in place that can competently receive a complaint, conduct an investigation, pursue a prosecution, provide for mechanisms for adjudication or convictions, and devise remedies.

Not all countries have the capacity to put such a system in place, however. Therefore it becomes all the more important for international financial institutions such as the World Bank, the Inter-American Development Bank, and the European Bank for Reconstruction and Development to create and maintain robust, independent, and credible investigative capacity. Because these institutions receive overwhelming numbers of complaints, heads of their investigative units can select cases for investigation and sanctioning that can then be leveraged to the maximum extent possible. By publicly exposing and sanctioning the wrongdoing of a range of firms—large, small, those that work in a single sector, and those that work in many sectors—these investigations can have an asymmetrical deterrent effect that encourages companies to take preventive action to reduce the likelihood of corruption in their operations.

Voluntary Disclosure Programs

To complement sanctions, international financial institutions can also set up voluntary disclosure programs, which allow contractors to report fraud and corruption in their operations.[23] Under such programs, a contractor that makes a complete, timely, and truthful disclosure would not be barred from bidding on future business contracts (Ware and Noone 2005).

Obtaining cooperation from parties involved in illicit behavior in exchange for immunity or reduced sanctions has won growing popularity because of the advantage given to law enforcement officials when an insider provides a detailed map of the proceedings. The practice of reducing sanctions in exchange for disclosure has increasingly been codified in many legal systems around the world. Among the countries providing some form of leniency for cooperating parties are Argentina, Brazil, France, Italy, Kosovo (Serbia), Pakistan, Poland, and the United States.[24] The United Nations Convention against Corruption (which has been signed by 140 members and ratified by more than 45 members) entered into force in December 2005, providing a powerful precedent by specifically encouraging states to consider implementing voluntary disclosure programs.[25]

Demand-Side Mechanisms

External Monitoring

In contrast to the use of investigators, which implies that a crime may have been committed, the use of monitors can closely scrutinize the procurement process from the beginning and thus help prevent the occurrence of corruption. Independent compliance monitors—governance experts retained by private sector companies or appointed by government regulators to monitor crucial control functions—are emerging as critical players serving oversight functions for controlling fraud and corruption.[26] The use of monitors in the procurement process has increased even in the United States. The U.S. Department of Defense and the Securities and Exchange Commission use monitors to observe the performance of contractors whose employees have engaged in wrongful or corrupt conduct in the past (Zucker 2004). In developing countries, innovative approaches suggest that the use of such monitors may be a promising avenue for restraining corruption despite weak enforcement.

In countries where corruption in public procurement is rife, civil society groups can be useful external allies in combating corruption. The appropriate civil society groups can be matched to the different phases of the procurement chain. For example, in a roads project, reputable associations of contractors or civil engineers, if any exist, might be asked to monitor the initial selection and design of the project as well as to review the project upon completion to ensure that it conformed to good construction practices, was cost effective, and otherwise met the specifications of the contract. Alternatively, if a local or regional university had an engineering school, engineering students might undertake the monitoring as part of a practicum program before graduation. For the steps of the bidding phase, as well as for payment, an appropriate monitor might be a nongovernmental organization (NGO) with a focus on anticorruption and some expertise in procurement, such as a local chapter of Transparency International. A religious organization might offer similar monitoring skills. These monitors could be given observer status on bids and awards committees.

Transparency International's integrity pact illustrates another avenue for engaging civil society in monitoring the procurement process. Introduced in the 1990s, the integrity pact is a formal agreement between the government procurement agency and the bidders, in which all participants pledge not to "pay, offer, demand or accept bribes, or collude with competitors to obtain a contract, or while carrying it out." A third-party monitor is engaged to oversee the proper implementation of the mutual agreement. In essence, the integrity pact was designed as a credible commitment device that could assure both bidders and the government that no one is "playing games" and the process is truly without bias.

The level of the pact's success is determined by the stage of the procurement process in which it is introduced. Ideally, the anticorruption commitment should be made at the planning stage and cover the design, construction, and installation or operation of assets in addition to the preselection of bidders, bidding, and contracting proper. An integrity pact that is in place at the beginning of a project and ends only when the project is complete ensures a strong and consistent monitoring presence throughout the entire process.

BOX 9.6 Using an Integrity Pact in Public Procurement of Garbage Collection Services in Argentina

In 2000, the municipality of Morón in Argentina included an integrity pact in its bidding process for garbage collection service, valued at $48 million. This specific pact was developed from recommendations and input from the 2000 International Workshop on Integrity Pacts in Bogotá, Colombia, and the latest pact used in Colombia. All four prequalified bidders signed the integrity pact, thereby committing themselves to the requirements set forth, which sought to eliminate the incentives for corruption in the procurement process. Transparency International's national chapter in Argentina, *Poder Cuidadono,* monitored compliance with the pact throughout the bid evaluation, award decision process, and implementation of the contract. Violations of the contract would lead to sanctions equal to 10 percent of the value of the contract, with the prospect of also being blacklisted for five years. A hearing to discuss the bidding document and terms of the contract brought more than 500 people together to provide an opportunity to modify or amend any of the documents. Following the hearing, the bidding documents were published on a Web site. In addition to eliminating the opportunities for corruption, the integrity pact also appeared to be cost effective: the awarded contract was valued at $32 million, well below the $48 million originally estimated.

Source: Transparency International (2002).

An integrity pact levels the playing field by assuring companies that their competitors are not participating in bribery. The government benefits not only because the pact fosters transparency and mitigates corruption but also because it results in a more cost-efficient procurement process that benefits the government financially and the country economically. Currently Transparency International's integrity pact is being used in at least 14 countries (Transparency International 2002). Successful cases in which the integrity pact was implemented in its entirety include Argentina and Colombia (for an example from Argentina, see box 9.6).

Reporting and Access to Information

The media and local and international NGOs play a critical role in monitoring and exposing corruption. Reporters and journalists should be educated on the public procurement process so that they can better understand where potential problems might lie as well as spot them when they appear. In this context, complementary national legislation should include a "freedom of information" act that allows the citizenry, watchdog groups, and the media access to the information they need to find out which firms are getting contracts under what terms and what the value of the contracts is.[27] The ability of published findings exposing corrupt actions of individuals and companies to reduce corrupt acts more generally cannot be underestimated (Zucker 2004).

NGOs also can play an important role in raising awareness of the dangers of corruption and the need to do something about it. In the Philippines, for example, Procurement Watch Inc. (PWI) was established to educate civil society organizations, the media, politicians, government officials, and the general public on the virtues of a well-functioning, noncorrupt procurement system and on the implications of a proposed overhaul of procurement legislation. Such a broad understanding of the benefits of the legislation was necessary to galvanize support for its passage (Campos and Syquia 2006). Once the law was passed, the PWI began conducting training workshops for NGOs interested in monitoring public procurement bidding in their respective regions, for media, and for small and medium enterprises interested in bidding on government contracts. PWI's experience suggests NGOs in other developing countries may need to undertake a similar role if public procurement reforms are to be enacted.

Information Sharing and Collective Action

Several international financial institutions have created investigative units designed to ferret out both internal and external fraud and corruption. However, these institutions do not share their information, nor do they engage in collective sanctioning. Two of the authors have suggested that the institutions cooperate in an information-sharing program that could be centered in a "transnational corruption information-sharing center" (Ware and Noone 2005). The center could process information that would be useful in business and loan decisions, investigations, and assistance with national law enforcement efforts. The shared information would also be useful in collective action that could be imposed on corrupt regimes, corporations, and individuals. Both activities would face considerable bureaucratic and political obstacles. Institutions may claim that the sanctioning action by another institution is politically motivated and fail to take collective action. Or one institution may be reluctant to rely on the investigative findings of other institutions out of concern for lack of integrity or thoroughness in the investigative process. These concerns might be overcome if information were widely shared among the institutions, and if each retained the right "to autonomously review the findings of other institutions and make independent determinations," Ware and Noone (2005, p. 42) write, adding that these collective actions could deter some of the greatest offenders in illicit procurement schemes.

Norms and Conventions: Addressing Cross-Border Corruption

The evolving international trends in minimizing corruption and fraud in the public procurement process include harmonization of norms, standards, practices, and vocabulary—all of which help foster greater transparency and predictability in the procurement process. Model procurement regulations and codes, such as those drawn up by the United Nations Commission on International Trade Law (UNCITRAL) and the American Bar Association, assist in the standardization of this field.[29] Another critical piece of this effort is the continued emergence of regional and international anticorruption conventions. Four such conventions claim scores of nations committed to fighting corruption: the Organization of American States Inter-American Convention Against Corruption, the Organisation for Economic Co-operation and Development (OECD) Convention on Combating Bribery of Foreign Officials in International Business Transactions, the Council of Europe's Criminal Law Convention on Corruption, and the recently ratified United Nations Convention against Corruption.[30] An added benefit of participation in multilateral conventions, as Sandholtz and Gray (2005) note, is that countries that are "more open to the international economy and participate more broadly in international organization (such as the IMF, OECD, UN and World Bank) tend to have lower levels of perceived corruption."

CONCLUSION: WHERE NEXT?

When environmental impact assessments were introduced in the 1980s, there were those who argued that the assessments would impair project progress, be too costly, and retard development. Today, however, environmental impact assessments are a fact of life in large public works projects.

The newest and most innovative idea in the field of fraud and corruption prevention is the Corruption Vulnerability Assessment (CVA). Like an environmental impact assessment, a CVA can be conducted before large development projects involving public procurement are begun. A CVA is an intelligence-driven assessment that can determine the likelihood of corruption occurring in a planned project. Before any funds are distributed, a CVA examines the environment in a particular country for corruption vulnerabilities that might put funds at risk. Completed assessments would give project designers and international financial institutions more information on which to base measures for ensuring that public money is used for its intended purposes. For example, if government officials or their families have widespread holdings in private companies, a mandatory financial disclosure program could be installed to ensure that officials do not steer contracts to their own business entities. If project monitors are active in a project, the results of the CVA can provide critical information for tailoring the monitoring protocol to specific circumstances.

Briefly, the CVA would contain the following elements:

- *Environmental and country risk assessment.* This tool would assess the country environment for its vulnerability to corrupt practices. Are bribes necessary to obtain contracts, licenses, and permits? If so, what are the methodologies and schemes most commonly employed? Are conflicts of interest between government officials and businesses common? What is the status of anticorruption programs at national, state, and local levels? Does the government have the capacity to detect and prosecute corruption at the highest level of government?
- *Systems and control review.* The systems and control review would assess the measures that are in place to prevent corruption from occurring within a given project. Are auditors trained to spot indicators of corruption? Are the government officials who manage the project required to make financial disclosure of their assets and outside ownership interests? Are appropriate hotlines established for reporting corruption by both government watchdogs and civil society? Are companies bidding on the project required to maintain corporate governance and compliance programs? Are investigative assets available to follow up on allegations of fraud and corruption?
- *Human factors.* This component would examine reputations, associations, activities, and ethics of individuals running the projects. Do they have undisclosed liabilities or questionable financial reporting? Have project officials been accused of corruption in the past, or do they have a reputation for obtaining bribes in their official capacity?

By obtaining comprehensive information—before funds are distributed—on the likelihood of corruption, the methods likely to be employed, and the actors likely to participate, advance control measures could be uniquely and specifically employed to ensure public funds are less susceptible to corruption.

Flowing from the CVA, project supervisors, fiduciary staff, and auditors and monitors should conduct routine *enhanced due diligence* throughout the project cycle. Enhanced due diligence would mean that project overseers would scan the environment throughout the project cycle based on the litany of yellow flags noted previously. To conduct enhanced due diligence, fiduciary staff need to be trained to be aware of corruption risks and able to spot early warning indicators throughout the project cycle. By having a control framework where all fiduciary staff are part of the anticorruption control, the risk of detection will increase the likelihood of reducing corruption.

Corruption in public procurement presents one of the most vexing social problems confronting governments. It weakens economies, creates entrenched cynicism among civil society, and in some cases, threatens the stability of the very governments that permit illegal schemes to continue unabated. To combat corruption, a clear and adequate legal and regulatory framework must be established. But that is hardly sufficient. Laws and regulations need to be enforced, and constant and consistent vigilance exercised in all corners of society.[31]

Corruption in public procurement manifests itself in recurring patterns of illicit behavior that present opportunities for intervention. This chapter has attempted to explore the common anatomy and vulnerabilities that occur in the public procurement process. By raising awareness of these vulnerabilities across disciplines, new approaches and methodologies for successful control interventions can be studied, implemented, and evaluated to find the most effective mechanisms for reducing corruption. We hope this chapter provides additional impetus to efforts to address one of the most serious obstacles to effective development throughout the world.

ANNEX 9A: THE SPECIAL CASE OF EMERGENCY PROCUREMENT: JUSTIFIABLE EXCEPTION OR AVENUE FOR CORRUPTION?

In times of emergency or in a postconflict environment, the need to speed funds to a region may be great, and an elaborate procurement system that can be mapped for vulnerabilities may therefore not be practicable in emergency procurements.[32] In an emergency, procurement funds must begin to flow quickly, but a system of checks must still be in place to ensure that it is spent appropriately. In natural or manmade disasters when the front-end controls are eased to speed distribution, continuous monitoring is essential and back-end enforcement becomes even more important.

After the devastating tsunami in the Indian Ocean in December 2004, there were many accusations of corruption on several different levels. Among the allegations: food diverted from victims to shopkeepers to be sold, or to officials' homes; military personnel taxing incoming aid trucks; and local officials taking a cut of employees' wages in exchange for referring them to employers for work (Batha 2005; Harvey 2005). In some locations, people registered themselves as victims in two or three different areas, in an attempt to receive compensation two or three times for what they had lost.[33] People take advantage of disasters much like computer hackers take advantage of an unprotected computer network.

One of the more serious cases of corruption in Aceh, Indonesia, resulted from shortcuts taken in the building of homeless shelters for tsunami victims. The shelters were long wooden barracks, and to save money on the structure, the contractor did not attach the wood to the concrete foundation. The concrete contained more sand (and less concrete) than is safe, and it was also too shallow. In short, the contractor stole money to enrich himself, or perhaps to pay off government officials, or both, while the victims were relegated to unsafe housing and were victimized again.[34]

In 2005, a group of experts, sponsored by multilateral development banks, went to Indonesia to study ways to reduce corruption in relief operations. This group identified a number of vulnerabilities to corruption associated with postdisaster situations, including:

- extreme urgency during the relief phase, with priority on saving lives
- logistical difficulties in delivering assistance to people in need
- massive inflows of funds from various providers, overwhelming recipient governments' ability to manage procurement and finance functions
- disruption of local administrative systems and control measures
- lack of coordination of responsibilities, with some donors insisting on managing funds and procurement themselves
- disruption of normal markets for goods and services
- special rules and incentives set by aid providers as a condition for receiving postdisaster assistance
- unfamiliarity of aid providers with local conditions.

Some suggestions for managing these increased risks of corruption include systematic and transparent needs assessment procedures; integration of affected people into assessment and decision-making processes; specific management systems to assess and sort all assistance offered and delivered, and to match this aid to assessed need; donor coordination to agree on common procurement approaches and guidelines; and channels for reporting suspicions of corruption (ADB/OECD/Transparency International 2005).

In the United States, thousands of people were displaced after Hurricane Katrina ripped across the Gulf Coast in late August 2005. In an effort to help as many people as possible, the American Red Cross quickly distributed cash to affected individuals and families who requested such assistance. Unfortunately, false claims were filed as part of an illicit scheme to steal relief money (CNN 2005). Thus, even in developed countries like the United States, a natural disaster provides tremendous opportunity for those with the incentive, opportunity, rationalization, and capability to be corrupt. But unlike less developed countries, the United States has tremendous back-end capacity to detect and prosecute fraudsters who take advantage of a slack control environment (Yen 2005). In developing countries, the lack of front-end prevention and control and back-end enforcement provides an unchecked breeding ground for corruption.

The experience of the tsunami in Asia and the hurricane in the United States clearly demonstrates that there is no working model yet in place that can prevent corruption from invading emergency relief.

ANNEX 9B: RELATED CORRUPTION SCHEMES

Two additional corruption schemes—embezzlement and misuse of public assets—are only indirectly related to procurement but are nonetheless problems that should be addressed.

Embezzlement occurs when government officials steal money from procurement projects. A variety of means can be used, some as straightforward as writing checks to themselves or their family members. The payments are typically made with fraudulent invoices or by having ghost employees on the payroll. At times, the siphoned funds are used to finance buildings and structures that are used not by the public but by government officials for their personal use.

Misuse of public assets occurs when government officials use official vehicles, planes, computers, credit cards, and facilities for their own gain or gain of their political party or personal interest group. These cases run from small misuse of office computer equipment to misuse of aircraft for private events and functions. In one case investigated by the authors, a government-owned jet was taken for personal use at a cost to taxpayers in the hundreds of thousands of dollars. The flight was mischaracterized as an "overland navigation training flight" in the aircraft logbook and on the official authorization government airlift request. In other cases, government officials may abuse their position of trust by structuring projects that favor their personal interests. For example, government managers of an urban transport project may ensure that roads are built or bus stops are placed in areas that favor businesses they own or that favor their families' interests.

In a number of development projects, investigators found misuse of project vehicles and theft of gasoline to be commonplace. While seemingly insignificant, the absence of a vehicle from a roads project may prevent governmental inspectors from traveling to a site to inspect the progress of the road construction. This resultant lack of oversight creates further vulnerabilities in the control architecture and permits more theft.

Red flags signaling possible misuse of public assets include:

- official vehicles being used for personal errands
- using government assets and personnel (such as computers, support staff) for personal matters
- unjustifiably high dining, lodging, and personal expenses while on government business
- appearance of governmental assets at personal residences
- paid overtime used for personal errands
- known reputation for abuse of assets
- appointment of friends, relatives, and even spouses to government positions
- unjustified consulting studies.

ENDNOTES

1. Public procurement usually accounts for 10–20 percent of a country's GDP. In the European Union, for example, the total value of public procurement (the purchases of goods, services, and public works by governments and public utilities) was €1.5 trillion,

or about 16 percent of the EU's GDP in 2002. http://ec.europa.eu/internal_market/publicprocurement/index_en.htm.

2. Federal Acquisition Regulation at http://www.arnet.gov/far/. In addition, the Defense Contract Audit Agency has over 4,500 staff designated to audit the massive defense procurement system on top of the thousands of inspectors general that exist at the defense and service agency level. https://www.jagcnet.army.mil/JAGCNETInternet/Homepages/AC/ArmyFraud.nsf/(JAGCNetDocID)/86DABEE8FC6CC4DA8525703F005519E9/$FILE/ISS%20Compliance%20Agreement.pdf.
3. P. Overby, "Boeing Moves Forward after Government Fine," National Public Radio's Morning Edition, May 16, 2006, http://www.npr.org/templates/story/story.php?storyId=5407530. See also *Congressional Quarterly,* August 1, 2006, "Boeing Global Settlement," Senate Armed Services Committee hearing testimony by Paul J. McNulty, Deputy Attorney General, U.S. Department of Justice. The Boeing chief financial officer, Michael Sears, was sentenced in U.S. federal court to four months in prison and fined $250,000 for violating federal conflict of interest law. S. J. Hedges, "Former Boeing Finance Chief Gets Four Month Sentence," *Chicago Tribune,* February 19, 2005. The Air Force official, Darleen Druyun, received a nine-month prison sentence. M. Sirak, "DoDIG: Druyun Impacted Air Force's KC-135 Depot Contract With Boeing," *Defense Daily,* May 26, 2006.
4. For an excellent and more extensive discussion of these principles, see Burton (2005) and Wittig (2005).
5. The red flags listed in this chapter came from a variety of sources, including the authors' field work, lessons provided by leading transnational investigators such as W. Michael Kramer, and a variety of publications. See, for example, http://www.bhutanaudit.gov.bt/contents/papers/asosai-pakistan/Overview%20of%20Fraud%20and%20Corruption%20Detection%20Process.pdf; http://www.srac.gpg.gov.za/Anti-corruption%20booklet.pdf and http://www.wmkramer.com/1basics.html.
6. One of the authors was retained by a large company to ensure that its 400 agents conducting business overseas are not engaged in corruption in violation of the U.S. Foreign Corrupt Practices Act of 1977.
7. U.S. contractors doing business with agents overseas are increasingly conducting due diligence investigations of their prospective foreign agents to determine if they have a reputation or known practice of paying bribes to obtain contracts for the companies they represent.
8. For example, Titan, a California-based military intelligence and communications company, was required to pay more than $28 million in civil and criminal fines for violating the Federal Corrupt Practices Act by funneling, through intermediaries, inappropriate payments to government officials in Benin and several Asian countries. The Titan case has been one of the most significant prosecutions of corruption involving an agent, as the company received the largest fine ever levied under the federal law. See *Securities and Exchange Commission v. The Titan Corporation,* Civil Action No. 05-0411 (U.S.D.C., D.D.C., filed March 1, 2005). See also "Titan Pleads Guilty to Bribery Under Foreign Corrupt Practices Act," *U.S. Fed News,* March 1, 2005.
9. It should be noted that local contractors, especially the large ones, may also engage brokers to insulate themselves from possible prosecution.
10. Not all bid rigging involves kickbacks. Because of the prevalence of bribery, it is increasingly possible to have a completely transparent bidding process with the winning bidder paying a bribe after contract signing. In such situations, the need for a bribe is well understood by all the bidders and their pricing reflects these fees.

11. In a recent case in Africa, forensic investigators found minutes of a meeting between government officials deciding who would win certain consulting contracts on a mega-million-dollar road construction project months before the bids were actually opened.
12. Rose-Ackerman (1978) writes that competition among service providers would reduce corruption.
13. For a thoughtful analysis on detecting bid rigging as a result of charges filed in Sweden for suspected bid rigging on road contracts, see M. Jakobsson, "Bid-Rigging in Swedish Procurement Auctions," June 2004. http://www.joensuu.fi/taloustieteet/ott/scandale/tarto/papers/Maria%20Jakobsson.pdf.
14. Secrecy jurisdictions are countries with very lax business registration requirements, bank regulations, and tax requirements.
15. In cases uncovered by the authors, the companies were registered corporations with government officials listed as directors, shareholders, or officers of the corporation.
16. For an interesting analysis and discussion of the front companies of cronies, children, and relatives of the late Ferdinand Marcos, and the impunity with which these companies were used to extract rents, see Manapat (1991).
17. See Mitchell (2005). "Structural holes" exist in procurement systems because the procurement process is made up of a network of people, and the holes that often result when multiple networks are linked are often exploited for personal advantage.
18. A responsive control adjustment is the affirmative act of closing system vulnerabilities, such as loopholes.
19. The vulnerabilities identified in this chapter come principally from the Forensic Services Unit of the World Bank's Department of Institutional Integrity. An assessment of the total number of vulnerabilities within the system can provide a metric that reflects the overall risk of corruption in the conduct of bidding and the implementation of government contracts.
20. Major investigations take the form of fiduciary reviews and are conducted by the Bank's internal investigation unit, the Department of Institutional Integrity. The U.S. Agency for International Development (USAID) has also developed a similar indicator base. See Fraud Indicators, Office of the Inspector General Investigations, USAID, http://www.usaid.gov/oig/hotline/fraud_awareness_handbook_052201.pdf.
21. On controlling administrative costs, see http://www.idea-knowledge.gov.uk/idk/core/ page.do?pageld=82701. For an extensive discussion of the potential impact of e-procurement on curbing corruption, see World Bank (forthcoming). In a recent report commissioned by the OECD, Korea's use of e-procurement provides encouraging news on the value of e-procurement platforms. See http://www.nibr.no/content/download/3663/17219/file/OECD-rapport+2005-+aase.pdf.
22. Some scholars suggest that three distinct policy approaches can be employed against corruption: status quo (that is, no additional resources for detection or punishment); individual-level deterrence (such as increasing resources for better detection and punishment); and alterations in the "structural conditions relevant to corruption" (such as reducing bureaucratic inefficiency or making legislation more congruent with social demands). See Nas, Price, and Weber (1986, p. 116).
23. The legal research on the existence of global disclosure programs was provided by Ms. Pascale Dubois, Senior Counsel, The World Bank Group.
24. In France, for certain offences, the French Criminal Procedure Code (*Code de Procédure Pénale)* allows the district prosecutor to implement alternative proceedings, called a *composition*, instead of a criminal prosecution. The defendant can avoid formal criminal proceedings altogether in exchange for an admission of guilt and the fulfillment of special

conditions (such as paying a fine or performing community service). See C. PR. PÉN. Arts. 41-1 to -3 (2004) (Fr.). In the United States, several agencies, including the Environmental Protection Agency, the Department of Justice Antitrust Division, the Securities and Exchange Commission, and the Department of Health and Human Services utilize voluntary disclosure programs. See Environmental Protection Agency, Incentives for Self-Policing: Discovery, Disclosure, Correction and Prevention of Violations, 60 Fed. Reg. 66706 (Dec. 22, 1995); see also Anne K. Bingaman, Assistant Attorney General, Remarks before the Antitrust Section of the American Bar Association (Aug. 10, 1993), reprinted in 6 Department of Justice Manual Section 7-2A.470 at 7-244.315 (1995); see generally Report of the Securities and Exchange Commission on Questionable and Illegal Corporate Payments and Practices (submitted to the Senate Banking, Housing and Urban Affairs Committee May 12, 1976); *In re Sealed Case,* 676 F.2d 793 (D.C. Cir. 1982); and see generally Richard A. Feinstein and Jonathan L. Diesenhaus, "Unmasking Health Care Fraud and Abuse," *Legal Times*, July 17, 1995. Pakistan's National Accountability Bureau Ordinance offers full or conditional pardons to persons who make full and true disclosures of their violations and provide the names of persons involved in the corrupt schemes. It also provides violators with potential amnesty from incarceration if they admit to their corrupt practices and return the assets or gains acquired through the corrupt practices. See National Accountability Bureau Ordinance, Pakistan Ordinance No. XVIII of 1999, §§ 25, 25A, and 26, as amended by Pakistan Ordinance Nos. XIX of 1999 and IV of 2000. To fight organized crime, Poland uses the *świadek koronny*, or crown witness, law in which a criminal who testifies against his or her accomplices receives immunity, as well as identity protection if he or she may suffer retaliation. See *Ustawa z dnia 25 czerwca 1997 r. o świadku koronnym.* Argentina fights drug-trafficking crimes by either reducing the punishment or dismissing the case against a person who helps authorities to uncover the identity of other wrongdoers or identify other drug shipments. See paragraph 29 ter of Law Nr. 23.737. Argentina also permits the reduction of penalties for a wrongdoer who provides the state with information leading to locating a kidnapping victim. See paragraph 41 ter of Law Nr. 25.742. Brazil's leniency program encourages voluntary communication of information on anticompetitive practices by guaranteeing the informant immunity from punishment as long as the Ministry of Justice had no knowledge about the illicit practice prior to the informant's disclosure. See Brazilian Antitrust Law, Law 10.149/2000 of Dec. 21, 2000. Italy's *pentiti* laws offer immunity from prosecution and/or reductions of penalties and witness protection to cooperating persons who provide information regarding subversion of the democratic order by violent means, terrorist activities, mafia-type organizations, kidnapping, drug trafficking, and smuggling. See, for example, Law No. 304 of May 29, 1982; Law No. 15 of Feb. 15, 1980; Law No. 34 of Feb. 18, 1987; Decree-Law No. 8/91; Law No. 45/01; Decree-Law No. 8 of Jan. 15, 1991; and Law. No. 45 of Feb. 15, 2001. Prosecutors in the United Nations–led interim civil administration of Kosovo may request full immunity from prosecution if a judge determines that a suspect or defendant will give evidence that is likely to prevent further criminal acts or lead to the successful prosecution of another suspect. See UNMIK Regulation No. 2001/21 on cooperative witnesses (Sept. 20, 2001); UNMIK Regulation No. 2003/26, Provisional Criminal Procedure Code of Kosovo, Arts. 298-303 (July 6, 2003).

25. Article 37(3) of the UN Convention against Corruption provides: "Each State Party shall consider providing for the possibility, in accordance with fundamental principals of its domestic law, of granting immunity from prosecution to a person who provides substantial cooperation in the investigation or prosecution of an offense established in accordance with this Convention."

26. See, for example, Homer E. Moyer, Jr., "Corporate Counsel-Law Firms, Voluntary Disclosure, Independent Compliance Monitors and Other FCPA Enforcement Issues," *Metropolitan Corporate Counsel,* June 2005. http://www.metrocorpcounsel.com/current.php?artType=view&artMonth=June&artYear=2005&EntryNo=3063.
27. The United Kingdom recently enacted such legislation, and the United States has similar legislation (http://www.epic.org/open_gov/foia/us_foia_act.html), as do numerous other nations; see http://www.freedominfo.org/.
28. See, for instance, the impact of lifestyle checks conducted by the Philippine Center for Investigative Journalism (http://www.pcij.org/stories/2003/bir.html).
29. See UNCITRAL Web site for Model Law on Procurement of Goods, Construction and Services with Guide to Enactment, http://www.uncitral.org/uncitral/en/uncitral_texts/procurement_infrastructure/1994Model.html; see also http://www.abanet.org/.
30. See Organization of American States (OAS) Inter-American Convention Against Corruption, Treaty Doc. No. 105-39; OECD Convention on Combating Bribery of Foreign Officials in International Business Transactions, Treaty Doc. No. 105-43, 1997 U.S.T. Lexis 105; and the Council of Europe, Criminal Law Convention on Corruption, ETS No. 173., entered into force July 1, 2002. The United Nations Convention against Corruption (UNCAC), UN Doc. A/58/422 (adopted October 31, 2003), entered into force December 15, 2005.
31. Soreide (2006) notes in a survey of firms in the OECD that "as many as 55 percent of the respondents did not think that tender rules could prevent corruption. Fifteen percent said that tender rules do function as an obstacle, while only six percent considered tender rules to be an *efficient* obstacle to corruption."
32. This annex was researched and written by Benjamin M. Cox.
33 See the International NGO Forum on Indonesian Development, March 23, 2005, http://www.infid.be/aceh_combating_corruption.htm.
34. See the International NGO Forum on Indonesian Development, March 23, 2005.

REFERENCES

ADB (Asian Development Bank). 1998. *Anti-Corruption: Policies and Strategies.* Manila: ADB.

ADB/OECD/Transparency International. 2005. *Curbing Corruption in Tsunami Relief Operations.* Proceedings of the Jakarta Expert Meeting, April 7–8. Manila: ADB.

Batha, E. 2005. "Corruption and Aid" Reuters, November 9. http://www.alertnet.org/thefacts/reliefresources/11315551833.htm.

Burton, Robert A. 2005. "Improving Integrity in Public Procurement: The Role of Transparency and Accountability." In *Fighting Corruption and Promoting Integrity in Public Procurement,* 23–28. Paris: OECD.

Campos, J. E., and J. Syquia. 2006. "Managing the Politics of Reform: Overhauling the Legal Infrastructure of Public Procurement in the Philippines." World Bank, Washington, DC.

CNN. 2005. "Dozens Indicted in Alleged Katrina Scam: Red Cross Contract Workers Accused of Filing False Claims," December 29. http://www.cnn.com/2005/LAW/12/28/katrina.fraud/index.html.

Harvey, R. 2005. "Corruption Challenge for Aceh Aid." *BBC News,* May 31. http://newsvote.bbc.co.uk/mpapps/pagetools/print/news.bbc.co.uk/2/hi/asia-pacific/ 4583557.stm.

Klitgaard, Robert. 1988. *Controlling Corruption.* Berkeley: University of California Press.

Manapat, Ricardo. 1991. *Some Are Smarter than Others: The History of Marcos' Crony Capitalism.* New York: Aletheia Publications.

Manning, Nick, and Neil Parison. 2004. *International Public Administration Reform.* Washington, DC: World Bank.

Merle, R., and J. Markon. "Ex-Pentagon Official Admits Job Deal." *Washington Post,* April 21, p. A1. Merle, R. 2004. "Long Fall for Pentagon Star: Druyun Doled Out Favors by the Millions." *Washington Post,* November 14, p. A1.

Mitchell, L. E. 2005. "Symposium: Corporate Misbehavior by Elite Decision-Makers: Perspectives from Law and Social Psychology: Structural Holes, CEOs, and Informational Monopolies—the Missing Link in Corporate Governance." *Brooklyn Law Review* 70 (Summer): 1313.

Mora, Jose Eduardo. 2004. "Central America: The High Cost of Corruption" Inter Press Service, http://www.worldrevolution.org/article/1624.

Mugazi, Henry. 2005. "Corrupt Public Procurement. Civil Society Should Be Involved More in Following Up Corrupt Officials." Newsletter 3, August. http://www.ms.dk/sw930/.asp

Nas, T. F., A. C. Price, and C. T. Weber. 1986. "A Policy-Oriented Theory of Corruption." *American Political Science Review* 80 (March): 107–19.

New York State, Office of Attorney General Eliot Spitzer. 2001. "Eleven School Custodians Arrested for Kickback and Bid Rigging Scheme." Press Release, December 11. http://www.oag.state.ny.us/press/2001/dec/dec11b_01.html.

Nunberg, Barbara. 1997. "Rethinking Civil Service Reform: An Agenda for Smart Government." Poverty and Social Policy Working Paper, World Bank, Washington, DC.

Odhiambo, Walter, and Paul Kamau. 2003. "Public Procurement: Lessons from Kenya, Tanzania, and Uganda." Working paper 208, OECD Development Centre, Paris. http://www.u4.no/document/literature/Odhiambo-public-procuremnt-Tz-Ug-Ky.pdf.

OECD. 2005. "Fighting Corruption and Promoting Integrity in Public Procurement." Paris: OECD.

Paine, L., R. Deshpande, J. D. Margolis, and K. E. Bettcher. 2005. "Up to Code: Does Your Company's Conduct Meet World-Class Standards?" *Harvard Business Review* 83 (12): 122–33.

Rose-Ackerman, Susan. 1978. *Corruption: A Study in Political Economy.* New York: Academic Press.

———. 1999. *Corruption and Government: Causes, Consequences, and Reform.* Cambridge, UK: Cambridge University Press.

Sacerdoti, Giorgio. 2005. "Forum Workshop on Identifying Risks in the Bidding Process to Prevent and Sanction." In *Fighting Corruption and Promoting Public Integrity in Public Procurement,* 153–60. Paris: OECD.

Sandholtz, W., and M. Gray. 2005. "International Determinants of National Corruption Levels." In *Transparency International Global Corruption Report 2005.* http://www.globalcorruptionreport.org/download.html#download.

Soreide, Tina. 2006. "Procurement Procedures and the Size of Firms in Infrastructure Contracts." Paper prepared for the World Bank ABCDE conference, Tokyo, May 29–30.

Stone, R. W. 2004. "The Political Economy of IMF Lending in Africa." *American Political Science Review* 98 (4): 577–91.

Thachuk, K. 2005. "Corruption and International Security" *SAIS Review* 25 (Winter-Spring): 143–52.

Transparency International. 2002. "Status Report on the Integrity Pact: The Concept, the Model, and Present Applications." Transparency International (December 31).

———. 2006a. Handbook: Curbing Corruption in Public Procurement. http://www.transparency.org./global_priorities/public_contracting

———. 2006b. *Global Corruption Report 2006.* http://www.globalcorruptionreport.org/download.html#download.

Trepte, Peter. 2005. "Transparency and Accountability as Tools for Promoting Integrity and Preventing Corruption in Procurement: Possibilities and Limitations." OECD, Paris.

(U.S. Department of Justice). n.d. "Preventing and Detecting Bid Rigging, Price Fixing, and Market Allocation in Post-Disaster Rebuilding Projects: An Antitrust Primer for Agents and Procurement Officials." http://www.usdoj.gov/atr/public/guidelines/disaster_primer.htm.

U.S. Department of the Treasury. 2004. "U.S. Identifies Front Companies for Saddam Hussein Regime." Press Release, Office of Public Affairs, April 15, Washington, DC. http://www.cpa-rqa.org/transcripts/20040415_front_companies.html.

U.S. Government Accountability Office. 2006. "Company Formations: Minimal Ownership Information is Collected." Report 06–376 (April).

Volcker Committee (Independent Inquiry Committee into the United Nations Oil-For-Food Programme, chaired by Paul A. Volcker). 2005a. *Report on the Manipulation of the Oil-For-Food Programme* (October 27). http://www.iic-offp.org/documents/IIC%20Final%20Report%2027Oct2005.pdf.

———. 2005b. "Third Interim Report" (August 8). http://www.iic-offp.org/documents/Third%20Interim%20Report.pdf.

Ware, G. T., and G. P. Noone. 2003. "The Culture of Corruption in the Post Conflict and Developing World. " In *Imagine Coexistence: Restoring Humanity After Violent Ethnic Conflict,* ed. A. Chayes and M. Minnow. San Francisco, CA: Jossey-Bass.

———. 2005. "The Anatomy of Transnational Corruption." *International Affairs Review* 14 (Fall): 29–52.

Wax, E. 2005. "Kenya Is Buffeted by Graft Scandals." *The Washington Post*, February 13.

Werlin, H. H. 2005. "Corruption and Foreign Aid in Africa." *Orbis* 49 (Summer): 517–27.

Wittig, Wayne A. 2005. "Linking Islands of Integrity to Promote Good Governance in Public Procurement: Issues for Consideration." In *Fighting Corruption and Promoting Integrity in Public Procurement,* pp. 109–14. Paris: OECD.

World Bank. Forthcoming. *Corruption vs. Technology in Public Procurement.*

Yen, H. 2005. "GAO Probes Katrina Credit Card Bills: Audits Examine Purchases by Federal Workers for Abuse, Overpayment." *Washington Post,* December 27, p. A23. See also http://www.cnn.com/2005/LAW/12/28/katrina.fraud/index.html.

Zucker, J. S. 2004. "The Boeing Suspension: Has Increased Consolidation Tied the Department of Defense's Hands?" *The Army Lawyer,* April. https://www.jagcnet.army.mil/JAGCNETInternet/Homepages/AC/ArmyFraud.nsf/(JAGCNetDocID)/86DABEE8FC6CC4DA8525703F005519E9/$FILE/The%20Boeing%20Suspension.pdf.

10

Combating Corruption in Revenue Administration

An Overview

TUAN MINH LE

Surveys in developing and transition countries indicate that revenue administration agencies are typically ranked among the most corrupt public institutions. Corruption in tax and customs administrations leads to both efficiency and equity problems. It is one of the leading causes for revenue leakage (see, for example, Martinez-Vazquez, Arze, and Boex [2004]). Empirical studies have shown that countries with a high incidence of corruption tend to have a larger shadow economy, which implies a depleted tax base and thus a serious loss of revenues (Schneider and Enste 2000; Johnson, Kaufmann, and Zoido-Lobaton 1998). Moreover, because it provokes unfair treatment of honest taxpayers and hurts their competitiveness, corruption drives more businesses out of the formal sector and generates a vicious circle that retards the development of the formal economy. In the case of customs, corruption may even compromise the national security by becoming a conduit for the transit of drugs and arms.

Empirical studies have also found that the magnitude of the impact of corruption varies by the type of tax, with a larger negative impact on direct taxes than on indirect taxes (Tanzi and Davoodi 2000). Corruption exacerbates the imbalances in the tax take from direct and indirect taxes; it reduces the tax collection from a certain group of taxpayers (normally those well-to-do businesses that have the ability to bribe tax officials) and increases the relative tax burden of the poorer groups of taxpayers.

MOTIVES AND OPPORTUNITIES FOR CORRUPTION IN REVENUE ADMINISTRATION

In revenue administration, motives for corruption are intense and opportunities plentiful. A revenue officer is likely to engage in corrupt behavior if his expected gains are greater than the expected cost of being caught and fined (Huther and Shah 2000).

The expectations regarding potential gains and costs are in turn determined by the specific governance environment in which tax and customs administrations operate.

Generally, the legal framework for revenue administration in many developing countries is characterized by complex tax and trade regimes including multiple discretionary exemptions, confusing and nontransparent procedures for tax compliance, and excessive discretionary power of tax inspectors. Furthermore, various reports show that tax and customs officers in many countries lack professionalism and work in institutional settings with inadequate reward and penalty structures and weak internal and external controls.

APPROACHES TO COMBATING CORRUPTION

The multifaceted causes of corruption suggest that successful anticorruption programs have to be comprehensive and targeted at the multiple incentives and opportunities for corruption. Das-Gupta, Engelschalk, and Mayville (1999) have proposed several reform measures that can potentially help redress the motives, incentives, and opportunities for corruption. These are summarized in table 1 below.

TABLE 1 Anticorruption Measures in Revenue Administration Reforms

Reform measures to address motives and incentives for corruption	*Reform measures to address opportunities for corruption*
Basic motivation • Mission and vision statements • Elite ethos and esprit de corps	Tax structure reforms • Low and few rates and limited exemptions • Withholding and presumptive taxes • Nondiscretionary penalties
Positive incentives • Organizational autonomy • Transparent budget procedures and performance-linked budgets • Performance-linked compensation • Intra- and interagency competition • Competitive base pay • Transparent and nonarbitrary reward procedures	Organization and management • Functional organization • Increased use of third-party data • Limited contact with taxpayers and suppliers • Arm's length, transparent, and nondiscretionary business procedures • Transparent human resource, procurement, and budgetary procedures • Computerization and automation • Privatization of selected functions
Negative incentives • Effective sanctions for corruption • Stronger taxpayer voice through independent surveys • Citizen review and oversight	Internal and external checks • Independent internal and external audits • Effective management supervision procedures • Citizen review and oversight • Internal anticorruption units
Supply-side elements • Effective sanctions for bribe payers • Independent institutions to protect taxpayers from harassment and extortion • Publicity for penalties	

Source: Das-Gupta, Engelschalk, Mayville (1999).

Isolated anticorruption programs for revenue administration rarely are sustainable. Instead, anticorruption reforms need to build on a broader set of governance initiatives. Since the late 1990s, World Bank technical assistance projects in revenue administration have adopted a comprehensive design framework with due attention paid to accountability, institution building, and cost-effectiveness. Chapter 10 presents one such example—the reform of the Bolivian National Tax Service. A similar effort has also been undertaken in Latvia, where tax reform activities have been aligned with broader public administration reform efforts. The Latvian reforms have included the establishment of a close relationship with the Corruption Prevention Council, the introduction of organizational and technological changes in the State Revenue Service, unification of the tax and social contributions collections as well as customs administration, the establishment of a broad set of performance indicators, and the setting up of transparent mechanisms for consultation with stakeholders.

A recent trend in reforming revenue administration, particularly in Latin America and Africa, has been the creation of semiautonomous revenue agencies (SARAs). The typical objective of these efforts has been to address the problem of corruption and poor collection performance (Kidd and Crandall 2006; Fjeldstad 2005.) In many instances, SARAs are viewed as catalysts for broader reforms or are regarded as a significant institutional component of the overall public sector reform strategy. However, several assessments of the experience with SARAs (see, for instance, Kidd and Crandall [2006]) conclude that the SARA as governance model is not a panacea and that success depends in large part on the existence of a comprehensive reform plan supported by strong and sustained political commitments.

Chapters 10 and 11 present a more detailed summary of the scope, determinants, and impact of corruption in tax and customs administrations. Both chapters focus on operationally tractable reform measures and explore the usefulness of mapping corruption risks in business process flows as a basis for designing suitable anticorruption strategies.

REFERENCES

Das-Gupta, Aridam, Michael Engelschalk, and William Mayville. 1999. "An Anticorruption Strategy for Revenue Administration." PREM Notes 33, Poverty Reduction and Economic Management Network, World Bank, Washington, DC.

Fjeldstad, Odd-Helge. 2005. "Corruption in Tax Administration: Lessons from Institutional Reforms in Uganda." CMI Working Paper, Chr. Michelsen Institute, Bergen, Norway.

Huther, Jeff, and Anwar Shah. 2000. "Anti-Corruption Policies and Programs: A Framework for Evaluation." Policy Review Working Paper 2501, World Bank, Washington, DC (December).

Johnson, Simon, Daniel Kaufmann, and Pablo Zoido-Lobaton. 1998. "Regulatory Discretion and the Unofficial Economy." *American Economic Review* 88 (2): 387–92.

Kidd, Maureen, and William Crandall. 2006. "Revenue Authorities: Issues and Problems in Evaluating Their Success." International Monetary Fund, Washington, DC.

Martinez-Vazquez, Jorge, F. Javier Arze, and Jameson Boex. 2004. "Corruption, Fiscal Policy, and Fiscal Management." Working paper prepared for the Fiscal Refrom in Support of Trade Liberalization Project, Development Alternatives, Inc. (October).

Schneider, Friedrich, and Dominik Enste. 2000. "Shadow Economies around the World: Size, Causes, and Consequences." IMF Working Paper WP/00/26, International Monetary Fund, Washington, DC (February).

Tanzi, Vito, and Hamid Davoodi. 2000. "Corruption, Growth, and Public Finances." IMF Working Paper WP/00/182, International Monetary Fund, Washington, DC (November).

10

Combating Corruption in Revenue Administration

The Case of VAT Refunds in Bolivia

JUAN CARLOS ZULETA, ALBERTO LEYTON, AND ENRIQUE FANTA IVANOVIC

"The problem of declining tax revenues is almost always associated with corruption. Addressing the problem of corruption necessitates a holistic approach. The integrated tax reform framework designed by the Bolivian government to address this problem covers both tax policy and tax administration reforms ranging from enacting a new tax code to establishing a new Tax Revenue Service. This is a good and concrete example of a real tax reform, one which focuses on the truly pressing issues in tax administration—performance and accountability."

Rene G. Banez, Former Commissioner,
Bureau of Internal Revenue, Government of the Philippines

Fighting corruption has become a major challenge for most revenue agencies in the world, mainly because corruption substantially reduces overall tax collections. Based on studies in several countries, Fjeldstad (2005b) has recently argued that at least half of the revenue that should be collected can be lost by government treasuries through corruption and tax evasion, decreasing the funding available for public service provision.[1] In addition, corruption and tax evasion reduce voluntary compliance with tax laws and regulations, demoralize honest taxpayers, and create an atmosphere of cynicism. Finally, corruption induces tax officials to resist reform of tax structures, which over the long term leads to an erosion of public trust and confidence in government institutions and undermines the legitimacy of government.

In theory, corruption occurs when agents (tax officers) enjoy monopoly power over clients (taxpayers), have discretionary control over provision of services (for example, in tax assessments), and operate under low levels of accountability and transparency (Klitgaard 1988). This analytical framework implies that tax officials confront both incentives and opportunities for engaging in corrupt activities. The expected gains from corruption will be higher, the greater the monopoly and discretionary power of tax officials. By contrast, the expected costs will be lower, the lower the levels of accountability and transparency tax officials face (Fjeldstad 2005b).

Hence, reforms of tax administration should aim to influence either the incentives or the opportunities for corruption. In particular, reform measures should reduce the expected gain while increasing the probability of being caught and the size of the sanction if detected (Rose-Ackerman 1999). If the expected gains from corruption are greater than expected costs, the agent will decide to be corrupt and vice versa.

This chapter has two objectives. First, to highlight the relative roles of various reform measures proposed for tax administration, it discusses the experience of the newly reformed National Tax Service (NTS) of Bolivia in carrying out a relatively successful anticorruption strategy involving value added tax (VAT) refunds as applied to exports. Typically, VAT refunds result from a long and often complex chain of tax credits generated by the VAT system, involving various stakeholders such as taxpayers, exporters, domestic suppliers, tax officers, and the central government. In a recent review of country experience, Harrison and Krelove (2005) have argued that refunding may be the Achilles heel of the VAT system because it gives rise to serious problems of implementation, including opportunities for fraud and corruption and denial of refunds by governments with cash shortages. In this context, this chapter presents a case study describing how corrupt tax officers can funnel unlawful VAT refunds to corrupt exporters in exchange for bribes. It also shows how the reform of Bolivia's revenue service, particularly improved inspection control processes, contributed to reducing corruption in the National Tax Service and stemmed the loss of public funds.

Second, through this case study, the chapter attempts to illustrate the utility of adopting a process flow approach for identifying corruption risks or threats in a particular area and the corresponding remedial measures that can potentially limit those vulnerabilities. Tax collection in general, and VAT refunds in particular, lend themselves naturally to this approach, which in turn provides the basis for a successful anticorruption strategy.

The chapter first describes the different forms in which corruption can take place in revenue administration as well as the factors affecting the behavior of the various stakeholders and patrimonial networks engaged in these actions.[2] It also discusses the policy environment in which the tax administration operates and shows the core business processes (and subprocesses) characterizing a modern tax administration as well as their vulnerabilities to corruption, early warning indicators of the presence of corruption, and possible reform measures for addressing those risks. The chapter then briefly summarizes the fundamental underpinnings of reforms in tax administration, focusing on political economy considerations and other institutional factors critical to combating corruption more generally in the public sector. Then, the case study of the institutional transformation of the Bolivian tax administration office is presented, followed by some general conclusions.

THE ANATOMY OF CORRUPTION IN REVENUE ADMINISTRATION

A typology of tax evasion and corruption in the revenue service is presented in table 10.1. At first glance, tax evasion appears to be confined to taxpayers, whereas the various types of corruption are related to different combinations of stakeholders

TABLE 10.1 Typology of Tax Evasion and Corruption

No.	Type of tax evasion/corruption	Mechanism of integrity violation	Stakeholders/patrimonial networks involved
1.	**Tax evasion (without the involvement of tax officers)**		
1.1	Taxable income/transactions that are not reported or are underreported in accounts	Several ledgers are often used, including one for taxation purposes that may show a deficit.	Business taxpayers
1.2	Underreporting of turnover	Common within retail and wholesale sectors.	Business taxpayers
1.3	Overreporting of expenditures	An accounting trick to reduce tax burden.	Business taxpayers
2.	**Collusion between revenue officers and taxpayers**		
2.1	Tax exemptions	In some cases, the taxpayer is not registered in the tax registers, but pays a lower tax "privately" to tax collectors.	Taxpayers, tax officers, politicians
2.2	VAT fraud	Falsified claims for VAT refunds that occur with the help of collaborators within the tax administration.	Taxpayers, tax officers, fictitious companies
3.	**Corruption without the direct involvement of taxpayers**		
3.1	Extortion	By taking advantage of taxpayers' incomplete knowledge of tax legislation, revenue officers (and eventually politicians) threaten taxpayers to pay above rates.	Tax officers and politicians
3.2	Embezzlement of collected revenue	Revenue officers steal money collected. May take place with the collusion of bank employees and/or auditors within the tax administration.	Tax officers, bank employees, patrimonial networks
3.3	Fraud	Falsifying tax receipts is common.	Tax officers, authorized printing house
3.4	Corrupt inspectors/auditors	Internal auditing may be inefficient and corrupt. Exacerbates the problems of corruption because it undermines the credibility of the monitoring policy. Yet tax officers working in this area may be supported by management and politicians.	Tax officers, politicians, patrimonial networks

Source: Adapted from table 1 in Fjeldstad (2005b).

(in which tax officers always seem to take part), including patrimonial networks in certain cases. Despite these distinctions, however, there are no clear-cut boundaries between the two concepts. Indeed, as is shown later, tax evasion may turn out to be sustained by corruption. Moreover, the table also depicts two broad manifestations of corruption. One is perpetrated by collusion between revenue officers and taxpayers, and the other discards the direct involvement of taxpayers but may include patrimonial networks. Finally, politicians are seen to participate in two types of corruption: tax exemptions and extortion.

TABLE 10.2 Factors Affecting the Behavior of Stakeholders and Patrimonial Networks in Corruption

Stakeholder/patrimonial networks	*Factors*
Taxpayers	1. Discretionary power of politicians and tax officers to grant exemptions 2. Likelihood of detection and punishment 3. High taxes 4. Trust in the government, which is in turn related to government's capacity to deliver services for taxes paid and perceived compliance by other taxpayers[a]
Tax officials	1. Corruption in networks, based on trust and reciprocity among network members, whereby both transaction and moral costs from corruption are reduced 2. Corruption ubiquity, a situation in which almost everyone is corrupt, thereby weakening any commitment to honesty 3. Low and high wages: low wages may create severe pressure to demand bribes to meet household expenditures, and high wages may provide an incentive for corruption where attractive jobs are likely to be bought and sold 4. Wage differentials among tax officers of different levels 5. Erosion of real wages 6. Likelihood of detection and punishment 7. Existence of alternative employment: firing corrupt staff may backfire because the former staff could be attractive to the private sector due to their knowledge of the inner workings of the system 8. Markets for attractive positions, undermining the recruitment process 9. Corrupt management that legitimizes corruption
Politicians	1. Tax exemptions granted to supporters 2. Political opponents harassed through audits 3. Political interference exerted over personnel hiring and firing processes as well as on taxpayers' compliance
Patrimonial networks	1. Tax officers with higher salaries could be confronted with increased social obligations and be more prone to corruption 2. Favors granted by revenue officials to members of the network may imply the forgiveness of corrupt acts 3. To the extent that the state is unreliable in delivering basic services, ordinary people may be forced to turn to kinship and other social relationships to get access to them, undermining tax compliance

Source: Adapted from Fjeldstad (2005b).

a. As recent survey data show, the problem of nonpayment of taxes should be addressed in terms of service delivery, better administration and information schemes, and community involvement (Fjeldstad 2004).

Table 10.2 describes the most important factors affecting corrupt behavior by stakeholders and patrimonial networks. The variety of factors affecting the different stakeholders and patrimonial networks, as well as the several interactions among them, highlight the complexity of solving the corruption problem.

The Policy Environment

Corruption in the revenue service is influenced by the legal, regulatory, and policy framework that governs the tax system. The operation of the tax system is established in a tax code. Tax codes are usually cumbersome and complex instruments that create both incentives and opportunities for corrupt activities by the different stakeholders. For instance, complex tax codes, together with the discretionary power of politicians and tax officers to grant exemptions, can motivate corruption among taxpayers. Likewise, cumbersome tax regulations and procedures together with high taxes may lead taxpayers to evade taxes or engage in corrupt acts. Also, the nature and complexity of the legislation setting up the tax system and of the tax structure itself provide wide discretionary powers to tax officers to interpret tax laws to allow or disallow expenses or charges. Weak legal sanctions when it comes to enforcing punishments on taxpayers or tax collectors who infringe the law do little to discourage corruption.

Vulnerabilities to Corruption in Revenue Administration

In general, three core business processes characterize a modern tax administration: taxpayer service and voluntary compliance; revenue service control; and tax refutation, recuperation, and charging.[3] Table 10.3 lists these processes (along with their corresponding subprocesses), together with their vulnerabilities to corruption, some early warning indicators that corruption is present, and remedial measures for addressing the problems.

As mentioned earlier and shown in this table, the boundaries between tax evasion and corruption are no longer clear, since tax evasion may, in fact, depend on corruption to perpetuate itself (see, for example, subprocesses 2.2 and 2.4). Moreover, the different remedial measures established in the third column of the table can be thought of as a minimum anticorruption program in tax administration, addressing both motives (incentives) and opportunities for corruption.[4] As depicted in the table, addressing corruption in the area of taxpayer service and voluntary compliance requires organizational and regulatory measures ranging from streamlining procedures to simplifying specific subprocesses through automation, which amounts to paying attention to the opportunities for corruption. Likewise, facing corruption in revenue service control involves installing smart controls and automated random checks, as well as providing incentives for high performance, sanctions for corrupt behavior, career development, and competitive salaries; all of this amounts to looking at both opportunities and motives for corruption. Finally, confronting corruption in tax refutation, recuperation, and charging requires reforms in the area of general and human resource management, which amounts to placing more emphasis on the motives for corruption. Interestingly enough, whereas automation seems to play a key role as both an efficiency instrument and an anticorruption measure primarily in taxpayer service and voluntary compliance and to a lesser extent in revenue service control, human resource development appears to be crucial in addressing efficiency and corruption in tax refutation, recuperation, and charging and to a lesser extent in revenue service control.

THE INSTITUTIONAL UNDERPINNINGS OF REFORMS

In general, political economy considerations constitute a key factor influencing the extent to which technically sound reforms can be introduced and implemented. In essence, the political economy of reforms pertains to overcoming the resistance of vested interests. As Koromzay (2004) argued, reforms are usually about reducing

TABLE 10.3 Risks and Remedies in Principal Processes in Tax Administration

Processes/subprocesses	Risk of corruption	Potential early warning indicators	Possible remedial measures
1. Taxpayer service and voluntary compliance			
1.1 Pretaxpayer education	• None	• None	• None
1.2 Taxpayer identification	• Accelerate the processing of document in exchange for a bribe	• Perception of corruption increases above a certain range	• Automation to speed up processing of document
1.3 Approval of fiscal documents (invoices)	• Falsify tax invoices in exchange for a bribe	• Perception of corruption increases above a certain range	• Automated random checks to detect anomalies; self-assessment
1.4 Taxpayer operations	• Provide specialized information on new procedures in place in exchange for a bribe	• Taxpayers perception of the quality of service	• New procedures are published on a regular basis and are accessible to everyone; taxpayer service is improved substantially
1.5 Taxpayer operations registration	• Accelerate registration of taxpayer operations in exchange for a bribe	• Time it takes to register	• Automation to speed up registration of taxpayer operations
1.6 Sworn tax statement (STS)	• Provide assistance to fill out complicated forms in exchange for a bribe	• Taxpayers perception of the quality of service	• Simplification of forms made readily available to everyone; automation.
1.7 Payment of taxes	• Provide assistance to facilitate payment of taxes in exchange for a bribe	• Time it takes to pay taxes	• Streamlining of tax payment procedure; automation
2. Revenue service control			
2.1 Taxpayer identification control	• Falsify the document in exchange for a bribe.	• Data inconsistencies above a given threshold (for example, set a certain percentage of error acceptable, say 5%, above which there is reason to worry about corruption)	• Smart controls and cross-checks with the National Identification Service; self-assessment
2.2 Taxpayer operations control	• Ignore taxable income/ transactions not reported or underreported in accounts in exchange for a bribe	• Data inconsistencies above a given threshold (for example, set a certain acceptable deviation from historical data, say 5%, above which there is reason to worry about corruption)	• Automated random checks to detect anomalies; self-assessment
2.3 STS control	• Ignore STS submission after deadline in exchange for a bribe.	• Data inconsistencies above a given threshold (for example, set a certain acceptable deviation from historical data, say 5% above which there is reason to worry about corruption)	• Automated random checks to detect anomalies; self-assessment
2.4 Control of consistency between STS and taxpayer payment	• Ignore underreporting of turnover or overreporting of expenditures in exchange for a bribe	• Data inconsistencies above a given threshold (for example, set a certain accceptable deviation from historical data, say 5%, above which there is reason to worry about corruption)	• Automated random checks to detect anomalies, self-assessment
2.5 Intensive control	• Ignore tax sanction in exchange for a bribe	• Number of tax sanctions falls below a given threshold	• Incentives for high performance; sanctions for corrupt behavior; career development; competitive salaries

TABLE 10.3 ***(Continued)***

Processes/subprocesses	Risk of corruption	Potential early warning indicators	Possible remedial measures
3. Tax refutation, recuperation, and charging			
3.1 Lawsuits and litigations	• Ignore deadlines and procedures in exchange for a bribe	• Number of lawsuits and litigations lost increases above a certain range	• Incentives for high performance; sanctions for corrupt behavior; career development; competitive salaries
3.2 Recuperation of and charging taxpayer debts	• Postpone recuperation of and charging debts without justification	• Percentage of debt recuperation and charging falls below a given range.	• Incentives for high performance; sanctions for corrupt behavior; career development; competitive salaries

Source: NTS, La Paz, Bolivia.

rents, so they will be opposed by those whose rents are at risk. In addition, the beneficiaries of the reforms are much less aware of the benefits and, for that reason, will be less willing to support them. Moreover, rent reductions may be seen and felt as unfair because beneficiaries of the rent will not usually bear the cost of the reductions. This is particularly relevant in developing countries with large informal sectors that are typically not included in the reform effort, at least in its very beginning. In this context, broad-based reforms may be possible only under a perception of crisis. However, the timing of the reform can also be influenced by political leadership to the extent that it manages to reflect a perception of the need for change. In any event, governments should move ahead in areas where the ground for reform has been best prepared.

Among all the factors influencing a reform aimed at combating corruption in the tax administration, three are essential: enforcement of laws and regulations and prosecution of offenders, management and human resources, and capacity constraints.

First, a successful anticorruption strategy requires the rule of law; this means not only that an adequate regulatory framework must be in place but also that it is reliably enforced and violators prosecuted. This, of course, pertains to the justice system and constitutes an external condition for reform.

Second, tax officials need more than competitive wages. They also require career development (including merit-based recruitment and promotion), support systems, and sufficient funds to do their jobs. In recent years, persistent problems with tax administration have led many developing countries (mostly in Latin America and Africa) to transfer this function from the finance ministry to a semiautonomous agency (Fjeldstad 2005a). Three fundamental problems contributed to this development. First, under pressure from fiscal deficits and demand for greater funding for public services, governments were disappointed with the low levels of efficiency and tax collections in the government revenue agencies. Second, perceptions of widespread corruption and tax evasion, together with high taxpayer compliance costs, led to demands for urgent reform in tax administration. Third, international aid donors encouraged creation of semiautonomous revenue authorities (SARAs), promising support for additional administrative reforms once the new agency was in place. As

William McCarten has recently argued, however, SARAs may enable the achievement of major improvements in combating corruption and attaining major efficiency gains, but by themselves they may not be sufficient.[5]

Third, to capture the benefits of SARAs, the agencies have to acquire good managerial skills and leadership, commit to reengineering work processes, establish effective vigilance systems, make some organizational changes to capture the gains of information and communication technology (ICT), establish rewards for good work, and ensure effective oversight of the SARA by an outside agent accountable to the public, such as the president of the legislative branch.[6]

IMPLEMENTING REFORMS IN REVENUE ADMINISTRATION IN BOLIVIA

Bolivia was a strong reformer of public governance throughout the 1990s.[7] With much donor support, successive governments undertook several initiatives to improve the public sector, building on the successful macroeconomic stabilization of the mid-1980s. A modern legal framework for government financial management and control (the Financial Management and Control Law [SAFCO]) was introduced, and several attempts were made to advance civil service reform, beginning in the early 1990s. But these attempts to reform the core public administration produced little, and a high degree of informality—the propensity of public servants to follow their own rules and regulations—continued to characterize both financial and personnel management. In September 1997, just one month after taking over office, the new government of Hugo Banzer was surprised by the announcement that, according to Transparency International's Corruption Perception Index for 1997, Bolivia was the second most corrupt country on a list of about 70 countries worldwide. The news was seen as an opportunity to prepare and launch the government's anticorruption initiative, which was to receive strong support from the whole population.

The National Integrity Plan

Despite (or perhaps because of) the frustrated reforms of the past, the government was strongly committed to implementing a comprehensive public sector reform and anticorruption measure. To that end, it designed a comprehensive governance reform program, called the National Integrity Plan (NIP). With World Bank support, an ambitious Institutional Reform Project (IRP) was prepared to implement key elements of the NIP. The World Bank also supported the reform effort through an innovative institutional and governance review, which assessed the political economy of government reform and the role of extreme forms of political patronage in undermining the efficiency and effectiveness of government agencies.[8]

After completing this review and several other studies, surveys, and consultation processes, the government announced its strategy for fighting corruption at the beginning of 1998. The president himself presented the NIP, which was met with high scepticism but a willingness to collaborate by other sectors and parties. The NIP was formulated as a long-term strategy to address structural issues in the public administration arena. It recognized corruption as the symptom of structural

FIGURE 10.1 The NIP

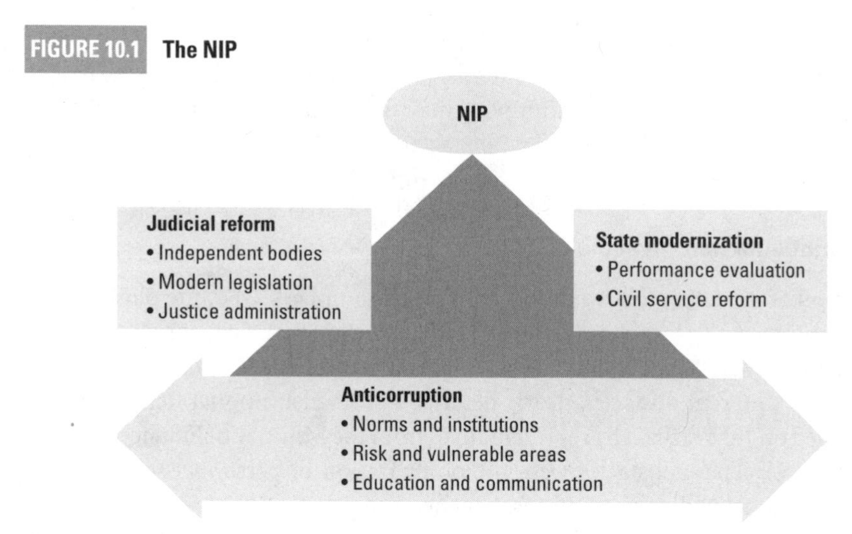

Source: Leyton and Matsuda (2004).

institutional weaknesses and identified the areas to be strengthened through enhanced capacities and transparency in order to overcome corruption. The NIP comprised three major components: judicial reform, aimed at improving the administration of justice as well as enhancing enforcement capacities; public administration reform, aimed at strengthening capacities by implementing modern systems for managing public expenditures and human resources; and a short-term anticorruption reform, aimed at implementing specific actions to build the credibility of the overall program (figure 10.1).

With a positive response from the whole donor community to the government's initiative, the vice president's office put together a proposal and sought financial support. An immediate response came from the World Bank, which prepared the IRP as the operational instrument to support the NIP implementation. The IRP became the basis for raising additional funding from bilateral donors, which pooled a significant amount of money to support the project.

The IRP recognized important advances made by the country in various areas of public administration and built on the existing institutional framework. At the same time, the IRP identified a number of measures, including the passage of new legislation, that were necessary to implement an effective institutional building process.

The approach consisted of supporting a number of "horizontal reforms," within a general normative and institutional framework, for core public administration functions such as personnel management, budget management, and procurement reforms. These reforms would then be gradually implemented through a series of "vertical reforms," using public agencies as pilot cases to test the reform processes.

The horizontal reforms were based on the general framework established since 1990 under SAFCO, recognized as a modern and adequate legal framework that had been very poorly implemented. Because politicization of the civil service was identified as a key problem to resolve, the strategy also stressed the need for enacting a similar framework to govern administration of human resources.

Vertical reforms were intended to give the reform process credibility as well as learning models on how to implement various instruments and norms geared to cleaning up selected agencies and improving their performance capacity. The NTS was one of several agencies to be chosen as pilot agencies.[9]

The Institutional Reform of the NTS

On December 22, 2000, following the promulgation of Law 2166, the old National Service for Internal Taxes was transformed into the new NTS. Of course, changing the agency's name was not enough to modify its performance. The NTS had to surmount a number of different obstacles clearly described in its Institutional Reform Agreement signed on July 2, 2002, by representatives from the Ministry of Finance, the IRP, and the NTS.[10] These obstacles were the politicization of personnel selection; tax policy aimed at providing exemptions, benefits, and preferences to specific taxpayer sectors; low quality of rules and procedures that conspired against an effective and efficient tax administration; poor relations with other public and private entities that hindered the exchange and exploitation of accounting and economic information for tax collection purposes; deficient human resources and lack of training; insufficient, untimely, and ill-distributed financial resources that made it difficult to meet institutional ends and goals; inadequate administrative and technical organization; lack of internal culture of customer service; and an undefined communication strategy for launching the NTS corporate image and promoting citizen tax compliance.

The major objectives of the reform agreement were to improve the efficiency of the tax administration; make a qualitative change in taxpayer service; promote the modernization, concord, and streamlining of norms; provide transparency to tax administration functions; increase citizen tax compliance; and institutionalize the NTS.[11] The reform strategy focused on three fundamental pillars: human resources development, streamlining of norms and procedures, and improvement of inspection and control processes and fiscal intelligence.[12] In what follows, an attempt is made to describe the general progress in each of these areas.

Human Resources Development

Until 2001, the tax administration had 991 public servants. Their average job tenure was eight months, and thus little institutional commitment was generated. Training was practically nonexistent, and the salary levels were extremely low, averaging $350 a month. A constant personnel rotation was accompanied by strong political intervention in the hiring process. There was no civil service (administrative career) system, and the absence of a career path for public servants undermined their job motivation and created the potential for corruption.

As a first step in the NTS reform process, several adjustments were made to its organizational structure. Office personnel were organized by function and job descriptions given a more technical profile. Salaries were increased by 36 percent, on average, relative to their levels before the reform. The tax agency then embarked on a comprehensive, merit-based hiring process aimed at renewing more than 80 percent of its management and front-line staff. Once these personnel were hired (with the help of specialized consulting firms), they were engaged in a process of induction and training; each staff member was expected to receive at least 80 hours of training.

Streamlining of Norms and Procedures

In general, norms and procedures and how they are applied are central to the problem of corruption. Before the reforms were enacted, the tax system was composed of hundreds of legal dispositions, many of them contradictory, granting exemptions and special treatment to many different types of taxpayers.[13] In August 2003, a new tax code was enacted, aimed largely at modernizing the tax system to keep pace with development of international trade and technology.[14] This new law also strengthened inspection and control facilities, called for new guidelines aimed at improving services to taxpayers, and laid a framework for developing new operational procedures. Once the reform process was under way, the NTS essentially threw out its old information system and started over again with modern technology designed specifically for the agency. With the aid of the international community, a new computing center was acquired under a new centralized approach to the use of information, and communication services were contracted from a private enterprise. The NTS not only increased its computing and data storage capacity by several orders of magnitude, it also installed a modern information and database system, including a new online tax collection system operated through the commercial bank network. Because about half of the country's taxpayers had not submitted tax statements in recent years or could not be reached at their last known address, the NTS decided to draw up a new registry of taxpayers that was keyed into the information system. Beginning in January 2005, the so-called large taxpayers (representing approximately 75 percent of total tax collections) were able to submit their sworn tax statements over the Internet.

Improvement of Inspection and Control Processes and Fiscal Intelligence

Nowadays, inspection and control processes constitute the cornerstone of an efficient tax administration. One of the most important drawbacks of the old tax administration was the lack of fiscal intelligence for determining which categories of taxpayers might be most likely to evade their taxes. Before the reform, taxpayers subject to audits by the tax administration were selected on a discretionary basis, and no objective criteria were used to identify possible tax evasion. As a result, the hydrocarbons sector, currently accounting for 30 percent of total tax collection, was not subject to any special audits. Nor were any inspectors trained to audit the strategic sectors. Likewise, there were no computerized applications available for monitoring the inspection processes or the results of actions in terms of cases and tax collection.

With the advent of the reform, a new approach to inspection was implemented, which made intensive use of information technology, third-party information systems, and fiscal intelligence to determine which taxpayers should be subject to what kind of audit. In June 2005, about 80 percent of all cases subject to inspection were selected through automatic methods without participation of tax officers. Just four year earlier, 75 percent of all inspection cases were selected on a discretionary basis, with no assistance from automated systems.

The NTS now uses automated processes to track several important kinds of transactions.

- *Informed purchases versus declared sales.* Declared sales by a supplier are compared with an aggregation of purchases declared by the supplier's clients.
- *Credit cards.* Verification processes use credit card sales information to detect taxpayers who have declared a lower amount of sales than the credit cards show, taxpayers with expired tax identification numbers that continue to accept credit card sales, and taxpayers who use the simplified regime and who accept credit card payments.
- *Purchases and sales books.* Taxpayers who do not submit their purchase and sales books required by the tax administration are subject to automatic sanctions.
- *Duplicated invoices.* The system can also detect invoices used by more than one taxpayer to obtain credit from the VAT.

Finally, beginning August 2005, a new investigatory *fedatario* unit was created on a national scale to identify evasion by using simulated purchasing procedures.

Figure 10.2 shows the overall impact of the reform on tax collections. Except for the complementary regime of VAT and the transitory program, all taxes collected by the revenue service reflect an outstanding performance. These findings are further

FIGURE 10.2 Tax Collections by Type of Taxes[a]

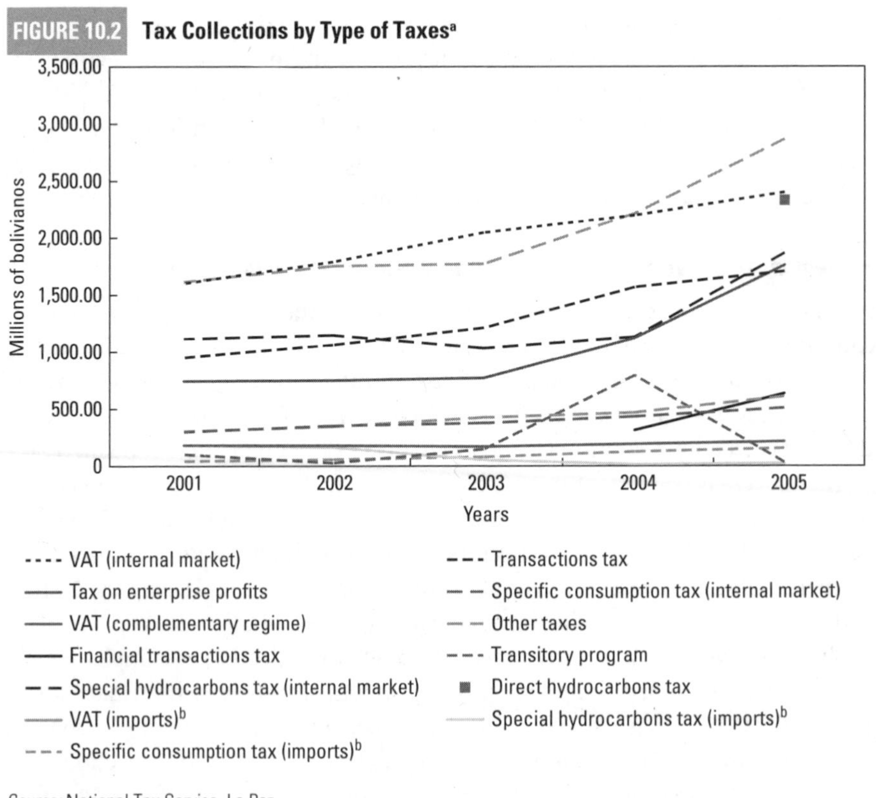

Source: National Tax Service, La Paz.

a. Includes taxes paid in cash and securities.

b. Taxes collected by Customs.

reinforced by VAT evasion figures, perhaps a better indicator of the efficacy of the tax administration. These show a significant downward trend, from 42 percent in 2001 to 39 percent in 2002, 35 percent in 2003, and 29 percent in 2004.[15]

COMBATING CORRUPTION: THE CASE OF VAT REFUNDS FOR EXPORTS

For a better appreciation of the nature of the reforms and their link to outcomes, it is helpful to look at a particular slice of the reforms. For this purpose, we have selected VAT refunds for exports, as the VAT has become the most important tax in developing countries over the past decade.

The Rationale for VAT Refunding

VAT refunding is defined as the process of reimbursement of taxes paid by exporters to obtain the export product and is based on the general international trade principle that "countries should not export taxes." [16]

Tax refunds are accepted as an international norm based on the following principles:

- *Final locality or destination* in the sense that taxes should be charged to final consumers. To the extent that the final locality or consumer of the exported merchandise is the importing country, the exporting country should not establish taxes on those goods, and any taxes paid by exporters should be refunded.
- *Tax neutrality* to avoid double taxation on capital goods, inputs, services, and other expenditures actually made by exporters and necessary for the production of export goods.
- *Competitiveness* to the extent that taxes are an important component of the cost of the merchandise and therefore of its competitiveness.

In this context, under Bolivian law, only three specific taxes are subject to refunding, namely, the VAT, the specific consumption tax, and the customs duty.[17] VAT refunds are made for up to 13 percent of the value of the merchandise, free on board, considering the maximum fiscal credit generated by the purchases and in proportion to exports versus internal sales, which are not subject to tax devolution.[18] VAT refund certificates can be sold to third parties, who can use them to pay their own taxes.

VAT refund securities are issued following either an ex ante or ex post verification of exporters' requests. In the first case, a review of documentation and tax facts precedes delivery of VAT refund certificates. In the second case, VAT refunds are granted to exporters once they present a warranty for an amount equal to that of the requested reimbursement, and inspection or auditing and control activities is to take place within 120 days after delivery of the VAT certificates.

The Corruption Risk Map of VAT Refunds before the Reform

The inspection and control processes and procedures applied to VAT refunds before the NTS institutional reform were characterized by extreme complexity,[19] heavy

FIGURE 10.3 Corruption Risk Map of VAT Refunds Procedure before the Reform

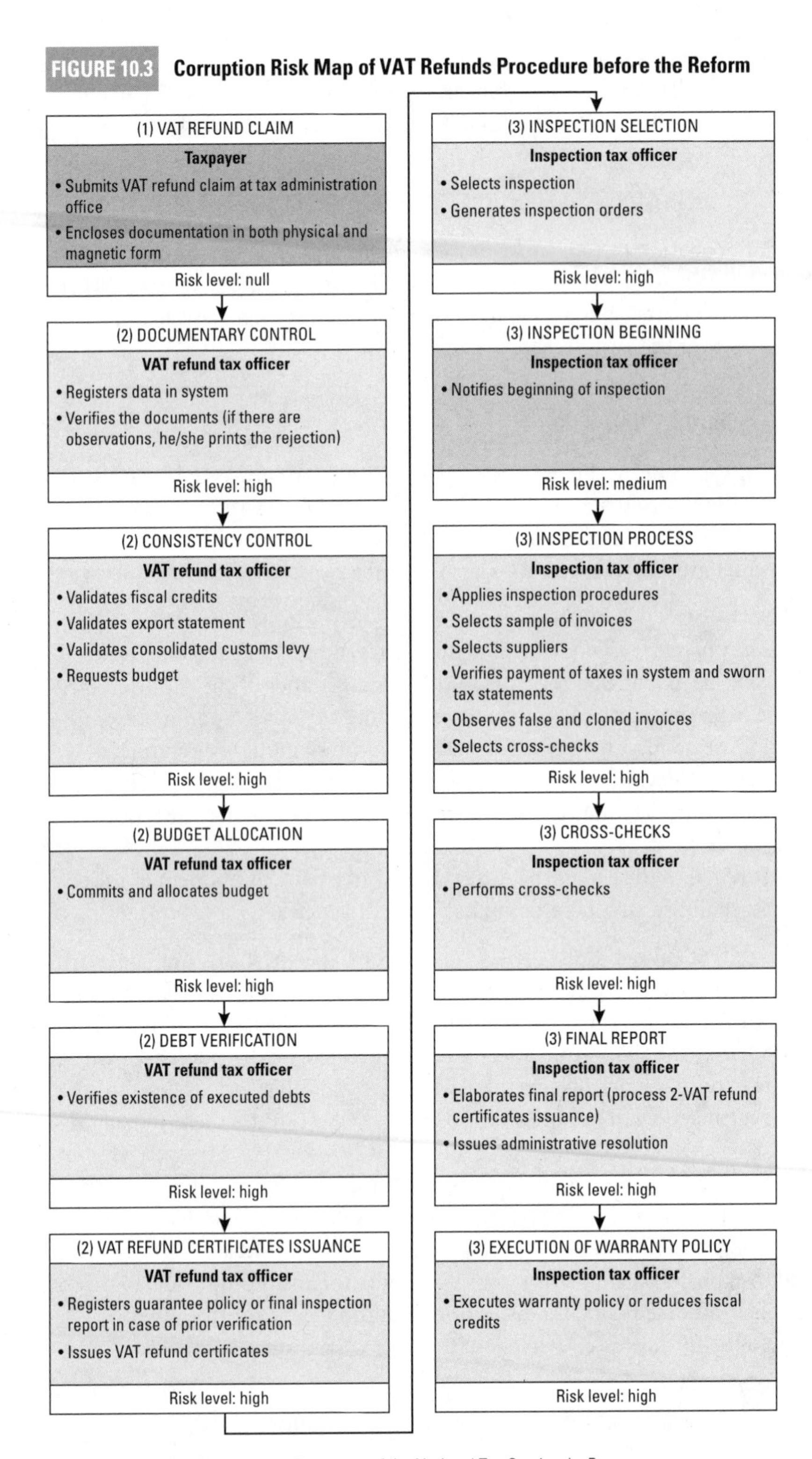

Source: Mario Arduz, former general manager of the National Tax Service, La Paz.

reliance on programming mechanisms and discretionary methods of verification, and scant use of information technology and systems.[20] As a result, they were prone to corruption. See the corruption map in figure 10.3, which identifies the vulnerable points of the VAT refund procedure before the reform. An important feature of this flow chart is that the whole procedure depended on two tax officers, the VAT refund tax officer and the inspection tax officer, both of whom enjoyed an enormous degree of discretion in their actions.

The Fraud and Corruption Chain in VAT Refunds

To receive a VAT refund under both the old and the new systems, exporters are required to submit the fiscal invoices obtained for acquisition of inputs, raw materials, or services necessary for the creation of the merchandise being exported. The invoice forms themselves must be authorized by the tax administration. Based on a number of inspection processes conducted by the Bolivian tax administration, the following types of fraudulent invoices were identified in VAT refunding[21]:

- *False and cloned invoices.* False invoices are those that were not authorized for circulation by the tax administration, whereas cloned invoices are copies of authorized ones applied to a fictitious sale of a good or service. These types of invoices are printed by underground or clandestine printing houses and commercialized by third parties.
- *Authorized invoices from fictitious suppliers.* Fictitious suppliers are persons of generally low economic condition who obtain a tax identification number under the pretense of being a supplier, receive authorized invoices from the tax administration, and sell or give them to fraudulent exporters.
- *Authorized invoices from false or nonexistent suppliers.* This type of invoice is obtained through a more complex procedure that involves registering nonexistent persons or persons with false identity in the tax registry; authorized invoices issued to these phony names are then used by fraudulent exporters to obtain VAT refunds.
- *Authorized invoices from registered suppliers.* These are invoices correctly obtained that can be used for fraud.

Even though all VAT refund claims must be accompanied by a unique export statement (UES) provided by Customs, exporting may or may not have taken place or the actual volume or quality of the merchandise exported may have been lower so that the actual value of merchandise was smaller than that registered in the UES. Moreover, making things worse, an exporting company could be fictitious. Fictitious exporters are often detected because they cannot provide documentation showing that they own or rent physical infrastructure or that they actually compete in the export market.

Given these distortions, at least three different types of VAT refund fraud can arise. First, a fictitious company may obtain false invoices or authorized invoices from false, nonexistent, or fictitious suppliers, which are then used to request and

BOX 10.1 The ARGOSUR Case

According to an investigation conducted by the NTS in 2003, a private exporting company named ARGOSUR had requested tax refunds for an approximate amount of Bs 25 million (more than $3 million) since 1998. The NTS simply paid the refunds because tax officers ignored expiration dates of warranty policies. (These policies are warrants issued by commercial banks for the amount of the tax refund claim as a guarantee that the tax refund claim is correct. Like any other document of the kind, they have expiration dates, after which they are simply useless.) Supposedly, this company was devoted to exporting gold sticks for aeronautical use, a high-technology product sold to South American Gold Traders, a fictitious American company. The specific characteristics of the exported goods generated some doubts among tax officers about the validity of these transactions.

The refund claim was based primarily on purported purchases from a supplier company named MIXCO, which claimed on its VAT refund forms that a private company named INCOBOL was its unique supplier of gold sticks. INCOBOL turned out to be a fictitious enterprise. Moreover, the invoices presented by ARGOSUR were found to be false, and the NTS eventually was able to identify the principal supplier of the gold sticks: a poor motorcycle taxi driver with a daily income of Bs 30 (less than $4), who would have had to sell more than Bs 150 million ($18.75 million) in gold to generate the Bs 25 million that ARGOSUR received as VAT refunds.

The investigation also discovered that five people were involved in a plot to sell VAT refund certificates, including a former tax officer from the inspection and control area of the old tax administration.[a] All the income from the sales of the certificates was deposited in this officer's bank accounts, which were then used to obtain bank warranty policies to request tax returns for 15 exporting companies. This person was able to maintain more than $2 million in his accounts, on a salary of just $312 a month. Several other former tax officers are currently under investigation for their alleged involvement in the scheme.

The NTS turned over all the evidence it collected to the attorney's office, which is undertaking its own investigation and has yet to file any charges. Meanwhile, NTS officers involved in the original investigation have faced all sorts of threats and intimidation.

a. According to recent information published by an important Bolivian newspaper, between 2002 and the first semester of 2004 and after a number of audits, the NTS discovered 207 tax officers involved in corruption, who were consequently fired from the revenue service. Of these, 134 were indicted, 60 were given administrative penalties, and four were found guilty of criminal actions. Moreover, for the first time since the institutional reform was implemented, two former tax officers were convicted on charges of extortion (see *La Prensa*, January 5, 2005).

obtain VAT refunds even thought the company has not exported anything (see box 10.1 and figure 10.4 for a concrete example).

Second, a real company can purchase inputs or services without any invoices and hence avoid making any tax payment on these inputs, then use false invoices or authorized invoices from false, nonexistent, or fictitious suppliers to request and obtain VAT refunds. And third, a real company may buy goods or services with an authorized invoice but sell those goods in the domestic market and still use the invoices to request and obtain VAT refunds. These three types of fraud are possible only with the collusion of unscrupulous tax officials who must authorize a fraudulent tax refund. Figure 10.5 illustrates these three typologies.

FIGURE 10.4 Gold Sticks Operation

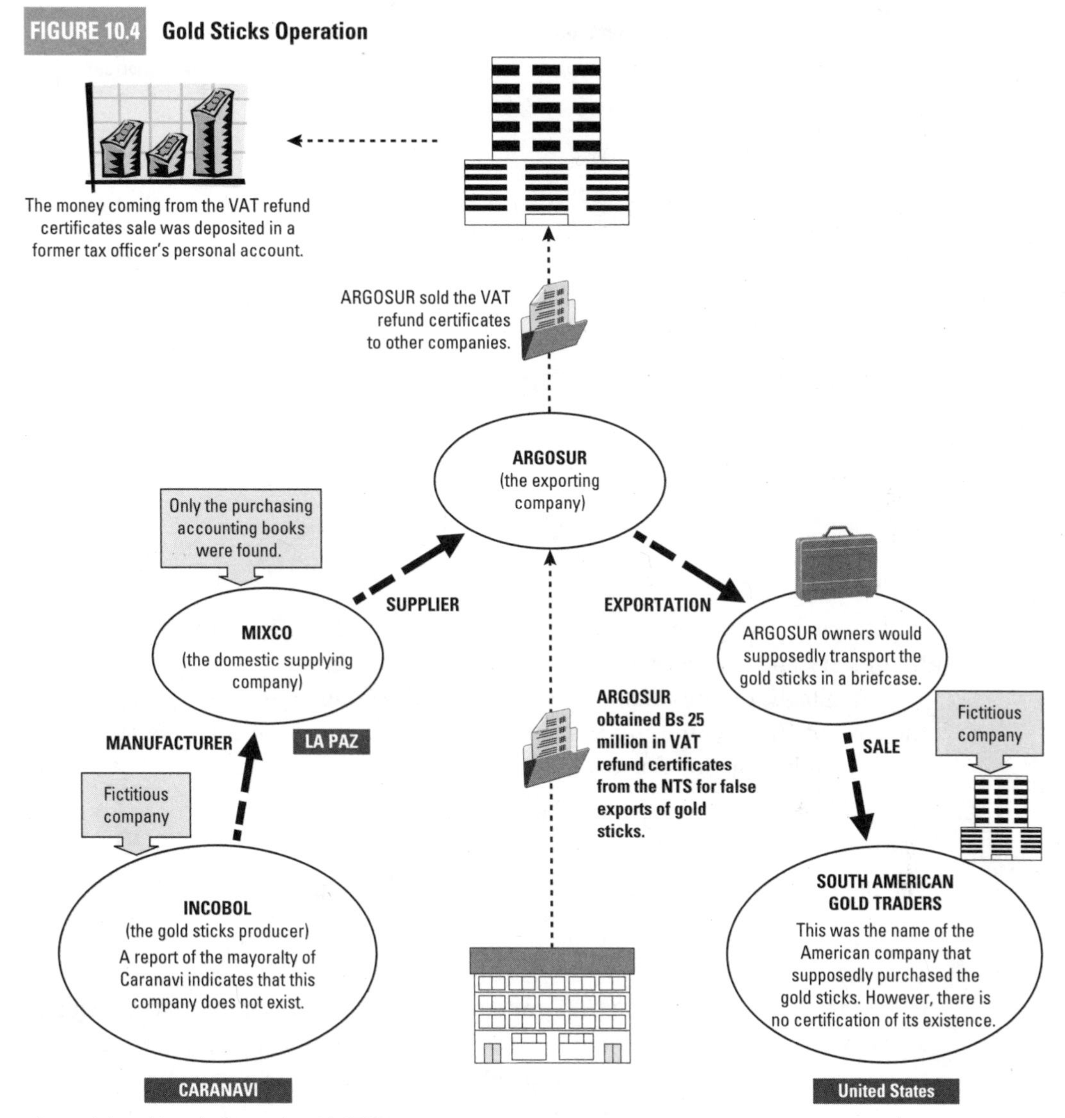

Source: Adapted from *La Prensa,* June 13, 2003.

The Corruption Risk Map of VAT Refunds after the Reform

During the first years of the reform, the tax administration learned from its own experience and developed new processes and procedures for issuing VAT refunds. Unlike the processes and procedures established before the reform, those put in place after the reform were much simpler, more reliable, and heavily supported by information technology and systems.[22] These measures basically reduce human contact between tax officials and taxpayers and make the process much more transparent. As figure 10.6 shows, under the new VAT refund procedure, there are fewer vulnerable points. An automated system replaces a number of processes previously controlled

FIGURE 10.5 **The Corruption Chain in VAT Refunds**

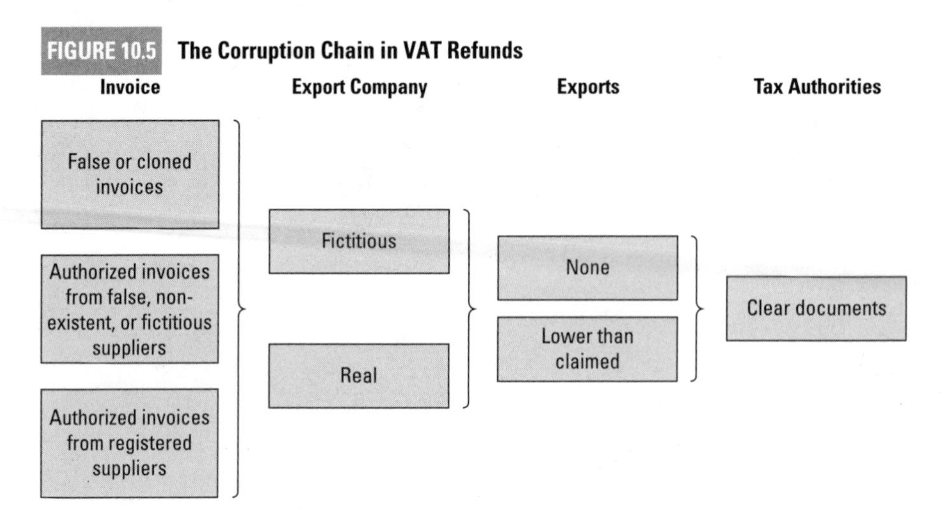

Source: The authors are greatly indebted to Ed Campos for the final version of this figure.

by just one or two persons; inspections and cross-checks are performed by different tax officers; and discretionary activities are drastically limited.

Despite the progress made thus far, some vulnerabilities to corruption persist in the current VAT refund process. Table 10.4 shows some remedial measures and warning indicators for the risk levels (vulnerabilities) of corruption identified in figure 10.6.

The Impact of the Reforms on VAT Refunds for Exports

In terms of outcomes, the reforms had a significant positive impact. Figures 10.7, 10.8, and 10.9 present data on exports (without hydrocarbons, personal effects, and reexports), VAT refunds, and VAT collections. Except for 1998, exports (as defined above) were quite stable over the 1994–2001 period. However, beginning in 2002, a clear upward trend can be observed. This contrasts markedly with the trend in VAT refunds, which remained rather stable. Note also that the growth of VAT refunds as a percent of exports dropped significantly during the NTS institutional reform period (2002–05) and that VAT refunds as a percent of VAT collections fell at the inception of the NTS reforms. Finally, VAT refunds as a percentage of collections likewise declined. All these developments suggest that unwarranted VAT refunds have been curtailed and, by implication, that corruption in the VAT refund process has been reduced.[23]

Despite this enormous progress, important constraints, weaknesses, and threats to the reforms persist. The most important constraints have to do with the deficiencies of the existing regulatory framework. As long as current rules and regulations applied to VAT refunding provide incentives to commit fraud and corruption, this unlawful behavior will not be eliminated, no matter what improvements are made in terms of processes and procedures.[24] VAT refunds amount to real export subsidies, which are very attractive not only to real, but also to fictitious and false

FIGURE 10.6 Corruption Risk Map of VAT Refund Procedure after the Reform

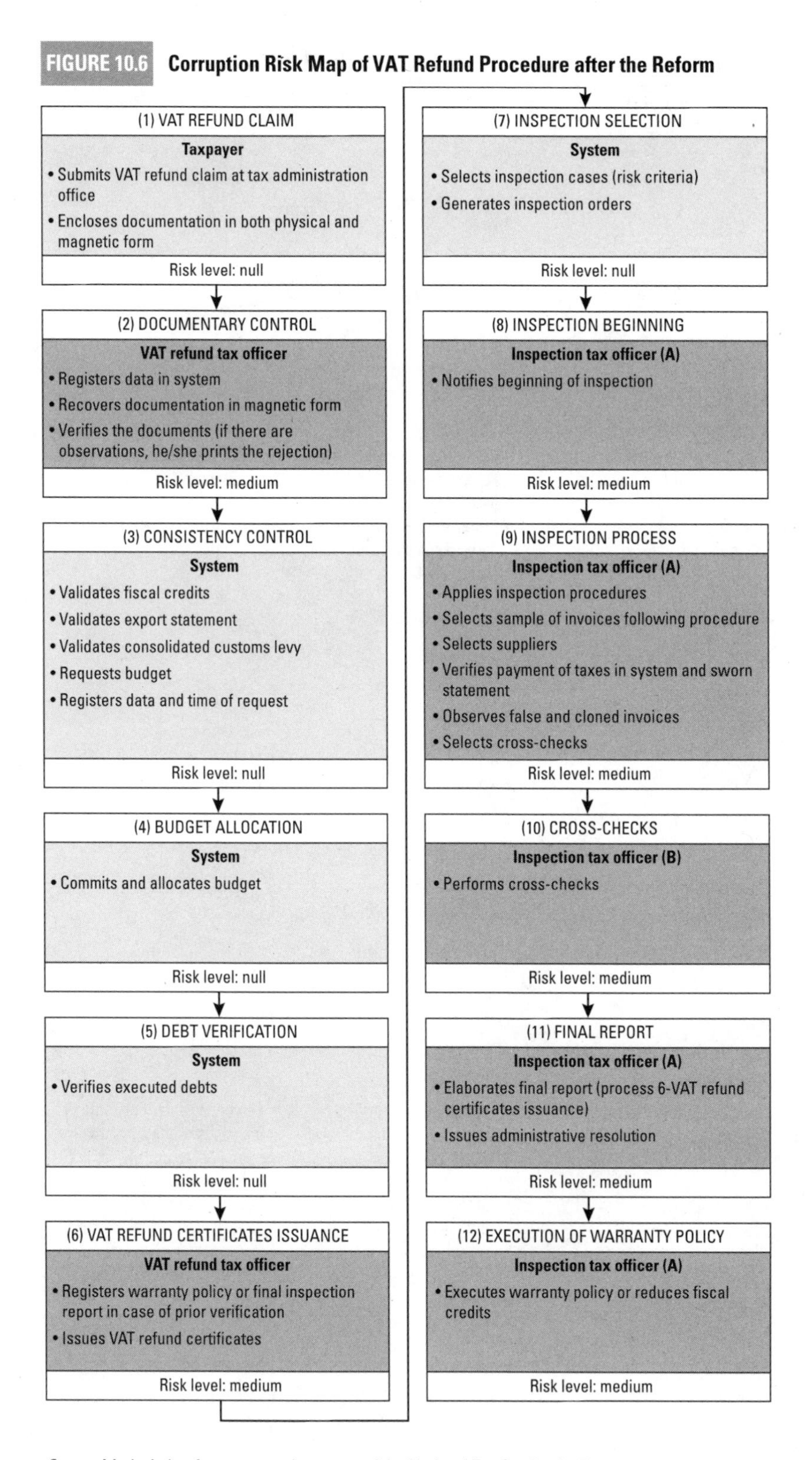

Source: Mario Arduz, former general manager of the National Tax Service, La Paz.

TABLE 10.4 Risks and Remedies in the VAT Refund Process after the Reform

Stages in VAT refund process	*Risk or threat of corruption*	*Possible remedial measures*	*Early warning indicators*
VAT refund claim			
Taxpayer:			
Submits VAT refund claim at tax administration office	• None	• None	• None
Encloses documentation in both physical and magnetic form	• None	• None	• None
Documentary control			
VAT refund tax officer			
Registers data in system	• Accelerates registration of data in the system in exchange for a bribe	• Automation to speed up data registration in the system	• Perception of corruption increases over a certain range
Recovers documentation in magnetic form	• Ignores errors or lack of documentation for a bribe	• Automated random checks to detect anomalies; self-assessment	• Data inconsistencies above a given threshold
Verifies the documents (if there are observations, he prints the rejection)	• Ignores observations in documents for a bribe	• Automated random checks to detect anomalies; self-assessment	• Data inconsistencies above a given threshold
Consistency control system			
Validates fiscal credits	• None	• None	• None
Validates export statement	• None	• None	• None
Validates consolidated customs levy	• None	• None	• None
Requests budget	• None	• None	• None
Registers data and time of request	• None	• None	• None
Budget allocation system			
Commits and allocates budget	• None	• None	• None
Debt verification system			
Verifies executed debts.	• None	• None	• None
VAT refund certificates issuance			
VAT refund tax officer			
Registers warranty policy or final inspection report in case of prior verification	• Accelerates registration of warranty policy or final inspection report for a bribe	• Automation to speed up registration of warranty policy or final report	• Perception survey of corruption increases over a certain range; number of refund claims increases over a given range
Issues VAT refund certificates	• Accelerates issuance of VAT refund certificates for a bribe	• Automation to speed up issuance of VAT refund certificates	• Perception survey of corruption increases over a certain range; issuance of VAT refund certificates increases over a given range
Inspection selection system			
Selects inspection cases under risk criteria	• None	• None	• None

TABLE 10.4 (Continued)

Stages in VAT refund process	*Risk or threat of corruption*	*Possible remedial measures*	*Early warning indicators*
Inspection beginning			
Inspection tax officer (A) Notifies beginning of inspection	• Delays beginning of inspection for a bribe	• Automation to notify beginning of inspection	• Number of days before inspection takes place after VAT refund certificates are issued, number of refund claims increases over a given range
Inspection process			
Inspection tax officer (A) Applies inspection procedures	• Overrides inspection procedures for a bribe	• Compliance of inspection procedures is subject to ex post review	• Ex post review determines deviation over a given threshold
Selects sample of invoices following procedure	• Overrides procedure for selecting sample of invoices for a bribe	• Compliance of sample selection procedure is subject to ex post review	• Ex post review determines deviation over a given threshold
Selects suppliers	• Overrides procedure for selecting suppliers for a bribe	• Compliance of suppliers selection procedure is subject to ex post review	• Ex post review determines deviation over a given threshold
Verifies payment of taxes in system and STS	• Ignores verification for a bribe	• Automation to verify payment of taxes in system and STS	• Data inconsistencies above a given threshold
Observes false and cloned invoices	• Ignores false and cloned invoices for a bribe	• Automation of random checks to detect anomalies	• Data inconsistencies above a given threshold
Selects cross-checks	• Overrides inspection procedures for selecting cross-checks for a bribe	• Compliance with cross-checks selection procedure is subject to ex post review	• Ex post review determines deviation over a given threshold
Cross-checks			
Inspection tax officer (B) Performs cross-checks	• Overrides inspection procedures for performing cross-checks for a bribe	• Compliance with cross-checks selection procedure is subject to ex post review	• Ex post review determines deviation over a given threshold
Final report			
Inspection tax officer (A) Drafts final report Issues administrative resolution	• Recommends issuance of tax refund certificates without justification	• Incentives for high performance, sanctions for corrupt behavior, career development, competitive salaries, automation	• Amount of tax refunds increases over a given range[a]
Execution of guarantee policy			
Inspection tax officer (A) Executes guarantee policy or reduces fiscal credit	• Ignores expiration dates of guarantee policy or refrains from reducing fiscal credit for a bribe	• Incentives for high performance, sanctions for corrupt behavior, career development, competitive salaries, automation	• Number of executed guarantee policies decreases over a given range

Source: Authors.

a. Compare this quantity with the number of VAT refund certificates that were issued. If the two are significantly different, it may be an indication of a problem.

FIGURE 10.7 Exports[a] and VAT Refunds

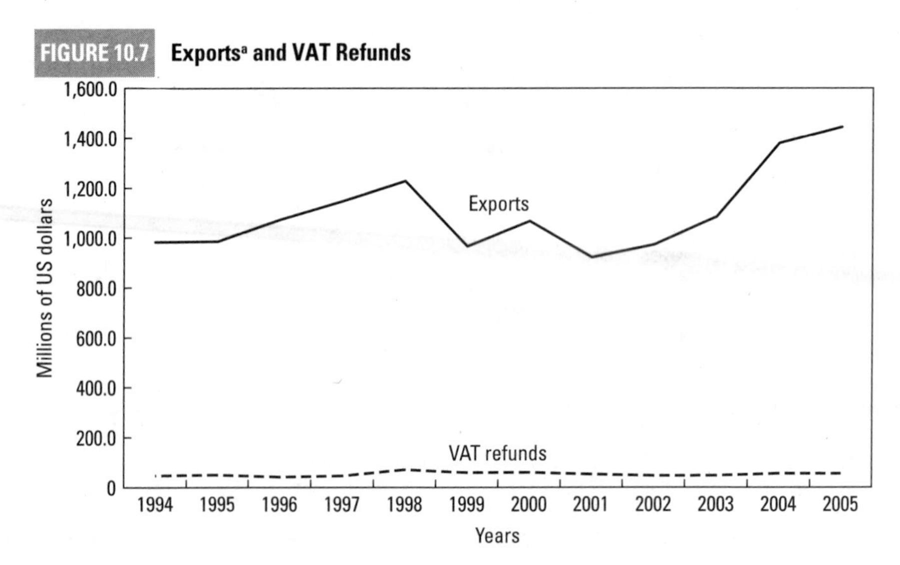

Source: National Tax Service and National Statistics Institute, La Paz.
a. Exclude hydrocarbon exports, personal effects exports, and reexports.

FIGURE 10.8 Exports[a] and VAT

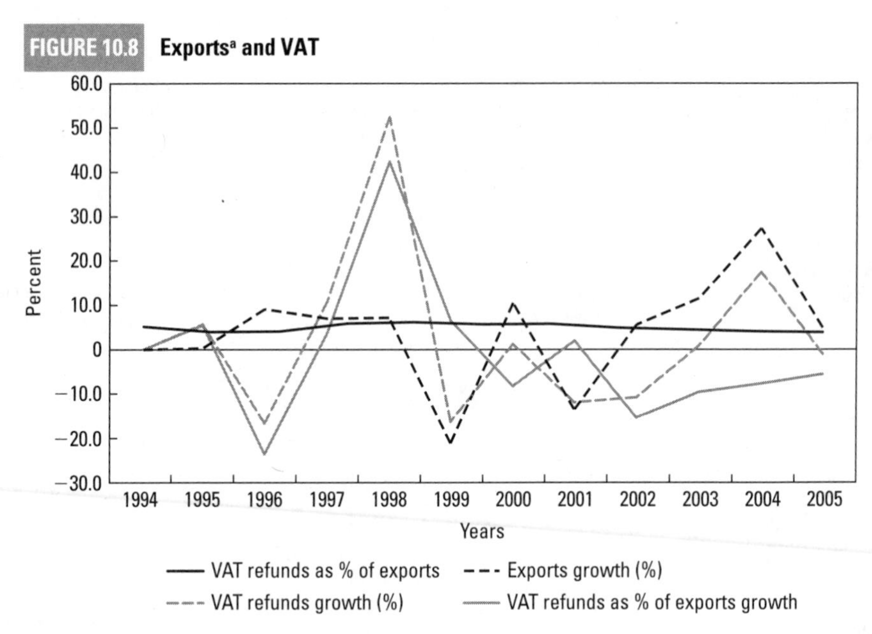

Source: National Tax Service and National Statistics Institute, La Paz.
a. Exclude hydrocarbon exports, personal effects, and reexports.

exporters. The principal weaknesses of the anticorruption strategy pertain to the still precarious coordination with Customs, even though most cases of fraud and corruption identified in this case study come from situations in which no real exportation occurs.[25]

FIGURE 10.9 **VAT Refunds as a Percentage of VAT Collections**

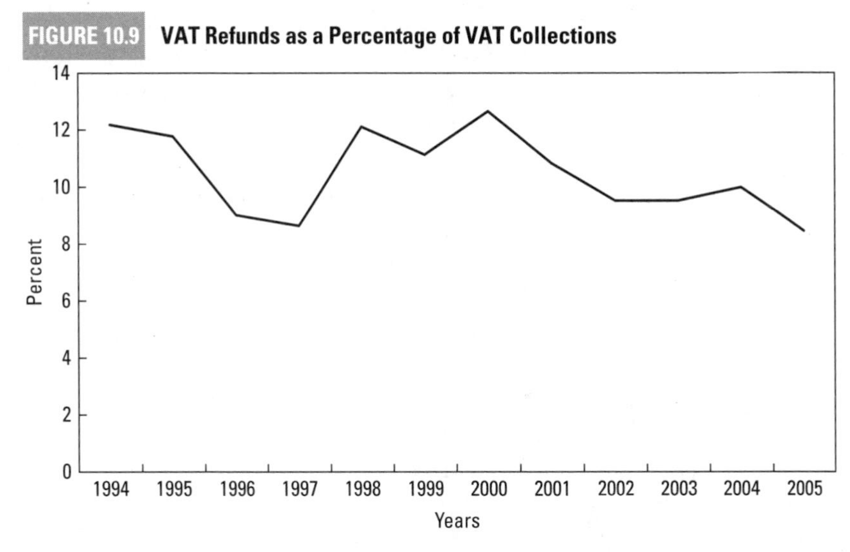

Source: National Tax Service and National Statistics Institute, La Paz.

CONCLUSION

The discussion and analysis in this chapter lead to several conclusions. First, the institutional reform carried out by the NTS beginning 2001 contributed to reducing the amounts of VAT refunds actually paid to exporters. By implication, this meant a reduction in corruption.[26]

Second, a successful anticorruption strategy such as the one described in this case study cannot be possible outside the context of a broader institutional reform of the tax administration. The design of a tax administration reform must be underpinned by a good integrated governance framework. Corruption is a symptom of bad governance; it cannot be effectively curtailed unless broader concerns of governance pertaining to transparency, accountability, and performance management are likewise addressed.[27]

It should be noted that the benefits of creating "an island of integrity," like the NTS, within a general environment of severe public sector governance problems may not be realized, and if they are, may not be sustainable. The NTS reform was a success mainly because of leadership and the support from the IRP. Latvia offers a similar case: the country conducted a successful tax administration reform in parallel with the reform of the state administration with a focus on reducing vulnerabilities of public institutions to corruption.

Third, improvements in VAT refunding procedures require intensive use of information technology. In tax collection, it is the face-to-face contact between tax officials and taxpayers that creates opportunities for bribery and corruption. Automation through appropriate applications of information technology reduces the discretion of tax officials and enhances the transparency of the VAT administration and refund processes.

Fourth, to maximize its effectiveness, an anticorruption program must engage all major stakeholders. The reform process in Bolivia covers a broad range of areas, including human resources development, business process reengineering, and streamlining of norms and procedures—all supported by information technology. However, a major institutional constraint remains: the inadequate coordination with other stakeholders, particularly with Customs, has constrained the ability of the government to fully exploit the potential effectiveness and efficiency of the reforms in the VAT refunds to exporters. Likewise, more effective integration and coordination with other external stakeholders such as the Ministry of Finance to ensure full consistency with the tax policy environment as well as with the comptroller's and prosecutor's offices and the judiciary to ensure adequate follow-up of enforcement-related actions are all tasks that need to be addressed.

Finally, there is no clear sense about whether the reform efforts will be sustainable under a new government. Most of the elements contemplated to ensure continuity are related to the establishment of a sound legal framework to prevent abuses and discretionary decisions over tax administration procedures, the setting up of institutional arrangements for appointing senior NST authorities to prevent capture by political or economic interests, and consolidation of a professionalization process for civil servants within the institution. These three elements will certainly play a role in sustaining the reform process but will prove insufficient in the absence of required political will.

Thus, the only element to maintain momentum and commitment to reform processes like this is the delivery of critical results. Given the impressive increases in revenue resulting from sounder administration of tax collection, it is now unlikely that critical aspects of the reform will be reversed. The reform process in this case has reached the point at which the cost, both political and fiscal, of reversing it would be too high for any new authority to undertake.

ENDNOTES

1. However, the relation between corruption and tax collection may not be so straightforward, particularly in more advanced countries. Mookherjee (1997), cited in Fjeldstad (2005a), for example, has argued that fiscal corruption may, at least in theory, contribute to an increase in tax revenues because the possibility to negotiate bribes from evasive taxpayers motivates tax officers to work harder to detect evasion. To the extent that taxpayers anticipate this behavior, they will try to avoid tax evasion because the probability of being caught has increased. Thus, by making tax evasion less attractive to taxpayers, corruption may indeed increase tax collection. Nevertheless, Fjeldstad and Tungodden (2003) have argued that using fiscal corruption as a means of collecting more taxes may not be sustainable in the long run.
2. Fjeldstad (2005b) refers to patrimonial networks as kinship and other social relationships of reciprocity that are used to mobilize effective ties combining moral obligations and emotional attachment and serving to perpetuate an ethic of appropriate redistribution that fuels corruption. These relationships may exert a strong influence on the behavior of tax officials, taxpayers, and politicians involved in corrupt activities. This emphasizes the need for a rather different approach to reform in certain developing countries (particularly in Africa), including measures aimed at establishing the basis for a "cultural change" in the public service.

3. Ideally, these processes could be applied to any type of tax, including the VAT.
4. For the distinction between motives and opportunities for corruption, see chapter 11 on corruption in customs administration.
5. McCarten's comments were made in an e-mail exchange with the authors. For more extensive discussions of SARAs, see Mann (2004) and Taliercio (2004), both of which indicate that the experience with them has been mixed.
6. From a different perspective, Di John (2006) argues that capacity building in tax administration has been seen merely as a "technical exercise" focusing on institutional designs (mainly concerning degree of autonomy) and administrative reform (raising wages of civil servants, more training, greater meritocracy), and ignoring the political nature of taxation. In this connection, a more sustainable approach to long-run consolidation of tax administration requires placing more emphasis on direct and progressive income and property taxes. This is particularly relevant to Latin American countries characterized by very unequal income distributions, Di John argues. Because direct taxes are more challenging to collect in both administrative and political terms, apolitical and ahistorical approaches to state capacity are inadequate. Thus a major challenge, Di John argues, is to develop a more strategic, historical, and politically informed basis to promote the more difficult tax reforms, which should take account of context and the stage of development of countries.
7. This section draws heavily on the paper by Leyton and Matsuda (2004).
8. The Bolivia institutional governance review was aimed at understanding the country's public sector and identifying challenges and possible directions for an ambitious and indispensable second-generation reform agenda. By exploring the concept and causes of informality, the review underscored the most significant obstacles facing the incipient Bolivian bureaucracy. Broadly defined as a set of actual behavioral patterns followed by public servants without taking into consideration the letter and spirit of the existing rules, informality was found in several areas of public administration, such as implementation of the SAFCO law, public expenditure, and personnel management. In general, its underlying causes were associated with the dynamics of politics. In addition, the review cited a weak private sector incapable of generating employment, politicians' interest in obtaining electoral support from and control of the government bureaucracy, and a fragmented party system that forced political organizations to negotiate coalition agreements as sources of patronage and clientelism. Finally, deficiencies in the formal rules and procedures, weakness of supporting institutions in the face of de facto "operational decentralization" in line agencies without corresponding development of institutional capacities for "normative centralization," the Ministry of Finance's traditional concern about fiscal discipline at the expense of strategic allocations and efficiency in resource use, and delays in the implementation of the Statute of the Public Officials were all found to present obstacles to the development of a well-functioning government. The review offered four central recommendations: depoliticization of public sector personnel management, strengthening of central oversight capacity in financial and personnel management, learning from the recent successful experience of the autonomous regulatory agencies (superintendencies) in an attempt to replicate it in other public sector entities, and use of "citizens voice" as a way to exercise social control over public administration (see Zuleta 2000).
9. Initially, the following public entities were selected as pilot agencies in the IRP: Ministry of Finance (including Customs and Revenue Service); Ministry of Housing and Basic Utilities; Ministry of Sustainable Development; Ministry of Agriculture, Cattle and Rural Development; Ministry of Education, Culture and Sports; and the prefecture of Oruro.

10. Even though the reform agreement was signed on that date, the institutional reform of NTS had already started on September 15, 2001, after its new executive president and board of directors were appointed by the president of Bolivia (and after being nominated by two-thirds of the members of the Chamber of Deputies). This date also marks the beginning of the NTS as a SARA (Fjeldstad 2005a).
11. Interestingly, in line with Koromzay's (2004) contention, this broad-based reform was launched in the middle of an economic crisis. In fact, during the period 1999–2003, on average and in constant 1990 prices, the Bolivian economy grew at a rate of 1.97 percent, whereas during the period 1993–98, its growth reached 4.74 percent (see http://www.ine.gov.bo).
12. The authors are indebted to Mario Arduz, former general manager of the NTS, for the information provided to describe the NTS reform strategy.
13. Notwithstanding the progress made in this area, exemptions obtained by socially and politically influential groups continue to fracture the tax system by means of special regimes (the simplified tax regime, the integrated tax regime, and the unified agricultural regime) that work against the proper application of the VAT. Another limitation of the current system is the lack of a proper income tax to substitute for the complementary regime of the VAT, which functions as a de facto income tax in Bolivia. This situation supports the argument advanced by Di John (2006).
14. In this connection, particular emphasis was placed on use of technology for receiving sworn tax statements through the Internet, notifications by e-mail, and the like.
15. See http://www.impuestos.gov.bo. Note that two factors appear to have played a major role in this outcome, namely, leadership and support from the IRP. First, the head of the agency was highly motivated and remained in the post for most of the reform process. Second, despite a lack of political will throughout the execution period of the reform (August 2002–December 2005), the technical unit of the IRP managed to provide effective, continuing technical and financial assistance to the NTS. In this context, competitive hiring and incremental salaries were crucial for a successful institutional change; for example, the coefficient of correlation between data on taxes collected by the NTS (in the internal market) and numbers of competitively hired personnel during the same implementation process was found to be relatively high (76 percent).
16. This section draws heavily on the technical document elaborated by Suárez (2004).
17. According to Harrison and Krelove (2005), exporters make all of the VAT refund claims in Bolivia.
18. This rule appears to be pervasive for the treasury because it entails a real export subsidy. Moreover, to the extent that certain operational costs incurred by exporters such as labor payments, social welfare contributions, and depreciation are not subject to VAT, this norm is also contradictory in its own terms because it implies that the exporter constitutes a simple intermediary incapable of generating value or making these expenditures.
19. The Instructions Guide DAF No. 02-09-07, enacted on April 5, 1997, was a confusing, 60-page document without a flow chart and including irrelevant information on specific functions of personnel in charge of inspection, auditing, and control activities.
20. The authors are indebted to Mario Arduz, former general manager of the NTS, for the information provided to develop this subsection.
21. Strictly speaking, these unlawful refunds are often based on types of fraud that are more closely associated with organized crime than with conventional tax evasion, "the main difference being that, unlike conventional VAT evasion, they rely on transactions that never actually take place" (Pashev 2005).

22. Technical Guide No. FIS-GT-CED-V01-019, enacted on July 10, 2003, is a straightforward, 21-page document with a flow chart including only relevant information on inspection, auditing, and control processes and procedures for VAT refunds. Under the new inspection procedures, the universe of invoices subject to verification is quantified, supplier invoices are grouped in order of importance, analysis criteria are applied, and at least half of all invoices are actually verified for validity.
23. Ron Myers has suggested, in an e-mail to the authors, that the fall in refunds may have been caused by policy changes or unfair treatment to exporters. However, during the reform period (2002–05), no significant policy changes regarding VAT refunds were made. The question of unfair treatment of exporters remains an important issue subject to further scrutiny.
24. An alternative regulatory framework for VAT refunds should be explored. One option may be to use a VAT retention system such as the one currently being applied in Argentina, Chile, and Peru. Harrison and Krelove (2005) describe a number of other approaches that other countries have adopted to deal with VAT refund problems.
25. Options for coordination between Customs and the NTS abound. Some examples are joint audits and exchange of information on fraudulent taxpayers, including importers and exporters; coordinated control activities; and delegation of tasks by the NTS to be performed by Customs (for example, issuance of tax identification numbers at the border between Bolivia and neighboring countries).
26. However, this conclusion should be taken with caution. As Harrison and Krelove (2005) suggest, the challenge for tax administrations is indeed "to strike a balance between applying effective controls to protect revenue, while ensuring that compliant taxpayers are not overburdened with compliance costs." In this connection, another important issue subject to further enquiry, particularly for a small and landlocked country such as Bolivia, may be whether Bolivian exporters face higher transactions costs than other developing countries, implying that effective controls to protect revenue could also have negative consequences for the economy as a whole.
27. Bolivia's experience is consistent with experiences elsewhere, such as the establishment of SUNAT, a semiautonomous revenue authority, in Peru. On SUNAT, see Taliercio and Engelschalk (2001); see Mann (2004) for other reasonably successful experiences. The creation of SARAs does not guarantee that corruption will be reduced. The experience with SARAs in some countries, including many in Africa, indicates that corruption may be reduced in the initial years but then quickly rise; see, for example, Kidd and Crandall (2006); and Fjeldstad (2005b).

REFERENCES

Di John, Jonathan. 2006. "The Political Economy of Taxation and Tax Reform in Developing Countries." UNU-WIDER Research Paper 2006/74. United Nations University–World Institute for Development Economics Research (July), http://www.wider.unu.edu/publications/publications.htm.

Fjeldstad, Odd-Helge. 2004. "To Pay or Not to Pay? Citizens's Views on Taxation in Local Authorities in Tanzania." WP 8, Chr. Michelsen Institute, Bergen, Norway.

———. 2005a. "Corruption in Tax Administration: Lessons from Institutional Reforms in Uganda." CMI Working Paper. Chr. Michelsen Institute, Bergen, Norway. http://www.cmi.no/pdf/?file=/publications/2005/wp/wp2005-10.pdf.

———. 2005b. "Revenue Administration and Corruption." U4 Issue 2:2005, Chr. Michelsen Institute, Bergen, Norway. http://www.u4.no/themes/pfm/u4issue2_05fjeldstad.pdf.

Fjeldstad, Odd-Helge, and B. Tungodden. 2003. "Fiscal Corruption: A Vice or a Virtue?" *World Development* 31 (8): 1459–67.

Harrison, Graham, and Russell Krelove. 2005. "VAT Refunds: A Review of Country Experience." IMF Working Paper WP/05/218, International Monetary Fund, Washington, DC (November).

Kidd, Maureen, and William Crandall. 2006. "Revenue Authorities: Issues and Problems in Evaluating Their Success." International Monetary Fund, Washington, DC.

Klitgaard, Robert. 1988. *Controlling Corruption*. Berkeley: University of California Press.

Koromzay, Val. 2004. "Some Reflections on the Political Economy of Reform." Comments presented to the International Conference on Economic Reforms for Europe: Growth Opportunities in an Enlarged European Union, Bratislava, Slovakia, March 18.

Leyton, Alberto, and Yasuhiko Matsuda. 2004. "Overcoming Informality in the Bolivian State: The First Generation Institutional and Governance Reviews and the National Integrity Plan." Paper prepared for the Ninth International Congress of the Latin American Center of Administration for Development, Madrid, November 2–4.

Mann, Arthur J. 2004. "Are Semi-Autonomous Revenue Authorities the Answer to Tax Administration Problems in Developing Countries?—A Practical Guide." Research Paper for the project "Fiscal Reform for Trade Liberalization," U.S. Agency for International Development, Washington, DC (August).

Mookherjee, D. 1997. "Incentive Reforms in Developing Country Bureaucracies: Lessons from Tax Administration." Paper prepared for the Annual Bank Conference on Developing Economics, World Bank, Washington, DC.

Pashev, Konstantin. 2005. "Corruption and Tax Compliance: Challenges to Tax Policy and Administration." Center for the Study of Democracy Report 16, Sofia, http://www.csd.bg/fileSrs.php?id=1411.

Rose-Ackerman, Susan. 1999. *Corruption in Government: Causes, Consequences, and Reform.* Cambridge: Cambridge University Press.

Suárez, Saúl. 2004. "Evaluación del proceso de devolución impositiva." National Tax Service, National Inspection Department, Technical Document, La Paz (June).

Taliercio, Robert. 2004. "Designing Performance: The Semi-Autonomous Revenue Authority Model in Africa and Latin America." Policy Research Working Paper 3423, World Bank, Washington, DC.

Taliercio, Robert, and Michael Engelschalk. 2001. "Strengthening Peru's Tax Agency." PREM Notes 60, Poverty Reduction and Economic Management Network, World Bank, Washington, DC.

Zuleta, Juan Carlos. 2000. "Preface." In *Bolivia: From Patronage to a Professional State, Bolivia Institutional and Governance Review*, vol. 1: *Main Report.* Report 20115-BO. Washington, DC: World Bank.

11

The Challenge of Combating Corruption in Customs Administrations

CARLOS FERREIRA, MICHAEL ENGELSCHALK, AND WILLIAM MAYVILLE

"The World Customs Organization Arusha Declaration for customs integrity proposes two elements to improve integrity: simplification of procedures, including automation, and adequate human resource management. The declaration, along with the Integrity Development Guide, a set of comprehensive integrity tools specifically designed to help customs administrations implement the principles contained in the Arusha Declaration, casts light on customs reform and modernization from the angle of fighting corruption, as improving integrity should be a cornerstone of any capacity building activities.

With regard to simplifying customs procedures, The WCO Revised Kyoto Convention provides a blueprint for modern customs procedures and administration in a comprehensive and structured manner. But we must help managers of customs take leadership in implementing the convention with strong political and business support.

Partnership with business is essential because it is necessary to address the dual problem of giving and receiving bribes. As such, the Revised Kyoto Convention urges customs administrations to take measures that will encourage business to improve their compliance with law, which should contribute to enhancing partnership with trade, including in fighting corruption.

The World Bank has been a reliable partner in the fight against corruption. I appreciate the joint approach in encouraging customs to intensify their efforts as well as calling governments, businesses, donors, and all other stakeholders for supporting customs efforts."

Kunio Mikuriya, Deputy Secretary General, World Customs Organization

Customs administrations play a vital role in the economic welfare of a country. For that reason, dysfunctional customs administrations can easily harm trade relations and curtail foreign investment. Tax revenue generated from trade generally is declining in importance in both developing and transition countries; nevertheless, customs revenue still represents a substantial share of total tax collection. For example, in the Russian Federation, customs duties accounted for nearly 34 percent of total federal budget revenues in 2001 and were approaching 40 percent by 2005.

In addition, the customs administration's role in the operation of value added tax (VAT) systems positions it as a core revenue collection agency—even when tariffs are low.

Customs operations pose several challenges for public sector management as well. In most countries, the customs agency is one of the largest public sector agencies because of its extensive office network and large number of staff. The business community frequently perceives customs as one of the most serious constraints to business investment (World Bank 2003) and cites it as one of the most corrupt government agencies. The Transparency International Global Corruption Barometer identifies customs as the third most corrupt government agency after the police and the tax administration (Transparency International 2005, p. 3). Corruption in customs agencies differs from that of other government bureaus, in that it may not even be understood as such by commodity importers and exporters. Bribes requested by customs officials to facilitate the clearance of import or export flows easily become tacitly accepted as another aspect of the cost of doing business and thus a normal part of overall clearance expenses of customs brokers; these expenses are then routinely passed on to the customer through increased service fees. What makes customs administrations so susceptible to institutionalized corruption?

This chapter identifies the reasons for corruption in customs administrations and the conditions under which such practices flourish. Generally preferred solutions, such as those recommended by the World Customs Organization (WCO), are implemented in organizational environments where corruption is a major challenge. Discussion centers on areas of vulnerability inherent in customs administrations and links between and among them. These vulnerabilities are highlighted through country examples, with tools provided to diagnose the root causes of corruption. Additional information on addressing vulnerabilities, including how to plan comprehensive customs reforms, can be found in the World Bank's *Customs Modernization Handbook* (De Wulf and Sokol 2005).

UNIQUE VULNERABILITY OF CUSTOMS

Few public agencies exist in which the classic preconditions for institutional corruption are as clearly present as they are in customs administrations. Administrative monopoly combined with broad discretionary power—particularly in a working environment where risk-based systems of control and accountability are absent or easily breached—generate corrupt practices (Shaver 1997). As Klitgaard (1988, p. 75) observed, corruption occurs when there is a monopoly plus discretion and no accountability. Moreover, because of its monopoly over the flow of goods, a customs agency can easily interfere with a firm's ability to do business. For this reason, the potential for corruption in the customs environment cannot be overstated (Lane 1998). A decision by a customs official to accept a fraudulent declaration can reduce significantly the duties and taxes owed and provide high rents both for the trader and the customs official, with the spoils divided at the expense of the treasury. And rents extracted can be high. For example, a report prepared for Bulgaria by the Centre for the Study of Democracy (2002, p. 11) found that the average bribe totaled nearly 30 percent of unpaid customs duties and other fees.

As a border protection agency, customs must endeavor to prevent the importation of illegal goods. Smuggling of drugs and weapons, plus large-scale smuggling of alcohol and cigarettes, places customs directly into the vortex of organized crime—with criminals using any means, from extensive bribery to intimidation and violence, to promote their illegal transactions. Given the high financial stakes, rent-seeking opportunities tend to multiply and become difficult to staunch. Lane (1998) cites the case of one U.S. Customs inspector who extorted approximately $1 million for arranging the entry of textiles to circumvent U.S. law. The heavy financial losses attributable to deviant customs decisions also can be exacerbated when linked to broad discretionary power given to low-paid customs officials, who can freely choose to accept or reject an import or export declaration or arbitrarily embargo an otherwise acceptable shipment for inspection. Absent an efficient postclearance control system, the chance that such discretionary practices will ever be detected becomes minuscule.

Unlike tax administrations, customs agencies operate in geographically dispersed, remote posts, frequently around the clock, with relatively few staff. In this environment, adequate supervision of a customs office or individual officer becomes problematic. The risk of corruption networks springing up like weeds increases commensurately, and collusion affecting an entire local customs office is not unknown. Staff transferred to offices permeated by corruption understandably find it difficult to refuse participation in illegal schemes—group intimidation takes hold and risk of refusal imperils individual well-being. Traditional control of remote offices through headquarters or regional internal audit units has proven ineffectual in the absence of systematic efforts to diagnose and eradicate the causes (box 11.1).

In too many countries, customs control still denotes substantial direct contact between customs officials and import agents. Even with modern, deliberately sophisticated clearance procedures, direct contact cannot be avoided while goods are being physically inspected. Customs checks carry the inherent risk of not being conducted by a team but rather an individual officer, especially in small offices and during night and weekend shifts, thereby cultivating the opportunity for rent-seeking behavior.

BOX 11.1 The Difficulty of Detecting Corruption Networks at Remote Customs Offices

In November 2004, Russian investigators revealed a major corruption network at the Rylsk customs office and arrested the head and deputy head of the office. The office is located in a small village in the Kursk *oblast* about five kilometers from the Ukrainian border, with only one road linking the village to the hinterland. Office staff was accused of having issued falsified customs documents to importers of electronics and clothes. Between December 2003 and March 2004 alone, between $3 million and $6 million in customs duties were evaded through this scheme. However, detection was particularly difficult, as all male inhabitants of the village were working at the customs office, and its remote location made a covert observation of its operations virtually impossible. When intelligence units first tried to inspect the Rylsk customs warehouse, they were prevented from doing so by 10 armed fighters from the Kursk customs agency, who were joined by local security officers with rifles.

Source: Center for Security Studies at the Swiss Federal Institute of Technology (ETF) and Transnational Crime and Corruption Center (TraCCC) 2004.

But not all cases of corruption at the border should be attributed to customs agents. Customs is the most prominent and visible government agency on the frontier, so it is frequently blamed for fraud actually committed by other border control agencies. In Russia, in addition to the customs service, standard border control of shipments entering the country by land requires checks by immigration, border police, transport inspection, sanitary inspection, and veterinary control. Corruption can germinate through actions of any of these border agencies; moreover, importers may be confused about which agency bears responsibility for any given step in border control processing—especially when requirements for multiple clearances arise before releasing goods. For this reason, any program aimed at facilitating cross-border trade and reducing corruption should focus not just on customs but on the entire border administration, mapping corruption risks in all other border control agencies.

CORRUPTION'S TELLING EFFECT ON PERFORMANCE

Modern customs administrations not only collect revenue but also play two other vital national roles: expediting cross-border trade to promote economic development and preventing international trafficking in illicit goods, such as weapons and narcotics, to protect the state. Corrupt practices often stand in the way of meeting these challenges, actively compromising revenue systems operations, trade facilitation, and internal security requirements.

Revenue System Operations

A sharp shortfall in the expected amount of customs duties and tax revenues collected is a clear signal that corruption is rampant. Pressure points include the collection of import duties—that is, customs duties, excises, and VAT—as well as the expected operation of the domestic tax system. Domestic VAT systems are most often breached by fraudulent VAT refund claims and improper initial valuation. Without proper controls, fraudulent refund claims can become widespread. Customs must ensure the legitimacy of refunds to exporters by checking the accuracy of export declarations and ensuring that certified copies of export declarations are provided only for goods that actually leave the country. A strong invitation to abuse the system arises if this control function is weak (see chapter 10 for a discussion of VAT export refunds in Bolivia).

Customs corruption also can undermine the entire VAT system—the consumption tax evaporates if the levy is not assessed and recovered across the production chain. For imports, the proper levy corresponds to the first production stage. Securing VAT collection on imports at the initial stage is crucial to effective collection of revenue throughout the production chain because it provides the foundation for the proper functioning of the VAT system in general (Ebrill and others 2001, p. 49).

Imported goods that bypass the VAT levy rarely enter the formal economy. With the tax burden lowered by this means, traders in the gray economy enjoy a comparative advantage over compliant importers. This occurs when the market is stocked with smuggled goods, thus distorting price signals and often forcing compliant local producers and importers out of legitimate business and into the shadow economy. So corrupt practices in customs directly influence the size of a country's informal economy and can effectively lower the ratio of tax revenue to gross domestic product (GDP).

Estimation of forgone revenues attributable to corruption in customs is complicated. It is nearly impossible to separate the consequences of customs inefficiency and the inability to prevent smuggling, to distinguish fraud from actual smuggling, or to identify fraud specifically linked to corruption. Empirically derived data and other estimates typically refer not only to customs revenue loss that stems from corrupt practices but more broadly to losses caused by inefficiency. Nevertheless, composite data indicate that customs corruption can have serious consequences for the federal budget. In Russia, the minister of economy complained that in 2004 the country was losing $4.5 billion in duties on goods imported from Europe, which the minister said could be attributed to false customs declarations linked mainly to organized corruption.[1] In Bangladesh in 2000, the forgone customs revenue traced to corruption and inefficiency, as well as to the income tax department, was estimated to exceed 5 percent of GDP (OECD 2003, p. 9). Fortunately, measures to deal systematically with customs corruption have produced dramatic results. In Ukraine, following a campaign initiated by the new government in late 2004 to combat corruption and reduce smuggling, revenues from import duties in the first half of 2005 increased by 61.5 percent over the same period in 2004. This occurred with no increase in tariff rates.[2]

Efficiency of International Trade Operations

Customs corruption impedes trade facilitation and consequently reduces a country's international competitiveness. From a business standpoint, corruption both reduces the predictability of customs operations and raises the cost of cross-border trade. In business sectors that depend on expeditious clearance processes, such as courier services and just-in-time manufacturing, substantial illicit payments may be required to operate a business efficiently. In one transition country, the representative of an international express delivery service reported that he had to "employ" a number of customs agents to meet operational targets. Traders reluctant to engage in corrupt practices experience a decided disadvantage. This takes the form of substantial delays in import clearance, extensive physical inspections, and the use of administrative discretion that works against the importer.

Corruption also can nullify efforts toward administrative simplification and become a prime mover for erecting administrative barriers and inducing efficiency losses. The United Nations Conference on Trade and Development (UNCTAD) and the World Bank observed in a 1996 joint review (de Castro 1996) that the key trade facilitation problem is not the danger posed by practices where irregular payments can move goods through even the strictest regulatory system; nor is it the extra "unofficial" charges levied on innocent as well as fraudulent traders. Instead, it is the maintenance of unnecessarily complicated procedures that foster chronic delays for the general run of consignments, thus providing the pretext for bribes for "exceptional" simplifications. In many countries, customs is open for extended hours, including round-the-clock seven days a week. The reduction of service hours for customs clearance is a typical practice that creates opportunities for extracting rents from importers. A particularly egregious example is that of Cambodia, in particular the entry points of the port of Sihanoukville and the city of Phnom Penh. Customs ends daily operations at 5:00 p.m., even though both the port and city are equipped to handle vessels and other carriers 24 hours a day. Only through informal payments could customs officials be persuaded to operate after 5:00 p.m. (Integrated Framework 2001). The diversion of imports to inefficient transportation routes—especially when corruption resides in the nearest customs clearance posts—is yet another example of efficiency loss resulting from corruption.

The consequences of corruption on trade facilitation extend far beyond the deleterious effects on individual importers and can seriously place the overall competitiveness of a country at risk. Competition to attract international trade and investment continues to grow unabated worldwide. The trade community is acutely aware of transaction costs and the need for predictability and efficiency in customs clearance to increase business profitability. Pervasive corruption in a customs agency can have direct economic consequences for a country in the form of a lower ranking in global investment climate surveys. International trade also provides the conduit for economic growth by enhancing technology transfer, so corruption in customs can significantly reduce this potential by inhibiting such transfers (Yang 2005, p. 2).

Security

Corruption in customs takes on new significance in the current climate of national security awareness. It plays a vital role in combating illicit trade in high-risk and prohibited goods, including drugs, weapons, and explosives. In Germany, more than 70 percent of the total amount of drugs seized every year can be attributed to detection by customs officers. Collusion of organized crime with corrupt customs officials poses a major security risk and can easily neutralize sophisticated security systems. For instance, a high-tech X-ray machine operated at a corrupt customs post can thwart all efforts to pinpoint potential terrorist activities. Integrity programs and related security systems provide the backbone to protect the international trade supply chain at all stages (Mikuriya 2005).

MAPPING RISKS AND OPPORTUNITIES FOR CORRUPTION

Customs is exposed to the risk of corruption in myriad ways. In extreme cases, an entire customs administration can be politically captured, with customs becoming an instrument to generate revenues for the political elite.[3] In such cases, senior politicians sanction corrupt practices, and there is no political will to increase integrity and transparency. Political corruption can be facilitated by a governmental arrangement that makes customs independent of the general government structure, treating it as a special revenue-raising agency reporting directly to the president or prime minister.

Apart from the special case of political capture, corruption risks may be generated or increased either by the external framework in which the customs agency operates or by weaknesses inherent in its own internal organization and procedures. The legal and regulatory base for customs operations can present a major corruption risk for the agency. Examples (Walsh 2003) include complex and restrictive tax and foreign trade systems that lead to rent-seeking and corrupt behavior, and high tax and tariff rates that create incentives to engage in corrupt practices to reduce the tax burden. Exemptions, in particular discretionary exemptions, which can be granted by the minister or the head of the customs service, create opportunities for negotiation, and ambiguities in the customs and tax laws, especially regarding the classification of goods, often lead to discretionary behavior. When a trade tariff scheme is highly diversified, customs officials often threaten importers with misclassification of goods into more heavily taxed categories unless a bribe is paid (Gatti 1999).

The overall human resource management system in a country also can become another external factor with strong influence on customs integrity. A key issue is whether the civil service system allows a suitably rigorous recruitment process for customs staff. Given the huge potential to extract bribes, it is not uncommon that positions in customs are bought by interested individuals who intend to use the position for rent seeking. In Cambodia, the value of the "concession fee" required to secure a customs post was rumored to have increased within a few years from $2,000 to $10,000 (Integrated Framework 2001). A second issue is whether the salary level is adequate to support an integrity initiative. If the regular salary of a customs official is below a living wage for the country, it may be virtually impossible for an official to resist soliciting bribes to supplement his income for basic needs. At the same time, the difference between a customs salary and the potential income from corruption will always be substantial (see below). Whether the civil service and the judicial systems permit quick and appropriate action against identified incidence of corruption is also a major factor and frequently encountered constraint on maintaining customs integrity.

Finally, the lack of an appropriate external accountability system contributes to customs corruption. Clear and sufficiently ambitious performance targets—which not only refer to the amount of duties and taxes collected but also determine trade facilitation and service standards to be achieved and which are monitored on a regular basis—permit customs stakeholders to evaluate trends in the quality of customs administration.

In the area of organization and processes, the development of a customs anticorruption strategy signifies determining the specific risks of corrupt behavior at the various stages of the customs clearance process. McLinden (2005) has prepared a risk map—a list of core customs functions and their vulnerability to corruption (table 11.1).

An analysis of the specific elements of the customs clearance process and the development of a risk map, outlining the extent to which existing processes facilitate the integrity violations delineated above, are prerequisites for the design of an anticorruption strategy. The risk analysis should identify unnecessary administrative steps in the clearance process, steps that lack sufficient transparency, and areas that promote extensive direct contact between customs officials and clients.

TABLE 11.1 A Customs Risk Map

Selected customs functions	*Examples of integrity violations*
Processing of import, export, and transit declarations	Soliciting or accepting payment to • accelerate the processing of documents • ignore the fact that some cargo listed on the manifest was not declared • certify the exportation of fictitious exports or provide for a wrong HS (harmonized system) classification • permit goods in transit to be released for domestic consumption.
Assessment of origin, value, and classification of goods	Soliciting or accepting payments to • permit underinvoicing of goods • not challenge the declaration of goods under a different HS that attracts a lower tariff rate • accept a false country-of-origin declaration, thus permitting the importer to benefit from a preferential tariff regime.
Physical inspection, examination, and release of cargo	Soliciting or accepting staff who would • ensure that an inspecting officer is chosen who will take an accommodating approach to the inspection • skip the inspection • influence the findings of the inspection • simply speed up the inspection.
Administration of concessions, suspense and exemption schemes, and drawback schemes	Soliciting or accepting payment to • permit traders to release, for domestic consumption and without paying the required import duties, goods that entered under suspense regimes or goods made with inputs that entered under such regimes • obtain a release of the bond that is to protect customs revenues in cases of temporary admission of imports without adequate documentation • permit traders to claim excessive input coefficients for exports produced with inputs that benefited from the suspense regimes • permit traders to claim drawbacks for fictitious exports • permit importers to transfer imports that benefited from duty relief to unauthorized users or for unintended purposes, or permitting them to import such goods in excess of the amounts agreed to.
Conduct of postclearance audits	Soliciting or accepting payments to influence the outcome of audit findings.
Issuing of import licenses, warehouse approvals, and authorized trader status approvals	Soliciting or accepting payments to obtain these licenses and certificates without proper justification.
Processing of urgent consignments	Soliciting or accepting payments to obtain preferential treatment or speedy clearance.

Source: McLinden (2005, p. 69).

STRATEGIES FOR REDUCING THE RISK OF CORRUPTION

Reducing corruption became a priority of customs reform efforts in many transition and developing countries in the 1990s. At that time, customs organizations worldwide made a commitment to increasing integrity; subsequently, a wealth of experience in the design and implementation of anticorruption strategies became available. In 1993, the WCO, at its annual meeting in Arusha, Tanzania, formulated a declaration (the Arusha Declaration) as a blueprint for implementing comprehensive measures that collectively could reduce the opportunities and incentives for corrupt practices in customs. The declaration was revised in June 2003, based on experience and practices found most efficacious in counteracting corruption in WCO member states.

The Revised Arusha Declaration on Integrity in Customs recommends 10 specific areas that must be addressed to create the necessary transparency for customs operations: leadership and commitment; regulatory framework, transparency, automation, reform and modernization, audit and investigation, code of conduct, human resource management, morale and organizational culture, and relationship with the private sector. The WCO has also developed other diagnostic tools, including the Integrity Development Guide, available on its Web site (http://www.wcoomd.org), and the Model Code of Conduct. In addition, the WCO recently compiled the Compendium of Integrity Best Practices that is available to the public with periodic updates. A database of the compendium has also been developed and placed on the WCO Web site.

An anticorruption strategy for customs operations also needs to mesh elements addressing the opportunities for corruption with those intended to reduce the motive for corrupt practices (Das-Gupta, Engelschalk, and Mayville 1999). Addressing the motive for corruption primarily requires addressing weaknesses in human resource policies and management in general; however, the need for reforms may go far beyond this (table 11.2). The development of an elite ethos and esprit de corps, as a human

TABLE 11.2 Measures Addressing Motive and Opportunities for Corruption in Customs Agencies

Measures addressing motives	*Measures addressing opportunities*
• Elite ethos and esprit de corps	• Clear legal framework reducing discretion
• Positive career development	• Clarified valuation procedures
• Competitive base pay	• Computerization
• Incentives for high performance	• Inspections based on risk analysis
• Sanctions for corrupt behavior	• Stronger supervision and controls
• Stakeholder surveys	• Arm's length transactions and reduction in discretionary powers
	• Transparent clearance requirements
	• Rotation of officers
	• Functional organization
	• Internal audit unit
	• Stakeholder surveys

Source: Das-Gupta, Engelschalk, and Mayville (1999).

resource and training issue, requires familiarizing staff with the importance of customs administration for the country, developing and communicating a proper vision and mission statement of the organization, and designing team-building strategies and related programs. However, making a customs official proud of being part of the organization also requires creating an adequate work environment, including suitable work conditions and proper uniforms. This may not always be easy because of limited administrative budgets. In some cases, the establishment of customs as a semiautonomous revenue agency may seem a reasonable option to address such constraints; however, international experience suggests that structural independence is no panacea for dealing with endemic corruption.

The development of an elite ethos in customs can be aided by drafting a special code of ethics and conduct. General codes of conduct for the civil service are often used in lieu of special codes for customs agencies. While such general codes provide overall guidelines for the ethical behavior and conduct that is expected of civil servants, the special integrity challenges in customs are better addressed by a specific code of ethics and conduct that delineates the high moral and behavioral standards to which all customs officials are expected to adhere in their unique work environment. Basic elements of a customs code are a credo or statement of beliefs; guidelines for decision making when faced with ethical dilemmas; specific rules that prohibit certain behaviors and require others; definitions, rationales, and illustrations of acceptable and unacceptable behavior in specific situations; and resources and hotline information.[4] Crucial factors to the success of any code of conduct include its full dissemination to staff, continuous monitoring of its implementation, enforcement of disciplinary sanctions in cases where violations of basic principles are detected, and periodic updating and training. Experience in a number of countries attests that codes of conduct quickly lose relevance if management takes no visible or concrete action when staff members deviate from the principles of the code.

Clearly, offering a competitive salary and benefits package is another major factor for effectively addressing the motive for corruption—especially for customs officials in decision-making positions who have frequent and direct contact with clients. Customs agencies should be able to offer a living wage to staff. Nonetheless, evidence of the effect of salary increases and bonuses on the level of integrity in an agency is not definitive. Experience in Nepal has shown that in a few months a corrupt customs official could collect bribes equal to 1,000 annual salaries.[5] These data suggest that even substantial salary increases beyond a competitively set wage cannot completely wipe out the temptation to seek rents by corrupt customs officials or guarantee ethical behavior. A living wage can be achieved not only through base pay but by functional and performance-related bonuses—assuming the flexibility to regularly supplement base pay exists, as it does in Pakistan's Central Board of Revenue. Of course, not all customs administrations possess the authority and the required budget resources to implement similar bonus schemes—which often conflict with civil service pay guidelines unless special concessions are granted to customs administrations.

One of the main challenges in implementing an anticorruption strategy is designing a human resources policy that reduces incentives for corruption and creates the necessary conditions for customs staff to act with integrity, that is, refuse to engage in corrupt practices. This goes substantially beyond providing adequate salaries to necessitate complementary reforms in staff selection, career development, and succession planning. The overall public sector human resource management system can create serious obstacles to reform in this area. In some cases the establishment of a semiautonomous revenue authority may be perceived as the only remedy to overcome these constraints, but this must be accompanied by other comprehensive reform measures as well.

Limiting the opportunities for rent seeking requires a combination of coordinated organizational and legal measures, ranging from simplifying and streamlining the overall legal operational framework for customs to streamlining and computerizing specific business processes. The customs legal and regulatory framework has already been identified as a core risk area for corrupt practices. Simplification of the customs code and streamlining secondary legislation are perhaps the most important ways to limit the opportunity for corruption; such actions can also increase economic efficiency. For example, lowering and harmonizing tariff rates, eliminating special exemptions, providing clear rules for the classification of goods, and reducing the number and type of supporting documents to be provided for customs clearance clarifies and brings transparency to the obligations of importers and reduces their compliance costs. Transparency, moreover, requires availability of up-to-date and easily accessible information on customs laws and procedures. Many customs administrations have put the relevant legislation and explanatory circulars on their Web site. In addition, a clear and efficient administrative and judicial dispute resolution mechanism provides a tool for ensuring the correct application of the legal framework and protects the importer from having to participate in corrupt practices as the sole tool to ensure his rights. Moreover, the outcome of the dispute resolution process should be made widely available internally as well as to the trading community to reduce further the opportunities for future rent extraction.

Modernization of procedures is closely linked to transparency and represents a sine qua non for successful customs computerization initiatives. Streamlining the customs clearance process, eliminating unnecessary administrative requirements, and reducing the number of customs officials involved in the clearance process can reduce substantially the opportunities for corruption. Experience from developing countries reveals that the scope for such streamlining can be considerable. The customs reform program implemented in the Philippines in the 1990s, with World Bank support, dramatically reduced the number of signatures required to release a shipment from a port from 92 to 5; this reduction entailed replacing nearly 30 documents with a single administrative document. Similarly, like the reform of the legal framework, such streamlining not only may reduce corruption but concomitantly lead to major economic benefits. In the Philippines, the by-product of the reform was a remarkable contraction of time required to process cargo—from eight days to about two hours (UNCTAD 2005).

In addition to the efficiency gains of accelerating clearance, computerization of streamlined processes substantially reduces the need for direct contact between customs officials and importers or their agents. Moreover, it improves the conditions for deploying and enforcing the use of uniform business practices by all customs offices, substantially reduces discretion, and deters any discretion remaining to customs officials. It also provides clear and auditable trails of the clearance process, forcing customs staff to follow well-defined rules and procedures. As experience in Mali and Senegal showed, the key institutional reform was perceived to be the computerization of the customs service (Stasavage and Daubree 1998, p. 31). Computerization clearly can be the most important technical instrument for implementing an anticorruption program. It remains a support tool, however, and should not be the driving force in a reform process that should be rooted in overall institutional development (Engelschalk, Melhem, and Weist 2000).

Direct contact between customs officials and importers or their agents appears inevitable and leads to one of the main risk areas of corruption: the physical inspection of goods. The corruption risk is duplicated if the clearance system mandates 100 percent physical inspection of imports in the absence of a risk-based approach—as is still the practice in some customs administrations. In practice, 100 percent physical inspection is unrealistic, especially at most ports and other customs posts that process a high volume of imports. Apart from the efficiency losses from wasting scarce resources to inspect low-risk imports, a legal requirement to inspect all imports creates a powerful means to extract bribes from all importers, for example, by threatening that otherwise the physical inspection would be subjected to protracted delays or the import agent required to off-load the entire contents of the truck or container. The introduction of an efficient, risk-based selection system for physical inspection allows most imports to be cleared without inspection. It also forces customs officials to select cases for physical inspection based on risk analysis results, instead of the payment of "facilitating" money as the reason for not conducting a thorough inspection.

Various supervision and control mechanisms are essential for counteracting the opportunities for corruption. As in any government agency, an internal audit unit needs to impose adequate controls to ensure that rules and procedures are actually followed. Especially in larger countries, the application and interpretation of customs rules and regulations, including the implementation of an anticorruption strategy, may differ dramatically from region to region. For this reason, complaints about corruption may be much more frequent in some regions than others (a case in point is the results of a regional survey in Russia discussed elsewhere in this chapter). Close and ongoing supervision of regional and local customs offices by headquarters is required to smooth out regional disparities, with an emphasis on implementing a special anticorruption strategy where a high incidence of corruption exists.

Finally, an open, transparent, and trusting relationship with the private sector, in particular business associations and associations of customs brokers, is crucial for the success of any integrity program. As a primary beneficiary of increased integrity, the private sector can mobilize support for integrity initiatives and lobby for sustainability of results. Private sector feedback—through periodic perception surveys or routine consultations between customs management and private sector representatives—can support the required measurement of the efficacy of an anticorruption strategy, highlight trends, and identify problem areas.

TARGETING SYSTEMIC CORRUPTION: THE CASE OF THE RUSSIAN CUSTOMS SERVICE

The Russian Federal Customs Service epitomizes every anticorruption challenge outlined in this chapter. The reform of the service focused on addressing an array of incentives issues and still faces daunting external and internal challenges. Like all such reforms, it is work in progress, but it exemplifies the increasingly comprehensive customs reforms the World Bank is undertaking based on lessons learned in previous reform programs.

As in other countries, the Russian Federal Customs Service is one of the largest government agencies, with over 60,000 staff operating across 11 time zones. The agency includes the Moscow headquarters, 7 regional directorates, 141 customs offices processing goods and vehicles, and 670 customs posts, of which 416 are border checkpoints and 216 are in-country posts. The remaining 38 are special posts, such as for energy exports, and posts inside premises of large importers, such as IKEA in the Moscow *oblast*. The business community has consistently perceived the Russian customs service as one of the major obstacles to trade facilitation. Long delivery time, compared with other countries, was thought to be caused by most goods and related documents being examined individually by customs officials. Even minor errors or spelling mistakes could stop the whole procedure. For this reason, some 10–15 percent of all shipments were estimated to be delayed by two weeks. Delays and additional costs for imports were estimated to add 12 percent to the total cost of imported products. Many companies employed a full-time person to deal with customs procedures to reduce the risk of delays (OECD 2005, p. 63).

The Federal Customs Service operates in an environment replete with opportunities for corruption, as suggested by this brief profile. In 2006, Transparency International's Corruption Perception Index ranked Russia near the bottom for corruption—121st among 163 countries surveyed. Businesses cite rent seeking by customs officials as one of the most serious problems affecting their operations (OECD 2005, p. 72).

The Customs Reform Program

In December 2000, the Russian government launched the Federal Targeted Program of Development of the Customs Service of the Russian Federation for 2001–2003. There was general agreement that in addition to a fundamental shift in the mindset of the customs service—from protecting the domestic economy from external exploitation to fostering international trade and private sector development—an urgent need existed for improving the integrity and professional skills of customs officers, as well as substantially reducing opportunities for rent seeking by both officers and traders.

The targeted program provided a strategic context for modernization based on facilitating customs clearance; bringing transparency and predictability to customs activities; and fostering a partnership attitude in the relationship between the customs service and the trading community, including the creation of efficient dispute resolution mechanisms. The Federal Targeted Program ultimately became the basis for a World Bank technical assistance project. The objective of the project, complementing the government's targeted program, sought to modernize the Federal

Customs Service on two fronts. The first was to promote internationally acceptable practices for processing of international trade flows by customs; this step would further integrate the country into the world trading community, improve the investment climate, and secure the benefits from foreign and domestic investments in the economy. The second front was intended to increase taxpayer compliance with the customs code and ensure uniformity in its application; this action would support macroeconomic stability and increase transparency, timely transfer of collected revenues to the federal budget, and equity and predictability in customs operations. The project was approved in March 2003 and is expected to be completed in June 2009.

The Anticorruption Strategy of the Customs Reform Program

Improving integrity became a key element both of the Federal Targeted Program and the World Bank project. The design of the anticorruption strategy has been guided by international practice, in particular the revised Arusha Declaration. Russia agreed to the development of an annex in the World Bank Project Appraisal Document that specifically dealt with the need to develop an integrated strategy to promote integrity in the (then) State Customs Committee. The strategy sought to address the motive and opportunity for corruption in the customs service and included the following core activities.

Harmonization and Simplification of the Regulatory Framework for Customs Operations

A new customs code was drafted and became effective January 1, 2004, providing the legal basis for the reform activities of the project. The new legislation clarified and simplified customs law and brought it in line with requirements for World Trade Organization accession, which was planned for 2006. The new code also incorporated the principles of the revised Kyoto Convention for the Simplification and Harmonization of Customs Procedures. All secondary legislation was reviewed and redrafted to reduce ambiguities and discretionary powers. The new code also stipulated documents required for clearance to reduce the scope of customs officials' arbitrary implementation and unreasonable requests for documents.

Simple and Transparent Procedures

The introduction of risk-based verifications was intended to greatly reduce opportunities for rent seeking by curtailing the extensive physical inspection practices undertaken by the Federal Customs Service. The service would adopt a multichannel, selective approach to the inspection and release of consignments. Increased transparency and easier access to information would speed the clearance process while increasing confidence in the integrity of the customs service. The service would also improve its Web site design and promote the site's use by domestic and international communities as a key source of information on relevant laws, regulations, judicial decisions, and administrative rulings relating to customs matters.

Automation of Customs Processes

Discretion was to be reduced by improving and ensuring data exchanges and cross-checks; automated discharge of sensitive operations, such as the transit of high-value cargo; uniform application of customs procedures; and use of selectivity and detection of misclassification and undervaluation of goods. Over the past several years, the customs administration invested heavily in information technology. It is now in the process of integrating several interdependent processes so that critical information would be available when needed at border posts and inland clearance depots, and to the banking system. This integration required a comprehensive telecommunications infrastructure as well as a significantly redesigned and improved, unified, automated information system for the Federal Customs Service.

Strengthening a Professional Customs Administration

This step was taken by using a three-pronged approach that includes human resource policies, organizational restructuring, and improved management systems. To buttress these measures, a revised code of ethics was developed. It must be signed by all personnel, who also receive specific training in its role and value in increasing integrity in the service. The project in its initial phase supported a review of the existing organizational structure. Thereafter, the Federal Customs Service made adjustments at all levels in response to the modernization of customs business processes, including a reconfiguration of organizational units along functional lines. Finally, the project assists the service in improving management systems to safeguard accountability and ensure integrity.

Reinforcing the Capacity of the Personnel Inspection Unit

This step focused explicitly on providing anticorruption safeguards by studying patterns of evasion, designing a strategy to prevent abuses, and detecting cases of misconduct and taking disciplinary action.

Ensuring an Independent Appeals Mechanism

This mechanism was directed to help clarify customs procedures, privileges, and exemptions as well as to help reduce the currently high number of cases referred to the judiciary.

Reinforcing External Feedback Mechanisms

The Federal Customs Service long recognized the importance of involving stakeholders in its operations. The chairman of the service heads two advisory councils to improve relations with traders, one including executives from public associations representing the Russian business community, and another including foreign companies and international financial institutions. These councils also help reinforce corporate transparency. Short-, medium-, and long-term strategies were developed to inform the public and trading community of the rationale for and efforts to improve the customs administration. This included sample user surveys to provide baseline data on stakeholders' perceptions of agency integrity. Surveys are to be conducted periodically during project implementation to give senior management in the customs service direct feedback from clients, traders, and enterprises on changes in service performance.

Tracing Integrity Improvements through Performance Indicators

Gradual institutional reform to improve integrity in the customs service is more realistic and effective in achieving sustainable results than an ad hoc, symptomatic approach. While the new business processes would have nationwide impact, the investment in technology infrastructure was initially limited to the offices that generate higher revenues. Eventually, the customs service is expected to modernize other offices as well, to avoid exposure to gray market operators who might seek out more vulnerable posts.

The full impact of the anticorruption measures in this project will need several years to take root. Systemic political and legal factors influence the climate for corruption in any country, and these affect but fall outside the control of the customs administration. To measure the positive impact of the integrity agenda, a series of indicators was developed and is being monitored on a periodic basis. The indicators include those that have an indirect rather than direct impact on corruption, such as:

- increases in the overall compliance level in the collection of taxes and duties
- increased enforced compliance in the collection of taxes and duties
- use of a risk-based approach and a reduced number of import declarations and nonenergy exports declarations selected for physical inspection
- reduced average customs processing and clearance time at the border and at import clearance terminals
- perceptions of traders and other stakeholders regarding the quality of service, responsiveness to complaints, and integrity of the customs administration, as indicated by periodic surveys.

Results Achieved to Date

Reducing corruption is a long-term process and the project is nearing the midpoint of implementation. Initial results are mixed but have had some positive consequences. In early 2005, the Russian business community rated the Federal Customs Service as the best government agency for openness and transparency. In contrast, foreign firms operating in Russia report improvements but still encounter legal and technical ambiguities.

Evidence from the customs service program to combat corruption indicates at least some initial success. In 2005, the Internal Control Departments, both headquarters and regionally, conducted 100 document checks and 42 cargo-specific checks. Financial violations detected accounted for some 47 million Russian rubles (about $1.5 million); 27 officials were subjected to disciplinary action and 14 to financial sanctions.

In addition, internal security units initiated 530 criminal cases, including 252 cases of corruption (compared with 413 and 218 cases in 2004, respectively). Of the total, 216 cases were initiated against customs officials. Notably, 107 officials pleaded guilty on criminal grounds, compared with 192 criminal cases, 188 cases of corruption, and 80 against customs officials, respectively, the previous year. Additionally, in

2005, there were 36 cases of attempts to bribe customs officials, with action initiated against 37 staff, and 16 persons who attempted to bribe customs officials pleaded guilty—an increase over 2004 totals.

To prevent corruption among customs staff, 9,432 persons went through rigorous background checks in 2005 as part of the recruitment and promotion procedure. Of these, 272 candidates were denied employment or promotion in the Federal Customs Service, including 35 persons found to be communicating with criminal organizations on customs matters. Also, 91 cases were detected of customs officials participating in business activities or supporting commercial ventures while performing official duties. Overall, 728 official inspections were initiated that led to the firing of 45 customs officials, disciplinary sanctions against 761, and 12 rotations to other positions.

The International Monetary Fund (IMF) found that the measures taken to reform customs present a major step in furthering transparency in the Federal Customs Service (IMF 2004, p. 15). Nevertheless, as the Transparency International Global Corruption Barometer for 2005 shows, the customs service is still perceived as having serious corruption problems. The Federal Customs Service received a rating of 3.7 on a scale ranging from 1 (not at all corrupt) to 5 (extremely corrupt) and thus is "cleaner" than the police (rating 4.2) but still far from satisfactory.

There is evidence that the level of corruption in customs differs substantially among regions, which is understandable in a country the size of Russia. The Centre for Economic and Financial Research (CEFIR) in Moscow conducted a survey of 510 companies in seven regions, measuring changes in customs performance during the first half of 2004. The results of the survey show that corruption was considered nearly nonexistent in Karelia but remained substantial in Kaliningrad and the Moscow *oblast* (figure 11.1).

The IMF (2004, p. 15) noted that the new customs code—the objectives of which are to clarify the rights and responsibilities of traders and customs officers and to significantly lessen the scope for discretion in customs valuation—together with the steps

FIGURE 11.1 Customs Performance in Selected Russian Regions, 2004

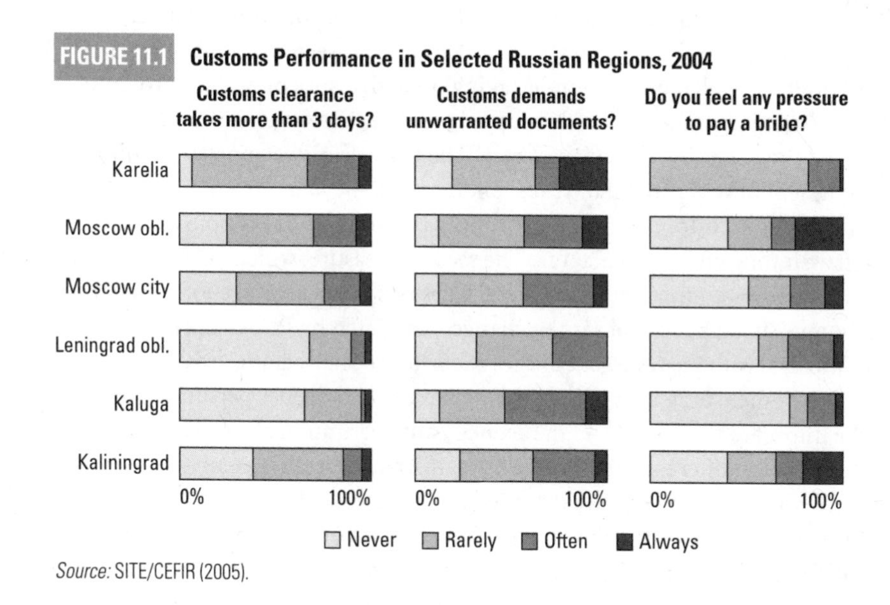

Source: SITE/CEFIR (2005).

BOX 11.2 Bribery in the Case of Cargo Escorting

An edict issued by the Russian cabinet provides for the escort of goods valued at more than $50,000 by customs officers at rates fixed by the government. In practice, however, customs officials frequently argue that they have only a few officers on duty and therefore cannot escort a shipment. They suggest that clients should use a commercial firm instead. But not only are the rates in this case 5 to 10 times the official rate, but in practice, the only certified agency that renders such commercial services is the Union of Customs Veterans.

Source: Vremya Novostei, October 27, 2005.

to automate customs procedures and standardize documentation requirements—represent a major step forward in furthering transparency in the customs service. Additional work will be required to improve the dissemination of information about the details of the code and to achieve consistency in interpretation by local customs posts, where interpretive variations persist (OECD 2005, p. 62).

Evidence also suggests that efforts to increase integrity will need to focus on the relationship between the customs service and private agents, in particular customs brokers, to avoid the risk that corruption will not be reduced but instead assume a new guise as bribes become replaced by fees to intermediaries. The CEFIR report (CITE/CEFIR 2005) suggests that while overall corruption in the Federal Customs Service might be decreasing, the costs to intermediaries were reported to have increased at the same time. The example of the International Road Union illustrates how such practices might work (box 11.2).

Recent Developments

The modernization reform of the customs administration in Russia has been central to the government's expressed desire to integrate with the global economy, attract direct foreign investment, and establish a sustainable basis for growth. Clearly, dealing with corruption in the Federal Customs Service was seen as a long-term, ongoing effort, as it is for all countries undertaking proactive anticorruption programs.

The Russian government recently adopted measures to reorganize the government that affected the State Customs Committee. The first was a sweeping reorganization and realignment of government bureaus, under which the State Customs Committee became the Federal Customs Service, reporting to the Ministry of Economy, with many of its staff assuming civil service status. The second measure, which occurred in May 2006, pertains to customs alone: the Federal Customs Service now reports directly to the prime minister. The reason for the change, mandated by Russia's president, was ostensibly to deal with the resurgence of corruption, especially along the China border posts, with commensurate top management changes and deeper personnel implications. The impact of this change on the agency's anticorruption efforts is still unclear. It is not unusual for different structural and organizational arrangements to occur with or without reform agendas that are intended to curb corruption in customs. As such, the Russian reform typifies the ebb and flow of reform in general and the shifting targets of anticorruption programs, especially in important revenue-generating agencies.

CONCLUSIONS

Anticorruption efforts in customs administrations take many forms and must be constantly monitored to ensure that they continue to produce results. Emphasis should be placed on institutional and organizational development, starting with such basics as the legal framework, human resource management and incentive systems, integrity training, and the commitment of headquarters and field managers to the integrity program. Highly automated systems also are an integral part of any anticorruption program. In fact, the robustness of business processes and systems is key to reducing opportunities for corruption and must accompany any efforts to address motive (by changing incentive systems, for example), which may prove insufficient otherwise. In the end, the opportunity and motive for corruption will vary with country circumstances; however, the common elements described in this chapter must receive systematic and persistent attention while reforms are taking place and remedies sustained over time—using international benchmarks.

The pressure to engage in corrupt practices will persist in customs administrations, and anticorruption efforts will need to be renewed from time to time. Abatement of corruption will depend on the ability of these agencies to severely limit opportunities by identifying flashpoints through risk mapping and then deliberately addressing them. Appropriate incentives also must be developed to curtail any rent-seeking motivation on the part of customs officials. The sustained efforts of governments to support anticorruption reform programs in customs is a sine qua non for even modest success in combating corrupt practices at the government, agency, and individual levels.

ENDNOTES

1. *RIA Novosti Moscow,* December 8, 2005.
2. SigmaBleyzer Kyiv. "Ukraine—Macroeconomic situation—July 2005." August 5, 2005.
3. An example of a scenario for political corruption in customs is Bolivia, in Hors (2001, p. 20).
4. For further information, see William Mayville, "Codes of Ethics and Conduct in Revenue Administrations: What Does International Practice Tell Us." http://www1.worldbank.org/publicsector/pe/Tax/CodesofEthics.doc.
5. Statements during a session on "Managing Integrity in Customs," Global Forum III on Fighting Corruption and Safeguarding Integrity, hosted by the government of Korea with the help of Transparency International and the International Anti-Corruption Conference (IACC) Council, Seoul, May 2003.

REFERENCES

Center for Security Studies at the Swiss Federal Institute of Technology (ETH) and the Transnational Crime and Corruption Center at American University (TraCCC). 2004. "Russia Regional Report" 9 (25). Zurich and Washington, DC.

Centre for the Study of Democracy. 2002. "Corruption, Trafficking, and Institutional Reform: Prevention of Trans-Border Crime in Bulgaria (2001–2002)." Sofia.

De Castro, Carlos F. 1996. "Trade and Transport Facilitation. Review of Current Issues and Experience." SSATP Working Paper 27, UNCTAD, Geneva, and World Bank, Washington, DC.

De Wulf, Luc, and José B. Sokol, eds. 2005. *Customs Modernization Handbook.* Washington, DC: World Bank.

Das-Gupta, Arindam, Michael Engelschalk, and William Mayville. 1999. "An Anticorruption Strategy for Revenue Administration." PREM Note 33, Poverty Reduction and Economic Management Network, World Bank, Washington, DC.

Ebrill, Liam, Michael Keen, Jean-Paul Bodin, and Victoria Summers. 2001. "The Modern VAT." International Monetary Fund, Washington, DC.

Engelschalk, Michael, Samia Melhem, and Dana Weist. 2000. "Computerizing Tax and Customs Administrations." PREM Note 44, Poverty Reduction and Economic Management Network, World Bank, Washington, DC.

Gatti, Roberta. 1999. "Corruption and Trade Tariffs, or a Case for Uniform Tariffs." Policy Research Working Paper 2216, World Bank, Washington, DC.

Hors, Irène. 2001. "Fighting Corruption in Customs Administration: What Can We Learn from Recent Experiences?" OECD Development Centre Working Paper 175, Organisation for Economic Co-operation and Development, Paris.

IMF (International Monetary Fund). 2004. "Russian Federation: Report on the Observance of Standards and Codes: Fiscal Transparency Module." Country Report 04/288, IMF, Washington, DC.

Integrated Framework for Trade-Related Technical Assistance. 2001. "Cambodia Integration and Competitiveness Study." Pilot study, Integrated Framework for Trade-Related Technical Assistance.

Klitgaard, Robert. 1988. *Controlling Corruption.* Berkeley: University of California Press.

Lane, Michael. 1998. "Customs and Corruption." Working paper, Transparency International, Berlin.

McLinden, Gerard. 2005. "Integrity in Customs." In *Customs Modernization Handbook*, ed. Luc De Wulf and José B. Sokol. Washington, DC: World Bank.

Mikuriya, Kunio. 2005. "Integrity: a Cornerstone for Economic Development and Security." Speech at Global Forum IV on Fighting Corruption and Safeguarding Integrity, Brasilia, June 6–9.

OECD (Organisation for Economic Co-operation and Development). 2003. "Trade Facilitation Reforms in the Service of Development." Trade Committee Working Paper TD/TC/WP(2003)11/FINAL, OECD, Paris.

———. 2005. "Regulatory Reform in Russia: Enhancing Market Openness through Regulatory Reform." OECD, Paris.

Shaver, James W. 1997. "Defeating Corruption in the International Trade Environment: A Global Vision." Paper presented at the Eighth International Anti-Corruption Conference, Lima.

SITE/CEFIR. 2005. "Russian Customs Reform." Centre for Economic and Financial Research, Moscow.

Stasavage, David, and Cecile Daubree. 1998. "Determinants of Customs Fraud and Corruption: Evidence from Two African Countries." Working Paper 138, OECD, Paris.

Transparency International. 2005. "Report on the Transparency International Global Corruption Barometer 2005," http://www.transparency.org/policy_and_research/surveys_indices/gcb.

UNCTAD. 2005. "Use of Customs Automation Systems." Trust Fund for Trade Facilitation Negotiations, Technical Note 3, United Nations Conference on Trade and Development, Geneva.

Walsh, James. 2003. "Practical Measures to Promote Integrity in Customs Administrations." In *Changing Customs: Challenges and Strategies for the Reform of Customs Administration*, ed. Michael Keen. Washington, DC: International Monetary Fund.

World Bank. 2003. Investment Climate Survey Database, http://www.enterprisesurveys.org/.

Yang, Dean. 2005. "Integrity for Hire: An Analysis of a Widespread Program for Combating Customs Corruption." Discussion paper 525, Gerald R. Ford School of Public Policy, University of Michigan, Ann Arbor.

PART 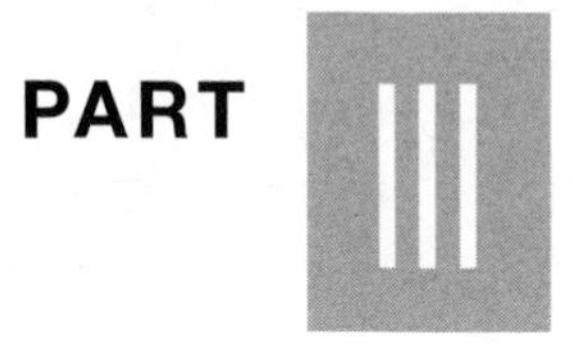

Where Goes the Money?

12

Money Laundering and Corruption

MICHAEL LEVI, MARIA DAKOLIAS,
AND THEODORE S. GREENBERG

"International efforts to control the flow of corrupt receipts into the international financial system should be strengthened. More needs to be done to encourage cross-border cooperation and to protect those who report and investigate corruption and money laundering. However, we lack solid information on which techniques are most effective."

Susan Rose-Ackerman, Henry R. Luce Professor of Law and Political Science, Yale Law School

"Money screamed across the wires, its provenance fading in a maze of electronic transfers, which shifted it, hid it, broke it up into manageable wads which would be withdrawn and re-deposited elsewhere obliterating the trail."

Linda Davies, *Nest of Vipers*

The previous chapters have discussed the kinds of corruption that take place in various sectors and the challenges that they pose. These chapters have detailed the cancer of corruption and how it affects development. But how is corruption financed? What happens once the corrupt act occurs? Where do the proceeds go?[1] Very often the corrupt act is a bribe in the form of cash or a wire transfer to a foreign account. Depending on the amount, some recipients use bribes for subsistence, while others use them for conspicuous consumption—cars, jewelry, gambling, drugs, "high living," or through domestic patronage networks to sustain power.

When the amount of money is substantial, the individual or group involved typically has to find a way to control the funds without drawing attention to the underlying criminal activity or the persons involved in generating the funds. In some cases, such proceeds may be invested domestically through the purchase of real estate and business ventures, such as casinos, in which large amounts of cash are commonly used. Alternatively, the cash may be kept abroad or laundered through a series of international transfers and investments before coming back into the country. The process of concealing or disguising the monetary proceeds from illicit activities and legitimizing their future use is called money laundering. Criminals wash their ill-gotten gains by disguising the origin and ownership of the funds, changing their form, or moving them to a place where they are less likely to attract attention.

Money laundering not only enables the criminal to avoid detection and to enjoy criminal profits without revealing their origins, but it also creates obstacles for regulatory and law enforcement agencies in identifying illegal proceeds, tracing the funds to the criminal activities, and confiscating the assets. Most corruption of the type discussed in this book involves some sort of bribe, in the broadest sense of the word. Bribe money can be generated through drug and arms trafficking as well as nontrafficking offenses such as fraud.[2] It can also be generated from legitimate business activities; an example might be a multinational corporation that uses money earned legitimately to bribe public officials to obtain access to a particular market or "win" an important contract. In these cases, the bribe payer has to find justification for making electronic payments or converting large amounts of cash, perhaps through "agents," that can then be used to corrupt public officials.

The need to launder corruptly obtained funds depends on the amount and how highly they are concentrated: the larger the volume and the fewer the number of people who receive the proceeds of corruption, the greater will be the need for laundering. Likewise, the lower the confidence of the corrupt in their own future security and that of their assets, the greater will be the desire to export their proceeds in liquid funds to what they consider a "safe haven."

No one really knows how much money is laundered every year.[3] Given that $1 million in $100 bills weighs only slightly more than 10 kilograms, cash can easily be transferred around the world in suitcases. The International Monetary Fund (IMF) has estimated that 2 to 5 percent of global gross domestic product is laundered each year (Camdessus 1998), but this is considered a rough estimate and cannot be substantiated. Looking only at corruption, Transparency International estimated in 2005 that the top 10 global kleptocrats of the 20th century "stole" between $25 billion and $60 billion (box 12.1). Although the amount of this money that was laundered

BOX 12.1 Transparency International Rankings

The anticorruption watchdog Transparency International has listed the 10 most self-enriching political leaders in recent years. Ranked by the amount each allegedly stole, in U.S. dollars, they are:

1. Former Indonesian president Suharto ($15–35 billion)
2. Former Philippine president Ferdinand Marcos ($5–10 billion)
3. Former Zairian president Mobutu Sese Seko ($5 billion)
4. Former Nigerian president Sani Abacha ($2–5 billion)
5. Former Yugoslav president Slobodan Milošević ($1 billion)
6. Former Haitian president Jean-Claude Duvalier ($300–800 million)
7. Former Peruvian president Alberto Fujimori ($600 million)
8. Former Ukrainian prime minister Pavlo Lazarenko ($114–200 million)
9. Former Nicaraguan president Arnoldo Alemán ($100 million)
10. Former Philippine president Joseph Estrada ($78–80 million)

Source: Transparency International (2004).

outside the home country cannot be determined, these numbers may be viewed as target amounts for reducing corruption through anti-money-laundering (AML) laws as well as other governance mechanisms.

These excesses of corruption have served as an impetus for AML efforts at both the national and international levels. Perceptions that grand corruption has harmed development efforts have motivated governments and international financial and development organizations to do something about corruption and money laundering (see, for example, Commission for Africa [2005]). Efforts to freeze funds (putting them beyond the use of the corrupt officials and their families) and return them to the countries from which they were looted have built on antidrug measures and have been complemented by antiterrorist measures.

Although there are no hard data, it would be surprising if the risk (cost) of money laundering had not increased since the 1980s, as the banking and legal environment has become much less hospitable to the proceeds of corruption. Opportunities for corruption and money laundering may have increased—there are ample examples of contemporary scandals in the extractive industries and in procurement, especially in those capital-intensive projects that, as Shleifer and Vishny (1993) remind us, are often selected precisely because they offer the greatest opportunities for rent seeking. But the world has become a riskier place both for those who accept or demand bribes and for those who pay them. At the same time, the complexities of national and international financial flows and their regulation have increased.

Bribery prosecutions remain modest in most countries, but some progress has been made. AML legislation, international cooperation, and expert evaluation have identified those jurisdictions that formerly offered banking secrecy and no mutual legal assistance. Launderers face greater risk in foreign jurisdictions, for example, in the finance centers of OECD (Organisation for Economic Co-operation and Development) member countries. Pressure points for anticorruption measures to be effective are being identified internationally and not just locally.

Efforts to evaluate the effectiveness of AML within a formal quantitative modeling framework present intractable methodological constraints when neither the stock of assets accumulated nor the flow of new funds being laundered are known. Nonetheless, AML regimes provide extensive tools to help identify, trace, and confiscate the proceeds of crime when they move through financial institutions. For this reason, AML measures must be considered as part of any anticorruption strategy. Even where countries have not yet enacted AML laws, the financial investigation techniques used to identify and track money laundering can be used to a great advantage in detecting, investigating, and prosecuting corruption and bribery cases. Both prevention as well as enforcement aspects of AML must be considered. Prevention includes establishing regulation and supervision of financial institutions, reporting requirements, customer due diligence, and civil and administrative sanctions for noncompliance. The enforcement side includes investigation, prosecution, freezing assets, confiscation, and punishment for money laundering and often for the underlying predicate crime (Reuter and Truman 2004). Of course, both prevention and enforcement are interdependent.

Fighting money laundering and corruption requires an interagency, interdisciplinary, and international approach. Developing countries are often unaware of how cooperation takes place between governments on money-laundering issues or how other governments can assist in providing evidence of the whereabouts of corrupt proceeds. For example, they may be unaware of the mechanisms available for overcoming bank secrecy laws. In addition to a well-trained staff of prosecutors and investigators, part of any anticorruption program must include training on how this cooperation takes place between governments. Clear, effective, and efficient channels are needed through which international cooperation can take place.

This chapter concentrates on corruption on the grand scale. It reviews the evidence of laundering the proceeds of corruption and discusses the role that prevention of money laundering and enforcement of laws prohibiting it might play in reducing corruption. It identifies key money-laundering vulnerabilities and pressure points associated with corruption and assesses how effectively AML policy can and does maximize the potential to constrain corruption as well as restrain and return proceeds. The chapter also raises several issues that have to be resolved before AML mechanisms can reach their full potential. The conclusions point to how countries can adopt frameworks and approaches that increase the effectiveness of AML reforms in combating corruption. A working list of indicators of potentially corrupt asset flows can help guide the adoption of specific policies.

WHAT IS MONEY LAUNDERING?

Money laundering is the transformation of illicit proceeds so that they can be used as if they had been legitimately acquired. Specifically, money laundering includes:

- the conversion or transfer of property, knowing that such property derives from some form of unlawful activity, for the purpose of concealing or disguising the illicit origin of the property;
- the concealment or disguise of the true nature, source, location, disposition, movement, or ownership of or rights to property, knowing that such property derives from some form of unlawful activity.

Laundering is a phenomenon with both ex ante and ex post links to corruption. Very few people pay large bribes using their own legitimately acquired funds. In most cases of bribery (except bribery for survival or low-level administrative corruption), the money that is generated to pay the bribes comes from some form of unlawful activity (such as fraud, including false or fictitious invoices on contracts). Except perhaps where they are confident in their own impunity, those involved in corruption take steps to hide the source of the funds and who receives them.

In legal terms, money laundering encompasses an enormous range of methods and skills, from simply remitting money to family members elsewhere or hiding cash under a mattress to sophisticated multijurisdictional mechanisms that make real-time and ex post facto tracing and pursuit difficult, expensive, and perhaps impossible (Reuter and Truman 2004).[4] Incentives to launder include large amount of proceeds that need to be hidden; low confidence in the security of assets in country; the existence of asset disclosure requirements; political instability or possible regime change; and high risk of detection, investigation, prosecution, or forfeiture of assets if they remain in their current form.

Laundered money often follows a complex and sophisticated path, depending on the assessment of the risks faced by those paying the bribes and those accepting them. Different forms of money laundering may be required for different forms of corruption and different countries. There is demand for both customized and wholesale laundering services. "Laundering problems" vary according to size, location, form, timing, and sensitivity of the corruption and underlying transaction.

Any given incident of money laundering may involve a variety of transaction types, including money orders, wire transfers to a foreign account, real estate purchases, establishment of new businesses, and more. Very often, businesses that require substantial cash flow are established to hide illegal proceeds as well as to generate profits to finance future illegal activities. Such businesses include hotels, casinos, restaurants, financial service firms, construction companies, and travel agencies. Real estate is another area where ill-gotten gains are often invested, sometimes using corporate nominees whose beneficial ownership may be hard to establish. A one-time opportunity for money laundering occurred in 2002, when several European countries converted from their individual currencies to the euro. Laundered cash held in the currency of participating European countries had to be converted to another currency; it is thought that the cash was usually sent abroad. One such example is Finland, where cash obtained illegally was either converted into U.S. dollars and Swedish kronor or transferred abroad and invested in real estate.[5] In Spain, the real estate sector had been especially attractive for transactions using money obtained illegally, and the Spanish government considered the introduction of the euro as an opportunity to control such money (Burgen 2006; Goodman 2002).

Money laundering can be divided into three basic stages: placement of funds generated by the predicate crime, layering of funds, and integration into business or financial activities. As a World Bank AML manual describes the process, once the predicate crime takes place, the illicit funds are separated from their illegal source and placed into one or more financial institutions domestically or internationally (World Bank 2006). For example, cash or checks from corruption are deposited into a regulated financial institution such as a bank or securities company or are used to buy goods or services. "After successfully injecting the illicit cash into the financial system, laundering the funds requires creating multiple layers of transactions that further separate the funds from their illegal source," the manual explains. "The purpose of this stage is to make it difficult to trace these funds to the illegal source." For example, part of the corrupt proceeds might be used to purchase goods later sold for legal cash, invested in shared portfolios, converted into foreign currency, or deposited into several foreign bank accounts that may be held by several shell companies.

The integration of the proceeds is the stage when illegal funds are reintroduced into the legitimate economy. "The funds now appear as clean and taxable income," the World Bank manual explains. "The purpose of the integration of the funds is to allow the criminal to use the funds without raising suspicion that might trigger investigation and pursuit. For example, cash-intensive businesses such as a restaurant or video rental shop are established where illegal funds can be injected into the business and reappear as fictitious profits or loan repayment."

Another example from the manual "is the establishment of a web of front companies with fictitious import/export businesses using false invoicing and transactions to integrate the funds as normal earnings from the trade." For purposes of illustrating the simple flow of laundered money, picture the "life cycle" of $20, $50, and $100 bills that constitute the proceeds of drug trafficking moving from the streets into the financial system. The complete process for a simple, corruption-based, money-laundering cycle is depicted in figure 12.1.

FIGURE 12.1 Money-Laundering Cycle

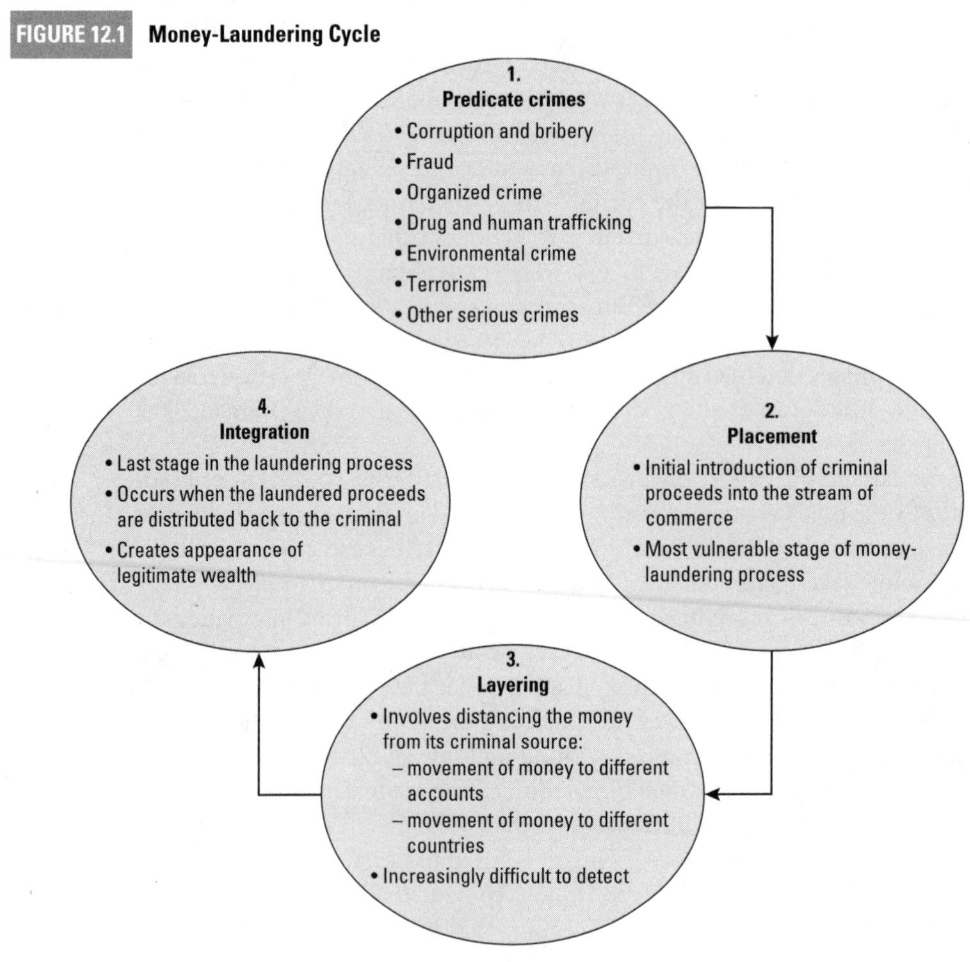

Source: Authors.

MEASURES TO ADDRESS MONEY LAUNDERING

Money laundering is truly an international mechanism to carry out and obfuscate corruption, because it almost always includes some international transaction and depends on the financial systems and business practices of other countries. Criminals have seized on the new opportunities created by globalization to vastly expand their activities. In turn, to combat money laundering, countries must work together to identify and enforce laws and seize assets that result from these criminal activities. Coordinated international efforts to fight money laundering are a relatively recent phenomenon. They began in the 1980s in an effort to reduce drug trafficking and soon extended to other forms of trafficking, terrorist financing, and corruption. The main purposes of AML measures are to make it hard for launderers (including corruptors and corruptees) to hide, move, store, and convert illegal assets; to deter them from doing so by increasing the chances of detection, conviction, and undesirable penalties; and to make it easier to find, freeze, confiscate, and return proceeds of corruption to their rightful owners.

Limiting the ways to legitimize the profits from corruption both domestically and internationally creates opportunities to weed out corruption. Among other things, AML laws

- provide for seizure and confiscation of the proceeds of crime, including corruption and bribery
- require financial institutions to file suspicious transaction reports (STRs) with financial intelligence units (FIUs), which are then analyzed and disseminated to law enforcement agencies[6]
- require financial institutions to identify the true beneficial owners of legal entities and establish enhanced identification procedures for senior government officials (including members of the parliament, the military, and the judiciary)[7]
- provide effective methods for the rapid and informal international exchange of financial data.

The international nature of most money-laundering transactions means that cooperation is needed among international financial systems and among countries to investigate corruption and track its proceeds. Some countries are the source of the funds and others are intermediaries; still others are considered safe havens for the final investment. Those countries that offer bank secrecy provide a means to conceal illicit criminal proceeds. Today, although much remains to be analyzed systematically and patterns can change over time, more and more is becoming known about which countries are involved in different stages of the process (UNODC 1998).

International money-laundering efforts can succeed only if individual countries also adopt and enforce strong domestic AML measures. Although many countries have adopted AML laws, many still need to back those laws with the resources and personnel necessary to enforce them. Many countries still need to enact legislation setting up effective regulatory supervision of the financial sector and allowing authorities to set aside bank secrecy laws and to impose due diligence, record keeping, and suspicious transaction reporting requirements on financial and certain nonfinancial businesses and professions. Adequate support and training must be given to anticorruption commissions, prosecution offices, and investigators if domestic AML measures are to be effective.

The following section first looks briefly at the international standards in place to combat money laundering. It then looks at some continuing vulnerabilities, before turning to reforms that individual countries can take to use AML measures to fight corruption.

INTERNATIONAL STANDARDS

Global standards on AML measures are set by the Financial Action Task Force (FATF), which was established in 1989 by the Group of Seven developed-country leaders to address drug money laundering. The FATF produced the 40 Recommendations on Money Laundering in 1990, which have since been revised and expanded. In October 2001, the FATF adopted eight special recommendations aimed at reaching financing of terrorist operations. A ninth recommendation was added later, and today these standards are generally referred to as the FATF 40+9. The result has been to force criminals "out of business" or "out of the country" into lax jurisdictions that can then be targeted at a diplomatic level and so pressed into taking action at both a regulatory and operational level. More than 100 countries have adopted the FATF 40+9 and have enacted or are enacting legislation to meet the standards. The FATF standards require countries to implement a minimum set of measures regarding criminal justice and regulatory systems, financial institutions, and international cooperation. The FATF also undertook an initiative to pressure reluctant governments to adopt the FATF standards (box 12.2).

The 1988 United Nations Convention against Illicit Traffic in Narcotic Drugs and Psychotropic Substances articulated the principle that disposition of confiscated proceeds and property is to be determined by the law and practice of the jurisdiction in which such confiscation finally takes place: asset sharing is encouraged but not required. This approach may be adequate for drug trafficking, but the extension of money laundering and confiscation regimes to an ever-broadening range of predicate offences, including bribery and corruption, calls into question the adequacy of this principle in meeting newer international needs.

An important step was taken in 2003 with the conclusion of the UN Convention against Corruption (UNCAC). This convention requires signatory countries to criminalize the laundering of the proceeds gained through a range of corrupt activities, including bribery of national and foreign public officials and the embezzlement and misappropriation of property. Building upon precedents in the spheres of drug trafficking and organized crime, the convention also provides for international cooperation in investigation, prosecution, and asset recovery. UNCAC incorporates a new and more sophisticated approach to the key issue of the ultimate disposal of confiscated criminal proceeds. States that ratify the convention are to consider taking measures to allow confiscation of property "without a criminal conviction in cases

BOX 12.2 Applying Peer Pressure

One major initiative undertaken by the FATF to combat international money laundering was a global "name and shame" exercise. The Non-Cooperative Countries and Territories (NCCTs) exercise began in 1998, when many countries did not have adequate AML measures in place. The goal of the initiative was to persuade all jurisdictions to adopt international standards to prevent, detect, and punish money laundering. In February 2000, the FATF published its initial report on NCCTs, which included 25 criteria identifying detrimental financial rules and practices that impede international cooperation in the fight against money laundering and that could be used to identify noncooperating jurisdictions. The report also contained a set of possible countermeasures that FATF members could use to protect their economies against the proceeds of crime. Of the 43 jurisdictions reviewed, a total of 23 jurisdictions were identified as NCCTs, 15 in 2000 and 8 in 2001. The NCCTs began immediately improving their AML systems after being listed and have since made significant progress. As of October 2006, no countries were on the NCCTs list.

The NCCTs exercise has led to an intensive, worldwide, peer-based program that has been complemented by the World Bank and IMF Anti-Money Laundering/Combating the Financing of Terrorism (AML/CFT) Financial Sector Assessments. Corruption-specific reviews are also conducted under Group of States against Corruption (GRECO)—with the Council of Europe Secretariat—and under the OECD monitoring of the OECD Convention on Combating Bribery of Foreign Public Officials in International Business Transactions 1997.[a] Compliance with FATF standards is now part of the World Bank's Financial Sector Assessment Program (FSAP) Reports and its Reports on Standards and Codes (ROSCs).[b]

a. Article 7 of the convention states that where a state has made bribery of its own public officials a predicate offense for the purpose of the application of its money-laundering legislation, the state shall do so on the same terms for the bribery of a foreign public official, without regard to the place where the bribery occurred.
b. The FATF recommendations were formally added as a standard for World Bank-IMF operational work on November 15, 2002, with the decision DEC No.12884-(02/114).

in which the offender cannot be prosecuted by reason of death, flight or absence or in other appropriate cases." The convention encourages, but does not require, state parties to assist each other in investigations of and proceedings in civil and administrative matters relating to corruption.

FATF Standards for National AML Efforts

FATF-based national approaches to using AML policies to fight corruption rest on the twin pillars of prevention and enforcement. The preventive pillar's aim is to raise the risks that financial institutions will either refuse to do business altogether with corrupters and corruptees or will monitor their accounts and pass on suspicions to investigative units at home or overseas.[8] The law enforcement pillar combines intelligence (with a view to ex ante intervention), investigation (usually to determine if money laundering has occurred), and evidence gathering (such as reconstruction of audit trails). Some jurisdictions have made it an offense to have undisclosed accounts overseas. This was one of many allegations made by the Chilean government against former president Augusto Pinochet for secret accounts held in Riggs Bank in the United States (box 12.3).

BOX 12.3 The Pinochet Case

In addition to charges of human rights abuses committed during his reign as Chile's president, Augusto Pinochet was also charged with personal corruption. On October 1, 2004, Chile's Internal Revenue Service filed a lawsuit against Pinochet, accusing him of fraud and tax evasion involving secret accounts held in the United States under false names between 1996 and 2002. In November 2005, he was indicted on charges of tax evasion and placed under house arrest. Pinochet was alleged to have hidden $27 million in these secret accounts; the amount was later reduced to $11 million. Pinochet died in December 2006, before the case was resolved

Pinochet's "partner" in the alleged crime was a Washington, DC, bank. Riggs Bank, with the knowledge and support of the its leadership, participated in money laundering for Pinochet, setting up offshore shell corporations in the names of those corporations to disguise Pinochet's ownership of the accounts, hiding his accounts from regulatory agencies, and accepting millions of dollars in deposits without following the procedures of "know your customers," that is, identifying and verifying the identity of the beneficial owners of legal entities and the source of the monies.

In particular, Riggs Bank's handling of Pinochet's corrupt monies included engaging in the following activities: After Pinochet was arrested in 1998 in London for possible extradition to Spain, Riggs transferred $1.6 million from Pinochet's accounts in London to the United States, ignoring the Spanish court order freezing his assets. Riggs Bank had concealed the existence of the Pinochet accounts from examiners for the U.S. Office of the Comptroller of the Currency (OCC) for two years, resisted OCC requests for information, and closed the Pinochet accounts only after a detailed OCC examination in 2002.

In January 2005, Riggs Bank pled guilty to one U.S. felony count of failing to report suspicious activity to law enforcement officials and paid a criminal fine of $16 million. In February 2005, to settle civil and criminal charges filed by Spanish authorities for the violation of the 1998 Spanish court order directing financial institutions to freeze Pinochet's assets, Riggs Bank and owners Joseph and Robert Allbritton paid about $1 million in court costs and legal expenses and another $8 million to a foundation established to assist victims of the Pinochet regime. Riggs was ultimately sold as a consequence of its deficient AML practices.

Source: U.S. Senate Minority Staff of the Permanent Subcommittee on Investigations (2004); U.S. Senate Permanent Subcommittee on Investigations (2005). See also *In the Matter of Riggs Bank, N.A. (No. 2004-01, FinCen, May 13, 2004), Assesment of Civil Money Penalty* http://www.fincen.gov/riggsassessment3.pdf.

Countries that have committed to the FATF 40+9 agree to enact a set of minimum measures aimed at reducing money laundering and combating the financing of terrorism. These measures include criminalization of money-laundering activities and financing of terrorist activities. Although the FATF's initial focus was on drug proceeds, the definition of money-laundering offenses has now expanded to include a minimum of 20 designated categories of offenses that should be included as predicate offences for money laundering. These offenses include human trafficking, arms trafficking, extortion, terrorist financing, corruption, and bribery.[9] The FATF also requires countries to adopt legislation that allows authorities to identify, trace, freeze, or seize, and confiscate the illegal proceeds; to create regulatory and supervisory agencies capable of and with the authority to implement and monitor the AML measures and to adopt appropriate measures that allow the country to cooperate with other countries on all aspects of enforcing AML measures, including exchange of information both formally and informally, preservation and confiscation of assets, and extradition.

The FATF minimum standards rely heavily on the private sector, particularly financial institutions, as the first line of defense against money laundering. To meet FATF standards, countries must impose on their financial institutions, and certain other nonfinancial businesses and professions, responsibilities to implement due diligence, enforce regulations, and maintain records. Financial institutions are required to know their customers and to abolish the use of anonymous accounts. Before entering into relationships with a customer, financial sector gatekeepers must verify the customer's identity, as well as the identities of any agents involved. They must also apply heightened scrutiny to politically exposed persons, or PEPs, defined as "individuals who have or have had positions of public trust such as government officials, senior executives of government corporations, politicians, important political party functionaries, and their families and close associates." [10]

Financial institutions are prohibited under the FATF standards from dealing with shell banks and are required to guard against establishing relations with foreign financial institutions that permit their accounts to be used by shell banks.[11] Some countries have gone even further; the USA PATRIOT Act, for example, provides for the forfeiture of funds in U.S. interbank accounts under certain circumstances. [12] The relevant section states that if funds are deposited into an account at a foreign bank that has an interbank account with a financial institution in the United States, the funds are deemed to have been deposited into the interbank account in the United States for the purpose of seizing the funds, and the U.S. government does not need to establish that the funds are directly traceable to the funds that were deposited into the foreign bank.

FATF standards also require certain nonfinancial businesses and professions to follow customer identification procedures. This requirement applies to lawyers, notaries, real estate agents, and other independent legal professionals and accountants when they prepare for or carry out transactions for their clients concerning activities such as buying and selling real estate and managing client money, securities, or other assets. The requirement also applies to casinos and dealers in precious metals and precious stones but only when the customer engages in a transaction equal to or above a designated threshold. Regulated firms must also be sufficiently familiar with their clients, their clients' pattern of business, and the pattern of business in their own sector to be able to spot unusual and suspicious activity.

Under the FATF minimum standards, countries must also require financial institutions to keep records on all transactions, to report all transactions that raise their suspicion without alerting the clients, and to adopt internal mechanisms that allow them to comply with the regulatory requirements.

These institutions must take on these responsibilities at their own expense. The sanction for failure to fulfill duties normally takes the form of fines on the institution rather than imprisonment of employees (although the latter may be applied in cases involving criminal intent).

Regulated institutions in the countries that follow FATF guidelines are often required by national legislation to appoint money-laundering reporting officers (MLROs). MLROs are responsible for establishing suspicious activity reporting (SAR) regimes and cooperating with the country's FIUs. MLROs depend on "relationship managers" and front-line staff who deal directly with customers.

The Private Sector and Approaches to Money-Laundering Regulation

As discussed above, AML regulations put responsibility on the private sector. In addition, pushed by reputational risk and scandals over looted state assets since the early 1990s—in the post-Abacha era, in particular—the private sector has become increasing involved in AML (Abacha case, box 12.4). Scrutiny of clients and actions affecting the clients or the institutions runs the gamut from rejecting someone as a client, to monitoring accounts of private clients and reporting suspicious activity to government authorities, to responding to requests for information from domestic and foreign investigators and to carrying out freezing orders.

Services such as private databases supplied by the private sector now help with identification and monitoring of PEPs and related parties, both individual and corporate.[13] These databases mainly rely on open public sources, but use them proactively to develop linked relationship charts that provide far more than a mere negative record check.

In 2000, 11 global banks[14] sought to complement the FATF recommendations by adopting a set of principles designed to cut across the multiplicity of jurisdictional issues, reduce their regulatory costs and reputational risk, and avoid the serious

BOX 12.4 The Abacha Case

General Sani Abacha, former president of Nigeria, was listed as the world's fourth most corrupt leader in recent history by Transparency International in 2004, having appropriated some $4 billion from Nigeria's treasury through a number of property crimes, including embezzlement, fraud, forgery, and money laundering. Abacha and his entourage invested most of the monies in accounts in Luxembourg, Switzerland, the United Kingdom, and the United States. After Abacha's death in June 1998, his wife was stopped at a Lagos airport with 38 suitcases full of cash, and his son was found with $100 million in cash.

In 1999, at the request of Nigerian authorities, the Swiss judiciary in Geneva initiated proceedings against Abacha's entourage on suspicion of money laundering. The Swiss judicial authorities indicted under Swiss law one of Abacha's sons and other members of his entourage for money laundering, fraud, and taking part in a criminal organization. According to a report by the Swiss Federal Banking Commission, Abacha-related funds were traced in 19 banks in Switzerland. At the end of 1999, the total sum of assets invested and frozen at Swiss banks was approximately $660 million. In 2005, the Federal Supreme Court authorized the repatriation of $505.5 million to the government of Nigeria, making Switzerland the first country to repatriate looted funds to an African country.

Banks in the United Kingdom and the United States were also implicated in the case. In September 1998, while the Nigerian government investigation of corruption was ongoing, the Abacha sons made a request to Citibank to transfer $39 million out of their London time deposit accounts. Citibank lent the sons $39 million so they could avoid the penalty for withdrawing the money prematurely and then satisfied the loan when the time deposit matured two weeks later.

The Financial Services Authority in the United Kingdom reported that of the 23 U.K. banks investigated because of possible links with Abacha accounts, 15 had significant money-laundering control weaknesses. The total turnover of Abacha accounts in the United Kingdom alone between 1996 and 2000 was $1.3 billion. These banks have since corrected the weaknesses through strengthening their AML controls under close supervision by the Financial Services Authority.

Source: Swiss Federal Department of Justice and Police (2000); U.S. Senate Permanent Subcommittee on Investigations (1999); World Bank (2006).

reputational damage some banks have suffered in connection with money laundering. The Wolfsberg Principles set common standards for the participating banks' private banking operations (that is, for very wealthy clients).[15] The principles include common due diligence procedures for opening and keeping watch over accounts, especially those identified as belonging to politically exposed persons who may sometimes combine corruption with drug money laundering and even financing terrorism. The international banks have developed sophisticated models of risk management that track ongoing transaction monitoring as well as improved initial customer identification. However, while some banks have been voluntarily improving standards, others, particularly those in developing countries, are restrained by limited resources and capacity.

Banks must also be protected from in-country threats from powerful forces. In general, countries have been better at dealing with the corruption of past leaders than the corruption of current elites. To whom will suspicious activity reports on current senior power figures be directed if not to the government, and who would have the courage and independence (as well as the financial resources) to investigate and prosecute?

Financial Intelligence Units and Suspicious Activity Reporting

One critical accomplishment of the FATF standards has been the creation of FIUs. More than 100 countries have established national FIUs whose job is to receive, analyze, and process suspicious transaction reports submitted by regulated institutions. FIUs use information from these reporting and record-keeping requirements to reconstruct financial transactions, establish links between individual clients and particular businesses, help establish facts and help identify the possible role of an individual in criminal activity (World Bank–IMF 2006).

Much effort has gone into building an infrastructure of FIUs, although highly corrupt countries tend not to have highly developed FIUs, if (until recently) any at all. As with anticorruption investigations generally, political independence is necessary, especially when investigating higher-level officials. (There is, however, also a need for performance evaluation in case the independent bodies are *in*active.) Independence is particularly vital where information is to be exchanged with international FIUs; otherwise, despite protocols in place that in principle protect the reporting institution or person, the corrupt may be able to deduce who has made the reports on suspected activity. This can then lead to financial or physical retaliation against the individual staff or the institution itself. Much recent effort has gone into the identification of weaknesses in reporting regimes and action upon reports.[16]

The effective use of suspicious transaction reports in corruption—especially foreign corruption—cases remains a largely unexplored issue in these evaluations, but it should not be forgotten that a key aim of the AML effort is to identify PEPs and to pressure financial institutions into close, proactive monitoring of their accounts, in advance of any known misconduct as well as in response to requests for legal assistance. The extent to which this monitoring inhibits the institutions may be affected by the mode and extent of bribery. In cases where PEPs and their families or friends are running businesses whose use is compulsory for those who wish to get government contracts, but that appear to have a legitimate area of activity (even if overpriced), it makes it more difficult for banks to detect suspicious financial transactions.

National FIUs are supported by an FATF-inspired policy environment of shared goals, prevention, and enforcement, and an evolving strategy of integrating the efforts of the many international agencies now involved.[17] Current AML policy demands that the financial intermediaries play a major initial role in scanning for suspicious subjects and behaviors, in addition to the enforcers relying on "intelligence" from their usual sources. The extensive resource and data-processing requirements have required delegation of primary prevention to the financial services industry, banks, and other regulated bodies, such as lawyers and accountants, who in most cases must report to their domestic FIUs any transactions they consider suspicious.

The FIUs can now pursue these reports and, where appropriate in international cases, pass their substance on to other FIUs and investigators elsewhere for action. What constitutes "reasonable grounds for suspicion" and how to raise the diligence, motivation, and consciousness of intermediaries preoccupies those in the financial centers of the OECD world who take corruption seriously.

INTERNATIONAL COOPERATION

Even with all the AML standards discussed above, fighting money laundering requires effective international cooperation. In a few recent cases, such cooperation has led to asset recovery. The Swiss response to the Abacha case (see box 12.4) and the Montesinos case are instructive. In addition, the Lesotho case provides an example of cooperation under a World Bank-financed project.

The Montesinos Case

In September 2000, Vladimiro Lenin Montesinos Torres, former head of the Peruvian National Intelligence Service, was charged with a host of illegal activities, including drug trafficking, arms dealing, embezzlement of public funds, and violations of human rights (U.S. Department of Justice 2005). He fled Peru but was later arrested in República Bolivariana de Venezuela and extradited to Peru, where he was sentenced to a 15-year prison term on corruption charges. In September 2006, Montesinos was sentenced to a 20-year prison term for his direct involvement in an illegal arms deal aimed at providing 10,000 assault weapons to Colombian rebels.

Thanks to the proactive attitude of the Swiss judicial and police authorities, the illegal assets Montesinos had deposited in Swiss accounts were frozen and the Peruvian authorities notified. They in turn submitted a formal request for legal assistance, with which the Swiss authorities complied. The Swiss started money-laundering proceedings involving $113.6 million in several different accounts. The investigations carried out by the Examining Magistrate's Office of Zurich revealed that the funds belonging to Montesinos originated from corruption-related crimes. Since 1990,

Montesinos had received "commissions" on arms deliveries to Peru and had this bribe money paid to his bank accounts in Luxembourg, Switzerland, and the United States. Montesinos received bribes for at least 32 transactions, each worth 18 percent of the purchase price. He also collected $10.9 million in "commissions" on the purchase of three planes bought by the Peruvian air force from the state-owned Russian arms factory. In return, Montesinos used his position to ensure that certain arms dealers were given preference when these orders were issued. On the basis of these facts, the Examining Magistrate's Office of Zurich issued a decision on June 12, 2002, ordering the transfer of the assets belonging to Montesinos to Peru. A total of $80.7 million was transferred to an account belonging to the Peruvian National Bank.

In addition, one of the arms dealers who enjoyed preferential treatment "voluntarily" repatriated from his Swiss bank accounts his $7 million commission from these transactions. General Nicolas de Bari Hermoza Rios also accepted bribes relating to arms deliveries to Peru and also agreed to return the money ($21 million). In August 2004, U.S. officials returned to Peru $20 million in funds embezzled by Montesinos that had been deposited in U.S. banks by two men working for him.

In a separate action, the Swiss Federal Banking Commission (SFBC) investigated the activities of five banks in connection with the Montesinos case: Bank Leumi le-Israel (Switzerland) Ltd., Fibi Bank Switzerland Ltd., Banque CAI (Suisse) Ltd., UBS Ltd., and Bank Leu Ltd. The SFBC wanted to examine whether the banks had acted in compliance with the Swiss money-laundering law and the commission's own directive on money laundering with regard to due diligence and reporting duties.

The SFBC found that after due diligence, UBS and Bank Leu had terminated their banking relationship with Montesinos before the criminal investigation had started. But the banking commission discovered that Bank Leumi le-Israel (Switzerland) Ltd. had several shortcomings in opening banking relationships with politically exposed persons. In an August 28, 2001, ruling, the SFBC said that the bank did not exercise due diligence with regard to Montesinos and had fallen short of clarifying the source of funds in cases of unusual transactions. Despite significant amounts deposited and indication of activities in arms dealing, the bank did not investigate any further. It failed to recognize Montesinos's PEP quality even though publicly accessible information would have enabled it to do so with reasonable effort.

Because of the general manager's position in the hierarchy of the bank's management, the SFBC held him responsible for the bank's organizational deficiencies. The general manager also was alleged to have personally approved the opening of accounts with Montesinos despite formal shortcomings in the opening procedure. Furthermore, he was held coresponsible for not recognizing Montesinos as a politically exposed person. The SFBC held that the general manager was not fit to hold his position and ordered that he be removed immediately; he left by September 15, 2001. The banking commission also ordered that a special audit of the bank be conducted by an outside auditor in 2002.

In a report issued on November 13, 2001, the SFBC offered the following conclusions based on its investigations into the Montesinos case (SFBC 2001).

- Careful investigation into the possibility of a customer's PEP quality is a precondition for compliance with the SFBC's PEP rules and guidelines. Customers will not always disclose such backgrounds or may make false statements. It is important for the bank to look into sources of information generally accessible to the public.

- With the exception of UBS Ltd., none of the banks involved contacted Montesinos directly but based decisions on opening accounts solely on information provided by third parties. The commission said that was insufficient in the case of significant private banking relationships.
- If a bank has doubts about the legality of a client's activities, it may be desirable for the bank to terminate the banking relationship even though those doubts need not be reported to the federal money-laundering reporting agency.

As a result of this investigation, the banking commission revised its code of conduct for Swiss banks in 2003.

The Lesotho Highlands Water Project

A very different case from that of Montesinos involved construction of a system of dams and tunnels in Lesotho to provide water to South Africa and electricity to Lesotho. The project was financed by the World Bank.[18] The Lesotho Highlands Development Authority (LHDA) was mandated to manage the entire project.

During the course of the project, it emerged that a large number of transnational corporations had paid money into bank accounts in Switzerland in the name of certain intermediaries, and that some of that money had subsequently passed into bank accounts held by the LHDA's chief executive officer, Masupha Sole. In the case of the key intermediary, one Z. M. Bam, investigations revealed that 60 percent of the money paid into Bam's account was transmitted to Sole very shortly thereafter. It was established in the Lesotho court[19] that Sole received 493,000 (Can$) between January and April 1991, as well as another Can$188,000 between June 1991 and January 1998. The source of this particular bribe was a Canadian company, Acres International, which wanted to secure the contracts for the construction of the Katse Dam. Other companies were also allegedly involved in paying Sole through a different route. Sole was sentenced to 18 years in jail for receiving more than R 7.5 million (South African rand; equivalent to $1 million) from international contractors and consultants. This was reduced on appeal to 15 years.

The forensic investigations revealed a trail of money leading from other transnational corporations to six intermediaries, all of whom managed banking accounts outside Lesotho, and then further on to a second tier of intermediaries and ultimately to Sole's accounts in Geneva. Transfers were traced further to an account in Sole's name at Standard Bank in Ladybrand, just across the border in South Africa.

As far as is known, the amount recovered from Sole in a civil judgment against him in October 1999, and confirmed on appeal in April 2001, was R 8.9 million (then worth a little less than $1.2 million). In addition, Acres International was fined R 22 million (slightly more than $2.9 million) on conviction in the Lesotho court and was placed by the World Bank on its blacklist.

In this case, the individuals involved employed relatively simple bribery mechanisms and little formal laundering. Simple payments were made to intermediaries who took their risk-based cut before passing funds on to ordinary accounts held offshore. It remains to be seen whether this pattern will change as potential corruptors and their intermediaries realize that the Swiss will cooperate[20] with corruption investigations overseas once they are convinced that there is clear evidence of corruption.

Challenges in Dealing with Illicitly Acquired Assets

Despite these examples, many challenges remain in dealing with illegally acquired assets. For one thing, in accordance with the international customary law principle of immunity, heads of state are exempt from criminal prosecution, as the Swiss Federal Supreme Court duly confirmed in the case of former Philippine president Ferdinand Marcos.[21] Although the financial intermediary and its officials have no immunity, in Switzerland and elsewhere, restitution is not easy, for several reasons:

- *Lack of cooperation in the area of legal assistance.* The requesting state fails to instigate internal criminal proceedings or is unable to conclude them (for political reasons or because of a lack of good governance). Even where there is no immunity, it is sometimes very difficult for a requesting state to collect sufficient evidence against a former head of state concerning violations committed during his or her term of office.

  The most recent Swiss examples are the cases of Mobutu and Duvalier. On December 15, 2003, the Federal Council ruled that the assets (totaling approximately 10.8 million Swiss francs [SwF]) of the deceased dictator of the Democratic Republic of Congo, Mobutu Sese Seko, were to remain blocked for an additional three years. The decision overruled Swiss judicial authorities, who had decided, because of a lack of cooperation on the part of the authorities in Kinshasa, to end the legal assistance procedure that had been in progress since 1997 and to release the blocked assets. The Federal Council based its ruling on the Federal Constitution, holding that it was not in Switzerland's interests to return assets to the Democratic Republic of Congo without an agreement having been reached between the parties involved. Similarly, in the case of the former dictator of Haiti, Jean-Claude Duvalier, the Federal Council ruled on June 14, 2002 that the assets (approximately SwF 7.6 million) that had been blocked to date on the basis of a request for legal assistance were to remain blocked for three more years. The legal assistance procedure that had been initiated in 1986 had to be discontinued as a result of a lack of cooperation on the part of the Haitian authorities and their failure to provide adequate guarantees concerning legal proceedings against Duvalier. These sorts of cases require a negotiated solution.
- *Corruption is widespread within the country concerned, which also lacks good governance. There is therefore a high risk that the returned assets will be misappropriated again.* This runs contrary to Switzerland's fundamental interest in ensuring that returned assets are used for the benefit of the general population.
- *Relationships of third parties claiming legitimate entitlement to the blocked funds have to be verified.* This may concern third parties who have claims against the holder of the blocked account, or victims who are claiming compensation, for

example, for human rights violations. This situation complicates efforts to find an acceptable negotiated solution and often leads to legal proceedings and numerous appeals in the state where the funds are lodged.

Gaps in geographic coverage exist, but the World Bank and IMF can assist by building capacity within borrowing countries to prosecute such cases. It is important to ensure the sensitization of anticorruption bodies to the importance of the laundering, confiscation, and repatriation of the proceeds of corruption. In particular, the detailed attention paid by UNCAC to the issue of asset repatriation broke new ground, as it was the first international legal instrument to recognize the need for all states to commit to asset repatriation. Preexisting conventions and arrangements in this area, such as the OECD bribery convention, did not consider this dimension of the anticorruption agenda. The most recent African Union Convention on Preventing and Combating Corruption of July 2003 addresses the issue of repatriation as a requirement under international cooperation.[22] Recovery and repatriation are now becoming far more central issues for all bodies, built into the routine activities of policy making, monitoring, and assessment in the anticorruption area.

KEY ISSUES IN AML

Before the 1990s, corrupt public officials wishing to launder money paid the generic cost of international services. Swiss banks paid very low interest rates, which depositors were willing to accept in exchange for both secrecy and the safekeeping of their funds—suggesting that these banks were the laundry of choice at that time. With the advent of AML laws creating financial and criminal risks for financial intermediaries, their awareness of laundering and their likelihood of reporting suspicious transactions to financial intelligence units increased. This may have had a perverse effect: corrupt public officials or their agents may now be more likely to bribe the employees of the overseas financial intermediaries to take the laundered sums.

A variation may be that instead of bribes to specific personnel, the corrupt depositor tolerates less prudent management or placement of the funds by the bank, in effect entering into an unwritten equity agreement. There are, of course, other methods of achieving cross-border "value transfers," often using items such as precious stones, bearer bonds, works of art, and metals, as well as false invoicing and alternative remittance. There is no firm evidence that these have become more common for laundering the proceeds of corruption, but it seems plausible that they would for some types of crime, and corruption should be no exception.

As shown earlier, there are examples of successful identification of money laundering activities. However, some countries are still less than transparent. Because laundering can happen anywhere in the world, no country can avoid its responsibilities and no part of the world is immune. The tighter the controls worldwide, the greater the expected concentration of crime proceeds in those jurisdictions that remain outside the control loop because of poor regulation or poor implementation. Such controls provide less opportunity for international laundering, and greater opportunities for proceeds held locally within a country to be discovered and returned to their rightful owners. AML efforts may also mean that informal banking systems, such as the *hawala*, are used to facilitate the laundering of illicit proceeds. Such systems allow quick transfers to take place without any paper trail and are particularly useful if bribes are made in cash.

Key issues that still need to be addressed in order to strengthen existing AML efforts:

Attempts at confiscating illegally obtained assets from public officials can be frustrated by the presence of certain forms of immunity that bar domestic prosecution. The more immunity granted to public officials, especially the level of immunity accorded to heads of state, the more difficult it is to bring civil actions against them, although governments can waive immunity. Paradoxically, where the confiscation of proceeds of crime depends upon conviction, the death of someone accused of grand corruption has traditionally protected their relatives and other beneficiaries, allowing them to keep any illegally gained proceeds without prosecution, contrary to the public interest.

There is no systematic analysis of money-laundering cases.[23] Because of the historically low priority afforded to issues relating to the proceeds of corruption, neither refined, replicated data sets nor evidence-based analyses are available for substantive areas of corrupt behavior and governance. One can aggregate notable instances over time, but no detailed, systematic account of the laundering of the proceeds of corruption through the financial systems of OECD countries exists. The extent to which AML has incapacitated crime networks, reduced the variety of their offenses, or reduced the scale of their growth as "criminal organizations" remains unknown and largely unanalyzed (Levi and Maguire 2004; Nelen 2004). The impact in the developing world is even more problematic.

Kaufmann's 2002 model, set out in figure 12.2, shows how the four stages of a standardized money-laundering cycle can be mapped to misgovernance and corruption in the public, financial, and corporate sectors. We would add the proviso (omitted from this diagram) that some of the proceeds of corruption will be consumed without ever being laundered, while others will be consumed after undergoing some but perhaps not all laundering stages. Corruption is specifically circled in dark grey at stage 1, but in some developing countries, every element of stage 1 may be controlled by relatives and friends of the PEPs.

Much of the media criticism and complaints from the developing countries impute responsibility for transnational corruption to OECD countries, both as the source of bribes and the site of the laundering of the proceeds. Widespread perceptions in developing countries that a double standard exists—one that targets PEPs in developing countries but looks the other way at OECD countries that may be both the source of bribes and the site of laundering operations—have had an adverse political impact, for example, on the implementation of the UNCAC and has informed the work of the Commission for Africa (2005). Because the profits of corruption are laundered through major financial centers in the OECD and through more obscure jurisdictions, corruption in poorer countries would be extremely difficult without access to such financial institutions.[24] Scandals reported by the media create reputational risk, both for the country itself and for individual banks and other businesses.

FIGURE 12.2 Not a Simple "Laundromat": Money Laundering in a Broader Framework

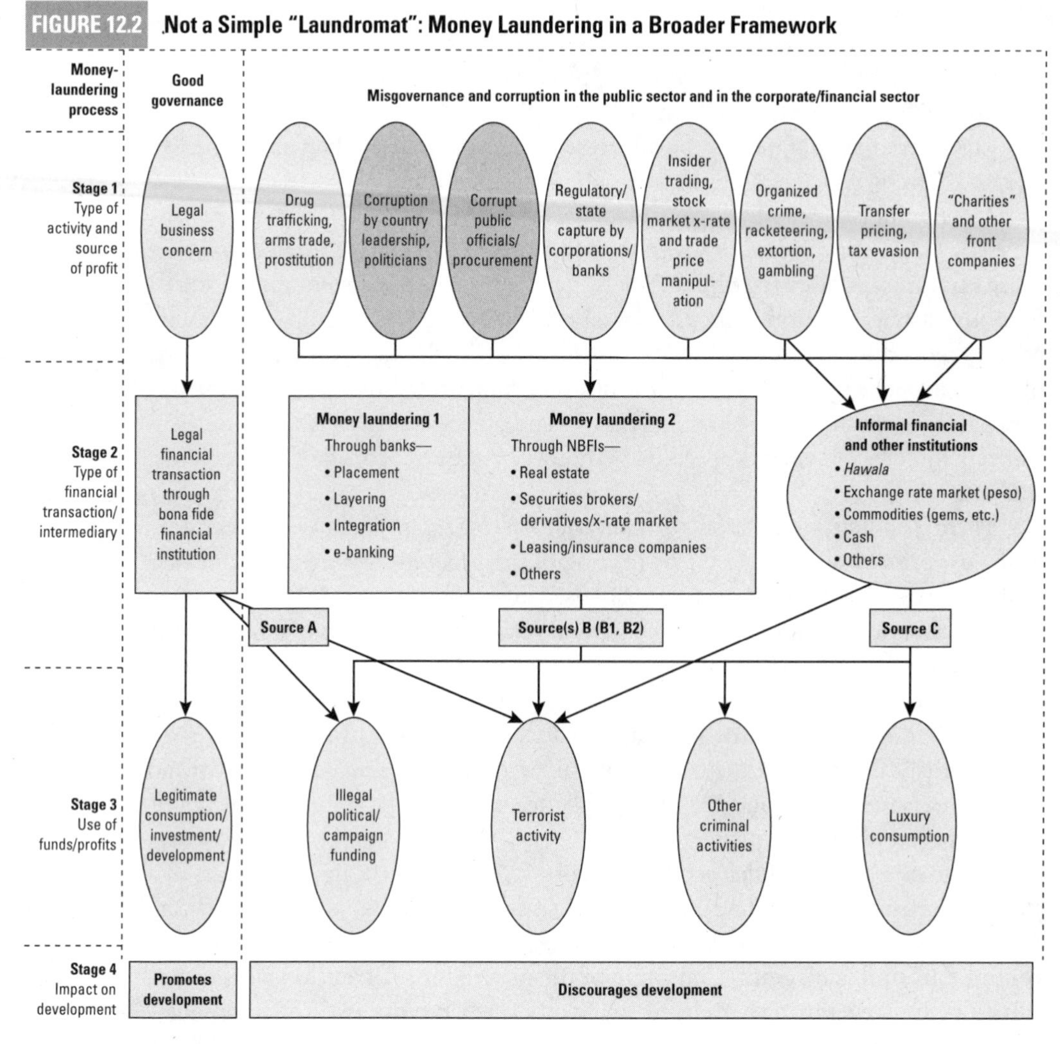

Source: Kaufmann (2002).

All OECD financial centers have experienced corruption and money-laundering scandals and there is no reason to suppose that they will not be implicated again. Indeed, the availability of "offshore laundries" constitutes an important enabler of corruption, since without them, funds might have to be stored "onshore," exposing them to detection and confiscation by a successor regime or an independent justice system.[25] There is now an opportunity to use AML regimes in OECD countries to complement anticorruption regimes in developing countries. Even with large and complex operations, it may only take one report from a financial institution or lawyer and one serious attempt to investigate for some schemes to unravel.

There are limits to the extent to which the police (or, for that matter, bankers or lawyers) can detect the purpose of suspected transactions without asking suspects (or, in the case of bankers or lawyers, clients), and this is a particular problem in corruption cases, including corrupt law enforcement as well as grand corruption. There may also be difficulty in getting countries to supply the information needed to conclude investigations overseas—for example, in Switzerland, where prosecutors are quite active in taking on cases whose predicate crime occurred elsewhere. However, improved recording of financial accounts and greater attention to beneficial ownership of assets should logically help with asset recovery compared with the postarrest or even postcharge financial investigations that were previously commonplace—in this sense, AML has an influence on law enforcement methodologies, from drugs to grand corruption.[26]

Moreover, there seems little doubt that the ability to prosecute for money laundering in, for example, Switzerland, has increased the risks for those who transact business via that country, so that control of law enforcement or prosecution in the particular developing country does not create total immunity worldwide for persons and/or the assets of the corruptor or the corruptee. Nevertheless, corruption has proved to be very expensive to investigate and prosecute, causing severe strains upon public funds. International funding for such cases may be necessary if small jurisdictions are to have the capacity to deal with them.

Judicial corruption and lack of judicial independence can also inhibit the prosecution and punishment of offenders. The judiciaries in Latin American countries, for example, have historically not acted as significant institutional counterforces to legislative and executive abuses of power for a number of historical, political, and structural reasons. Lack of judicial independence and judicial corruption often go hand-in-hand—judges who may be susceptible to pressure from other branches of government may also be more likely to sell themselves to litigants and lawyers. In Chile, under the Pinochet regime, judges who did not obey were fired, persecuted, or had their careers frozen (Dakolias and Thachuk 2000, p. 362). If a government wants control of the judiciary, it will appoint corrupt or subservient judges. Hungary's experience, outlined in box 12.5, suggests that where countries establish only a limited enforcement capacity for combating corruption, only grand corruption attracts investigative resources and because intense political controversy usually surrounds such cases, the judicial process is at high risk of becoming politicized. Hungary's example also emphasizes how, to be effective, political will is needed not just for embarking on both anticorruption and AML reforms, but also for seeing them through. Prosecutions, timely and impartial trials, and risk-based sanctions send a very clear signal that the closely linked forms of corruption will not be tolerated.

The Limitations of AML Policy in Stopping Corruption

AML measures have several limitations as a policy for stopping corruption as it is defined in this book—the use of public monies for private gain. For one thing, AML regulation is not specific to corruption but is aimed primarily at stopping a broad class of crime that involves moving large amounts of money. While that may cover grand corruption by top political leaders, much corruption takes place on much smaller scale. In some countries, the suspicion of even medium-scale corruption may not be considered important enough to merit the allocation of scarce financial

BOX 12.5 Anticorruption Reform in Hungary

Hungary provides an interesting case study of anticorruption reform not least because part of its efforts in this area were initiated under the UN Global Program against Corruption in 1999 and therefore closely monitored. It is also useful as an example of a former Communist country that is now a member of the European Union (EU). Hungary is a party to the OECD antibribery convention and has ratified the Council of Europe's Criminal Law and Civil Law Conventions on Corruption. It is also a member of GRECO. In 1999, Transparency International's Corruption Perception Index put Hungary's score in the low 30s, making it a regional leader in resistance to corruption.[a] Under UN guidance, Hungary developed a 27-point anticorruption strategy.

During the late 1990s, the FATF blacklisted Hungary for noncompliance with the FATF+40 recommendations then in force. One of the reasons was the persistence of passbook accounts (though with little evidence of their widespread use for money laundering), which Hungary had been slow to phase out. The impact of blacklisting and its potential implications for pending EU accession, together with the September 11, 2001, terrorist attacks on the United States and their aftermath, focused the government on the problem. An interministerial panel was formed to oversee the drafting of a new AML law as well as to set up a media campaign, training courses, and outreach to industry efforts. By the time Hungary joined the EU in May 2003, it had some of the most up-to-date AML legislation in Europe. It was one of the first countries in Europe to extend AML provisions to the high-value-goods sector.

Two points in this history stand out. Because Hungary used the "all crime" definition of predicate offense, its AML laws include corruption. On a deeper level, the FATF blacklisting brought home to Hungary the need to set its house in order and avoid the type of practical problems and adverse publicity caused by an inadequate regime for detecting money-laundering activities. The AML laws were passed seamlessly despite a change of government halfway through the process, and Hungary complemented its ratification of the Council of Europe's anticorruption conventions with the enactment of a 2003 "glass pocket" statute that authorized the State Audit Office of Hungary to examine contracts between the public and private sectors. Previously, such contracts had been considered a confidential business matter. Public interest in this area was high because of a number of real or alleged scandals linked to the privatization process in the 1990s, another scandal involving the bribing of the agriculture minister, and a controversy over the use of the national development bank to award contracts without going to tender.

Hungary took other actions to combat corruption and laundering of the proceeds, including limiting the involvement of civil servants in private companies and requiring members of parliament to disclose their interests, income, and assets. Other laws sought to limit petty corruption, such as placing curbs on collecting fines on the spot and granting immunity for reporting requests for bribes. During this period, several ministers, senior civil servants, and business people were forced to resign, and several were prosecuted.

Despite these efforts, however, key corruption perception ratings have stayed stable or deteriorated. A 2005 survey of corruption in Europe conducted by the European Bank for Reconstruction and Development suggested that kickbacks in Hungary had risen 10 percent over three years. The Freedom House rating for corruption has remained unchanged at 2.75. How can this be the case? One explanation could be that attracting foreign business and greater investment increased the supply of funds available for corruption. Competition to construct the large-scale infrastructure projects linked to EU accession and new facilities for large multinationals also may have offered new opportunities for corruption. However, both the rating reports and an assessment conducted under the auspices of the OECD antibribery convention emphasize that the high-level reform of the legal framework has not been followed through with effective internal institutional reforms, especially enforcement.

a. http://www.transparency.org/policy_research/surveys_indices/cpi/previous_cpi__1/1999.

resources to investigation or evidence gathering. In other countries, the prosecution of small-scale corruption may result in small penalties for the precursor offense but disproportionately large penalties for money laundering, which may lead to a reluctance to apply the law, especially where local and cultural differences in the definition of corruption exist.

Another limitation of AML regulation, particularly global regulation, is its reliance on gatekeepers for its effectiveness. That means that the gatekeepers' knowledge of and attitudes toward corruption are a critical factor for success. To be effective, AML measures require what is now a wide section of the public to see a possible connection between a commercial transaction and a corrupt act and to be motivated, or sufficiently afraid of sanctions, to report suspicions. One side effect of this reliance is that the regulations may create the preconditions for more corruption of financial institutions and gatekeepers themselves than would be necessary if "laundering" were legal.

A third limitation is that AML rules are skewed toward detection of the corruptee rather than the corruptor. There are no statutory checks for money laundering at a critical weak point—inside the organization undertaking the act of corruption. This is especially important in large organizations with sophisticated finance departments and in international treasuries that have the resources, ability, and judgment to apply complex checks for corruption but that, despite (variable) whistleblowing protection legislation, may not see it is their role to prevent corruption by the firm in pursuit of its narrow economic interests (as opposed to embezzlement from it).

At the global policy level, it can be expected that higher barriers to money laundering in advanced economies lead to higher prices for money laundering. In other words, money laundering will continue but through more devious and costly laundering mechanisms. In addition, where heads of state or their families are involved in grand corruption (including embezzlement, illicit trafficking, and other major crimes), it is far from obvious to whom either domestic or foreign institutions should report without fear of retaliation, or who has sufficient motivation to take serious action. In this respect, the national FIU model, like most national crime investigation and prosecution models, breaks down when confronted by key elites, even where they have no formal immunity for acts performed in office. The resulting vicious circle simply leads to a situation where the more corrupt political power and the machinery of state become, the harder it is to establish an environment in which effective AML controls can address the situation.

To break the vicious circle of corruption, better provision must be made for protecting those who report and investigate corruption and money laundering. There are limits to what OECD country banks can be expected to do, even with goodwill. For example, the SFBC, using information received from the committee investigating corruption in the UN Oil-for-Food Program in Iraq (see box 12.6), concluded that the banks had used acceptable levels of due diligence in vetting the oil contracts they financed and did not have access to information that would have shown that some of these contracts involved bribes, "called commissions," to Iraqi officials (SFBC 2005).

BOX 12.6 UN Oil-for-Food Program in Iraq

To relieve the suffering of Iraqis caused by a worldwide embargo on Iraqi oil in the 1990s after Iraq's thwarted invasion of Kuwait, the United Nations set up a program to allocate certain volumes of crude oil for sale on international markets. The proceeds were earmarked to purchase food and other necessities for Iraqis. The UN determined a fair market price at which the Iraqi crude oil could be sold, but the Iraqi government, not the United Nations, chose the buyers.

In a relatively large number of these transactions, the purchasers selected by the Iraqi government lacked the financial resources to pay for the oil or did not have the necessary expertise to commercialize the oil allocated to them. Purchasers therefore turned to true oil traders, who purchased the Iraqi oil for their own account but in the name of the approved purchasers. For the purposes of these transactions, banks issued letters of credit in the name of the approved purchaser in favor of the United Nations, but under the financial responsibility of their clients, the oil traders. These clients, regarded as contract holders, were duly identified and known by the banks.

This "contract holder" practice is fairly widespread in free oil trading, where it has a legitimate commercial purpose. For instance, among groups of trading companies, some entities are responsible for identifying purchase opportunities, and others deal with financing the resulting transactions. In addition, information currently available to the SFBC indicates that the practice has not prevented the United Nations from receiving the full price it set.

Therefore, on the basis of the information available to the SFBC and the information that the banks could access at the time, the oil transactions financed by the Swiss-based banks were in line with the applicable business practices and generally did not require a higher level of due diligence.

INSTITUTIONAL UNDERPINNINGS OF ANTICORRUPTION REFORMS

Given these limitations, there are several steps that can be taken to improve the effectiveness of AML measures in individual countries.

Setting Clear Ground Rules

Educating legislators to develop policy goals that include money-laundering controls as part of an anticorruption package is essential. To ensure the accurate and effective transposition of goals into law, legal draftspeople need to frame laws so that they fit into the legal structures and institutions of the country (rather than adopting "one-size-fits-all" models). Having clear ground rules on acceptable and unacceptable behavior, as well as clear penalties for unacceptable behavior, puts regulators in a good position to select the appropriate instruments with which to engage target groups and target behavior. Reviews by the FATF, World Bank, and the IMF have generated significant success in drawing up recommendations to address those issues. The ratification of the UNCAC, which has substantial AML and asset recovery components, should carry that effort forward. Compliance with these and similar regimes indicates awareness not only that the corruption laundering supports is wrong in itself but also that noncompliance is bad business for government leaders and for their societies.

Controls, Enforcement, and Sanctions

Implementing an effective AML regime is likely to require significant resources. AML controls are only as effective as the people who undertake them and their quality of supervision. This almost inevitably means substantial investment in the training of investigators, prosecutors, and judges. The advantages of increased detection are soon lost if there are failures in prosecuting, trying, and punishing offenders.

Money laundering is notoriously hard to prosecute, especially in complex cases. In addition to training deficits, the state simply may not be able to afford a judiciary and prosecution of as high a quality as the defense, particularly where international corporations with much to lose are targeted. A number of strategies can be adopted in such instances. States trying corruption cases where money has flowed into more developed foreign jurisdictions may be able to provide those jurisdictions with evidence to support a request for extradition. Another response is to separate the removal of the money from the conviction of the person, an approach undertaken in Ireland, the United Kingdom, and the United States, to decrease criminals' incentives with the prospect of pain for little or no gain. One problem that has arisen in relation to the declaration of assets of politicians prior to their appointment is the alleged overstatement of their assets (and claims of family inheritance) so that later enhancements can be discounted and concealed. To the extent that criminal convictions can be secured, penalties need to be carefully balanced to reflect the relative importance of money laundering and corruption in relation to other crimes.

Some AML regimes' principal use has been to increase the penalties that can be imposed on predicate offenders and therefore increase the incentives for them to cooperate with prosecutors. To date, AML regimes have apprehended few professional money launderers or high-level criminals. In Europe, there has been some activity against professionals such as lawyers as well as against bankers, though more by regulatory than by criminal sanctions.

Institutional Architecture and Internal Arrangements

Countries with severe corruption problems do not always have the same range and depth of legal, financial, and administrative systems from which AML controls were developed. For controls to be successful in developing countries, allowance has to be made for what can be very different systems for handling money. A high-level example of this would be alternative remittance systems, which play an essential role in ensuring financial certainty and integrity in areas usually associated with low levels of law enforcement.[27] Closing down such systems on the grounds that they infringe on money-laundering regulations would be a very indirect way of tackling corruption and would create economic hardship by interrupting what are mostly legal flows.

Thus, in low-capacity countries, where legal, financial, and administrative systems are not well developed, AML reforms are likely to focus, for example, on cash handling and wire transfers.[28] In countries where these systems are more developed, the emphasis is more likely to be on monitoring complex financial products and high-value goods. All jurisdictions should focus on transfers of money and other items of value through false invoicing, including invoicing for ill-defined consultancy services and hard-to-check technological components, and on simple smuggling of low-volume, high-value items such as precious stones.

By extension, efforts to improve AML measures influence the type of institutions that need to be developed and their level of staffing and sophistication. In establishing these institutions, a key issue is their sustainability and ability to deliver change over what may involve an intergenerational period of time and constantly changing background variables.

A successful AML regime is rarely operated successfully by a single agency or even by multiagency public sector bodies. Invariably, it requires cooperation from a relatively large number of agencies and private sector bodies, including the police, tax authorities, security services, customs agencies, FIUs, prosecutors, regulators, representatives of regulated sectors, and the court system.

Moreover, the increasing number of nonstate actors involved in recovering proceeds of corruption on behalf of owners (such as security firms, lawyers, insolvency practitioners and receivers, and credit reference agencies) should be taken into account, both as powerful potential allies and as potential creators of barriers to national and transnational initiatives if their activities are executed irresponsibly. Left uncoordinated, public and private sector actors have only a random chance of forming a coherent national AML system. Coordination is essential and is best done at a national level, through an AML commission, for example. This also provides the best chance of targeting specific crimes, including corruption, that drive laundering.

Capacity

Passing AML laws and setting up the apparatus to oversee their implementation are necessary but not sufficient conditions for progress. Another necessary condition is an appropriate number of competent staff and the financial and technical resources to enable them to perform their functions to a sufficient standard. Enhancing financial intelligence and investigation capacities means that investigators can deal better not only with corruption but also with other AML concerns. That will not happen, however, where there is a substantial lack of local investigative resources and prosecutorial competence and independence, especially when senior personnel in a current administration are targets of investigation.

FIUs and, in some countries, independent anticorruption commissions are the formal institutional agencies responsible for implementing anti-corruption and AML measures. Over 100 national FIUs meet FATF criteria for receiving, analyzing, and processing reports, including suspicious activity reports, from regulated institutions.[29] The FIUs are authorized by national legislation to exchange suspicious transaction reports and related information. Despite having very different locations—some are housed within finance ministries, others in the police, and others still in central banks—as well as different relationships with law enforcement agencies, FIUs follow procedures laid out by the FATF and other international AML measures for following funds and pursuing a financial intelligence trail for use as evidence against suspects.

Many developing countries—especially former British colonies—have independent commissions against corruption that jealously guard their independence from government. These commissions often have small budgets, however, which limit their travel both internally and internationally, as well as their ability to make the international telephone calls and faxes essential to a major laundering investigation. Tensions also may develop between the commissions and chief prosecutors, whose consent is typically required to pursue corruption prosecutions and who may find it difficult to develop the expertise or independence necessary for high-level cases.[30]

RED FLAGS

Extensive and costly effort has been invested within financial services firms and regulatory bodies to develop red flags that alert people, sometimes through intelligent software, to phenomena associated with the crimes sought to be prevented. So far, most of this effort has been directed at detecting mainstream crimes rather than grand corruption or terrorist financing, but there is pressure for more red flags aimed at corruption.

Calibrating the red flags so that they neither over- or underpredict is also an issue. Too many reports waste scarce resource time on investigating things that turn out not to be money laundering (or the proceeds of corruption). The scarcer investigative resources are (partly political, partly economic prioritization issues), the more that bureaucracies can be drowned in processing rather than investigation.

Below is a summary of generic red flags used by FIUs and banks to detect possible money laundering activity (Howell 2006, appendix 4). Some of these flags have been adapted somewhat to make them relevant to corruption. It should be remembered that what is "normal" behavior in one country may be "suspicious" in another. For example, residents of developing countries and many transition economies typically use more cash than do citizens in developed countries, especially in the United States. This cultural difference has often created tensions over what is "suspicious" behavior.

Use of Cash

- invoices settled by cash or wire transfers between unrelated companies
- payments with small-denomination notes, transferred by postal orders, or payment for flights, hotels, and consumer goods just below the cash limit for currency transaction reports
- frequent or large deposits of currency and dealing only in cash equivalents
- asking for exemptions from regulations on deposit of cash and cash equivalents
- use of notes by a politically exposed person
- frequent changing of large notes for small ones by PEPs
- repeated use of automated cash deposit machines or purchase of travelers' checks for sums just below threshold
- repeated cash transfers to or from foreign banks or companies
- repeated cash receipts or payments by a customer who normally makes or receives transfers by check or bank

- sudden interruption in bank withdrawals
- sudden increase in deposits or withdrawals, attributed, for example, to "playing the lottery."

Know the Business

- establishment of a business without real knowledge of how the sector operates
- transactions lack business sense, a clear strategy, or are inconsistent with the customer's objectives
- high turnover of funds, at little or no risk, with no apparent substantive business
- indifference to high risk and high transaction costs
- dealing in high-risk securities (legitimate but associated with fraud)
- dealings with high-risk areas without clear rationale
- repeat transactions for amounts just under the reporting limit
- frequent receipt of electronic funds transfers, with balance drawn down by check or debit card without any apparent business purpose
- sudden large payment to or from abroad without apparent reason
- transfers to unrelated third parties
- deposit of a large sum for a stated purpose where the amount is suddenly paid away for different ends or with no explanation
- unduly complex arrangements
- inconsistencies in an account's activities such as size, destination, and timing of payments, especially international transfers
- inconsistency of business with businesses of similar size in the same industry
- intermingling of personal and firm funds
- pressure exerted to avoid record keeping or reporting requirements
- requests to process transactions in a way that avoids the firm's normal documentation requirements.

Know Your Customer

- name of past client is used as an introduction, but the past client now has a new address or is unreachable
- company address is that of a service company or agent
- identity documents are from foreign countries, especially less well-known countries, or are diplomatic passports or photocopies (with or without excuse)
- unreadiness, unwillingness, or inability to provide information and verifiable documentation about self, business organization, key officials, owners or controllers, or business plans
- false or misleading statements, or no statement, about origins of funds, especially after specific request
- customer shows unusual interest in the firm's compliance with AML policies and suspicious transaction report procedures when discussing identity, type of business, and source of assets

- negative background checks on customer and known associates
- evasiveness about links to a suspected principal in the transaction
- unusual or suspicious identification or business documents
- business is alleged to be part of a confidential venture involving a blue chip organization, a government body, or well-known, high-net-worth individual
- the business supports a particular charity
- opening multiple accounts with similar names
- inconsistent information provided with usual business practices
- the business is run by someone who has inside knowledge of a highly lucrative market.

Insurance Red Flags

- request for an unsuitable product with no adequate reason
- more interest in the cancellation or surrender terms than in the return
- request to use a large lump payment to upsize small policies or transactions based on regular payments
- acceptance of unfavorable terms in relation to health or age
- contract for life insurance of fewer than three years
- request made through an unknown broker or a broker in region with light regulation
- the first premium is paid from a bank account overseas, especially from lightly regulated countries
- purchase of insurance products using a third-party check
- use of a performance bond resulting in a cross-border payment
- frequent changes to beneficiaries
- attempt to borrow maximum cash value of a single-premium policy soon after purchase
- client cancels investment or insurance soon after purchase, especially where reimbursement is requested to a third party.

Measuring Progress

It is possible to define and measure inputs that contribute to success in implementing AML measures. Definition and measurement allow thresholds of adequacy and inadequacy to be established and the situation in any given country to be mapped. The status of a country (or key institution) can then be monitored over time or compared with peers' scores according to the same criteria. This mapping also helps highlight where gaps need closing and the comparative cost of closing specific gaps. Resources can then be allocated to where they will have greatest effect.

Having measures in place does not result per se in effectiveness, however. Monitoring should be designed to relate performance of AML activities to their effects on money laundering and corruption. Insufficient attention has been paid to the kinds of performance indicators that enable an assessment of those effects and the relationship of AML inputs to anticorruption outcomes. Indicators that can demonstrate results are important given that implementing AML measures is costly.

In the late 20th century, the links between anticorruption efforts and the development of AML systems were modest. As a consequence of some major scandals in the late 1990s, most notably those involving Sani Abacha of Nigeria, financial institutions (especially those involved in high-net-worth wealth management) and other regulated bodies now use large, usually public, databases to check their client base, and private investigators check connections of business people for relationships with publicly identified "organized criminals" or terrorists.[31]

On the governmental side, there has been a major shift in emphasis on building up infrastructures that support criminalization of money-laundering activities and, to a lesser extent, the investigation and incapacitation of offenders and key players in laundering networks, as well as common procedures for providing mutual legal assistance and dealing with suspicious activity reports locally and internationally. People who pay and accept bribes or other corrupt payouts face heightened risks of detection in a climate where the serious investigation of one component in a money-laundering scheme can result in major consequences for all those involved. The challenge is to learn some positive lessons from those cases that have been investigated and to deepen and extend AML mechanisms in both developing and developed countries to reduce, if not eliminate, the scale of middle to grand corruption and to recover more assets for those who are looted.

CONCLUSION

Enhancing the culture of integrity, transparency, and accountability will help fight all forms of corruption. Grand corruption has an enormous impact on the culture of impunity and the local and international public's perception of corruption within a country. Political leaders who have been entrusted to make decisions on behalf of the public, but who instead abscond with millions of dollars, create distrust in the government. Lack of confidence in government and the courts may then result in political as well as economic instability or at the very least in a lack of confidence by foreign investors, narrowing the range of businesspeople willing to invest in the country. Legitimate investors may not be able to compete with businesses backed by illicit investments. A reputational risk results from being perceived as a country that permits money laundering. This risk has the potential to cause macroeconomic distortions, misallocate capital and resources, increase the risks to a country's financial sector, and hurt the credibility and integrity of domestic financial sectors and the international financial system.[32]

Large-scale impunity in a country results in, and reflects, the lack of rule of law. Good governance necessitates transparency, predictability, and the rule of law. Money laundering is one mechanism by which criminals avoid being held accountable for their corrupt behavior. It is for this reason that anticorruption programs need to consider not only local efforts to curb opportunities for corrupt behavior but also international mechanisms to detect moves to hide the proceeds. In some states, commercial transparency is little more than an opportunity for a more perfect market in extortion possibilities. In others, suspicious activity reports have assisted those motivated to investigate in linking intercompany transfers to corrupt individuals and have facilitated prosecutions or at least the identification of proceeds of corruption and the assets of those suspected of corruption, which can then be frozen and, where there is a legal basis for doing so, returned.

AML measures can assist in uncovering predicate crimes, especially where financial institutions comply with the requirements to know their customers. For example, banks that follow the requirement to know their customers (including identifying and verifying identity of the beneficial owners of legal entities) and that report suspicious financial transactions can help detect and combat illegal logging (Setiono and Husein 2005). Given that illegal logging tends to involve corruption by government officials, enhanced customer due diligence requirements that financial institutions must follow when dealing, for example, with politically exposed persons increase the probability that their illegal activity will be discovered. Other regulations, including those governing seizure and confiscation of the proceeds of crime, as well as opportunities for expanded formal and informal international cooperation and mutual legal assistance provided by AML laws, will greatly enhance the fight against illegal logging and other forest crime. Using these and other tools, countries could consider setting up a special strike force of investigators and prosecutors to target a select number of significant illegal logging cases involving money laundering and corruption for investigation and prosecution.

Bank surveillance of their PEP customers may assist in preventing further corrupt behavior, especially if such surveillance is expanded to domestic as well as foreign officials. PEPs should also be subject to a more senior level of approval than would otherwise be required for standard customers. However, corrupt bank tellers, account managers, and others involved in the process may create obstacles to exposing the money laundering. These key players must be equipped with the proper tools through awareness raising and training exercises to identify, report, and investigate cases that raise suspicions of money laundering. They must also believe or know that they will be held accountable if they fail to display due diligence. This is important since criminals may try to develop relationships with some of these professionals as a counter to the controls, thereby corrupting the very institutions that are meant to regulate money laundering. Some banks have been fined for not having the appropriate safeguards in place to detect money laundering. For example, the Bank of Ireland was fined £375,000 in 2004 for not detecting the misuse of bank drafts in one of its branches in violation of AML regulations (Financial Services Authority 2004). In another example, the Arab Bank was fined $24 million for violating the AML regulations at its New York branch because it did not apply safeguard controls to wire transfers (U.S. Department of the Treasury 2005).

In addition, many multinational corporations are working to ensure that their local foreign offices are behaving in a manner consistent with anticorruption standards. It would be helpful if all international corporations, not just financial institutions, adopted compliance and ethics programs. Banks, insurance companies, securities dealers, lawyers, real estate agents, and many other financial and nonfinancial businesses and professions can be at high risk for abuse by criminals and must put necessary preventive measures in place to guard against money laundering. The private sector can also be helpful in raising awareness among the public about the importance of these issues and can demonstrate the benefits of a strong AML system.

If enforcement is aggressive, there may be a greater degree of self-regulation by the private sector itself. However, such enforcement would require an efficient and effective judiciary and prosecution office as well as cooperation from foreign governments.

There is now a plethora of legislation and international conventions making bribery a crime. This includes the OECD Anti-Bribery Convention, the Inter-American Convention against Corruption, the Criminal Law Convention against Corruption of the Council of Europe, the EU Joint Action of December 22, 1998, on corruption in the private sector, the Convention of the EU on the fight against corruption involving officials of the European Communities or officials of member states, the Council of Europe Directive on the Prevention of the Use of the Financial System for the Purpose of Money Laundering and Terrorist Financing, and the UN Convention against Illicit Traffic in Narcotic Drugs and Psychotropic Substances. The payment of a bribe in most countries is a crime, and false entries into company books and records are also crimes in more and more countries. Such false entries are very often how money is generated to finance a bribe. Enforcement is necessary from both sides to ensure that not only the individual but also the high-powered politicians and corporations will be subject to the same standards. In this way, there will be greater trust and, therefore, greater cooperation with law enforcement when investigating corruption and money laundering.

How can governments develop greater synergies between AML and anticorruption? First, anticorruption and AML assessments should each be aware of all the measures taken to prevent and combat corruption or money laundering. For example, FATF/FSRB mutual evaluations and World Bank–IMF AML/CFT assessments could look at the impact of corruption laws and their impact on a jurisdiction's implementation of AML measures. Understanding the process that corrupt proceeds undergo to become legitimate is central to understanding how impunity occurs. Second, national AML laws should be brought into line with the FATF recommendations. Third, countries should make their own assessment of money-laundering and corruption vulnerabilities, especially the type, magnitude, and geographic location within their borders, and design a proactive national strategy as well as law enforcement targeting priorities based on the assessment rather than solely as a by-product of following up on the usual suspects. Fourth, anticorruption commissions, prosecution offices, and the judiciary should have adequate training on international as well as domestic legislation related to money laundering and on mechanisms for requesting international cooperation. There should be training in identifying and monitoring the flow of illegal proceeds overseas as well as freezing, confiscation, and repatriation of these assets. Education and training of parliamentarians, the press, and the public about the relationships between corruption and money laundering are also important. Fifth, interagency and interdisciplinary cooperation should be developed within a government to facilitate investigation and prosecution as well as adequate supervision. Sixth, global, regional, subregional, and bilateral cooperation should be forged among the judiciary, law enforcement agencies,[33] FIUs, and financial regulatory authorities to address corruption and money laundering. Seventh, investigators, prosecutors, and the judiciary need capacity building in AML financial investigation techniques as well as technical assistance in developing and prosecuting grand corruption cases. Eighth, the results of those prosecutions should be well publicized in the media to build public confidence in enforcement of the laws. Ninth, aggressive efforts should be made to recover corrupt proceeds and those proceeds then used in a transparent way either to compensate the victims or for the benefit of the public. Finally, both sides (briber and bribed) are more likely to be exposed when there are a free press, an independent judiciary, and political diversity. There is little doubt that both developed and developing countries could strengthen AML measures to make it more difficult for bribe payers and bribe takers to do business.

ENDNOTES

1. This chapter does not attempt to address the separate issues relating to the connection between money laundering and the financing of terrorism.
2. Proceeds are generated by carrying out predicate offenses that include fraud, corruption, and bribery; organized crime; trafficking in human beings and drugs; and environmental crime (such as illegal logging). Money laundering is a separate crime from the predicate offense, and a person can be convicted for money laundering even though he or she did not carry out the predicate offense.
3. Reuter and Truman (2004). The Financial Action Task Force and several member countries tried to measure the magnitude of money laundering, but they were unsuccessful. There was no agreement on the methodology to be used and how to measure money moving at various stages of the laundering process.
4. Money is sometimes laundered through brokerage firms, insurance companies, money remitters, real estate agents, lawyers, and accounting professionals. Levi and Reuter (2006) estimate that only at an income of around $50,000 a year and above do offenders really launder money, that is, do more than simply store it in a bank account in their own names. However, this estimate is derived only from the affluent OECD countries, where nominal and real costs of living and incomes are high. One might expect that for those trying to avoid conspicuous consumption in developing countries, the level of criminal income at which money is laundered would be lower than in OECD countries. See Levi and Reuter (2006) for further information.
5. See http://www.worldpress.org/specials/euro/1119web_Helsinki.htm and FATF Typologies Report 2001–2002, pages 21–23. http://www.fatf-gafi.org/dataoecd/29/35/34038006. pdf.
6. The requirements for STRs and FIUs could be considered the most important and innovative part of the FATF *40 Recommendations on Money Laundering.*
7. Financial institutions are defined in the FATF+40 recommendations glossary as covering one or more of the 13 activities or operations listed. http://www.fatf-gafi.org/dataoecd/46/48/34274813.PDF.
8. In international banking, accounting, and lawyering, the constructs of "home" and "overseas" are sometimes difficult to define, as there may be group as well as local compliance officers tasked with monitoring.
9. It is important to understand the distinction between the predicate crime and money laundering. Money laundering can be prosecuted as a separate crime only if it is included as a separate criminal offense. The FATF states in its Recommendation 1 that: "Countries should apply the crime of money laundering to all serious offences, with a view to including the widest range of predicate offences. Predicate offences may be described by reference to all offences, or to a threshold linked either to a category of serious offences or to

the penalty of imprisonment applicable to the predicate offence (threshold approach), or to a list of predicate offences, or a combination of these approaches." http://www.fatf-gafi.org/dataoecd/7/40/34849567.PDF.

10. The definition of PEPs is not intended to cover middle-ranking or more junior individuals in these categories; see http://www.fatf-gafi.org/dataoecd/ 7/40/34849567.PDF. The international banks have developed some important guidelines explaining how to go about recognizing who is and is not a PEP; see also "Wolfsberg Frequently Asked Questions on Politically Exposed Persons" at http://www.wolfsberg-principles.com/faq-persons.html and "Wolfsberg AML Principles for Correspondent Banking," Principle 4: Risk-Based Due Diligence, http://www.wolfsberg-principles.com/ corresp-banking.html. Various firms also sell lists of identified PEPs to financial institutions to assist them in their due diligence on clients.
11. A shell bank is a bank incorporated in a jurisdiction in which it has no physical presence and which is unaffiliated with a regulated financial group. See FATF (2003).
12. The Uniting and Strengthening America by Providing Appropriate Tools Required to Intercept and Obstruct Terrorism Act of 2001, PL 107-56, 2001 HR 3162, section 319. The U.S. Department of Justice has used section 319 in several significant cases. One example is the Gibson case: On January 18, 2001, a federal grand jury indicted James Gibson for offenses including conspiracy to commit money laundering as well as mail and wire fraud. Gibson had defrauded his clients by fraudulently structuring settlements. Gibson fled to Belize, depositing some of the proceeds in two Belizean banks. Following the passage of the USA PATRIOT Act, a seizure warrant was served on the Belizean bank's correspondent account in the United States pursuant to section 319, and the funds were recovered. See U.S. Department of Justice (2004).
13. Business relationships with family members or close associates of PEPs involve reputational risks similar to those of PEPs themselves.
14. Initially there were 11 banks participating in the association: ABN AMRO, Barclays Bank, Banco Santander Central Hispano, S.A., The Chase Manhattan Private Bank, Citibank, N.A., Credit Suisse Group, Deutsche Bank AG, HSBC, J.P. Morgan, Société Générale, and UBS AG. The number increased to 12 when Bank of Tokyo, Mitsubishi UFJ joined the association.
15. Wolfsberg AML Principles for Private Banking: "1. client acceptance: general guidelines; 2. client acceptance: situations requiring additional diligence/attention; 3. updating client files; 4. practices when identifying unusual or suspicious activities; 5. monitoring; 6. control responsibilities; 7. reporting; 8. education, training, and information; 9. record retention requirements; 10. exceptions and deviations; 11. anti-money-laundering organization." http://www.wolfsberg-principles.com.
16. For the most recent analysis, see the "Review of the Suspicious Activity Reports Regime" at http://www.soca.gov.uk/downloads/SOCAtheSARsReview_FINAL_Web.pdf.
17. If they meet certain criteria of competence and independence, they may be admitted to the Egmont Group, which at the end of 2006 has 102 members, nearly two-thirds of UN membership.
18. In the High Court of Lesotho held at Maseru. In the matter between: The Crown versus Acres International Limited, indictment (charged that for June 1991–January 1998, Acres transferred approximately $433,900 into a Swiss bank account for the benefit of LHDA CEO; and that for January 31, 1991–April 3, 1991, Acres transferred approximately $165,664 into a Swiss bank account for the benefit of LHDA CEO). This case also led in 2004 to Acres being banned by the World Bank Sanctions Committee for three years from participating in Bank-financed construction projects. See World Bank (2004).

19. In the Lesotho High Court, in the matter between The Crown versus Masupha Ephraim Sole, CRI/T/111/99.
20. In 1997, the Swiss authorities began investigating Sole's bank accounts in Geneva and Zurich after the government of Lesotho applied to the Swiss Supreme Court for disclosure of the Swiss bank accounts belonging to Sole.
21. *Marcos and Marcos v Federal Department of police* (1989) ILR 198. The court stated that,

    "The privilege of the immunity from criminal jurisdiction of head of state . . . has not been fully codified in the Vienna convention (on Diplomatic Relations) . . . but it cannot be concluded that the texts of conventions drafted under the aegis of the United Nations grant a lesser protection to heads of foreign states than to the Diplomatic representatives of the state which those heads of state lead or universally represent. . . . Article 32 and 39 of the Vienna Convention must therefore apply by analogy to the heads of state."
22. The AU Convention on Preventing and Combating Corruption of July 2003, articles 16.1 (c) and 19.3.
23. For a discussion, see Levi and Reuter (2006, n. 6). Kaufman (2002, p. 1) states, "While the bulk of money laundering in many countries still tend[s] to use the formal banking system, money laundering through non-banking financial institutions (NBFIs) appears to be growing in importance—through real estate transactions, security brokers, derivatives, the exchange rate market, leasing insurance companies, and others." However, in our view, it is not readily knowable whether this does indeed represent a trend (presumably via displacement from the banking sector) or simply a greater focus on those latter issues, picking up more of the "dark figure" of undetected money laundering than was appreciated previously. This can be an important point, if causal displacement hypotheses are important to policy, but given data imperfections, it may be more practical simply to be aware that such displacement *can* exist and that the existing detection mechanisms are unable to pick up the signs, despite the excellent work done on remittances and informal value transfer systems. See also Maimbo (2003); Maimbo and others (2005); and Maimbo and Passas (2004).
24. Some assessment needs to be made of the magnitude of corruption proceeds that remain in developing countries and are invested in real estate and domestic businesses.
25. Provided, of course, that the accused does not have head-of-state immunity for offenses carried out while in office, even though not committed in pursuit of legitimate state objectives. Such criminal and procedural immunities are more common in developing countries but they also appear in developed countries, as may be deduced from corruption investigations in OECD countries.
26. Issues such as drugs and the smuggling of illicit commodities are relevant here because they are often associated with corruption.
27. There are many terms used to describe alternative remittance systems, including underground banking and ethnic banking. Geographically, the terms used to describe informal remittance systems include *hawala* (India and Middle East), *padala* (the Philippines), *hui kuan* (Hong Kong, China), and *phei kwan* (Thailand). Alternative remittance systems involve informal money or value transfer services that run parallel to, but generally independent of, the formal banking system. See World Bank–IMF (2006).
28. See FATF Revised Interpretative Note to Special Recommendation VII: Wire transfers http://www.fatf-gafi.org/dataoecd/34/56/35002635.pdf.
29. These FIUs also meet the criteria of the Egmont Group of Financial Intelligence Units (Egmont Group), an informal organization of FIUs "commit[ed] to [encouraging] the development of FIUs and co-operation among and between them in the interest of combating money laundering and in assisting with the global fight against terrorism financing." Egmont Statement of Purpose, 2004, available at http://www.egmontgroup.org/.

30. This is not merely a problem for developing countries. Some EU countries (and candidate countries) have also experienced difficulties, and the role of special prosecutors and independent counsel in the United States has not been without criticism. There is in this sense a tension between granting political autonomy to law officers and ensuring their accountability for efficiency and for integrity purposes.
31. The issue of the private sector's access to undeclared suspects' identities in intelligence files remains a deeply contentious issue, since for the most part such "data" are inaccessible.
32. In 2001, Citigroup was caught up in the corruption investigation surrounding one of its wealthy customers, Joseph Estrada, the ousted president of the Philippines; see "Through the Wringer," *The Economist,* April 12, 2001.
33. For example, The International Criminal Police Organization (ICPO/Interpol), and the World Customs Organization, as well as Europol and Eurojust at the EU level.

REFERENCES

Burgen, Stephen. 2006. "Pirates of the Mediterranean" (July 30). *The Sunday Times.* http://www.timesonline.co.uk/tol/life_and_style/article690365.ece.

Camdessus, Michael. 1998. "Money Laundering: The Importance of International Countermeasures." Address to the Financial Action Task Force Plenary Meeting, Paris, February 10.

Commission for Africa. 2005. *Our Common Interest: Report of the Commission for Africa.* London: Commission for Africa.

Dakolias, Maria, and Kimberly Thachuk. 2000. "Attacking Corruption in the Judiciary: A Critical Process in Judicial Reform." *Wisconsin International Law Journal* 18 (Spring): 353–406.

Financial Action Task Force on Money Laundering (FATF). 2003. "The Forty Recommendations" (June 20). http://www.fatf-gafi.org/dataoecd/7/40/34849567.PDF.

Financial Services Authority (FSA). 2004. "FSA Fines Bank of Ireland 375,000 for Breaches of Anti-money Laundering Requirements." FSA/PN/077/2004 (February 9). http://www.fsa.gov.uk/pages/Library/Communication/PR/2004/077.shtml.

Goodman, Al. 2002. "Black Money: Spain's 'Euro Effect.'" CNN.com, January 2. http://archives.cnn.com/2001/WORLD/europe/12/24/spain.black.money/.

Howell, J. 2006. *Guide to the Prevention of Money Laundering and Terrorist Financing* Publication 669. Paris: International Chamber of Commerce (ICC).

Kaufmann, D. 2002. *Governance in the Financial Sector: The Broader Context of Money Laundering and Terrorist Financing.* Washington, DC: World Bank. http://info.worldbank.org/etools/docs/library/108443/aml_Kaufmann.pdf.

Levi, M., and M. Maguire. 2004. "Reducing and Preventing Organized Crime: An Evidence-Based Critique." *Crime, Law and Social Change* 41(5): 397–469.

Levi, M. and P. Reuter. 2006. "Money Laundering: A Review of Current Controls and Their Consequences." In *Crime and Justice: A Review of Research,* vol. 34, ed. M. Tonry 289–375. Chicago: University of Chicago Press.

Maimbo, S. M. 2003. *The Money Exchange Dealers of Kabul: A Study of the Informal Funds Transfer Markets in Afghanistan.* Washington, DC: World Bank.

Maimbo, S. M., R. Adams, R. Aggarwal, and N. Passas. 2005. *Migrant Labor Remittances in the South Asia Region.* Washington, DC: World Bank.

Maimbo, S. M., and N. Passas. 2004. "The Regulation and Supervision of Informal Remittance Systems." *Small Enterprise Development* 14 (1): 53–62.

Nelen, H. 2004. "Hit Them Where It Hurts Most? The Proceeds-of-Crime Approach in the Netherlands." *Crime, Law and Social Change* 41: 517–34.

Passas, N. 2006. *Legislative Guide for the Implementation of the United States Convention against Corruption.* New York: United Nations.

Reuter, Peter, and Edwin M. Truman. 2004. *Chasing Dirty Money: The Fight against Money Laundering.* Washington, DC: Institute for International Economics.

Setiono, Bambang, and Yunus Husein. 2005. "Fighting Forest Crime and Promoting Prudent Banking for Sustainable Forest Management—The Anti-Money-Laundering Approach." Center for International Forestry Research (CIFOR) Occasional Paper 44, Bogor, Indonesia.

Shleifer, Andrei, and Robert Vishny. 1993. "Corruption." *Quarterly Journal of Economics* 108 (3): 599–617.

SFBC (Swiss Federal Banking Commission). 2001. "SFBC Orders Removal of Bank's General Manager: Investigation by Supervisory Authority in Montesinos Case Concluded" (November 13). http://www.ebk.admin.ch/e/archiv/2001/pdf/m1113-01e.pdf.

————. 2005. "Report on the Activity of Swiss-Based Banks in the United Nations Oil-for-Food Programme" (October 27). http://www.ebk.admin.ch/e/archiv/2005/20051027/051027_02_e.pdf.

Swiss Federal Department of Justice and Police. 2000. "Abacha Funds at Swiss Banks." Report of the Swiss Federal Banking Commission (August). http://www.ebk.admin.ch/e/archiv/2000/pdf/neu14a-00.pdf.

Transparency International. 2005. *Global Corruption Report 2004.* Berlin: Transparency International.

United Nations. 2004. *United Nations Handbook on Practical Anticorruption Measures for Prosecutors and Investigators, Annex: The Lesotho Corruption Trials: A Case Study*, 136–210. United Nations: Vienna:

UNODC (United Nations Office on Drugs and Crime). 1998. *Financial Havens, Banking Secrecy and Money Laundering.* Technical Series Issue 8. New York: United Nations.

U.S. Department of Justice. 2004. "Report from the Field: The USA PATRIOT Act at Work" (July). http://www.lifeandliberty.gov/docs/071304_report_from_the_field.pdf.

————. 2005. "International Narcotics Control Strategy Report" (March). http://www. state.gov/p/inl/rls/nrcrpt/2005/vol2/html/42382.htm; http://en.wikipedia.org/wiki/Vladimiro_Montesinos.

U.S. Department of the Treasury. 2005. "Assessment of Civil Money Penalty." 2005-2. http://www.fincen.gov/arab081705.pdf.

U.S. Senate Minority Staff of the Permanent Subcommittee on Investigations. 2004. *Money Laundering and Foreign Corruption: Enforcement and Effectiveness of the PATRIOT Act. Case Study Involving Riggs Bank.* Washington, DC, http://www.senate.gov/~govt-aff/_files/ACF5F8.pdf.

U.S. Senate Permanent Subcommittee on Investigations. 2005. *Money Laundering and Foreign Corruption: Enforcement and Effectiveness of the PATRIOT Act.* Supplemental Staff Report on U.S. accounts used by Augusto Pinochet. Washington, DC, http://hsgac. senate.gov/ _files/PINOCHETREPORTFINALwcharts0.pdf.

U.S. Senate Subcommittee on Investigations. 1999. "Private Banking and Money Laundering, a Case Study of Opportunities and Vulnerabilities," http://frwebgate.access.gpo.gov/cgi-bin/getdoc.cgi?dbname=106_senate_hearings&docid=f:61699.pdf.

World Bank. 2004. "World Bank Sanctions Acres International Limited." Press Release 2005/33/S. http://web.worldbank.org/WBSITE/EXTERNAL/NEWS/0,,contentMDK:20229958~menuPK:34463~pagePK:64003015~piPK:64003012~theSitePK: 4607,00.html.

————. 2005. "The World Bank Capacity Enhancement Program on Anti-Money-Laundering and Combating the Financing of Terrorism, Module 1, Workbook." World Bank, Washington, DC.

World Bank, with cooperation from the Swiss Federal Ministry of Finance. 2006. "Utilization of Repatriated Abacha Loot." http://web.worldbank.org/WBSITE/EXTERNAL/COUNTRIES/AFRICAEXT/NIGERIAEXTN/0,,contentMDK:21169888~menu PK:3287725~pagePK:141137~piPK:141127~theSitePK:368896,00.html.

World Bank–IMF. 2006. *Reference Guide to Anti-Money Laundering and Combating the Financing of Terrorism* (Second Edition). Washington, DC: World Bank.

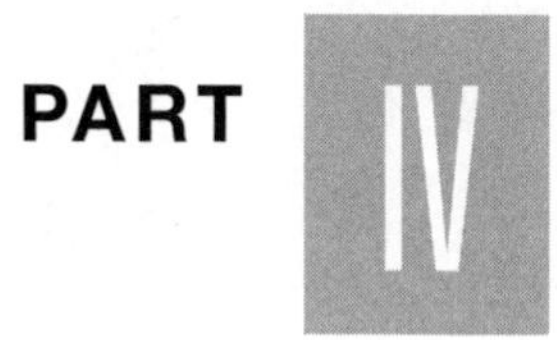
PART IV

The Challenges Ahead

Conclusion

Where to Next?

J. EDGARDO CAMPOS, SANJAY PRADHAN,
AND FRANCESCA RECANATINI

After so many years, Sanjiv and his family finally have electricity in their modest home. His children can now do their homework every evening with the benefit of light. His wife can now cook with a little more comfort as the breeze of an electric fan cools their small kitchen. And Sanjiv can now enjoy watching television, albeit in black and white, after a long day's work. But many of their neighbors and friends in the community still long for the day when they too can enjoy these little benefits. Unlike Sanjiv, they do not have the wherewithal to save enough to pay the speed money to jump the 10-year queue. But something is brewing in this little town. A group of concerned elderly citizens has petitioned the mayor to hold a public forum to discuss the difficulties of obtaining critical public services, especially electricity. Why is it that most families in the next town enjoy at least several hours of electricity a day, while here only a handful have access? Why do we have to pay speed money to get public services? These are the questions they are asking. And they are going door to door to persuade their fellow citizens to add their voices to the slowly mounting public dissatisfaction with the status quo.

On the opposite side of the globe, Carlos has won the latest contract from the municipal government to construct a five-kilometer stretch of road around the outskirts of the town. As always, he and four of his fellow contractors drew lots to determine who would be the "winning" bidder. This time he was the lucky one. But there is a growing concern among all five about the future of their cozy arrangement. They have just learned that the central government will be setting up an electronic procurement system. When this is completed, all public contracts, including those of local government, will have to be posted on a government Web site that will be accessible to any contractor in or outside the country. Carlos and his compatriots are now worried that their cartel will lose control over construction contracts in their municipality. With the increased transparency in the invitations to bid, outside contractors will likely bid for municipal contracts. That could mean 10 or more new competitors for a contract, which would make it impossible to spread the gravy across all of bidders. The days of easy money may be coming to an end.

In still another country thousands of miles across the ocean from Carlos' municipality, the husband of the president has finally secured the "entry fees" from four international firms to prequalify for the contract to construct the country's new international airport, an ambitious $300 million project that hopes to make the country an international hub for the continent. In private, the four firms have started to voice concerns about the escalating cost of bidding for contracts in this country and many others as well. They all recognize that each would be better off if the playing field were leveled, with no one having to pay entry and negotiation fees. Moreover, as multinationals, they are also getting nervous about more rigorous enforcement of the OECD Convention on Combating Bribery of Foreign Public Officials. The first gentleman has also begun harboring some concerns as well, but of a different kind. Several major donor countries have just signed an agreement to establish an international fund dedicated to combating corruption among world leaders. One country has already pledged close to $200 million and others are set to follow soon. What are the implications of this for him; his wife, president; his children; and his cronies? Coming on the heels of this agreement, could the under-the-table arrangement on this huge project backfire on him? Might it even lead to impeachment of the president? Or might there be some point in the near future that his family's assets abroad could be confiscated and he imprisoned in another country?

Sanjiv, Carlos, and the first gentleman have each witnessed, experienced, or perpetrated different manifestations of the world's most virulent social disease. Corruption indeed comes in varied forms and shapes and truly has many faces. This volume has attempted to chart a potentially promising path toward understanding the deeper crevices of corruption: where are the vulnerabilities at the sector level, and how might they be recognized and tracked? But it is just the beginning of a long journey. The road ahead leads to challenging tasks including, among other things, the development of sophisticated corruption vulnerability assessment tools, the conduct of detailed field studies to distill lessons of what works and what does not at the sector level, and ultimately the formulation of operationally tractable sectoral anticorruption strategies.

Existing work has typically focused on macro-level analysis to identify major impediments to growth and poverty reduction. At best, this work identifies those sectors that are the most corrupt or where corruption has been most harmful to development efforts.[1] While this work is useful as a first-tier analysis, the problem of corruption begs for more nuanced analyses that drill down to the sector level. The road-map approach adopted by this volume provides an avenue for undertaking such analyses and paves the way for the development of sector-specific vulnerability assessments.

To move forward on such assessments, it would be useful to start with pilot efforts in a few countries and selected sectors. These pilots can be used to develop quantitative indicators of vulnerabilities that can then be applied to the selected sectors in a larger number of countries. This process can lead to the development of a cross-country database of actionable indicators to benchmark, compare, and track progress of countries in combating corruption in various sectors.

Within any given sector, the procurement process is perhaps the single most corruption-prone area. But it also presents the most promising area for which a set of concrete, quantifiable indicators can be developed, from the initial planning phase all the way through to contract award and implementation.[2] Hence, focusing on the procurement process in one or two key sectors, such as roads, could be a good jumping-off point for the development of actionable indicators. Procurement offers three advantages in this regard. First, the basic procurement process is very much the same across countries, so the indicators developed through the pilots are likely to work for other countries as well. Second, these pilots can lead to a large database of indicators that do not suffer from what Johnston (2001) calls "the single number problem." Each indicator would reflect the state of governance of a particular aspect of a country's procurement system, such as the prequalification phase. Moreover, a composite indicator consisting of a weighted sum of the various indicators could conceivably be constructed that would reflect a very specific slice of a country's governance system—procurement. There would be little question as to what the indicators represent. And third, there is a slowly growing body of theoretical work on public procurement based on the economics of information that could help guide the construction of indicators (see, for example, Laffont and Tirole [1993] and Manelli and Vincent [1995]). Theoretically derived indicators tend to provide better insights into the design of appropriate reform measures—theory helps determine where to look for answers to problems.

Detailed corruption road maps and sector-specific indicators can offer many possibilities for fine-tuning evolving anticorruption reform measures and tailoring them to different sectoral contexts. The central insight of this volume is that sectors and subsectors differ considerably in the nature of their value chains and processes and consequently that reform strategies need to be tailored to tackle those specific areas of vulnerability.

New tools and instruments are in fact continuously being developed to help manage, control, and hinder the spread of corruption. These new instruments tend to fall into three general categories: strengthening the demand side of good governance (the post-Sanjiv saga), using information and communications technology strategically (Carlos's concern), and building global partnerships (the first gentleman's nemesis). While enforcement (investigation, prosecution, litigation, civil and criminal penalties) is important and necessary, the thrust of these instruments is primarily on prevention. Prevention targets opportunities for corruption. If these doors can be closed, then the incidence of corruption will necessarily fall, and enforcement can focus on a few critical areas where it can then be more effective.

In this context, the main challenge lies in matching these new instruments to sector vulnerabilities in the formulation of reform strategies. For example, in the case of demand-side mechanisms, a variety of promising options include report card surveys, community monitoring of projects or programs, and media-driven lifestyle checks. Report card surveys have been helpful in improving the delivery of basic services and reducing the corruption that typically plagues these services. But they might not be as well suited to improving the quality of road construction and maintenance. That requires some form of random testing of the finished product and thus could be better served by some suitable form of community monitoring of completed road projects.[3] Similarly, for oil and gas, such surveys are unlikely to curtail corruption, since the problems generally need to be addressed at the international level, which will require a different mechanism to raise demand-side pressures for reform. The matching of demand-side mechanisms to sector-specific vulnerabilities is still not very well understood. Given its promise as an instrument of reform, it deserves more attention from researchers interested in pushing the knowledge frontier on governance and anticorruption.

Experiences around the world on the use of modern information and communications technology (ICT) in improving the efficiency and effectiveness of government suggest that a judicious and appropriate application of such technology can have a significant impact on corruption and more generally on improved governance.[4] Early efforts to apply modern ICT were not particularly encouraging because they were indiscriminately applied, typically involved "computerization" of inefficient business processes, and in many cases, were simply imposed from above without adequate attention placed on managing the change process (World Bank 2005). Much has been learned over the years.

One emerging approach turns the table upside down: instead of technology being applied to existing processes, processes are restructured and reforms designed around the technical capabilities of new technologies. The World Bank, the Asian Development Bank, and the Inter-American Development Bank have collaborated on a report on the application of ICT to public procurement. As the report (World Bank forthcoming) states:

> . . . these technologies do more than simply provide access to information: the effective application of these technologies requires that processes be formally defined, lines of authority clearly specified, and procedures and terms and conditions be standardized. Thus, e-procurement is not simply the application of technology to existing processes, but *a reform process in itself that requires in many instances, that traditional processes be modified or abolished*—that management processes, protocols and procedures be standardized, reformatted and often simplified in order that they become compatible with the digital environment.

New technologies open up possibilities that were not available in the past and thus, if applied appropriately, can potentially help improve the design and implementation of governance reforms.

But, like demand-side mechanisms, ICT must be adapted to sector-specific characteristics. E-procurement systems, for instance, hold considerable promise as an anchor around which transparency and accountability in government contracting can be strengthened, particularly in the purchase of standard goods and services and the construction and maintenance of roads. Global satellite systems offer new possibilities for restructuring monitoring processes and systems in managing forests that can potentially constrain illegal logging operations and consequently the grand corruption that often afflicts forest management.

Grand corruption is indeed a serious problem in the forest sector. But it afflicts other areas as well—typically in international trading of extractive resources or the awarding of huge government contracts (predominantly in infrastructure)—and is often difficult to contain at the country level. Invariably, multinational firms or developed-country governments, or both, are involved in these types of transactions, a situation that raises difficult coordination problems. For example, in the competition for large government contracts that only big firms can potentially service, firms are pressed to bribe government officials for fear that, if they do not, competitors will likely do so and hence they will lose out: ironically, bribes level the playing field. Sector reforms in these cases must go beyond borders; the more typical reforms, such as procurement reforms, while helpful, are not sufficient to hold corruption in check. Examples of cross-border initiatives, such as the Extractive Industries

Transparency Initiative, focused primarily on petroleum and mining, the Forest Law Enforcement and Governance ministerial processes, and the OECD Convention against the Bribery of Foreign Officials are beginning to emerge. But such initiatives will need to be strengthened considerably to be able to manage the complex and difficult coordination problems that are often at the core of corruption in these areas.

A recent announcement by the government of the United Kingdom that it was establishing a special fund to support efforts to curb corruption among world leaders offers genuine possibilities for stemming the flow of grand corruption.[5] Such a fund can potentially be used to support detailed investigations of global investments and assets of so-called politically exposed persons. Where solid evidence of laundering can be established, prosecution can perhaps then be pursued in the country where the suspected assets or investments are located. Not surprisingly, many such assets and investments are typically located in countries where the rule of law is observed and robust: even thieves worry about the security of their property. Hence investigations and prosecutions have a fair chance of leading to convictions and repatriations. This approach will indirectly strengthen the enforcement capacity of countries. But, more important, if it is successful in putting a few big fish behind bars and getting the involved assets repatriated, the initiative would likely dampen the appetite for megabribes of influential but unscrupulous individuals.

The potential impact of this arrangement depends in part on the extent to which other countries decide to contribute to the fund.[6] The size of the fund by itself can potentially act as a deterrent. A billion dollars, for example, set aside exclusively to conduct investigations and prosecutions (in "rule of law" countries) of a few targeted individuals, significantly increases the probability of conviction and thus imprisonment and the loss of ill-gotten wealth. As theory and experience suggest, that expectation would tend to discourage individuals from engaging in grand corruption. Like most international agreements, this arrangement carries with it complexities and challenges that will take time to iron out. But it is a promising avenue that can potentially yield benefits many times its cost.

With grand corruption come issues in and problems of political economy. This volume has purposely eschewed any extensive discussion of the interface between corruption and politics. Its primary purpose is to argue for the adoption of a roadmap approach toward unpacking corruption at both the sector (value chain) and process (process flow) levels and to illustrate its usefulness in addressing corruption in an operational context. However, this approach invariably brings up the need for serious work on political economy at the sector and process levels. Sectors in particular differ as well in terms of their underlying political economy, not just in their value chains. Each sector can potentially have a different profile of key stakeholders, and the internal political logic that feeds corruption could differ as well. The challenge in this instance is to determine what sector vulnerabilities lend themselves more easily to reforms in the short to medium term and what if any can be done in the long run to address those that may be at the heart of the sector's political economy. This determination invariably demands a good understanding of sector politics and its links to the broader political environment. To be sure, there has been excellent work in the political economy at the sector level. Bates's (1981) seminal research on the agriculture-grains sectors in select countries in Africa—Kenya, Uganda, and

Ghana—and Ross's (2001) acclaimed work on the politics of timber in Indonesia are good examples. However, in most countries, such in-depth, sector-focused political economy analyses are not generally available. To formulate feasible and sustainable reform strategies, such studies and analyses are necessary. Hence, in the context of reform strategies, political economy analysis at the sector level is a consequential twin of the value chain approach. The two in combination are likely to imply a logical, temporal sequence of reforms.

Corruption is very much like a cancer. It manifests itself in a multitude of ways, continuously morphing into new shapes. But just like the proverbial medical researcher laboring every day in the laboratory until the early hours of the morning, social scientists and practitioners continue to search for new ways to address and contain this disease. This volume has attempted to open up new avenues of research and investigation that its authors hope will lead to more effective sector-specific antidotes that can keep different strands of the disease in permanent remission.

ENDNOTES

1. The country assistance strategies of the World Bank typically address the first. Investment climate surveys address the latter. The two need not necessarily point to the same sectors as the source of the problems. Often, however, the two overlap considerably.
2. In fact, this can logically build on the performance indicators being developed by the OECD–Development Assistance Committee Joint Venture on Procurement. http://www.oecd.org/document/40/0,2340,en_2649_ 19101395_37130152_1_1_1_1,00.html.
3. Several nongovernmental organizations have in fact developed simple methodologies for testing the quality of road construction. These groups include the Public Affairs Centre in Bangalore and Abra Citizens for Good Government in the Philippines.
4. See, for instance, chapter 9 on procurement and chapter 10 on tax administration.
5. *The Guardian,* 2006, July 14. http://www.guardian.co.uk/guardianpolitics/story/0,,1820152,00.html; as reported in Reuters, August 10, 2006.
6. The U.S. government announced on August 10, 2006, that it would support the effort to fight grand corruption at the international level.

REFERENCES

Bates, Robert. 1981. *Markets and States in Tropical Africa.* Los Angeles: University of California Press.

Johnston, Michael. 2001. "Measuring Corruption: Numbers versus Knowledge versus Understanding." In *The Political Economy of Corruption,* ed. Arvind Jain, pp. 157–79. New York: Routledge Press.

Laffont, Jean-Jacques, and Jean Tirole. 1993. *A Theory of Incentives in Procurement and Regulation.* Cambridge, MA: MIT Press.

Manelli, Alejandro, and Daniel Vincent. 1995. "Optimal Procurement Mechanisms." *Econometrica* 63 (3): 591–620.

Ross, Michael L. 2001. *Timber Booms and Institutional Breakdown in Southeast Asia.* Cambridge, UK: Cambridge University Press.

World Bank. 2005. "Improving Public Sector Governance: The Grand Challenge?" In *Economic Growth in the 1990s: Learning from a Decade of Reform,* 275–301. Washington, DC: World Bank.

———. Forthcoming. *Corruption and Technology in Public Procurement.* Washington, DC: World Bank.

Index

Boxes, figures, notes, and tables are indicated by *b, f, n,* and *t,* respectively.

Eco-Audit

Environmental Benefits Statement

The World Bank is committed to preserving endangered forests and natural resources. The Office of the Publisher has chosen to print *The Many Faces of Corruption* on recycled paper in accordance with the recommended standards for paper usage set by the Green Press Initiative, a nonprofit program supporting publishers in using fiber that is not sourced from endangered forests. Using this paper, the following were saved: 22 trees, 15 million BTUs of total energy, 1,948 pounds of CO_2 equivalent of greenhouse gases, 8,085 gallons of waste water, 1,038 pounds of solid waste. For more information, visit www.greenpressinitiative.org.